The Design
of Cost Management
Systems

Text and Cases
Second Edition

Robin Cooper

Peter F. Drucker
Graduate School of Management

Robert S. Kaplan

Harvard Business School

Prentice Hall, Upper Saddle River, New Jersey 07458

Executive Editor: Annie Todd
Editorial Assistant: Fran Toepfer
Editor-in-Chief: P. J. Boardman
Executive Marketing Manager: Beth Toland
Production Editor: Susan Rifkin
Permissions Coordinator: Monica Stipanov
Managing Editor: Dee Josephson
Senior Manufacturing Supervisor: Paul Smolenski
Manufacturing Manager: Vincent Scelta
Design Manager: Patricia Smythe
Composition: Progressive Publishing Alternatives

THE ROBERT S. KAPLAN SERIES IN MANAGEMENT ACCOUNTING
Robert S. Kaplan, *Consulting Editor*

The text portion of this book draws from Robert S. Kaplan and Robin Cooper, *Cost and Effect: Using Integrated Cost Systems to Drive Profitability and Performance* (Boston: Harvard Business School Press, 1998). Used with permission.

Library of Congress Cataloging-in-Publication Data
Cooper, Robin,
    The design of cost management systems: text, cases, and readings
  / Robin Cooper, Robert S. Kaplan.
     p. cm.
    ISBN 0-13-570417-0
    1. Managerial accounting. 2. Cost accounting. I. Kaplan, Robert
S. II. Title.
  HF5657.4.C65   1998
  658.15'11—dc21   98-37654
                                    CIP

Prentice-Hall International (UK) Limited, *London*
Prentice-Hall of Australia Pty. Limited, *Sydney*
Prentice-Hall Canada Inc., *Toronto*
Prentice-Hall Hispanoamericana, S.A., *Mexico*
Prentice-Hall of India Private Limited, *New Delhi*
Prentice-Hall of Japan, Inc., *Tokyo*
Pearson Education Asia Pte. Ltd., *Singapore*
Editora Prentice-Hall do Brasil, Ltda., *Rio de Janeiro*

Printed in the United States of America

10 9 8 7 6 5 4 3

To our children
M-J, Brie, and Alex
Jennifer and Dina

Contents

3   STAGE III SYSTEMS FOR LEARNING AND IMPROVEMENT   136

4   ACTIVITY-BASED COSTING: INTRODUCTION   208

5   MEASURING THE COST OF RESOURCE CAPACITY   243

6 OPERATIONAL AND STRATEGIC ACTIVITY-BASED MANAGEMENT IN MANUFACTURING COMPANIES   277

7 STRATEGIC ACTIVITY-BASED MANAGEMENT FOR CUSTOMERS AND SUPPLIERS   341

8 STRATEGIC ACTIVITY-BASED MANAGEMENT: PRODUCT DEVELOPMENT   395

Preface

During the last 15 years a revolution in the practice of cost management has occurred. First, activity-based costing (ABC) emerged in the 1980s as a replacement for the traditional standard cost systems that had remained essentially unchanged since the turn of century. Second, activity-based management (ABM)—the operational improvements and strategic actions taken with ABC information—became integrated with other cost-management techniques, such as kaizen and target costing, to produce new ways to reduce costs both across the value chain and over the life of the product. At the same time, the importance of nonfinancial measures to inform and motivate performance improvements became apparent. This book illustrates the conceptual leap from feedback to feedforward cost management, leading to powerful programs for strategic cost management.

This book provides a comprehensive treatment of the various innovations in cost and performance management. Students will learn the individual concepts and, more importantly, how they fit together, enabling companies to reduce costs while maintaining or increasing revenues. Underlying this integration are two powerful concepts: first, the accurate measurement of activity costs; and second, the reduction of costs by continuous and discontinuous improvements. As the organizational integrator, the finance function shifts from being the passive reporter of the past to a proactive influencer of the future. This migration enables cost and performance measurement systems to become embedded in the formulation and implementation of strategies and operational improvements.

We identify three primary functions of cost management systems:

1. measure cost of goods sold and value inventory for the financial reporting function
2. estimate costs of activities, products, services, and customers
3. provide economic feedback to employees and operators about process efficiency.

Using a four-stage model of cost system evolution, we document the evolution of cost-management systems for these three functions. We start with stage I systems. These systems cannot perform any of the three primary functions well. Next, we explore stage II systems that can perform the first function, financial reporting, effectively but not the two managerial functions. Third, we explore the use of multiple stand-alone stage III systems, each capable of performing one function effectively. Finally, we introduce the concept of stage IV, where new enterprise resource planning (ERP) systems integrate the capabilities of the stand-alone stage III cost systems into a single system capable of performing all three primary functions. We conclude by documenting the application of activity-based management to budgeting and transfer pricing. These final applications demand such intense information exchanges between the ABC system and other organizational systems that they require the integration capabilities of an ERP-based stage IV system.

Textual material at the beginning of each chapter presents the themes and general principles that will emerge from the study of the cases in the chapter. The cases, written from actual company experience, explore the properties of cost systems. They reveal how the design of cost systems determines the type of information management receives about the costs of its product, production processes, customers, suppliers, and other organizational units. More than 50 percent of the cases are new to this second edition.

The book has been written primarily for classroom use. For MBA and undergraduate courses, we believe the study of multiple cases with each chapter allows the concepts to be learned inductively. Our companion book, *Cost and Effect: Using Integrated Cost Systems to Drive Profitability and Performance* (Boston: Harvard Business School Press, 1998), was written for executives and practitioners, and contains more illustrative examples and in-depth discussion. For executive programs, with fewer sessions per course, the two books can be combined by having the students read the textual chapters of *Cost and Effect* while analyzing representative cases from this book.

Even beyond classroom use, practitioners including financial and operational managers, management accountants, and consultants should find much useful material in the second edition. The innovative approaches to cost management have evolved so rapidly and recently that the cases in this book represent the most available and comprehensive presentation of how these emerging concepts are applied in practice. Practitioners who study the cases carefully will learn much about the sources of failure in existing systems and the opportunities for innovative approaches in their own organizations.

The cases have been selected to explore the evolution of cost systems from the stage I systems, that were surprisingly common only 20 years ago, all the way to stage IV systems that are only now beginning to emerge. Chapter 1 introduces the concepts of cost and performance measurement and presents the four-stage model of cost system evolution. The cases for this chapter deal specifically with the failures from stage I and stage II systems that fail to perform all three primary functions of cost measurement systems. Several of the cases show the rudiments of emerging stage III cost systems.

In chapter 2, we learn in more detail about the specific limitations of traditional costing systems for serving managerial purposes. From this start, we can see how innovative systems can provide adopting companies with more responsive, more accurate, and more relevant information for making operational improvements and strategic decisions. The cases in this chapter illustrate effective stage II systems that can accurately value inventory and measure cost of goods sold for financial reporting purposes but provide poor or only limited support for the two managerial functions of cost management systems. The last two cases in the chapter describe how standard costing systems have been made more timely and responsive for providing feedback on financial expenses.

Chapter 3 illustrates how Japanese and US companies are using new financial and nonfinancial measurement systems to drive employees' learning and improvement activities. The chapter shows innovating Japanese and US companies using kaizen costing and pseudo profit centers for their continuous improvement efforts.

Chapters 4–9 provide a comprehensive treatment of activity-based costing and activity-based management (ABM). Chapter 4 describes the foundations of activity-based costing. The cases involve relatively simple ABC systems, most designed at the very beginning of the ABC movement. Chapter 5 treats the measurement of capacity costs comprehensively, and it illustrates how ABC can switch from being an historic to a prospective costing system. The cases explore the various issues that surround costing unused capacity. Some of the cases deal with traditional systems whereas others explore capacity-adjusted ABC, including the integration of ABC with the theory of constraints.

Chapter 6 and its associated cases explore ABM, both operational ABM, where managers use the ABC information to make better decisions about improving activity and process efficiency, and strategic ABM, which focuses on decisions about product pricing and mix. In addition to the managerial uses of ABC information, the cases in this chapter provide a marvelous learning experience about the implementation issues that arise when installing ABC systems in actual organizations. Chapter 7 extends ABC and ABM out of the factory to encompass the economics of customer and supplier relationships. Students will learn how companies are using ABC information to manage their total value and supply chain more effectively. Chapter 8 and its associated cases illustrate how cost information can be used productively during the product design and development process. The cases show product engineers using both target costing and activity-based cost information to make better product design and development decisions.

Chapter 9 extends the application of ABM principles to nonmanufacturing settings, such as banks and hospitals. By the end of chapter 9, we have documented the current state of the art in operational control and activity-based cost systems. Chapter 10 provides the ultimate destination for the book. It describes the vision for the future: cost and performance measurement systems, tightly integrated together to provide managers with valid, timely information for managerial purposes, as well as for external reporting. The cases in this chapter illustrate the risks of attempting such integration before the principles of stage IV systems are fully understood, and they help to identify the design characteristics for effective stage IV systems.

Chapter 11 builds upon this vision to describe how the ABC system can be used as the foundation for budgeting, on a rational, analytic basis, the organization's future expenses and resource supply. In addition, it explores the application of activity-based principles to transfer pricing. Since stage IV systems are just now emerging at this time, we do not have cases to illustrate these applications.

In developing the ideas in this book, we are obviously indebted to the many individuals and organizations in North America, Europe, and Japan with whom we have worked during the past 15 years. We were fortunate in receiving permission to present many of these cases in undisguised form. The several dozen case studies, drawn from innovative companies willing to share their experiences in implementing new cost management systems, required the cooperation of hundreds of people. We have learned from each of them, and rather than list them individually, we wish to thank them collectively for allowing us to enhance our research by studying their experiences.

We also have benefited from support of the Harvard Business School and the Claremont Graduate University. A combination of teaching assignments and support for the extensive fieldwork and case studies enabled us to learn from and influence practice. With this book, we can leverage this support to share the knowledge with faculty, students, and practitioners around the world. We also appreciate the permission from Harvard Business School Press, and its president, Carol Franco, to use text from our trade book, *Cost and Effect: Using Integrated Cost Systems to Drive Profitability and Performance* (Boston: Harvard Business School Press, 1998) in preparing the second edition.

Jenica Flores at Harvard Business School gave us great administrative assistance in the preparation of the book. We appreciate the contributions of Professor V. G. Narayanan for use of three of his newest cases. At Prentice-Hall, P. J. Boardman provided continual encouragement to share our latest work in a second edition of the book; Annie Todd, as editor, coordinated our contributions and kept us moving forward, and Susan Rifkin gave careful attention to the quality and speed of the production process. We profited from the reviews of William D. J. Cotton, SUNY at Geneseo; Susan S. Hamlen, SUNY at Buffalo; Monte R. Swain, Brigham Young University; and Y. Robert Lin, California State University, Hayward.

In summary, the material in this book presents a state-of-the-art view of the emerging principles of cost management system design. We have observed, after teaching this material, that our students and executives are capable of leading the change in their organizations to redesign their cost management systems. Thus, we feel confident that the material is actionable and practical. However, the material is not a cookbook that can be followed unthinkingly. Students must master the underlying design principles for cost management systems and learn how to apply these principles sensibly and in a cost-effective fashion, recognizing the competitive environment, product and customer mix, process and information technology, and organizational situation in their individual companies.

Robin Cooper
Atlanta

Robert S. Kaplan
Boston

1

Cost and Performance Management Systems

Companies' cost systems perform three primary functions. First, for manufacturing companies, the systems assign production expenses each period to the output produced, so that the expenses can be partitioned between cost of goods sold and inventory. This is the financial reporting function. Second, cost systems provide economic feedback to employees and operators about process efficiencies and expense control. Finally, cost information is used to estimate the costs of activities, products, services, and customers.

The financial reporting function is driven by the needs of constituencies that are *external* to the organization: investors, creditors, regulators, and tax authorities. The procedures for performing this external financial reporting function are governed by a myriad of rules and regulations established by tax authorities, governmental agencies, private standard-setting bodies, and public accounting societies. The two other functions arise from the needs of managers *internal* to the organization for accurate and timely cost information for the strategic decisions and operational improvements that will enhance profitability. Managers require valid information for strategic decisions such as:

- Designing products and services that both meet customers' expectations and can be produced and delivered at a profit;
- Making product mix and investment decisions;
- Choosing among alternative suppliers;
- Negotiating about price, product features, quality, delivery, and service with customers; and
- Aligning efficient and effective distribution and service processes to targeted market and customer segments.

Managers also use accurate, timely information for operational improvements, such as

- Continuous and discontinuous (reengineering) improvements in quality, efficiency, and speed; and
- Assisting front-line employees for their learning and continuous improvement activities.

In the past, many companies attempted to meet their financial reporting, strategic costing, and operational control and improvement functions with a single costing system. In an environ-

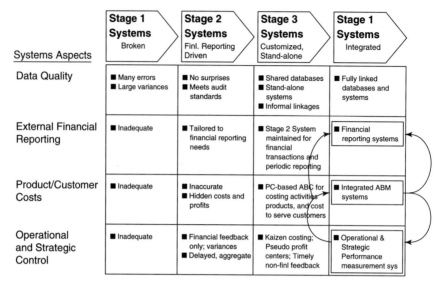

Systems Aspects	Stage 1 Systems Broken	Stage 2 Systems Finl. Reporting Driven	Stage 3 Systems Customized, Stand-alone	Stage 1 Systems Integrated
Data Quality	■ Many errors ■ Large variances	■ No surprises ■ Meets audit standards	■ Shared databases ■ Stand-alone systems ■ Informal linkages	■ Fully linked databases and systems
External Financial Reporting	■ Inadequate	■ Tailored to financial reporting needs	■ Stage 2 System maintained for financial transactions and periodic reporting	■ Financial reporting systems
Product/Customer Costs	■ Inadequate	■ Inaccurate ■ Hidden costs and profits	■ PC-based ABC for costing activities, products, and cost to serve customers	■ Integrated ABM systems
Operational and Strategic Control	■ Inadequate	■ Financial feedback only; variances ■ Delayed, aggregate	■ Kaizen costing; Pseudo profit centers; Timely non-finl feedback	■ Operational & Strategic Performance measurement sys

EXHIBIT 1-1   Cost Systems Typically Pass Through Four Stages

ment of limited product and process variety, and where excellence in operating processes was not critical for success, a single costing system might have sufficed. This is no longer possible. In general, a company cannot accomplish all its financial and managerial accounting functions with a single cost system. Exhibit 1–1 provides a framework for thinking about the status of a company's multiple cost measurement and management systems. Managers can view the development of their integrated cost and performance measurement systems as a journey through four sequential stages.

STAGE I SYSTEMS: INADEQUATE FOR FINANCIAL REPORTING

Some companies have cost systems that are inadequate even for financial reporting purposes. Inadequacies arise from poor internal controls for recording transactions so that transactions are either not recorded or are recorded with error. Stage I systems can arise in newly emerging companies that have not yet had the time or resources to install an excellent financial system. But they can also arise in mature companies that continue to use financial systems installed decades earlier on what are called legacy systems. These systems are now technologically obsolete and almost impossible to maintain since the original designers have left the company and so many undocumented changes and updates have occurred that no one fully understands the mechanics or the logic of the existing system. But the system cannot be scrapped in the short run since it is the only mechanism for recording and maintaining financial transactions.

Some Stage I systems have incorrect algorithms for allocating overhead costs to products as they pass through different processing stages and for updating old standard costs to current price levels. The incorrect algorithms introduce errors into the accounts so that book values of inventory are virtually guaranteed not to be reconcilable to physical inventory. Other companies' cost systems do not recognize all the outputs that a company produces during a period. Consequently, periodic production expenses get assigned only to a subset of the outputs that an organization produces each period. For example, the costs of producing prototype or experimental products may not be recorded, or the costs associated with the production of peripheral products may be allocated arbitrarily to the main product line.

Even companies that once had adequate systems for financial reporting may now have inadequate systems because of acquisitions. Usually, the financial systems in the newly acquired companies or divisions will be independent of and inconsistent with each other. The diverse systems have different general ledgers and classify the same type of financial transactions in different ways. They likely make different assumptions about the way factory and indirect costs are assigned to products for inventory valuation.

Symptoms of Stage I cost systems are:

- Extensive amounts of time and resources are required to consolidate different reporting entities within the company and to close the books each accounting period,
- Some of the company's products or services have no costs assigned to them,
- Unexpected variances occur at the end of each accounting period when physical inventories are reconciled against book values,
- Auditors consistently require writedowns of inventory after internal and external audits,
- Accountants perform many ad hoc post-closing adjusting entries to the financial accounts, and
- Managers lack faith in the integrity and auditability of the financial system.

These legacy systems have become obsolete over time and can no longer function adequately for even the simplest of the three primary functions of cost systems, namely to value inventory and measure cost of goods sold for financial and reporting purposes. Given that they fail this objective, they cannot hope to satisfy the requirements of the other two primary functions; estimating cost of activities, products, services, and customers and providing economic feedback to employees and operators about process efficiencies.

Fortunately, most companies do not have Stage I cost systems, and those that do can acquire and install modern general ledger systems that avoid all the problems identified above.

STAGE II SYSTEMS: FINANCIAL REPORTING DRIVEN

Most cost systems today fulfill the financial reporting function adequately. The systems have common data and account definitions across different business units so that financial managers can readily compare and consolidate financial results across multiple units, divisions, and operating companies. The systems can prepare complete financial statements shortly after the close of an accounting period that require few if any post-closing adjustments. They prepare statements consistent with standards established by financial reporting, government, regulatory, and tax authorities, and the system of data recording and processing have excellent integrity so that they satisfy stringent auditability and internal control standards.

Stage II financial systems (see Exhibit 1–2), however, also report individual product costs with the same simple and aggregate methods used for external financial reporting, to value inventory and measure cost of goods sold. For example, some companies continue to use cost systems with simple direct labor overhead allocations, perhaps with only a single rate, despite operating with plants containing diverse processes, including both manual assembly and highly automated machining. Even with overhead rates reaching 500–1,000% of direct labor cost, however, auditors, regulators, and tax authorities remain perfectly content with the methods used to allocate manufacturing overhead to products. Companies receive clean audit opinions since auditors are more concerned with consistency in method from year to year than with accuracy of costs at the individual cost center or product level. As long as the reported inventory and cost-of-goods sold numbers are roughly correct in aggregate, external users are satisfied.

Such aggregate methods, however, for allocating factory overhead costs to products, provide poor information to managers. In addition, the costs of many organizational resources, especially those used for product design and development, marketing, sales, and distribution, may

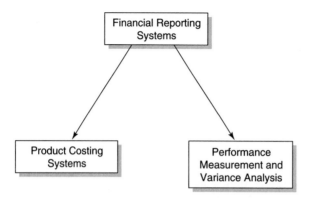

EXHIBIT 1–2   Stage 2 Cost Systems Depend upon the External Financial Reporting System

not be assigned to cost objects at all because such costs are not "inventoriable" in financial statements. Even though these resources clearly help the organization meet the demands of individual customers, channels, and markets, the financial system does not assign their costs to users. Such a calculation is neither necessary nor allowable for financial reporting purposes.

Many companies, recognizing the arbitrary nature of factory overhead allocations in their inventory valuation system, have shifted to direct costing systems for facilitating managerial decisions. Direct costing systems assign just the materials and direct labor costs to individual products and ignore overhead costs when calculating the profitability of products, services, and customers. Direct costing methods are fine if the ignored indirect and support costs are a small fraction of total costs, or if, as direct costing advocates claim, they are "fixed" costs. Yet organizations have found that not only were the indirect and support costs not fixed, they are not even variable. For many organizations, these costs are "super-variable;" they have been increasing at a faster rate than production or sales volume.

In addition to limitations for measuring product and customer costs, managers have also found that their traditional, standard costing systems are inadequate for providing feedback to responsibility center supervisors and employees. Historically, management accountants were scorekeepers; they were neutral observers, sitting on the sidelines, distant from the action, and often not even observing the processes that produced and delivered products and services. The management accountants issued periodic reports, derived from their financial accounting system, which reconciled actual with budgeted (or standard) expenses. The accounting and finance staff issued these periodic performance reports according to the monthly financial reporting cycle, so they appeared days or weeks delayed from the actual events they reported on. And the reports were filled with cost accounting jargon—allocations and variances calculated many different ways—that were incomprehensible to the people performing the work.

Apart from the delays and difficulty in interpreting these reports, their philosophic underpinnings were inconsistent with the demands of the new operating environment. These traditional cost controlling systems, with their standards and variance reporting, emphasized stability, control, and efficiency of isolated machines, workers, and departments. Such an emphasis was not responsive to today's competitive world that stresses the continuous and discontinuous (i.e., reengineering) improvement and the cross-functional integration required to provide quick response, high-quality processes geared to customer demands.

Thus, Stage II cost systems are completely inadequate for the two key managerial purposes:

1. Estimating the cost of activities and business processes, and the cost and profitability of products, services, customers, and organizational units; and

2. Providing feedback useful for improving business processes.

STAGE III SYSTEMS: DEVELOP CUSTOMIZED, MANAGERIALLY RELEVANT, STAND-ALONE SYSTEMS

Many companies today are developing customized approaches for their financial reporting, cost measurement, and performance management functions (see Exhibit 1–3). Stage III cost systems contain:

- A Stage II system for periodic financial reporting to external users;
- One or more activity-based cost (ABC) systems that take data from the "official" financial system, as well as from other information and operating systems, for strategic costing; and
- Operational feedback systems that provide operators and all front-line employees with timely, accurate information, both financial and nonfinancial, on the efficiency, quality, and cycle times of business processes.

In Stage III, companies retain their existing (Stage II) financial system to prepare financial reports for external constituencies, such as shareholders, regulators, and tax authorities. Companies need a basic financial system to capture the transactions occurring continually through their operations, to assign these transactions to accounts in a general ledger system, and to aggregate and process these transactions to prepare the statutory periodic financial statements. Given that many companies already have financial systems that are adequate for this purpose, it seems foolish to scrap these systems just because they are inadequate for managerial decision-making and for employees' learning and improvement activities. Companies, however, may want to simplify their Stage II systems, because the managerial functions of responsibility center reporting and individual product costing will be performed by newer, customized systems. For external reporting, companies can get by with using one or only a few cost centers in a facility, and with simple allocation bases such as labor dollars, machine hours, and material dollars.

Given the availability of powerful microcomputers and networked client-server systems, available information can be processed into specialized managerial accounting systems without much difficulty. Development times are measured in months, not years, and total resource costs

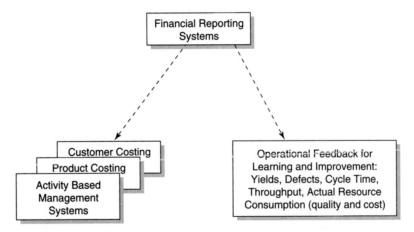

EXHIBIT 1–3   Stage 3 Cost Systems Break the Linkage from Financial Reporting Systems

are in the tens to hundreds of thousands of dollars, not the millions that would be required for entire new financial systems.

One of these customized systems will be activity-based for strategic costing. We will discuss extensively, in chapters 4 to 9, the role for activity-based cost systems to help managers make strategic decisions and to establish priorities for process improvement activities. But ABC systems are not useful for short-term operational decisions and control. Also needed is a second type of managerial financial system for day-to-day feedback on the performance of business processes. In chapter 3, we identify how some companies are deploying innovative cost and performance measurement systems for learning and improvement.

STAGE IV SYSTEMS: INTEGRATED COST MANAGEMENT AND FINANCIAL REPORTING

In Stage IV, the two primarily managerial cost and performance measurement systems developed during Stage III (ABC and operational feedback) become integrated and together provide the basis for preparing external financial statements (see Exhibit 1–4). The integration can be accomplished with enterprise resource planning (ERP) systems that integrate and coordinate all the major business functions: purchasing, manufacturing, marketing, sales, logistics, and order fulfillment, plus support services such as human resources and accounting. For example, with an ERP system, a salesperson's order anywhere in the world triggers a shipment from a regional warehouse or schedules the order into production in an appropriate factory. The system then automatically updates inventory levels, material purchases, production schedules, customer information, and accounting data.

ERP systems will enable companies to contemplate having an integrated set of operating, financial, and management systems. ERPs have a common data structure and a centralized, accessible data warehouse that permits data to be entered and accessed from anywhere in the world. With this technology, managers can envision bringing together all their stand-alone ABC and operational improvement and learning systems into a single integrated system. The integration can provide new capabilities not realizable when financial reporting, product, customer and process costing, and operational feedback and learning systems were separate.

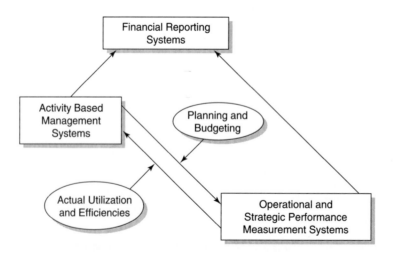

EXHIBIT 1–4   Stage 4: Integrated Cost Systems

We describe this integration in chapter 10, after we have established more of the design foundation for both ABC and operational feedback systems. For now, we can summarize the findings that the ABC system will become the basis for organizational budgeting, authorizing the supply of (and spending on) resources in all organizational units. These activity-based budgets are then used by the operational feedback system to compare and analyze the actual expenses incurred by each organizational unit throughout the year. In return, the operational feedback system provides the ABC systems with information about the most recent efficiencies and capacity utilization of operations. This enables the ABC to update cost driver rates when the organization has made demonstrable, sustained changes in operating efficiencies and practical capacity. This feedback enables activity cost driver rates to track operating improvements quickly and reliably.

SUMMARY

In this book we will study the innovations in cost management systems to improve the information that managers and employees receive about their organizational economics. Companies today can contemplate using three distinct types of cost systems:

1. A simple, standard costing system that meets financial reporting requirements for calculating cost of goods sold and valuing inventory each accounting period;
2. Local operational control and learning systems for promoting continuous improvement and efficiencies; and
3. One or more activity-based cost systems to measure the cost of activities and processes, and the cost and profitability of products, customers, suppliers, regions, and responsibility centers.

We will start in chapter 2 by studying the basic structure used by all cost systems, especially the traditional cost systems that existed prior to the development of systems for continuous improvement and for activity-based costing. We then study, in chapter 3, the new systems for operational control and learning. We examine systems of financial and nonfinancial measurement that enable employees not just to stabilize and control their operations, but to make continual improvements and enhancements. In chapters 4 to 9, we will explore the structure and use of ABC systems. We study the first historical activity-based cost systems applied in manufacturing companies and continue the journey with the ABC extensions to managing customer and supplier relationships and service companies. We complete our journey by looking at ways that ERP systems enable companies to integrate their cost and performance measurement systems and give them new capabilities for budgeting and authorizing their supply of resources.

CASES

The first case, *Bridgeton Industries,* explores the implications of management making product mix and outsourcing decisions with an obsolete cost system. The outcomes from these decisions are not what they expect. The *Colorscope* case illustrates the role for cost information in a small, entrepreneurial business. The *Union Pacific* series describes the role for different systems for operational control and for product costing. In addition, it illustrates how many service companies pose some special challenges for product and customer costing, such as the low percentage of direct, traceable costs. Cost management issues in service companies are addressed in more depth in chapter 9. The *Brookwood Medical Center* case illustrates the poor condition of cost systems at many hospitals. Such primitive, essentially nonexistent systems were common in regulated industries where profits were "guaranteed" by legislation. Finally, the *Indianapolis (A)* case shows how activity-based costing can be applied in a government setting. The case demonstrates how ABC information should be used both to stimulate process improvement and for making strategic decisions, such as outsourcing.

BRIDGETON INDUSTRIES AUTOMOTIVE COMPONENT AND FABRICATION PLANT

The union has worked with us and has even led in cost reduction programs. Now corporate is talking about outsourcing additional products. What more can we do to keep the business?

Mike Lewis, Plant Manager

The Automotive Component and Fabrication Plant (ACF) was the original plant site for Bridgeton Industries, a major supplier of components for the domestic automotive industry. The history of the plant dated back to the 1840s when the adjoining river attracted mills that processed the rich lumber resources in the area. The site progressed through several industrial uses, including an early wagon works, until it was finally purchased by the founder of Bridgeton. He opened his first office there in the early 1900s.

All of ACF's production was sold to the Big Three domestic manufacturers. Competition was primarily from local suppliers and other Bridgeton plants. As long as the market was growing and dominated by U.S. manufacturers, this strategy worked. It became less effective when foreign competition and scarce, expensive gasoline caused domestic loss of market share. Suppliers found themselves competing for a shrinking pool of production contracts. Throughout the 1980s, ACF experienced serious cutbacks due to this competitive pressure. However, as the 1989/90 model year budget approached, ACF was still considered a critical plant. Model years ran from September 1 to August 31 and were the basis for budgeting. Production contracts were usually awarded for a model year.

The Engine Plant Shutdown

ACF first felt the effects of domestic loss of market share in 1985. After the first oil crunch in the mid-1970s, Bridgeton had built two plants for manufacture of fuel-efficient diesel engines in anticipation of a continued growth in the market. One of these plants was at

This case was prepared by Patricia J. Bost, Research Associate (under the supervision of Associate Professor Robin Cooper).

Copyright © 1990 by the President and Fellows of Harvard College. Harvard Business School case 190-085.

the ACF facility. When the growth in diesel-powered cars was not sustained, one of the operations had to be shut down.

Special studies were made of the relative costs of the two plants, and ACF's facility was the one chosen to be closed. When the production workers at ACF were told they were not cost competitive, they took actions to reduce unit product cost, brining it down to within a few cents of the competing quote. Despite these efforts, ACF's facility was closed. "Management told us we were not cost competitive. We worked ourselves into the ground and lowered the unit cost, and still lost the business," recalls Ronald Peters, a long-time production worker in the old engine facility.

When the engine plant closed at the end of 1985/6 model year, all of the related production jobs were eliminated. The skilled trades positions were eliminated where possible. However, tradespeople who had unique skills that were needed in other areas of the plant were retained. The physical machinery, equipment, and building were written down and taken off the plant books.

Strategic Analysis

During the 1986/7 model year, the corporation hired a strategic consulting firm to examine all of Bridgeton's products and classify them in terms of world-class competitive position and potential. Four criteria were considered: (a) quality, (b) customer service, (c) technical capability (engineering and sophistication of plant processes), and (d) competitive cost position.

The data used to evaluate quality included warranty failure rates, product rejects per million, percent scheduled maintenance versus breakdown maintenance, customer complaints per million, and published user rating service scales.

To evaluate customer service, in addition to interviews, the study examined percent on-schedule production and shipments, percent variation in these schedules, time to respond to requests for information, time to respond to customer complaints, lead-time from design of concept to production of product, and degree of manufacturing flexibility.

Technical capability was largely estimated by interviewing customers. Internal data were gathered about product feature innovations, degree of technological proprietary, and depth of engineering expertise.

Competitive cost position was evaluated by interviewing financial, purchasing, and engineering personnel and undertaking a cost analysis which examined the cost of production by breaking each product cost into three elements: materials, direct labor and benefits, and overhead. The product costs used for the study were total full-factory costs based on examination of the manufacturing cost reports generated by the facility's cost system. The details were provided by the plant financial personnel. Comparative competitive costs were obtained through plant tours and interviews with engineering and purchasing people at other Bridgeton plants (internal competitors), information from competing component suppliers (external competitors), and discussions with financial personnel.

The budgeted unit costs provided by the plant for the 1986/7 model year study included overhead (burden) applied to products as a percent of direct labor dollars. The overhead percentage was calculated at budget time and used throughout the model year to allocate overhead to products using a single overhead pool. The overhead rate used in the study was 435% of direct labor dollars.

Product costs were analyzed by the consultants to classify products by degree of cost competitiveness. Product classification was finished and reviewed at the corporate level with little plant adjustment or involvement after initial data collection. Products classified as world class (having costs equal to or lower than competitors' manufacturing costs) were considered Class I. Products which had the potential of becoming world class (having costs 5% to 15% higher than competitors' costs) were classified as Class II. Products which had no hope of becoming world class (having costs more than 15% higher than the major competitor) were classified as Class III.

The other criteria (quality, customer service, and technical capability) were weighted into a factor that determined the final classification of the products. The consultants recommended that Class I products should remain at their present locations. Class II products were to be watched closely for improvement or deterioration. Class III were designated to be outsourced (i.e., the business was awarded to another Bridgeton location, or purchased from an outside competitor) or eliminated.

The consultants advised ACF's management that their products fell into the following classifications (for a description of these products see Exhibit 1): (a) Class I: Fuel tanks; (b) Class II: Manifolds, front and rear doors; and (c) Class III: Muffler-exhaust systems, and oil pans.

Product Outsourcing

At the end of the 1987/8 model year, oil pans and muffler-exhaust systems were outsourced from ACF. This outsourcing resulted in a loss of 60 direct labor (production) jobs and 30 indirect (skilled) jobs. These 90 people were transferred to a retraining job pool, which was administered and paid by the union. The job pool cost was not part of plant burden costs.

With this second major cutback, plant management and labor moved toward more cooperation and openness in efforts to retain the remaining business. Several programs were introduced to improve product quality and increase productivity. These programs stretched the traditional union/management boundaries as both sides worked toward creative solutions to meet these challenges.

One of these efforts, led by Fred Simmonds, an experienced die maker, involved union formation of teams to lower the time required to change dies, a major constraint in the production process. By combining union labor classes and skill levels on press line die change teams, ACF lowered the required time to change dies from 12 hours to 90 minutes. This was the best in Bridgeton. Other locations averaged between four and five hours. The world-class times of Japanese assembly lines, approximately 10 minutes, required special plant layouts.

Another productivity improvement program created by Simmonds and Peters used "hourly to time hourly." In this program, hourly workers kept track of the causes of downtime and categorized them as being related to personal time, tools and equipment, or startup. People from the retraining job pool formed by the union at the time of the prior layoffs were asked to time the lines. Production personnel's knowledge of the process and experience on the line resulted in highly accurate activity times for the operations they observed. Their reporting emphasized the positive side of the information using uptime reports to show progress toward the world-class goal of 80% uptime set by the Japanese. Through identifying problem areas and working with industrial engineers, they increased their uptime from an average of 30% to 65%, the best in Bridgeton.

In spite of these improvements in the production process, manifolds, designated Class II in the initial study, were downgraded to Class III in the 1989/90 model year budget and identified as candidates for outsourcing (for the 1986/7 through 1989/90 model year budgets, see Exhibits 2 and 3). Any decision to outsource manifolds was complicated by the possibility that increased emission standards would require new vehicles be fitted with lighter weight, more efficient manifolds. If this occurred, the demand for stainless steel manifolds could increase dramatically and so, probably, would its selling price.

Reacting to the change in status of the manifolds, Lewis called together his plant superintendents and union representatives. "This doesn't make sense. I know we are more competitive. We have made all kinds of improvements, but our costs keep going up and we're still losing business. What more can we do?"

EXHIBIT 1

BRIDGETON INDUSTRIES
Product Lines in 1990 Budget

Fuel tanks: These are produced on six stamping lines from coated sheet metal, which is stamped in halves and then placed together and automatically seam welded.

Manifolds: Stainless steel exhaust manifolds are produced in a highly automated production process. The parts are loaded on fixture and robotically welded. These manifolds are superior to the older technology cast iron manifolds in pollution control. The disadvantage of using stainless steel is its high relative cost.

Front and rear doors: These are the front doors and rear cargo doors for vans. They are produced on four press lines with up to six presses per line.

Muffler-exhaust systems: These are formed from sheet metal that is bent to shape and robotically welded.

Oil pans: These are small steel stampings. They are produced on two lines containing one press each.

EXHIBIT 2

BRIDGETON INDUSTRIES
1986/7 through 1989/90 Model Year Budgets
$(000)

	MODEL YEAR			
	1986/87	1987/88	1988/89	1989/90
Sales				
Fuel tanks	70,278	75,196	79,816	83,535
Manifolds	79,459	84,776	89,323	93,120
Doors	41,845	45,174	47,199	49,887
Muffler/exhausts	62,986	66,266	0	0
Oil pans	75,586	79,658	0	0
Total	330,154	351,071	216,338	226,542
Direct material				
Fuel tanks	15,125	15,756	16,312	16,996
Manifolds	31,696	33,016	34,392	35,725
Doors	14,886	15,506	16,252	16,825
Muffler/exhausts	28,440	29,525	0	0
Oil pans	32,218	33,560	0	0
Total	122,365	127,363	66,956	69,546
Direct labor				
Fuel tanks	4,169	4,238	4,415	4,599
Manifolds	5,886	6,027	6,278	6,540
Doors	2,621	2,731	2,884	2,963
Muffler/exhausts	5,635	5,766	0	0
Oil pans	6,371	6,532	0	0
Total	24,682	25,294	13,537	14,102

(continued)

EXHIBIT 2 *(cont.)*

Overhead by account number

1000	7,713	7,806	5,572	5,679
1500	6,743	6,824	5,883	5,928
2000	3,642	3,794	2,031	2,115
3000	2,428	2,529	1,354	1,410
4000	8,817	8,888	7,360	7,433
5000	24,181	24,460	20,063	20,274
8000	5,964	5,946	3,744	3,744
9000	6,708	6,771	5,948	5,987
11000	5,089	5,011	3,150	3,030
12000	26,954	28,077	15,027	15,683
14000	9,733	9,784	8,025	8,110
Total	107,954	109,890	78,157	79,393
Factory profit	75,153	88,524	57,688	63,501

EXHIBIT 3

BRIDGETON INDUSTRIES

Description of Chart of Accounts

ACCOUNT NUMBER	DESCRIPTION
1000	Wages and benefits for nonskilled hourly personnel such as janitors and truck drivers
1500	All plant salaried personnel expense, including benefits, except industrial engineers (included in account number 11000)
2000	Production supplies such as gloves, safety goggles, and packing material
3000	Small wearing tools such as grinding wheels, hammers, and screwdrivers
4000	All purchased utilities including coal and compressed gas
5000	Wages for nonproduction employees with specialized skilled classifications used for plant maintenance and rearrangement; the benefits associated with these wages are in class 14000
8000	Depreciation, on a straight-line basis, and property taxes
9000	Various relatively constant personnel-related expenses including items such as training, travel, and union representation
11000	Project expense for one-time setup and some rearrangement of new equipment and machinery
12000	Benefits and overtime premium for production hourly workers including COLA (Cost of Living Adjustment), state unemployment, and pension (Wages are in direct labor.)
14000	Benefits for skilled hourly workers similar to those for production workers (Wages are in account 5000.)

COLORSCOPE, INC.

Introduction

Andrew Cha, the founder of Colorscope, Inc., a small, vibrant firm in the graphic arts industry, had seen his business change dramatically over the years. The rapid development of such technologies as desktop publishing and the World Wide Web as well as the consolidation of several major players within the industry had radically altered his company's relative positioning on the competitive landscape. Preparing to celebrate the company's twentieth anniversary in March 1996, Cha pondered the issues involved in moving Colorscope ahead.

Company History   Born in Anhui, China in 1938, Andrew Cha immigrated to the United States in 1967 to seek a better life. Originally planning to settle in New York City, where he would pursue his craft as a painter and his wife would attend New York University, his funds ran out in Los Angeles, forcing him to work as a cook and busboy in a downtown Chinese restaurant. Through fortune and hard work, however, Cha eventually found jobs that took advantage of his artistic skills in draftmanship and photography; a succession of promotions within one graphic arts company convinced him that his abilities would enable him to start his own business. Founded on March 1, 1976, Colorscope Inc. was established as a special-effects photography laboratory serving local advertising agencies in southern California.

As Cha's reputation grew, so did the business. Sales increased steadily over the years, peaking in 1988 at $5 million dollars. The company served agency giants such as Saatchi & Saatchi, Grey Advertising, and J. Walter Thompson and large retailing and entertainment companies such as The Walt Disney Company and R. H. Macy & Co. To improve service to these customers, Cha invested in expensive proprietary computer equipment to continue providing ever more complicated print special effects.

During 1988, Cha was approached by R. R. Donnelley & Sons Co. about a possible acquisition. Donnelley, the largest printer in the world with roughly $4.3 billion in sales at the time, was interested in acquiring Colorscope for approximately $10 million. The interest in

Joseph Cha, HBS MBA class of 1996 and Assistant Professor V.G. Narayanan prepared this case.
Copyright © 1996 by the President and Fellows of Harvard College. Harvard Business School case 197-040.

Colorscope was twofold. First, Cha had built solid relationships with highly valuable print and pre-press buyers in the marketplace. Every pre-press dollar he sold was worth several more in printing. By owning Cha's pre-press business and employing him as a sales consultant, Donnelley hoped to secure large print contracts, which at the time were still subject to open bidding. Second, Cha's operation was considered one of the most efficient in the business. Donnelley employees had previously visited his operation and modeled some of his workflows, adapting them into the design of one of their own pre-press facilities. As a result, Donnelley considered Cha's business processes as well as his training methods an operational advantage they could leverage to other pre-press facilities in their network of operations across the country.

After considering his options and his belief in the potential of the business, however, Cha grew dissatisfied with several of the contingency and non-compete clauses built into the agreement, and eventually decided against the sale of his company. The timing of this decision proved costly. While serving his existing base of high-margin clients, Cha ignored certain trends in the business, particularly the price pressures brought on by cheaper PC- and Mac-based microcomputers. As these devices, equipped with increasingly sophisticated page layout and color correction software, proliferated and increased in functionality, small ad agencies and print shops began to take pieces of business away from larger graphic art companies like Colorscope. Cha, however, had felt protected from the trend by the strong personal relationships he had built with key clients over his career.

Nevertheless, by 1990, technology and the pace of change in the desktop publishing industry forced significant changes in his business. The first impact was on pricing. Although he emphasized the quality and reliability of his work, market pressure forced him to reduce his own basic prices which previously had held up against industry trends. (See Exhibit 1). This, however, proved to be insufficient. In May 1994, his largest account, representing about 80% of his business, announced that it was purchasing its own graphic design and production equipment, replacing Colorscope with an internal group. The process was to be phased in over the following year. After losing his most significant and long-term client, Cha thought that to rebuild the business he had to reevaluate the industry, his company's position in the pre-press segment, its pricing policy, and its operations.

The Pre-press Production Process

Although technology dramatically changed the means by which production was conducted as well as the corresponding values to each phase, the basic process for print material, known in the industry as pre-press or color separations, remained essentially the same over the past 20 years. (See Exhibit 2). A content provider, such as a magazine or direct mail cataloger, designed and laid out a "book" or "project" for distribution. Once the book's layout was approved, a photographer captured and developed the images, received approvals from the client, and sent them to the pre-press house or "color separator," in this case Colorscope. Once in production, images were processed or digitized via laser scanner and compiled with text and other graphics to form a master file for the printer.

During this process, the magazine or direct mail client saw iterations, or proofs, of their "book" with digital and conventional proofing devices. At these intervals, the clients could ask for changes, ranging from simple price and copy adjustments to sophisticated special effects, adjusting colors or clearing blemishes in products and people. A very important qualitative component of the separator's task was understanding the product's desired "look and "feel" and translating the direction the client desired into the actual images on each page. Typically, the pre-press house charged a base rate for digitizing, assembling, and proofing each page, with an additional fee for the special effects. When the "books" were ultimately produced on paper, the images were filed and stored in the separator's database for future use.

After the project gained final approval, Colorscope sent the "master book," or file, to the printer either electronically or by large sheets of four-color master film. At this point, the separator had converted all of the client's information, digital text, graphics, and photographs (described in a postscript or dpi format) into a printer-acceptable (line screen) format. Once at the printer, the film or information was converted to physical plates of various materials (metal, alloys, or plastics) specific to the size of the item and the number to be printed. These plates were mounted on drums, and the information became imprinted via an offset or

gravure printing process with multiple ink types onto a wide ranging array of papers depending again on the size of the item and order size of the project. After the printer finished the pieces (i.e., cutting, binding, and addressing), the final "books" were ready for shipment to the magazine or direct mailer's subscribers.

Industry Dynamics   The overall market for commercial printing services in the United States topped $66 billion in 1995. Because of the highly diverse range of printed material produced, companies in the print industry tended to specialize in market subsets like greeting cards, business forms, financial reports, newspapers and newspaper inserts, magazines, direct mail catalogs, coupons, directories, etc. This evolved specialization led to a highly fragmented competitive landscape, where most companies served a few primary clients, highlighting an operational expertise in an area narrow enough to discourage other competitors. Thus, if a client planned an advertising campaign that involved several media, e.g., point-of-sale stands, packaging, and direct mail catalogs, it might use several different printers and print distributors for the different products. As a result, in the commercial printing business for catalogs, there were only a handful of printers with the necessary capacity and marketing strength to compete effectively for large print customers. (See Exhibit 3.)

The pre-press market mirrored the print industry but on a smaller scale. Given the highly fragmented nature of the business as well as a paucity of published information about actual pre-press sales on a national level, it was difficult to quantify the exact market size for pre-press services. Because the typical catalog pre-press job represented approximately 10% to 20% of the printing price charged to the client, however, the U.S. pre-press market in 1995 could have been as large as $6 billion (See Exhibit 4). Specialization among competitors, similar to the print business, was common. Although a client might choose a single pre-press firm to house all of its images to interface with several printers, many larger graphics customers employed several separators to handle different projects if they had different expertise with specific print products. Those clients would, for example, use separators specialized in video box (i.e., packaging for VHS video cassettes), posters, or printed books.

For the individual pre-press firm the market had drastically changed. Thus Colorscope's previous position as a high quality, high service player appeared unsustainable in a marketplace full of service providers that claimed the same quality at lower prices (See Exhibit 5). While in the past prosperous relationships could last several years, with customers consistently able and willing to pay for top quality separations, current technology blurred the clear distinctions in quality of the actual film output. As a result, some previously loyal customers looked at pre-press services as more of a commodity product; correspondingly, personal relationships alone no longer seemed to ensure the livelihood of Cha's business. As more pre-press houses bought desktop equipment and lowered their prices, customers in the catalog arena defected to even lower-cost providers. By 1995, the base price for a typical direct mail catalog had stabilized around $500–$600 per page, roughly half the rates charged only five years before. Given that the basic scanning and proofing functions of a pre-press house could be easily replicated on a smaller scale with minimal investment,[1] and given the significant overcapacity in the industry, Cha knew that the downward pressure on prices was likely to continue.

Direct Competition   Although the number of larger direct mail clients had remained flat for several years, the competition for them was intense. Cha's competitors were no longer other local craftsmen with conventional cameras and artistic skills; rather, they came in three main types. First were larger, more technically savvy printing companies with professional salespeople pushing bundled pricing, integrating pre-press services with printing in a single package. Rivals here consisted of national printers with multimillion dollar and billion dollar-plus revenues like R. R. Donnelley & Sons Co. and Quad Graphics, which had integrated backward into pre-press services over the last decade. Another significant rival type was represented by the horizontally integrated national pre-press houses or "trade shops" such as American Color and Wace/Techtron—highly entrenched, multi-million dollar pre-press service providers backed by national sales networks of service professionals and multiple physical plant locations across the United States. These companies competed in several different submarkets beyond catalogs, e.g., inserts, comic syndications, and coupons. A third rival type comprised other standalone firms that competed

with loose affiliations to other printers or advertising agencies, or that literally set up shop next door to their largest accounts to fend off potential competitors. Cha currently lacked a sales infrastructure similar to that of these competitor types, however.

Work Flow Organization at Colorscope   A "job" at Colorscope began when the customer placed an order. Customer Service representatives interacted with the customer on the phone and recorded the job specification details. Each order was "owned" by a particular representative, who, based on the specifications, did a "job preparation." A separate "job bag" was opened for each set of four pages for the order. The template of the job was created by physically cutting and pasting text, graphics, and photographs; extensive markings on the template specified the changes in font, color, shading, and layout. The next step in the production process was scanning, whereby the pictures were digitized and output as a computer file. Colorscope had three laser scanners.

The following step was assembly, performed on nine high-end, souped-up Macintosh computers, each with 256MB RAM and oversized computer terminals. The computers were networked and hooked up to the scanners, output devices, and a powerful file server with 40 gigabytes memory that contained archives of optical images. Operators worked on the computers composing the "job" with scanned images and text input from the keyboard. At this stage the operators changed colors and shades of the scanned picture to the exact specifications the customer demanded. Once a job was fully assembled, it was output on one of two high-end output devices. The output was a large sheet of four-color film that was then developed.

The "job" then flowed to Quality Control (QC) for proofing. Proofing involved comparing the hardcopy output with customer specifications. Reworks were initiated at this stage. QC might, for instance, require the job to be rescanned if it determined that the original scanning was flawed. Then the rescanned image would then have to be reassembled, re-output, and pass QC all over again. Once a job passed QC, it was shipped to the customer's printer either on a computer disk or, more usually, on film.

Colorscope's operators were cross-trained and could work on any stage of the production process. Work flow and production procedures were standardized but not documented. Colorscope relied instead on the institutional knowledge of its employees and frequent supervi-

---

[1]Local service bureaus could scan color film, layout pages, and output printer specified film with a minimal capital investment of less than $100,000.

sion by Andy Cha to maintain and improve operational efficiency.

The Future   By the spring of 1996, Cha realized that Colorscope had to capitalize on its biggest assets, its employees, who were all well trained and worked effectively as a team to meet deadlines. (See Exhibits 6 and 7.) The short-term strategy was to increase marketing efforts to drum up new business for the lean months that preceded the huge rush of orders to do pre-press for catalogs in the fall season before holiday shopping started. Exhibit 8 gives details of jobs completed in June 1996 and revenue generated from each customer. Revenue per page, however, was unlikely to improve due to competitive pressures. Cost containment and improving operational efficiency were, therefore, critical, particularly in reducing the amount of rework. This effort required the cooperation of its workers, and Cha was considering sharing the gains of such improvement with its employees. With this objective in mind, Colorscope began tracking hours spent on rework, which was broken down into hours spent on rework initiated by customer due to change in specifications, and rework caused by errors in-house. Colorscope compensated its line workers on an hourly wage basis. To keep track of hours worked, employees logged the hours spent on various jobs into a centralized computer from remote terminals.

(Exhibit 9 gives the hours spent at different workstations by different jobs in June 1996.) So tracking rework hours was fairly straightforward; employees recorded both types of rework hours separately for each job. (Exhibit 10 gives the rework hours recorded during June 1996.)

Another area for improvement was product pricing. At present Colorscope quoted more or less the same per-page price for different customers, plus additional charges for special effects. Yet different customers placed different demands on organizational resources, and this was not appropriately reflected in the price charged. However, Colorscope could not afford expensive accounting systems or to hire consultants to design a state-of-the-art activity-based cost system. Exhibit 11 gives selected financial information while Exhibit 12 gives materials expense, broken down by jobs, for the month of June 1996.

Questions for the Future   As Andrew Cha anticipated the celebration of Colorscope's twentieth year in business, he jotted down three questions that summed up the areas of improvement he felt were needed. How could Colorscope improve its operations? How could it change its pricing strategy? What accounting and control system should his company install?

EXHIBIT 1   Price Trend of Color Separations to Scan, Assemble, Proof and Output Printer Specified Film for a Hypothetical Direct Mail Catalog Page with One Image

Price/Page of work ($):		1991	1992	1993	1994	1995
Colorscope		1,100	900	750	650	600
Service-Bureau[2]		400	425	450	475	500

[1] Service -Bureaus such as Kinko's and Alphagraphics typically do jobs that are cheaper, and involve fewer and/or smaller pages.

EXHIBIT 2 How Technology Has Changed the Prepress Process.

Up until the early 1990s, before the dawn of desktop publishing, print production "end to end" for a hypothetical book required (excluding client approval times for merchandising) approximately 8 weeks on average. The average catalog client would hire different vendors to provide each service and coordinate the production process. The diagram below outlines how four separate companies would act in concert to produce a typical book.

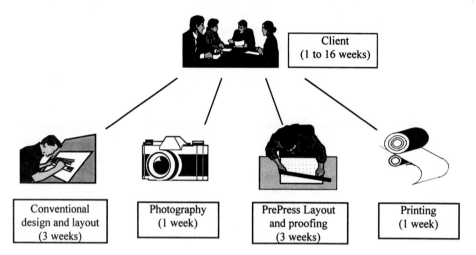

With the advent of desktop publishing, print production "end to end" times shrank on average by two weeks. Savings come mainly from time saved in the artists' and production technicians' capacity to make changes quickly and easily. Digital photography has potential to shrink photography times even further.

EXHIBIT 3 Top 25 American Printers and Specialization's

Rank	Company	Sales (Million $US)	Primary Business
1	R. R. Donnelley & Sons Co.	4,800	BK, CAT, DIR, FIN, INS, PUB
2	Hallmark Cards, Inc.	3,800	GC, SPC
3	Moore Corp. Ltd.	2,401	BF, SPC
4	Quebecor Printing, Inc.	2,116	BK, CAT, COM, INS, PUB
5	American Greetings Corp.	1,870	GC, SPC
6	Deluxe Corporation	1,748	BF, GC
7	World Color Press, Inc.	970	CAT, COM, DIR, PUB
8	Banta Corporation	811	BK, CAT, COM, PUB, SPC
9	Treasure Chest Advertising Co.	807	INS, SPC
10	Quad/Graphics, Inc.	801	CAT, COM, INS, PUB
11	Standard Register	767	BF, COM
12	UARCO, Inc.	599	BF, SPC
13	Wallace Computer Services, Inc.	588	BF, COM, SPC
14	American Business Products	563	BF, BK, PKG, SPC
15	AT&T Systemedia Group	560	BF
16	Gibson Greetings, Inc.	549	GC, SPC
17	Valassis Communications, Inc.	543	INS, SPC
18	John H. Harland Co.	521	BF, SPC
19	Taylor Corporation	488	COM
20	Sullivan Communications	475	BK, INS, PUB
21	Ringier America, Inc.	471	BK, CAT, INS, PUB
22	Reynolds & Reynolds	426	BF
23	Transcontinental Printing, Inc.	416	CAT, COM, INS, PUB
24	Western Publishing Co.	398	BK, CAT, DIR, PUB, SPC
25	Brown Printing Co.	384	CAT, INS, PUB

Business Category Abbreviations:

BF	Business Forms	DIR	Directories	PKG	Packaging
BK	Book Publishing	FIN	Financial	PUB	Publications
CAT	Catalogs	GC	Greeting	SPC	Specialty Printing
COM	Commercial	INS	Cards Inserts		

Source: American Printer, 1995

EXHIBIT 4 Time/Cost Breakdown for the Catalog Producer

Direct mail catalogers constituted over 90% of Colorscope's customers. To produce an average project run, in this example, 1 million copies of a 52-page catalog, costs would break down as follows:

Design (3 weeks), writing copy, producing layouts, gaining management approvals.	Photography (2 weeks), 200-300 images, studio and location shots.	Prepress (2 weeks), 2 rounds of proofs to the project manager.	Printing (3 days), cutting, binding, addressing for national distribution	Distribution (2-3 weeks), second class bulk rate post.
$10,000	$50,000	$30,000	$1,300,000	$120,000

EXHIBIT 5 Top American Pre-press Competitors (does not include printers that have integrated forward)

Company	Sales (M$US)	Employees	Facilities (sites)	Primary Business
WACE USA	200	1,850	20	magazines, direct mail, packaging
Applied Graphics Technologies	130	1,060	13	magazines, direct mail, packaging
Black Dot Group	109	900	12	mags, dir. mail, packaging, books
Schawk, Inc.	104	729	12	mags, dir. mail, packaging, agency
American Color	76	840	16	mags, dir. mail, pkg, agncy, newsp
Intaglio Vivi-Color	60	450	13	packaging
Enteron Group	56	400	4	mags, dir. mail, pkg, agncy, books
Kwik International	41	110	1	packaging, agency
Color Associates	37	390	1	packaging, publishing, catalogs
TSI Graphics	27	313	4	mags, dir. mail, packaging, books
Blanks Color Imaging	24	230	1	mags, dir. mail, packaging, agency
Kreber Graphics, Inc.	22	165	2	mags, dir. mail, pkg, agncy, retail

EXHIBIT 6 Key Personnel at Colorscope

Andrew ("Andy") Cha - founder and president, since 1976. In charge of operations and sales. Plays "bad cop" on the shop floor to make sure productivity stays ultra high. Major contribution to the business is his experience base which he leverages to close new sales.

Agatha ("Aggie") Cha - VP Marketing, since 1976. Works with her husband to nurture all client relationships and customer and prospect needs. Functions as head of human resources, making all hiring, firing, and salary recommendations. Also keeps the pulse of workers, keeping track of birthdays, anniversaries, etc.

Joe Cha son of Andrew and Agatha, HBS MBA 1996; Stanford BA in Economics 1991 and MA in Sociology 1992. Worked at Colorscope in marketing during 1993-94, bringing in several new customers; would be spending the summer of 1996 in improving operations and customer relations before moving to Shanghai to pursue a career in consulting.

John Gibson - controller, since 1981. Manages working capital, payroll, and all financing necessary to fund the business. Actually lives with the Cha family.

Ruth Fukushima - head of customer service, since 1980. Manages quality control and customer satisfaction while playing "good cop" on the shop floor to keep operators from burning out under Andrew Cha's management. Organizes company picnics, parties, and other celebrations.

Don Chin - technology director, since 1992. Manages data servers and keeps Andrew Cha on top of new technologies. Handles all new software training issues and is general fix-it man for all hardware problems. A technology whiz and Joe Cha's friend from their undergraduate days together at Stanford, Chin also helps to increase customers' comfort levels with new platforms and technologies.

EXHIBIT 7 Organization Chart

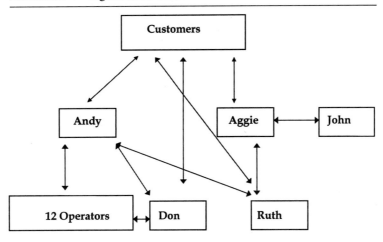

EXHIBIT 8 Jobs Completed in June 1996*

Job #	Customer #	Pages	Revenue
61001	10	16	$ 9,600
61002	10	16	9,600
61003	10	32	23,000
61101	11	16	12,000
61102	11	16	11,000
61201	12	16	11,000
61202	12	32	23,000
61203	12	32	22,000
61204	12	32	20,000
61301	13	128	50,000
61401	14	16	7,800
61402	14	16	8,000
61403	14	16	8,000
61404	14	16	9,000
61405	14	16	9,800
61501	15	16	11,000
61502	15	16	11,000
61601	16	32	20,000
61602	16	4	2,000
61603	16	4	1,400
61701	17	16	8,000
61702	17	16	10,000
61801	18	4	4,000
61901	19	4	2,000
61902	19	16	12,000
62001	20	1	0
Total		**545**	**$315,200**

* All figures are disguised

EXHIBIT 9 Hours Clocked at Different Workstations in June 1996*

JOB #	Job Preparation	Scanning	Assembly	Output	Quality Control	Total
61001	4	32	42	8	7	93
61002	3	24	38	8	8	81
61003	7	40	75	16	8	146
61101	4	16	30	4	4	58
61102	4	16	28	4	4	56
61201	4	16	32	4	6	62
61202	7	32	58	8	5	110
61203	6	34	64	8	6	118
61204	6	30	58	8	8	110
61301	15	130	250	32	30	457
61401	5	14	32	4	4	59
61402	4	19	32	8	7	70
61403	4	20	34	4	3	65
61404	4	22	36	4	5	71
61405	4	20	36	4	4	68
61501	4	21	39	4	4	72
61502	4	20	40	8	7	79
61601	7	26	60	8	9	110
61602	2	5	10	1	1	19
61603	2	5	11	2	1	21
61701	4	20	39	4	3	70
61702	4	20	41	4	5	74
61801	1	5	11	2	1	20
61901	2	5	12	1	1	21
61902	5	19	42	4	5	75
62001	1	1	2	1	1	6
Idle Time	43	28	128	37	13	249
Capacity	160	640	1280	200	160	2440

Hours clocked in different work stations include rework hours given in **Exhibit 10.**

* All figures are disguised

EXHIBIT 10 Rework Hours*

Rework due to change in specifications by customer

JOB #	Job Preparation	Scanning	Assembly	Output	Quality Control	Total
61001	0	16	10	4	2	32
61002	0	8	6	4	3	21
61301	2	5	10	2	2	21
61502	1	4	8	1	0	14
61801	0	1	3	1	0	5
61901	1	1	4	0	0	6
Total	**4**	**35**	**41**	**12**	**7**	**99**

Quality Control initiated rework of house errors

JOB #	Job Preparation	Scanning	Assembly	Output	Quality Control	Total
61301	1	3	4	1	1	10
61402	0	9	16	2	2	29
61403	0	10	14	2	1	27
61603	1	3	3	1	0	8
Total	**2**	**25**	**37**	**6**	**4**	**74**

In all four jobs that were subsequently reworked because Quality Control initiated rework, the original defects were introduced in the scanning stage of the operation. However, when a job is rescanned, assembly, output, and quality control all have to be redone.

---

* All figures are disguised

EXHIBIT 11 Selected Financial Information for June 1996*

Description	Job Preparation	Scanning	Assembly	Output	Quality Control	Idle	Total
Wages	$8,000	$32,000	$64,000	$10,000	$11,000		$125,000
Depreciation	$500	$25,000	$10,000	$14,000	$500		$50,000
Rent							$30,000
Others							$20,000
Total Overhead							$225,000
Floor Space in sq. ft.	1000	1000	4000	2000	500	6,500	15,000

*All figures are disguised

EXHIBIT 12 Materials Expense in June 1996*

Job #	Total Materials expense[3]	Customer initiated rework	Correction of house error
61001	$ 5,400	$2,700	
61002	3,500	1,100	
61003	4,500		
61101	1,800		
61102	1,500		
61201	1,500		
61202	3,300		
61203	3,400		
61204	3,200		
61301	13,000	1,000	$1,000
61401	1,800		
61402	3,100		1,000
61403	3,900		1,000
61404	2,100		
61405	2000		
61501	2200		
61502	3,600	1,500	
61601	3,300		
61602	600		
61603	1,000		500
61701	2100		
61702	2,500		
61801	1,600	1,000	
61901	1,700	1,000	
61902	2,200		
62001	200		
Total	$75,000	$8,300	$3,500

*All figures are disguised
[3]Includes materials for rework.

UNION PACIFIC (A)

Introduction

The cost numbers we get from the Planning and Analysis Group will be the bottom line, and no salesperson will quote a price below estimated cost. We need to have confidence in the numbers provided to us. Cost accounting is too complex a subject for me to be comfortable having marketing managers developing their own formulas or rules of thumb.

George Craig, Senior Vice-President for Marketing and Sales for the Union Pacific System, was commenting on the highly competitive environment for railroads in the deregulation era. Success in this environment mandated much tighter linkages between accounting

and marketing than had ever been required during the first 100+ years of railroading.

A railroad sells only three things: equipment, service, and price. Before 1980, price was determined by tariffs filed with the Interstate Commerce Commission (ICC) and therefore was not an issue except when we competed against other forms of transportation. Probably less than 15% of customers' decisions were determined by price. After the Staggers Rail Act, while service and equipment are still factors, 85% of our business is now won by being the low-price bidder. Even in our Intermodal business, in which we believe delivery time and service is critical, we recently lost a contract on only a $25 per trailer differential despite offering delivery 24 hours faster than our competitor. Now that really hurts.

We also enter into many long-term contracts, and we had better be sure that our prices cover our costs. We have over 5,000 contracts whose duration ranges from six months to

This case was prepared by Professor Robert S. Kaplan.
Copyright © 1985 by the President and Fellows of Harvard College. Harvard Business School case 186-177.

20 years. If we price too low on these contracts, we're going to put ourselves out of business.

On the other hand, if we price too high because our cost estimates are too conservative, we will lose lots of bids and sacrifice future growth. Some opportunities for bidding, especially for large utility companies, may arise only once every 15 years. That's why it is really critical for us to understand and know our true costs.

Cost Accounting

All accounting reports are subject to ICC reporting requirements which were modernized effective January 1, 1978.

Rail Form A, the venerable costing formula developed earlier this century by the ICC, takes the total operating expenses for a railroad and links them to the activities (service units) that are felt to best explain the incurrence of these expenses. Examples of such service units are gross ton miles, locomotive unit miles, train miles, car days, and engine switching minutes. ICC cross-sectional statistical studies of the railroad industry have estimated the average percentage that is variable of any given cost category (see Exhibit 1). The variable cost is then allocated among the various service units. After a long sequence of calculations, the total cost per service unit is obtained; that is, the cost per gross ton mile, cost per engine switching minute, etc. (see Exhibit 2 for a simplified format of Rail Form A). Appendix A contains an excerpt from an ICC publication describing the assignment of railroad operating expenses to service units.

The accounts specified in Rail Form A provided the chart of accounts used by Union Pacific to collect and control its costs into the 1960s. At that time, two major efforts were undertaken to improve its cost measurement system.

Cost Out All Traffic (Coat) System

In 1965, the company initiated an effort to develop the COAT (Cost Out All Traffic) system. The COAT system worked from the waybill for each carload move.

The waybill provided information on origin, destination commodity, lading tons, car type, and car ownership (whether a system, private, or a foreign[1] car). For any given move, the shortest distance between origin and destination was estimated. The system averages computed in Rail Form A were then used to cost out the

move. For example, costs that were assumed variable with gross ton miles were assigned based on the length of the move and the weight of the shipment. Costs based on car miles or carloads could similarly be apportioned. The cost of using a private or foreign car was estimated based on time and mileage charges applicable to that car, whereas depreciation, maintenance, and repair of system-owned cars were calculated based on Rail Form A averages. The Rail Form A averages of frequency of intertrain switches, interchange (between two roads) switches, and pickup and delivery costs were also included and costed to the move.

Union Pacific management recognized that the move-by-move cost and profitability information provided by COAT was not very accurate. Any time system-wide or industry-wide averages were used to cost out individual moves, the data could only provide a very rough estimate of the actual costs. Train size could vary greatly from the assumed average size, road conditions differed over the system and had a major impact on running costs, and switching time could vary by yard and by region. Also, the Rail Form A costs could understate the cost of special features which had been provided to attract certain forms of traffic. For example, along certain lines, extra-strength rail had been installed to carry the anticipated heavy traffic.

Thus, the COAT data could provide only a flag, a signal, for where more detailed analysis should be undertaken. But the more detailed analysis required an enormous work effort to determine whether the Rail Form A assumptions were valid in particular circumstances.

Despite these limitations, cost and profitability information from COAT alerted the company to instances where it could seek rate increases from the ICC on currently unprofitable business. Occasionally, Union Pacific tried to exit markets where it felt it was losing money, out-of-pocket, and where it could not get rate relief. Conversely, the COAT system also signaled which business looked highly profitable. Special attention was then devoted to keep that business and to make sure that rates were not raised which would jeopardize losing that business to other transportation forms.

Management Cost Control System

In 1968, a project to develop a Management Cost Control System (MCC) was initiated. MCC was a responsibility accounting system designed for the hierarchy of

---

[1] A system car is one owned by Union Pacific, a foreign car is owned by another railroad, and a private car is owned by a shipper or a private car line.

cost centers in the railroad. Approximately 5,000 cost centers were identified throughout the system; the operational definition of a cost center was either who spent money or who authorized an expense. About 1,500 different cost codes were used to accumulate expenses for all the cost centers.

Each cost center manager received a monthly report summarizing actual expenses in the cost center, with a comparison to budget and last year's expenses. (Exhibit 3 shows the first page of a monthly report for a locomotive repair facility.) Summary reports could be prepared by grouping cost codes into more aggregate categories and also by grouping similar cost centers within the same district.

Exhibit 4 shows the summary, by major expense categories, of the costs of the locomotive repair facility detailed in Exhibit 3. Exhibit 5 is the monthly summary of costs for all locomotive repair facilities, by location, and Exhibit 6 summarizes locomotive repair costs by major expense category. Similar cost reports are prepared for subunits in the engineering and transportation departments.

Special reports summarizing monthly and year-to-date operations were prepared for senior managers at the railroad's headquarters in Omaha. Exhibit 7 shows a monthly summary for the mechanical department featuring the cost of administration, diesel fuel, locomotive maintenance, and freight car maintenance. These costs are shown normalized by various activity measures: power unit miles, horsepower miles, serviceable locomotive and cardays, freight car miles, and gross ton miles. Exhibit 8 shows freight crew costs per thousand gross ton miles by geographical district. Exhibit 9 is the first page (of a nine-page report) showing operating statistics by train symbol; a train symbol denotes a particular regularly scheduled train that runs between two hubs. The following monthly train statistics are displayed and compared to the corresponding month in the prior year:

- Average tons/train
- Average horsepower/train
- Average initial terminal delay (ITD) minutes
- Average final terminal delay (FTD) minutes
- Average road speed
- Crews called

These monthly and year-to-date summaries were frequently accompanied by extensive tables and charts to facilitate analysis of unusual conditions and trends.

The MCC system was first installed in the early 1970s. For several years, it was run in parallel with the ICC system (used to generate data for Rail Form A and other ICC reports). Eventually, as the system became accepted and actively used as a management reporting tool, MCC became the sole internal system.

The Future

As deregulation loomed over the horizon in the late 1970s, Union Pacific management knew that many old ways of doing business would not survive. More aggressive attention to marketing and pricing would clearly be necessary. MCC and COAT were among the most advanced cost systems in the entire industry. But would they be adequate for the turbulent years ahead?

EXHIBIT 1

UNION PACIFIC (A)

Variability Percents Used in Rail Form A Application

(Based on Study by ICC Section of Cost and Valuation)

FREIGHT EXPENSE VARIABLE	RELATED OUTPUT (%)	
Maintenance of way and structures		
Yard and way switching tracks	Yard and train switching hours	55%
Running tracks	Gross ton miles	57
Other	Tons of revenue freight	60
Maintenance of equipment:		
Yard locomotive repairs	Yard switching locomotive unit miles	82
Train locomotive repairs	Freight gross ton miles	68
Freight car repairs	Freight car miles	86
Other	Tons of revenue freight	79
Transportation—rail line:		
Yard expenses	Yard switching hours	96
Train expenses	Freight train miles	97
Station employees—platform	Not applicable	100
Other	Tons of revenue	44
Freight tax accruals	Tons of revenue	72
Traffic, miscellaneous operations, and general	Other operating expenses	70

EXHIBIT 2

UNION PACIFIC (A)

Rail Form A Formula Costs

COST CATEGORY	VARIABILITY (%)	VARIABLE COST	GROSS TON MILES (GTM)	LOCOMOTIVE UNIT MILES (LUM)	ENGINE MINUTES (EM)
Transportation					
Yard switching fuel	96	xxx			xxx
Train fuel	97	xxx	xxx	xxx	xxx
Yard enginemen	96	xxx			
.	.	.	.		
.	.	.	.		
.					
Maintenance of equipment					
Locomotive repairs—yard	82	xxx			xxx
Locomotive repairs—road	68	xxx	xxx	xxx	xxx
.	.	.	.	.	.
.	.	.	.	.	.
.					
Maintenance of way					
Rail yard switching track	55	xxx			xxx
Rail running track	57	xxx	xxx	—	—
Total expense			xxx	xxx	xxx
Total activity (units)			GTM	LUM	EM
Unit cost:					
Total expense/number of service units			$/GTM	$/LUM	$/EM

EXHIBIT 3 Union Pacific (A): Form 3860—Final Management Cost Control Report
Detail of Costs for December 1976

NORTH PLATTE DIESEL FACILITY — LOCO DEPT.

CURRENT MONTH VARIANCE FROM					YEAR TO DATE VARIANCE FROM		
ACTUAL	BUDGET	LAST YEAR	COST CODE	DESCRIPTION	ACTUAL	BUDGET	LAST YEAR
17,148	2,748*	44,931*	1100	Officers	185,713	12,913*	42,144*
69,945	11,065	9,016*	1111	Supervisory Personnel—Agrmnt.	816,406	134,693	115,084*
3,199	1,523*	1,686*	1112	Supervisory Personnel—Non Agrmnt.	27,097	6,985*	1,504*
1,382	27*	199*	1114	Chief and Assistant Chief Clerk—Non Agrmnt.	15,108	1,153	1,484*
2,491	653	1,032*	1122	Professional and Administrative—Non Agrmnt.	36,448	1,291	6,242*
2,682	1,337*	1,469*	1124	Technical and Clerical—Non Agrmnt.	23,243	7,103*	9,405*
10,996	56	76*	1137	General Clerical Personnel—Agrmnt.	136,050	6,205*	27,919*
76,336	11,912	2,434	1201	Rep & Mntce Loco—Propulsion Engines	986,130	73,427	157,523*
2,242	758*	1,089	1202	Rep & Mntce Loco—Turbochargers	26,138	10,714*	5,201*
18,258	3,145	1,019	1203	Rep & Mntce Loco—Traction Mtrs.—Excl Gears	224,852	26,418	31,209*
101,812	22,519	24,839*	1204	Rep & Mntce Loco—Other Electrical	1,194,245	153,803	310,544*
24,301	5,706	919*	1205	Rep & Mntce Loco—Running Gear	288,823	56,970	41,463*
149,838	86,504	13,556*	1206	Rep & Mntce Loco—Other repairs	1,721,891	1,028,900	223,272*
11,865	7,662	517	1208	Rep & Mntce Loco—Painting	168,249	58,408	25,113*
34,194	37,646	1,713*	1211	Rep & Mntce Loco—Federal Inspections	411,342	417,067	61,717
16,034	1,065*	1,692*	1212	Rep & Mntce Loco—Lubrication	189,172	15,398*	71,099*
15,051	4,532	480*	1213	Rep & Mntce Loco—Wheel Truing	155,880	76,747	11,796
1,429	1,347*	1,141*	1221	Rep & Mntce Cabooses—General	6,246	5,280*	5,424*
79	79*	79*	1231	Rep & Mntce Frt Cars—Car Body & Underframe	90	90*	40
			1233	Rep & Mntce Frt Cars—Couplers & Craft Gears			68
		39	1234	Rep & Mntce Frt Cars—Brake Equipment	185	185*	369
35	35*	35*	1236	Rep & Mntce Frt Cars—Interior Loading Device	35	35*	35*
			1239	Rep & Mntce Frt Cars—Other Repairs	57	57*	10
			1241	Rep & Mntce Frt Cars—Inspection	21	21*	21*
			1242	Rep & Mntce Frt Cars —Lubrication			45
9,508	8,454	319*	1251	Shop Order Labor	108,890	99,859	13,017
			1252	Store Order Labor	54	54*	54*
56	38	141	1371	Rep & Mntce Automotive Equipment	496	616	257
769	646*	387*	1380	Rep & Mntce Work Equipment	6,505	5,062*	3,996*
8,181	7,253*	1,830*	1390	Rep & Mntce Shop & Power Plant Machinery	89,750	5,138	15,057*
			1403	Cleaning Covered Hoppers	623	623*	623*
			1406	Cleaning & Servicing Cabooses	81	81*	45*
			1409	Freight Car Servicing	577	577*	532*
			1500	Dismantling Road and Equipment Property	22	22*	22*
			1510	Cleaning Wrecks	83	83*	83*
104,207	26,989*	11,191*	1530	Fueling & Servicing Locomotives	1,264,974	391,842*	580,647*
			1540	Transfer or Adjust Loads	571	571*	412*
8,670	1,631*	3,144*	1630	Equipment Operators	77,157	4,117	26,001*
			1640	Power Plant Labor	78	78*	36*
26,675	1,796*	3,301*	1691	Miscellaneous Labor—Agrmnt.	299,636	11,136*	94,279*
			1699	Undistributed—Payroll Errors			25
39,350	2,895	4,883*	1740	Hostlers	446,306	47,680	62,555*
			1791	Bak Pay—Non Operating	356,294	356,294*	213,857*
			1792	Back Pay—Operating			11,507
		38,382	1793	Accrued Liabilities—Non Operating	313,773	313,773	627,545

*Variance—Unfavorable

26

EXHIBIT 4

UNION PACIFIC (A)

Mechanical Department—North Platte Diesel Shop

Detail of Expenses

(December 1976)

Date Prepared 01-12-77

Time Prepared 20.42.03

| CURRENT MONTH | | | | | | YEAR TO DATE | | | | |
ACTUAL ($)	DEVIATION BUDGET ($)	(%)	LAST YEAR ($)	(%)		ACTUAL ($)	DEVIATION BUDGET ($)	(%)	LAST YEAR ($)	(%)
					% Payroll & related expenses:					
758	153	16.8	82*	12.2*	Straight time	8,913	1,813	16.9	1,771	24.8*
39	15	28.2	3*	10.5*	Overtime	480	110*	29.7	23	4.6
			38	$$$	Accrued liabilities and back pay	42	42*	$$$*	425	90.9
40	23	36.4	1	4.6	Health & welfare	629	121	16.1	184*	41.3
47	5*	14.0*	25*	117.5*	Vacation accruals	577	53*	10.1*	139*	31.8*
66	66*	$$$*	37*	125.9*	Holiday	319	319*	$$$*	82*	34.8*
1	1*	$$$*	*	48.3*	Sick leave	27	27*	$$$*	5*	24.6*
4	*	2.2*	3*	176.4*	Other allowances	72	17*	32.2*	30*	72.8*
159	13*	9.2*	34*	27.1*	Payroll taxes	1,763	47*	2.7*	410*	30.3*
	37*	$$$*			Vacation pay—Actual		410*	$$$*		
$1,119	66	5.6	146*	15.1*	Total	$12,826	906	6.5	2,175*	20.4*
					Less credits:					
	*	$$$*	1*	$$$*	Investment accounts	.—	*	30.3*	2*	73.8*
9—	11	54.8*	2	26.7	Other credits	122—	125*	50.5*	36*	23.0*
9—	11*	55.1*		3.4	Total credits	123—	125*	50.4*	39*	24.1*
1,109	55	4.7	146*	15.2*	Net payroll & related expenses	$12,703	780	5.7	2,214	21.1*
					Material & supplies:					
392	9	2.3	3	.8	Repair parts & material	4,924	164*	3.4*	836*	20.4*
217	13*	6.6*	63*	41.2*	Lubricants	2,618	216*	9.0*	335*	14.7*
1	1	56.9		16.3	Gasoline	11	17	60.3	7	37.7
31	4	12.4	28	47.4	Shop supplies	380	48	11.2	1*	.3*
6	5	46.6	15	70.3	Locomotive & train supplies	84	61	42.2	39	32.1
40	3	7.9	25	38.0	Miscellaneous materials & supplies	730	208*	39.9*	210*	40.5*
689	11	1.5	8	1.2	Total material & supplies	8,750	462*	5.5*	1,336*	18.0*
26	17*	217.7*	5*	24.1*	Utilities	249	165*	197.3*	126*	103.3*
	*	241.3*		50.1	Repair & maintenance contracts	7	4*	195.8*	3*	79.1*
3	1*	152.2	2*	226.5*	Miscellaneous contracts	16	1*	8.4*	2*	21.9*
		$$$		$$$	Travel & entertainment	6	1*	33.1*	2	24.3
20	15*	324.7*	12*	146.5*	Miscellaneous expenses	96	37*	64.5*	160*	250.5*
					Less credits to operating expenses:					
	3*	95.6*	*	61.1*	Investment accounts	6	50*	114.2*	34*	122.5*
	2*	$$$*	2*	$$$*	Other credits	1—	24*	93.6*	20*	92.4*
					Car cleaning trans to transportation	.—		$$$		$$$
					Cab clean & service TFD to transportation	.—		$$$		128.6
	5*	97.2*	2*	93.4*	Total credits	3	74*	105.6*	54*	107.8*
1,850	24	1.3	158*	9.3*	Total mechanical operating expenses	21,833	33	.1	3,896*	21.7*
1,850	24	1.3	158*	9.3*	Total North Platte diesel shop	21,833	33	.1	3,896*	21.7*

EXHIBIT 5

UNION PACIFIC (A)

Mechanical Department—Locomotive Facilities

Summary of Expenses

(December 1976)

Date Prepared 01-12-77
Time Prepared 20.42.03

CURRENT MONTH						YEAR TO DATE				
	DEVIATION						DEVIATION			
ACTUAL	BUDGET		LAST YEAR			ACTUAL	BUDGET		LAST YEAR	
($)	($)	(%)	($)	(%)		($)	($)	(%)	($)	(%)
13,813	11,980*	653.3	11,880*	614.7*	Locomotive facility—Omaha	35,843	14,050*	64.4*	20,302*	130.6*
1,850	24	1.3	158*	9.3*	Locomotive facility—No. Platte	21,833	33	1	3,896*	21.7*
1,006	67	6.3	44*	4.6*	Locomotive facility—Salt Lake	12,272	1		1,731*	16.4*
555	76	12.0	1	.3	Locomotive facilities—East Dist.	7,247	94*	1.3*	725*	11.1*
1,378	134*	10.7*	28	2.0	Locomotive facilities—West Dist.	16,887	2,141*	14.5	2,315*	15.8*
18,604	11,945*	179.3*	12,053*	183.9*	Total locomotive facilities	94,084	16,251*	20.8*	28,972*	44.4*

EXHIBIT 6

UNION PACIFIC (A)

Mechanical Department—Locomotive Facilities

Detail of Expenses

(December 1976)

CURRENT MONTH						YEAR TO DATE				
	DEVIATION						DEVIATION			
ACTUAL	BUDGET		LAST YEAR			ACTUAL	BUDGET		LAST YEAR	
($)	($)	(%)	($)	(%)		($)	($)	(%)	($)	(%)
					% Payroll & related expenses:					
3,040	480	13.6	325*	11.9*	Straight time	35,757	5,409	13.1	6,451*	22.0*
146	29	16.9	90	38.1	Overtime	2,109	615*	41.1*	41*	2.0*
			170	$$$	Accrued liabilities and back pay	174	174*	$$$*	1,836	91.3
162	83	34.0	8	5.0	Health & welfare	2,522	359	12.4	678*	36.8*
229	23*	11.2*	120*	110.2*	Vacation accruals	2,965	298*	11.1*	516*	21.0*
264	264*	$$$*	149*	130.2*	Holiday	1,280	1,280*	$$$*	313*	32.4*
9	9*	$$$*	1*	20.8*	Sick leave	113	113*	$$$*	7	6.0
24	6*	33.1*	8*	51.0*	Other allowances	350	131*	59.9*	140*	66.6*
643	80*	14.2*	133*	26.2*	Payroll taxes	7,159	573*	8.6*	1,560*	27.8*
	199*	$$$*			Vacation pay—actual		2,163*	$$$*		
4,521	11	.2	469*	11.5*	Total	52,435	418	7	7,858*	17.6*
					Less credits:					
32−	11	57.1	2*	5.8*	Investment accounts	335−	92	38.1	28	9.2
78−	72*	48.1*	23	42.5	Other credits	989−	764*	43.5*	213*	17.7*
110−	61*	35.4*	21	23.9	Total credits	1,324−	672*	33.6*	185*	12.2*
4,410	49*	1.1*	448*	11.3*	Net payroll & related expenses	$51,110	253*	.4*	8,043*	18.6*
					Material & supplies:					
1,700	663	28.0	661	27.9	Repair parts & material	31,138	3,081*	10.9*	8,110*	35.2*
385	105	21.5	50	11.6	Lubricants	5,245	252	4.5	181*	3.5*
4	4*	$$$*	.	6.6	Fuel	54	54*	$$$*	24*	85.4*
15	1*	9.2*	1	6.6	Gasoline	143	20	12.2	4	3.2
97	2	2.6	81	45.6	Shop supplies	1,486	243*	19.6*	246*	19.8*
21	7	26.2	22	50.9	Locomotive & train supplies	266	78	22.7	36	12.0
259	48*	23.1*	25	8.8	Miscellaneous material & supplies	3,096	604*	24.2*	612*	24.6*
2,483	725	22.6	842	25.3	Total material & supplies	41,431	3,632*	9.6*	9,134*	28.2*
92	22*	31.3*	23*	33.9*	Utilities	972	150*	18.3*	155*	18.9*
8	1	15.1	6	43.9	Repair & maintenance contracts	104	17	14.1	1*	.9*

13	,	.3	*	2.9*	Miscellaneous contracts	197	40*	25.8*	48*	32.1*
3	.	3.4	3	46.4	Travel & entertainment	59	11*	22.8*	5	8.1
34	19	122.2*	14*	68.2*	Miscellaneous expenses	326	138*	73.6*	244*	297.6*
					Less credits to operating expenses:					
	*	$$$*	*	$$$*	AAR billing credits	1−	4*	67.7*	1*	46.1*
11,563	12,562*	$$$*	12,395*	$$$*	Investment accounts	24	11,828*	99.7*	11,035*	99.7*
2−	24*	90.4*	23*	89.9*	Other credits	58−	285*	83.0*	325*	84.8*
−	*	40.7*	.	23.9	Car cleaning trans to transportation	8−	3	90.5	2	48.0
2−	2	252.7	.	9.0	Cab clean & service TFD to transportation	24−	15	162.2	8	50.0
11,557	12,586*	$$$*	12,418*	$$$*	Total credits	117−	12,099*	99.0*	11,351*	98.9*
18,604	11,949*	179.5*	12,053*	183.9*	Total mechanical operating expenses	94,084	16,309*	20.9*	28,972*	44.4*
	4	$$$			% retirements		57	$$$		
18,604	11,945*	179.3*	12,053*	183.9*	Total locomotive facilities	94,084	16,251*	20.8*	28,972*	44.4*

EXHIBIT 7 Union Pacific (A): Union Pacific Railroad Company, Mechanical Department Cost Report—October 1983

	OCTOBER 1980	NET CHANGE FROM LAST YEAR* ( ) —INCREASE		YEAR-TO-DATE 1980	NET CHANGE FROM LAST YEAR*		TWELVE MONTH AVERAGE 11/79–10/80	CHANGE %
		AMOUNT	%		AMOUNT	%		
Administratives								
CMO—Staff & Admin.	$1,104,926	$(47,916)	(5)	$10,329,793	$(255,692)	(2)	$ 993,778	(4)
R&S Engr.—Staff & Gen.	144,439	(20,600)	(19)	1,290,845	(27,212)	(2)	122,367	3
Total Administrative	$1,249,365	$(66,516)	(7)	$11,620,638	$(282,904)	(2)	$1,116,145	(3)
Diesel Fuel								
Cost Per Power Unit Mile	$ 2.20	$ 0.17	9	$ 2.16	$ 0.11	8	$ 2.01	13
Million Horsepower Miles	$ 730.81	$ 11.10	2	$ 699.24	$ 14.62	3	$ 648.95	19
Power Unit Hour	$ 61.32	$ 1.20	2	$ 59.47	$ 1.14	3	$ 54.95	9
Service Loco. Day	$ 518.46	$ 40.71	9	$ 490.26	$ 22.15	7	$ 459.99	11
Locomotive Maintenances								
Cost Per Power Unit Mile								
Direct (Labor & Matl.)	$ 0.8189	$ 0.0465	6	$ 0.7577	$ 0.0606	8	$ 0.7330	11
General	0.1091	0.0697	42	0.1516	0.0326	20	0.1519	18
Lubricants	0.0778	0.0059	9	0.0657	0.0028	5	0.0609	9
Total Cost/Power Unit Mile	$ 1.0058	$ 0.1221	12	$ 0.9750	$ 0.0980	10	$ 0.9458	12
Cost Per Million Horsepower Miles								
Direct (Labor & Matl.)	$ 271.66	$ (3.22)	(1)	$ 246.69	$ 8.64	4	$ 235.91	8
General	36.22	19.15	37	49.14	8.09	16	48.88	15
Lubricants	25.84	0.40	3	21.31	0.13	1	19.59	6
Total Cost/Mil. Horsepower Miles	$ 333.94	$ 16.33	5	$ 317.14	$ 16.66	6	$ 304.38	9
Cost Per Power Unit Hour								
Direct (Labor & Matl.)	$ 22.81	$ (0.16)	1	$ 20.90	$ 0.69	4	$ 19.98	7
General	3.04	1.63	37	4.18	0.68	15	4.14	15
Lubricants	2.17	0.04	3	1.81	0.01	1	1.66	5
Total Cost/Power Unit Hour	$ 28.02	$ 1.51	5	$ 26.89	$ 1.38	5	$ 25.78	9

continued

EXHIBIT 7 *(continued)*

	OCTOBER 1980	NET CHANGE FROM LAST YEAR* ( ) —INCREASE AMOUNT	%	YEAR-TO-DATE 1980	NET CHANGE FROM LAST YEAR* AMOUNT	%	TWELVE MONTH AVERAGE 11/79–10/80	CHANGE %
Cost Per Serviceable Loco. Day								
Direct (Labor & Matl.)	$ 192.88	$ 11.21	7	$ 172.26	$ 11.67	7	$ 167.04	9
General	25.69	16.48	42	34.46	6.98	10	34.61	16
Lubricants	18.33	1.41	9	14.94	0.51	4	13.87	7
Total Cost/Serviceable Loco. Day	$ 236.90	$ 29.10	13	$ 221.66	$ 19.36	9	$ 215.52	10
Freight Car Maintenance								
Cost Per Hundred Freight Car Miles								
Direct (Labor & Matl.)	$ 3.9080	$ 0.1607	4	$ 4.1538	$ 0.1253	3	$ 3.9282	8
General	1.0314	(0.0124)	(1)	0.9862	0.0638	7	0.9538	8
Lubricants	0.0107	0.0041	34	0.0163	0.0039	24	0.0165	25
Total Cost/Hund. Freight Car Miles	$ 4.9501	$ 0.1524	3	$ 5.1583	$ 0.1930	4	$ 4.8985	8
Cost Per Thousand Gross Ton Miles								
Direct (Labor & Matl.)	$ 0.5764	$ 0.0289	5	$ 0.6114	$ 0.8269	5	$ 0.5796	10
General	0.1521	(0.0006)	—	0.1452	0.0114	8	0.1407	10
Lubricants	0.0016	0.0006	34	0.0024	0.0060	25	0.0025	26
Total Cost/Thou. Gross Ton Miles	$ 0.7301	$ 0.0289	4	$ 0.7590	$ 0.8443	5	$ 0.7228	10
Cost Per Serviceable Car Day								
Direct (Labor & Matl.)	$ 4.3282	$0.3032	7	$ 4.5222	$ 0.0038	—	$ 4.3162	3
General	1.1423	0.0168	1	1.0737	0.0374	4	1.0481	3
Lubricants	0.0119	0.0050	36	0.0178	0.0037	21	0.0181	21
Total Cost/Serviceable Car Day	$ 5.4824	$ 0.3250	6	$ 5.6137	$ 0.0449	1	$ 5.3824	3

EXHIBIT 8

UNION PACIFIC (A)

Through and Local[1]
Comparison of Through and Local Freight Crew Cost
per Thousand Gross Ton Miles after Deflation
for Wage Increases Granted

	JAN. 1978 CREW COSTS PER 000 GTM	JAN. 1978 DEFLATED FOR WAGE INCREASES[2]	JAN. 1977 CREW COSTS PER 000 GTM	VARIANCE AMOUNT	PERCENT
Nebraska	.537	.504	.509	−.005	−1
Wyoming	.628	.589	.566	+.023	+4
Kansas	.602	.565	.662	−.097	−15
Eastern district	.581	.545	.554	−.009	−2
Utah	.776	.728	.680	+.048	+7
California	.896	.841	.773	+.068	+9
South Central district	.816	.765	.711	+.054	+8
Idaho	.816	.765	.838	−.073	−9
Oregon	.934	.876	.911	−.035	−4
Northwestern district	.868	.814	.869	−.055	−6
Total system	.674	.632	.647	−.015	−2

[1] Does not include zone locals.
[2] Compound wage inflation effect of 6.6% removed.
− favorable, + unfavorable.

Appendix A

RAIL FORM A

ASSIGNMENT OF EXPENSES TO SERVICES AND
ASSOCIATION OF THE EXPENSES WITH SERVICE UNITS

EXPENSE GROUP AND SERVICE TO WHICH ASSIGNED	SERVICE UNIT WITH WHICH ASSOCIATED	EXPENSE GROUP AND SERVICE TO WHICH ASSIGNED	SERVICE UNIT WITH WHICH ASSOCIATED
Maintenance of Ways and Structures		Depreciation, freight-train cars	
		Mileage portion (70%)	
Yard and way switch tracks:		Running	Car miles
Related to distance	Car miles	Switching	
Unrelated to distance	Cars	Related to distance	Car miles
		Unrelated to distance	Cars
Running tracks	Gross ton miles	Time (car-day) portion (30%)	
		Running	Car miles
Station and office buildings		Switching	
Running	Gross ton miles	Related to distance	Car Miles
Station platform	Carload tons	Unrelated to distance	Cars
Other station (clerical)		**Transportation—Rail Line**	
Line-haul traffic	Carload		
Terminal switching	Cars	Dispatching: running	Gross ton miles
Other structures		Station platform labor	Car load tons
Running	Gross ton miles		
Switching		Station labor, nonplatform	
Related to distance	Car miles	Train work, running	Gross ton miles
Unrelated to distance	Cars	Station clerical	
		Carload traffic	Carload shipments
Maintenance of Equipment		Switching	Carload cars
		Special services	Carload shipments
Locomotive repairs			
Running	Gross ton miles	Yard and train expenses	
Switching		Running	Gross ton miles
Related to distance	Car miles	Switching	
Unrelated to distance	Cars	Related to distance	Car miles
		Unrelated to distance	Cars
Freight-train car repairs		**Traffic, General, and Miscellaneous**	
Mileage portion (70%)			
Running	Gross ton miles	General office clerks—waybills	
Switching		Station clerical	
Related to distance	Car miles	Line haul	Carload shipments
Unrelated to distance	Cars	Switching	Carload cars
Time (car-day) portion (30%)			
Running	Car miles	General office clerks—claims	
Switching		Loss and damage	
Related to distance	Car miles	Line haul	Carload tons
Unrelated to distance	Cars	Switching	Carload cars switched
Depreciation, locomotives		Loss and damage	Apportioned over all other expenses
Running	Gross ton miles		
Switching			
Related to distance	Car miles	Traffic, general office	Apportioned over all services
Unrelated to distance	Cars	expenses, taxes, miscellaneous	

EXHIBIT 9 Union Pacific: Train Statistics Change Report: October 1978 vs 1977, Report No. 01, 11/21/78

		AVERAGE TONS/TRAIN			AVERAGE HP PER TON			AVERAGE ITD MINUTES		
DIRC	SYMBOL	CURRENT YEAR	PRIOR YEAR	% CHANGE	CURRENT YEAR	PRIOR YEAR	% CHANGE	CURRENT YEAR	PRIOR YEAR	% CHANGE
E	ABNP	6,023	4,699	28%	1.7	2.5	− 32%	49	52	− 6%
E	ACKP	8,610	7,307	18%	1.9	2.0	− 5%	109	18	506%
E	ACUE	2,875	2,918	− 1%	4.7	4.9	− 4%	24	18	33%
E	AFCCP	7,142	4,935	45%	1.3	2.0	− 35%	12	4	200%
E	AKO	5,227	4,919	6%	1.2	1.7	− 29%	2	36	− 94%
E	ARIP	7,110	6,691	6%	2.0	1.7	18%	63	74	− 15%
E	RKL	7,727	7,857	− 2%	1.8	1.9	− 5%	19	19	0%
E	ABV		5,530		0.0	2.4			3	
E	ABPX	4,134	4,652	− 11%	3.4	3.1	10%	15	15	0%
E	AXPX	5,912	4,999	18%	1.9	2.5	− 24%	41	21	95%
E	BAX	2,852	2,802	2%	3.6	4.5	− 20%	15	24	− 38%
E	ERG	7,946	8,006	− 1%	1.1	1.1	0%	30	28	7%
E	BKL	7,546	8,297	20%	1.1	1.4	− 21%	28	30	− 7%
E	FNCA	3,761			3.2	0.0		49		
E	BNNP	4,159			2.9	0.0		25		
E	ENP	5,675	3,400	67%	1.7	3.8	− 55%	60	45	83%
E	BNBL	3,527			3.1	0.0		35		
E	YNVG	3,177			3.9	0.0		79		
E	SPUE		13,263		0.0	0.7			11	
E	FUS	4,040	4,381	− 7%	3.5	3.0	17%	8	6	33%
E	CN	4,532	4,307	5%	3.0	3.4	− 12%	29	25	16%
E	CNWP	5,639	5,884	13%	1.4	1.7	− 18%	66	85	− 22%
E	CDALE	8,922	6,175	44%	1.1	1.8	− 39%	11	12	− 8%
E	CONTR		2,981		0.0	4.9			27	
E	CPUE	13,398	13,635	− 2%	0.7	0.7	0%	30	19	58%
E	CRP	8,746	7,544	16%	1.8	1.9	− 5%	29	92	− 68%

EXHIBIT 9 *(continued)*

DIRC	SYMBOL	AVERAGE FTD MINUTES			AVERAGE ROAD SPEED			CREWS CALLED		
		CURRENT YEAR	PRIOR YEAR	% CHANGE	CURRENT YEAR	PRIOR YEAR	% CHANGE	CURRENT YEAR	PRIOR YEAR	% CHANGE
E	ABNP	43	36	19%	48	46	4%	31	30	3%
E	ACKP	51	5	920%	44	45	− 2%	28	58	− 52%
E	ACUE	13	21	− 38%	31	27	15%	62	60	3%
E	AFCCP	8	3	187%	37	42	− 12%	92	90	2%
E	AKO	6	37	− 84%	24	24	0%	23	59	− 61%
E	ARIP	96	83	16%	40	41	− 2%	25	31	− 19%
E	RKL	21	30	− 30%	30	30	0%	350	257	36%
E	ABV		11			44			167	
E	ABPX	28	22	27%	39	40	− 3%	216	245	− 12%
E	AXPX	28	23	22%	31	36	− 14%	61	172	− 65%
E	BAX	20	24	− 17%	53	56	− 5%	102	111	− 8%
E	ERG	25	30	− 17%	33	39	− 15%	98	89	10%
E	BKL	62	36	72%	33	39	− 15%	89	83	7%
E	FNCA	47			26			24		
E	BNNP	27			30			59		
E	ENP	32	26	23%	47	42	12%	32	32	0%
E	BNBL	48			27			39		
E	YNVG	63			21			14		
E	SPUE		20			32			20	
E	FUS	71	51	39%	30	27	11%	33	41	− 20%
E	CN	35	28	25%	32	37	− 14%	310	342	− 9%
E	CNWP	71	74	− 4%	43	44	− 2%	30	31	− 3%
E	CDALE	20	26	− 23%	30	27	11%	89	27	230%
E	CONTR		36			48			10	
E	CPUE	23	16	44%	37	34	9%	13	28	− 54%
E	CRP	22	43	− 49%	48	56	− 14%	43	29	48%

Union Pacific (B)

By the late 1970s, Union Pacific executives realized that a new competitive era would soon be unleashed. In addition to its traditional competition from other transportation forms, primarily trucking, and from surviving railroads after a wave of consolidations and mergers, the expected sharp reduction in ICC rate regulation would radically change the nature of competition. In this new environment, effective cost measurement systems would be essential if Union Pacific were to remain a vigorous competitor.

In late 1980, the CEO of Union Pacific asked John Rebensdorf, the head of the planning and analysis department, to develop a new system to measure the railroad's profits by line of business. The goals of the new system were easily explained.

> In a regulated environment, prices are set to cover the costs of the least efficient producers. With deregulation, prices will be established by the most efficient producers. We need to know our costs if we are going to be able to price aggressively, meet our competition, and maximize our profitability.

The recently developed Management Cost Control (MCC) system (see Union Pacific, A) provided valuable information on cost incurrence at detailed cost center levels. These data could be aggregated up to provide overall cost and productivity information on the railroad's transportation, engineering, and mechanical departments. While useful for cost control, MCC was not directly helpful to marketing managers, who wanted cost information on individual carload moves as they attempted to win business away from trucks and other railroads.

The Cost Out All Traffic (COAT) system provided estimates of the cost of each move, but the estimates were based on system- or industry-wide averages, with some of the parameters arising from studies done decades earlier. The estimates, therefore, did not reflect particular traffic patterns, train sizes, and operating procedures of Union Pacific, much less the considerable variation that existed within the Union Pacific system.

Basically, the railroad operated with two completely independent financial systems. The revenue system was

driven by the waybills produced for each move. The tariff on a waybill was a function of the origin and destination of the move, the type of commodity being moved, the weight of the shipment, the type of car used, plus any special features associated with the move. The specific costs, however, of a particular move could not be easily computed since the MCC system collected data only by the operating functions of the railroad: transportation, engineering, mechanical, and general and administrative.

Both systems, the revenue and the MCC system, performed effectively the functions for which they were designed. Overall railroad profits could be computed by subtracting all incurred costs from the revenues produced. But computing profits only on a system-wide basis was not very helpful in the emerging competitive environment for railroads. Management knew that certain of its business must be highly profitable whereas other lines of business were close to breakeven or losing money. Some individual moves were costed manually to reflect specific movement parameters, but this approach was cumbersome and time consuming. Without being able to relate specific costs incurred to the revenues produced on an individual move, product-line, or customer basis, it would be difficult for Union Pacific to use its new pricing freedom effectively.

Train and Car Movement Cost Systems

By 1985, the cost and profit planning area of the planning and analysis group had developed an integrated set of systems to cost out prospective and actual car moves. Extensive statistical studies had been performed to understand cost behavior and to choose service units that could be used to compute unit costs. These unit costs, derived from operating expenses and operating statistics, were combined with actual car and train moves to provide cost estimates for individual carload moves. Three separate systems had been developed and linked together.

Train Unit Cost System The goal of the Train Unit Cost (TUC) System was to develop train-related expenses on a train symbol and location specific basis. For example, costs would be collected for train ABC running from Los Angeles to North Platte, Nebraska. For each such train, the entire run was broken down into crew districts. A crew district is a segment of 100 to 300

This case was prepared by Professor Robert S. Kaplan.
Copyright © 1985 by the President and Fellows of Harvard College. Harvard Business School case 186-178.

miles that represents the basic unit of measurement for transportation, train, and engine crew expenses. The data input to TUC are daily train symbol operating statistics and specific crew wages by location. The train symbol operating service units include number and type of cars, number of locomotives, carload weights, gross ton miles, locomotive horsepower, locomotive miles, and train miles. These data are entered from each crew district via an on-line work order system and run in a batch mode on the system's central computer during the late night/early morning shift to prepare a daily Train Statistical Record.

Depreciation and repair costs for freight cars, locomotives, and cabooses were computed from the UP unit cost systems. Basically, these unit costs provided estimates of locomotive repair and depreciation costs per locomotive unit mile. These locomotive costs could then be allocated to freight carried by each train. Freight car repair and depreciation expenses were computed by another unit cost system and were directly allocated to a particular freight movement.

Fuel consumption was measured for each train and location based on locomotive units, train speed, gross ton miles, track conditions, and geography. The allocation was accomplished by an engineering model that predicted fuel consumption. At present, it was considered too expensive to measure actual fuel consumption by specific train symbol and location.

Finally, each train-related expense was divided by the gross ton miles for each train symbol to calculate train unit costs by symbol and location. The train-related costs per gross ton mile were transmitted to the two-car movement costing systems: Consolidated Profit Measurement System (CPMS) and Network Cost System (NCS). Appendix A provides a sample calculation from the Train Unit Cost System.

Consolidated Profit Measurement System

The Consolidated Profit Measurement System (CPMS) estimated the cost and profit of every railroad shipment. The system started with the estimated revenue of each shipment as collected by the waybills. The shipment was matched against actual car and train movements, as collected in the Train Unit Cost System and another car movement history system, to determine the actual operating parameters and service units for the shipment. That is, the system located the train used to carry the shipment and determined the actual train characteris-

tics: horsepower of locomotives, number of cars, tonnage, car miles, transit time, and routing.

Additional operating features were identified such as whether the car was leased or owned, whether the move resulted in an empty car return trip, the switching locations, and whether location-specific costs such as drayage and ramping were required. The planning and analysis group identified 21 primary cost categories to be measured when computing the total cost of a move. A summary of these 21 cost components is presented in Exhibit 1. An example of a sample CPMS computation appears in Appendix B.

By early 1985, the CPMS was able to match successfully shipment revenues with actual car moves more than 95% of the time. When a match with an actual car movement could not be made, averages for the previous month for that type of car movement were used to cost out the move. By using actual train movements to cost out a move, the CPMS calculation accounted for the variation in actual operating decisions. The estimated cost of a particular move was a function of the number and type of locomotives used, train weight, the speed of the train, the particular routing chosen, the number and location of switching activities, car type and ownership, and lading weight.

CPMS reports indicated where the railroad was and was not profitable and why, down to a detailed car-by-car basis. Profitability could be measured by the following:

- Market manager responsibility
- Shipper
- Commodity
- Traffic corridor
- Ramp
- Location (origin, destination, interchange)
- Equipment type

The CPMS cost calculations were run daily based on the automated revenue reporting system for completed trips and the Train Unit Cost System. By mid-1985, CPMS was costing out 6,000 to 8,000 carload movements each day plus almost that many movements of empty cars. Even though CPMS costed records on a daily basis, a summary profitability report was prepared only on a monthly basis. This monthly report consisted of four large books of printouts plus an executive summary. It was distributed only to the most senior management of the railroad. The estimated costs and profits by commodity, location, and train symbol were considered highly valuable and sensitive information. Hence, access to CPMS was restricted. Marketing people could, by request, get CPMS information move-by-move. An on-line system was being developed to permit access to the CPMS data base.

The CPMS was a retrospective system, providing monthly feedback on the profitability of actual carload moves. While a great advance over the highly aggregate and average cost-based COAT system, additional information was needed to support marketing and sales personnel. Marketing and sales managers needed cost estimates to price bids for prospective movements. In the old (regulated) days, special studies would be performed to cost out a particular move. Five full-time people performed these special studies, but they could not handle very many such requests. With deregulation, the planning and analysis group could envision receiving hundreds of requests each day from marketing and sales for cost estimates or rate changes.

Network Cost System

The Network Cost System (NCS) was a recently developed on-line model that permitted the cost of prospective moves to be estimated. It was designed to support the marketing department in preparing bids for new business. NCS developed both historical and projected cost estimates for specific moves based on detailed movement parameters specified by users.

In principle, the NCS would have required estimating costs between every possible origin and every possible destination. But the number of possible origin and destination combinations was so high that a simplified network approach was used for the system. With the network approach, each possible origin and destination was associated with its nearest hub. Any move to an origin or destination was assumed to go through its nearby hub. With this assumption, it was only necessary to calculate costs along the branch from each station to its neighboring hub and then to compute costs between adjacent pairs of hubs. The network approach permitted a considerable savings in computer code and running time.

A request by the marketing department for a cost estimate from the Network Cost System needed to contain at least the following information:

- Movement type (TOFC/COFC, manifest) and service level
- Origin
- Destination
- Routing (branches and main routes: hub to hub)
- Commodity type (STCC code)

- Car type (box, covered hopper, refrigerator [reefer], TOFC, automobile; also owned versus foreign car)
- Empty return assumption
- Commodity (lading) weight
- Time period for costs (today, in six months, one year from now)

For TOFC/COFC:

- Number of trailers/containers on flatcar
- Type of trailer/container

After receiving such a request, the Network Cost System estimated the costs of the proposed move. Exhibit 2 shows the format for output from NCS.

The total cost of a move was broken down into major cost categories: car, locomotive/caboose, overhead, train, terminal, and loss and damage. Each of these major cost categories was further broken down into subcategories (e.g., train cost included the costs of fuel, wages, maintenance of way, roadway depreciation, and line haul). All costs were summed to produce a total cost per car.

Because of the different time periods over which costs were incurred and the inherent jointness of many of a railroad's costs, the costs of prospective moves were prepared under various assumptions. The most-used classification was long-term variable cost. Even within this classification, NCS prepared two estimates. The ledger cost figure estimated depreciation and repair expense based on the book value of long-term assets (e.g., freight cars, locomotives, fixed plant, and track). The replacement cost figure used estimates of the replacement cost of long-term assets when computing depreciation, repair, and maintenance expenses. A fully allocated cost, again both ledger and replacement, was also computed.

The collection and allocation of costs for a particular move followed the same method used to prepare a CPMS estimate (see Appendix B).

The NCS cost estimate of a proposed commodity movement could vary significantly based on actual operating decisions such as the number and horsepower of locomotives, assumed train speed, routing used, and number of cars per train. Line-specific historical averages were used to estimate these parameters with the data coming from the actual operating parameters collected and stored in the Train Unit Cost System. Sensitivity analysis on train sizes, routing, car type/ownership, lading weight, and time period could be performed.

Most of the requests to NCS were to cost out the move of a carload shipment which would be part of a larger train. In addition, however, NCS had the capability to estimate the cost for a unit train; that is, a train entirely dedicated to a particular shipment. Unit train requests were most common for coal trains, TOFC, and intermodal operations.

Greg Broderick, director of the cost and profit planning area in the planning and analysis group, commented on the use of the NCS system.

By the summer of 1985, we were getting about 500 requests per day from the marketing people for cost analyses from NCS. In the current commercial environment, marketing and sales people need the capability to change rates every day. Without NCS, we would have needed 65 people doing nothing but preparing cost studies for bids, and probably doing these with lots of errors.

EXHIBIT 1

UNION PACIFIC (B)

CPMS Cost Components

(Primary Components)

COST COMPONENT	DESCRIPTION
1. Wage	1. Train crew wage costs. Actual wage costs by train symbol, including fringes.
2. Fuel	2. Train fuel consumption cost for train movement between origin/destination terminals. Fuel consumption estimated for each train reflecting actual train operating characteristics
3. Locomotive repairs/depreciation	3. Repairs reflect cost of maintaining locomotives including both labor, fringes, and material. Depreciation represents the recovery of the purchase cost over the economic life.
4. Maintenance of way	4. Consists of the costs of maintaining track and roadway, including labor, fringes, and material.
5. Roadway depreciation	5. Includes recovery of ownership costs on road property such as roadway buildings, office buildings, and other miscellaneous depreciable structures.
6. Other line haul	6. Major items include costs of dispatching trains, signal operation and maintenance, servicing locomotives, shop machinery, repairs/depreciation, and car inspection.
7. System car—repairs/depreciation	7. Repair costs of maintaining system cars, including labor fringes and material. Car depreciation reflects the purchase cost of a car and the recovery of the recovery of the cost over its economic life.
8. Foreign/private car—mileage and per diem	8. Cost reflects the per diem and/or per mile charge for foreign or private cars while on company's lines.
9. Car overheads	9. Includes wages of car department supervisory personnel (e.g., shop foreman) and other indirect costs associated with repair of cars.
10. Locomotive overheads	10. Wages of locomotive department supervisory personnel and other indirect costs associated with the repair of locomotives.
11. Transportation overheads	11. Wages and supplies of local transportation supervisory personnel and other transportation department staff.
12. General overheads	12. Costs of mechanical, engineering, and transportation department activities as well as other general and administration, traffic, and support functions.
13. Joint facility cost	13. Charges incurred for movement of car within or over facilities of another or group of railroads.

continued

14. Reciprocal switching	14. Charges incurred when the industry is located on another railroad and the terminal is open to reciprocal switching.
15. Switching	15. Switching costs are incurred when a car is (1) switched from a train to an industry, (2) switched from one railroad to another railroad, or (3) switched from one train to another. Costs include wages and fringes, supplies, fuel, locomotive repairs and depreciation, and maintenance and depreciation on yard tracks.
16. Other terminal	16. Major costs include expenses associated with preparing waybills and paperwork involved with car movement and cleaning cars.
17. Loss & damage costs	17. Loss and damage costs are claims paid out to shippers for commodities lost or damaged during shipment.
18. Drayage	18. Drayage includes the costs of moving a van over the road from the industry location to the ramping point, or vice versa. Costs include driver wages, fuel, and maintenance and depreciation on tractors.
19. Other TOFC/COFC costs	19. Includes ramp/deramp expense (labor and fuel) and depreciation on specialized equipment (cranes) used in the loading/unloading process.
20. Van rental	20. Rental cost for vans while on UP system.
21. Appurtenance rental	21. Rental on multilevel racks on a flatcar.

EXHIBIT 2

UNION PACIFIC (B)
Format for Network Cost System Estimate

	LONG-TERM VARIABLE		FULLY ALLOCATED	
	LEDGER	REPLACEMENT	LEDGER	REPLACEMENT
Car—System				
Repairs				
Depreciation				
Locomotive/caboose				
Repairs				
Depreciation				
Overhead				
Car				
Transportation				
Locomotive				
General				
Train				
Fuel				
Wages				
Maintenance of way				
Roadway depreciation				
Line haul				
Terminal				
Switching				
Other terminal				
Reciprocal switch				
Joint facility				
Loss & damage				
Total/car				

APPENDIX A

Development of train unit costs

I. System developed unit costs
   Locomotive depreciation per locomotive unit mile
   Locomotive repairs per locomotive unit mile
II. Train symbol operating costs by location
   System developed unit cost × train symbol operating statistic
   Crew wage cost from accounting department information
   Train fuel estimate × price per gallon
III. Train symbol unit costs by location
   Train symbol operating costs ÷ train symbol gross ton miles

Train unit cost per gross ton mile locomotive repairs

I. System developed unit cost
   Locomotive repair cost per locomotive unit mile—$.7407
II. Train unit cost system
   A. Train statistics:
      Z200 train of February 3, 1985
      Locomotive unit miles—300
      Gross ton miles—500,000
   B. Locomotive repair cost per gross ton mile

1. SYSTEM DEVELOPED UNIT COST		LOCOMOTIVE UNIT MILES		TOTAL TRAIN LOCOMOTIVE REPAIR COST
$.7407	×	300	=	$222.21

2. TOTAL TRAIN LOCOMOTIVE REPAIR COST		GROSS TON MILES		LOCOMOTIVE REPAIR PER GROSS TON MILE
$222.21	÷	500,000	=	$.000444

APPENDIX B

Sample train and car movement

TRAIN

Symbol	: Z200, XZ, Z400
Date	: February 1985
Origin city	: City A
Destination city	: City E

CAR

Identification	: ABX 003301
Date	: February 1985
Origin city on Z200 train	: City A
Destination city on Z400 train	: City D

(continued)

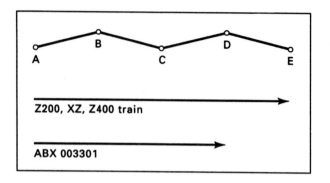

Train symbol operating statistics from train costing system

TRAIN SYMBOL Z200, ZX, Z400

CREW DISTRICT	TRAIN MILES	LOCOMOTIVE UNIT MILES	TRAIN WEIGHT	GROSS TON MILES	NUMBER OF CARS
A-B	100	300	5,000	500,000	90
B-C	50	150	5,500	275,000	100
C-D	150	300	4,500	675,000	80
D-E	200	600	4,000	800,000	70

TRAIN SYMBOL CREW WAGES
FROM ACCOUNTING DEPARTMENT

TRAIN SYMBOL Z200, ZX, Z400

CREW DISTRICT	CREW WAGES
A-B	$1,050
B-C	440
C-D	1,283
D-E	1,500

Car movement operation statistics

Identification	: ABX 003301
Date	: February 1, 1985
Train symbol	: Z200, XZ, Z400
Origin city	: City A
Destination city	: City D
Car gross weight	: 90 tons
Number of terminals	: 2
Terminal switching minutes	: 7 minutes
Miles by crew district	

A-B	100
B-C	50
C-D	150

Application of unit costs in the car movement costing systems

UNIT COSTS DIRECTLY FROM UNIT COST SYSTEMS

UP SYSTEM DEVELOPED UNIT COST		CAR MOVEMENT OPERATING STATISTICS	TOTAL COST
DESCRIPTION	VALUE		
Station clerical cost per terminal	$ 5.75	× 2 terminal minutes =	$11.50
Terminal switching cost per minute	$ 3.20	× 7 terminal minutes =	$22.40

UNIT COSTS REFINED THROUGH THE TRAIN UNIT COST SYSTEM

TRAIN UNIT COST DESCRIPTION	CREW DISTRICT	UNIT COST VALUE	CAR MOVEMENT OPERATING STATISTICS	TOTAL COST
Fuel cost per gross ton mile	A-B	$.0017	× (90 tons × 100 miles) =	$15.30
	B-C	$.0021	× (90 tons × 50 miles) =	$ 9.45
	C-D	$.0007	× (90 tons × 150 miles) =	$ 9.45
Wage cost per gross ton mile	A-B	$.0021	× (90 tons × 100 miles) =	$18.90
	B-C	$.0016	× (90 tons × 50 miles) =	$ 7.45
	C-D	$.0019	× (90 tons × 150 miles) =	$25.65

Example of CPMS computation of car movement cost and profit

COMPLETED CAR CYCLE

```
Car ID:  ABX 003301      CSN: 0027421902      Own:  P
Type:  B       AAR:  B300      L/E:  L      STCC:  XXXXXX      Lad:  034
Tare:  056      Start:  850201 13 52      End:  850206 05 20
Consignor:  ABC Company      Consignee:  XYZ Company
Orig:  City A      Dest:  City D      CGTM:  27,000
Per diem:  0.00      Milg-amt:  0.6300      Transit:  46.00      Car mi:  300
Orig-switch:  7.0      Orig-dtn:  128.0 hrs.
Des-switch:  7.0      Des-dtn:  79.6 hrs.
Intermed-switch:  City B 2.2      Dtn:  14.2hrs.
Intermed-switch:  City C 2.2      Dtn:  17.5 hrs.
```

CAR MOVEMENT DATA

EVENT	DATA	TIME	CITY	STATE	TRAIN
Release	02/01/85	1352	A	XX	—
Term. depart	02/03/85	2200	A	XX	Z200
Term. arrive	02/04/85	0430	B	XX	Z200
Term. depart	02/04/85	1845	B	XX	XZ
Term. arrive	02/04/85	2210	C	XX	XZ
Term. depart	02/05/85	1545	C	XX	Z400
Term. arrive	02/05/85	2000	D	XX	Z400
Act placed	02/06/85	0520	D	XX	—

(continued)

Car movement costed history (cost detail)

LOADED MOVEMENT—CITY A TO CITY D

Wage	$52
Fuel	34
Maintenance of Way	48
Locomotive repairs	12
Locomotive depreciation	6
Line haul	21
Car—mileage	189
Car—per diem	0
Term. switch—origin	22
Term. switch—destination	22
Term. switch—intermediate	12
Transportation overhead	10
Locomotive overhead	2
Car overhead	1
General overhead	56
Roadway depreciation	1
Other terminal	49
Total	$537

CPMS: car movement contribution calculation city A to city D

A. Loaded movement revenue		$1,000
B. Loaded movement cost (city A to city B)	$537	
C. Empty movement cost (city B to city A)	150	
Total cost of movement		$ 687
Movement contribution		$ 313
Movement profitability indicator (PI)		1.45

BROOKWOOD MEDICAL CENTER (A)
A COST EFFECTIVE HEALTH CARE SYSTEM

"In 1990, a major insurer asked us to bid on performing all of their open-heart surgeries in the Southeast United States. We prepared a bid by pulling charges on all (not just Medicare) patients we had treated in the four diagnostic related groups (DRGs) and applying the hospital-wide cost-to-charge ratio. We did not get the bid and had *no idea* whether to be disappointed or relieved. From talks with third-party payers and major employers, we believed that by the mid-1990s we would be bidding for portions of business, like open-heart surgeries, on a reg-

ular basis. We realized that we needed a much better understanding of costs at the DRG and individual patient levels if we're to be able to compete effectively."

Carolyn Johnson, Vice President of Finance

Introduction

By the end of the 1980s, cost management had become one of the most important issues faced by Brookwood Medical Center (BMC) administrators. BMC faced pressure from managed care providers such as health maintenance organizations (HMOs) and preferred provider

This case was prepared by Thomas L. Albright, University of Alabama, and Robin Cooper, Claremont Graduate School.
Copyright © 1998 by Institute of Management Accountants, Montvale, NJ.

organizations (PPOs) to keep medical costs low while continuing to provide high-quality health care services. For the first time, BMC was asked to bid on specific health care services for members of managed care insurance plans. To provide bids that were competitive yet profitable, hospital administrators needed detailed cost information about specific health care procedures. In addition, Medicare and other insurance providers moved to fixed fee reimbursement schedules, paying a defined fixed rate depending on a patient's diagnostic related group (DRG) and severity level. The use of fixed payment rates provided incentives for BMC to identify costs associated with providing health care to specific patients in each DRG. Health care providers realized that reductions in the average length of stay (ALOS) as a result of shorter inpatient hospital stays and increased outpatient services could decrease costs without decreasing the quality of care.

The New Cost System

As more payers moved to a fixed fee form of reimbursement, BMC administrators determined the existing cost system was not providing sufficiently accurate or detailed cost information. The old methodology provided aggregated cost data by department; but no reliable method existed to trace costs to individual patients or diagnostic groups. The new health care environment required hospitals to compete for managed care contracts and to make strategic decisions based on a solid understanding of costs.

Jan Kelly, director of cost accounting, identified the following issues to support the need for a new cost management system:

- *Unexplained variation in practice patterns.* Physicians largely drove the health care delivery process through treatment protocols and medical orders that determined patient charges and length of stay. A new cost system could help identify costs associated with specific physician practice patterns.
- *Concern with costs and more appropriate care.* BMC recognized the opportunity to reduce tests and procedures for patients (e.g., ordering a component test rather than a whole profile on bloodwork). Some inpatient testing and care could be effectively done on an outpatient basis due to advances in medications and other technology. Many diagnostic tests and longer inpatient stays may not result in better patient outcomes.
- *Questions regarding effectiveness.* Questions concerning the effectiveness of care, especially when evaluating new technology or treatments, were becoming increasingly

commonplace. Thus, BMC required more sophisticated cost management tools.

- *Beliefs regarding cost vs. value of care.* Balancing the quality of care with the costs of providing care was a fundamental concern for BMC. For example, if a new surgical procedure allows early discharge or little scarring but costs 10 times more than an old procedure, is it necessary for the hospital to offer the new procedure and incur additional costs? Executives had to identify a strategy for new technology and the existing methodology, management began to explore alternatives to the old cost accounting methodology. They required a cost system that would provide a product-line focus, i.e., open heart surgery, diabetes care, rehabilitation, or respiratory therapy, and that would permit segmentation of the patient population. Details of Mason's oncological study were reviewed, and the results reinforced the belief that costs calculated on a facility-wide basis were not helpful for making decisions that were DRG-specific.

In March 1991, BMC executives hired an Atlanta-based CPA firm to work with Kelly to gain an understanding of departmental operating costs and to build cost standards. They backloaded cost data for 20 months and identified two types of costs, direct and indirect. Meetings were held twice a week with key hospital administrators and clinicians to determine activities that caused costs.

BMC used a computerized information system known as Transition I (TSI) to assist with standard costing, financial modeling, and forecasting. The software allowed cost managers at BMC to identify activities, link activities to costs, and categorize costs based on predetermined or specific allocation bases. The system also generated simultaneous algebraic equations used to allocate indirect costs to revenue-generating departments. TSI allowed the creation of a database with cost and demographic information that could be sorted by both traditional and nontraditional demographic elements. Detailed information allowed BMC to obtain more accurate measurements of costs to provide care and to monitor and improve the quality of care provided to patients. For example, the patient number, length of stay, total charges, direct costs, and indirect costs for all appendectomy patients treated during a specific time period were summarized by the TSI system (see Table 1).

Direct Costs

Direct costs could be traced to a patient or procedure and included resources consumed in providing testing services, supplies, pharmaceuticals, and nursing care. Costs for patient testing and procedures (including

X-ray, laboratory services, operating room costs, labor and delivery room costs) were associated with each patient, using the internally calculated direct cost for each test or procedure. Major supplies and pharmaceuticals were individually assigned to the patient based on the actual cost of the supply or drug.

Nursing care costs were driven to the patient level through daily patient classification and room rate charges. These charges were based on the nursing skill level required to care for patients in each specialty area, as well as the average acuity levels in each specialty area. Nursing staff skill levels were divided into three classifications as follows: registered nurse (RN), licensed practical nurse (LPN), and aide. Example of specialty areas were obstetrics, surgical, psychiatric, and cardiovascular. BMC divided six acuity levels according to the level of clinical attention required by the patient. For example, a direct cost of $123 per day was incurred in the Nursing-MED/SURG department for acuity level 1 (see Table 2).

The cost system produced departmental reports identifying the daily rate by acuity level and the underlying assumptions of the allocation routine (see Table 3). Because the number of minutes required to attend patients varied across acuity levels, the estimated (budgeted) volume of patient days was adjusted for daily service levels, expressed in minutes. The department's budgeted cost was allocated to each acuity level as a percentage of total budgeted minutes. Finally, a daily rate for each acuity level was calculated by dividing the allocated costs by the budgeted volume of days within each acuity level.

Indirect Costs

Indirect costs such as depreciation, administrative, and general were allocated to revenue-producing activities using simultaneous algebraic equations. The calculations were performed by BMC's computerized accounting system using allocation percentages based on the amount of services provided to other departments. The system allocated costs among several departments with reciprocal service relationships. For example, assume an organization has two support departments, housekeep-

ing and information systems (IS), and two revenue-producing departments, operating room (OR) and emergency room (ER). The IS department manager estimated the housekeeping department consumed 10% of the IS department's activities, while the ER and OR required 40% and 50%, respectively. Thus, the IS department's direct costs of $100,000 were allocated to housekeeping, OR, and ER consistent with the resources demanded (see Table 4). Next, the housekeeping department's direct ($60,000) and allocated ($10,000) costs of $70,000 were allocated to IS, OR, and ER using 30%, 40%, and 30%, respectively. Though the IS department had allocated all costs totaling $100,000 in the first step, the housekeeping department transferred costs ($21,000) back into the IS department that had to be reallocated in the second iteration. Iterations continued until the costs remaining in the support departments were too small to be significant. Thus, after multiple iterations, all support department costs were transferred to the OR and ER (see Table 4).

The cost system used by BMC simultaneously allocated costs associated with all indirect activities to revenue-producing activities based on cost drivers identified by BMC. For example, the education department allocated its costs to various departments including pain management, diabetic services, and emergency room using the percentage of paid hours within each department as the allocation base. Though the process required multiple iterations (see Table 4), the cost management system produced reports after each allocation iteration (see Table 5). When the allocation procedure had completed the final iteration, all costs for support-related departments were contained in the accounts of revenue-producing departments. Thus, education costs were included in the emergency room indirect cost per hour of $142 (see Table 2).

As the health care environment changed, new information demands were placed on the cost reporting system. The Mason study added length of stay as well as direct costs within DRG categories to the cost-to-charge ratio. According to Kelly, "TSI represented a significant step toward understanding and managing the costs of delivering health care services at BMC."

TABLE 1 Brookwood Medical Center

Appendectomy Patient Listing

Patient Number	Length of Stay	Total Charges	Direct Cost Variable	Direct Cost Fixed	Indirect Cost	Total Cost
1	3	$ 8,486	751	164	1,187	2,102
2	4	18,394	2,960	566	3,106	6,631
3	2	7,297	926	245	1,280	2,451
4	2	12,350	2,069	258	1,556	3,884
5	2	5,854	765	210	1,152	2,126
6	3	14,574	1,966	395	2,160	4,522
7	2	14,289	2,440	332	1,577	4,349
8	1	5,772	856	102	661	1,619
9	2	11,589	1,404	325	1,553	3,282
10	2	8,398	1,192	365	2,045	3,601
11	2	8,771	1,033	225	901	2,159
12	3	14,920	2,626	295	2,546	5,466
13	3	10,320	1,751	487	2,644	4,882
14	3	8,871	1,097	178	1,460	2,735
15	1	9,103	1,998	221	1,647	3,865
16	2	8,365	1,563	168	1,050	2,781
17	5	13,355	2,195	687	3,237	6,119
18	2	11,235	2,414	258	2,195	4,867
19	1	8,976	1,170	201	1,067	2,438
20	5	18,033	3,123	563	3,457	7,143
21	4	11,756	1,739	229	1,279	3,247
22	1	8,068	1,698	210	1,350	3,258
23	1	8,133	1,669	247	1,257	3,174
24	1	7,396	1,232	160	825	2,217
25	1	6,926	911	147	637	1,695
26	1	7,558	1,268	188	1,141	2,598
27	5	20,140	3,151	468	3,419	7,037
28	2	6,211	718	167	843	1,728
29	2	8,740	1,324	189	1,212	2,724
30	1	6,931	779	140	736	1,656
31	1	8,493	1,345	152	1,013	2,510
32	1	6,580	1,041	153	863	2,056
33	2	8,646	1,328	195	1,200	2,723
34	2	11,319	1,214	247	1,424	2,885
35	1	7,435	1,042	161	817	2,020
36	2	11,765	1,564	267	1,647	3,478
37	1	9,822	1,443	165	1,143	2,752
38	2	10,354	1,929	184	1,669	3,782
39	3	9,117	1,117	126	1,309	2,552
40	1	11,097	1,623	348	1,847	3,818
41	1	9,030	900	141	859	1,901
42	1	7,659	1,558	112	1,045	2,716
43	2	9,943	1,619	174	1,217	3,010
44	2	11,238	1,177	202	1,273	2,651
Grand Totals	91	$443,309	67,688	11,017	66,506	145,210

Source: sample of appendectomy patients from TSI data.

TABLE 2 DRG 470—Appendectomy Utilization Report

Department Description	Product Description	Direct Cost	Indirect Cost	Quantity	Total Cost
NURSING - MED/SURG	Acuity level 1-- daily rate	$123.00	$190.00	1	313.00
	Acuity level 2 -- daily rate	140.00	229.00	2	738.00
OPERATING ROOM	Major surgery -- 1 hour	174.00	170.00	1	344.00
OPERATING ROOM SUPPLIES	Sutures	17.00	7.00	5	120.00
	Basic surgical pack	17.00	6.00	1	23.00
	Additional OR supplies*	118.00	50.00	1	168.00
RECOVERY	Recovery level II -- 1/4 hour	24.00	11.00	3	105.00
CENTRAL STORES	Central store supplies*	25.50	58.00	1	83.50
LABORATORY SERVICES	Blood profile, potassium, renal profile	29.50	11.00	2	81.00
CARDIOLOGY/EKG	EKG 3 channel w/o physician in	13.00	12.00	1	25.00
PHARMACY	Pharmaceuticals*	163.50	133.00	1	296.50
RESPIRATORY THERAPY	Incentive spirometer	4.00	3.00	5	35.00
	New start spirometer & oxygen	6.00	4.00	1	10.00
EMERGENCY ROOM	ER visit level II -- intensive	80.00	142.00	1	222.00
DIETARY	Daily hospital service	24.00	18.00	3	126.00
LAUNDRY/LINEN	Daily hospital service	9.00	6.00	3	45.00
					$2,735.00

*Detail of specific items charged collapsed into one line item.

TABLE 3 Brookwood Medical Center, Department 6103, Nursing MED/SURG

Budget $95,759

Description	Budgeted Volume in Days	Minutes Daily Service	Budgeted Minutes	Percent Allocation	Allocation	Daily Rate
Acuity level 1	18	346	?	?	?	?
Acuity level 2	264	394	?	?	?	?
Acuity level 3	199	464	92,336	0.343	$32,864	$165
Acuity level 4	25	547	13,675	0.051	4,867	195
Observation	165	40	6,600	0.025	2,349	14
Observation	133	30	3,990	0.015	1,420	11
All others	211	200	42,200	0.157	15,020	71
Total			269,045	1.000	$95,759	

TABLE 4 Calculations for Reciprocal Service Department Allocation

| | Service Departments | | Revenue Departments | |
	IS	Housekeeping	OR	ER
Beginning balance	$100,000	$60,000	$0	$0
IS allocation	(100,000)	10,000[1]	50,000[2]	40,000[3]
Balance after allocation	*$0*	*$70,000*	*50,000*	*40,000*
Housekeeping allocation	21,000[4]	(70,000)	28,000[5]	21,000[6]
Balance after allocation	*21,000*	*0*	*78,000*	*61,000*
2nd IS allocation	(21,000)	2,100	10,500	8,400
Balance after allocation	*0*	*2,100*	*88,500*	*69,400*
2nd housekeeping allocation	630	(2,100)	840	630
Balance after allocation	*630*	*0*	*89,340*	*70,030*
3rd IS allocation	(630)	63	315	252
Balance after allocation	*0*	*63*	*89,655*	*70,282*
3rd housekeeping allocation	19	(63)	25	19
Balance after allocation	*19*	*0*	*89,680*	*70,301*
Transfer minimal balances	(19)	0	10	9
Ending balance	0	0	$89,690	$70,310

[1] $100,000 x 10%   [4] $100,000 x 40%   [5] $70,000 x 40%
[2] $100,000 x 50%   [6] $70,000 x 30%   [6] $70,000 x 30%

TABLE 5 Brookwood Medical Center, Education Allocation to Emergency Room

Allocation base: paid hours
Budget—$500,000

Department	Paid Hours	Percentage of paid hours by department	Amount allocated
Pain Management	2,083	?	?
Diabetic Services	8,993	?	?
Emergency Room	124,212	?	?
Monitoring Services	40,634	?	?
Quality Assurance	21,314	?	?
Dietary	167,411	?	?
Collections	13,650	.279320	$1,396.60
Outpatient Registration	19,776	.404677	$2,023.39
All others	4,488,783	91.854210	$459,271.05
Total	4,886,856	100.00%	$500,000.00

INDIANAPOLIS: ACTIVITY-BASED COSTING OF CITY SERVICES (A)

Introducing competition and privatization to government services requires real cost information. You can't compete if you are using fake money.

Stephen Goldsmith, Mayor of the City of Indianapolis

The City

The City of Indianapolis is located in the center of Indiana, about 200 miles southeast of Chicago. For the past 25 years the city had enjoyed a healthy economy and steady population growth. When Stephen Goldsmith took office in 1992, Indianapolis had a population of 800,000 and was the 13th largest city in the country. Historically, the city was known mainly for one weekend a year when cars raced 500 miles around an oval track at speeds in excess of 200 miles per hour. The city was shedding its reputation as a sleepy midwestern town by building strength in a number of industries including health care (Eli Lilly), automotive (Cummins Engine) and professional and amateur sports (the city had major league football and basketball teams, and hosted more Olympic governing bodies than any other).

The 1992 city government employed about 5,600 people and the budget was approximately $480 million dollars. The city's budget was divided among six operating departments whose responsibilities ranged from sewage treatment and trash collection to police and fire protection. Prior to Stephen Goldsmith's election in November 1991, the budget had grown at a 6% compounded annual rate since the mid-1980s. In every year since 1987, budgeted expenses had exceeded revenues by between $8 and $14 million dollars and the projected annual deficit when Mayor Goldsmith first took office was a record $20 million dollars.

Robomayor

"No more business as usual for many cities." Indianapolis' Goldsmith, a former Republican prosecutor dubbed "Robomayor" by the local press, pushed 60 city services into free-market competition in three years. City "business agencies" now bid against private firms on everything from filling potholes to handling welfare clients.

USA *Today (February 16, 1995)*

During the election campaign in 1991, Stephen Goldsmith, a former Republican prosecutor, had pledged to reduce the size of government, hold the line on taxes, and re-invest in the city's infrastructure. Unfortunately, during his first year the mayor would also have to deal with the prior leadership's largely unfunded commitments to two of the largest capital projects in the history of the city: the construction of a $250 million downtown shopping mall, and the opening of a new $500 million United Airlines maintenance terminal at the airport. Additionally, the local chamber of commerce had recently completed a report identifying over $1 billion dollars in badly needed infrastructure improvements. Not only was the city running in the red on an operating basis, but it had a $1.75 billion dollar gap in needed capital funds.

Aside from the financial challenges confronting him, Mayor Goldsmith was generally unhappy with the way government conducted business. After spending 12 years as a prosecutor within Indianapolis government the mayor had seen many problems:

> While the private sector attempts to improve services while reducing cost, the public sector generally spends more money each year while providing the same or lower quality service to the public. Traditional public management tools were clearly incapable of solving the problems our government faced. The staff organizations in the city were worthless; they impeded progress, and subtracted value. The multi-layered bureaucracy was out of control. Lots of unnecessary people were on the payroll because of the patronage process.

> Although on many measures Indianapolis was a good deal better off than other cities, we shouldn't be benchmarking ourselves against a failing industry, government. This seemed to be a particularly curious way to approach improving the system.

Mayor Goldsmith established several guiding principles for his administration:

- People governed least are governed best.
- Government should be a rudder, not an engine.
- People know better than government.
- Government should be measured the same way every other enterprise is measured: by its results.

This case was prepared by Professor Robert S. Kaplan, with assistance from Matt Ridenour, '95 MBA student.

The mayor wanted to make government smaller, to make it more responsive, and to make its managers think about value—the cost and quality of services delivered to its customers, the citizens. A senior manager in the new administration reinforced this philosophy:

> Smaller government is a core philosophy. We believe that individual choice, individual freedom and a lack of intrusiveness are important values; to the extent we can limit government's role or shrink the size of government, then in most cases we are probably doing good.

> Now at some point the core philosophy runs up against reality. If you were to eliminate, for example, all police officers, even if you return 100% of the tax dollars back to the citizens, would they be in a better position? Probably not. But there are hundreds of millions of dollars in opportunity before you ever begin to intrude on the essential missions of government.

Pressure from the Mayor   After the election but before entering office, the mayor called the current department leaders and asked them for management and financial reports about their departments' performance. He commented on the responses to this request:

> All people had were the income and expense numbers for this and last year's budget. Nothing was broken down by activity and they had no performance-based measurements, so it was impossible to measure anything. Although we were anxious to get in and make changes, we couldn't manage without data.

In the past few years the city had installed a "work management system." This system tracked how many people went out on particular street repair projects, how many hours they worked, and the equipment they used. But the data did not allow city managers to know how much, in total, they had spent to repair roads or to collect garbage.

Upon taking office, Mayor Goldsmith replaced many senior managers and requested that his new team install better systems to measure the performance and efficiency of government, "down to the unit." The mayor wanted to attack the problems of government from two directions. First, he demanded that departments describe and measure the services they provided as well as the cost of providing these services. Second, he established a new office, Enterprise Development, to create competition for the provision of city-supplied services.

Skip Stitt, the first director of the Enterprise Development office, articulated the new philosophy of city government:

> Competition was our core strategy—we defined service quality and price with private-sector marketplace measures. If there were rigorous competition for filling potholes, what would it cost? How would it be done? For some services, such as managing public golf courses, we would ask ourselves if taking a tax dollar out of John Public's pocket to subsidize golf was appropriate at all. If it's not, perhaps we should get out of that business and let the private sector fill the void.

Stitt's office would oversee initiatives to increase the competitiveness of the municipal departments, and to privatize services where these services could be delivered more efficiently by a private service company.

The Department of Transportation   Mitch Roob, a former management consultant, was appointed as the new head of the Department of Transportation. The department had a $50 million annual budget, most of it committed to two operating divisions: maintenance and construction. Roob was immediately struck by the lack of planning in the department:

> Programs were not linked to dollars. Management had no idea about the value of the city infrastructure. There was no balance sheet, no capital plan, no maintenance plans. The department simply did what they did the year before and requested a 10% higher budget. We went back through the archives and discovered that their current activities were descendants of priorities established in the mid 1970s. These were not necessarily bad plans, but they were no longer appropriate in the mid-1990s.

Roob faced some long-term issues. How should money be spent among road reconstruction and enhancement, repaving, resurfacing, or simply pot-hole filling? He began by asking the senior managers in the Department of Transportation for a list of their current activities and their cost.

> It seemed like these were simple questions. But we couldn't begin to answer them. We didn't have any relevant data and we had no costing system. No one had ever focused on what they did, on how much it cost to do whatever it was they did, and, certainly, on whether whatever they were doing was being done effectively and efficiently.

Roob also asked the managers what they believed the desired outcome should be from street repair work. The question seemed obvious, but it had not been asked before. Roob believed that the objective of the street maintenance division should be smooth streets, and that any activities that did not help to reach that objective were probably unnecessary.

Roob called a number of accounting firms to help him measure the costs of the Department's activities. One accounting firm said that it could start work on the project in six weeks. Another, KPMG Peat Marwick, said it could start the next day. Time was of the essence. The Mayor wanted rapid results to build momentum for the reforms. Thus, Roob chose KPMG Peat Marwick for a six-week pilot project. KPMG brought experience with implementing activity-based costing (ABC) in local manufacturing firms. Bridget Anderson, a Peat Marwick manager, was assigned to the project and began meeting with Roob and other DOT employees to determine where the costing study should begin.

The Pothole Repair Contract The newly formed team wanted to focus on a service that was highly visible and important to the average citizen. The cost study was scheduled for completion in early Spring, just when the maintenance division would be repairing streets damaged by the freezing and thawing cycle during the winter. The team quickly decided to study the cost of filling potholes. Roob set a tight deadline for completing the study and he announced publicly that pothole maintenance would be put out for open bid after the study's results had been received. On a certain date, private sector bids would be solicited and the cost system would provide the basis for the bid submitted by the city to keep doing the work. The department's cost team had the burden of both understanding the current cost of filling potholes and then working to lower its cost to compete with the bids that would be forthcoming from the private sector.

Bridget Anderson described her introduction to municipal accounting.

> We started by asking people how much it cost them to provide services. People couldn't answer that question. Lots of data were available but none of it was useful for management decisions. No data could be traced to the cost of the activities that delivered services, like filling potholes or keeping streets clean for citizens.

Anderson formed a project team, that included several representatives from the unionized work force and the non-unionized management team, to perform the costing study. Peat Marwick developed a training program that every member of the street maintenance division attended. The goal was for each employee to understand why ABC was being used and how the cost estimates would be determined. Anderson described her working relationship with the city union:

The mayor and Mitch Roob made it very clear that the union would have to be heavily involved in the process of costing the work activity. In essence, we would be working with the union to help them understand what it cost for them to do a certain job. Then, once they knew the cost, and made efforts to improve it, they would face a bid process. So, both the union and the private sector would have to believe ABC costing was legitimate because it would be the basis of the union's bid. The union's initial reaction to our presence, however, was very cautious, even hostile.

Anderson and her team applied a five-phase approach to implement activity-based costing at the city (see Exhibit 1).

> In Phase 1, we interviewed the people in street maintenance to find out what they did. This was an interesting process. Once they got over their surprise that we were asking them about what they did, they began by telling us they only did 5 or 6 major things for street maintenance—things like "fix a pothole, seal cracks on the street, or paint a curb." After much discussion and some process mapping we helped them to discover the literally hundreds of activities that go into providing these services. In the end, we were able to consolidate similar activities and ended up with a list of about 35 basic activities that we described in an Activity Dictionary (see Exhibit 2).

In Phase 2, Peak Marwick and the city team gathered data from the controller's office, from the work management system, and from interviews to determine the cost of performing each of the basic activities. Most of the effort was spent estimating how people spent their time among the 35 defined activities since, by far, the largest cost and resource in city government was people. Anderson recalled some of the difficulties at this stage:

> We quickly found out that the data in the work management system weren't all inclusive and had input errors as well. We went through some reconciliation procedures back to payroll registers to try and make the information as credible as it could be.

The team also had to identify the indirect and support costs associated with the 35 primary activities. Support costs included indirect labor, supplies, fixed assets (trucks and buildings), and the cost of services in city offices—human resources, payroll, legal, information systems, and controller. Much of the indirect cost assignments were available from an indirect cost recovery plan performed for reimbursement on federal grants. All the direct and indirect cost data were entered into a personal computer using ABC software.

In Phase 3, the team selected a cost driver, such as

hours worked or pounds of material, for each of the 35 activities. The cost driver would be used to assign activity costs to the output of the activities. The team initially had difficulty defining outputs for some of the activities. For example, potholes, unlike standard manufactured products, are all different. They don't come in standard sizes and shapes. The team realized quickly that attempting to find out what it costs to fill potholes would be answering the wrong question. They decided to measure the cost of putting a ton of asphalt in potholes, so the "cost object" of the study was the fully loaded cost of filling potholes with a ton of asphalt.

In Phases 4 and 5, the team reviewed the preliminary ABC cost reports and made refinements to the model and to the data after checking against the controller's records to assure that all costs were captured. Exhibits 3A and 3B show the total and unit costs for filling potholes in Indianapolis's five geographic sectors. The collection of costs for each of the five sectors allowed variations in terrain and work procedures in the five sectors to be reflected in the calculated cost of filling potholes.

Some people questioned the tracing of the fixed asset and indirect support costs to pothole filling. They acknowledged that the equipment and vehicles used directly for pothole filling were costs that should be included. But Anderson argued for including the cost of all assets that the city owned:

> What about all the desks, chairs, and computers being used by support people throughout the city? We found that the city did have a fixed asset accounting system that could produce reasonable depreciation figures. Even though the city did not calculate depreciation in its financial statements, we felt that in order to have a true cost to provide services, we needed to adjust out the current year capital purchases, and then add back the cost (depreciation) of having fixed assets like vehicles and equipment of all types, as well as the maintenance and repair of these fixed assets. The mayor wanted to have his departments compete against the private sector and these calculations would put city services on a more level playing field with private sector companies.

The team decided, however, not to assign the headquarters expenses to the costs for pothole filling. The rationale was that these expenses would remain in the city, whether the pothole filling was done by municipal workers or private contractors. So only the costs of resources expected to be directly affected by the decision were included in the contract costs.

The ABC team did decide to load the depreciation and maintenance costs of unused equipment into a line item, "unused equipment," in the pothole-filling cost calculation. The cost of unused equipment ranged up to 10% of total costs for some city services. Anderson described how this problem arose:

> The city workers all liked having vehicles available, just in case. We talked with them about only having equipment that they needed on a regular and routine basis; that for the couple of times each year they needed the back-up equipment, because the regular equipment had broken down, it would be cheaper to rent than to maintain the stand-by reserve capacity. Also, they might get better utilization by acquiring multiple-use equipment. Many of the crews may not need a different vehicle for each separate use. The departments could realize savings by sharing their equipment and vehicles with each other. At present, each department had a lot of excess equipment in their fleets.

After six weeks, the work team arrived at an average cost of $445 per ton of asphalt placed in potholes (see Total column in Exhibit 3A).

Skip Stitt recalled the surprise from seeing all the costs associated with performing city services:

> It was fascinating. Prior to activity-based costing, employees and their managers only thought about the number of hours that employees spent filling a pothole that day. Nobody ever thought about unproductive time, excess equipment, real estate, inventory, or about overhead, including management. When we began seeing the results from the early ABC studies, it was astonishing. You could look at a specific pothole-filling team and see how many take-home vehicles had been allocated to them, what their annual supplies budget was, and their costs for rent and maintenance of both their facilities and their vehicles. People weren't used to thinking of all the costs that get buried with the asphalt in a pothole. In many cases, employees' hourly wages were only 20% of the fully loaded cost. Before ABC, management might have placed that number at 80%–90% of the cost.

> Senior management and line employees suddenly came to the same question: how could they reduce or eliminate costs. As one example, they began to scrutinize the cost to maintain a vehicle, which was done in another division, because the inefficiencies in the equipment-maintenance group and their expensive oil changes were hitting the union employees' and DOT's bottom line cost of fixing potholes.

Bob Larson, a supervisor (and union member) in the Maintenance Department, recalled how the employees started to work to reduce costs:

> Both management and the union sat down and admitted that we had to do better. We shouldn't be going out with a five or six-man repair crew, plus a supervisor, if we could do the job, safely, with a three or four-man self-managed

crew. When you had 75 hourly employees out on a street with 36 supervisors, that ratio was not right. A supervisor should be able to handle ten people. It's ridiculous to have that many supervisors. That's why the overhead got so high, paying salary and benefits to all these people. The guy in the front line doesn't need 20 people to support him.

Steve Fantauzzo, the state executive director of AFSCME,[1] the municipal workers' union, commented on the results of the cost study:

> The ABC system really highlighted the amount of overhead, particularly managers, that existed on the city side. We urged city management to "get these guys off our backs." We didn't want to lose bids because the city made us carry managers who don't help us fill potholes.

Mitch Roob responded by dismissing half the supervisors, most of whom had been placed in those jobs by the local Republican party. The union was surprised by this action and Roob recalled its impact:

> They now realized that they had no choice. If we were willing to fire half of our guys, we would certainly be prepared to fire all of their guys.

In the following weeks every line item on the ABC report was closely examined and there was tremendous pressure on support groups to justify their expense. The union reconfigured its approach to filling potholes by reducing manpower on each team and changing the type and amount of equipment used. Larson explained how he worked with his union crews to get the cost down:

> I move around quite a bit. I just take my laptop loaded with the ABC model out to a work site and say, "OK, suppose we get rid of that single-axle dump, delete that extra mixer off there, take the truck driver off, now look what it would cost you to do a ton a day." The guys know that the next time they show up on a job they better have those improvements made or they'll lose a bid to the private sector and be out of a job.
>
> We also got some benefits by doing multiple tasks with the same resources. While the patching crew was waiting for the asphalt to be picked up and delivered to the pothole, I had them doing other jobs, like sweeping a bridge or picking up limbs. Those were all activities in the ABC model so we could charge their time to those tasks. This way our

people are kept busy doing useful tasks, and the pothole filling activity is not charged for unproductive time.

As the improvements in staffing, equipment utilization, and work processes were being made, management and the union recalculated the savings. Soon they would be submitting bids for pothole filling in competition with private sector contractors. Ray Wallace, Assistant to the Mayor, was the liaison for the activity-based costing initiative.

> Initially, I was viewed as a bad guy by the union people because I was "management" and a lot of the employees thought this was the mayor's way to break the union. There was a lot of uncertainty and animosity not only towards the process but to Mitch Roob, myself, the consultants, and anyone else from management involved in the process. But when we put together the bid with them, we were all working together, eating pizza at 10:00 in the evening, and staying until 3:00 in the morning. The last night, we worked from 6:00 A.M. through the next day without going home to sleep. So they saw us working just as hard as they were, committed to putting together a quality bid. Somewhere in the middle of that process, the barriers started to lift and we began to win the trust of the people.

By eliminating half the supervisors, changing the crew assignments for filling potholes, from eight down to four or six, and gaining efficiencies in the use and assignment of trucks and other equipment, the union team could realize significant cost reductions. The first test would come when they submitted bids for two pothole filling contracts that would be awarded; one in the Northwest sector and one in the Northeast sector of the city. The union estimated the resources—people, materials, and equipment—they now felt they would need to fill potholes using the revised work procedures and submitted their estimates to Bridget Anderson for verification (see Exhibit 4). Anderson, who had been monitoring how the new work procedures were being implemented, concurred that the union's estimates of resources required to do the job were reasonable and consistent with current practice. The union workers submitted a bid based on their revised cost estimates and waited anxiously for the announcement of whether they had won the business against the several private contractors who had also submitted bids for the pothole filling business.

---

[1]American Federation of State, County, and Municipal Employees.

EXHIBIT 1 Five-Phase Approach to Activity-Based Costing (ABC)

Phase 1: **Define project objectives and establish department activities and outputs.**
    The first phase focuses on familiarizing the project team with department operations, personnel, and means of quantifying data. The most effective means of identifying activities and outputs, the foundation for the ABC model, are determined.

Phase 2: **Collect and analyze appropriate costs and cost drivers.**
    Collect relevant cost information. Choose appropriate cost drivers for the activities defined in Phase I. Determine the most effective means of measuring departmental outputs.

Phase 3: **Collect remaining direct and indirect cost information**
    Establish resource cost pools on PC-based spreadsheets. Resource cost pools include personnel, direct materials, vehicles and equipment, fixed asset and facility costs, and administrative overhead.

Phase 4: **Develop an ABC Model**
    Develop an ABC model. First, assign resource costs to activities, and second, use cost drivers to assign activity costs to departmental outputs.

Phase 5: **Summarize cost information; expand departments' capabilities to continue to use the ABC model.**
    Hold training session to assist departmental personnel to learn how to use the ABC model on an ongoing basis.

EXHIBIT 2 Activity Listing: City Services

MAINTENANCE SECTION (9)	ASSET MANAGEMENT DIVISION (10)
Snow control	Bridge rehabilitation
Curb repair	Bridge replacement
Guardrail repair	Intersection improvements
Crack sealing	Road widening
Strip patching	Street reconstruction
Special maintenance	Street rehabilitation
Mowing and brush cutting	Signal interconnects
Alley repair	Signal upgrades
Drainage repair	Resurfacing
	Curbs and sidewalks

TRAFFIC MANAGEMENT (11)	PARKING MANAGEMENT DIVISION (5)
Pavement markings	Administration and planning
Sign installation	Parking lot and garage operations
Sign repair	Parking meter enforcement
Signal installation	Collections
Signal maintenance	Adjudications
Street cleaning	
Sidewalk repair	
Berm repair	
Pothole patching	
Street paving	
Sidewalk paving	

EXHIBIT 3A Pothole-Filling Costs: Five Districts, 1992 Actual (Jan.–March)

ACTIVITY	NORTHWEST	NORTHEAST	CENTER	SOUTHWEST	SOUTHEAST	TOTAL
C Labor (laborers)	27,455	27,927	83,482	41,954	25,162	205,980
C Labor overtime	462	2,658	1,558	1,210	908	6,797
D Labor (truck drivers)	175,608	181,869	354,628	188,468	163,748	1,064,322
D Labor overtime	5,225	10,183	16,133	6,192	6,057	43,790
E Labor (equipment oprs.)	43,604	90,373	27,038	20,089	35,844	216,949
E Labor overtime	2,693	6,162	1,067	7,201	3,579	20,702
Supervisors	41,893	47,085	60,008	55,790	38,267	243,044
Transp. supervisors	47,997	89,372	33,440	18,798	43,855	233,463
Personnel costs	$344,939	$455,629	$577,354	$339,703	$317,421	$2,035,046
Binder		432			83	514
Cold mix	6,185	7,266	3,265	4,659	5,589	26,964
Hot mix	14,901	21,644	51,301	23,175	56,987	168,009
Special mix	11,028	11,271	7,320	21,864	17,289	68,772
Tack	2,578	1,070	1,601	484	3	5,735
Direct materials costs	$34,692	$41,683	$63,487	$50,183	$79,950	$269,994
Central admin. expense	99,774	134,680	160,199	89,172	91,152	574,977
Central operations	38,206	51,573	94,792	52,765	34,908	272,244
Central maintenance	34,588	46,688	55,548	28,480	31,604	196,908
Facility expense	14,554	42,218	29,129	8,007	12,278	106,187
Fixed assets	1,098	828	1,536	1,029	936	5,428
Maintenance admin.	17,375	23,456	27,891	14,280	15,885	98,888
Operations admin.	18,172	24,544	29,193	14,946	16,601	103,456
Overhead costs	$223,767	$323,987	$398,290	$208,679	$203,364	$1,358,080
Cargo van				3,086		3,086
Crew cab		11,167				11,167
Crew: Cab pickup 86	12,369			11,699	14,150	38,218
Grader		2,727		4,236		6,963
Hotbox	16,276	4,954	11,396	13,272	18,335	64,233
Loader	1,457	8,958	1,024	1,271	358	13,067
Paver		207				207
Pickup mini	1,815	11,478		4,014		17,307
Roller		69				69
Roller VIB: 2 ton	104			2,541	330	2,976
SAD	40,090	35,607	25,203	41,853	45,535	188,287
SADA	9,005	20,833	19,953	12,243	9,333	71,367
Sedan		6,990				6,990
Tack wagon		777				777
TAD	5,607	1,225	7,213	95	1,432	15,571
TADA	29,397	38,542	18,971	37,940	16,738	141,588
Trailer			5,314			5,314
Truck: 1-ton dump	4,647	11,909	11,054	13,716	10,847	52,173
Truck: Patch 91	11,514		3,713			15,227
Unused equipment	3,769	6,127		7,402	20,537	37,836
Rolling stock costs	$136,050	$161,571	$103,840	$153,367	$137,595	$692,423
Total cost	$739,447	$982,871	$1,142,971	$751,932	$738,330	$4,355,549
Tons filled	1,156	1,726	2,134	2,017	2,753	9,786
Cost per ton	$639.66	$569.45	$535.60	$372.80	$268.19	$445.00

EXHIBIT 3B Pothole-Filling Costs per Ton: Five Districts, 1992 Actual (Jan.–March)

ACTIVITY	NORTHWEST	NORTHEAST	CENTER	SOUTHWEST	SOUTHEAST
C Labor (laborers)	23.75	16.18	39.12	20.80	9.14
C Labor overtime	0.40	1.54	0.73	0.60	0.33
D Labor (truck drivers)	151.91	105.37	166.18	93.44	59.48
D Labor overtime	4.52	5.90	7.56	3.07	2.20
E Labor (equipment oprs.)	37.72	52.36	12.67	9.96	13.02
E Labor overtime	2.33	3.57	0.50	3.57	1.30
Supervisors	36.24	27.28	28.12	27.66	13.90
Transp. supervisors	41.52	51.78	15.67	9.32	15.93
Personnel costs	$298.39	$263.98	$270.55	$168.42	$115.30
Binder		0.25			0.03
Cold mix	5.35	4.21	1.53	2.31	2.03
Hot mix	12.89	12.54	24.04	11.49	20.7
Special mix	9.54	6.53	3.43	10.84	6.28
Tack	2.23	0.62	0.75	0.24	0.00
Direct materials costs	$30.01	$24.15	$29.75	$24.88	$29.04
Central admin. expense	86.31	78.03	75.07	44.21	33.11
Central operations	33.05	29.88	44.42	26.16	12.68
Central maintenance	29.92	27.05	26.03	14.12	11.48
Facility expense	12.59	24.46	13.65	3.97	4.46
Fixed assets	0.95	0.48	0.72	0.51	0.34
Maintenance admin.	15.03	13.59	13.07	7.08	5.77
Operations admin.	15.72	14.22	13.68	7.41	6.03
Overhead costs	$193.57	$187.71	$186.64	$103.46	$73.87
Cargo van				1.53	
Crew cab		6.47			
Crew: Cab pickup 86	10.70			5.80	5.14
Grader		1.58		2.10	
Hotbox	14.08	2.87	5.34	6.58	6.66
Loader	1.26	5.19	0.48	0.63	0.13
Paver		0.12			
Pickup mini	1.57	6.65		1.99	
Roller		0.04			
Roller VIB: 2 ton	0.09			1.26	0.12
SAD	34.68	20.63	11.81	20.75	16.54
SADA	7.79	12.07	9.35	6.07	3.39
Sedan		4.05			
Tack wagon		0.45			
TAD	4.85	0.71	3.38	0.05	0.52
TADA	25.43	22.33	8.89	18.81	6.08
Trailer			2.49		
Truck: 1-ton dump	4.02	6.90	5.18	6.80	3.94
Truck: Patch 91	9.96		1.74		
Unused equipment	3.26	3.55		3.67	7.46
Rolling stock costs	$117.69	$93.61	$48.66	$76.04	$49.98
Total cost per ton	$639.66	$569.45	$535.60	$372.80	$268.19

EXHIBIT 4 Union Estimates of Resources Required for Two Pothole-Filling Contracts

	NORTHWEST		NORTHEAST	
	QUANTITY	RATE*	QUANTITY	RATE*
Personnel Cost Pool				
C Labor (laborers)	2.60 hours/ton	$23.25/hour	2.60 hours/ton	$11.18/hour
D Labor (vehicle drivers)	2.60 hours/ton	20.00/hour	2.60 hours/ton	23.08/hour
E Labor (eqpmt. operators)	0.35 hours/ton	44.49/hour	1.15 hours/ton	28.01/hour
Materials Cost Pool				
Hotmix for potholes	1 ton	$22.00/ton	1 ton	$22.00/ton
Tack	2.5 gallons/ton	1.54/gallon	2.5 gallons/ton	1.54/gallon
Vehicle Cost Pool				
Crew cab	1 hour/ton	$8.65/hour	1 hour/ton	$8.60/hour
Hotbox	1 hour/ton	17.65/hour	1 hour/ton	11.26/hour
One-ton truck	.6 hours/ton	15.20/hour	.6 hours/ton	18.22/hour
Arrowboard	1 hour/ton	2.00/hour	1 hour/ton	2.00/hour
Indirect Cost Pool	5.55 hours/ton	$17.06/hour	6.35 hours/ton	$19.56/hour

Labor rates based on projections from union contract; material rates based on actual contractor price quotes.

2

Traditional Stage II Cost Systems: Linking Resource Expenses to Cost Centers and Cost Objects

One of the primary functions of cost systems is to estimate the costs of objects such as activities, products, services, and customers. For example, companies that manufacture discrete, customized products, such as machine tools, use their cost system to measure the costs of all the resources used to produce each item. To perform this function they must identify the resources that each object consumes, estimate the cost of each resource, and then sum the cost across all resources used. This information determines the profitability of producing different product lines and helps to determine the prices that would be offered, particularly for customized products, to prospective customers.

DIRECT ASSIGNMENT

Cost systems can assign resource costs either directly or indirectly. When costs are assigned directly, the equation $C = P \times Q$ is used to assign costs to objects. Here C is the cost of the resource consumed, P is its purchase price (or acquisition cost) per unit, and Q is the quantity of that resource consumed by the object. For example, in calculating the materials cost of a product, P represents the price per kilogram of the materials and Q equals the number of kilograms used in each product unit. The cost of material for each product is given by multiplying the price per kilogram by the number of kilograms consumed.

The process of direct assignment consists of five steps:

1. Identify all the directly assigned resources that are consumed by the object.
2. Estimate the price per unit for each of those resources (typically from purchase orders).
3. Estimate the quantity of those resources that the object consumes (typically from engineering specifications or managerial estimates).
4. Multiply the price of a unit of resource by the quantity of that resource used by the object.
5. Sum up all the directly assignable resource costs to obtain the direct cost of the object.

Historically, in manufacturing settings the costs of two (and only two) resources were assigned directly. These resources were "direct" materials and "direct" labor.[1] The costs of these

---

[1] In fact, the term *direct labor* became so ubiquitous that it was used to describe the labor that worked on the production floor irrespective of the way that those costs were assigned.

resources were assigned directly for several reasons. First, they accounted for the majority of the costs of products. Second, the scientific management movement believed that it was important to control the usage and consumption of these expensive resources. Finally, the consumption of these resources by individual products was fairly easy to measure. These characteristics justified the measurement costs for estimating the price per unit and the quantity of materials and labor consumed by each product. For all other resources, the cost of estimation was considered greater than the benefits associated with direct assignment. These resources were designated as overhead or burden and their costs were assigned to products indirectly. These costs were (and still are) called indirect costs for obvious reasons.

INDIRECT COST ASSIGNMENT

Direct assignment for all resources can be a complex, costly process, because of the difficulty of estimating P and Q for each resource. Indirect assignment avoids these high measurement costs, but at the risk of reducing the accuracy of the resulting cost estimates. For example, if the cost of a resource represents only a small percentage of the total cost of the object, any errors from using approximations in the cost estimation process will be insignificant. Also, since the quantity of that resource consumed by each object is difficult to measure, the approximation avoids the high measurement costs required for direct assignment.

When costs are assigned indirectly, the equation $C' = R \times Q'$ is used to assign costs to objects. Here C' is the estimated cost of the resource consumed, R is the rate per cost driver unit of the resource being consumed, and Q' is the quantity of the cost driver consumed by the object. For example, if the cost driver, direct labor hours, is used to indirectly assign supervision costs, then R is determined by identifying the total cost of supervision and dividing it by the total number of direct labor hours consumed to give the cost of supervision per direct labor hour. Q' is the quantity of direct labor hours (the indirect cost driver) consumed by the object. The estimated cost of the resource is determined by multiplying the rate per cost driver unit by the quantity of cost driver units consumed.

The process of indirect assignment thus consists of six steps.

1. Identify all the indirectly assigned resources that are consumed by the object.
2. Identify an appropriate cost driver for each of those resources.
3. Estimate the cost driver rate for each cost driver–resource pair (typically the costs of the resources are obtained from purchase orders).
4. Estimate the quantity of those cost drivers that the object consumes (typically from engineering specifications or managerial estimates).
5. Multiply the cost driver rate for each resource by the quantity of the cost driver consumed.
6. Sum up the resource costs to obtain the indirect costs assigned to the object. Add the indirect costs to the sum of the direct costs to determine the total cost of the object.

The savings from adopting indirect assignment can be significant, especially when the same cost driver can be used for many resources. For example, direct labor hours can be used to assign the cost of any resource that is consumed in approximately the same proportion as direct labor, such as the electricity to run machines operated by a single person. The costs of all such resources can be collected into a single cost pool and divided by the total number of direct labor hours to give the combined rate for these resources. Multiplying this combined rate by the quantity of direct labor hours each object consumes gives the estimated cost of those combined resources.

Indirect assignment, however, produces less accurate cost estimates. For example, if only some of the direct labor force requires supervision, then the use of direct labor hours as the cost driver will incorrectly assign supervision costs to objects. Those objects that actually consume relatively little or no supervision will be overcosted and those that actually require relatively high levels of supervision will be undercosted. Only those objects that actually consume supervision and direct labor hours in the same ratio as the average rate will be correctly costed. Consequently, cost system designers should attempt to choose a cost driver that all objects consume in about the same proportion as the resource whose costs are being assigned.

When objects consume resources in different ratios, no single cost driver can accurately assign all indirect costs. Consequently, most cost systems use multiple cost drivers for their indirect cost assignment. Each cost driver captures a different pattern of resource consumption. In general, as more cost drivers are used in a system, the designer can develop a more accurate cost system. Every additional cost driver, however, increases the cost of measurement because the designer must specify the usage of that cost driver by each cost object. Therefore, the design of cost systems reflects a cost-benefit trade off between the cost of errors caused by relying upon inaccurate cost estimates (when using only a few cost drivers) and the cost of measurement (which increases when new cost drivers are added to the system). The optimum cost system is one that minimizes the total cost of errors and measurement.

A NUMERICAL EXAMPLE

A numerical example will be used to illustrate direct and indirect cost assignment. Consider a firm producing two products (the cost objects) P_1 and P_2.

Direct Assignment

The two products are produced from the same material, a stainless steel alloy costing $15 per kilogram, and are built with the same labor force, which is paid $10 per hour. Exhibit 2–1 shows the consumption and costs of the directly assigned resources, material, and labor:

EXHIBIT 2–1

	P_1	P_2
Materials (kg.)	5	3
Direct Labor (hours)	5	10
Materials Cost	$75	$45
Direct Labor Cost	50	100
Total Direct Costs	$125	$145

The assignment of direct costs is not always this easy. Often companies have difficulties measuring the quantity of resources consumed by each item. The most common solution to this problem is to build the correction into the $C = P \times Q$ equation by adjusting upwards either the price per unit or the quantity consumed. The first correction is typically used for labor and the second for material. So in the previous example labor costs $8 per hour for a forty-hour week but the workforce only produces products for 32 of those 40 hours. During the other eight hours, workers are involved with training, lunch, coffee breaks, and downtime. The typical solution in such a situation is to increase the rate per hour from the nominal $8 to $10 to adjust for the nonproductive time ($8 per hour $\times$ 40 hours/32 hours = $10 per hour). For materials,

EXHIBIT 2–2

INFORMATION	P_1	P_2	TOTAL
Volume	20 Units	40 Units	
Direct Material/Unit	5 kilograms	3 kilograms	
Total Direct Material	100 kilograms	120 kilograms	220 kilograms
Direct Labor Hours/Unit	5 hours	10 hours	
Total Direct Labor Hours	100 hours	400 hours	500 hours
Supervision			$1,000
Cooling Fluid			$2,000
Electricity			$1,500
Rags			$200

suppose the company must start with 3 kilograms of metal to end up with 2 kilograms of material in the final product (one third of the material is lost as waste or scrap or is consumed in the process). A typical solution in this situation is to include the cost of the scrapped material in the quantity consumed. For example, even though the finished product only weighs 2 kilograms, the material specification calls for 3 kilograms of material to be consumed in the process of producing a unit of output; thus $Q = 3$ in the cost equation.

Indirect Assignment

The two products consume four other resources: supervision of direct labor, cooling fluid for the cutting process, electricity for the machines, and rags to clean the products after machining. Analysis of the patterns of resource consumption show that supervision and electricity are consumed by the two products in essentially the same ratio as direct labor hours and that the other two resources are consumed in the same ratio as material weight. The ratios of direct labor and machine hours are different for the two products. Exhibit 2–2 provides the information required to complete the estimation of the costs of P_1 and P_2.

   The cost of the supervision and electricity resources are combined to create a direct labor-related cost pool of $2,500, and the cost of the cooling fluid and rags resources are combined to give a material-related cost pool of $2,200. The cost driver rate for direct labor hours is calculated by dividing the supervision and electricity pool by the total number of direct labor hours (500) in the facility. This calculation gives a rate of $5 per hour. The material weight cost driver rate is determined by dividing the cooling fluid and rags cost pool by the total weight of material consumed (220 kg) in the facility. This calculation gives a rate of $10 per kilogram.

   The indirectly assigned costs of supervision and electricity are determined by multiplying the cost driver rate for direct labor hours by the number of direct labor hours consumed by each product. This calculation assigns $25 to P_1 and $50 to P_2. The indirectly assigned costs of cooling fluid and rags are determined in the same way, as $50 and $30 respectively. The total indirect costs of the two products are $75 for P_1 and $80 for P_2. Summing the direct and indirect costs gives the total cost of the two products as $195 for P_1 and $225 for P_2.

TWO-STAGE DIAGRAMS

Cost systems can be graphically illustrated using a two-stage diagram. At the first stage, the system establishes the cost driver rate; at the second stage, the system uses the cost driver rate to assign resource costs to cost objects. When drawing the two-stage diagram, directly assigned

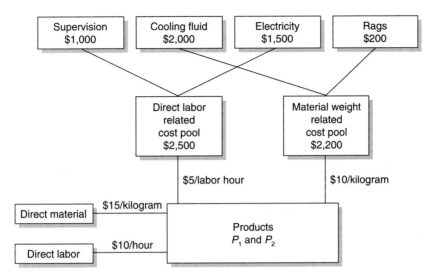

EXHIBIT 2–3   Example of a Two-Stage Diagram

costs (e.g., materials and labor) are represented horizontally; indirectly assigned costs are represented vertically. Boxes represent cost pools and cost objects, and arrows represent assignments of costs. Only one arrow can connect from a cost pool to another cost pool or to a cost object. When multiple arrows enter a cost pool or cost object, the costs flowing into the cost pool or object have to be summed to give the total cost of the pool or object. The two-stage diagram for the numerical example is illustrated in Exhibit 2–3.

Assigning Costs of Service and Support Departments

Not all costs can be directly or indirectly assigned to cost objects so easily. Some costs, particularly those incurred in many service and support departments—such as product engineering, plant administration, finance, information systems, and human resources, plus plant-level expenses including property taxes, building depreciation and insurance, heat, and light—cannot be directly assigned to products. Instead, these costs have to be assigned first to the production departments and subsequently to the products. The process of getting these costs to the production departments can be broken into four steps.

1. Identify the demands placed on the support department by other organizational units, including production centers and other support departments.
2. Develop a quantifiable measure (cost driver) for those demands.
3. Calculate a rate for each cost driver by dividing the cost of supplying the demanded services by the total quantity of the driver.
4. Assign the support department's costs by multiplying the driver rate by the driver quantity demanded by each of the other organizational units.

Many support or service departments in companies can provide support to other support and service departments, as well as to production departments that directly benefit products. For example, consider a human resources or payroll department that provides services for people in both production and support departments throughout the organization. Or consider the resources that provide space, heat, light, and air-conditioning throughout the plant, to both production areas and support areas.

To illustrate how to handle this situation, let us assume that the demands placed on support departments can be summarized into three activities:

- Provide space for people, machines, materials, and products;
- Provide CPU cycles of information processing; and
- Provide employee support (e.g., training, advising, hiring).

The resource expenses from various support departments assigned to the activity *Provide Space* include building depreciation, insurance, taxes, and the expenses of heat, light, air-conditioning, security, internal housekeeping, and maintenance of surrounding grounds outside the factory. The output from this activity is square meters of usable floor space.[2] The cost of this activity would then be assigned to the space occupied by production departments and the space used by the two other support departments: information systems (IS) and human resources (HR) (which perform the two other support activities). After assigning the cost of the *Provide Space* activity, the costs of the IS and HR departments will include not only their own traceable department costs but also the assignment of occupancy costs. The HR department costs, associated with the activity *Support Employees*, has, as its cost driver, the number of employees.[3] Since the IS department has a significant number of employees, it would receive a cost assignment from HR. The cost assignment would include its pro-rata share of HR expenses as well as an occupancy charge that HR received from the *Provide Space* activity. Thus two of the support activities, *Provide Space* and *Provide Employee Support* would assign some of their expenses to production departments, and some to other support activities, like *Provide CPU cycles*. At the final round, the costs in the *Provide CPU Cycle* activity (which include space and HR costs) would be assigned to production departments, based on the number of CPU cycles used by each department. So, the expenses of support activities ripple through and eventually find their way to production cost centers.[4]

A further complication arises when reciprocal relationships exist among service departments. For example, a personnel department hires and oversees people for all departments in the organization; a utility department provides heat and light to all departments (including the personnel department and itself); a data processing department provides computer services and output to many service departments; a housekeeping department cleans all facilities; and a maintenance department repairs machinery throughout a facility. With such interactions, an analysis that charges all the costs of each service department directly to production departments does not give an accurate picture of cost dependency.

We have already described how to attribute the costs of each service department to all departments, both production and service, that use its output. But once the process begins, just what *the costs* of a service department include is no longer clear. Besides its own traceable costs, each service department will start to accumulate charges based on the services it receives from other service departments, and these must be reassigned back to its user departments.

---

[2]In many factories, not all space is equally costly to supply. For example, in semiconductor wafer fabrication facilities the expense to provide clean room space is much higher than the expense to provide normal space. In such cases, the analyst should have at least two activities: *Provide Normal Space* and *Provide Clean Room Space*. The *Provide Clean Room Space* activity would attract much higher utility expenses because of the need to recirculate and filter air continuously. Similarly, space provided for warehousing raw materials and finished goods may be less expensive to supply and support than the temperature and humidity-controlled space required for sophisticated electronics-controlled equipment.

[3]Again, this treatment assumes that all employees demand the same time and other resources from the HR department. It would be straightforward, but more complicated, to allow for the HR activities to be more focused on some employees than on others. One could either construct a weighted HR service index to represent the complexity of demands by different individuals, or one could split what is now a homogeneous activity, *Provide Employee Support*, into two or more separate categories, *Provide Complex Support*, *Provide Average Support*, and *Provide Basic Support*, with employees associated with one of these three mutually exclusive activities.

[4]Exactly the same procedure can and should be performed in the activity-based cost systems to be described in chapter 4. With ABC systems, instead of tracing the costs of support activities just to production cost centers, the costs of support departments will be assigned as well to primary activities, those that directly benefit the production and sales of products.

Three major alternatives have been proposed to deal with this interacting or reciprocal service department situation:

1. The direct method, in which all service department costs are assigned only to production centers, ignoring the use of service department costs by other service departments and their support activities.
2. The step down method, which has the potential of only partially considering the reciprocal services. This method was illustrated previously when first the space costs were assigned to human resources and IS, and then the HR costs were assigned to IS. In this process, we ignored reciprocal or feedback relationships between the support activities. For example, we ignored the assignment of IS costs to the HR and *Provide Space* activities, and the assignment of HR costs to the people who participated in the *Provide Space* activity.
3. The reciprocal method, which models the reciprocal relationships among service departments exactly.

Extending our simple two product example illustrates the way these costs are treated in the second stage and driven to products. Suppose that the: *Provide Space* assignment process increases the direct-labor cost pool by $1,500 and the weight-related cost pool by $750. Similarly, the *Provide CPUs* assignment process increases the cost pools by $1,750 and $350 respectively. Finally, the *Support People* assignment process increases the two cost pools by an additional $1,750 and $1,100. The two cost pools now contain $7,500 and $4,400 respectively. The new driver rates are therefore $15 per direct labor hour and $20 per kilogram. This gives new product costs of $295 for P_1 and $355 for P_2.

Flexible Budgeting Systems for Cost Control

Traditional systems for cost control of responsibility centers incorporate two additional principles. First, responsibility (cost) centers become the focal point for cost planning, cost control, and product costing. This focus enables managers to monitor and control the efficiency of responsibility centers. The second principle establishes clear distinctions between fixed and variable costs at every individual cost center. These two principles are incorporated in companies' cost planning and control systems. Annually, financial managers conduct an analytical process to plan each cost center's expenses (e.g., labor wages and salary, consumable supplies, equipment depreciation). They then establish monthly budgets for each cost component at each cost center. The budgeted costs are set at standard levels, based on estimates of efficient resource consumption, as determined by industrial engineers.

Flexible budgeting systems then calculate separate rates for assigning the production cost center's variable costs (which includes the variable costs assigned by indirect cost centers, as well as the variable costs incurred within the production cost center) and fixed costs. Some systems may not assign any fixed costs to products, except for a separate calculation used to value inventory for financial reporting purposes. These companies are using what they interpret as a marginal costing approach in which only short-term variable costs are assigned as product costs.

During the year, the cost system records and assigns actual expenses to all responsibility centers. The standard cost system records efficiency (inefficiency) variances (favorable [unfavorable] spending and usage variances in a cost center) at the cost center where they arise, rather than allocating the variances either from indirect centers to direct (production) centers, or from direct production centers to products. Thus, costs are transferred between departments at budgeted levels, representing standard levels of efficiency. With this procedure, managers are held accountable for costs they can control—spending and usage variances within their cost center, and quantities of services they use from other cost centers, valued at standard prices. They are not assigned costs they cannot control.

The flexible budgeting system assigns the budgeted fixed costs of a support department to the other cost centers at a predetermined budgeted rate, calculated annually. The variable costs of the support department are assigned based on actual usage and standard prices.

A standard cost, flexible budgeting system also calculates product and part costs at standard levels of efficiencies. Inefficiencies, as reflected in unfavorable spending and usage variances, are calculated each period and can be highlighted for management attention. They should not be rolled forward into product costs; otherwise sales and marketing personnel may attempt to recover the costs of internal inefficiencies by raising prices to customers.

LIMITATIONS OF STANDARD COST, FLEXIBLE BUDGETING SYSTEMS FOR PRODUCT COSTING

Even the best standard cost, flexible budgeting systems, however, have two limitations that severely impair their value for companies today. First, they do not report accurately on the costs of processes, products, and customers. Second, they provide inadequate information to support organizations' continuous learning and improvement activities.

For product and customer costing, the systems may identify the short-term variable costs associated with producing one more or one less unit of a product for a customer order. But the systems fail to capture and trace accurately many other costs triggered by designing, producing, delivering, marketing, selling, and servicing individual products. Large categories of costs—in design and development, in logistics and distribution, in marketing and selling, and in post-sales service—are not traced to individual products and customers with these traditional cost systems. Largely because these other categories of costs are not considered inventoriable or part of the "cost-of-goods-sold" calculation in the periodic income statement, little attention has been given to trace these categories of costs to individual products and customers. They are expensed each period on the income statement, appearing "below the [gross margin] line" as elements within large agglomerations of period expenses.

But even beyond the failure to trace nonfactory costs to individual products, traditional cost systems treat many indirect factory expenses as "fixed" or period expenses. These period expenses are either ignored entirely, as in direct costing systems, or allocated using the same cost drivers (e.g., materials weight, labor hours, machining hours) used to assign indirect variable expenses to individual products. Unfortunately, the period or fixed expenses are not fixed with respect to the volume and mix of individual products manufactured within a plant. Plants producing a wide range of products—high volume and low volume, new and mature, standard and customized—have much higher levels of period costs than plants producing only one or two products in high volumes.[5]

Traditional systems are inadequate for assigning expenses to products, services, and customers. The methods used to allocate factory overhead and other indirect costs to products for inventory valuation may be adequate for the aggregate inventory accounts on the balance sheet and the cost-of-goods-sold account on the income statement. Errors in product costing at the individual product unit level cancel each other out as products are agglomerated together at the balance sheet and income statement levels. Also, whatever defects exist in the method of cost assignment, the systems at least use the same method consistently each year. As we noted in the previous chapter, auditors and financial accountants prefer consistency to accuracy when assigning costs to products.

---

[5]We will develop this point in considerable detail when we introduce activity-based cost systems in chapter 4.

LIMITATIONS OF TRADITIONAL COST SYSTEMS FOR FEEDBACK AND LEARNING

Traditional cost systems may be adequate for cost monitoring and cost control, particularly when companies use the standard cost, flexible budgeting systems described earlier in the chapter. But even the best of these systems do not promote learning and improvement activities. The new competitive environment requires that operators and managers have timely and accurate information to make processes more efficient and more customer-focused. As noted earlier in the chapter, traditional financial systems prepare and issue summary financial feedback according to a financial reporting cycle (typically monthly or every four weeks). Because of the complexities associated with closing the books, the reports are delayed for several days or weeks after the close of the accounting period, certainly too late for operators and managers to take corrective actions. So the feedback information to responsibility center managers and supervisors is delayed and covers an extensive time period of operations.

In addition, the monthly performance reports for many operating departments can contain extensive cost allocations, so that managers will be held accountable for performance that is neither under their control nor traceable to them. The costs of corporate- or factory-level resources, such as the heat and lighting in the building or the landscaping outside, are allocated arbitrarily to individual departments even though the departments are not responsible for these costs. For example, think about having the accountants, after a ball is thrown down each of an establishment's 35 bowling lanes, count all the pins knocked down in the entire establishment, divide by 35, and report back the average, say 8.25714,[6] to every bowler. Such a number may be quite accurate (it does represent the mean number of pins knocked down per alley), but it is completely useless to every individual bowler. Bowler wants to see the number of pins they each knock down, so that they might improve on the next toss. Bowlers do not want this number contaminated or influenced by the actions of others over which they have no control.

Traditional systems, operating with the same frequency as the financial reporting system, provide feedback via monthly variances, based on a system of engineered work standards and standard costs that was developed a century ago by engineers in the scientific management movement. The system of work and cost standards represents a philosophy in which engineers and managers determine operators' tasks. Operators are instructed to keep following these procedures, and the system of measurement—including cost variances that compared actual results to the predetermined standards—is used to check whether the workers are following the prescribed procedures. But performance that just meets historical standards is no longer adequate. Employees must now make continuous improvement to ongoing processes to reduce and eliminate waste, improve quality, and reduce defects.

Managers have learned that perhaps their best source of new ideas for continually improving performance comes from their operators, the people who are closest to the work being performed. These operators see firsthand the types of defects that occur and the principal causes of these defects. Front-line employees, not engineers or managers, are expected to devise new approaches for how to perform work and satisfy customers.

For these new responsibilities, the operators need information to assist their problem-solving activities, not to control them against preset and soon-to-become-obsolete standards. For operational control, companies need to shift away from their traditional standard cost—

---

[6]Many accountants like to report all results using six significant digits. It makes them feel that they are very accurate. In truth, they are merely being precise but are usually quite inaccurate (the first digit may be wrong). In management accounting, we prefer to be vaguely accurate (get the first digit correct) rather than precisely wrong.

flexible budgeting systems since these systems emphasize performance against historical standards. Front-line employees need new and more timely forms of feedback information to assist and empower them for their continuous improvement activities. We turn to systems designed to provide such information to front-line employees in chapter 3.

SUMMARY

Traditional standard cost systems have worked well for many decades, and continue to be useful today for the financial reporting functions to value inventory and measure cost of goods. Using a two-stage assignment process, the systems provide aggregate, periodic information for decentralized cost monitoring and cost control. But, by themselves, they are inadequate for managers and employees in today's competitive environment.

CASES

The *Seligram, Inc.: Electronic Testing Operations* case provides a simple introduction to two-stage system design. The firm has realized that its current system is obsolete and is exploring new designs which contain multiple cost centers. The next case, *Komatsu (B)*, looks at how cost systems become obsolete over time.

We continue our exploration of the evolution of cost systems by looking at several traditional systems. These systems vary from being quite simple to highly sophisticated. While they all provide important financial accounting information, they fail to perform adequately the profitability and performance evaluation functions required of cost management systems. Since the ability to perform the financial reporting function is a critical requirement, it is important to understand how effective traditional systems operate.

Mayers Tap (A), *(B)*, and *(C)* provide hands-on design experience by using the associated computer software. The objective is to design a new traditional cost system for the firm. *Mueller Lehmkuhl* exposes students to the strategic implications of cost system design. The firm has designed its cost system to support its strategy but the outcomes are not now what management intended. The *Mitsubishi Kasei* case explores what happens when a cost system is designed to report product line as opposed to product costs. Such systems are becoming more common as firms convert to cellular manufacturing and the factory becomes a collection of cells dedicated to single product lines.

Digital Communications Inc. introduces the issues that arise from support departments providing service to each other as well as to production centers. *Metabo* describes a typical German cost system employing extensive use of standard costs and flexible budgeting. These systems are extremely sophisticated and provide much information for detailed cost control. The *Peoria Engine Plant (A)* case illustrates a U.S. version of Metabo, and explores the benefits from more frequent (daily) reporting of labor and overhead to enhance cost control.

SELIGRAM, INC.: ELECTRONIC TESTING OPERATIONS

We put in a piece of automated equipment a year ago that only fits the requirements of one customer. This equipment reduced the direct labor required to test his components and, because of our labor-based burden allocation system, substantially reduced his costs. But putting a $40,000 machine into the general burden pool raised the costs to our other customers. It just doesn't make sense shooting yourself in the foot at the same time you are lowering the company's cost of operations.

Paul Carte, Manager

Introduction

The Electronic Testing Center (ETO), a division of Seligram, Inc., provided centralized testing for electronic components such as integrated circuits. ETO was created as a result of a decision in 1979 to consolidate electronic testing from 11 different divisions of Seligram, Inc., provided centralized testing for electronic components such as integrated circuits. ETO commenced services to these divisions in 1983. It was estimated that centralization would save Seligram in excess of $20 million in testing equipment investment over the next five years.

ETO operated as a cost center and transferred products to other divisions at full cost (direct costs plus allocated burden). Although ETO was a captive division, other divisions within Seligram were allowed to use outside testing services if ETO could not meet their cost or service requirements. ETO was permitted to devote up to 10% of its testing capacity to outside customers but chose to work mainly with other Seligram divisions due to limited marketing resources.

ETO employed approximately 60 hourly personnel and 40 administrative and technical staff members. Budgeted expenses were $7.9 million in 1988 (see Exhibit 1).

Testing Procedures

ETO expected to test between 35 and 40 million components in 1988. These components included integrated circuits (ICs), diodes, transistors, capacitors, resistors,

transformers, relays, and crystals. Component testing was required for two reasons. First, if defective components were not caught early in the manufacturing cycle, the cost of repair could exceed the manufacturing cost of the product itself. Studies indicated that a defective resistor caught before use in the manufacturing process cost two cents. If the resistor was not caught until the end product was in the field, however, the cost of repair could run into the thousands of dollars. Second, a large proportion of Seligram's work was defense related. Military specifications frequently required extensive testing of components utilized in aerospace and naval products. By 1988, ETO had the ability to test 6,500 different components. Typically, however, the division would test about 500 different components each month and between 3,000 and 3,500 per year. Components were received from customers in lots; in 1988 ETO would receive approximately 12,000 lots of components.

ETO performed both electrical and mechanical testing. Electrical testing involved measuring the electrical characteristics of the components and comparing these measurements with the components' specifications. For example, the specifications for an amplifier may have called for a 1-volt input to be amplified into a 10-volt output. ETO would deliver a 1-volt input to the component. By measuring the amplifier's output, ETO gauged its conformance with specifications.

Mechanical testing included solderability, component burn-in, thermal shock, lead straightening, and leak detection. Solderability involved the inspection of components to see if they held solder. Burn-in was the extended powering of components at high temperature. Thermal shock involved the cycling of components between high and low temperatures. Lead straightening was the detection and correction of bent leads on components such as axial components. Leak detection examined hermetically sealed ICs for leaks.

Components varied significantly in the number and type of electrical and mechanical testing procedures they required. This variation resulted in about 200 different standard process flows for the division. Process flows were determined by the different combinations of tests and specifications requested by the customer. Based on these combinations, ETO planners determined the routing of components between testing

This case was prepared by Professor Peter B. B. Turney, Portland State University, and Christopher Ittner, doctoral student (under the supervision of Professor Robin Cooper).

equipment and the type of tests to be performed at each station. ICs, for example, could follow six different flows through the facility. While some ICs only required electrical testing at room temperature, solderability, and leak detection, others also required thermal shock and burn-in.

Each type of component required separate software development, and custom tools and fixtures were often required. Software, tools, and fixtures were developed by the engineering group, which was made up of specialists in software development, equipment maintenance, calibration and repair, tooling and fixturing, and testing equipment operation. Software engineers developed programs for specific applications. The programs were then retained in a software library for future use. ETO had 6,500 different software programs on file, of which 1,300 were programs developed in the past year. ETO also had an inventory of 1,500 tools and fixtures, of which 300 had been developed in the past year. The large number of tools and fixtures allowed the testing of components with a wide variety of leads, pin combinations, and mating configurations.

The testing facility was divided into two rooms. The main testing room contained the equipment used for electrical testing. The mechanical room contained the equipment used for mechanical testing, plus incoming receiving and the stockroom. A total of 20 people worked in the two rooms on each of two main shifts, and 10 people worked on the night shift.

Cost Accounting System

The cost accounting system measured two components of cost: direct labor and burden. Burden was grouped into a single cost pool which included burden associated with each of the testing rooms, as well as the engineering burden costs relating to software and tooling development and the administrative costs of the division. Total burden costs were divided by the sum of testing and engineering labor dollars to arrive at a burden rate per direct labor dollar. The division costed each lot of components. Burden was calculated for each lot by multiplying the actual direct labor dollars associated with the lot by the 145% of burden rate. The resulting burden was then added to the actual direct labor costs to determine the lot's total cost. In 1988, the facility-wide burden rate was 145% of each direct labor dollar, of which more than 25% was attributable to equipment depreciation (see Exhibit 2).

Signs of Obsolescence

Several trends pointed to the obsolescence of the labor-based burden allocation process. Since the founding of the division in 1983, direct labor hours per lot tested had been declining steadily. This trend was aggravated by an increased dependence on vendor certification. Vendor certification was a key component of just-in-time (JIT) delivery. With vendor certification, Seligram's suppliers did the primary testing of components. ETO then utilized statistical sampling to verify that the supplier's production process was still in control. Thus, while JIT led to an increased number of smaller lots being received by ETO, vendor certification reduced the number of tests performed. Early indications were that JIT deliveries would account for 30% of Seligram's shipments within the next five years.

In addition to declining direct labor content and fewer test lots, the obsolescence of the labor-based allocation system was intensified by a shift from simple inspection services to broader based test technology. On complex parts requiring screening, environmental conditioning, and testing, the division was consistently cheaper than outside services. Where only elementary testing was required, however, low-tech outside laboratories were often cheaper, especially on large lots. The advantage that the division brought customers over the outside labs was that the latter provided essentially no engineering support, whereas ETO with its resident engineering resources was able to support such service on a rapid and cost-effective basis. The shift to more technically sophisticated services prompted a shift in the labor mix from direct to indirect personnel. The division expected to see a crossover between engineering head count and hourly head count early in the 1990s.

Finally, the introduction of higher technology components created the need for more automatic testing, longer test cycles, and more data per part. Digital components, for example, were currently tested for up to 100 conditions (combinations of electrical input and output states). The new generation of digital components, on the other hand, would be much more complex and require verification of up to 10,000 conditions. These would require very expensive highly automated equipment. This increase in automation would, in turn, lead to a smaller base of direct labor to absorb the depreciation costs of this new equipment.

There were fears that the resulting increase in burden rates would drive some customers away. ETO had already noticed an increase in the number and frequency of complaints from customers regarding the rates they were charged for testing.

The division's accounting manager proposed a new cost accounting system to alleviate the problem. Under this new system, burden would be directly traced to two cost pools. The first pool would contain burden related to the administrative and technical functions (division management, engineering, planning, and administrative personnel). This pool would be charged on a rate per direct labor dollar. The second pool would include all other burden costs and would be charged based on machine hours. Exhibit 3 provides the proposed burden rates.

Shortly after the accounting manager submitted his proposal, a consultant hired by Seligram's corporate management prepared an assessment of ETO's cost system. He recommended the implementation of a three-burden pool system utilizing separate burden centers for each test room and a common technical and administrative pool. Burden would be directly traced to each of the three burden pools. Like the accounting manager's system, burden costs in the test rooms would then be allocated on a machine hour basis. Technical and administrative costs would continue to be charged on a rate per direct labor dollar.

To examine the impact of the two alternative systems, ETO management asked that a study be conducted on a representative sample of parts. Exhibit 4 provides a breakdown of actual direct labor and machine hour requirements per lot for the five components selected for the study.

Technological Future

In 1988, the division faced major changes in the technology of testing that required important equipment acquisition decisions. The existing testing equipment was getting old and would not be able to keep pace with developments in component technology. Existing components, for example, had between 16 and 40 input/output terminations (e.g., pins or other mating configu-

rations), and ETO's equipment could handle up to 120 terminations. Although the 120-termination limit had only been reached a couple of times in the past few years, a new generation of components with up to 256 terminations was already being developed. Similarly, the upper limit of frequency on existing components was 20 MHz (million cycles per second), whereas the frequency on the next generation of components was expected to be 50 MHz.

The equipment required to test the next generation of components would be expensive. Each machine cost approximately $2 million. Testing on this equipment would be more automated than existing equipment, with longer test cycles and the generation of more test data per part. It was also likely that lot sizes would be larger. The new equipment would not replace the existing equipment but would merely add capabilities ETO did not currently possess. Additionally, the new equipment would only be needed to service the requirements of one or two customers in the foreseeable future. Exhibit 5 provides a summary of the new equipment's economics and operating characteristics.

The impact of this new equipment would be an acceleration in the decline in direct labor hours per lot of components. At the same time, burden would increase with the additional depreciation and engineering costs associated with the new equipment. This would result in a large increase in the burden rate per direct labor dollar. As Paul Carte, Manager of ETO, saw it, the acquisition of the new equipment could have a disastrous effect on the division's pricing structure if the labor-based allocation system remained in use:

> We plan on investing $2 million on a large electronic testing machine to test the chips of one or two customers. This machine will be very fast and will require little direct labor. Its acquisition will have a significant effect on our per direct labor dollar burden rate, which will result in an increase in charges to our other customers. It is clear that a number of customers will walk away if we try to pass this increase on. I am afraid that we will lose 25% of our customer base if we don't change our cost system.

EXHIBIT 1

SELIGRAM, INC.:
ELECTRONIC TESTING CENTER
1988 Budgeted Expenses

Direct labor	$3,260,015
Indirect labor	859,242
Salary expense	394,211
Supplies & expenses	538,029
Services[1]	245,226
Personnel allocations[2]	229,140
Service allocations[3]	2,448,134
Total budgeted expenses	$7,973,097

[1]Includes tool repair, computer expenses, maintenance stores, and service cost transfers from other divisions.
[2]Includes indirect and salaried employee fringe benefits, personnel department, security, stores/warehousing, and holidays/vacations.
[3]Includes building occupancy, telephones, depreciation, information systems, and data control.

EXHIBIT 2

SELIGRAM, INC.:
ELECTRONIC TESTING OPERATIONS
Calculation of Burden Rate
Based on 1988 Plan

BURDEN ELEMENT		
Indirect labor		$859,242
Salary expense		394,211
Supplies & expenses		538,029
Services		245,226
Personnel allocations		229,140
Service allocations		2,448,134
Total burden[1]		$4,713,982
Burden rate	$=$	$\dfrac{\text{TOTAL BURDEN \$}}{\text{DIRECT LABOR \$}}$
	$=$	$\dfrac{\$4,713,982}{3,260,015}$
	$=$	144.6%
Effective rate		145%

[1]*Cost Breakdown*

Variable	$1,426,317
Fixed:	
Depreciation	1,288,000
Other fixed:	1,999,665
Total burden:	$4,713,982

EXHIBIT 3

SELIGRAM, INC.:
ELECTRONIC TESTING OPERATIONS
Proposed Burden Rates
Based on 1988 Plan

MACHINE HOUR RATES

	MACHINE HRS	**BURDEN $[1]**
Main test room	33,201	$2,103,116
Mechanical test room	17,103	1,926,263
Total	50,304	$4,029,379

$$\text{Machine Hour Rate} = \frac{\text{Burden \$}}{\text{Machine Hrs}} = \frac{\$4,029,379}{50,304} = \$80.10$$

Effective machine hour rate = $80.00

Rate per Direct Labor Hour

Total engineering & administrative burden $ = $684,603[2]

Total direct labor dollars = $3,260,015[3]

$$\text{Burden rate} = \frac{\text{Engr \& admin \$}}{\text{Direct lbr \$}} = \frac{\$684,603}{\$3,260,015} = 21\%$$

Effective burden rate per direct labor $ = 20%

[1]Burden $

		Fixed		
	Variable	*Depreciation*	*Other*	*Total*
Main test room	$ 887,379	$ 88,779	$1,126,958	$2,103,116
Mechanical test room	443,833	808,103	679,327	1,926,263
Total burden	$1,331,212	$896,882	$1,801,285	$4,029,379

[2]Cost Breakdown

Variable	$ 95,105
Fixed:	
Depreciation	391,118
Other	198,380
Total	$684,603

[3]Includes all direct labor costs, including direct labor costs incurred in both test rooms as well as engineering.

EXHIBIT 4

SELIGRAM, INC.:
ELECTRONIC TESTING OPERATIONS
Direct Labor and Machine Hour Requirements
Actuals for One Lot

	DIRECT LABOR $	**MACHINE HOURS**		
		MAIN ROOM	**MECH. ROOM**	**TOTAL**
IC A	$ 917	8.5	10.0	18.5
IC B	2051	14.0	26.0	40.0
Capacitor	1094	3.0	4.5	7.5
Amplifier	525	4.0	1.0	5.0
Diode	519	7.0	5.0	12.0

EXHIBIT 5

SELIGRAM, INC.:
ELECTRONIC TESTING OPERATIONS
New Testing Equipment Economics and Operating
Characteristics

Cost	$2 million
Useful life	8 years
Depreciation method	Double declining balance (first-year depreciation costs of $500,000)
Location	Main test room
Utilization	10% first year, rising to 60% by third year and in all subsequent years, based on 4,000 hours per year availability (2 shifts × 2000-hour/year)
Direct labor requirements	Approximately five minutes per hour of operation; average labor rate of $30 per hour
Engineering requirements	$75,000 in installation and programming costs in first year
Estimated overhead (nonengineering depreciation)	$250,000 ($100,000 variable, $150,000 fixed)

KOMATSU, LTD. (B): PROFIT PLANNING AND PRODUCT COSTING

Komatsu, Ltd., was one of Japan's largest heavy industrial manufacturers. Founded in 1917 as part of the Takeuchi Mining Co., Komatsu Ironworks separated from its parent in 1921 to become Komatsu, Ltd. In 1991, Komatsu was a large international firm with revenues of ¥989 billion and net income of ¥31 billion. The company was organized along three major lines of business: construction equipment, industrial machinery, and electronic-applied products. Together, these three lines of business generated about 80% of corporate revenues. Other operations, which accounted for the remaining 20% of corporate revenues, included construction, real estate, unit housing, chemicals and plastics, and software development. Construction equipment and industrial equipment were considered core businesses while electronics-applied products and other operations were considered new businesses.

In 1989, the company adopted a "3G" strategy of growth, globalization, and group diversification. The growth objective required all divisions to expand aggressively, with 1995 sales expected to reach ¥1.4 trillion. The globalization objective was to achieve worldwide production by the year 2000. In 1993, the firm's equipment was used in over 160 countries and was manufactured on three continents in eleven countries. The group diversification objective sought to aggressively develop three new business areas: electronics, plastics, and robotics. By the year 2000, the firm expected all nonconstruction products, including these three areas, to account for 50% of group revenues.

Professor Robin Cooper of the Peter F. Drucker Graduate Management Center at The Claremont Graduate School prepared this case.

Profit Planning Process

Komatsu's profit planning process consisted of three major stages: policy making, profit planning, and evaluation. Prior to 1990, profit planning at Komatsu was undertaken semi-annually. However, an annual planning horizon was adopted in 1990. Three major reasons drove this decision. First, annual preparation reduced the work load on the profit planning group. Second, management felt that semi-annual plans engendered a short-term perspective. Finally, given the fluctuation in sales levels between the two semi-annual periods, the allocation of fixed costs between them was considered too arbitrary to be meaningful.

Policy-Making Stage The process of profit planning began with the development of the firm's long-term plan, which consisted of the sales, production, and product development plans. This long-term plan provided strategic direction to the corporation for the next 5 to 10 years. It was updated from time to time to reflect current conditions and any changes in anticipated future conditions.

The development of the long-term plan began with the preparation of a preliminary long-term plan by the corporate planning and control department. This preliminary plan was submitted to the board of directors for approval. After the preliminary plan was accepted, a process that often required considerable discussion and amendment, long-term profit plans were prepared by each division. The development of these plans was coordinated by the corporate planning and control department to ensure that when aggregated they would support the preliminary long-term plan.

These long-term divisional plans were submitted to the board for approval. Upon their acceptance, a process that again often required considerable negotiation, the annual company policy was announced by the president. This policy, which was developed under the umbrella of the firm's 3G strategy, provided strategic direction for the year.

After discussion about the implications of the annual company policy, the corporate planning and control department prepared the firm's annual profit plan. This plan identified Komatsu's profit objective for the year. The acceptance of the annual profit plan by the board of directors initiated the preparation of the annual divisional profit plans. These plans were developed using sales and cost targets prepared by the sales and production departments.

Profit Planning Stage The divisional profit plans were the basis of negotiations between headquarters and the divisions regarding production and sales volume. From these negotiations emerged the sales and production plans for each division, which were used to develop more power and equipment investment plans. The plans were combined to produce the preliminary divisional cost plans. The aggregation of the divisional sales and preliminary cost plans produced the all-Komatsu sales plan and a preliminary profit estimate. This estimate was compared to the target profit of the annual profit plan, and after a period of negotiations, the divisional plans were approved by the board. The final budget and cost plans resulted from this board review.

The final budget and cost plans were used as the basis for preparing more detailed budgets for each division (such budgets included general and administration, research and development, sales expense, warranty, and overhead). These budgets were used by the firm's cost system to generate product costs and transfer prices. The reported product costs and transfer prices were used to check the budget and to develop the execution cost plan and the profit plan by product.

The budget plans and profit plans by product were used to develop the all-Komatsu profit plan. This plan was sent to the board for approval, and after negotiations, the divisional execution plans were prepared. These execution plans were monthly profit and loss plans that were used as a benchmark against which to evaluate divisional performance.

Evaluation Stage Actual sales revenue, sales quantities, and costs were compared to their execution plan equivalents on a monthly basis. Two reports were prepared for the board. The first report identified profit differences and the second analyzed in detail the reasons for the difference between actual and expected performance. Significant differences between actual and expected performance triggered the development of secondary plans, or countermeasures, as they were known. These countermeasures were designed to ensure that profit and sales shortfalls were as small as possible. For example, one year when sales of excavators and bulldozers were below budget, the sales of attachments were increased by introducing a number of new designs to create additional demand. Prior to their implementation, countermeasures were submitted to the board for approval. The execution plans were updated to reflect the effects of any counter-measures.

Product Costing The evaluation stage relied heavily upon Komatsu's standard cost system. Five different variances were computed every month. Some of these variances were computed more frequently, but divisional reporting occurred once a month. These variances were the raw material and purchased parts price variances, the budget and operation volume variances, and the inventory variance. The two purchase price variances captured the difference between expected and actual prices. The raw material purchase price variance was determined upon purchase of direct and indirect raw materials. These materials were placed into inventory at standard costs. The purchased parts price variance was determined when the parts were used in the production process. Purchased parts were placed into work-in-process at actual and relieved at standard.

Labor costs and overhead expenses were debited to the production overhead account as they were incurred. As the production of a product was completed in each cost center, production overhead was transferred to the work-in-process account at actual volume and standard price. The monthly difference between the labor and overhead expenses was charged to the production overhead account and divided into two variances: the budget and operation volume variances. The budget variance was a spending variance that captured the difference between the budgeted and actual level of expenses. The operation volume variance was the production volume variance, which captured the unabsorbed overhead due to actual production volume being different from planned.

As production was completed, the work-in-process account was relieved using standard volume and standard price. At the end of the month, the work-in-process account was closed out by evaluating the ending inventory at standard volume and standard price. The remaining balance in the work-in-process account was the inventory variance, which captured unexpected material usage of procured parts and production overhead.

The five variances—inventory, operation volume, budget, and the two purchase price variances—were aggregated into a production overhead and material cost variance. The material cost variance contained both of the purchase price variances and the direct material portion of the inventory variance. The production overhead variance contained the other variances.

Treatment of Manufacturing Overhead Costs

In the late 1980s, Komatsu had experienced significant growth in its manufacturing overhead costs relative to its direct costs. The firm identified several factors that were causing overhead to increase:

1. Increases in indirect labor wage rates that were not being offset by increases in productivity.
2. Automation, especially the introduction of flexible machinery systems and computer-integrated manufacturing, that decreased the direct labor content of products while increasing their indirect content, including machine depreciation and technical support costs.
3. Increases in product diversity, which led to increases in the relative importance of indirect costs.
4. The shift to offshore production for some components and products, which increased their administration costs.

Reacting to this growth in indirect costs, Komatsu changed the treatment of these costs in its plant cost system.

Old Cost System Under the old system, plant overhead costs were split into three major categories: direct manufacturing overhead, indirect manufacturing overhead, and production overhead (see Exhibit 1). Direct manufacturing overhead costs were those expenses consumed in the production departments. Indirect manufacturing overhead costs were expenses consumed in support departments whose outputs were consumed directly by the production departments. These support departments included manufacturing engineering, machine and equipment support, fabrication inspection, administration, and general staff. Production overhead costs included the expenses of support departments whose outputs were not consumed by the production departments. These support departments were purchased parts inspection, purchasing, warehousing, production control, engineering, data processing, and accounting administration.

The costs of the indirect manufacturing departments were allocated to the direct departments on the basis of several factors: head count (the number of people in the production department), labor hours, electricity consumption, tool consumption, direct manufacturing overhead costs, and machine hours (see Exhibit 2). These costs were then combined with the costs of each manufacturing department and allocated to the product models. Four direct manufacturing departments were identified: casting, machining, welding, and assembly. The costs of these departments and the allocations from the indirect manufacturing departments were allocated to the product models using three different bases: weight, machine hours, and labor hours. Production overhead was allocated to the product models based upon their manufacturing costs (material, labor, plus both direct and indirect manufacturing overhead costs). Exhibits 3 and 4 illustrate how the production overhead was allocated to the product models.

New Cost System   The new cost system was a simplified version of the old one (see Exhibit 5). Analysis of how the old cost system allocated indirect manufacturing overhead costs to the product models indicated that reported costs were inaccurate. When the old system was designed, the number of production engineers supporting the shop floor labor force was relatively small; therefore, inaccuracies in how these costs were assigned to products was considered acceptable. Over time, as both overhead as a percent of total cost and the degree of automation increased, the use of direct labor hours as the only allocation basis for overhead produced greater inaccuracies. Eventually, the distortions in reported costs became unacceptable.

Management decided to simplify the old cost system by combining indirect manufacturing overhead costs and production overhead costs into a single category called plant control overhead, and by allocating these costs to the product categories. Product categories consisted of end products, attachments, spare parts, prototypes, and an "other" category that contained miscellaneous items such as castings. The product category "end products" contained product lines, such as bulldozers and excavators. The product lines contained product models, such as bulldozers D85 and D155 and excavators PC100 and PC200 (see Exhibit 6). Three different allocation bases were used to drive plant control overhead to the five product categories: production yen (including material and outside processing costs), adjusted production yen, and cost of in-house processing (i.e., the direct manufacturing overhead costs).

The most commonly used allocation base was production yen. It was used to allocate the costs of the gen-

eral, administration, and inspection departments and the technical center. The costs of the technical center consisted of the cost of design and warranty maintenance associated with current models. The adjusted production yen base was used to allocate the costs of planning and coordination and purchasing. Production yen was adjusted to allow for the more complex management required for attachments, spare parts, and prototypes. For example, it usually took longer to manage the attachments, spare parts, and prototypes because unlike excavators, they were not produced continuously but intermittently, and also because the customer frequently required rapid service.

A special two-stage procedure was used to allocate the costs of the planning and coordination and purchasing departments. In the first stage, the costs of the planning and coordination and purchasing departments were driven to the "end products" category using adjusted production yen. In the second stage, the costs of the end product category were driven to the different end product lines (bulldozers and excavators) using head count (here defined as the number of people in the overhead department dedicated to that product line). For the other four product categories, the planning and coordination and purchasing costs were allocated on the basis of adjusted production yen. No equivalents to product lines were identified. The only minor exception was for spare parts, which were purchased from a separate department; the cost of this department was directly charged to the spare parts category. The cost of in-house processing was used to allocate the costs of manufacturing engineering and manufacturing control to the product categories.

The allocation procedure used in the new cost system to assign the indirect plant control overhead costs to product models used the reported direct manufacturing costs of the product models (material, labor, plus direct manufacturing overhead). This allocation procedure is illustrated in Exhibits 7 and 8. The new system was designed to be accurate at the product category and line levels but not at the product model level. Its primary objective was to provide better cost control. Consequently, production floor managers were only held accountable for the direct manufacturing costs of the products. Support department managers were held responsible for indirect costs. Management was aware that the new system did not relate overhead to individual product models in ways that captured the consumption of overhead. However, the system was much simpler to understand, highlighted the importance of managing overhead departments, and was less expensive to maintain.

Despite concerns about the accuracy of the product model costs reported by the new cost system, Komatsu management relied upon these costs when making several product-related decisions, including transfer pricing, product mix management, and turning down orders. The cost information used in making these decisions included the allocation of indirect manufacturing and production department overhead. It was this use of reported product costs that caused management to be concerned with the new cost system. There was consensus that products and models differed in how they consumed overhead, and that these differences were not captured by either the old or new systems. Over time, the company planned to implement a new cost system that could better assign all manufacturing costs to products, thereby increasing management's ability to control overhead. Exhibit 9 illustrates the seven major categories of overhead in the new cost system.

EXHIBIT 1 Contents of the Three Major Categories of Overhead in Old Cost System

OLD CATEGORY	CONTENTS
Direct Manufacturing Overhead Costs	Casting
	Machinery
	Welding
	Assembly
Indirect Manufacturing Overhead Costs	Manufacturing Engineering
	Machine and Equipment Support
	Inspection of Fabrication
	Administration
	General Staff
Production Overhead Costs	Inspection of Purchased Parts
	Purchasing
	Warehousing
	Production Control
	Engineering
	Data Processing
	Accounting Administration

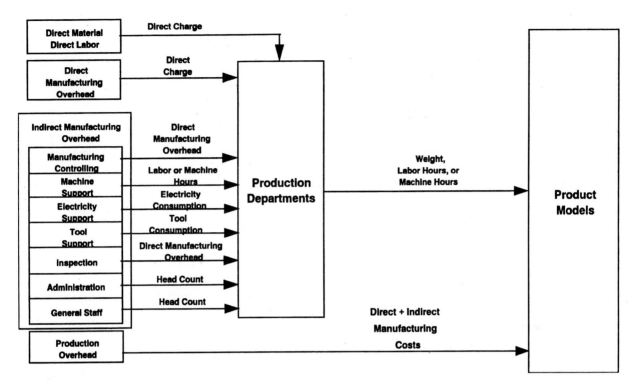

EXHIBIT 2   Komatsu's Old Cost System

EXHIBIT 3 Determination of Production Overhead Ratio in Old Cost System

PRODUCT MODEL	DIRECT MATERIAL COST	DIRECT MFG. O/H PER UNIT	INDIRECT MFG. O/H PER UNIT	TOTAL MFG. COST PER UNIT
1	¥80	¥7	¥3	¥ 90
2	¥90	¥8	¥4	¥102
3	¥70	¥5	¥5	¥ 80

PRODUCT MODEL	TOTAL MFG. COST PER UNIT	PRODUCTION VOLUME	TOTAL MFG. COST
1	¥ 90	4	¥ 360
2	¥102	3	¥ 306
3	¥ 80	6	¥ 480
Total Manufacturing Costs			¥ 1,146
Total Production Overhead			¥ 100
Total Production Costs			¥ 1,246
Production Overhead per Manufacturing Cost			¥0.0873

EXHIBIT 4 Allocation of Production Overhead Costs to Product Models in Old Cost System

PRODUCT MODEL	TOTAL MANUFACTURING COST	PRODUCTION OVERHEAD RATIO	PRODUCT OVERHEAD	TOTAL COST PER UNIT
1	¥ 90	0.0873	¥7.85	¥ 97.85
2	¥102	0.0873	¥8.90	¥110.90
3	¥ 80	0.0873	¥6.98	¥ 86.98

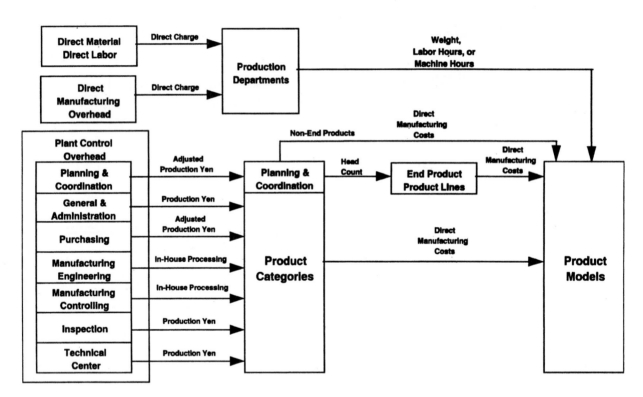

EXHIBIT 5   **Komatsu's New Cost System**

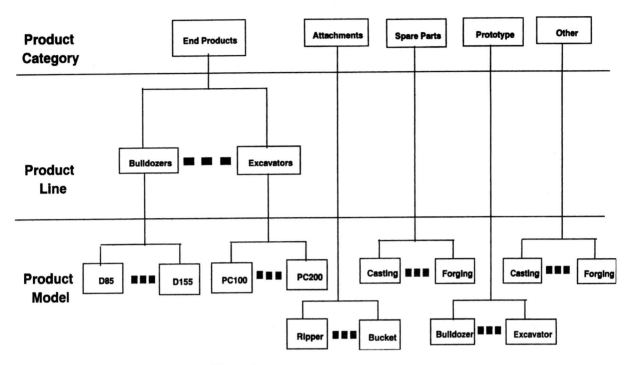

EXHIBIT 6   Komatsu's Product Hierarchy

EXHIBIT 7 Determination of Production Control Overhead Ratio in New Cost System

PRODUCT MODEL	DIRECT MATERIAL COST	DIRECT MFG. O/H PER UNIT	TOTAL MFG. COST PER UNIT
1	¥80	¥7	¥87
2	¥90	¥8	¥98
3	¥70	¥5	¥75

PRODUCT MODEL	TOTAL MFG. COST PER UNIT	PRODUCTION VOLUME	TOTAL MFG. COST
1	¥87	4	¥ 348
2	¥98	3	¥ 294
3	¥75	6	¥ 450
Total Manufacturing Costs			¥1,092
Total Indirect Manufacturing Overhead (All Products)			¥ 54
Total Production Overhead (All Products)			¥ 100
Plant Control Overhead			¥ 154
Total Production Costs			¥1,246
Plant Control Overhead per Direct Manufacturing Cost			¥0.1410

EXHIBIT 8 Allocation of Production Control Overhead Costs to Product Models in New Cost System

PRODUCT MODEL	DIRECT MFG. COST PER UNIT	PRODUCTION CONTROL O/H RATIO	PRODUCTION CONTROL OVERHEAD	TOTAL COST PER UNIT
1	¥87	0.1410	¥12.26	¥ 99.26
2	¥98	0.1410	¥13.82	¥112.82
3	¥75	0.1410	¥10.58	¥ 85.50

EXHIBIT 9 Contents of the Seven Major Categories of Overhead in New Cost System

NEW CATEGORY	CONTENTS
General and Administration	Administration
	Accounting Administration
Planning and Coordination	Product Control
	Data Processing
Purchasing	Purchasing
	Warehousing
Manufacturing Engineering	Manufacturing Engineering
	Machine and Equipment Support
Manufacturing Controlling	General Staff
Inspection	Inspection and Fabrication
	Inspection of Purchased Parts
Technical Center	Engineering

MAYERS TAP, INC. (A)

Mayers Tap, Inc., (MTI) is a subsidiary of the Mayers Corporation, a manufacturer of machine tools and cutting tools. The parent company was founded in 1910 by Helen G. Mayers to produce drill bits and was first known as St. Louis Drill Manufacturers. The name was later changed to the Mayers Corporation in honor of the founder.

During the early 1960s, the Mayers Corporation embarked on an aggressive 10-year expansion plan to capitalize on rapid growth in the cutting-tool industry. In 1966 a tap manufacturing plant was built in Denver, Colorado, and in 1976 a second plant was built in Albany, New York. All selling and administrative activities were consolidated at the Albany facility upon its com-

pletion, and a separate subsidiary, Mayers Tap, Inc., was formed to manage the company's tap business. MTI was headed by John Mayers, the 31-year-old grandson of the company's founder. MTI was entirely family owned, and the majority ownership was held by John's father, who had run the company until his retirement in 1978. MTI was proud of its employee relations; Mayers claimed this was the major reason that MTI was one of the few nonunion firms in the industry.

In the fall of 1983 John Mayers decided to replace MTI's cost accounting system. The old system was not providing enough data to price MTI's products competitively or identify cost control problem areas effectively. For example, the company sometimes lost bids to its competitors with similar productive facilities even when MTI had quoted what it considered close to break-even prices. In other cases, the firm quoted high to avoid business because it was at capacity, and yet it was the

This case was prepared by Professor Robin Cooper.
Copyright © 1984 by the President and Fellows of Harvard College. Harvard Business School case 185-111.

low bidder by quite a large margin. Another major problem was the continuous discrepancy between the profits predicted by the cost accounting system and those reported by the financial accounting system. In 1983 this difference amounted to nearly $200,000, with the cost system predicting higher profitability. These and other symptoms indicated to Mayers that MTI did not know what its products cost to make.

Part of the problem was the impact of changes in the production process. Although many of the machines were typical metalworking equipment, MTI had started to invest in new automatic loading machinery that substantially changed the way taps were produced. It was clear to Mayers that the cost accounting system had to be designed with the manufacturing process in mind.

The existing cost system used a single burden rate in both the Albany and Denver plants for all labor and overhead costs. The standard cost was found by multiplying the burden rate by the total standard production hours for each product and then adding the standard raw material costs.

Three questions faced Mayers in replacing the cost system:

1. How to allocate overhead costs;
2. How many cost centers to have; and
3. Whether to drop one or more products if the new cost system showed them to be uneconomical.

MTI Products

Mayers Tap, Inc., produced a small variety of taps and had become known for high-quality output. Taps were used to cut threads into a drilled hole. These threads allowed a bolt to be screwed into the hole without requiring a nut to hold it in place. The taps were made from hardened high-speed steel, and the production process basically involved a series of precise, specialized metal-grinding operations. The principal parts of the tap are as follows:

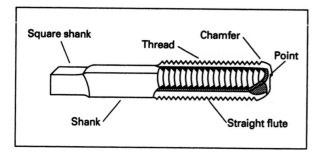

The tap shank was squared off on one end so that it would be held securely in the tapping machine. Flutes were ground lengthwise in the tap to permit removal of the metal chips produced during tapping and to allow lubricating oil to reach the cutting surfaces. The point end of the tap was chamfered (tapered) so that the amount of thread-cutting surface gradually increased at the beginning of the tap. This increased the life of the tap by reducing the amount of heat generated during tapping.

MTI's 1984 product line consisted of 11 products. Five of the products were considered standard design taps while the remaining six taps had very specialized designs. A list of the products appears in Table A.

Table A.   MTI Product Line, 1984

PRODUCT NUMBER	TAP TYPE	DIAMETER (IN.)	FLUTES	THREADS PER INCH
1	Standard	1 1/4	4	7
2	Pilot	1 1/4	5	2
3	Pilot	1/4	4	20
4	Pipe	3/4	5	14
5	Standard	5/8	4	11
6	Reamer	1/4	4	20
7	Reamer	3/8	4	16
8	Forming	5/8	0	16
9	Standard	1/4	4	20
10	Standard	3/8	3	16
11	Standard	5/8	4	13

The Tap Industry

Sales in the tap industry as a whole amounted to about $86 million in 1983 (see Exhibit 1). The industry was very mature. There had been relatively few new tap styles developed in the past 30 years, and except for increased automation, there were no fundamental changes in production techniques during the same period. More than 20 firms produced taps, and the largest had a 15% market share. In the last few years there had been some reduction in the conventional tap market. First, the four-cylinder engine had become more common in U.S. automobiles at the expense of the eight-cylinder engine. A four-cylinder engine requires about 50% fewer tapping operations. Second, new materials and alloys allowed for an expanded use of self-tapping screws.

MTI accounted for about 10% of the industry sales. It marketed its taps to large end users on the basis of high quality at a low price. Price competition was heated in the tap industry. Each manufacturer published list prices for its taps, but discounts of up to 50% were often given to secure a customer. Discounts were determined on a customer-by-customer basis, depending on the size of the customer and the competition.

Manufacturing operations MTI's highly automated Denver plant was designed for high-volume production of the most common taps but could only machine taps smaller than 5/8″ in diameter. The Albany plant produced taps 5/8″ and larger in diameter, taps of special design, small-volume orders, and urgent orders. MTI's operations were separated in this manner because Mayers felt that two fundamentally different types of manufacturing operations were necessary for MTI's product line. He felt that this not only helped to hold down costs but made management easier, because managers in each plant could focus on one specific philosophy of manufacturing operation.

The Denver plant, which Mayers characterized as an automated production line factory, had been built using the latest machining and heat-treating equipment available. It was staffed by lower-paid machine operators, who required relatively little training to operate the equipment. Operators in Denver were trained to operate most of the machinery in the plant and therefore could be transferred among the machines as required by the production schedule. Unlike the Albany machinery, the Denver equipment could generally operate unattended. An important difference between the machines in the two plants was that the Denver equipment had autoloaders. The operator merely had to load a stack of tap blanks into a machine, and it would pick each one up and machine it automatically. The Denver equipment required longer setup times, but the machining speed of the equipment in each plant was roughly the same.

Albany was considered a specialized job shop. Most of its machinery was multipurpose metal-machining equipment such as lathes, milling machines, and grinders that averaged about 25 years old. For the most part, the production equipment was manually controlled and required skilled machinists; few machinists were trained to operate more than one type of machine. As a result, Albany's per-hour labor costs were substantially higher than Denver's.

The two plants contained 31 different types of machines and 47 machines in total (Exhibit 2 lists all 31 classes of machine). The type of labor required was dependent on the machine class in question. For example, many of the Denver machines required unskilled operators while the Albany machinery required skilled machinists.

The two-plant system allowed MTI to offer 24-hour delivery on a broad range of tools. Fast delivery was a major marketing plus for MTI. Customers were offered two levels of service, QIK and QIK-24. QIK was the normal delivery time (usually only a few working days) and provided the most competitive prices. QIK-24 orders were shipped within 24 hours for a premium price competitive with the prices of other manufacturers offering 24-hour service.

Tap Production

Tap production, while varying from tap to tap, consisted of several distinct steps:

1. Cutoff—The bar stock was cut into proper lengths and, for large taps, the shank was square milled.
2. Heat treatment—The cut lengths were immersed in molten salt at 1,000° centigrade to harden the parts.
3. Grinding—The outer diameter of the part was ground to tolerance and the shanks of larger taps were center lapped to allow the part to fit into standard tapping equipment.
4. T-1 blanks—At this point in the process, some of the parts made in Denver were called T-1 blanks. These could be machined into a number of different products in either of the two plants (see Table B).
5. Flute grinding—The flutes were ground into the part, one at a time.
6. Thread grinding—The fluted parts were now thread ground using diamond wheels.
7. Chamfering—The end of the tap was tapered so that cutting begins gradually.

Each of the grinding or cutting machines was lubricated by MTI's high-pressure oil system. The system pumped lubricating oil to each of the machines and sprayed the oil on the cutting surfaces to cool them and to remove steel chips. The oil was then pumped back to a filtering system that removed the steel chips.

All tap production was done in fixed volumes known as EPQs (economic production quantities). The EPQs were designed to provide the most cost-effective tradeoff between the setup costs, the inventory levels, and the production scheduling requirements. Taps were produced for inventory, and when the inventory level of a given tap dropped below a predetermined level, manufacturing would produce another EPQ batch of that tap.

Table B. Products Made from T-1 Blanks

PRODUCT NUMBER	FINAL MANUFACTURE	TAP TYPE	T-1 (IN.)
5	Albany	Standard	5/8
6	Albany	Reamer	1/4
7	Albany	Reamer	3/8
8	Albany	Forming	5/8
9	Denver	Standard	1/4
10	Denver	Standard	3/8
11	Denver	Standard	5/8

EXHIBIT 1

Tap Industry Sales

	1976	1977	1978	1979	1980	1981	1982	1983
Total sales ($000s)	$48,304	$52,171	$56,829	$61,789	$67,466	$68,043	$72,475	$86,162
Total units sold (000s)	27,761	29,146	30,553	33,015	33,565	32,871	33,942	35,168
Average price[a]	$1.74	$1.79	$1.86	$1.93	$2.01	$2.07	$2.15	$2.45

[a]As a specialty tap producer, Mayers had an average tap cost much higher than the industry.

EXHIBIT 2

Machine Descriptions

Albany

TYPE NO.	QUANTITY	TYPE OF MACHINE	YEAR PURCHASED	NATURE OF MACHINE	OPERATOR
K-40	3	Flute grinder	1979	Semiautomatic, manual loading	Specialized machinist
F-10	4	Thread grinder	1979	Automatic loading	Specialized machinist
J-22	1	Butt grinder	1970		General machinist
G-58	2	Chamfer grinder	1970		General machinist
D-34	3	OD grinder	1967		General machinist
N-68	1	Cutter grinder	1970		General machinist
C-50	2	Salt-bath furnace	1978	Manual loading	Unskilled labor
N-72	2	Cutter grinder	1960		General machinist
C-86	1	Buffing wheel	1965		Unskilled labor
N-78	1	Split-point grinder	1970		General machinist
A-39	2	Template lathe	1977	Manual operation	Specialized machinist
A-40	1	Turret lathe	1977	Manual operation	Specialized machinist
B-79	1	Milling machine	1953		Specialized machinist
C-45	2	Straightening press	1962	Hand-operated	Unskilled labor
B-86	1	Cutter grinder	1977		Specialized machinist
A-44	1	Cutoff machine	1953		Unskilled labor
A-76	1	Centering machine	1963	Specialized type of lathe	Specialized machinist
B-81	1	Milling machine	1953	Multiple head (gang)	Specialized machinist
C-59	1	Center lap	1962	Cleans and machines centers, hand-operated	Unskilled labor
F-07	2	Thread grinder	1970	Manual loading	Specialized machinist
Total	33				

continued

Denver

TYPE NO.	QUANTITY	TYPE OF MACHINE	YEAR PURCHASED	NATURE OF MACHINE	OPERATOR
D-43	3	Flute grinder	1978	Fully automatic	
E-01	3	Thread grinder	1977	Fully automatic	
F-32	1	Chamfer grinder	1975	Fully automatic	
G-05	1	Butt grinder	1979	Fully automatic	
A-06	1	Cutoff machine	1981	Automatic operation, manual loading	
B-03	3	Salt-bath furnace	1982	Automatic loading/unloading for heat treating	Unskilled labor
C-03	1	Centerless grinder	1976	Fully automatic	
D-02	1	Square grinder	1977	Fully automatic	
A-41	1	Cutoff machine	1975	Manual loading, automatic operation	
C-31	1	Centerless grinder	1978	Fully automatic	
A-51	1	Cutoff machine	1980	Automatic loading, automatic operation	
Total	17				

MAYERS TAP, INC. (B)

John Mayers, president of Mayers Tap, Inc., (MTI) asked Lee Rhodes, controller, to conduct a major review of the company's cost accounting system [see Mayers Tap, Inc. (A) for background on the company]. Mayers was concerned that the current methods of allocating fixed and variable costs might have made unprofitable taps look profitable and vice versa.

Under the old accounting system, the company distributed overhead at only one rate. This rate was calculated by dividing the sum of the nonmaterial costs for both plants by the expected total number of direct labor hours. The resulting rate per direct labor hour, called the burden rate, was then used to allocate nonmaterial costs to the taps produced. In 1985 the direct labor burden rate was expected to be $30. Therefore, for a tap that required five hours of direct labor to produce, $150 ($30/hour × 5 hours) would be added to the raw material cost to arrive at the total cost for the tap. (Exhibit 1 shows the expected price, standard cost, and budgeted volume for MTI's 11 principal products.) Certain products were currently selling at very low prices, and Mayers thought they were close to their variable cost of production. Although the firm did not know the exact variable cost, it was thought to be about 60% of the total cost.

Mayers hoped that the new system would help MTI determine which taps were most profitable by allowing more than one burden rate. If more accurate cost information was available through the use of multiple burden rates, it would be possible to reprice the taps. Alternatively, MTI might drop some existing products and replace them with new ones. In addition, the new cost system would help MTI focus management attention on high-cost operations.

Rhodes had been asked to develop a plan to create the new cost system. He had broken it down into three major steps:

1. Determine allocation bases for each principal cost category and then allocate these costs to products, differentiating between fixed and variable costs.
2. Check whether the resulting cost data would be more accurate if each machine class was used as a cost center or whether a single rate or two plant-specific rates would be sufficient.
3. If plantwide rates were not sufficient, attempt to minimize the number of cost centers required without sacrificing the accuracy of the cost data.

Rhodes's first step was to prepare a list of the direct labor, variable overhead, and fixed overhead costs for each of the factory machines and to identify the allocation bases that should be used to allocate the costs to each machine. He started by obtaining a copy of the 1985 budget (see Exhibit 2) and a description of the

This case was prepared by Professor Robin Cooper.
Copyright © 1984 by the President and Fellows of Harvard College. Harvard Business School case 185-111.

contents of each of the line items in the budget (see Exhibit 3).

Obtaining an appropriate allocation base was an extremely tedious task. It required going back through MTI's accounting records to break down the costs in the necessary detail. In many instances, budget estimates had been based on only one year's data because of the amount of work required to break down the information from the existing accounting records. Often the records were not sufficiently detailed to split transactions, and Rhodes had to guess what the costs were. Although this work would allow vast improvements in the precision of MTI's cost information, the controller estimated that he would need two to three years to adequately revise and update the input data used for the system. Even then, annual adjustments would be necessary to reflect changes in factory operations and the company's product line. After several months of effort, Lee had identified 13 potential allocation bases (see Exhibit 4) and the ratios for each of the machine classes (see Exhibit 5).

Rhodes decided to develop allocations for each of the 31 machine classes. There seemed little point in differentiating among identical machines since they necessarily had very similar costs and were used interchangeably in production.

The Denver heat treatment process (machine class B-03) was used to heat-treat all products made by the firm. The Albany products were completed to a stage just prior to heat treatment, shipped to Denver, heat-treated, and returned to Albany for completion. It cost less to transport the parts than to continuously operate a second heat treatment plant in Albany. Albany had a small heat treatment facility (machine class C-50) that could be switched on and off as needed. It was used when small volumes of parts had to be completed quickly for shipment. This facility was also used to surface-treat certain products.

The cost of heat treatment at Denver was handled like any other machining operation. Consequently, the apparent budgeted expense for heat treatment in Denver was zero, since heat treatment costs were included with other line items (such as direct labor, power, and heat). The same approach was originally planned for Albany heat treatment costs, but the problems associated with allocating costs to products that only occasionally used a process were considered too difficult to overcome for a $9,000 line item. Consequently, Albany heat treatment costs were treated as an overhead item, and the operations costs were set to zero.

EXHIBIT 1

Fiscal 1985 Product Budget

	PRODUCT	EXPECTED SELLING PRICE	STANDARD COST[a]	BUDGETED VOLUME (000s)
1. Standard	(1¼″– 7 4FL)[b]	$25.25	$17.17	6.0
2. Pilot	(1¼″– 2 5FL)	83.80	124.46	28.8
3. Pilot	(¼″ – 20 4FL)	35.15	24.94	8.0
4. Pipe	(⅝″ – 14 5FL)	15.00	9.04	75.0
5. Standard	(⅝″ – 11 4FL)	6.90	4.42	46.2
6. Reamer	(¼″ – 20 4FL)	4.50	3.17	24.0
7. Reamer	(⅜″ – 16 4FL)	4.75	3.40	165.0
8. Forming	(⅝″ – 16 OFL)	5.75	8.41	66.0
9. Standard	(¼″ – 20 4FL)	3.35	1.46	324.0
10. Standard	(⅜″ – 16 3FL)	1.50	1.87	255.0
11. Standard	(½″ – 13 4FL)	7.30	4.49	360.0

[a]Existing single burden rate system standard cost.
[b]FL signifies flute.

EXHIBIT 2

Fiscal 1985 Financial Budget

		ALBANY	DENVER	
Budgeted sales				$9,657,070
Budgeted expenses				
	Raw materials	$1,122,536	$705,846	
	Direct labor[a]	1,182,012	671,172	
	Nonproductive labor	110,000	68,000	
	OT and night labor	82,500	51,000	
	Power and heat	175,000	240,000	
	Repairs and maintenance	150,000	175,000	
	Grinding wheels	225,000	300,000	
	Other factory supplies	50,000	80,000	
	Depreciation, machines	120,000	250,000	
	Depreciation, buildings	160,000	150,000	
	General factory supplies	30,000	40,000	
	General factory maintenance	150,000	125,000	
	Factory support expenses	400,000	350,000	
	General plant costs	150,000	125,000	
	Oil filtration expenses	300,000	600,000	
	Inspection center costs	90,000	90,000	
	Heat treatment costs	9,000	0	
		$4,506,048	$4,021,018	8,527,066
Selling, general, and administrative				500,000
Net income				$ 630,004

[a]Direct labor hours budgeted: 131,778 (Albany) and 83,897 (Denver).

EXHIBIT 3

Description of Factory Costs

Raw Materials	Raw material consisted of steel bar stock purchased as needed in 25-foot lengths. The raw material cost for each tap was calculated by dividing the number of tap blanks to be cut from the bar stock by the total cost of the bar.
Direct Labor	Direct labor included wages and employee benefit costs. Labor costs varied by machine. Some machines, such as the milling machines and thread grinders, were operated by skilled machinists paid at higher rates. Other machines, such as the flute grinders, were simpler and could be controlled by operators with relatively little training who earned lower wage rates. If one machinist ran several machines at once, only a fraction of that person's hourly costs were charged to a given machine. Consequently, much of the difference in the wages of machinists versus operators was not apparent on a per-machine basis.
Nonproductive Labor	MTI hourly workers used computerized time clocks to record the amount of time they spent on each job. When a job was begun, the operator or machinist entered his or her employee number and the job number into the clock. Any paid work time (idle time, meetings, breaks, etc.) that was not directly charged to a job was considered nonproductive labor time. This usually accounted for slightly less than 10% of the total direct labor hours. The amount of nonproductive time varied by machine because of uncertainties in the availability of work for machines in the final stages of the production process.

(continued on next page)

Overtime and Night Labor	Overtime was determined much like nonproductive time. A percentage of direct labor cost for each machine was determined based on historical overtime requirements. MTI ran two eight-hour day shifts, the early shift (6 A.M.–2 P.M.) and the late shift (2 P.M.–10 P.M.). A third night shift was sometimes used for the machines that were capacity bottlenecks. Night labor hours were computed by subtracting the available daytime hours from the total required operating hours for each machine. Night labor was paid the day rate plus 10%.
Power and Heat	Electricity and gas were the only elements of power and heat. Most power was consumed by the production machinery. The factory was not heated because the heat given off by the machines and heat treatment facility was sufficient to keep the building warm. The other principal power user was the oil system. The oil was pumped at 150 psi, which required large pump motors. The administrative offices were heated by baseboard electric heat and cooled with electric air conditioners in the summer. The company received one electric bill for each building. MTI estimated that the administrative office area in Albany consumed $5,000 of electricity annually, and this was excluded from the power and heat account. The general rule for the rest of the power cost was 75% allocated to the machinery and 25% to the oil system. This was based on detailed testing of power use.
Repairs and Maintenance	Repairs and maintenance included labor and the cost of parts and supplies used in regular maintenance. No worker did repair and maintenance work exclusively. Some of the machinists that ran the production equipment regularly maintained and repaired the production equipment. MTI would subcontract particularly difficult repair work. Maintenance time was recorded by MTI workers through the computerized time clock, and parts and supplies used for repair were recorded by machine when taken from the stockroom. A machine's maintenance budget was estimated by the production manager based on historical expenses with consideration for any special maintenance that might be needed.
Grinding and Diamond Wheels	Grinding wheels and diamond wheels were one of the largest factory expenses. Grinding wheels were large abrasive stone wheels used to remove steel from the taps. The diamond wheels were small diamond-coated metal wheels that were used to reshape grinding wheels when they wore down. The amount of grinding wheel used depended on the volume of steel that had to be removed on a tap, so larger taps used much more of the grinding wheels than smaller taps. The stockroom kept track of the grinding wheels used by each machine. The budgeted expense was based on historical experience adjusted for changes in the overall estimated production volume of taps for the budgeted year.
Other Factory Supplies	Other factory supplies included all supplies used by the factory machines (other than grinding and diamond wheels), such as grease, abrasive cutoff wheels, milling cutters, and lathe bits.
Depreciation, Machines	Most of the Albany machines were over 10 years old and had been fully depreciated. The Colorado plant's newer equipment still had depreciable life remaining. All machines were depreciated on a straight-line basis over 10 years.
Depreciation, Buildings	Depreciation of the factory portion of the buildings and other equipment not directly related to the production machines was classified separately. The buildings were depreciated on a straight-line basis over 30 years.
General Factory Supplies	These consisted mostly of small general merchandise items, such as rags, nails, and glue. The budgeted amount was estimated by the production manager based on historical experience.
General Factory Maintenance	These were mostly the labor costs of the janitors who cleaned and maintained the factory area. It also included cleaning and maintenance supplies used in the factory. Three full-time janitors worked in Albany, two in Denver. The budgeted amount consisted of the janitors' salaries plus an amount for supplies estimated by the production manager.
Factory Support	Factory support was the labor costs (including benefits) of the factory's salaried workers, including the production manager, product engineers, production control supervisors, and shipping and stockroom staff.

(continued on next page)

EXHIBIT 3 *(continued)*

General Plant Costs	General plant costs included the property taxes, rental expenses, general building maintenance, outside services such as garbage collection, the cost of employment ads, and other miscellaneous expenses. For the Albany building only, the factory share of these expenses is included. The budgeted general plant costs were estimated by the plant manager based on the historical expenses and adjusted for expected cost increases.
Oil Filtration Expenses	These were the costs incurred by the high-pressure oil system that was used to lubricate the production machines and remove the metal chips during processing. There were three major elements of cost associated with the oil system: equipment costs, oil and oil filter replacement costs, and power costs. The same oil system was used in both plants. It had been purchased in 1976 at a cost of $150,000 per plant. The oil and filter replacement costs were directly dependent on the level of production. The power cost depended on the number of hours that the system was operating and the production level. The power was consumed by the pumps used to maintain the 150 psi pressure. Some pumping was required to maintain the pressure even if no production equipment was operating, but more power was required as the number of production machines in operation at any given time increased. There was wide variation in the amount of oil required for the operation of each machine. For example, the flute grinders removed a large amount of steel relatively quickly and required much more oil than the butt grinders over an equal amount of operating time. In 1983 the power expenses of the Albany and Denver plants were $18,000 and $20,000, respectively. The oil and filter replacement costs amounted to $24,000 and $29,000.
Inspection Costs	Each plant employed one person per daytime shift to oversee the quality control of the manufacturing operations. Machine operators were responsible for checking the output of their machines. When they discovered a flaw in a tap, they would take the tap to the inspector on duty. He would record the production process, operator, and machine, and would help the operator correct the problem, if necessary. The inspector would also make periodic quality checks of the finished taps. MTI placed a great priority on its quality reputation. All of the expensive pilot taps were individually inspected. The inspection also identified machines that needed unscheduled maintenance or repair.
Heat Treatment Costs	The Colorado heat treatment equipment was a relatively new, automated, salt-bath process. It was used to harden and temper the high-speed steel used for all the taps and tap blanks produced in Colorado. The Albany equipment consisted of two old heat treatment tanks that were manually loaded and unloaded. The Albany equipment was used only for taps from Albany stock. The heat tanks in Colorado were used continuously and were maintained at the necessary temperature on a 24-hour, seven-day basis. The Albany tanks were used only when a batch of taps was produced in the Albany plant that required heat treatment. The heat tanks required almost a full day to heat up to the required temperature and would often be used for just a few hours. The biggest cost of treatment was the natural gas used to heat it. Additional salt would be added as needed, but little was consumed and the cost was minimal. To heat-treat a tap required only a few minutes in the salt bath, and little additional energy was required to maintain the tank temperature when the tank was in use.

EXHIBIT 4

Description of Overhead Allocation Bases

Budgeted Production (units)	The budgeted number of taps produced by each of the machines was easily determined.
Budgeted Raw Material Dollars	This was calculated by multiplying the unit production by the unit cost of the raw steel for each type of tap. This differed from the unit production basis because it allocated more cost to the larger taps.
Budgeted Direct Labor Hours	The number of budgeted direct labor hours was the sum of the number of operating hours (hours that the machinist was running the machine) plus the total setup time for the machine (hours that the machinist was setting up).
Budgeted Direct Labor Dollars	This basis was the budgeted direct labor hours multiplied by the respective wage rates. It allocated more cost to those machines that required highly paid labor.
Budgeted Machine Hours	This was the number of budgeted production hours. It was derived by multiplying the number of taps produced and the amount of time required to produce each tap by machine.
Nonproductive Labor	MTI hourly factory workers recorded the amount of time they spent on each job through a system of computerized time clocks. Any paid work time (idle time, meetings, breaks, etc.) that was not directly charged to a job was considered nonproductive labor time. The system recorded this by machine class.
Overtime and Night Labor	MTI ran two main factory shifts during the day. A third limited night shift was used for the machines that represented the capacity bottlenecks in the plant.
Maintenance Allocation	When the budget was prepared, MTI's production manager estimated the maintenance costs for each machine. This estimate included labor and supplies by machine and was based on both historical costs and specially scheduled maintenance.
Power Consumption	MTI machinery was powered by electric motors. To track power consumption, the company recorded the size of each machine's motor(s) as measured by wattage. This wattage multiplied by the expected run time gave the power consumption.
Oil System Usage	Due to the large costs associated with the oil system, the company identified the oil consumption of each of the machines. This was done by measuring the fluid flow rates of each of the machines when they were operating in a normal mode.
Grinding Wheel Costs	The cost of the grinding wheels used by each machine.
Floor Space	The total floor space directly associated with each of the production machines.
Machine Book Value	The net book value of the production machinery and the remaining depreciable life.

EXHIBIT 5

Overhead Allocation Ratios (%)

Albany

ALLOCATION BASES	K-40	F-10	J-22	G-58	D-34	N-68	C-50	N-72	C-86	N-78
Production (units)	13.32	14.18	15.457	14.50	4.84	1.18	0.00	1.51	0.00	7.77
Raw materials cost ($)	3.65	9.60	2.546	10.31	9.86	6.66	0.00	7.36	0.00	0.33
Direct labor hours	9.89	20.42	0.748	11.00	11.83	0.73	0.00	7.72	0.18	1.23
Direct labor cost ($)	8.69	20.71	0.808	8.81	12.31	0.76	0.00	8.05	0.20	0.99
Machine hours	9.83	20.39	0.734	10.97	11.89	0.74	0.00	7.79	0.18	1.22
Nonproductive labor	9.08	24.06	0.845	9.20	1.43	0.80	0.00	8.41	0.23	1.03
OT and night labor	12.43	26.67	0.463	12.60	0.88	0.76	0.00	8.06	0.20	1.41
Maintenance	22.00	16.50	1.100	5.50	8.80	1.10	0.00	11.50	0.10	1.80
Power	9.70	12.90	1.800	7.80	12.00	1.70	0.00	18.40	0.00	2.90
Oil system	10.40	37.50	0.400	7.20	14.00	0.40	0.00	4.10	0.00	0.60
Grinding wheel	20.50	12.90	1.800	5.60	12.60	1.80	0.00	18.60	0.00	3.00
Floor space	6.98	22.32	1.395	4.19	6.98	1.40	0.00	2.79	0.18	1.40
Machine book value	18.36	56.60	0.000	0.00	0.00	0.00	0.00	0.00	0.00	0.00

	A-39	A-40	B-79	C-45	B-86	A-44	A-76	B-81	C-59	F-07
Production (units)	4.84	1.18	1.18	0.00	1.18	3.66	3.66	3.66	4.84	3.04
Raw materials cost ($)	9.86	6.66	6.66	0.00	6.66	3.20	3.20	3.20	9.86	0.70
Direct labor hours	3.11	0.49	5.63	8.41	5.49	0.44	0.61	0.44	0.48	11.16
Direct labor cost ($)	3.37	0.54	6.20	9.09	6.04	0.47	0.66	0.48	0.52	11.32
Machine hours	3.07	0.49	5.54	8.52	5.54	0.43	0.61	0.33	0.48	11.25
Nonproductive labor	3.91	0.62	7.20	10.56	7.01	0.55	0.76	0.56	0.60	13.14
OT and night labor	3.37	0.54	3.55	9.10	3.45	0.47	0.66	0.28	0.52	14.58
Maintenance	2.30	0.40	4.20	6.20	8.20	0.20	0.50	0.30	0.30	9.00
Power	3.70	0.60	6.70	0.00	13.10	0.30	0.70	0.50	0.00	7.20
Oil system	0.60	0.10	1.10	0.00	2.90	0.35	0.10	0.10	0.00	20.15
Grinding wheel	0.90	0.10	1.60	0.00	13.20	0.00	0.20	0.10	0.00	7.10
Floor space	9.77	0.56	5.58	6.98	1.40	1.40	2.09	0.49	0.42	23.72
Machine book value	14.22	5.16	0.00	0.00	5.66	0.00	0.00	0.00	0.00	0.00

Denver

ALLOCATION BASES	D-43	E-01	F-32	G-05	A-06	B-03	C-03	D-02	A-41	C-31	A-51
Production (units)	12.00	12.001	12.00	12.00	4.45	4.45	4.45	15.85	5.37	11.40	6.03
Raw materials cost ($)	0.00	0.000	0.00	0.00	2.56	2.56	2.56	32.48	7.54	29.92	22.38
Direct labor hours	26.04	25.152	5.43	2.54	2.16	20.41	1.34	4.31	1.75	3.53	7.35
Direct labor cost ($)	26.04	25.152	5.43	2.54	2.16	20.41	1.34	4.31	1.75	3.53	7.35
Machine hours	26.25	25.339	5.41	2.55	2.10	20.66	1.26	4.30	1.69	3.41	7.03
Nonproductive labor	26.04	25.152	5.43	2.54	2.16	20.41	1.34	4.31	1.75	3.53	7.35
OT and night labor	26.04	25.152	5.43	2.54	2.16	20.41	1.34	4.31	1.75	3.53	7.35
Maintenance	51.50	18.100	2.40	3.40	1.00	13.50	0.90	2.80	0.80	2.30	3.30
Power	27.30	17.300	4.20	6.50	1.60	26.10	1.50	4.70	1.30	3.90	5.60
Oil system	30.10	50.900	3.90	1.50	0.30	0.00	1.70	5.60	0.30	4.60	1.10
Grinding wheel	60.60	17.900	3.10	6.80	0.10	0.00	1.60	5.10	0.10	4.20	0.50
Floor space	16.48	21.978	2.20	1.65	3.85	21.98	1.37	3.85	3.02	8.24	15.38
Machine book value	16.48	49.451	3.30	2.20	1.10	14.84	3.30	2.75	1.10	3.30	2.20

Note: Allocation bases total 100.

MAYERS TAP, INC. (C)

John Mayers, president of Mayers Tap, Inc. (MTI), and Lee Rhodes, company controller, were reviewing the burden rates for each of MTI's machines. MTI was revising its cost accounting system [see Mayers Tap, Inc. (A) for background on the company], and obtaining more detailed burden rates had been the first major step. Major budgeted cost items had been allocated to the machines based on a number of operating factors, and the total budgeted costs for each machine were divided by the budgeted number of direct labor hours to arrive at a direct labor hour burden rate per machine [see Mayers Tap, Inc. (B) for a description of the overhead rate calculation]. Using the most recent budget figures (see Exhibit 1), in June 1984 Mayers had prepared a final set of burden rates for each machine that MTI would use for the coming year.

Historically, the company had treated both plants as a single aggregate cost center. The new cost accounting system allowed MTI to treat each of the 31 machine classes as a separate cost center. Mayers believed that having one cost center per machine class would provide him with the most accurate data, but he was concerned that it was not worth the cost of the extra record keeping and analysis required. It would be burdensome for management to review 31 separate reports on a monthly basis, and it might be confusing for management to determine what action to take based on these reports. Mayers was convinced, however, that consolidating the machines into fewer than 31 cost centers would make an assessment of the standard costs of MTI's products less accurate. Both Mayers and Rhodes believed that industry conditions required accurate costing so that products would not be sold below variable cost.

As a first cut, Mayers and Rhodes decided to try one cost center, the old system, and then two cost centers, one per plant, to see if either of these would provide sufficient accuracy.

Rhodes pointed out that the new system allowed them to separate the variable and fixed costs. Under the old system, these were not differentiated. Mayers agreed that this was a benefit but thought that the same results could have been achieved with much less effort.

Mayers identified three products, numbers 2, 8, and 10, that would provide the acid test. These were high-volume, low-margin products. They were currently used to "fill the plant" and were priced at what the management team felt was just above variable cost. The sale price for these products varied dramatically with economic conditions. At the moment, demand was low, so prices had dropped to rock bottom. Industry competition on these items was fierce, and any attempt to raise prices would simply result in sales of the product dropping to almost zero. Fortunately, when economic conditions improved, the demand would rapidly outpace supply, the price would rise, and MTI could reenter the market. Dropping one or more of these products would not affect the sales of other products.

Although Mayers and Rhodes agreed that dropping these products without identifying substitutes was not realistic at this time, they wanted to understand the economics of maintaining the products if they were selling below variable costs.

Rhodes's first step in the analysis was to determine the three products' standard costs using 1, 2, and 31 cost centers. His goal was to determine if the resulting standard costs varied sufficiently to affect the product discontinuance decision.

For each decision scenario he decided to calculate two net income numbers. The first, standard net income, simply took the standard costs of production and multiplied them by the volume of product manufactured. The second, budgeted net income, differed from the standard net income because it kept the fixed costs at their budgeted level. It was based on a flexible budget.

This case was prepared by Professor Robin Cooper.

Copyright © 1984 by the President and Fellows of Harvard College. Harvard Business School case 185-111.

EXHBIT 1

Direct Labor Hour Overhead Burden Rates

Albany	K-40	F-10	J-22	G-58	D-34	N-68	C-50	N-72	C-86	N-78
Direct labor	7.88	9.10	9.70	7.18	9.34	9.35	0.00	9.35	9.70	7.18
Variable overhead	11.61	8.86	12.04	5.71	8.55	12.10	0.00	12.02	2.47	11.89
Fixed overhead	8.50	10.25	9.54	6.05	6.54	9.65	0.00	6.00	7.49	7.82
Total[a]	27.99	28.21	31.28	18.94	24.43	31.09	0.00	27.38	19.67	26.89

	A-39	A-40	B-79	C-45	B-86	A-44	A-76	B-81	C-59	F-07
Direct labor	9.70	9.70	9.87	9.70	9.87	9.70	9.70	9.87	9.70	9.10
Variable overhead	5.19	5.18	5.20	2.68	12.03	5.11	5.24	5.05	2.55	8.81
Fixed overhead	16.69	17.30	7.48	7.10	6.69	12.69	13.24	7.78	7.21	10.15
Total[a]	31.58	32.17	22.55	19.48	28.59	27.50	28.17	22.70	19.46	28.07

Denver	D-43	E-01	F-32	G-05	A-06	B-03	C-03	D-02	A-41	C-31	A-51
Direct labor	8.00	8.00	8.00	8.00	8.00	8.00	8.00	8.00	8.00	8.00	8.00
Variable overhead	26.08	22.86	12.69	26.31	6.62	7.41	20.34	20.38	6.88	20.44	6.80
Fixed overhead	11.17	15.93	10.35	11.92	14.58	12.91	17.92	12.04	14.74	17.63	14.97
Total[a]	45.26	46.79	31.04	46.23	29.20	28.32	46.26	40.42	29.61	46.08	29.77

[a]Column entries may not sum to total due to rounding effects.

MUELLER-LEHMKUHL GMBH

According to Dr. Richard Welkers, president of Mueller-Lehmkuhl:

The merger with Atlas has significantly increased our ability to compete with the Japanese. As we are now the largest single manufacturer of apparel fasteners in Europe, we can reap the benefits of economies of scale. At the moment, we are cost competitive with the Japanese. While the Japanese have lower wages and overhead, we are closer to the market and have lower selling costs. Historically, the Japanese have been most successful when they were the low-cost producer.

Currently, the Japanese are pricing 20% below us. It is not enough to offset our quality advantage, but if they can match our quality or drop prices even further, we could have a problem.

Company Background

Mueller-Lehmkuhl (ML), a West German producer of apparel fasteners, was founded in 1876 as a manufacturer of shoe accessories. Soon after, other products were added, including the single-post snap fastener. Production of these items increased substantially when the company merged with a Hannover firm called Weiser. In 1929 Mueller-Weiser merged with Felix Lehmkuhl to become Mueller-Lehmkuhl. Sales growth and product diversification continued, and in 1938 the firm was acquired by the Moselhammer group.

In 1982 ML formed a joint venture with the German subsidiary of the Atlas group, an American multinational. Atlas was a conglomerate of six major businesses, one of which—Apparel Fasteners—complemented ML. At that time ML dominated a relatively small segment of the market, while Atlas Germany serviced a broader customer base. The objective of the merger was to integrate ML's technological superiority and higher margins with Atlas's access to the market. While substantially increasing its sales volume, one effect of the merger was to limit ML's potential markets

This case was prepared by Research Associate Dagmar Bottenbruch (under the supervision of Professor Robin Cooper).

Copyright © 1986 by the President and Fellows of Harvard College. Harvard Business School case 187-048.

to Europe and Africa: the rest of the world was serviced by other Atlas divisions. In 1986 ML had estimated revenues of $103 million[1] (see Exhibit 1).

Product Description

Snap fasteners are used by the garment industry to replace buttons and buttonholes. ML produced about 700 different fasteners in five major product lines: s-spring socket snap fasteners, ring socket snap fasteners, two open prong snap fasteners (brass and stainless steel), and tack buttons.

In 1985 ML introduced a new fashion line of products. These consisted of snap fasteners and tack buttons that were manufactured from a wider range of materials in a broader variety of shapes. The company's marketing manager wanted to convince the market that snap fasteners could be fashionable and could be used to replace conventional buttons in a wide array of clothing.

Each product line was designed for a specific application. The s-spring fasteners were used for medium-thick materials (1.4 mm to 2.0 mm). They could not be used for stretch materials, since they were attached centrally (through one stud) and would damage the material. The ring spring fasteners were used for thicker materials (up to 6.5 mm) and could be used on materials exposed to heavier strains. The open prong fasteners were especially well suited for use on thin (.25 mm to .75 mm) and stretchy materials, since they did not damage the materials. All fasteners could be washed, dry cleaned, and ironed. Tack buttons were used to replace conventional buttons and were usually used on blue jeans. Fasteners were customized either by applying various colors of finishes or by embossing the customer's logo on the cap.

As part of its strategy of being an integrated manufacturer, ML also manufactured attaching machines. In 1986 ML manufactured six attaching machines—three manual and three automatic. All of the machines could be modified to attach any of the company's fasteners. An operator using a manual machine placed the two parts of the fastener into the machine by hand, positioned the material, and operated the machine. In an automatic machine, one or more of the parts was positioned automatically. The operator still had to position the material manually (for characteristics of the machines, see Exhibit 2).

Over the years, the firm had developed a policy of selling the manual machines and renting the automatic ones. Manual machines were sold because, unlike automatic machines, they did not cost much, did not require service, and were easily and inexpensively modified to allow them to attach different fasteners. Automatic machines were rented on an annual basis, though the company was willing to take them back at any time. About 10% of the 7,000 rented machines were returned in the average year. The company inventoried these machines until new orders arrived. It then modified the old machines to enable them to attach a different fastener. Modification was expensive, since it required replacing all components specific to the fastener. The company estimated that an average modification cost $2,000.

Although the rental contract did not specify free service, it was industry practice to provide preventive maintenance and emergency service at no charge. Even though most large customers had downtime insurance, ML viewed reliability and fast service response as an important sales tool. Consequently, it was not unusual for service personnel to be flown to a customer site within hours of an emergency call. In 1986, service was expected to cost about $4.5 million. To partially make up for the cost of providing this service, ML attached two conditions to the rental of a machine: (1) only ML fasteners were to be used on the machine, and (2) at least $10,000 worth of fasteners were expected to be purchased during the year. However, due to uncertain demand and overly optimistic customers, the average rented machine attached only about $7,000 worth of fasteners per year.

Market Conditions

ML had positioned itself in the large-volume market, where automatic machines were required. Large volume referred to the quantity of a given fastener sold, not to the overall fastener consumption by a given firm. ML's preferred target market could be broken into two major segments: (1) large companies purchasing large volumes of a number of different fasteners, and (2) smaller companies needing major quantities of a single fastener. Large-volume customers accounted for 85% of fastener sales.

The European market could be characterized as a stable oligopoly consisting of four firms that together accounted for 65% of the European fastener market (Exhibit 3). An additional 13 firms (including the

---

[1]In 1986, the exchange rate was $1 = DM 2.1.

Japanese) accounted for the rest of the market. Most of these firms sold fasteners and attaching machines. In addition to the fastener manufacturers, there were several companies that produced only attaching machines. Their machines were usually cheaper and of inferior quality to ML's. ML's fastener sales to customers using third-party equipment were thought to be about 10%. The exact percentage was unknown because ML could not be certain on which machines its products were actually used.

The four major players, all providing equivalent services, had over the years settled into peaceful coexistence. They never initiated price wars and rarely tried to steal each other's customers. Customers had helped achieve this stability by sourcing from multiple suppliers. Customers normally identified a primary source but ordered from at least one other firm. If ML attempted to move from a secondary supplier to a primary supplier by price cutting, the adversely affected company could easily retaliate by trying to become the primary source for one of ML's customers.

There were several other factors that helped reduce the level of competition between the major players. First, the companies developed longstanding personal relationships with their customers. These relationships, coupled with high customer satisfaction, made it difficult to lure away any business. Second, the policy of renting machines, coupled with designing the fasteners so that they could be used only in the supplier's own machines, made switching an expensive undertaking. Third, there were virtually no standard prices. Each customer paid a different amount for its fasteners, making it difficult to compete on price.

Despite these limitations, the firms did compete on three dimensions:

1. The quality of the fasteners and, in particular, the tolerance to which they were manufactured (the higher the tolerance, the less likely fasteners were to cause machine downtime and the longer their life expectancy once fastened).
2. The performance of the attaching machine (in particular speed, reliability, safety, noise level, and ability to attach fasteners without scratching the surfaces).
3. The quality of service provided.

ML sold its products in approximately 20 countries. These countries differed in language, safety regulations, labor costs, taste, tariff barriers, payment terms, and currency. Even the smallest product required marketing materials, product descriptions, and labels to be in every language, adding to overhead and production costs. In some countries tariffs could add up to 100% of cost to the product, rendering a foreign producer uncompetitive with local producers. In other countries, labor costs were so low that even for large-scale production the use of manual attaching machines was still economical. In some countries, it was impossible to succeed without at least one salesperson fluent in that country's language.

To deal with these local differences, ML used agents in some countries, distributors in others, and regional sales offices in yet others to sell fasteners. Attaching machines were always purchased or rented directly from Mueller-Lehmkuhl. Agents generally represented a range of associated but noncompetitive products. They promoted ML products and were paid a 6% to 10% commission on fastener sales. Agents did not maintain inventories. Distributors differed from agents by maintaining inventory, thus reducing the uncertainty of local supply. Like agents, they enabled the local customer to deal with a fellow national. Overall, agents and distributors accounted for about 75% of sales. Product purchased through a distributor usually cost about 10% to 15% more than when purchased directly. In countries where local differences were not a major factor or ML maintained a regional sales office, large customers could purchase directly from the firm at reduced prices.

The European market was relatively mature, with overall growth expected to be 1% per annum (Exhibit 4). This low growth rate had caused ML to look for new markets, in particular Africa. The African market was more price sensitive than the European market. Low-cost producers had a significant advantage because quality was not important and no premium for a better product could be charged, making it difficult for quality-oriented producers to penetrate those markets. Since the textile industry was continuously shifting its production into less-developed countries, low-cost producers could position themselves well to service these growing markets. Unfortunately, the merger with Atlas had reduced ML's opportunities for geographic expansion, since the continuing offshore movement of the garment industry was moving ML's business into areas serviced by other Atlas divisions.

Production Process

ML's production facility was a four-story building located next to the head office in Düsseldorf, West Germany. The top floor of the building, which contained the machining and tooling departments, was primarily dedicated to the production of attaching machines. All design and prototype work for the attaching machines was completed in-house. This represented about 30% of the engineering staff's activities. Purchased parts, consisting of motors, engines, and all electrical parts, constituted about 30%[2] of the total cost of an automatic or semiautomatic attaching machine. Metal parts were cast according to ML's specifications by a local cast-iron business. After these parts were delivered to the company, they were prepared for welding, then welded, and finally the machines were assembled. Welding and final assembly required highly skilled labor, especially for the automatic and semiautomatic machines.

All product-specific parts (i.e., those that had to be changed if a machine was modified to attach a different fastener) were produced by ML. Precision was crucial to make the machine fit a customer's specifications. Therefore, testing was a major part of the production process. Frequently, up to 10,000 pieces of product had to be run through a machine before it could be delivered to the customer.

In addition to attaching machines, the company manufactured some of its own production machines. In early 1986 the company announced that it would start producing a new line of automated material-handling machines. These new machines relied heavily on the technology developed for attaching machines.

The machining department labor force was split into two groups—one producing attaching and production machines and the other refitting returned attaching machines. Management estimated that 80% of the labor force that was producing machines was dedicated to attaching machine production.

The tooling department, which was also located on the top floor, manufactured and repaired tools that were used in the production of both fasteners and machines. Tools used in the production of fasteners were very costly and were frequently reworked, whereas tools used in the production of attaching machines were relatively inexpensive and usually replaced when they showed signs of wear. No attempt had been made to determine how the tooling department's capacity was split between production and attaching machine tools.

The other three floors of the factory were dedicated to fastener production. Fastener production consisted of three major steps: stamping, assembly, and finishing. Each floor was primarily dedicated to a single step. In stamping, the material components were stamped out of large coils. If the fastener was being produced in very large quantities, then automated machines were used that could produce up to 12 components with a single stamp. These high-volume machines required expensive tooling, often costing up to $50,000. At low production volumes, less-sophisticated machines were used. The stamping department contained 47 different types of machines. In the stamping department, it was not unusual for a single operator to run several machines simultaneously.

In assembly, the stamped components were combined by machine. The tack button, for example, consisted of five components—three in the button and two in the underpart. The button was assembled from a cap (often with a logo stamped in the surface), a plastic insert that formed the locking mechanism, and a socket plate. These three parts were crimped together to form the button. The underpart consisted of two components, a stud and a cap, which were crimped together. The type of machine used to assemble the components again depended on the production volume. Altogether there were 112 different types of machines in assembly.

Once assembled, the parts were then washed and, if required, heat-treated before being sent to finishing. Several different finishes were produced. These included plating (the part was plated to make the surface smooth and shiny), painting or enameling (the part was spray-painted in a variety of colors), tumbling (to produce a matte surface), and polishing (to produce a smooth surface). There were 15 different types of machines in the finishing department.

Finished parts were packed ready for shipping. Only minimum work-in-process and finished goods inventories were maintained, because most fasteners were produced to order.

On the surface, fasteners seemed to be simple products requiring fairly low technology; in fact, however, they had to be machined to within a hundredth of a millimeter. This required precision stamping and high quality control. Similarly, the attaching machines were on the forefront of automated material handling technology. To maintain its technological superiority, the firm maintained a strong research and development department. The introduction of the fashion line required significant R&D resources. Management estimated that at least two-thirds of current R&D projects were related to

---

[2]This percentage was considerably smaller in the manual machines, since they did not contain any electrical parts.

fastener production, with the new high-fashion fasteners accounting for about 50%.

Cost Accounting System

The cost accounting system had recently been overhauled. According to the corporate controller, the old system, which consisted of about 70 cost centers, failed to differentiate appropriately between automatic and manually operated machines. The new system contained more cost centers: one per machine class.

Material, after adjustment for scrap, was charged directly to the product. The new cost system also identified a material overhead charge. This included the costs associated with purchasing, material handling, and inventory storage. Products were allocated material overhead on the basis of the material dollars they consumed.

In the stamping and assembly departments, labor costs, after dividing by the number of machines the operator was running, were charged directly to each product. Setup labor costs, after dividing by the lot size to produce a per-part setup charge, were also charged directly. Overhead was divided into two sections: machine costs and general overhead. Machine costs were those costs that could meaningfully be allocated directly to the machine: floor space, energy, maintenance, depreciation, and an interest charge for invested capital. The total cost of these items for each machine class was divided by the projected direct labor dollars (including setup) expected to be worked on that machine class to give the machine class overhead burden rate per direct labor dollar for the coming year. The resulting machine class burden rate was multiplied by the standard direct labor dollar content of each product to give the machine-related overhead portion of product cost.

General overhead consisted of factory support, factory supplies, technical administration, support department costs, machining department costs, and tooling department costs (Exhibit 5). Where possible, general overhead costs were traced directly to the fastener production departments; otherwise they were allocated to each department on the basis of direct labor dollars (including setup dollars). The general cost pool for each fastener production department was then divided by projected direct labor dollars (including setup dollars) for each department for the coming year to give the machine overhead burden rate per direct labor dollar. The resulting departmental burden rate was multiplied by the standard direct labor dollar content of each product to give

the general-overhead-related portion of product cost.

Batch costing was considered the most appropriate approach for costing products in the stamping and assembly departments. In the finishing department, process costing had been adopted. Each finish process was treated as a cost center, and all of the costs associated with that center were aggregated into a single cost pool. These costs were then allocated to the products, using equivalency factors that reflected the value of resources consumed by the products.

In summary, the cost system reported standard product costs using the cost of a component in the following manner (the unit of measurement was a "mil," which was equal to 1,000 pieces):

Material	standard cost + material-overhead
Stamping and Assembly	
Labor	standard labor hours × standard pay rate/number of machines operated
Setup	standard setup labor hours × standard pay rate/lot size
Machine OH	standard labor dollars × machine burden rate
General OH	standard labor dollars × departmental burden rate
Finishing	total departmental cost × equivalency factor

While the different products appeared relatively similar to the inexperienced eye, they could actually have significantly different cost structures (see Exhibit 6 for the cost structures of five representative products).

Japanese Competition

Hiroto Industries (HI), the major Japanese competitor in Europe, was a trading company that sold a broad range of fashion accessory products to the shoe, leather goods, and garment industries. Typical products included belts, buckles, and zippers. HI was approximately 10 times larger than ML, and the two firms competed in only 20% of HI's markets. Unlike ML, HI purchased approximately 85% of the products it sold. The 15% it produced were all high-volume, low-diversity product lines. HI's stated objective was to become number one in Japan and be a major worldwide competitor. It wanted about 25% of its business to be European based.

The existing fastener technology, which exhibited significant economies of scale, required a base market size of approximately 200 million people to support several competitors. Japan, with 120 million people, and Germany, with 60 million people, were not large enough to support domestic producers without significant international sales. The larger Japanese market provided Japanese producers with a significant economic advantage. The high price that Japanese garment manufacturers had to pay for their fasteners (120% of German prices) reflected the isolation of the Japanese market.

HI entered the European market in 1973. It faced substantial entry barriers, in particular the longstanding relationships of European companies with customers, its lack of high-quality attaching machines, and the absence of a network of distributors and service personnel. In Welkers' opinion, to help mitigate these barriers, HI had focused on the high-volume products, such as workwear, leather goods, and babywear, where the market consisted of a few customers ordering very large volumes of products.

In 1982, as part of the rationalization program between Atlas and ML, several service personnel were laid off. To strengthen its ability to deliver service in the European market, HI hired these personnel. This move enabled HI to penetrate the market even further. When ML rehired the most critical person in HI's team, this strategy failed and HI lost most of its newly acquired customers.

To compensate, HI adopted a new marketing strategy (Exhibit 7). Rather than rent the attaching machines themselves, HI identified distributors that were willing to purchase attaching machines and then rent them to its customers. These machines were purchased from the companies that manufactured only attaching machines because the firms that manufactured both attaching machines and fasteners would sell or rent their machines only to the end user.[3] HI then supplied these dealers

_____

[3]If no suitable European machines were available, HI would ship its own machines and sell them to the distributor.

with fasteners at about a 20% discount on the prevailing European prices. This strategy had several advantages for HI. First, HI did not own the machines and consequently did not have to provide service. Second, invested capital was kept to a minimum; and, finally, HI did not bear the risk of returned machines.

The dealers benefited because they could now compete with companies like ML. They had a significant price advantage and could "steal" those customers who were not contractually obligated to use a specific firm's fasteners.

HI's new strategy threatened two segments of ML's market. The first was the small-volume customer who used fasteners that were very popular. Several such firms were effectively equivalent to a large-volume customer. However, given that these customers owned their own equipment, they were free to purchase fasteners from whomever they chose.

The second, a more worrisome trend, was when a large-volume customer decided to use Japanese fasteners on ML equipment. Although most fasteners were customized, some of the really high-volume fasteners, such as stainless steel spring fasteners, were standardized and could run on anybody's equipment. Certain ML customers, even though contractually obligated to purchase product from ML, were beginning to experiment with the Japanese product. ML had threatened to cancel the equipment leases if it caught any firm violating the contract. In fact, one firm had been caught, but immediately agreed to stop "experimenting" with Japanese fasteners.

HI's new strategy met with some success and by 1986 HI had achieved about a 6% overall market penetration (Exhibit 8).

ML's European sales manager voiced his opinion:

My biggest concern is keeping price levels as high as possible in the face of Japanese competition. We do not want to lose market share to them, but the problem is that their prices are so much lower than ours that matching them would be too expensive. They do not present an immediate threat because our quality is so much higher. However, even though our customers carefully analyze the situation and decide to stay with us, they are left with the feeling that they would be better off if they bought Japanese.

EXHIBIT 1

Budgeted Income, 1986 ($000)

Sales			$103,000
Cost of goods			
Materials (including material overhead)		$31,000	
Direct labor (including setup labor)		1,610	
Machine overhead		4,500	
General overhead			
Factory support	$3,020		
Factory supplies	470		
Technical administration	6,500		
Support departments	6,500		
Machining department	13,350		
Tooling department	3,050		
		$32,890	
Total			$70,000
Sales, general, and administration			
Research and development	$5,810		
Administration	2,760		
Marketing	7,930		
Shipping	3,170		
Commission	3,830		
			$23,500
Net Income			$9,500

EXHIBIT 2

Characteristics of Attaching Machines

NUMBER	M1	M2	M3	A1	A2	A3
Operation mode	Manual	Manual	Manual	Semi-automatic	Automatic	Automatic
Motive force	Hand	Foot	Pneumatic	Pneumatic	Pneumatic	Electric
Price[a]	$200	$250	$500	—	—	—
Annual rental fee[b]	—	—	—	$300	$500	$1,500
Attachment speed[c]	5/min	6/min	15/min	15/min	25/min	50/min
Application (volume)[d]	Low	Low	Low	Low/medium	Medium/high	High
Budgeted production, 1986	35	70	105	350	280	420
Budgeted rental base, 1986[e]				1,350	2,250	3,500
Life expectancy (years)	20	20	15	10	10	10

[a]Manual machines are sold, not rented.
[b]Automatic machines are rented, not sold. Rental fee equals average paid for all outstanding models.
[c]Average number of fasteners attached per minute.
[d]Low volume is fewer than 50,000 fasteners per year. High volume is greater than 300,000 fasteners per year.
[e]Includes machines manufactured in earlier years and still on rental contracts.

EXHIBIT 3

Competitive Analysis-Predicted Sales by Fastener Product Line ($ millions)

NAME	COUNTRY OF ORIGIN	S-SPRING	RING	PRONG	TACK	TOTAL
ML	Germany	$12	$9	$60[a]	$15	$96
Piloni	Italy	44	30	16	2	92
Berghausen	Germany	63	11	11	2	87
Yost & Co.	Germany	12	21	46	4	83
Other		61	46	63	23	193
		$192	$117	$196	$46	$551

[a]$30 million prong brass + $30 million prong stainless steel.

EXHIBIT 4

Country Demographics

COUNTRY	POPULATION (000,000)	ESTIMATED MARKET ($000,000)	ML BUDGETED SALES ($000,000)	ML SHARE (%)	ESTIMATED MARKET GROWTH (%)	ML SALES THROUGH DISTRIBUTORS (%)
France	54	$84	$24	29%	+1%	100%
Germany	62	82	30	37	−1	20
U.K.	56	56	19	34	+1	0
Finland	5	12	4	33	+2	60
Netherlands	14	82	4	5	+1	50
Belgium	10	9	4	44	0	0
Spain	38	14	3	21	+1	100
Italy	57	138	2	1	+1	65
Yugoslavia	22	23	2	6	+2	60%
Other	362	51	4	8%	+1%	—
Total	680	$551	$96			

EXHIBIT 5

Description of General Overhead Accounts

Factory support included the unallocated supervision, floor space, and janitorial services that were consumed by fastener production. Production management was also contained in this account.

Factory supplies included oil, grease rags, and miscellaneous tools used in the fastener production departments.

Technical administration included attaching machine service costs and those engineering costs not included in R&D.

Support department included costs for production scheduling, fastener inventory control, the apprentice workshop, and the worker council.

Machining department included material labor, and overhead for the manufacture of production and attaching machines.[a]

Tooling department included material, labor, and overhead costs for the manufacture of tools.

[a]Under German accounting principles, given the nature of the lease agreement, the entire cost of the attaching machines was written off to general overhead in the year in which the machines were manufactured.

EXHIBIT 6 Product Cost Structures of Representative Products ($ per 1,000 units)

	S-SPRING	RING	PRONG (BRASS)	PRONG (SS)	TACK BUTTON
Average Selling Price	$46.75	$39.83	$15.28	$20.32	$38.40
	Total	Total	Total	Total	Total
Material					
Raw Material	$ 9.70	$ 8.88	$ 6.04	$ 5.74	$11.88
Material O/H	0.54	0.50	0.34	0.32	0.67
	10.24	9.38	6.38	6.06	12.55
Stamping					
Setup	0.12	0.25	0.01	0.03	0.03
Labor	0.68	0.48	0.04	0.21	0.25
Machine O/H	1.31	1.27	0.17	1.13	1.11
General O/H	22.40	14.64	0.94	5.64	8.42
	24.51	16.64	1.16	7.01	9.81
Assembly					
Setup	0.14	0.05	—	—	0.01
Labor	0.10	0.24	—	—	0.18
Machine O/H	0.25	0.45	0.00	0.00	0.26
General O/H	1.56	3.55	0.00	0.00	2.51
	2.04	4.29	0.00	0.00	2.96
Finishing	5.66	8.28	1.88	0.56	3.84
TOTAL	$42.46	$38.59	$ 9.42	$13.63	$29.17
Total DL (inc. setup) for All Departments (incl Finishing)	$1.32	$1.43	$0.14	$0.27	$0.66

EXHIBIT 7

Comparison of Mueller-Lehmkuhl and Hiroto Industries Product Distribution Approaches

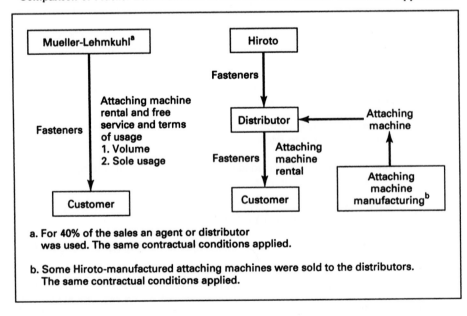

a. For 40% of the sales an agent or distributor was used. The same contractual conditions applied.

b. Some Hiroto-manufactured attaching machines were sold to the distributors. The same contractual conditions applied.

EXHIBIT 8

Estimated Japanese Market Share of European
Market in 1986

S-spring snap fastener	8%
Ring snap fastener	8
Open prong snap fastener (stainless steel)	2
Open prong snap fastener (brass)	9
Tack button	9%

MITSUBISHI KASEI CORPORATION: PRODUCT LINE COST SYSTEM

The Mitsubishi Kasei Corporation, formerly known as Mitsubishi Chemical Industries, Ltd., was Japan's largest integrated chemical company. Its revenues in 1992 were ¥710 billion and its net income ¥5 billion. The company consisted of three major groups: carbon and inorganic chemicals, petrochemicals, and functional products. The major products of the carbon and inorganic chemicals group were coke, synthetic rubber, carbon black, and fertilizers. The petrochemical group produced products such as ethylene, polyethylenes, and vinyl chloride monomer. The majority of the products produced and sold by these two groups could be characterized as high volume, mass-produced, and having a low value-added content. In contrast, the functional products group produced electronics, pharmaceuticals, and pesticides, products manufactured in relatively low volumes with high value-added content.

The current organizational structure, which was introduced in 1987, reflected the successful implementation of a strategy to add functional products to the firm's traditional product offerings. This product diversification, started in 1982, marked a significant shift in the firm's product mix, which had historically been dominated by high volume, mass-produced, low value-added items. Top management adopted this new strategy because the firm's traditional products had become less profitable due to the appreciation of the yen, an increase in the variability of input prices, and a downturn in the industry.

The appreciation of the yen had significantly reduced the profitability of the low value-added products be-

cause it increased the cost of any processing performed in Japan. Profit margins on these products had always been very narrow, and the increased processing costs made it more economical to produce these products elsewhere in the world. Simultaneously, increased variability in input prices caused the profits earned on these products to become highly volatile. With such thin profit margins, it did not require large swings in input prices to turn profits into losses.

Shifting to functional products with a high value-added content was expected to increase the firm's profitability for several reasons. First, these products had historically earned higher returns than the firm's traditional products. Therefore, all things being equal, switching sales between the two types of products would increase reported profits. Second, the high value-added content of functional products made their profits much less sensitive to changes in input prices and fluctuations in exchange rates. Third, the markets for functional products were expected to grow rapidly, while the markets for the firm's traditional products were expected to grow slowly. Finally, with their high value-added content, functional products were candidates for cost reduction programs. Over time, by becoming more efficient at their production, the firm could become even more profitable.

The stated objective of the new strategy was to have functional products contribute at least 30% of total net sales by 1990. However, in the first two years of the strategy, sales of functional products increased more rapidly than originally planned while sales of the mass-produced carbon and inorganic chemical products fell unexpectedly by about 15%. The major cause of these lost sales was a significant reduction in the domestic demand for coke caused by a slump in Japan's steel industry. Over the next three years, the percentage of sales

Professor Robin Cooper of the Peter F. Drucker Graduate Management Center at The Claremont Graduate School prepared this case.

due to functional products remained relatively constant; the growth in sales of functional products was matched by the recovery of the domestic steel industry, and hence coke sales. In 1992, the ratio of sales for the three groups was 24.6% carbon and inorganic chemicals, 37.7% petrochemicals, and 37.7% functional products.

Mitsubishi Kasei's rapid diversification into functional products caused a rapid increase in costs of service functions, such as investment planning, budgeting, quality control, engineering for improvements in production efficiency, and production management. Unfortunately, the existing cost system was not designed to control these costs. Rather, it was designed to report accurate product costs primarily for determining selling prices and attaining maximum profitability by adjusting the firm's product mix.

Old Cost System

Mitsubishi's old cost system identified three major categories of costs: factory costs, direct selling costs, and administrative expenses. Factory costs included the costs of the raw material, utilities, labor, and overhead consumed in the production process; direct selling costs included transporting, loading, and insuring the finished products; and administrative costs included the costs of marketing, distribution, and corporate administration.

Factory costs were identified as being either variable or fixed in nature. Variable costs included the costs of raw materials, receiving those materials, and the utilities consumed in the production process. The variable costs were directly charged to products unless the production process, such as the cracking or naphtha, resulted in joint products, in which case some form of allocation was unavoidable. Fixed costs included the costs of the direct labor work force, depreciation, repair costs, and production overhead. These costs were split into two types: direct and indirect. Direct fixed costs, such as direct labor, depreciation, and repair, were charged directly to the production processes and hence products that consumed them. Indirect fixed costs (which were further split into two categories: departmental overhead and factory burden) were allocated to the production processes. Departmental overhead, which included the salaries of the departmental general managers and the cost of the coordination and technical sections within the departments, was charged directly to the production cost centers and then allocated to the products. Factory burden, which included the costs of wastewater treatment and central planning, was allo-

cated to the production cost centers and subsequently to the products (see Exhibit 1).

The treatment of plant maintenance expenses illustrates how the system handled indirect production expenses. Plant maintenance expenses were split into direct and indirect categories. Direct maintenance expenses, such as those related to the repair and maintenance of the equipment in a given production center, were directly charged to the appropriate production cost centers. These costs were also directly charged to the products that caused them. Indirect maintenance expenses, such as those related to the central planning of the maintenance function, were treated as factory burden and allocated to the production cost centers in the production departments using the ratio of directly assigned maintenance costs. Thus, a production center that consumed a relatively large proportion of the direct maintenance expenses would have a correspondingly large proportion of the indirect maintenance expenses allocated to it. These costs were subsequently allocated to products using the ratio of direct maintenance expenses for each product. For example, if three products passed through a center and their direct maintenance expenses were ¥150, ¥300, and ¥50, then the ratio of indirect maintenance expenses that would be allocated was 30%, 60%, and 10%, respectively.

Because direct selling expenses could be identified by product, they were directly charged to products. Administrative expenses were allocated to the production centers. The administrative functions, such as general affairs, personnel, and accounting, were split into a number of separate service cost centers. For example, the personnel function was divided into five centers, including organization support, labor union support, accounting for wages, welfare, and training. The expenses of these service cost centers were allocated to the production centers using a basis that was thought to capture the work load created by the production centers. For example, the expenses of the welfare department were allocated to the production cost centers using a head count because the number of individuals in the production center captured approximately the amount of welfare support each center required (see Exhibit 2).

The departmental overhead, factory burden, and administrative expenses were allocated from the production cost centers to the products in two distinct steps. There were seven production cost centers at Mitsubishi Kasei, one for each of the firm's domestic production plants. These plants contained multiple facilities, each producing a different product line; for example, the Mizushima plant contained facilities that produced ethylene, polyethylene, polyvinyl chloride, and hard and optical computer disks (see Exhibit 3). Some of these facilities, such as the vinyl chloride monomer one at Mizushima, only produced a single product while others, such as the hard disk facility, produced multiple products.

The indirect costs were allocated first to the facilities within each production cost center and then subsequently to products. Thus, the system required up to three distinct allocation steps: to the production cost center, to the facility, and then to the products (see Exhibit 4). Cost allocation from the production center to the facility level was typically achieved by using the same basis as was used to allocate the costs to the production centers. For example, the welfare costs were allocated to the facilities using head count. Frequently, for the final allocation step, the quantities of the allocation basis used in the earlier steps were unavailable at the product level; therefore, these allocations relied upon a different basis, usually direct labor hours or a managerial estimate of usage.

Reported product costs included all of the costs directly charged and allocated to the products. Thus, reported costs included manufacturing, direct selling, and administrative costs (see Exhibit 5). The primary purpose of these reported product costs was to help fine-tune the firm's strategy by optimizing the product mix. For example, the grade of polyethylene produced would determine both its selling price and its cost of production. When demand exceeded capacity, the firm would determine which grades had the highest profitability and then produce the mix of products with the highest reported profit. Similarly, reported costs were used to identify products for introduction and discontinuance.

The intensive use of allocations in the old cost system, coupled with the way service costs were aggregated, made it virtually impossible to explicitly attribute responsibility for these costs to individual managers. Unfortunately, there was no other source of cost information to help management control these costs. When the old system was designed in the 1960s, computerization was still in its infancy and separate financial and managerial accounting systems were considered too expensive. Therefore, the cost system was designed to perform both financial and managerial accounting functions. For example, the system was also used to determine the cost of goods sold and inventory valuations for

financial reporting purposes and to help identify which cost reduction programs should be initiated.

As service costs increased in importance because of changes in the firm's product line makeup, the system's inability to assign responsibility for those costs to individuals became a serious limitation that had to be addressed. In addition, the existing system could not generate useful information in a timely manner.

New Cost System

In 1987, the firm's old cost system was replaced by a computerized system designed to overcome many of the limitations of the old system. In particular, the new system was designed to achieve four major objectives:

1. To allow explicit attribution of responsibility for all costs
2. To increase the firm's ability to control service costs
3. To allow departmental and section managers to control costs according to planned objectives
4. To allow individual product costs to be determined as required

The primary objective of the new system—explicit attribution of responsibility for all costs—required that the new cost system contain the minimum number of allocations possible. As the firm had discovered from its old system, allocations made it impossible to hold managers responsible for costs; instead, they allowed them to make excuses. To reduce the number of allocations to the absolute minimum, the new cost system was designed around cost centers that were associated with a single product line (see Exhibit 6). For example, the costs of production, distribution, marketing, and administration for a specific product line were charged directly to production and service cost centers that were responsible only for that product line.

The new cost system did not refer to costs as fixed or variable. Instead, it identified five distinct cost categories:

1. Raw material and energy costs: expenses of raw material and energy consumed in the production process
2. Direct value-adding costs: direct costs of processing and manufacturing departments
3. Service costs: costs of various support services
4. Interest costs: costs of funds procurement, determined by interest payable minus interest receivable
5. Future costs: costs whose benefits are expected in the future

The relationship between the cost categories in the old and new systems is shown in Exhibit 7.

Four types of service costs were identified: production, sales, distribution and marketing, and central administration and coordination. Production services comprised factory support and factory administration. Factory support included the costs of activities such as product analysis and the coordination and technical support sections of the production departments. Factory administration included the costs of general affairs, personnel, and accounting. Sales services included customer support, market development, and commissions. Distribution and marketing services included transportation, loading and shipment, and transportation insurance. Central administration and coordination services included such administration functions as personnel, accounting, and general affairs that were performed at headquarters.

Both direct and indirect elements of service costs were recognized. Direct service costs were costs associated with actually providing services, while indirect service costs were the costs of supporting the provision of services. For example, the costs of providing technical support were treated as direct service costs while the costs of administering and coordinating that function were treated as indirect service costs. The direct service costs were directly charged to the cost center performing the services; the indirect service costs were allocated using an applicable standard, such as the head count for the personnel department and the repair cost for the repair department. For departments where there was no obvious way to allocate the costs, a complex standard, formed by equally combining head count and facility investment, was used to assign costs to products (see Exhibit 8).

The cost system did not directly charge or allocate costs to products. Even raw material and energy costs that could be directly charged to products were only measured at the product line level. This meant that the new cost system could not report individual product costs. It could, however, report product line costs. There were two primary advantages to reporting product line instead of product costs. First, a second cost assignment step from the cost centers to the products was avoided. Because cost centers only serviced a single product line, reported product line costs could be determined by simply summing the costs of the appropriate cost centers. Second, the number of allocations required was minimal. Because most product lines at Mitsubishi Kasei represented a major proportion of the production volume of the plant that produced them, it was usually possible to identify responsibility centers that only serviced a single product line.

Sometimes it was not possible to identify a single product line cost center. Some services were provided on a centralized basis and responsibility for several product lines was unavoidable. The costs of such services were charged directly to these multiproduct-line cost centers and then subsequently allocated to the individual product lines serviced. These allocations, where possible, used bases that captured the underlying reasons for consumption by the product lines. For example, the costs of wastewater treatment were allocated to product lines based upon the volume of wastewater and the level of pollution they produced.

These unavoidable allocations were carefully chosen to be both understandable and believable by the product line managers. These characteristics were considered important because they ensured that even though some allocation was involved, pressure to reduce costs was created on product line managers. For example, with respect to wastewater treatment, incentives were created to reduce the volume of wastewater and level of pollutants produced.

When required, individual product costs could be determined, but not using the new cost system. Product costs were determined on an ad hoc basis outside the formal cost system. There were three major reasons why individual product costs were required. First, they helped determine individual product prices when the same product line was used in various ways. For example, polyethylene was injection-molded to form products such as beer crates, buckets, and plastic toys. It was also blow-molded to produce products such as detergent bottles, and extrusion-molded to create films. Each application required different types of resin, and these resins had different production costs. For the sales force to be able to sell these resins, they had to know their costs. Second, individual product costs were important to decisions about what grades of a product line to manufacture Product mix decisions of this class were usually made when a plant reached capacity and orders had to be turned down. Under these conditions it made sense to accept the most profitable orders where possible. Finally, individual product costs were used to check the profitability of individual products by comparing the product's costs to its selling price. Individual product costs were compared to selling prices when there was a risk that they were being sold below variable cost. Export sales were often made at prices that were much lower than domestic prices. The higher domestic prices were due to tariffs and special services provided to domestic customers. Mitsubishi Kasei accepted these low prices to keep plants busy. However, accepting such business only made sense if the variable costs of the products sold exceeded their selling prices.

When individual product costs were required, an engineer was asked to estimate the cost of an individual product based upon his or her experience with the production process. To determine individual product cost estimates, the engineer would develop cost factors for each of the five cost elements identified by the cost system. These cost factors were used to estimate the magnitude of the cost elements associated with the individual product. Summing these cost elements gave the estimated product cost (see Exhibit 9). Inventory was valued for financial accounting purposes using the product line cost information as a proxy for average product costs.

The new system increased the firm's ability to control costs by reporting to each general manager the actual costs of the resources consumed by the center for which he or she was responsible. For example, section managers received reports about the production processes for which they were responsible and departmental general managers received reports for the sections within their departments. Departmental reports were generated by simply summing the appropriate section reports (see Exhibit 10). These reports were generated monthly, and were available on the fifth day of the next month. Additional reports were generated for the manager of each major cost component (raw material and energy, direct value added, production service, sales service, and distribution service). These reports did not contain any allocated costs, only those that were directly charged. However, costs for indirect expenses that could be directly charged to production processes, such as wastewater treatment, were included in these reports.

The wastewater department was treated as a pseudo profit center. Each production process that created wastewater was levied a service fee based upon the volume and degree of contamination of the wastewater created. This service fee was "paid" to the wastewater department on a monthly basis via general ledger entry. The manager of the wastewater department received a monthly report that identified the difference between his costs and fees (see Exhibit 11).

To ensure that explicit responsibility for all costs was achieved, the number of cost centers in the new system was much higher than in the old one. In the old system, cost centers were either production plants that con-

tained multiple facilities or service centers that were responsible for providing services to the entire firm. These cost centers were so large that numerous cost allocations were unavoidable. In contrast, cost centers in the new system were predominantly production facilities and service centers that were responsible for only a single product line. Management called these cost centers "cost boxes" because they were concerned not with *how* costs were incurred within the centers but with the total amount of costs consumed within them. Yoshikazu Miyabe, a vice president who designed the system while he was managing director of the accounting, finance, and information systems department, stated, "To the worker in the field, controlling single cost elements, such as entertainment costs, is virtually meaningless. In the field, all that matters is total cost."

The new cost system, like the one it replaced, was an actual and not a standard cost system. A standard cost system was not considered appropriate by management because of the large unavoidable variances that it would have generated. There were two primary reasons why a standard cost system would have reported major variances at Mitsubishi Kasei. First, the changes in the price of raw materials (such as oil) and fluctuations in exchange rates would have caused the raw material price variances to be large. Second, the yield would decrease for a couple of months after each production process' annual overhaul until the process was brought back under control. This reduction in yield could not be estimated with any accuracy. Therefore, for the two months after the overhaul, the material usage variances would be large because the performance forecasts were too inaccurate to be useful.

Cost Reduction Program

Incentives to reduce total costs were created by setting cost reduction targets for every cost box manager. These targets were set in one of five different ways:

1. Voluntarily established by the cost box manager
2. Set using across-the-board percentage reductions
3. Calculated from a desired target margin and selling price
4. Set using an experience curve
5. Set using a prior index established by some external body

The actual technique used depended upon the nature of the cost reduction activity. The voluntary approach was used by the production managers to reduce their total production costs. For example, the self-assigned target might be to reduce the consumption of ethylene to 1.05 kilograms from 1.10 kilograms per kilogram of polyethylene product or to reduce head count for a given section from 12 to 10.

The across-the-board approach was used in company-wide campaigns to reduce costs, usually when the company was going through a bad period. Examples of such campaigns included reducing entertainment fees by 5% or reducing the cost of business trips by 10%. Occasionally, a plant general manager might use the approach for a plant-wide cost reduction program. The across-the-board approach was typically used to reduce fixed costs.

The mass-produced products divisions used the calculated approach. They set their cost reduction targets based on the worldwide prices of their products. For example, a division would have to reduce costs by ¥10 per kilogram to maintain its profit margins if there was a high probability that the selling price would decrease by ¥10 per kilogram the following year.

The experience curve approach was commonly used in the functional products divisions; for example, it was used in the floppy disk, optical disk, and hard disk facilities. The technique was particularly applicable to the mass production of discrete products.

And the prior index approach was used when managers could not identify the best cost reduction approach or did not have a standard against which to identify an appropriate cost reduction target. For example, managers of the indirect departments such as personnel did not have any objective measure of the appropriate head counts for their departments. Therefore, it was very difficult for them to set cost reduction objectives. Instead, they might refer to the index of direct to indirect costs for other firms or the industry as a whole. They would then use this benchmark to set their own cost reduction targets.

The overall cost reduction targets for a product line were called action plans (see Exhibit 12). For each cost box, a single target cost figure was identified. The difference between the target and the prior period actual costs was called the "amount of targeted improvement." Thus, each cost box manager was given a single cost reduction target. Every year, each cost box's cost reduction achievements were compared to budgeted targets; managers were neither rewarded nor punished for their performance against these targets. However, how well the cost box achieved its cost reduction and other targets was taken into account when making promotions. Once every three years, the overall performance of each cost box was evaluated by comparing it to the firm's medium-range plan, which covered a three- to five-year time period.

Every business general manager developed an action program that identified the counter-measures required to achieve the targeted cost reductions (see Exhibit 13). In addition, these action programs identified the time of execution for each countermeasure, the amount of facility investment required, and any impact on the head count at the facility. Separate action programs were developed for the administrative and coordinating service cost centers. Two programs were required because the general business manager was not held responsible for the administration and coordination costs associated with the facility; these expenses were the responsibility of the general managers of the administration and coordination departments.

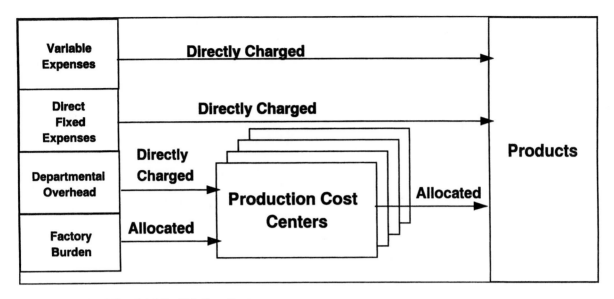

EXHIBIT 1   Mitsubishi's Old Cost System

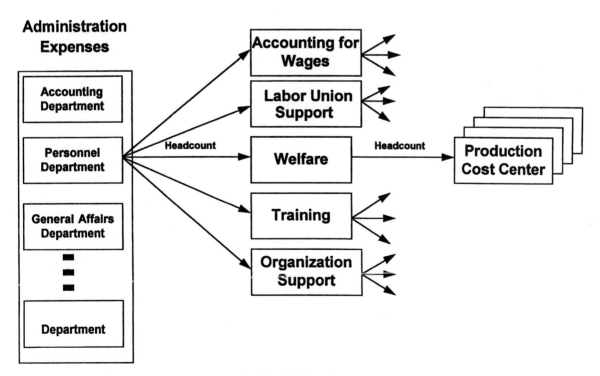

EXHIBIT 2   Administration of Mitsubishi's Old Cost System

EXHIBIT 3 Mitsubishi Kasei's Organization Structure of the Mizushima Plant

Administration Department

Production Department I
  Ethylene Section
  Gas Section
  Octanol Section
  Alpha Olefin Section
  Nonanol Section
  Tank Yard Section
  Coordination and Technical Section

Production Department II
  Aldehyde Section
  Nitrile Section
  Aromatics Section
  Organic Acids Section
  Chlor-Alkali Section
  VCM Section
  Coordination and Technical Section

Production Department III
  Polyethylene Production Section I
  Polyethylene Production Section II
  PVC Section

Production Department III *(Continued)*
  Plastic Products Section
  Soy Milk Section
  Coordination and Control Section

Information Media Products Department
  Hard Disk Section
  Technical Evaluation Section
  Quality Assurance Section
  Coordination and Technical Section

Power Department
  Power Section I
  Power Section II
  Coordination and Technical Section

Engineering Department

Planning and Coordination Department

Quality Assurance Department

Security and Environment Department

Development Center

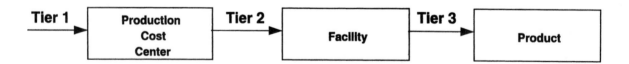

Directly Charged

Managerial Estimate   **Managerial Estimate**   **Managerial Estimate**

Direct Labor   **Direct Labor**   **Direct Labor**

EXHIBIT 4   Three Tiers of Allocation in Mitsubishi's Old Cost System

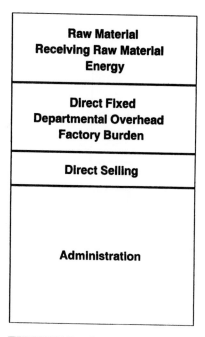

EXHIBIT 5   Structure of Reported Costs in Mitsubishi's Old Cost System

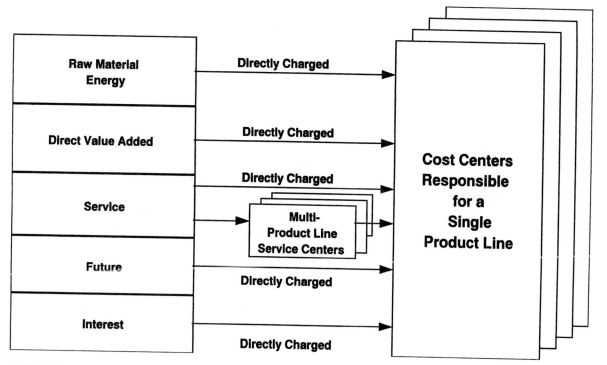

EXHIBIT 6   Reporting Product Line Costs in Mitsubishi's New Cost System

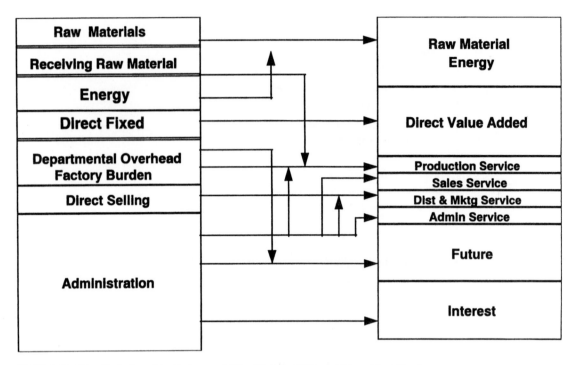

EXHIBIT 7 Relationship Between Mitsubishi's Old and New Cost Systems

EXHIBIT 8 Mitsubishi Kasei's Allocation to Products Using Complex Standard

| COMPLEX | HEAD COUNT (1/2) | | FACILITY COSTS (1/2) | | STANDARD |
	#	%	¥	%	%
Product A	10	20%	10	20%	20%
Product B	20	40%	5	10%	25%
Product C	10	20%	20	40%	30%
Product D	10	20%	15	30%	25%
Total	50	100%	50	100%	100%

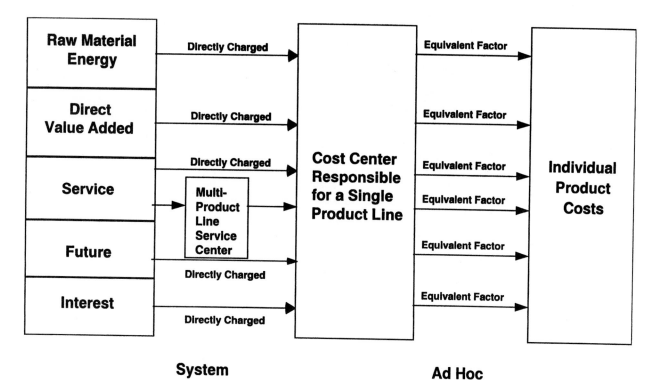

System   **Ad Hoc**

EXHIBIT 9   **Reporting Individual Product Costs in Mitsubishi's New Cost System**

EXHIBIT 10 Mitsubishi Kasei's Generating Section and Departmental Reports

	SECTION A	SECTION B	SECTION C	TOTAL DEPARTMENT
Repair Cost	XXXXX	XXXXX	XXXXX	XXXXX
Labor Cost	XXXXX	XXXXX	XXXXX	XXXXX
Depreciation	XXXXX	XXXXX	XXXXX	XXXXX
■				
■				
▬				
■				
Total	XXXXX	XXXXX	XXXXX	XXXXX
	Reports for Section Managers			Report for Department Manager

EXHIBIT 11 Mitsubishi Kasei's Wastewater Treatment Department Report

EXPENSE ITEM	¥
Raw Materials	XXXXXX
Energy Costs	XXXXXX
Repair	XXXXXX
Labor	XXXXXX
Depreciation	XXXXXX
Service Fee	(XXXXXX)
Total	Nearly Zero

Responsible Unit	Responsibility Cost						Future Costs	InC osts Interest	Total	Admin. & Coord. Costs	Total Cost
	Plant				Head Office						
	Production Department				Branch Offices						
Cost Item	Raw Mat'l & Energy	Direct Value Added	Total	Prod'n Service Costs	Sales Service Costs	Distrib'n Service Costs					
Basic Cost											
Target Cost											
Target Improvement			a	b					Ⓐ	Ⓑ	Ⓒ

EXHIBIT 12 Action Plan

Responsible Unit		Counter-Measure	Amount of Improvement	Time of Execution	Facility Investment	Labor +/-
Production Department						
			a			
Others						
			b			
a + b						
Targeted Improvement			Ⓐ			

EXHIBIT 13   Action Program

DIGITAL COMMUNICATIONS, INC.: ENCODER DEVICE DIVISION

Introduction

Digital Communications, Inc., a Connecticut-based company, produced a wide range of communications devices ranging from portable typewriters and hand-held walkie-talkies to complex voice and data encoding devices. Their primary customers were federal, state, and local government agencies, and 1988 sales were expected to be $100 million.

The Encoder Device Division (EDD) of Defense Communications, located in Hamden, Connecticut, specialized in classified government communication products to be used on the battlefield. There were four different basic products, each of which encoded different communication transmissions: data, video, voice ratio, and variable wire. Sales in 1988 were expected to be $30 million.

Because the four products manufactured at EDD were classified, all were produced in a factory-within-a-factory environment. That is, although the products were similar in some respects, they did not share any manufacturing facilities or staffs, for it was believed that a compartmentalized structure minimized exposure to the risk of security violations. The four production departments were Data Encoding (DE), Video Encoding

(VE), Voice Ratio Encoding (VRE), and Variable Wire Encoding (VWE).

There were a few exceptions to compartmentalization. The general support departments—personnel, financial, information services, and plant engineering—and the material departments—shipping and receiving, inventory control, and receiving inspection—serviced all four production departments. None of these staffs, however, had contact with classified information.

The other exceptions were the production support departments: product engineering, machine maintenance, quality control, program security, and program management and supervision. These represented hybrid departments; the people within them were completely dedicated to one of the four production areas. Nonetheless, they maintained an independent departmental structure like the other support departments.

EDD Accounting System

EDD's cost system directly charged all material, labor, and production support department costs to the production departments incurring the costs. The material support department's costs were allocated to the four production departments based on the fraction of EDD's direct labor hours worked in each department. Each department used approximately equal quantities of direct labor to produce its annual production volume, and all direct labor earned the same hourly wage.

This case was prepared by Shannon Weems, doctoral student (under the supervision of Professor Robin Cooper).

The general support department's costs were allocated on several factors. Prior to 1985, all costs had been allocated to production departments based on direct labor hours. Several studies indicated, however, that this did not reflect the departments' usage of these resources. Consequently, personnel costs were allocated to production based on head count; plant engineering costs were allocated on square feet of production space; and financial and information services were allocated based on a special study of the usage of their services by the production departments. Exhibit 1 details the accounting system's treatment of all 1987 costs and the resulting total annual costs of the four production departments.

The Subassembly Contract

Customers purchased products through a lengthy, sealed bid and negotiation process. Normally the final price was based on cost plus a negotiated profit. Once the contract was finalized, the manufacturer was responsible for providing internal security during all phases of manufacture. Contracts usually extended over several years and, in most cases, included any maintenance or upgrading of the product in the field that was necessary.

Occasionally, new technology would make it advantageous to upgrade a product in the middle of the contract. The upgrade to units in the field was achieved via a modification kit supplied by the manufacturer.

In 1987 a new microprocessor was developed which offered significant advantages to VRE device customers. Although the original product was otherwise acceptable, the replacement contract was subject to a sealed bid and negotiation process. The contract would entail making replacement subassemblies for the units in the field and substituting the new subassembly for the old subassembly in all future production.

EDD was particularly eager to win the contract because it was committed to making and servicing completed products. In the past it had avoided piecemeal jobs that would include subcontracting large pieces of production to other firms.

The problem for management was how to bid for the new contract. Although they had experience in constructing ground-up bids for entire programs, this was the first time they had been faced with manufacturing a single subassembly for resale.

Management was confident that they understood the total cost of each program quite well, largely because

of the factory-within-a-factory environment, which yielded few shared costs. However, they felt they lacked detailed information about the costs associated with individual subassemblies.

Bidding the Job

The VRE device was composed of six distinct subassemblies: three printed wire assemblies (PWAs), one of which was the mother board; two wire harnesses that connected the PWAs; and a case and cover assembly that housed the other subassemblies. Purchased materials included the case and cover, wire to make the harnesses, the bare printed wiring boards, and the components added to the PWAs during production, such as resistors and capacitors. The production process and labor and machine utilizations are detailed in Exhibit 2.

The VRE subassembly for the microprocessor upgrade (identified as board 2) was one of the PWAs, not the mother board. The replacement board would be configured differently from the compromised board but would be virtually identical in its manufacture and its components.

EDD had sufficient capacity in the PWA production process to accommodate production of the replacement PWAs in addition to those needed for future production of complete units. The volume of replacement PWAs for units in the field was approximately equal to one year's production of the PWA. Hence, EDD proposed to produce twice as many of the one PWA as required in completed units and to do so without altering its investment in equipment. The only additional costs to producing the part would be the labor and material costs, which were expected to remain virtually unchanged on a per-unit basis.

In early 1988, the top staff members of the VRE production group convened to discuss how they would develop cost estimates to bid the job. Representatives from the financial staff felt that the most expedient method of costing was to utilize detailed time reporting data to determine what fraction of departmental labor hours were used to produce board 2. The advocates of this system proposed to apply that fraction of the departmental overhead to board 2, in addition to its labor and material costs, to arrive at total cost. Exhibit 3 was submitted for review as the basis for a bid proposal.

Several production supervisors balked at this idea. In reviewing the financial department's proposal, they were shocked to learn that all three PWAs were thought to cost approximately the same. Intuition led them to believe that the PWAs should have very different costs. Although the three PWAs used similar amounts of direct labor in the whole production process, they had very different production characteristics.

"Wouldn't it be a better idea if we studied these overhead costs that we're talking about to learn how to apply them to the three boards?" asked the director of quality control. "I know my staff has almost nothing to do with direct labor. Their job is to identify quality problems, and we all know that usually means machinery problems." A number of the other support department directors felt similarly; much of their staff actions had little to do with the direct labor content of the PWAs.

After further discussion, the VRE staff decided to undertake a study to determine how costs should be allocated to the PWAs. From the findings of this study, they decided to modify the financial department's proposal. They believed that by using two additional allocation bases, machine hours, and material dollars, they could arrive at a reasonable estimate of what it cost to produce board 2.

They agreed on the following scheme for allocating VRE support department costs to the VRE subassemblies:

Machine hours:	Product engineering
	Machine maintenance
	department
	Quality department
	Plant engineering
	Information services
Direct labor hours:	Product security
	Product management
	and supervision
	Personnel
	Financial
Material dollars:	Shipping and receiving
	Inventory control
	Receiving inspection

After the results of the VRE study were presented, EDD controller Don Bryant began to worry whether the costs that the support departments were charging to the production departments were sufficiently accurate.

The financial department had reviewed and updated its methods for allocating general support department costs in 1985, so a number of new allocation bases replaced the previous direct labor hour allocation base.

Bryant recalled an issue that had arisen at the time of that study that was dismissed as having little impact on allocations: the reciprocal use of support departments. It was evident at the time that two of the major users of information systems support were the financial department and the personnel department. Similarly, personnel provided service to both financial and information services.

At the time of the detailed study of the service departments, the reciprocal usage of the general support departments, as well as their usage by production, was estimated (Exhibit 4). Given the workload of the finance department at that time, it was decided to ignore these reciprocal costs and to concentrate on accurately tracing production costs to the four production departments.

The justification for ignoring reciprocal usage was that the costs associated with reciprocal services were minimal and would not significantly change the costs of any product. Consequently, these costs were allocated to production in the proportion that production used the department's services directly. For instance, all of personnel costs were allocated to production based on head count in the production departments, even though 30% of personnel services were consumed by other support departments.

In light of the new subassembly contract and the need for more accurate product costs, Bryant decided that it was worth knowing the potential impact of using more accurate allocation procedures for reciprocal costs on product costs. He hired a business school student with accounting experience for the summer and assigned her the task of evaluating different treatments of joint expenses and their impact on product costs.

The student, Rebecca Wills, consulted a number of accounting texts and learned that one common treatment of such costs was the step-down method. This allocation method was a sequence of allocations that could be ordered based on the dollars in the departments, the number of services provided by the departments, or other criteria. Once the order was determined, all dollars from the first department in the sequence were allocated to the remaining departments. Then all dollars in the second department, including dollars allocated to it by the first department, were allocated to successive departments in the sequence.

The process would continue until all support department costs reached a production department. The key to the step-down method was that it did not permit costs to be allocated to a support department that preceded it in the sequence. It effectively broke one link of the reciprocal charge so that eventually all costs were allocated to productive departments.

Wills applied the step-down method using both magnitude of dollars and number of departments serviced as her criterion for sequencing the support departments (Exhibits 5 and 6). She was surprised at the size of the difference between the two approaches. She knew that when she reported her findings to Bryant, he would ask her advice about which approach was more appropriate. The VRE assembly contract was soon to be bid, and Wills realized that her assessment was of major importance.

EXHIBIT 1

DIGITAL COMMUNICATIONS, INC.: ENCODER DEVICE DIVISION
Current Financial System's Overhead Charging Mechanism

SUPPORT DEPARTMENT	DOLLARS	CHARGE MECHANISM	% USAGE OF SUPPORT SERVICE BY PRODUCTION DEPT.			
			VWE	VRE	DE	VE
General Support						
Personnel plant	$2,190,251	Headcount	25.00%	25.00%	25.00%	25.00%
Engineering building occupancy	3,011,960	Sq ftg	25.00	37.50	12.50	25.00
Information services	2,738,860	Usage	16.60	50.00	16.70	16.70
Finance & administration	1,682,000	Usage	33.30	16.70	33.30	16.70
Production Support						
Product management & supervision	$205,009	Usage	17.10%	34.44%	18.19%	30.28%
Machine maintenance	153,756	Usage	21.03	35.25	15.23	28.49
Product engineering	205,009	Usage	19.48	32.00	24.90	23.62
Product security	410,017	Usage	25.42	29.56	20.43	24.58
Quality control	256,260	Usage	13.45	32.00	19.70	34.86
Material Support						
Shipping & receiving	$221,492	Labor hours	25.00%	25.00%	25.00%	25.00%
Inventory control	110,746	Labor hours	25.00	25.00	25.00	25.00
Receiving inspection	332,239	Labor hours	25.00	25.00	25.00	25.00

Dollars Charged From Support Departments to Productive Departments

SUPPORT DEPARTMENT	DOLLARS	VWE	VRE	DE	VE
General Support					
Personnel plant	$2,190,251	$547,563	$547,563	$547,563	$547,563
Engineering building occupancy	3,011,960	752,990	1,129,485	376,495	752,990
Information services	2,738,860	454,651	1,369,430	457,390	457,390
Finance & administration	1,682,000	560,106	280,894	560,106	280,894
Production Support					
Product management & supervision	$205,009	$35,050	$70,603	$37,288	$62,068
Machine maintenance	153,756	32,333	54,202	23,421	43,800
Product engineering	205,009	39,929	65,603	51,050	48,427
Product security	410,017	104,235	121,215	83,780	100,787
Quality control	256,260	34,463	81,993	50,471	89,333

continued

Material Support

Shipping & receiving	$221,492		$55,373	$55,373	$55,373	$55,373
Inventory control	110,746		27,687	27,687	27,687	27,687
Receiving inspection	332,239		83,060	83,060	83,060	83,060
Total overhead	$11,517,599	52%	$2,727,439	$3,887,107	$2,353,683	$2,549,371
Direct wages	3,543,877	16	885,969	885,969	885,969	885,969
Raw materials	7,087,753	32	1,107,461	2,214,923	1,550,446	2,214,923
Total firm costs	22,149,229					
Total program costs			4,720,869	6,987,999	4,790,098	5,650,263
% of division expenses			21.31%	31.55%	21.63%	25.51%

EXHIBIT 2

DIGITAL COMMUNICATIONS, INC.: ENCODER DEVICE DIVISION

Percentage of VRE Dollar Hours (DLHRS) and Machine Hours (MCHRS) by Component, by Process

PROCESS SEQUENCE	MCHRS OR DLHRS WORKED	BOARD 1 (MOTHER BOARD)	BOARD 2	BOARD 3	FINAL & HARNESS
Automatic insertion	Dlhrs	0.82%	2.04%	1.22%	
Kit & prep	Dlhrs	0.82	3.27	4.08	
Semi-automatic insertion	Dlhrs	4.08	1.63	2.45	
Wave solder	Dlhrs	1.39	1.35	1.35	
Touch-up I	Dlhrs	1.53	5.61	3.06	
anual insertion	Dhlrs	0.61	2.45	3.06	
Test I	Dlhrs	0.69	0.67	0.67	
Test II	Dlhrs	0.00	0.61	1.43	
Mask & boot	Dlhrs	6.12	2.04	2.04	
Conformal coat	Dlhrs	1.40	1.35	1.35	
Touch-up II	Dlhrs	1.84	1.02	1.22	
Harness build	Dlhrs				12.24%
Assembly	Dlhrs				20.41
Test III	Dlhrs				4.08
Total % dlhrs		19.30	22.04	21.93	36.73
Automatic insertion	Mchrs	7.00	17.00	10.00	
Wave solder	Mchrs	11.00	11.00	11.00	
Conformal coat	Mchrs	11.00	11.00	11.00	
Total % mchrs		29.00	39.00	32.00	0.00

EXHIBIT 3

DIGITAL COMMUNICATIONS, INC.: ENCODER DEVICE DIVISION
VRE Component Costs

COST ELEMENT	VRE $'S	BOARD 1 (MOTHER BOARD)	BOARD 2	BOARD 3	FINAL & HARNESS
VRE material $'s	$2,214,923	18.00%	45.00%	27.00%	10.00%
VRE labor wages	885,969	19.30	22.04	21.93	36.73
VRE production & general support	3,720,988	19.30	22.04	21.93	36.73
VRE material support	166,119	19.30	22.04	21.93	36.73
Total cost	6,987,999	1,319,890	2,048,701	1,644,765	1,974,643

EXHIBIT 4

DIGITAL COMMUNICATIONS, INC.: ENCODER DEVICE DIVISION
Matrix of Reciprocal Usage of Support Departments

ORIGINATING BUDGET	$	DESTINATION DEPARTMENT PERCENTAGES				
		FINANCE	INFORMATION SERVICES	PERSONNEL	PLANT ENGINEERING	PRODUCTION
Finance	$1,682,000	0%	10%	5%	20%	65%
Information services	2,738,860	50	0	20	0	30
Personnel	2,190,251	13	11	0	6	70
Plant engineering	3,011,960	10	6	4	0	80

EXHIBIT 5

DIGITAL COMMUNICATIONS, INC.: ENCODER DEVICE DIVISION
Step-Down Allocation: Ordered by Dollars in Original Budget

Matrix of Reciprocal Usage of Support Departments

ORIGINATING BUDGET	$'S FROM:	$'S TO:	FINANCE	INFORMATION SERVICES	PERSONNEL	PLANT ENGINEERING	PRODUCTION
$1,682,000	finance		0%	10%	5%	20%	65%
2,738,860	information services		50	0	20	0	30
2,190,251	personnel		13	11	0	6	70
3,011,960	plant engineering		10	6	4	0	80
$9,623,071							

Step-Down Matrix Based on Dollars Charged Out

ORIGINATING BUDGET	$'S FROM:	$'S TO:	PLANT ENGINEERING	INFORMATION SERVICES	PERSONNEL	FINANCE	PRODUCTION
$3,011,960	plant engineering		0%	6%	4%	10%	80%
2,738,860	information services		0	0	20	50	30
2,190,251	personnel		0	0	0	16	84
1,682,000	finance		0	0	0	0	100

STEP 1: ORIGINATING BUDGET	$'S FROM:	$'S TO:	PLANT ENGINEERING	INFORMATION SERVICES	PERSONNEL	FINANCE	PRODUCTION	DOLLARS CHARGED TO PRODUCTION DEPARTMENTS			
								VWE	VRE	DE	VE
$3,011,960	plant engineering		0	$180,718	$120,478	$301,196	$2,409,568	$602,392	$903,588	$301,196	$602,392
2,738,860	information services		0	0	0	0	0	0	0	0	0
2,190,251	personnel		0	0	0	0	0	0	0	0	0
1,682,000	finance		0	0	0	0	0	0	0	0	0

EXHIBIT 5 *(continued)*

DIGITAL COMMUNICATIONS, INC.: ENCODER DEVICE DIVISION

Step-Down Allocation: Ordered by Dollars in Original Budget

STEP 2: ORIGINATING BUDGET	$'S FROM:	$'S TO:	PLANT ENGINEERING	INFORMATION SERVICES	PERSONNEL	FINANCE	PRODUCTION	DOLLARS CHARGED TO PRODUCTION DEPARTMENTS			
								VWE	VRE	DE	VE
$0	plant engineering		$0	$0	$120,478	$301,196	$2,409,568	$602,392	$903,588	$301,196	602,392
2,919,578	information services		0	0	583,916	1,459,789	875,873	146,271	437,936	146,271	145,395
2,190,251	personnel		0	0	0	0	0	0	0	0	0
1,682,000	finance		0	0	0	0	0	0	0	0	0

STEP 3: ORIGINATING BUDGET	$'S FROM:	$'S TO:	PLANT ENGINEERING	INFORMATION SERVICES	PERSONNEL	FINANCE	PRODUCTION	VWE	VRE	DE	VE
$0	plant engineering		$0	$0	$0	$301,196	$2,409,568	$602,392	$903,588	$301,196	$602,392
0	information services		0	0	0	1,459,789	875,873	146,271	437,936	146,271	145,395
2,894,645	personnel		0	0	0	463,143	2,431,502	607,876	607,876	607,876	607,876
1,682,000	finance		0	0	0	0	0	0	0	0	0

STEP 4: ORIGINATING BUDGET	$'S FROM:	$'S TO:	PLANT ENGINEERING	INFORMATION SERVICES	PERSONNEL	FINANCE	PRODUCTION	VWE	VRE	DE	VE
$0	plant engineering		$0	$0	$0	$0	$2,409,568	$602.392	$903,588	$301,169	$602,392
0	information services		0	0	0	0	875,873	146,271	437,936	146,271	145,395
0	personnel		0	0	0	0	2,431,502	607,876	607,876	607,876	607,876
3,906,128	finance		0	0	0	0	3,906,128	1,300,741	652,323	1,300,741	652,323
Total allocated to productive departments from support departments							9,623,071	2,657,280	2,601,723	2,356,084	2,007,986

EXHIBIT 6

DIGITAL COMMUNICATIONS, INC.: ENCODER DEVICE DIVISION

Step-Down Allocation: Ordered First by Number Serviced, Second by Dollars

Matrix of Reciprocal Usage of Support Departments

ORIGINATING BUDGET	$'S FROM:	$'S TO:	FINANCE	INFORMATION SERVICES	PERSONNEL	PLANT ENGINEERING	PRODUCTION
$1,682,000	finance		0%	10%	5%	20%	65%
2,738,860	information services		50	0	20	0	30
2,190,251	personnel		13	11	0	6	70
3,011,960	plant engineering		10	6	4	0	80
$9,623,071							

Step-Down Matrix Based Number of Departments Serviced and on Dollars Charged Out

ORIGINATING BUDGET	$'S FROM:	$'S TO:	PLANT ENGINEERING	PERSONNEL	FINANCE	INFORMATION SERVICES	PRODUCTION
$3,011,960	plant engineering		0%	4%	10%	6%	80%
2,190,251	personnel		0	0	14	12	74
1,682,000	finance		0	0	0	13	87
2,738,860	information services		0	0	0	0	100

STEP 1: ORIGINATING BUDGET	$'S FROM:	$'S TO:	PLANT ENGINEERING	PERSONNEL	FINANCE	INFORMATION SERVICES	PRODUCTION	DOLLARS CHARGED TO PRODUCTION DEPARTMENTS			
								VWE	VRE	DE	VE
$3,011,960	plant engineering		$0	$120,478	$301,196	$180,718	$2,409,568	$602,392	$903,588	$301,196	602,392
2,190,251	personnel		0	0	0	0	0	0	0	0	0
1,682,000	finance		0	0	0	0	0	0	0	0	0
2,738,860	information services		0	0	0	0	0	0	0	0	0

EXHIBIT 6 *(continued)*

DIGITAL COMMUNICATIONS, INC.: ENCODER DEVICE DIVISION

Step-Down Allocation: Ordered First by Number Serviced, Second by Dollars

STEP 2:

ORIGINATING BUDGET	$'S FROM:	$'S TO: PLANT ENGINEERING	PERSONNEL	FINANCE	INFORMATION SERVICES	PRODUCTION	VWE	VRE	DE	VE
$0	plant engineering	$0	$0	$301,196	$180,718	$2,409,568	$602,392	$903,588	$301,196	$602,392
2,310,729	personnel	0	0	323,502	277,287	1,709,939	427,485	427,485	427,485	427,485
1,682,000	finance	0	0	0	0	0	0	0	0	0
2,738,860	information services	0	0	0	0	0	0	0	0	0

STEP 3:

ORIGINATING BUDGET	$'S FROM:	$'S TO: PLANT ENGINEERING	PERSONNEL	FINANCE	INFORMATION SERVICES	PRODUCTION	VWE	VRE	DE	VE
$0	plant engineering	$0	$0	$0	$180,718	$2,409,568	$602,392	$903,588	$301,196	$602,392
0	personnel	0	0	0	277,288	1,709,940	427,485	427,485	427,485	427,485
2,306,698	finance	0	0	0	299,871	2,006,827	668,273	335,140	668,273	335,140
2,738,860	information services	0	0	0	0	0	0	0	0	0

STEP 4:

ORIGINATING BUDGET	$'S FROM:	$'S TO: PLANT ENGINEERING	PERSONNEL	FINANCE	INFORMATION SERVICES	PRODUCTION	VWE	VRE	DE	VE
$0	plant engineering	$0	$0	$0	$0	2,409,568	602,392	903,588	301,196	602,392
0	personnel	0	0	0	0	1,709,940	427,485	427,485	427,485	427,485
0	finance	0	0	0	0	2,006,827	668,273	335,140	668,273	335,140
3,496,737	information services	0	0	0	0	3,496,737	583,955	1,748,369	583,955	580,485
Total allocated to productive departments from support departments						9,623,072	2,282,105	3,414,581	1,980,909	1,945,475

METABO GMBH & CO. KG

When our old cost system was designed and implemented, it was state of the art. But it no longer provided us with accurate numbers. The reported numbers were too aggregated to provide direct feedback on the performance of shop floor workers. Our new system, in contrast, is the best available.

Mr. Häussler, controller, Metabo

History and Products

Metabo, located in Nurtingen, about 15 miles outside of Stuttgart in the Swabian region of West Germany, was founded in 1924 as the Schnizler Werke company. Initially it produced hand drills and subsequently expanded its product line into hand and electric tools for craftsmen, eventually offering the world's largest do-it-yourself product line of hand-operated power tools. The company is still controlled by the three founding families (Closs, Rauch, and Schnizler), although in 1978 its legal status was changed to a limited partnership with a limited company as general partner.

Today Metabo produces a full line of power tools including saws, rotary and impact drills, screwdrivers, hammers, grinders, polishers, planers, and routers. Products are sold to do-it-yourselfers, professionals, and industrial workers. In addition to hand tools, Metabo manufactures bench- and column-mounted drilling machines, belt polishing and buffing machines, and grinding machines. Altogether, Metabo produces 500 basic and about 2,000 different final products. The company manufactures 45,000 standard parts plus customer-specified products. About 85% to 90% of turnover occurs in standard products, the remainder in special orders. All products are developed internally.

Metabo is considered the Rolls Royce of the hand-tool industry and has been able to command a price premium compared to its competition. The company's main competitors, also offering full product lines, are Bosch and AEG, two West German manufacturers, and Black & Decker. Bosch, the market leader, and AEG, the number two, offer good quality, good image, and slightly lower prices. Black & Decker competes in the lower end of the market. Recently, Japanese competitors have entered Metabo's home market. While they offer good quality and lower prices, they lack Metabo's full product line.

This case was prepared by research associate Dagmar Bottenbruch and Professor Robert S. Kaplan.

The Production Process

Despite being a relatively small company, Metabo is completely vertically integrated and builds all critical components and subassemblies in-house. One of the company's founders believed, "You get quality only if you do it yourself."

Power tool production starts with raw material treatment, including components made in the aluminum foundry, by plastic injection molding, and in-steel treatment. About three metric tons of aluminum are melted daily in the foundry and cast into various small components that are subsequently cleaned, polished, and inspected. In the plastic injection molding department, granular material is fed from large storage silos into various machines to be heated and injected under pressure into molds to form plastic components (e.g., handles) for the hand tools. The molding machines come in different sizes and have different manpower requirements, ranging from one operator for one machine to one operator for six machines.

Steel treatment produces machined parts such as wheels, chucks, and armature shafts. Two types of treatment occur: bar feeding, where treated bars are cut after treatment, and piece feeding, where precut parts are machined. Because of the considerable diversity of parts (about 1,500) processed through steel treatment, a large inventory of 1,000 to 1,200 metric tons of steel, worth about DM 900,000, is maintained for the area.

In the bar feeding process, the steel bars are taken by crane to the appropriate turning machine for processing. Two types of turning machines are used: six-spindle machines, which process six steel bars simultaneously, and single-spindle machines. About 1,000 different parts are produced in this department—60% on the six-spindle machines. Setup times depend on the dimensions of the components. Components with similar specifications might require only minor adjustments to the machines. If the components are completely different, setup times can range between 2 and 14 hours, even with extensive preparation work performed while the previous part is running on the machine. Twelve setup people work exclusively in the department.

Other employees in the department feed the raw material and remove the finished parts and byproducts. Because of the long setup times, production of standard parts is scheduled in large batches. For example, one part which takes 13 seconds of machining time is produced in a lot size of 20,000 pieces. The large batch would then go into inventory and be released for further processing in smaller lot sizes, depending on final demand. Some components are produced continuously; others run for between 2 to 10 shifts.

Tool preparation is another major activity in this department. A setup schedule provides information on the need for tools and machine parts. The same people do the setups and prepare the tools. Tool preparation takes an average of 2.5 hours but can, of course, be done while the machine is running. An average of 7 of the 35 machines would be in the setup stage each day. Nearly DM 6 million of inventory of fixtures and tools support the turning machines. After a part leaves a turning machine, it is hardened in a furnace, heat-treated, and inspected.

Steel parts and other components are brought together in the electrical motor production line. This department contains a fully automated line that winds wire, attaches a fan and insulators, and tests and balances the component that becomes the motor for the hand tool. This highly automated process is replicated on a smaller scale by hand for certain custom applications and for spare parts no longer in standard production.

In final assembly, purchased parts and manufactured components are manually assembled into finished products. The finished product parts list contains 80 to 100 items, all of which must be available at the right time. The finished product receives a final electrical test and is then packaged and shipped through a fully automated distribution center.

The throughput time from casting aluminum to the finished product is 6 to 8 weeks. Grinding wheels, customized special machines, and in-house tool making and production machinery are produced in separate production areas.

The Old Cost System

Metabo provided a complex information management environment (see Exhibit 1). The complexity was difficult to track even with extensive use of computers by the old cost system. The system's main task was to compute actual total costs. It contained the three classic cost accounting elements: accumulate costs by accounts, by cost centers, and by products. Subsystems, such as materials control and wage control, provided inputs into the product costing module. Costs were distributed from 200 different cost accounts to 250 cost centers or work orders.

Product costs were built up from material master accounts, parts lists, and work plans. Secondary (support) center costs were allocated to primary (production) cost centers, using causal relations as much as possible, such as through internal work orders. The overhead allocation was done manually twice a year (in September for budgeting purposes and to compute standard costs for the year, and at year end to eliminate errors and use actual rather than budgeted amounts). The task required three to four weeks for a highly qualified person.

Product cost components were as follows:

Materials	
Materials overhead	Applied as a percentage of materials cost
Reemployed parts	The term for subassemblies
Direct Labor	
Fringe benefits	Applied based on direct labor cost
Production overhead	Applied using machine-hour rates based on capacity utilization
Special costs	Such as tooling

An analytic study was conducted once per year to determine individual machine-hour rates. Costs arising at the individual cost centers were assigned to each machine in the center and divided by the machine's estimated annual volume. The rates were estimated at the beginning of each year using the actual experience from the prior year. Metabo had 1,500 such machine-hour rates. Häussler noted that many companies continued to allocate overhead to products based on direct labor. Metabo had been using machine-hour rates since the early 1970s.

Six categories of traceable costs could be directly allocated to the machines:

Depreciation	Straight line based on replacement value[1]
Imputed interest	Based on 50% of machine's replacement value[2]
Space	
Energy	Based on run time and machine horsepower
Maintenance	Estimated based on experience and industry averages (including oil and grease)
Tooling	

---

[1]The calculation based on replacement costs was done for internal purposes only since historical costs were mandated for financial and tax reporting.

[2]A long-term (three- to five-year) bank lending rate was used to charge interest expense on inventory and fixed assets. Currently this rate was in the range of 5% to 6%.

Costs that could not be traced directly to machines were aggregated at the cost center and allocated to individual machines as a percentage markup of the traceable costs. The rates had ranged between 200% to 300% of traceable costs, but this procedure caused problems by heavily burdening expensive, automated machines. To avoid overburdening such newly purchased machines with large components of nontraceable costs, a compromise solution was adopted to allocate 50% of the nontraceable costs based on machine hours and 50% based on traceable costs.

Problems with the Old System

Despite the sophistication and care taken when designing Metabo's old cost system, it no longer satisfied top management's requirements. First, the manual processing of the data at the beginning and end of year was inefficient and costly. Second, long-time lags occurred between data collection and feedback, so operators could not get timely information about what was happening in their cost centers. Thus, operators were not very cost conscious. Also, since the machine rates were only calculated once a year and not split into variable and fixed components, major errors were introduced by fluctuations in capacity utilization. After a very good year, machine burden rates would plummet, and after a bad year the rates became much more expensive. While Mr. Häussler, based on his personal experience, tried to make some adjustments to dampen extreme variations in rates, the results were not satisfactory.

No budgets were prepared, so actual results could not be compared against a standard. Even with a budget, the information would have been meaningless to cost center managers because of the inability to control for the actual level of activity in a period. The degree of aggregation at a cost center produced additional problems. For example, the aluminum foundry and injection molding department were treated as a single cost center even though several different machines with different degrees of automation and labor intensity were used in each facility. In the steel treatment area, all six-spindle machines were in the same cost center; and in the motor production area, the fully automated and the hand assembly operations were included in the same cost center.

Also producing errors was the practice of charging fringe benefits (a very high cost component in Germany) to the cost center where a worker was originally assigned, while the actual direct labor charge was made to the cost center where he or she performed the work. German workers could perform a variety of skilled tasks and were rotated frequently among cost centers.

Since batch sizes varied from process to process, the job order accounting approach presented another serious problem. In the aluminum foundry, a job order could be written for 4,000 pieces of a component. If the process were running smoothly, the supervisor could decide to produce enough to release 4,500 good pieces to the next stage. Omitted from this count would be items produced in the batch but which had been set aside as scrap or rework. On the other hand, a few hundred pieces could have been added to the batch after they had been reworked from a previous batch.

With the old system, all the costs of working on the order would be accumulated and then divided by the number of good parts that left the production stage when computing a cost per unit. To get any useful information from such data, one person had to spend a month on a special study to track down the production costs associated with a single end product.

Häussler explained as follows:

You can't expect a production supervisor or technician to explain a total product cost variance. He needs information that relates directly to the process he is controlling. Only if you show him things like excess tooling expense, indirect materials, and the actual quantity produced at that stage can he start to respond on the source of the deviation.

A final flaw in the system was the difficulty of integrating cost accounting with financial accounting. The product cost figures used internally were different from those needed for financial reporting because of differing methods of depreciation (straight-line versus accelerated, and replacement value versus historical cost), and the use of imputed interest for internal measurement of product costs that was not allowed for external reporting. The reconciliation between the two systems was tedious and painful.

In Search of the Perfect System

Mr. Häussler still gets a tortured look on his face when thinking of the old system. He was pleased when top management decided that a new cost system was needed. His background included extensive shop floor experience starting, after school, as an apprenticeship at a machine tool company. While a machining apprentice, he had to fill in for the purchasing manager who be-

came sick. In this position he learned how little office and staff people knew of actual operations. He decided to do a second more technical apprenticeship, which occurred at Metabo. After one-and-a-half years in the technical service division of a construction machinery producer, he pursued studies in business. In 1972 he joined Metabo's control department.

Häussler, because of his technical background and his excellent relationship with the people on the shop floor, was put in charge of developing the new control system. Häussler concurred as follows:

It is easier to familiarize an engineer or technician with some basic economic principles than the other way around. An engineer has a feeling for the production process, can relate to it. Many corporate controllers can't do that.

While the old system was certainly better than no system at all, top management decided that they needed something better. They began their search and came across the Plaut/Kilger system and SAP software.

The Plaut/Kilger and SAP systems

Plaut—a German-based consulting firm—was a leader in developing and installing sophisticated cost systems for major industrial clients in West Germany and throughout Europe. SAP was founded in 1972 by four former IBM computer scientists to design efficient software for data processing in business and manufacturing applications. One SAP founder, Dr. Plattner, had met Plaut in 1984, and the two companies decided to combine Plaut's sophisticated cost control systems with SAP's leading-edge main frame software. Plaut would do the consulting work for the client's specific problems, and SAP would install and integrate its system with the client's operations. Mr. Häussler found that the SAP/Plaut system could satisfy the criteria top management had specified for a good system.

Implementation

The new cost management system used flexible, standard costing for cost budgeting, accounting, and control. The following functions were included:

1. Cost center accounting for manufacturing overhead cost control;
2. Production costing for product cost control;
3. Planning/simulation for strategic costing on a what-if basis.

Overhead cost control was the initial area of implementation. New cost centers had to be defined and appropriate activity bases selected for manufacturing, service, and support centers. Only similar machines with an identical relationship between incurred costs and the chosen activity base were grouped into the same cost center. Thus, highly automated machines, such as in a computer-integrated manufacturing (CIM) center, were placed in a separate cost center from operator-controlled machines. The number of cost centers had to increase from 250 to 600.

Activity bases for each cost center were chosen from operating parameters such as machine hours, labor hours, setup hours, kilograms of material, number of pieces, kilowatt-hours, and square meters of material. Occasionally, multiple activity bases, such as machining hours and setup hours, were used in the same cost center to distribute costs.

Once new cost centers and activity bases were defined, flexible budgets were prepared for each cost center. Budgeted costs were estimated, using analytic—not historical cost—methods for each manufacturing, service, and support cost center. Each cost center had about 70 different input resources identified, leading to more than 40,000 entries.

Primary costs, such as direct and indirect labor, indirect materials, energy consumption, machine costs, and outside services, were traced directly to each individual cost center. Secondary costs were allocated from service and support cost centers based on the quantities of secondary department resources used by the manufacturing (primary) cost centers. The budgeted secondary cost rates were determined by planned, not actual, volumes of consumption of secondary support resources. The budgeted cost rates were applied ex post, based on the actual volume of demands made by production cost centers, as a function of their operating activities, on the support and service cost centers. The details of this calculation are illustrated in the Appendix to this case. For the secondary cost centers where the output could not be measured easily by quantities, percentage allocations were used.

Each primary and secondary budgeted cost was split into variable (proportional) and fixed components, based on the relation between the cost element and the chosen activity base for the cost center. The final fixed and variable cost rates were used both for product costing and to authorize overhead costs at the cost center level.

Overhead cost control was accomplished with the cost center *budget performance report*. Actual costs incurred at the cost center, including both primary and secondary costs, were compared with the authorized cost for the cost center, based on the actual activity base volume at the cost center. A variety of variances—usage, price, rate, and volume—were computed and displayed.

Standard product costs could now be computed. The bill of materials and routing sheets supplied information on standard material quantities and processing times. The cost standards for material prices and manufacturing cost rates at each cost center could then be applied to obtain standard product costs for all product codes—parts, subassembly groups, and finished products—based on standard performance and standard rates. These frozen standards were used for profit planning and for inventory valuation. Updated for changes in the bills of materials, input prices, or changes in processing routes and times, they could be used for current manufacturing cost control; that is, costs would be authorized based on production work orders.

Product cost control was evaluated with the *production work order performance report*. Actual costs incurred—including direct materials use and manufacturing resource consumption—were compared with the authorized cost, which equaled the current standard product cost per unit multiplied by the actual quantity produced. Price (materials, cost rate) and performance (materials usage, manufacturing efficiency, and alternative routing) variances were separately identified. Absorption of product cost into inventory was accomplished using current standard product cost rates so that all production cost variances were expensed as period costs. In addition, management accounting cost procedures—such as straight-line depreciation based on replacement costs—which were not allowable for financial (external) accounting purposes were offset in a reconciliation routine when preparing the semiannual financial reports.

The new cost system maintained highly detailed records to measure accurately the actual activity volume at each manufacturing operation and at each of the 600 cost centers. Performance reports were produced monthly to summarize actual versus authorized performance, but the information behind these reports was continuously available, on-line, for immediate feedback. The detailed and accurate record keeping enabled manufacturing variances to be explained easily. For example, an unfavorable cost center variance could be traced either to events at the center itself or back to a secondary service/support center that had been reallocated to it.

Planning and simulation analysis could be performed easily because all costs, at both primary and secondary centers, could be flexed with respect to fluctuations in product volume and mix assumptions. What-if simulations could be based on changes in activity base or production quantity volumes and with respect to changes in labor rates, material prices, energy costs, tariffs, etc. Structural changes affecting the split of costs into fixed and variable components, or on resource and activity base consumption, would be entered manually before performing the simulation study.

Payoffs to Metabo

Häussler felt that Metabo's new cost system provided several major benefits to the company. The visibility and traceability of costs down to the lowest level in the organization enabled problems to be uncovered that had been hidden or averaged across units by the prior system. The information on marginal costs made it possible to compute accurate flexible budgets. The more accurate and detailed system gave all employees much greater confidence in the validity and reliability of the cost data. Costs could now be predicted as a function of production volume thereby eliminating a major source of uncertainty in the previous system. Problems could be traced to their source and remedied immediately. Operators had to accept responsibility for costs charged to their cost centers, whereas previously they had argued that excessive costs were introduced at previous stages, were the consequence of overcharges from the secondary cost centers, or arose from errors introduced by the average, total cost system.

The ability to reconcile data between the financial accounting and the cost accounting systems was another major advantage. The two systems were now compatible, which made tax planning and audits much easier. Auditors who questioned the minutest detail could access and investigate the underlying transactions record. Thus, Metabo now enjoyed the advantages of an effective cost control system driven by the underlying production process, while still being able to produce product cost information acceptable for the financial accounting statements.

The flexibility and power of the SAP software system made complex simulations and scenario planning possible. But the system had yet to be used to make product-related decisions. Pricing, product introduction, and product elimination decisions had been unaffected by the information from the new system.

Häussler emphasized the following:

Pricing is determined in the marketplace. We cannot use product cost information to determine our pricing. Also, we must offer a full product line. Previously, our brand position was so strong that customers would purchase only Metabo products. Now, however, if we do not offer a particular product model, the consumer may purchase a competitor's product. Compromising our full product line is not a good option.

Häussler summarized his feelings about the new system as follows:

Knowing, finally, what is going on and not tapping in the dark with a pile of information that could be more damaging than beneficial has given me an incredibly good feeling.

EXHIBIT 1
METABO GMBH & CO. KG
Summary of Operations

CATEGORY	QUANTITY
Material units	45,000
Routing sheets	15,000
Parts lists	15,000
Internal work orders	2,500
Production orders	3,000
Suppliers	3,000
Orders per month	2,300
Customers	21,000
Bills per month	17,000
Average inventory moves per month	160,000
Labor inputs per month	60,000

Appendix

Budgeting and Charging for Secondary Center Costs   Consider the secondary (support) center 55, Inspection of Production Batches. This center inspects the output from injection molding machines in three different primary (operating) cost centers.

Step 1: Develop the annual budgeted costs for center 55.

COST ELEMENT	BUDGETED COSTS		
	FIXED	VARIABLE	TOTAL
Personnel	50,000	250,000	300,000
Supplies	300	1,200	1,500
Tools		4,000	4,000
Maintenance	1,000	3,500	4,500
Capitalized services	20,000		20,000
Occupancy	24,000		24,000
Energy		3,500	3,500
Total costs	95,300	262,200	357,500

Step 2: Distribute planned costs from center 55 to primary cost centers.

The costs planned in cost center 55 are distributed to the three molding cost centers based on expected annual operating levels of the three centers.

OPERATING COST CENTER	ANNUAL OPERATING HOURS	PERCENTAGE
22	4,350	38.3%
25	1,870	16.5
27	5,130	45.2
	11,350	100.0%

Determine the budgeted variable cost rate for center 55.

$$\frac{\text{variable}}{\text{cost rate}} = \frac{\text{budgeted variable costs (center 55)}}{\text{planned operating hours (centers 22, 25, 27)}}$$

$$= \frac{262,200}{11,350} = 23.10 \text{ per hour worked}$$

Develop the monthly budget for the three operating cost centers.

	PLANNED COSTS		
	FIXED	VARIABLE	TOTAL
22	36,500	100,500	137,000
25	15,700	43,200	58,900
27	43,100	118,500	161,600
Total planned costs	95,300	262,200	357,500

Step 3: Determine monthly actual costs in support center 55 and activity levels in the three operating cost centers.

COST ELEMENT	ACTUAL COSTS
Personnel	27,000
Supplies	200
Tools	300
Maintenance	400
Capitalized services	1,667
Occupancy	2,000
Energy	297
Total actual costs	31,864

OPERATING COST CENTER	ACTUAL HOURS WORKED
22	415
25	90
27	460
Total hours worked	965

Step 4: Analyze actual costs in support center 55.

Budgeted fixed costs equal annual budgeted costs divided by 12. Authorized variable costs equal budgeted variable cost per hour worked multiplied by the actual hours worked in the three operating cost centers in the month.

COST ELEMENT	ALLOWED COSTS		ACTUAL COSTS	VARIANCE
	FIXED	VARIABLE		
Personnel	4,167	21,258	27,000	1,575
Supplies	25	102	200	73
Tools		340	300	(40)
Maintenance	83	298	400	19
Capitalized services	1,667		1,667	—
Occupancy	2,000		2,000	—
Energy		297	297	—
Total allowed costs	7,942	22,295	31,864	1,627

Note that the total allowed variable cost for center 55 can be computed as follows:

$$\frac{\text{allowed monthly}}{\text{variable}} = \frac{\text{actual monthly hours}}{\text{worked} \times 23.10}$$

$$= 965 \times 23.10$$

$$= 22,295$$

Under this system, all spending (or usage) variances that arise in the support center (55) remain in that center as the responsibility of the support center manager. Only budgeted fixed and authorized variable costs for the actual hours worked would be charged to the three operating cost centers. In a second step, the variances of the support center are charged to operating cost centers to get actual costs to these cost centers. But these charged variances are displayed separately in the cost center operating report.

Step 5: Distribute monthly Inspection Department costs to the three molding cost centers.

Fixed costs are distributed to the three cost centers based on planned annual usage (percentages computed in step 2). Monthly variable costs are distributed based on the annual planned variable rate (23.10 per hour) multiplied by the actual hours worked in each center.

COST CENTER	TARGETED COSTS		
	FIXED	VARIABLE	TOTAL
22	3,042	9,589	12,631
25	1,308	2,081	3,389
27	3,592	10,625	14,217
	7,942	22,295	30,237

PEORIA ENGINE PLANT (A): ABRIDGED

Labor and Overhead represent 20% of our costs, but we spend 90% of our perspiration monitoring and attempting to control them. Perhaps we have too much emphasis on what we traditionally have believed are our most controllable costs.

Lee Thomas, Supervisor of Operations Analysis
Peoria Engine Plant, Worldwide Motors

The Peoria Engine Plant

The Peoria Engine Plant (PEP) was one of six engine suppliers in the North American division of Worldwide Motors. PEP was an old plant on a three-square-mile area of land shared with several other Worldwide Motors plants. The main production facility of PEP was in a building more than one mile long and one-half mile wide.

During the first half of 1992, PEP produced about 2,500 engines per day, an annual rate in excess of 600,000 engines (423 engines per hourly employee per year). Annual sales were approximately $1.33 billion per year. Cost of goods sold were about $1.2 billion per year, of which about $960 million was direct material, $60 million direct labor, and $180 million manufacturing overhead. Most materials were purchased from other divisions of Worldwide Motors, and virtually all sales were made to Worldwide assembly divisions.

PEP produced two basic engines:

1. a 5.9 liter engine used in trucks, and
2. a 3.6 liter model used in a popular car model.

Sales for the car and truck models using the PEP engines were currently strong, and the plant was working

overtime to keep up with demand. Under terms of the union agreement, hourly employees were guaranteed pay for 80% of a 40-hour work week. Supervisors could send workers home if they were not needed during the shift and could call in workers early, or have them work later, if they were needed to meet extra production demands. Bob Jones, PEP controller, remarked:

> Direct labor is treated as 100% variable by our system, but this is probably not completely accurate. You can't get below one person to monitor machines. Direct labor is really a step function since volume may have to drop by 20% before we can start to see some real labor savings.

Plant Organization

The line organization of Peoria Engine Plant consisted of a plant manager, an assistant plant manager, superintendents for each of the three production areas, and managers of five staff departments (see Exhibit 1 for an organization chart). Nine production departments were defined within the three production areas. Department superintendents were responsible for the direct and indirect labor, direct materials, tools and supplies, and maintenance materials used within their departments. Departments were further subdivided into manufacturing sectors.

Information and Cost Systems

PEP's finance group maintained a plant ledger containing a companywide chart of accounts. Actual direct labor and indirect labor hours were recorded each day for payroll purposes. These were multiplied by actual wage rates and debited to departmental labor cost accounts. Supplies, tools, and maintenance materials were charged to the requesting department as they were withdrawn from the appropriate inventories. Scrap was

Professors Robert S. Kaplan and Amy Patricia Hutton prepared this case. Copyright © 1997 by the President and Fellows of Harvard College. Harvard Business School case 197-099.

recorded on the basis of "scrap tickets" that were prepared each time a part was scrapped.

During the second half of each year, PEP's finance group developed an expense budget for the following year for every account in the plant ledger. The budget base for individual accounts was the prior year's budget. This budget base was adjusted for expected changes in volume, mix, and product design for the upcoming year. The adjusted expense budget for each account was then decreased to reflect a targeted annual improvement factor. The annual improvement factor represented the implementation of one of Worldwide Motor's basic strategies: to maintain a competitive cost advantage.

Daily Reporting

Shop floor supervisors, at the end of each shift, entered the quantity of every part produced. The finance staff combined this information with direct labor and indirect labor record and prepared a daily performance report on direct labor usage (see Exhibit 2). In this report, Actual Hours represented the direct labor hours worked and recorded the previous day (this quantity was also sent to the payroll system). The Budgeted Work Standard (BWS) labor hours was the quantity of direct labor hours authorized for the actual parts produced that day. The system calculated the daily BWS labor hours for an area by:

1. multiplying the quantity produced of each part by the part's standard direct labor hours; and
2. summing the quantity calculated in step (1) across all the parts produced in the area that day.

The variances (total and percentage) between actual and BWS hours were calculated and reported in the daily performance report (Exhibit 2). The last column in the report displayed the week-to-date (W-T-D) percentage labor usage variance (the sum of the daily variances).

A similar report (see Exhibit 3) was prepared daily for the indirect labor worked at the plant. Indirect labor included people who performed maintenance, cleaning, materials handling, and inspection. The report showed the actual hours worked by indirect labor in each department and compared this quantity to the daily authorized indirect labor hours (labeled as BWS Hours in Exhibit 3). The authorized indirect labor hours were calculated as a percentage of the department's BWS direct labor hours. The authorized indirect labor hours percentage differed for each department.

The daily direct and indirect labor reports were available on the computer at the beginning of each day, with hard copies also printed daily. Supervisors, department superintendents, and managers could access their performance reports for the previous day from terminals on the plant floor.

Hal Green, superintendent for the largest production department at PEP, described the various factors that influenced daily labor variances:

> Sometimes, we have shortages of parts to work on because previous departments have produced less than scheduled. If I learn of these shortages early enough, I can send people home midway through a shift, but then I have to bring the next day's shift in early to make up for the shortfall from the previous day.
>
> Some days, we lose time because of machine breakdowns and repairs, or because not all the output we produced met quality standards. Other days, more people show up to work than expected. I can loan some people to other departments, but occasionally I send excess people home. Days when fewer people show up than I need to run the machines, I have to take salaried people and put them on the line.

Green did not feel that the daily direct labor performance report gave him much useful information:

> I can't wait until the next day to find out what my supervisors are doing with their labor force. I get a report hourly on the production output and labor hours worked from each section in my area [Exhibits 4 and 5 are copies of Green's handwritten reports on hourly production and labor hours worked]. I hold my general supervisors responsible for the actual and overtime hours worked in their departments, as shown in the Daily Report on Time [Exhibit 5].

Green expressed similar doubts about the daily indirect labor report:

> I probably "manage" the report more than I manage by the report. I generally maintain indirect labor below authorized levels by not replacing people who are on vacation or absent. I try to downsize the indirect labor force gradually, perhaps 1% every few weeks. My maintenance foreman, however, does watch the daily report closely to make sure that we are only charged for what we actually used.

Bill Walker, an area superintendent in the same production zone as Green, commented on his explanations of variances in the daily labor performance reports:

> There are lots of reasons why direct labor could be overspent. With just-in-time production, we're now more vulnerable to parts shortages. Other times, machines become idled because the powerplant shut down so that a new production line could be installed. But, problems are not al-

ways due to external events. Machines break down because of mistakes in loading materials. We can also produce more scrap than expected so that we have to work extra hours to reach our production targets.

Even in the best of circumstances, however, some of the labor standards have become difficult to meet because of all the performance tasks that have been rolled in. We'll only be making the engines we're currently producing for a few more years so management is reluctant to make significant capital investments for this line. Without new capital, additional productivity improvements may not be possible.

Walker reflected on the information he would like to have to manage his department:

The information I would look at daily are the number of pieces produced, machine up-time, quality, and a comparison of the actual direct labor hours with the Budgeted Work Standard hours authorized.

Bob Jones, PEP controller, questioned the value of the short-term reports:

If managers respond too closely to hourly or daily fluctuations, they may introduce more variation into the process and increase variances further. Also, the daily variance reports generate lots of excuses about the lack of funds for improvement programs. It may not be that useful to show costs to shop-floor people. I agree with Bill that the key drivers of plant performance are quality and machine up-time.

Weekly Reporting

Each Friday, senior plant management met with the superintendents to review the cost performance of the past week. Bob Jones explained that the agenda for the 90-minute meeting was set by the finance staff. Key issues were identified, and responsibility for each issue was assigned to individuals.

Lee Thomas and his Operations Analysis staff prepared and distributed weekly cost performance reports in advance of the meetings. Exhibit 6 shows a weekly performance report for the entire plant. Comparable reports were prepared for each production department. Graphs were included to highlight trends in Total Manufacturing Expense.[1] The variances in the weekly reports represented the difference between actual and authorized dollars for each account. Authorized direct labor dollars were calculated by multiplying the weekly

BWS labor hours by a moving average wage rate.[2] The authorized dollars for each variable overhead account were calculated by multiplying the BWS labor hours by an authorization rate for that account.

Lee Thomas described how he used the reports at the weekly meetings:

Susan Johnson [Plant Manager] wants people talking about future plans for problem solving, not explaining their past performance. So, at the weekly meeting, I might point to the negative 485 variance for indirect labor [see MTD column in Exhibit 6] and ask the superintendents how are we going to get under budget for the rest of June, July, and August? Do we need to review authorized levels of indirect people? Should we attempt to reduce weekend overtime or cut back on overtime during the week?

Bill Walker, Department 4's superintendent, cited several examples of explainable variances that might show up on his department's cost performance report:

Sometimes I get hit with things beyond my control, like the time a truck driver fell asleep at a truck stop with a load of parts. Another time a husband and wife driving team had an argument and abandoned a truck full of parts. Both times, with no parts to work on, I had to send the assembly line home.

Walker admitted that the weekly cost reports did direct his attention to potential problems but added that they also caused him to juggle resources. He explained that if a machine needed to be refurbished, he would buy parts over four weeks to smooth the purchases so he would not be in the red in any given week. Walker felt that some superintendents might allow their machines to run at less than "high performance" rather than purchase all the needed parts at once and have a cost overrun in their weekly performance report.

Hal Green, Department 7's superintendent, commented on his use of the weekly cost reports:

I don't use the weekly cost charts. I look at them to become familiar with them and to think about how I can explain them to upper management. Basically these reports are for upper management, not for me.

Susan Johnson expressed her preference for weekly reports over daily reports:

I don't think it's useful for me to react to short-term blips. But, if the blips form a trend, I notice. With trends I can

---

[1] Total Manufacturing Expense is reported in the last row of the first panel of numbers in Exhibit 6, labeled TOT MFG EXP.

[2] The moving average wage rate was calculated by dividing the sum of the three prior weeks' actual direct labor dollars by actual direct labor hours.

identify a big improvement or shortfall and ask questions about why it happened. Not all the inquiries are negative. If I see an improving trend, I want to know what the superintendent is doing and whether we can try his approach elsewhere.

Weekly direct labor usage graphs for each area were also displayed and discussed. Actual and BWS hours were graphed along with the planned hours. Planned hours were based on forecasted volume projections made during the budget process. Management recognized that the direct labor usage plots could look very different depending on whether the plant was operating with excess capacity or using overtime.

The weekly meeting also reviewed weekly scrap reports for each area. The scrap rate was calculated as the dollars of scrap per engine produced. Green commented that he wanted his departmental supervisors to pay attention to the weekly fluctuations in scrap:

> I send information on scrap down to each supervisor. Formerly, I had only a single individual acting as the champion of scrap. This person focused on the top five scrap issues. Now, all nine supervisors in my department must work on the top three scrap items in their respective departments. We have reduced scrap by 10% to 20% a year for the last four years.
>
> Today, our main source of scrap is caused by outside suppliers. I want supervisors to identify which particular suppliers are causing problems, and I want supervisors to talk directly to them. Problems with internal suppliers I try to handle privately. I am willing to take a beating in one weekly meeting from an internal supply problem, but then the supplier had better clean up his act.

To realize the 7% improvement target over last year's budget, each department superintendent developed Cost-Reduction Plans (CRPs). The CRPs identified specific plans of action to achieve cost savings. When superintendents failed to meet the planned date of implementation, the weekly meeting discussed the reasons for the delay.

Monthly Reporting

Each month, all North American plants of Worldwide Motors prepared a summary report, Direct Labor and Manufacturing Overhead Budget Performance Report. The report was reviewed by central finance staff at corporate headquarters. The report had extensive variance analysis to compare actual costs in 26 labor and overhead categories to both the calendarized budget (the annual budget, divided into 12 monthly components) and

the authorized budget (the costs authorized based on actual volume and mix of production). The report also summarized information on actual production and project spending. Everyone at the plant believed that this report was mainly for corporate's benefit. Senior plant management received a weekly version and hence already knew about the information that would appear in the monthly labor and overhead report.

The finance staff also produced a monthly productivity report that showed the number of engines produced per person and the cost per engine.[3] The plant received a report from corporate that showed the cost-per-engine produced in each of Worldwide's ten North American engine plants. This report was used internally to compare PEP's performance with the production of similar engines in other facilities. No data were provided to benchmark comparable costs for domestic and international competitors.

Bill Walker commented that the monthly summaries gave him a better perspective on his cost and productivity performance than the weekly or daily reports:

> I look at costs first; budgets are secondary and sometimes arbitrary, deriving from conditions that occurred more than two years ago or from arbitrary assignment of performance tasks. Over the long run, I can make substitutions that increase costs in one category, leading to reported variances, but that lower overall costs. For example, I shifted to a coolant that was 3 times more expensive than what we had been using, but the new coolant lasted about 10 times as long. The labor savings from less frequent changes amounted to $36,000 over two years. So, I personally set priorities on reducing costs rather than meeting budgets. If I am effective in lowering costs, the actuals will eventually fall within the budget.

Hal Green also preferred the longer-term perspective:

> The information that's most useful to me is the historical trends of actuals versus actuals. I watch the monthly reports for the trends on engines per person, actual hours worked, and the productivity/efficiency numbers. The outcomes from my work as a superintendent can take one to two years to realize. I have to maneuver within the system to get people the equipment they need. I try to get one year ahead of the improvement targets, but I'm beginning to fall behind now because money for capital improvements is scarce with the line phasing out.

[3.] This number was obtained by dividing the number of completed engines of each type by the number of fulltime-equivalent direct and indirect labor workers (overtime hours were converted into the equivalent additional workers). Workers in the Powerhouse, Training, and Project Launch were excluded from the calculation.

Susan Johnson, plant manager, watched the report that compared PEP's engine costs with those of the other Worldwide Motors plants:

> I compare the components in the cost-per-engine set report. I look at supplies, tools, maintenance materials, and scrap. The departmental superintendents look at these as well and call their colleagues at other plants if they see large discrepancies.

Lee Thomas was sympathetic to the concerns voiced by the operating people but defended the budgeting system:

> We may spend too much time classifying costs and not enough on reducing them. We could put more emphasis on actual costs, especially by improving our presentations on

cost trends. But I still believe that budgets and reporting on budgets are necessary. The cost classifications give us insights about the underlying cost elements, where problems are, and where priorities for cost improvement should be placed.

Susan Johnson believed that senior managers of Worldwide Motors emphasized the labor and overhead budget mainly because they believed that these cost components were the most controllable:

> Materials are very critical in overall costs. But plant people find it tough to control these costs since purchasing people have almost complete responsibility for materials acquisition.

> Achieving 7% controllable cost improvements in a mature product line is not easy.

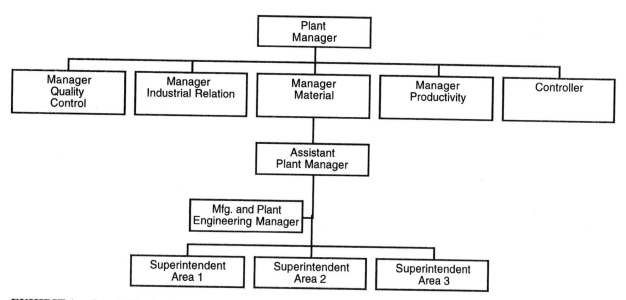

EXHIBIT 1   Peoria Engine Plant Organizational Chart

EXHIBIT 2 Peoria Engine Plant Daily Direct Labor Performance Report Area Summary—Wednesday July 29, 1992

	ACTUAL HRS.	BWS HRS.	BWS VARIANCE HRS.	BWS VARIANCE %	W-T-D %
Dept. 1	560	513	−47	−9.1	−17.8
Dept. 2	722	774	53	6.8	−6.6
Dept. 3	2,877	2,619	−258	−9.9	−6.8

continued

	ACTUAL HRS.	BWS HRS.	BWS VARIANCE HRS.	BWS VARIANCE %	W-T-D %
Area 1	4,158	3,906	− 252	− 6.5	− 8.2
Dept. 4	1,004	702	− 302	− 42.9	− 14.8
Dept. 5	744	641	− 104	− 16.2	− 26.0
Dept. 6	1,017	978	− 39	− 4.0	− 8.9
Dept. 7	3,692	3,849	158	4.1	− 5.2
Area 2	6,456	6,170	− 287	− 4.6	− 9.4
Dept. 8	95	107	12	11.3	− 2.0
Dept. 9	855	656	− 200	− 30.4	− 25.2
Area 3	950	762	− 188	− 24.6	− 21.6
Area 4 — Materials Control	63	74	11	14.3	13.3
Plant Total Daily	11,627	10,911	− 716	− 6.6	
Plant Total W-T-D	35,225	32,141	− 3,084	− 9.6	
Plant Total M-T-D	159,782	143,235	− 16,547	− 11.6	

Notes: BWS = Budgeted Work Standard labor hours
W-T-D = week to date
M-T-D = month to date

EXHIBIT 3 Peoria Engine Plant Daily Indirect Labor Performance Report Area Summary — Wednesday July 29, 1992

	ACTUAL HRS.	BWS HRS.	BWS VARIANCE HRS.	BWS VARIANCE %	W-T-D VARIANCE	W-T-D %
Dept. 1	353	233	− 120	− 51.6	− 316.5	− 46.9
Dept. 2	452	303	− 149	− 49.0	− 438	− 51.6
Dept. 3	770	612	− 158	− 25.7	− 288	− 15.7
Area 1	1,574	1,148	− 426	− 37.1	− 1,042.5	− 31.0
Dept. 4	414	389	− 26	− 6.6	268.5	18.4
Dept. 5	408	326	− 83	− 25.3	− 204	− 21.2
Dept. 6	504	347	− 158	− 45.5	− 424.5	− 41.2
Dept. 7	548	600	53	8.8	25.5	1.6
Area 2	1,874	1,661	− 213	− 12.8	− 334.5	− 6.6
Dept. 8	81	81	0	0.0	72	26.4
Dept. 9	578	239	− 339	− 142.1	− 1,087.5	− 150.8
Area 3	659	320	− 339	− 106.1	− 1,015.5	− 102.2
Area 4 — Materials Control	1,142	870	− 272	− 31.2	− 789	− 29.0
Area 5 — Quality	279	254	− 26	− 10.1	− 39	− 5.1
Area 6 — Plant Engineering	551	456	− 95	− 20.7	− 241.5	− 17.6
Area 7 — Cutter Grind	302	402	101	25.0	318	26.1
Area 8 — Central Maint.	1,700	1,205	− 495	− 41.1	− 2,001	− 55.5

continued

	ACTUAL HRS.	BWS HRS.	BWS VARIANCE HRS.	BWS VARIANCE %	W-T-D VARIANCE	W-T-D %
Plant—Project/Def. Maint.	210	210	0	0.0	0	0.0
Plant—Committee Reps	375	375	0	0.0	0	0.0
Plant—Fixed Fringe	3,675	3,675	0	0.0	0	0.0
Plant Total W-T-D	36,669	31,524	– 5,145	– 16.3		
Plant Total M-T-D	188,849	168,563	– 20,286	– 12.0		

Notes: *BWS = Budgeted Work Standard labor hours*
W-T-D = week to date
M-T-D = month to date

EXHIBIT 4 Peoria Engine Plant Hourly Production

	A	B	C	D	INTAKE CONVYR	E	DRESS UP	H/T SOLD	H/T REJ	A/T SOLD	A/T REJ	M/R REP	HEAD ASSY.	X	P&R ASSY	MICRO
1	200	263	145		171	165	199	162	10	334	0	26				
2	191	198	160		155	149	201	168	10	212	0	13				
2A	291	461	305	300	326	314	399	328	20	546	0	39				
3		125	133		128	134	214	178	8	112	0	3				
3A		586	438		454	449	513	506	28	658	0	42				
4	209	189	306		146	213	192	90	3	190	0	1				
4A	610	775	644	637	600	661	705	596	31	848	0	43				
5	206	205	746	200	135	175	201	178	2	177	0	3				
5A	816	990	840	837	755	836	906	774	33	1025	0	46				
6	206	207	198	200	204	203	194	182	2	175	0	11				
6A	1022	1197	1038	1037	959	1039	1100	956	35	1200	0	57				
7	120	123	100	98	77	89	106	181	8	97	0	5				
7A	1142	1310	1138	1135	1036	1128	1206	1137	43	1297	0	62				
8	220	198	174	195	162	191	178	91	3	186	1	4				
8A	1362	1508	1312	1310	1198	1319	1384	1228	46	1483	1	66				
9					75			153	0							
9A					1273			1381	46							
TOTAL	1362	1508	1312	1310	1273	1319	1384	1381	46	1483	1	66	1509	X	1510	X

FLOATS A&B		
	352	102
	272	189
	ø	ø
	ø	ø

TYPE OF FLOAT A&B		
REG	ø	ø
HO	ø	ø
TRK	272	189
MARINE	ø	ø

INTAKE FLOATS	
T/BIRD	
H.O.	
TRUCK	
AUST.	
ECONO.	

MAJOR REPAIRS AND TEARDOWNS			
MSC REJ	5	T/D'S	5
RETURNS	—	OTHER:	—

AHEAD HOT TES	AHEAD AIR TEST	AHEAD DROPS
125	65	140

HEAD FLOATS	
TRK:	1700
MUST:	100
SPEC:	200

HR	#1	#2	#3
1	197	230	
2	39	44	
3	72	90	
4	81	88	
5	84	109	
6	60	82	
7	67	85	
8	94	96	
9			
TOTAL	1490		

	VAR	REASON FOR VARIANCE
	-48	BAD BLOCKS NO MACHINED LOCATOR PAD FOR PALLET
2	-64	CARRYOVER
3	-0	NONE
4	-0	NONE
5	-38	SAME AS ABOVE
6	-10	NO HEADS FOR CHANGEOVER
7	-45	EI REP. BAY-BENT TRANSFER
8	-22	C10 (-10) / PALLET LOADER CONVEY OR SAMMED (-12)
9		

SLAT LINE

	VAR	REASON FOR VARIANCE
1	-25	STA. 17#1 BROKEN ANCHOR SLOT.
2	-34	WAITING ON MARINE BLOCKS...
3	-10	STA. 54- PLUGS JAM IN SLIDE
4	-16	CLEANING OUT REP. BAY FOR...
5	-19	STA 11- FALSE- REJ. STA-54
6	-19	STA 59 DOWEL PINS NOT FEEDING
7	0	NONE
8		EMPTIED WASHER
9		

PISTON HOOK-UP

HR	VAR	REASON FOR VARIANCE
1	263	—
2	198	—
3	125	—
4	189	—
5	205	—
6	207	—
7	123	—
8	198	—
9		

EXHIBIT 5   **Peoria Engine Plant Labor-Hours Worked**

D/L STD	ID/L STD	TTL AUTH	TOTAL ON DROT	INDR −	AWOL −	MED −	PER −	VAC −	DIS −	OTH −	O/S XTRA −	EARLY OUT	INSIDE BORR +	INSIDE LOAN −	OUTSIDE BORR +	OUTSIDE LOAN −	TOTAL DIR LAB =	D/L HRS AUTH	ACT
14	1a	15	16	1		1											14	112	127.3
19		19	23			1								1			21	152	177.5
16	1a	17	23	2			1				1					3	17	128	138.0
24	1a	25	32	1	1	2	1				3						27	232	193.7
29	1a	30	34	1			1	3									29	312	242.0
39*		39	43			2	6				1						35	104	220.3
13*	1b	14	16			2	1					1	1				13	104	114.0
26	1a	27	32	2		3	1			1			1				26	208	201.0
21	1a/1c	23	26	1		1	1	1								1	21	168	156.5
16		16	20	1			1							1			17	128	164.0
11		11	13	1	2									1			11	88	97.0
24		24	35		1	2	3							1			30	192	242.0
7	1a	8	✕														✕	56	✕
7	1a	8																56	
13e	1f	14	17	1	1			1									15	104	132.0
4/1g		5	5	1		1											3	40	32.0
277 / 7	11 / 1	228 / 8	335	12	5	15	16	5		1	5	1	4	6			278	2216 / 56	2304.8

hrs schd	hrs wrkd
8	8

ENGINE BLD 1319

ENGINE LST −227

HOURS AUTH 2235

HOURS USED 2305

VARIANCE 70

DROP COUNT #2 1490 #3 0

TOT 1490

Cleaner; (b) Coordinator; (c) Paint Mixer; (d) Scrap & Salvage; (e) Final Inspectors; (f) Floor Inspectors
Major Repair Co-ord. (*)E2 Incl. 6 For HO Std. TTL (37) /7 For Trks TTL (39)
E3 Incl. 1 for Trk. Stds TTL (13)

MANPOWER VARIANCE/OFF-STANDARD CONDITIONS

	TOTAL	QUALITY
BACKING UP STA 204	1	BLOCKLINE CHECKING MOTOR LOCATING LUG AT ST. 149 100%
CHECKING BLOCKS	1	
HD. GASKETS	2	① BLOCK W/NO WATER JACKET LIKE RIGHT BANK
ANDROIDS	1	
		DOCK BEING CHECKED 100% FOR FUEL RAIL BOLT – BLUE DOT OR WHITE DOT ON FRONT OF UPPER INTUBE IN BUYOFF

EXHIBIT 6   Peoria Engine Plant Weekly Performance Report

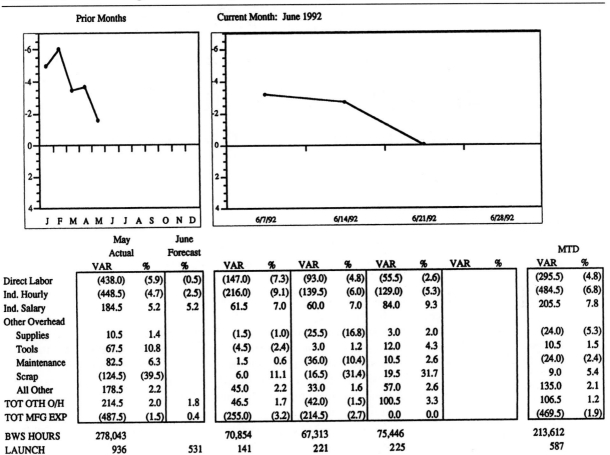

	May Actual		June Forecast										MTD	
	VAR	%	%	VAR	%	VAR	%	VAR	%	VAR	%	VAR	%
Direct Labor	(438.0)	(5.9)	(0.5)	(147.0)	(7.3)	(93.0)	(4.8)	(55.5)	(2.6)			(295.5)	(4.8)
Ind. Hourly	(448.5)	(4.7)	(2.5)	(216.0)	(9.1)	(139.5)	(6.0)	(129.0)	(5.3)			(484.5)	(6.8)
Ind. Salary	184.5	5.2	5.2	61.5	7.0	60.0	7.0	84.0	9.3			205.5	7.8
Other Overhead													
Supplies	10.5	1.4		(1.5)	(1.0)	(25.5)	(16.8)	3.0	2.0			(24.0)	(5.3)
Tools	67.5	10.8		(4.5)	(2.4)	3.0	1.2	12.0	4.3			10.5	1.5
Maintenance	82.5	6.3		1.5	0.6	(36.0)	(10.4)	10.5	2.6			(24.0)	(2.4)
Scrap	(124.5)	(39.5)		6.0	11.1	(16.5)	(31.4)	19.5	31.7			9.0	5.4
All Other	178.5	2.2		45.0	2.2	33.0	1.6	57.0	2.6			135.0	2.1
TOT OTH O/H	214.5	2.0	1.8	46.5	1.7	(42.0)	(1.5)	100.5	3.3			106.5	1.2
TOT MFG EXP	(487.5)	(1.5)	0.4	(255.0)	(3.2)	(214.5)	(2.7)	0.0	0.0			(469.5)	(1.9)
BWS HOURS	278,043			70,854		67,313		75,446				213,612	
LAUNCH	936		531	141		221		225				587	

3

Stage III Systems for Learning and Improvement

Cost systems for operational learning and improvement must provide timely feedback about the consequences from the most recent actions employees have taken with processes under their control. The feedback information should incorporate both nonfinancial and financial information so that employees can simultaneously work to improve process quality, cycle time, and cost. The information should encourage front-line employees, working in teams, to take informed actions based on their task-specific knowledge to modify and improve processes. The information should also be directed to achieving outstanding, even breakthrough, performance improvements in critical internal processes.

Several advocates of the new total quality management (TQM) approach claim that financial control systems should be discarded entirely—that financial information is at best irrelevant and at worst dysfunctional to the continuous improvement philosophy underlying TQM. Such a claim presents a stark challenge to management accountants. Has the new basis of competition in the information era outpaced the financial measurement and control systems that have proven so vital to success in industrial-age competition? Initially, the answer to this question was not clear. What was clear was that any financial information system that could meet the information needs of employees attempting to improve customer-focused, quick response, high-quality processes would be very different from the periodic variances calculated by traditional standard costing systems. Stage III performance measurement systems should enable organizations to provide feedback to employees about the actual cost, efficiency, quality, and timeliness of the business processes they perform.

ROLE FOR NONFINANCIAL MEASURES[1]

Cost reduction is an important managerial objective. But cost improvement alone may not be sufficient. Customers want not only lower prices and costs; they also greatly value quality, responsiveness, and timeliness. Consequently, employees must receive information about both the

---

[1] A more comprehensive treatment of nonfinancial measures, particularly those derived from strategic, not just operational, improvement considerations, can be found in R. S. Kaplan and D. P. Norton, *The Balanced Scorecard: Translating Strategy Into Action* (Boston: Harvard Business School Press, 1996), especially chapters 4–6.

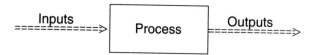

EXHIBIT 3-1

cost consequences of their activities and the quality and cycle time of processes under their control. Stage III systems for learning and improvement must supplement their financial feedback with information on critical non-financial measures, especially measures of process quality and time.

One can think of a process as converting a set of inputs to a set of outputs (Exhibit 3–1). Assuming that the output of the process meets the functionality requirements of customers, we can describe such a process with three parameters:

1. *Quality*:   *Defect rates*—for every 1,000,000 inputs, how many defective items are produced?

    Yields—what is the percentage of zero-defect finished items to total items started into production?

2. *Timeliness*:   *Cycle Time*—from the time an item starts into production, how long until it is completed?

    Lead Time—from the time an item has been ordered, how long until it starts production?

    On-Time Delivery—is the finished item delivered at the time promised?

3. *Cost*:   For each item produced, what are the costs of resources used (materials, labor, energy, machine time, indirect and support resources) for its production?

Stage III cost systems, reporting on a cycle corresponding to the underlying process rather than the financial reporting cycle, can provide timely and accurate answers to the third question, measuring the cost or resources used in operating processes. But they can certainly not provide information about the first two parameters: quality and timeliness. For this, Stage III systems must also include an appropriate set of nonfinancial indicators.

Process Quality Measurement

Organizations operating under the TQM philosophy have introduced a broad array of nonfinancial measures to monitor and improve the quality of their products and processes. These include:

- Process part-per-million (PPM) defect rates
- Yields[2] (ratio of good items produced to good items entering the process)
- Waste
- Scrap
- Rework
- Returns
- Percentage of processes under statistical process control

Motorola, a leading company in applying the TQM philosophy, adopted an aggressive approach to quality, setting a quality target of 6σ for its manufactured product, a level representing fewer

---

[2]The best yield measure is *first-pass yields*, the percentage of items completed that make it all the way through production, without any rework required. Some companies measure *total yield* (good items produced divided by items started into production) but count items that have been reworked into acceptable finished goods in the numerator of the yield ratio. This measurement indicates that customers may not be getting defective items, but does little to signal improvements in the underlying production process.

than 12 defects per 1 million parts. General Electric has now also embraced the 6σ philosophy for all of its operations.

Service organizations also need to identify the defects in their internal processes that could adversely affect costs, responsiveness, or customer satisfaction. Some companies have developed customized measures of quality shortfalls, for example:

- Long waiting times
- Inaccurate information
- Access denied or delayed
- Request or transaction not fulfilled
- Financial loss for customer
- Customer not treated as valued
- Ineffective communication

Front-line employees in any manufacturing or service organization must receive signals on process quality, not just on the cost of performing their task or process.

Western managers were slow to recognize the benefits from higher quality processes. Their financial model did not incorporate how improved quality could lead to higher profits. Many companies felt that defect rates in the parts per 100 were optimal. For example, Texas Instruments, before it bought into the TQM philosophy, emphasized financial control measures and expected a certain amount of defective product to be returned by the customer. But financial measures are lagging indicators. Employees, if they are to lower the cost of their processes, need leading indicators that they can control, such as defect rates and yields, not reports about the cost performance of last period's production.

Process Time Measurement

Managers in the 1980s learned that competition was taking place along a time dimension as well as a quality dimension. New time-based competition strategies were being deployed by superb Japanese manufacturers to compete both on rapid time-to-market for new products as well as short lead times and highly reliable delivery times for existing products.[3] For example, Olympus Optical reduced its product development cycle from 10 years (1970) to 18 months (1990), a reduction that enabled it to compete more aggressively on product functionality. Nissan Motor Company adopted a policy of delivering its cars "while the paint was still wet" a euphemism for extremely rapid order-manufacture-delivery response times. Nissan could now compete based on its short delivery time performance. Customers could order a car and have it manufactured and delivered to their residences in about the same time that it took to get a parking permit from the Tokyo City government. Many customers also value reliable lead times, as measured by on-time delivery. Thus, reducing cycle and throughput times of internal processes becomes a critical internal process objective.

Clearly, in the new competitive world, employees must receive feedback on the quality, timeliness, and responsiveness of processes under their control. Companies wanting to foster a spirit of continuous improvement in their employees often espouse a rhetoric of employee empowerment. Senior managers urge employees to take actions every day to improve quality, reduce cycle times, increase yields and output, and lower costs. But unless the employees are provided with timely and accurate feedback about the results from their continuous improvement experiments, employee empowerment is rhetoric, not reality.

---

[3]See T. M. Hout and J. L. Bower, "Fast-Cycle Capability for Competitive Power," *Harvard Business Review* (November–December 1988) and G. Stalk, Jr. And T. M. Hout, *Competing Against Time* (New York: Free Press, 1990).

FINANCIAL INFORMATION FOR CONTINUOUS IMPROVEMENT

A remaining question is whether employees receiving extensive nonfinancial information on quality, cycle time, and throughput also need to see financial information. Traditional cost feedback from standard costing systems emphasizes variances against standards. Such information promotes a controlling, not a learning, view. The variances are not easily understood by front-line employees, do not promote an integrated process view of the organization, and do not directly encourage continuous improvement activities.

Some companies have replaced variance reports from standard costing systems with kaizen costing or pseudo profit center systems to provide direct financial feedback to employees. These new systems are designed based on the actual production processes in the organization and have been explicitly customized to promote specific learning and improvement opportunities by front-line employee teams. They, like many contemporary feedback systems, use extensive nonfinancial information so that employees can improve process quality and cycle time. But their distinguishing characteristic is that financial information is also provided to empowered employees so that they can develop more efficient processes. Underlying all these systems is a common philosophy that the systems have been designed to provide *information* for local team improvement activities, not to *control* the employees and teams and monitor their adherence to preset standard operating practices.

KAIZEN COSTING[4]

Kaizen is the Japanese term for continuous improvement:

> gradual, unending improvement, doing 'little things' better; setting — and achieving — ever-higher standards.[5]

Most Western observers first became familiar with kaizen by studying the Japanese approach to improving quality and cycle time performance. The observers are somewhat less acquainted with how Japanese companies apply kaizen to reducing cost. We define *kaizen costing* as:[6]

> continuous improvement applied to cost reduction in the manufacturing stage of a product's life.

Kaizen costing is used to reduce the cost of producing existing products by finding ways to increase the efficiency of the production process used in their manufacture.[7] In many firms with very short-lived products, the life of production processes is longer than the life of products. Therefore, greater savings can be achieved by focusing on the production processes in the manufacturing phase of a product's life than on the product itself.

Work teams use continual information on actual costs to direct their attention to areas where improvements will have the largest impact on product and organizational profitability. The cost information also helps the teams assess the impact of their implemented improvements

---

[4]For a more detailed description of kaizen costing see R. Cooper and R. Slagmulder, *Confrontational Cost Management Volume 3*; *Kaizen Costing and Value Engineering* (Portland, OR: Productivity Press, 1998).

[5]M. Imai, *Kaizen: The Key to Japan's Competitive Success* (New York: McGraw-Hill, 1986).

[6]R. Cooper, "Kaizen Costing," chapter 11, pp. 239–254, in *When Lean Enterprises Collide: Competing Through Confrontation* (Boston: HBS Press, 1995).

[7]In practice, there are two types of kaizen costing. The first type focuses on reducing the cost of specific products. It is used when a product enters production above its target cost or when long-lived products become or are at risk of becoming unprofitable. The second type, general kaizen costing, focuses on production processes and sets out to find ways to reduce their costs and thus the cost of the products that require those processes. In this book, we describe only general kaizen costing.

since the reductions in resource requirements are denominated in a common unit (¥1,000 or $ saved). And knowing the cost of processes under their control, the work teams can generate investment proposals that balance the front-end costs of new equipment against the ongoing cost savings from improved processes when using the new equipment.

Kaizen costing systems have several important characteristics in common:

- The focus is to inform and motivate process cost reduction, not to obtain more accurate product costs.
- Cost reduction is a team, not an individual, responsibility.
- *Frequent*, even batch-by-batch, *actual* costs of production are calculated, shared, and analyzed by the front-line employees. In many instances the team itself collects and prepares the cost information, not the accounting staff.
- The cost information used by the teams is customized to their production environment, so that learning and improvement efforts are focused on the areas for highest cost reduction opportunities.
- Cost standards are continually adjusted to reflect both past reductions in actual costs and targeted improvements in future costs. This insures that proven innovations in process improvement will be sustained, and will set a new level for further improvements.
- Work teams are responsible for generating ideas to achieve the cost reduction targets; they have authority to make small-scale investments if these can be demonstrated to have cost-reduction paybacks.

The goal under kaizen costing is not stability of a production process to predetermined work standards. The goal is to constantly improve critical processes so that costs can be continually reduced even in product lines that are mature, highly price sensitive, and not amenable to product innovation.

PSEUDO PROFIT CENTERS

Some companies go beyond just providing financial feedback on traceable and controllable costs to their front-line employees. They motivate their employees by providing them with *profit* information about their operations. Profit is a more comprehensive financial signal than cost, and profit enhancement is proving to be a more powerful motivator for improvement than cost reduction. These systems provide real psychological benefits by focusing the teams on the positive action of increasing profits as opposed to the negative action of decreasing or avoiding costs.

An operating or financial manager who wishes to create a pseudo-profit center must supply a standard cost for each input to a production process and an approximate price for each output produced. Often, an output product can be purchased or sold in external markets, so prices in these markets provide a convenient reference point. In some pseudo-profit centers, managers even include the cost of capital by estimating the daily or weekly mortgage payment (based on the book value or an estimate of the replacement value of the assets employed, the division's cost of capital, and the expected useful life) required to pay back the company for use of the asset. Front-line employees may find depreciation an obscure concept, but most will be familiar with repaying loans for assets like cars, trucks, and homes.

In some pseudo-profit centers, managers also estimate a penalty for poor quality production. In this procedure, employees only earn the full revenue from production of output products if the output is within statistical control limits ($\pm 3\sigma$). Output outside the control limits, but still within rated specifications (still usable), can be priced at only 50% of the standard price (a 50% penalty). Output that is unusable will be hit with a 100% penalty so that no revenue credit is earned for output with critical parameters outside rated specifications. This procedure enables the pseudo-profit center to internalize the cost it might be causing either to downstream operations or in customer dissatisfaction by poor quality output. Rather than treating quality as something different from output, the financial penalty integrates quality considerations into the aggregate performance of the pseudo-profit center. This procedure allows seemingly intangible (to financial accountants) parameters, like quality and timeliness, to be incorporated into a profit figure. For example, if on-time delivery of an intermediate product from a pseudo-profit center is important, the "revenue" figure from the center can be penalized by a cost of late delivery. This would internalize to the pseudo-profit center the future revenue losses incurred by a downstream department because of late deliveries of finished products to customers.

Having pseudo-prices for the output from the department provides an alternative way to control for variations in the mix of outputs produced during a period. Historically and traditionally, variations in product mix are handled through a standard cost system where input allowances are determined for each product produced. Each period, an overall flexible budget is calculated based on the expected consumption of inputs for the product mix actually experienced. With pseudo-profit centers, as a more complex product mix is produced actual expenses may rise, but so would the revenue credit for the product mix produced. Thus, by pricing intermediate outputs, managers can encourage continuous reduction in the actual consumption of input resources to produce a given quantity and mix of output, without operating a standard costing system.

The output prices, in a pseudo-profit center system, give additional information to employees beyond the cost information available from a standard costing or kaizen costing system. Knowing the approximate prices of their outputs, employees can understand the value from lost output. Cost control or cost reduction treats the output as predetermined and asks employees to control or reduce resources required to produce that output. The profit figure, while still retaining the benefits from such cost reduction activities, also encourages employees to increase yields and throughput, and avoid unexpected downtime or other situations that limit the production of outputs.

Companies that use profit as a signal for continuous improvement do not necessarily organize their employee work teams into true profit centers. Employees typically are not given authority for pricing, product mix, or output. These decisions remain a higher management responsibility. The prices, in a pseudo-profit center, serve to signal the relative importance of different outputs, as well as the relative costs of the different inputs. The profit calculation provides a convenient summary measure of team profitability, and helps the team to see the alignment of its actions with overall firm performance. A summary income number is simple to understand and communicate. It provides a rapid guide to short-term actions to increase quality and throughput.

With both kaizen costing and pseudo-profit centers, the financial feedback enables employees to see the cost and revenue impact of their actions. They can set priorities for their continuous improvement efforts, evaluate trade-offs that may have to be made, and understand the opportunities for investments that can reduce future operating expenses, or improve quality and cycle time performance. Most importantly, the financial signals empower the employees to take local actions that maximize overall company performance. Companies, in Stage II, use standard costing systems to control employees to meet standards set high in the organizational hierarchy. In Stage III, managers provide relevant, customized cost, financial and nonfinancial information that empowers employees to continually improve their operating performance.

CASES

The cases in this chapter describe Stage III systems that are designed to enhance the firm's ability to learn and improve. Such systems augment the capabilities of Stage II financial reporting systems. The first case, *Romeo Engine Plant (A)*, illustrates the greatly expanded role for nonfinancial measurement to drive continuous improvement by front-line work teams. The *Analog Devices* case introduces the concept of the half-life approach, the metric for continuous improvement. It demonstrates the power of nonfinancial measures to motivate and guide process improvements in ways that financial measures cannot achieve.

The next two cases illustrate kaizen costing. Both firms are Japanese and have had their kaizen systems for many years. These systems are mature and have been incorporated into the culture of the firm. The cases vary according to the nature of the product and production processes utilized at the firms. The *Citizen Watch* case explores kaizen costing in an environment of discrete parts production of products that have long lives. The *Sumitomo Electric Industries* case describes the process when the products are long-lived but the production processes are continuous.

The last three cases illustrate pseudo-profit centers. These firms are both American and Japanese. The pseudo-profit center systems in the Japanese firms are used to augment their kaizen costing programs. The first two of the pseudo-profit centers cases, *Texas Eastman* and *Higashimaru Shoyu (A)* demonstrate how two managers separated by thousands of miles, different cultures, and different products, arrived at virtually the same solution for the same problem. The final case, *Olympus (B)*, illustrates the application of the technique in discrete, as opposed to continuous, production settings. The case also demonstrates how the approach can be applied to nonmanufacturing settings.

ROMEO ENGINE PLANT (ABRIDGED)

The Purpose of the Romeo Engine Plant is to produce the highest quality production engines in the world that meet all of our customers' requirements at a cost lower than the competition, and to develop teams of employees who are the best engine builders in the world.

Mission and Operating Philosophy, Manufacturing Handbook
Romeo Engine Plant, August 1989

The Romeo Engine Plant (REP), located in a rural area about 50 miles north of Detroit, was one of six North American engine suppliers of Ford Motor Company. From the early 1960s to mid 1980s the Romeo production facility had been used by Ford Motor Company to produce tractors. During this period, the Romeo Tractor Factory employed 2,000 unionized workers to produce about 10,000 tractors per year. In early 1984, corporate headquarters decided to phase out tractor production because of declining demand and increased foreign competition. In June 1987, the doors of the tractor factory were closed and locked for the last time. The 2,000 laid-off employees of the Romeo Tractor Factory had little hope of ever returning to their jobs.

In early 1986, Ford Motor Company began searching for a site to locate a new engine plant. Several management teams submitted proposals for the new engine production facility. George Pfeil, plant manager of the Dearborn Engine Plant, submitted a proposal to re-open the Romeo site for this purpose. After an extensive evaluation process, Romeo was selected as the new site, with George Pfeil appointed to become the plant manager. In 1993, the line organization (see Exhibit 1) of REP consisted of the plant manager (George Pfeil); two area managers, Lonnie Prater for machining and Bill Yowan for assembly, who reported directly to Pfeil; and 26 teams that reported to either Prater or Yowan.

The main production facility of REP was in a building covering more than 1.1 million square feet. During 1992, REP produced 400,000 engines in two engine models: a 4.6 liter, 2 valve engine used in the Lincoln Town Car, Ford Crown Victoria, and Mercury Grand Marquis, and a 4.6 liter, 4 valve engine used in Ford

Motor Company's Lincoln Mark VIII luxury car. Sales of these automobiles were strong and Ford Motor Company was continually introducing new car models that would use the Romeo engines. By 1996 REP expected to produce more than 800,000 engines per year.

Cost of goods sold in 1992 was about 75% direct material, 23% manufacturing overhead, and 2% direct labor.

The Romeo Quality Process

The Romeo Quality Process (RQP) was established to ensure that customer expectations about product performance were understood, deployed and controlled in the manufacturing and assembly processes. The RQP was a disciplined approach to total process design and planning that would minimize in-process variation and virtually guarantee that customers would get Zero Defect Parts with minimum variation. The primary elements of the RQP included:

- Forming teams that were responsible for product and manufacturing engineering, quality, production, systems, and supplier relationships (for materials, machine tools, and gauging equipment).
- Establishing target levels for product/process characteristics reflecting customer expectations and the required process capability levels.
- Defining the process to meet or exceed the process capability requirements.
- Selecting process control methods consistent with the nature of the process and sources of variation identified by the RQP planning process.
- Implementing the control plan on the production floor.

To emphasize the importance of a Zero Defects Philosophy, George Pfeil had eliminated incoming inspections and rework at the plant. If a supplier provided a defective part that was subsequently detected, the supplier was billed for the full loss caused by the defective part. Three years ago, a supplier had to pay for a $6,600 engine repair that was caused by a broken valve spring (an item that cost about $.05). The no rework policy required that a defective part had to be scrapped as soon as the problem was detected, with the scrap costs assigned to the work team responsible for the defective part.

Romeo had extended this no rework philosophy outside the factory as well. Under its *Engine Exchange*

Professors Robert S. Kaplan and Amy Patricia Hutton prepared this case. Copyright © 1997 by the President and Fellows of Harvard College. Harvard Business School Case 197-100.

Program, dealers or assembly plants who detected a problem with an engine that could not be fixed with a minor repair, were requested to pull the problem engine out of the vehicle, replace it with a new engine, and ship the defective engine back to REP. Romeo's quality personnel tracked daily any quality problems reported by assembly plants and the more than 5,000 dealers worldwide. Since production began back in 1990, only about 1,500 engines (out of 1 million produced) had been returned to Romeo and only in about 10% of these returned engines could Romeo's quality assurance personnel confirm the defect reported by the customer.

The RQP goal of satisfying customers' expectations required departments to respond to every quality problem reported by a customer, including internal customers. Quality problems were logged onto a complaint form and Action Plans had to be prepared in response to the complaints. For example, since machining's customers were engine assembly operations, an engine assembly team could reject an engine coming from machining and issue a complaint form. The machining department then had to prepare an Action Plan within 24 hours in response. The Action Plan had to identify the source of the problem, how machining planned to solve it, and how machining planned to prevent it from recurring. Quality problems originating from outside the plant or quality problems of a critical nature required immediate, not 24 hour, responses. Weekly quality meetings chaired by quality personnel reviewed complaint forms and corresponding Action Plans filed over the past week. Action Plans that had not been fully implemented were highlighted for special attention.

But the RQP process began long before production began. Production team members worked closely with product and manufacturing engineers on the design of parts and production processes. The plant-floor employees knew, from first-hand experience, what could and would go wrong with particular designs or processes. The goal was to influence the design of the engine parts and associated production processes to yield high quality, "producible" engines. Chris Hineman, Plant Controller, explained how these relationships had begun to payoff:

> The close working relationships between our line people and our engineers is one reason we have had the most successful launches in Powertrain's history.

New Vehicle Quality Surveys were used to benchmark Romeo's engines against other Powertrain engines and against the engines used in competitor's luxury cars. Romeo's two engine launches (in 1991 and in 1993) had the best quality rating among all Powertrain engines. The quality ratings in Romeo's 4.6 liter engines were approaching worldwide best-in-class levels.

None of the excellent results in the quality of internal processes and finished engines could have been achieved without a substantial investment in education and training of all employees. The newly-rehired REP employees had created a Life Education Center by renovating a deserted building located behind the main production facility. The Life Education Center operated from 2:00–4:00 P.M. every weekday, offering courses ranging from high school equivalency to graduate level technical and management skills. The operating committee taught four courses that were required for all employees: Mission/Team Concept, Quality 101, Team Problem Solving, and Productivity 101. Each employee had to complete a minimum of 300 hours of training.

Work Team Organization

Romeo assigned work teams to production areas that corresponded to a major engine component or assembly operation. Romeo's managers had established a work team organization because they believed that team work was essential to being able to produce, with consistently high quality, the complex 4.6 liter engines. The teams were designed to include people who needed to work together and who could learn from each other. Many of the processes at Romeo were fully automated so that fewer people were required to supervise machines than if an individual worker were assigned to each machine (the common practice in traditional machining operations). The team members were not to be machine operators; they were to use their specific expertise to continuously improve production and quality processes. Team members performed tool checks, quality checks, and problem solving. Chris Hineman summarized how the work team organization at Romeo was fundamentally different from the organization of other engine plants in the Powertrain division:

> When George [Pfeil] asked me to come to Romeo as controller, we decided to do things differently. From the beginning we told our people, "The machines build the parts. The machines are designed to run automatically. Your job is to think, to problem solve, to ensure quality, not to watch the parts go by."

Each of the 13 work teams operated as a separate business unit, with its own team manager, and its own support staff, including engineering, maintenance and administration. Work teams were given the authority, information, resources, and training needed to make decisions and implement them. They operated and maintained their own facilities which included work spaces, locker rooms and meeting rooms. Teams were responsible for safety, quality, engineering, productivity improvements, and maintenance of equipment. No housekeeping department existed at REP; each work team cleaned its own area.

Barriers to flexible work assignments had been eliminated. Romeo had only 11 labor and 2 skilled trades classifications, a sharp contrast with other Ford Motor Company Powertrain plants that had more than 200 labor classifications and at least 8 skilled trades classifications. The traditional barriers between laborers and management had also come down. All employees (including George Pfeil) wore the same Romeo Team Work Uniform, with a shirt patch embroidered with the individual's first name serving as an employee's only identification.

Management wanted to encourage initiative, creativity, and prudent risk taking in the work teams to support growth in capabilities and continuous improvement. George Pfeil believed that "failure based on prudent risk should not be punished, but should be treated as part of the learning experience." Rich Carter, hourly mechanical coordinator for the C line work team in engine assembly, described Romeo's learning and risk-taking environment:

> At Romeo, we do what the teams decide. George [Pfeil] wants team managers and coordinators to support the team's decision, even if we feel it's wrong, until they get it right. We can stop a decision if it is too costly to implement. But, if we stop a decision, then we have to give a reason and an alternative.

> Everybody cares about failing, but we do not make a big deal of it. We do not finger point if a wrong decision has been made. We are a team. If we fail, we fail together. If we succeed, we succeed together. We agree that a decision is our decision and we all live with the consequences.

Carter described the autonomy and responsibility vested in team members:

> I see all my people as managers who can influence their production environment. When we get a new part to produce or an existing part has changed, I guarantee that the new part does not go into production until my people sign

off on it. They have to commit to its production. They examine the process and must agree that it can be done. If they do not like the new part then they tell me. They give suggestions and alternatives to improve the part.

Work team members recognized and appreciated the differences in Romeo's work team environment relative to the other production environments where they had worked:

> In the old production environment, we were not always asked to contribute suggestions. The foreman told us what to do and sometimes it was done even if it was wrong. Here at Romeo, the team decides what to do. Now our voices are heard. All middle management has been cut out, foremen, superintendents, and general superintendents. Management relies on us, the team members, to make decisions. Salary people help us make these decisions; the production and manufacturing engineers work for us. They are always saying, "We work for you. What do you need." And, they listen to us.

Sam Nammo, machine operator on the connecting rod team, described his commitment to the team organization at Romeo:

> I came to Romeo in December of 1990 with the option of returning to my former plant whenever I wanted. I will never go back. I drive 60 miles each way to work at Romeo.

Chris Hineman provided his perspective on the Romeo work environment:

> In traditional factories, the financial system viewed people as variable costs. If you had a production problem you sent people home to reduce your variable costs. Here, we do not send people home. At Romeo, people are viewed as problem solvers, not variable costs.

Information Systems

A vast investment and deployment of information technology resources were essential for Romeo's work team and quality processes. REP had 5 Digital Equipment Corporation VAX computers to process information about machines, test parts, and disseminate information about processes and parts to more than 400 pagers and approximately 350 personal computers in the plant. The software for these computers had been developed mainly for Romeo applications.

The most important of the real time systems was the *Machine Monitoring System* (*MMS*). This system signaled when a defective piece had been made or when a machine had stopped. Machines were laid out along long rows. A neon marquee hung from the ceiling between each pair of machines. When machines were operating normally, a green light appeared on the marquee. Thus a single operator could look down a long row of unmanned machines and verify that all were functioning normally. If a machine stopped, either because materials had become jammed or because a defective part had been detected by the automatic gauging equipment, the signal light for that machine would change from green to red, and the marquee would display the status of the machine and a fault code indicating the reason for the shutdown. Simultaneously, this information was also sent to the VAX cluster to record the time of the stoppage, the machine ID number, and the fault code. The computer immediately sent an automatic page to the operator assigned to that machine cluster, signaling that a failure had occurred, the machine ID, and the fault code.

The Paging System   The paging system was used extensively for communicating inside the plant. Each day between 12,000 and 16,000 pages were placed, 60–70% were machine generated to page an operator when a machine had unexpectedly stopped working. In addition, if the computer sensed that significant repairs would be needed, it would also send a page to a skilled trades person. The team manager would be paged if the machine had previously been identified as a critical or bottleneck resource. If the machine was not restored to running condition within 30 minutes of the work stoppage, then the plant manager would be automatically paged.

In addition to these automatic pages sent after a machine failure, each team manager and area manager could program the system to automatically send a page every hour and report critical information. For example, an area manager concerned with output through a critical process could receive an hourly page that reported the production quantity through that process during the preceding hour. Also the paging system could be used to facilitate authorization of purchase or maintenance by team managers. Someone needing authorization could send the request to an area or team manager via the paging system and the manager could reply using one of the 350 terminals located throughout the plant.

Ren Falzon, an hourly maintenance coordinator on the engine assembly team, explained how the MMS and paging systems saved time and allowed him to focus on productivity issues:

> In a regular plant I would be running all over the floor just trying to gather the information that the MMS and paging systems provide. With this information already provided and with the improved communications, I have more time to devote to quality planning, productivity group meetings, and team meetings. Instead of running around the plant floor putting out fires, I now have time for preventive, long-term strategic planning to solve our maintenance problems.

Use of the Information Systems

Every employee had been trained on the MMS and had easy access to the system via one of the 350 computer terminals distributed about the plant. Employees could query MMS to obtain the time of a particular breakdown and the code for its cause. Employees obtained, from MMS, summaries of the number of occurrences and the time lost per occurrence by fault code. This information could be viewed in real time or accumulated for daily, weekly and monthly tracking.

Ken Bernek, a machine operator on the connecting rod team, explained the usefulness of the MMS system to him:

> When a machine breaks down, we do not have to stand around and guess at what had gone wrong. The fault codes tells us what is wrong. So, we can focus our attention on the problem and solve it quickly. In my old plant when a machine stopped running, there would be three managers standing around guessing at what the problem was. And none of them would know for sure what the problem was. Here, we work with the facts provided by MMS. This information is very accurate and reliable.

Rich Carter gave his perspective on the usefulness of MMS:

> MMS focuses our discussions. For example, when we started producing the four valve engines, we had a problem on the C line. Everyone in the assembly area was sure that the C3 operation was causing the problem, because this operation is very labor intensive. We looked at MMS and discovered that we were down twice as much on the C1 operation. Without MMS we just have opinions, with MMS we work from facts.

Team members concurred that the daily information from MMS was the most informative and actionable:

> The best information we get are the fault codes from MMS. MMS helps us to focus our efforts. Without it, we would not know where to start. For example, the bottle-

neck analysis determines which operation is the bottleneck. We then go to the Pareto fault charts to see what problems are creating downtime there and start a problem-solving team to fix them. The team takes some actions and we watch if the trend on that fault code starts to go down. Then we could put our priorities on another problem.

Bottleneck Operations   George Pfeil wanted the teams to focus their efforts on improving operations at bottleneck machines and processes. He believed, "Unless you are improving your bottleneck operations, you are not improving machine efficiency." Pfeil's philosophy had been implemented in the design of MMS by having the system prepare a report to help the work teams identify the operations that were currently the bottlenecks in their area. The teams also received a report from MMS that ranked the causes for shutdowns at the bottleneck. This Pareto analysis encouraged problem-solving teams to concentrate on the principal causes for shutdowns on critical resources.

Lonnie Prater, an Area Production Manager, concurred with this focus on bottleneck resources:

> The plant is manned thinly. We must focus our resources on the bottleneck operations in each area. Everyone knows which is the current bottleneck operation. If it goes down, everyone runs over to solve the problem.

The teams tracked trends in downtime caused by fault codes to verify that their approaches were indeed fixing the problem and reducing downtime on the bottleneck resource. Prater met daily with the problem-solving teams to learn about their progress in reducing and eliminating recurring faults with machines. The teams had been taught that if they were successful in improving bottleneck processes, then the bottleneck process should move to the next constraining process in the department. Prater recalled:

> We formed a small problem-solving team five months ago for one bottleneck operation that was producing only 105 pieces per hour on a machine that had an ideal rated capacity of 200 pieces per hour. The output soon improved to 160 pieces per hour. Frequently, however, the improvement in capability outstrips machine output because the bottleneck will have shifted.

Scrap   Anytime a defect was detected in a part, an employee filled out a red tag form to record the causal factor for the defect. The employee attached the form to the part and also entered the defect information into the nearest computer terminal. The computer removed the item from inventory and, from this information, produced daily, weekly, and monthly scrap reports for each team. Summary scrap reports could be prepared by fault code and by part. A weekly meeting discussed the trends and principal causes for scrap and defective material at the plant. As with monitoring throughput, the teams performed Pareto analysis on the defect causes and generally concentrated on attacking the top-3 causes. As needed, teams solicited information from suppliers and product engineering. At the weekly meetings, teams reviewed 8-D reports designed to guide their analysis of defect causes.[1]

If a consistent pattern of problems could be traced to supplier defects, the labor and overhead that had accumulated until the defect was detected was billed back to the supplier. A monthly quality meeting at the plant, at which both internal (Powertrain) and outside suppliers could be invited to participate, discussed major unsolved problems.

The Checkbook System   Each team received an authorization for how much they could spend on indirect materials such as supplies, tools, scrap, and maintenance material. The authorization was calculated based on the number of parts produced each day. Spending on these items had been placed under the direct control of the team. Each day the team could see the authorization they had generated, based on that day's production, as well as the requisitions they had.

The authorization rate for indirect materials was based on a targeted overhead allowance for each area derived from the budgeted overhead per engine specified by the Romeo controller's office. The long-run goal was to continually reduce overhead spending per unit of output. Prater was proud that the plant's teams had beaten the initial spending goal for the 4.6 liter engine by $30 per engine, but acknowledged that sometimes teams over-spent their allowance:

> The authorization operates more like a charge card with a nominal daily limit than an actual checkbook that you could not over-draft.

Several teams attempted to lower expenses by negotiating directly with suppliers for their indirect materi-

---

[1]The eight disciplines employed to analyze and fix defect causes were: (1) identifying the team members responsible for the analyses; (2) providing a concern description; identifying (3) containment actions, (4) root cause(s), and (5) corrective actions; implementing the (6) permanent corrective actions and (7) actions to prevent recurrence; and finally, (8) congratulating the team members.

als. Prater recalled that some teams discovered they could get discounts if they bought a high quantity of certain supplies. Subsequently, if the production part changed or a production problem was solved, the demand for these supplies was greatly reduced, and the team got charged for the excess inventory. Area managers tried not to intervene in these local decisions, feeling that, in the long run, it was better for the teams to take responsibility for and learn from such experiences than to expect management to check and approve each of their decisions.

Teams also received a weekly report on the total overhead expenses charged to their department, including telephone, utilities, indirect labor, and salaries of engineering and technical assistants. Dick James, the financial analysis team manager, noted that the Romeo system assigned to areas and teams many expenses that were sometimes considered "fixed" costs by other plants.

> The teams are responsible for their own expenses. They are billed for everything, including power, water, and telephone. If they leave the lights on, their costs go up.

Romeo's managers wanted to have their teams see the cost of having salaried employees, like process engineers and technical assistants, available to perform tasks in the team's area. The managers encouraged teams to make suggestions that would influence the use of salaried people. For example, teams could ask salaried people for help in increasing productivity or to use less overtime. Teams also had the option to not replace salaried people who left due to retirement or attrition.

Members of the teams were not completely sure how to use the financial information they were now seeing for the first time.

> The checkbook helps us keep track of our spending against our target but it is a little difficult for everyone to relate to these numbers. The machine operators, in particular, don't have any feeling about whether or not we are making our target. About the cost reports, the numbers are there and we have to understand them but they're not really useful. We're focusing now on productivity improvements; perhaps in the future we might concentrate more on cost analysis to reduce tooling costs.

Weekly Meeting   Each week, George Pfeil met on a rotating basis with one of the departmental teams to discuss opportunities for improvement. Wendy Coscia, the connecting rod team manager, described her team's weekly meetings:

> In our weekly meetings, we fucos on quality, productivity, and scrap. George Pfeil allows us to focus on these instead of variances. He recognizes that the old-style weekly variance meetings were negative discussions about spending too much. Here, we focus on ways to spend wisely to improve quality and productivity.
>
> If our discussion indicates that there is a recurring machine problem or quality issue, I ask for volunteers to form a small problem solving team to resolve the issue. If the issue is a concern for both shifts, then we set up a common problem solving team with members from each shift. I have found that my team members like to get involved; they like to have a voice; and they are willing to take ownership of the problem solving process.

Unit Costs versus Labor & Overhead Reporting

Historically, Ford's Powertrain plants relied on an extensive reporting system that compared actual labor and overhead expenses, by account, to budgeted amounts.[2] Dick James commented:

> We believe that the Labor and Overhead report is sometimes contrary to the continuous improvement philosophy we operate under at Romeo. The trend of actual costs is a better indicator. Cost is a result of all the other actions we do at the plant; it's a sanity check, not the driver.

The Labor and Overhead (L&OH) reporting system was fresh in area manager Bill Yowan's mind since he had only recently transferred to Romeo from another Powertrain plant:

> The L&OH system was a tremendously time consuming process to track budgets and variances. I spent 30–45 minutes each day learning about what happened yesterday so that I could respond to questions in this report. Also, when you encountered problems, you began to do all types of things to get back within your budget. Some of these were counter-productive. The pressure was to stay within budget not to identify what had gone wrong and attempt to improve it.

Lonnie Prater concurred with his colleague:

> Problems were revealed but, because of budget constraints, you sometimes delayed taking corrective action. In order to accomplish something permanent you had to circumvent the system. You spent the money where you knew it was needed but it took 6–7 months to begin to get the payback in lower costs. Meanwhile you made up excuses to explain the variances.

---

[2]The Labor & Overhead reporting system is described in Peoria Engine Plant (A), HBS Case # 9-193-082.

Yowan described how his behavior changed after assignment to the REP:

> At Romeo, I spend my time **improving** actions, not **tracking** actions. Instead of focusing on how much my area spent yesterday on tooling and overhead, I am coaching and problem-solving with teams on how to enhance line productivity. Though, to be honest, I am still not completely comfortable with this new environment. I keep thinking that I might be challenged at any time to respond to a query from the division, from people outside the Romeo world, about how much was spent on the last shift.

Chris Hineman described his experiences with the Labor & Overhead system:

> In a traditionally organized plant, people focus on the variance percentage, the percent deviation of actual cost from budget or standard. They soon learn that there are two ways to avoid unfavorable variances: reduce actual costs or increase your budgets. Initially people work hard to reduce costs, but at some point the demanding improvement factors and the lack of investment capital prevent a manager from achieving the budgeted costs. A manager then develops a case and argues for an increased budget allowance because of product design, mix changes, economics and machine deterioration. The increased allowances might be agreed to but how has this process helped to reduce spending in the plant?
>
> Costs have to go up with volume and down with volume, with unit costs constantly improving. With a budget system we concentrate too much on complexity and volume shifts, and look for excuses to explain away any increase in costs.

Recently, however, the Romeo plant had started to produce a new 4-valve aluminum block engine in addition to the much simpler 2-valve cast iron engine. Some of the managers wondered how actual cost reductions could be accomplished when a much more complex engine was introduced into the plant.

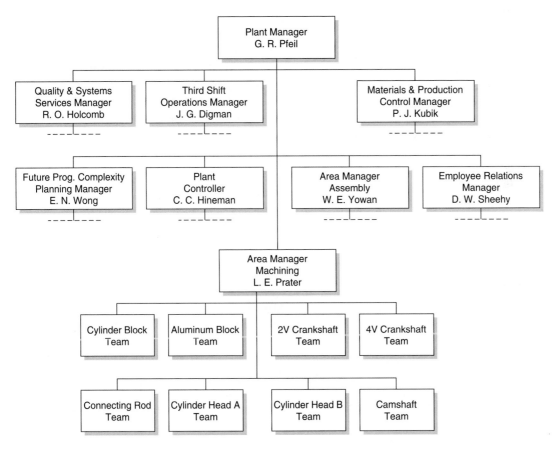

EXHIBIT 1

ANALOG DEVICES: THE HALF-LIFE SYSTEM

A problem with management information systems is that they are strongly biased toward reporting financial information to stockholders and government agencies. Unless quality improvement and other more fundamental performance measures are elevated to the same level of importance as financial measures, when conflicts arise, financial considerations win out. To address this issue, we designed a division scorecard that reports only the barest of financial information and places greater emphasis on quality improvement goals.

Ray Stata, chairman and president, Analog Devices, Inc.[1]

Company Background

Analog Devices, Inc. (ADI), headquartered in Norwood, Massachusetts, produced integrated circuits and systems for the high-end data acquisition market. The devices converted between physical and digital data in equipment such as high performance computer disc drives, aircraft sensors, medical instruments, and sophisticated consumer electronics (compact disc players, digital audio tape players and high definition television). As a senior ADI executive remarked, "The real world is not digital; it's analog. Someone has to measure temperatures, pressures, and velocity and convert these data into digital form."

ADI, with 5400 employees and seven manufacturing sites worldwide, had 1988 sales divided among the United States (56%), Europe (28%), and Asia (16%, principally Japan and Korea). Its customers were in the military/avionics, telecommunications, computer, instrument, and industrial market segments. Summary financial data appear in Exhibit 1.

Recently, the company had dedicated itself to an ongoing Quality Improvement Program. Ray Stata described the motivation for the effort:

For more than fifteen years, Analog Devices grew consistently at a rate of about 25 percent per year. Then for the first time, between 1982 and 1987, we missed our five-year goals—and by a country mile. Like other semiconductor companies we were affected by the malaise in the U.S.

electronics industry and by the strong dollar. But the external environment was only part of the problem: something was also wrong internally, and it had to be fixed.

But what was the problem? We had the largest share of our niche market in high-performance linear integrated circuits. We had the best designers and technologists in our business. We had excellent relations with a highly motivated workforce. We were not guilty of underinvestment, nor of managing for short-term profits. The only conclusion was that there was something about the way we were managing the company that was not good enough.

Motivated by systems dynamics concepts articulated decades earlier by Jay Forrester at Massachusetts Institute of Technology (M.I.T.), Stata came to focus on organizational learning as the key management concept: *"I would argue that the rate at which individuals and organizations learn may become the only sustainable competitive advantage, especially in knowledge-intensive industries."*

Improved performance in customer service, product quality, yield, and cost were becoming key strategic goals for ADI. Historically, the company had played a niche strategy, focusing its attention on being the first to the market with new products whose unique performance enabled it to earn substantial margins. These applications usually required only modest production volumes. But several of the newer applications for ADI's products had developed substantial high-volume potential. For high-volume applications, customers were demanding lower prices and better delivery performance. ADI decided to concentrate on penetrating the higher-volume markets developing in computers, communications networks, and consumer products and to use the lower-cost structure from serving these markets to maintain and increase penetration in its traditional lower-volume industrial and military markets.

Stata recalled what he believed was necessary in order to penetrate the high-volume markets:

We decided to focus our attention on product quality, on-time delivery, lead time, yields, and new-product time to market. We went to seminars, read books, gave speeches, and introduced information systems to measure our performance. But three years into the mission we were not getting very far very fast.

We knew all about error detection and correction and about doing it right the first time. But we did not have any

---

[1]Comments by Ray Stata throughout this case were extracted from his article, "Organizational Learning—The Key to Management Innovation," *Sloan Management Review* (Spring 1989): 63–74.

This case was prepared by Robert S. Kaplan.

Copyright © 1990 by the President and Fellows of Harvard College. Harvard Business School Case 190-061.

notion of what rate of improvement was satisfactory or what we could do to accelerate the improvement process.

The Quality Half-Life Concept

ADI believed strongly in operating with a small corporate staff, and that line managers had to take the lead in improving quality. But frustration with the slow rate of improvement led to the hiring of Art Schneiderman as vice president for quality and productivity improvement. Schneiderman, with mechanical engineering and management degrees from M.I.T., had worked for many years as a consultant for Bain & Co. His consulting experience had focused on case histories of successful quality improvement programs. Schneiderman was a follower of the Juran philosophy[2] that believed quality goals had to be incorporated into incentive and reward systems. But to be part of the reward system, Schneiderman knew that the quality goals needed to be realistic:

> The basic flaw in current goal setting is that specific goals should be set based on knowledge of the means that will be used to achieve them. Yet the means are rarely known at the time goals are set. The usual result is that if the goal is too low, we will underachieve relative to our potential. If the goal is too high, we will underperform relative to others' expectations. What's really needed to set rational goals is a means of predicting what is achievable if some sort of standard means for improvement were used.[3]

Schneiderman had recently made an important discovery:

> I had inadvertently made a transformation of some data provided by Yokogawa Hewlett Packard (HP) [see Exhibit 2] that suggested a simple model for the results of Quality Improvement Process (QIP) activity. Any defect level, subjected to legitimate QIP, decreases at a constant rate so that when plotted on semilog paper against time, it falls on a straight line. At the Japanese HP plant, the continuous improvement process produced a 50% reduction in the failure rate every 3.6 months over a two-year period. After reducing defects by a factor of more than 250, the process eventually slowed down probably due to inherent equipment limitations.
>
> After this initial discovery, I gathered data on every quality improvement program reported in the literature. The reports came from a wide variety of sources including my experience, various publications, presentations from the Ju-

ran Institute and the American Society for Quality Control, and a wide variety of textbooks on quality improvement.

> In analyzing this data, I used the word "defect" in its most general sense: any measurable quantity that is in need of improvement.

Among the "defects" studied by Schneiderman were errors, rework, yield loss, unnecessary reports, cycle times in manufacturing, design and administrative processes, unscheduled downtime, inventory, employee turnover, absenteeism, lateness, unrealized human potential, accidents, late deliveries, order lead time, setup time, cost of poor quality, and warranty costs. Exhibit 3 shows the graphs for five of the quality improvement programs.

In each QIP, Schneiderman measured the *half-life* for improvement. For each increment of time that equals this half-life, the defect level drops by 50%. For example, if the initial defect level was 10%, and the defect half-life was six months, then after the first six months, the defect level would be down to 5%; after the next six months, 2.5%; and so on. Schneiderman proceeded to test his half-life concept at ADI:

> One of the key corporate goals was to reduce the percentage of orders shipped late. We assembled a team from various organizations involved with customer service to analyze the causes of lateness. For each late shipment, we determined the cause, and then we plotted their distribution. We found that a relatively small number of causes was responsible for 50% of the problems.
>
> Next we assembled problem-solving teams to attack these major causes of lateness. When the cycle was completed, we repeated the process by prioritizing the causes for 50% of the remaining problems and then eliminating those causes. This cycle was repeated again and again; each time the most important remaining problems were identified, and resources were focused on solving them.

Under Schneiderman's leadership, the company had implemented a total QIP that stressed continual problem solving. The process was described as the PDCA cycle (see Exhibits 4 and 5): Plan, Do, Check, Act. This formulation emphasized that a quality program is not something an organization does for a year or two to correct some problems and then moves on to something else. Rather, the QIP embodied a continual problem-solving commitment in which the half-life method served as the *speedometer* for measuring how fast the organization was traveling around the PDCA cycle (see also Exhibit 6).

---

[2]J.M. Juran, *Quality Control Handbook,* 3rd Ed. (New York: McGraw Hill, 1979).

[3]Comments from Schneiderman in the case were obtained both from direct interviews and from his article, "Setting Quality Goals," *Quality Progress* (April 1988): 51–57.

Schneiderman commented on factors that influenced the improvement half-life:

> The slope of the learning curve seems to be determined by how long it takes to identify and prioritize the causes of the problem and to eliminate those causes. The required time for each cycle of improvement is largely a function of the complexity and bureaucracy of the organization [see Exhibit 7]. Ray Stata likes to rephrase this by saying that the half-life is determined by the rate of organizational learning.

Implementing the Half-Life Concept at ADI

The ADI five-year plan for fiscal year (FY) 1987 to FY 1992 called for:

Sales Growth	20% to 25% per year
Operating Profits	17% of Sales
Profit After Tax	9.4% of Sales
Return on Capital	15%

The sales growth target was particularly challenging since the worldwide projected growth rates for electronic equipment was only 11% per year and for semiconductor sales, 13% per year. ADI would have to grow profitably at a rate considerably higher than its competitors if it were to meet its objectives. Stata felt this could only be achieved if ADI was thought by its customers to be number one in terms of total value delivered. Rather than allow individual department and division managers to establish their own metrics and goals for customer performance, the senior executives of ADI established a top-down performance measurement system. In addition to continuing to turn out high-performance products that met customers' functional needs, specific targets were established for on-time delivery, defect levels, and lead time:

	1987	1992	Half-Life (months)
On-Time Delivery	85%	> 99.8%	9
Outgoing Defect Level	500 PPM	< 10 PPM	9
Lead Time	10 wks.	< 3 wks.	9

The 1992 goals were derived by asking key customers what kind of performance they expected from their number one supplier. Frequently, customers' purchasing people specified only modest improvements from 1987 performance. Customers' operations people were much more demanding, since they compared ADI to all their suppliers, not just to linear IC manufacturers. Some goals specified from the toughest customers were too demanding; ADI felt it could not reasonably expect to meet them. It then looked to see what its best competitor was currently doing and could be expected to be doing in 1992; and this became the target. Only if ADI could not meet its toughest competitor with its currently projected half-life improvement rate was the 1992 target specified by extrapolating from current half-lives.[4]

Schneiderman knew that these ambitious goals for customer service could be met in only two ways. One way involved building and holding inventory and using lots of inspection to meet the delivery, quality, and lead time goals. Schneiderman felt, however, that this way led to bankruptcy. The second way was to make continuing, fundamental improvement in manufacturing processes. Four measures of internal performance were established for every division and five-year goals for improvement of these measures specified:

	1987	1992	Half-Life (months)
Manufacturing Cycle Time	15 wks.	4–5 wks.	9
Process Defect Level	5000 PPM	< 10 PPM	6
Yield	20 %	> 50 %	9
Time to Market	36 months	6 months	24

The half-lives for improvement of both the external and internal measures had been estimated from Schneiderman's data base of 64 improvement examples. Schneiderman also pointed out that while the detailed tracking of improvement measures depended on making a quantity (such as % late deliveries) smaller, for motivational purposes the company executives liked to emphasize the positive aspects such as the on-time delivery percentage increasing from 60% to greater than 95%.

Stata recalled the introduction of the new performance measurement targets:

> The challenge of making continuous improvements with nine-to-twelve month halflives over an extended period is awesome. The first reaction of our organization was to recoil from what looked like unrealistic objectives. But if a

---

[4]Some in ADI felt that if the performance of its best competitor could not be met, then perhaps ADI should consider exiting that line of business.

company really gets its quality improvement act together, there is no fundamental reason why these goals cannot be achieved. There were companies in Japan already operating at these levels on some of these measures.

Schneiderman designed a quarterly scorecard (see Exhibit 8) so that the predicted performance of each division on the external and internal metrics could be conveniently displayed:

> Each year, I fill in the scorecard for the next year with benchmarks based on half-life improvement rates. Then the division managers come up with their bottom-up targets. We negotiate differences, usually ending up in the middle between our proposals.
>
> The Corporate Scorecard [Exhibit 8] is divided into five panels. The top panel, Financial Performance, presents information of interest to stockholders. The second panel, QIP indicators, presents data on how we look to our customers and employees. The measures, such as lead time, on-time delivery, and employee turnover, indicate what's important and what we need to improve. The third and fourth panels present measures of internal manufacturing performance. These measures are what we believe drive the external measures shown in the first two panels. The fifth panel shows how well we are doing in introducing new products and achieving the strategic goals specified in our five-year plan.

During the year, the trends on all key indicators are reported monthly and quarterly (see Exhibit 9 as a sample report for on-time delivery performance of the seven ADI divisions). Stata emphasized the importance of the reporting process:

> How information is displayed makes an incredible difference. The simple summary of on-time delivery [Exhibit 9] replaces pages of information that used to be circulated to managers. With all these pages, the most crucial information—the half-life trend—was missing. For management purposes, displaying all divisions together on a single page has great motivational value. A high level of internal competition exists to generate the fastest learning curve; it is obvious and embarrassing when you are not performing.

Schneiderman reviewed the trend performance of each division quarterly:

> By statistical analysis of the improvement curve, I can estimate upper and lower control limits for each observation. I circle any major variance, a red circle for an unfavorable variance and a green circle for a favorable one. When a "green variance" occurs, managers are asked to share their insights which led to a more rapid rate of improvement than had been historically achieved. For "red variances," managers must explain what was controllable versus non-

controllable, and give suggestions about how to make further improvements.

> Over time, managers have learned that there are right answers and wrong answers for explaining unfavorable variances. The wrong answer is to claim that lots of little reasons combined to produce the bad outcome. The right answer is to identify the two or three key problems that contributed to 80% to 90% of the bad performance and to describe the program that will lead to reducing the impact of these problems in the future.

The QIP Quarterly Scorecard soon became accepted at ADI, but a new unforeseen conflict had developed. Operating managers continued to receive extensive financial summaries of their monthly performance. Frequently, the QIP Scorecard and the Financial Performance summaries pointed in opposite directions; a manager might be performing well by one scorecard and performing poorly with the other scorecard. Gene Hornsby, director of product assurance, described the problem:

> We were trying to get managers to keep inventory down, improve quality, and match production to customer deliveries. But with the monthly financial reports, the operating people got stroked when volume was high and beat up when volume was low. They're not unresponsive. They soon figured out that getting stroked felt better than getting beat up. The accounting system seems to be a barrier to our attempts to implement just-in-time and short cycle times.

Active discussions and debates ensued attempting to reconcile the conflicting signals.

Monthly Financial System

The ADI financial system was a traditional process-oriented system that tracked expenses to each of the major production cost centers and allocated cost center costs to products. Each production center had a direct cost center (for materials and labor) and a fixed cost center. Most of the indirect expenses were considered fixed. Material, labor, and variable overhead costs were assigned to each batch of wafers started through the fabrication process. Fixed expenses were allocated to products only when preparing external financial statements to conform to generally accepted accounting practices.

The key determinant of the cost of an individual die was the wafer yield, defined as the ratio of good die produced on a wafer to the total number of die that can be printed and produced on the wafer. All the wafer fabrication costs were assigned to the good die based on estimated yield percentages. Currently, yield was averaging about 35%.

Labor and overhead expenses were assigned to wafers based on estimates of machine utilization and efficiency. Russ Brennan, semiconductor divisional controller at ADI, remarked:

It's been normal to have unfavorable variances equal to 20% to 25% of standard direct cost. The standards overstate the efficiency of machines and their utilization. For example, a machine may only be working for two hours per day, but the standard for the machine could be six hours of operation each day. Also, we frequently find there's a big gap between what we thought a machine's performance would be and what it is actually delivering.

But the big issue is yield. Each quarter, planners make assumptions about yield, and these assumptions drive the production schedule. The planners' estimates of yield can be different from the existing standard and also different from recent actual experience. They are evaluated by customer-service levels, not inventory levels, so that they have been reluctant to change production schedules based on short-term improvements in yield.

For example, as some of the continuous improvement activities took effect recently, yields increased dramatically. A planner eventually noticed the large buildup of die inventory and started to slow down the number of wafer starts. The slowdown caused overhead to be underabsorbed. Yield variances were favorable, but our absorption variances were unfavorable, since labor and overhead rates had been based on a higher number of wafer starts.

Weekly financial reports summarized new bookings, shipments (referred to as billings), and the key semiconductor industry ratio—"bookings to billings." A book-to-bill ratio larger than one signaled sales growth and a ratio less than one indicated a potential industry slowdown. Also reported weekly were scrap dollars, yield percentages, yield variances from standard and plan, and detailed inventory positions by product type and production stage.

A monthly income statement (see Exhibit 10) reported bookings, backlog, sales, and several levels of profit margins. Managers focused especially on the contribution margin line, which represented gross margin less fixed manufacturing and divisional fixed expenses (marketing, engineering, and general and administrative expenses). Monthly spending summaries, by detailed account type, were prepared for each department. The monthly report also summarized absorption variances of labor and variable overhead, purchase and usage variances for materials, and efficiency and rate variances for labor and variable overhead. Brennan acknowledged:

We use a pretty conventional costing system that was designed more for inventory measurement and valuation than for performance measurement. Line managers look mostly at yield and more at percentages than the dollar variances. They also keep track of completed goods each period. As the company moves forward with its continuous improvement activities, we will need to decide when we have enough confidence in the recent operating results to incorporate them into the financial numbers and the production build plan. Historically, our product volumes have been small, and process yields can change quickly when products are not produced in a smooth learning environment.

The Impact on Operating Managers

Goodloe Suttler, formerly a product-line manager at the Wilmington facility, had recently been appointed general manager of the Semiconductor Division. Suttler was skeptical about the value of financial information for semiconductor manufacturing:

Two years ago, we were producing one product for a very large computer manufacturer. Every day, I was looking at the die yields from the test and probe cost center. It was the best predictor for process efficiency and for meeting the customer's delivery schedule. A handful of key results, not the accounting system, tell you what you need to know to operate in real time. With timely and accurate local indicators at critical control points, we obtain orders-of-magnitude improvements in our ability to control. You can never get the official accounting system to provide the necessary timely, relevant information.

Suttler was asked his opinion of the recently introduced half-life system:

The half-life measurements provide the context for long-term problem solving. It made us realize that we had several chronic problems that we had learned to live with for a long time without fixing. With thousands of problems arising in our complex production environment, we can't address the most serious ones without a comprehensive measurement system. The metrics now being used will be much more useful than installing a better cost accounting system.

In the past, the ADI culture was design and marketing; manufacturing was a necessary evil in order to get customers to part with their money. Cost-reduction programs never seemed to work; they were boring, not meaningful. They didn't address how we were adding value for customers.

The QIP changes the emphasis from boring cost reduction to making improvements in measures that people can get really excited about. We are now following a three stage program. First, identify what matters to customers. This sets the objectives for our efforts. Second, we develop metrics for these objectives, and third, we analyze the metrics to develop problem-solving activities. We try to determine what problems exist that affect our ability to improve performance along each metric and form teams to address the problems with the highest priorities.

Suttler recalled the recent incident described by Brennan, when yields had increased substantially.

The production planners were determining wafer starts based on historic average yields, and they didn't slow down starts initially. They had seen ups (and downs) in yields many times before, but this time we had really fixed some problems and yields kept increasing. A lot of extra good die started piling up in inventory, but no real-time system was tracking it. The wafer fab manager figured out that the inventory must be building up somewhere, but he kept quiet for a while because he didn't want the unfavorable volume variances and pressure to idle workers that would result from slowing down starts. Eventually, he reported the buildup to me, but I waited another month to verify the buildup so that we produced even more inventory before finally ordering a major cutback on starts. We could have been producing the wrong mix for inventory and risking considerable obsolescence. Now we look weekly at our yields and schedule starts based on the most recent data. But until we worked off the inventory we had built, we had lower cost absorption. Wall Street analysts called us about the reductions in our short-term margins, not about the long-term improvement in die yield from wafer production.

An unexpected problem from the improvement in yields was a decreased demand for workers. ADI did not want to lay off workers because of the improvement in its production processes. Suttler speculated that perhaps the future QIP improvement targets should be matched with attrition and hiring rates to avoid the pressure for layoffs. Suttler recognized, however, that a big benefit from improved yield was to increase the effective capacity of the facility and therefore to defer, perhaps indefinitely, capital additions. Suttler was asked to describe occasions when financial measurements and operating improvements conflicted:

We always knew that manufacturing cycle time was a critical factor for improving customer service. A few years ago, however, our cycle times increased from 22 to 24 weeks to 30 weeks. When we investigated, we learned that we were using inventories to generate rapid earnings growth. We have a cost system with only a few inventory recognition points. Any material that starts into production is treated as WIP (assumed to be about halfway finished). At the end of one quarter, we had started lots of wafers into production, and they all got valued at the midway WIP point; this really helps earnings. In a high sales growth sit-

uation, you, in effect, pull third-quarter results into the first quarter. But all the wafers in WIP sat in front of new orders and had to be processed before we could get any of the new orders through the system.

Art Schneiderman described a second conflict:

There's an obvious tradeoff between OTD [on-time-delivery] and short-term financial performance. In the past, we have occasionally delayed many low revenue shipments that were near completion at the end of a quarter and substituted high revenue shipments that were due the next month. So the daily OTD deteriorated sharply; about a third of our late deliveries were caused by this revenue acceleration effect. And at the beginning of the next quarter, we had to go out and find all the small orders that had been delayed and reschedule them. The OTD statistics were lousy for another two weeks. Many companies, not just ADI, seem to go through this hockey-stick shipment phenomenon at the end of months or quarters. We have to decide whether we're going to be revenue-recognition driven or OTD-performance driven.

Lou Fiore, an operations manager in the semiconductor division, commented on his disdain of periodic financial summaries:

Cost variances are useless to me. I don't want to ever have to look at a cost variance, monthly or weekly. Once you've decided to run a product, you don't have many choices left. Resources are already committed regardless of how the cost system computes costs among alternative processes.

Asked about what information he finds useful to look at, Fiore responded:

Daily, I look at sales dollars, bookings, and OTD—the percentage of orders on time. For OTD, a late order is counted only once, on the day it was not shipped on time.

Weekly, I look at a variety of quality reports including the outgoing QC report on items passing the final test before shipment to the customer, in-process quality, and yields. Yield is a good surrogate for cost and quality.

Monthly, I do look at the financial reports. I want to see the bottom line P&L for the period and the *actual* direct margin percentages. I look closely at my fixed expenses and compare these to the budgets, especially on discretionary items like travel and maintenance. I also watch head count. But the financial systems still don't tell me where I am wasting money. I expect that if I make operating improvements, costs should go down, but I don't worry about the linkage too much. The organizational dynamics make it difficult to link precisely cause and effect.

The biggest challenge is OTD. We work on this continually. We meet once a week and discuss the data on missed deliveries. We develop a Pareto diagram for the reasons and decide whether there's anything important that we're not yet focusing on or were the problems already being addressed by actions underway but not yet completed.

The hot button we're working on now is cycle time. If we can continually reduce cycle time, the efficiency of the whole operation will increase. The previous production manager liked to run large lots because the system told him this reduced costs. My approach is exactly the opposite. We reorganized the test area from a job-shop functional layout to 30 production cells that match most of our routings. Out of the 30 groups, only 3 are really constraints. I focus on these cells, closely monitoring their efficiencies and making sure they don't go out of service.

I also try to size production lots so that they can be completed in eight hours on the slowest (gating) operation in the process. This enables us to finish a lot in one shift and makes production scheduling a lot easier since we can schedule work in one shift units. By reducing the lot size, we reduced both cycle time and the variance of cycle times. This led to dramatic decreases in WIP inventory while greatly improving our ability to spot quality problems. Production now matches customer demands more closely, and the number of expedited and late orders has decreased.

Russ Brennan, the divisional controller, defended the role for financial measurements. He felt that when conflicts between QIP and financial measures occurred, the financial measurements were not always at fault.

> For much of last year, overall chute yields were increasing, and yield variances were favorable, so the two signals were consistent with each other.[5] Then in the last quarter, actual chute yield continued to increase, but we reported an unfavorable yield variance. This caused considerable confusion among the operating people.
>
> After investigating, we found that the mix of our business had changed in the last quarter. We were building less low-volume, high ASP [average selling price] products and much more high-volume, low ASP products. The standard yields on the low ASP business are higher than on the high ASP products, so the reported improvement in chute yield was due more to the favorable mix change than to fundamental improvements in the production processes. Actual yields did not increase as much as they should

---

[5]Chute yield equals the ratio of good die released from final testing to the number of total die started into production.

have, an effect only revealed by our financial measure, the yield variance.

Current Developments

The QIP program was proceeding under a three-phase program. Phase I, worked on in 1989, concentrated on on-time delivery performance (OTD), measured relative to ADI's committed shipping date.

Phase II, beginning in 1990, would add two new measures of customer responsiveness: (1) the Percentage of Time ADI met customers' lead-time requests, and, when customer lead-time requests were not met, (2) Weeks of Excess Lead Time, measured as the difference between the lead time requested by the customer and the lead time committed to by the factory. The Phase II measurements (see Exhibit 11) would be added to the division scorecards. The causes of missed-OTD were also broken down by responsibility:

Source	Possible Cause
Factory	No product available
Warehouse	Handling error
Credit	Customer on credit hold
Customer	Closed for holiday
	Requested shipment hold

In Phase III, ADI hoped to use lead time as a strategic weapon. Schneiderman wanted to be able to offer lead times even below those requested by customers.

ADI had recently introduced an additional incentive bonus plan to increase attention paid to its operating indicators. It retained a corporatewide performance bonus tied to meeting ADI's financial goals. The plan was supplemented for divisional personnel with a bonus tied to surpassing a Divisional Net Income Benchmark while achieving an OTD percentage of 90% or better and operating with defect rates of less than 500 PPM (these target levels were to be raised each year). Annual performance reviews of professional staff highlighted setting and achieving goals that were linked to departmental or organizational objectives in support of the Benchmark and Five-Year Plan.

EXHIBIT 1 Selected Financial Statistics for Analog Devices, Inc., from 1979 to 1988

	SELECTED FINANCIAL STATISTICS ($000,000)									
	1988	1987	1986	1985	1984	1983	1982	1981	1980	1979
Sales	$439	$370	$334	$322	$313	$214	$174	$156	$136	$100
Net Income	38	19	23	30	37	18	10	5	9	7
Total Assets	449	397	369	348	296	223	163	145	126	84
Capital Expend.	49	43	37	69	58	19	19	16	20	8
Sales	100%	100%	100%	100%	100%	100%	100%	100%	100%	100%
Gross Margin	54%	54%	55%	53%	57%	54%	52%	48%	52%	50%
R&D	14	15	13	12	9	9	9	8	7	6
Operating Income	13	9	12	14	18	15	13	11	16	15
Return on Sales	9	5	7	9	12	9	6	3	7	7
Debt-to-Equity	0.09	0.13	0.14	0.23	0.17	0.21	0.65	0.76	1.11	0.96

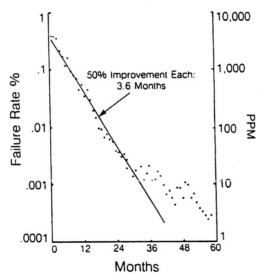

**EXHIBIT 2   Yokogawa Hewlett-Packard:
Dip Soldering Failures**

A. Signetics, Orem, Utah

Aluminum Smears from IC Test Pads

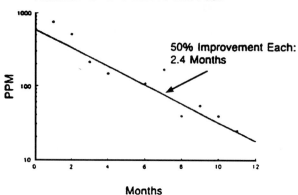

B. Eastman Kodak Copy Products Division

Average Defects per Unit, All Products

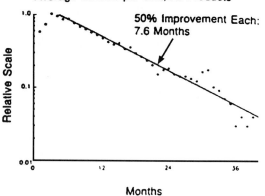

C. Rank Xerox Mitcheldean

Defect Index

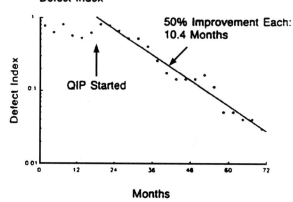

D. Japan Steel Works, Ltd., Hiroshima Plant

Absenteeism Due to Accidents

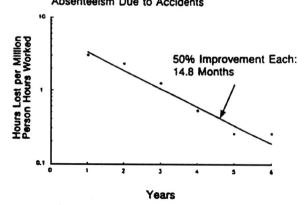

E. IBM

Vendor Quality

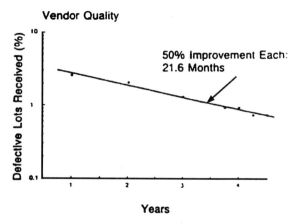

EXHIBIT 3   Five Quality Improvement Programs

THE DEMING CYCLE

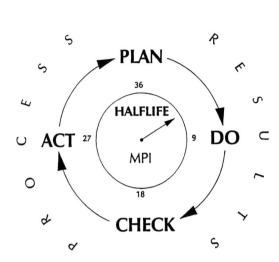

EXHIBIT 4   The Deming Cycle

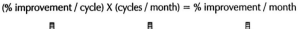

(% improvement / cycle) X (cycles / month) = % improvement / month

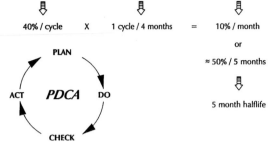

40% / cycle   X   1 cycle / 4 months   =   10% / month

or

≈ 50% / 5 months

5 month halflife

EXHIBIT 6   The "Half-Life"—A Metric of Continuous Improvement

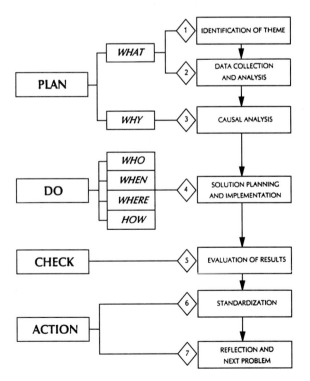

EXHIBIT 5   The PDCA Cycle and The 7 Steps

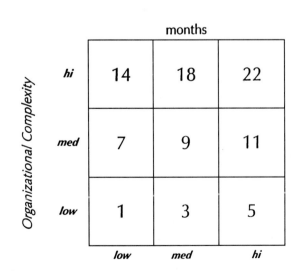

EXHIBIT 7   Target Half-Lives

	End FY89	Q190		Q290		Q390		Q490		FY90	
FINANCIAL	ACT	BHMK	ACT	BHMK	ACT	BHMK	ACT	BHMK	ACT	BHMK	ACT
REVENUE											
REVENUE GROWTH											
PROFIT											
ROA											
QIP											
ON TIME DELIVERY (to FCD)											
% CRDs NOT MATCHED											
EXCESS LEADTIME											
LABOR TURNOVER											
MANUFACTURING METRICS: IC PRODUCTS											
OUTGOING PPM											
PROCESS PPM											
CYCLE TIME											
YIELD											
MANUFACTURING METRICS: ASSEMBLED PRODUCTS											
OUTGOING PPM											
PROCESS PPM											
CYCLE TIME											
YIELD											
NEW PRODUCTS	ACTUAL	FY87 PLAN	ACTUAL	FY87 PLAN	ACTUAL	FY87 PLAN	ACTUAL	FY87 PLAN	ACTUAL	FY87 PLAN	ACTUAL
BOOKINGS PRE-86 PROD											
BOOKINGS POST-85 PROD											
TOTAL BOOKINGS											
1992 RATIO (FY90PLAN/FY87PLAN)	FY89 PLAN	FY87 PLAN	FY90 PLAN			FY87 PLAN	FY90 PLAN			FY87 PLAN	FY90 PLAN

EXHIBIT 8   FY 1990 Corporate Scorecard

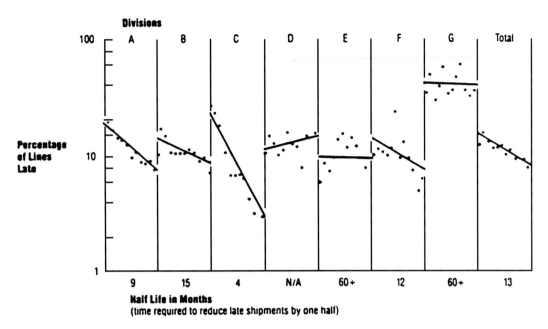

EXHIBIT 9   **Analog Devices, Inc., On-Time Customer Service Performance**

EXHIBIT 10   Analog Devices, Inc., Income Statement, June 1989 (QTD)

	1Q88	2Q88	3Q88	4Q88	YEAR 1988	1Q89	2Q89	2 MOS QTD	VAR ROLL	ROLL 3Q89
Bookings—Trade & Affil.	103,479	115,486	114,583	111,567	438,206	113,182	117,336	70,027	(765)	115,021
Sales—Total	101,207	109,608	113,284	115,107	439,206	114,145	115,003	74,800	2,542	117,420
Standard Margin	80,257	87,248	89,041	91,185	347,711	91,430	92,692	59,391	1,657	93,819
% of Sales	79.3%	79.6%	78.6%	79.2%	79.2%	80.1%	80.6%	79.4%		79.9%
Variances	(1,007)	(1,818)	(1,629)	(1,974)	(7,220)	(1,519)	(463)	(19)	979	(1,622)
Direct Margin	78,450	85,430	87,412	89,191	340,483	89,911	92,209	59,372	2,636	92,197
% of Sales	77.5%	77.9%	77.2%	77.5%	77.5%	78.8%	80.2%	79.4%		78.5%
Gross Margin	53,134	59,617	62,906	61,007	236,843	60,497	62,677	38,597	(134)	62,937
% Sales	52.5%	54.4%	55.5%	53.0%	53.9%	53.0%	54.5%	51.6%		53.6%
Division Fixed	44,936	46,912	48,486	50,992	191,326	51,137	54,741	38,896	(5,368)	54,483
% Sales	44.4%	42.8%	42.8%	44.3%	43.6%	44.8%	47.6%	52.0%		46.4%
Total Fixed	57,507	60,613	62,646	65,381	246,227	65,405	69,117	48,246	(5,368)	69,160
% Sales	56.8%	55.3%	55.3%	56.8%	56.1%	57.3%	60.1%	64.5%		58.9%
Contr Margin	20,863	24,817	24,766	23,810	94,256	24,506	23,093	11,126	(2,732)	23,036
% Sales	20.6%	22.6%	21.9%	20.7%	21.5%	21.5%	20.1%	14.9%		19.6%
ROA	15.3%	19.9%	20.2%	18.8%	18.6%	19.6%	17.4%	13.2%		17.2%
Deferred OH & Other Income	(810)	(877)	(906)	(921)	(3,514)	(913)	(920)	(598)	20	(939)
Operating Prof.	21,673	25,694	25,672	24,731	97,770	25,419	24,013	11,725	(2,753)	23,976
% Sales	21.4%	23.4%	22.7%	21.5%	22.3%	22.3%	20.9%	15.7%		20.4%

GOAL:
IMPROVE CUSTOMER SERVICE

CUSTOMER SERVICE METRICS

ON TIME
% late
% early   ▥▥▷   % on time

RESPONSIBILITY
factory   credit
warehouse   customer

LATENESS/EARLINESS
shipped late, how late?
shipped early, how early?
still late, how late?
    months to ship late backlog

LEAD TIME
customer requested lead time
% CRD s matched
excess lead time

RESPONSIVENESS
time to schedule an order

EXHIBIT 11   Phase II Measurements

CITIZEN WATCH COMPANY, LTD.: COST REDUCTION FOR MATURE PRODUCTS

Citizen, founded in 1930, was the world's largest watch manufacturer, producing over 146 million units in 1990. Citizen comprised Citizen Watch Company, Ltd., which was responsible for manufacturing, and Citizen Trading Company, Ltd., which was responsible for marketing and sales. In addition to watches, Citizen manufactured and sold numerically controlled production equipment, flexible disk drives, liquid crystal displays for televisions and computers, dot matrix printers, and jewelry.

Citizen's non-watch products resulted from more than 20 years of carefully planned diversification. In 1990, almost half of Citizen's revenues were generated by the sale of products other than watches (see Exhibit 1). All of the non-watch products relied heavily upon

technology that was critical to watch manufacture. For example, the decision to enter the flexible disk drive market in 1984 reflected the firm's ability to miniaturize electromechanical products. This expertise allowed Citizen to be the first firm to break both the "1 inch" and "3/4 inch" flexible disk drive barriers. Developing such thin disk drives was considered critical if the firm was to establish a strong foothold in the notebook computer disk drive market. Similarly, the liquid crystal display products (such as liquid crystal televisions, introduced in 1984) reflected the firms's expertise in producing LCD watches, which began with the introduction of digital watches in 1974.

The Watch Industry

From about 1970 to 1990, the watch industry underwent a number of significant changes. Historically, the industry was dominated by the Swiss. Prior to the emergence of electronic versions, watch movements were tiny me-

Professor Robin Cooper prepared this case. The assistance of Ms. May Mukuda of KPMG Peat Marwick is gratefully acknowledged.

chanical devices that required considerable skilled labor to manufacture. The Swiss had gained world dominance through a long history of technological developments that allowed them to be the low-cost producers of mechanical watch movements. At the heart of these developments was the ability to manufacture watch components, in volume, to the high tolerances required to produce accurate timepieces. These production processes relied upon a mixture of craft and mass-production techniques. The high skill and capital investment required to produce mechanical watch movements led to the consolidation of movement manufacture into a very small number of companies, each specializing in a limited number of parts. In contrast, the manufacture of the watch case and the assembly of the completed watch, which was manually intensive and required a relatively low-skill work force, was done by a large number of small firms.

The Japanese watch industry, however, was vertically integrated. The difference between the structure of the Japanese and Swiss industries reflected Japan's lack of experience in precision mechanics. As the fledgling Japanese industry developed, it proved that the best way to mass-produce quality watches was through vertical integration and concentration of the industry. In 1970, the Japanese industry contained only four firms: Citizen, Seiko, Orient, and Ricoh.

The National Aeronautics and Space Administration's (NASA's) development of the digital electronic watch allowed mass-production techniques to be applied throughout movement manufacture, thereby removing the need for a highly skilled labor force. The Swiss industry's unique mix of both centralized and decentralized firms was poorly configured to adapt to the new technology, which changed both the movement and case design. This structural handicap, particularly relating to movement production, coupled with both a reluctance to switch to a new technology that invalidated their historical competitive advantage and a lack of true mass-production experience, caused the Swiss to hesitate before adapting to electronic movements. This hesitation created an opportunity for the Japanese watch industry to break the dominant position of the Swiss.

The Japanese quickly adopted the new technology. Their vertical integration and heavy mass-production experience had created a work force capable of switching from mechanical to electronic production relatively easily. This ease of transition, combined with a strategic disadvantage in the mechanical movement market,

caused the Japanese industry to view the new technology as an opportunity, not a threat. The application of true mass-production procedures to watch manufacture, and rapid advances in electronics, allowed the cost of digital watches to fall rapidly. Whereas the first digital watches sold for ¥100,000, by 1990 they were selling for under ¥1,000.

The digital watch craze was short-lived, however, because Japanese consumers felt that digital watches looked inexpensive. Consequently, quartz analogue watches rapidly came to dominate the industry. These watches, while identical in appearance to mechanical ones, were about 50 times more accurate and could be mass produced. Highly skilled workers were not required and production volumes soared. World capacity soon exceeded demand and prices fell dramatically. The impact on the industry was enormous. As the selling price of electronic watches fell below that of mechanical ones, the Swiss industry collapsed.

Japanese watch firms, while in better shape than their Swiss counterparts, faced a future of low profits. Realizing that the only way to survive was through volume, Citizen adopted an aggressive strategy of continuous price reductions matched by equivalent cost reductions. This strategy depended upon the average consumer increasing the number of watches he or she owned. This strategy proved successful: by 1990 the average Japanese adult owned three watches, compared to only one in 1970.

Despite success in changing consumer buying behavior, the watch industry continued to experience downward price and profit pressures. At Citizen and its primary competitor, Seiko, a culture of continuous expansion and cost reduction evolved. Until 1985, Seiko was larger than Citizen. Seiko had dominated primarily because of its decision to adopt quartz technology somewhat earlier than Citizen.

Citizen had chosen not to adopt quartz technology because in 1970 it had entered a joint venture with Bulova, a Swiss firm, to produce Accutron watches. These watches relied upon miniature tuning forks for their accuracy. Because the Accutron technology was protected by patent, Seiko was forced to find an alternative technology: it chose quartz. Over the next three years, the inherent superiority of the quartz technology became apparent and Citizen was forced to shift from Accutron to quartz technology. The delay, however, had caused Citizen to lose significant market share to Seiko.

In 1979, Citizen adopted a new strategy of selling

watch movements as well as completed watches. This decision created a major conflict within Citizen. Citizen Watch Company, the manufacturing arm, favored this decision because it would significantly increase its scale of production. Citizen Trading Company, the trading arm that sold completed Citizen watches, opposed the strategy because it felt that the new strategy would create additional competition for its products. Because the highest profit margins were on completed watches, the Trading Company argued that the new strategy would cause overall profits to fall. At Citizen, the parent company (and hence the dominant one) was Citizen Watch Company; Citizen Trading Company was a subsidiary of the watch company. Consequently, after considerable debate, the new strategy was adopted.

At Seiko, in contrast, the parent company was the trading arm. Consequently, Seiko chose not to follow Citizen's lead. Citizen's decision to sell movements was extremely successful and in 1986 Citizen overtook Seiko in watch movement production worldwide. By 1990, Seiko, accepting the inevitable, began to sell watch movements.

Manufacturing Process

The Tanashi plant, built in 1935, was Citizen's primary watch movement manufacturing facility. Located in a suburb of Tokyo, it was responsible for producing approximately 20% of all watch components and all domestic watch movement assembly. The other 80% of components' manufacture was undertaken at 10 other sites spread throughout Japan. Complete watch assembly was undertaken at three domestic and three overseas facilities. In addition, the Tanashi plant designed all of the specialty tools and dies required by the firm. The tiny size of the components used in watch movements had required Citizen to develop an expertise in small die manufacture. This expertise had allowed it to profitably sell dies to other companies. Other products produced at Tanashi included flexible disk drives and liquid crystal displays.

The Tanashi plant contained two distinct manufacturing areas dedicated to watch movement production: component production and assembly. Several different technologies were used in the component production area, including wire turning, pressing, and plating. Wire turning machines were used to produce mainly pins and pinions. The press facility produced some five billion pressed parts per year, primarily wheels, springs, and

levers. The plating department was responsible for all nickel plating operations for rust protection operations.

The assembly area assembled watch movements in a highly automated and clean room environment. The Tanashi plant and associated plants of subsidiary companies contained 40 automated assembly lines. Each line was dedicated to a major family of movements, which on average contained more than three different movements. The average line assembled 35 components into a movement using 130 robots. Production ran 24 hours per day. Daily output per line was about 550,000 units. The high robot-to-component ratio reflected the use of robots to perform 100% testing of every movement after each assembly operation and to oil the movements at numerous stages in the assembly process.

Through its automation and kaizen (continuous improvement) programs, Citizen had significantly reduced the cost of watch movement production. Much of this reduction had been accomplished by designing movements with fewer components and by achieving very high quality production standards. The culmination of this automation/parts reduction program was the introduction, in 1980, of the Caliber 2000 line of products. This line contained 38 different models, was used in low- to mid-range watches, and in 1990 accounted for approximately two-thirds of Citizen's unit production. It was expected to remain in production until changes in market demand made the line obsolete. Citizen management did not expect this line to become obsolete in the near future. The long product life cycle of the Caliber line indicated the maturity of quartz watch technology.

Current defect rates were well below 1 per 1,000 movements produced. These rates had been achieved by automatically stopping any assembly operation that was out of tolerance. With 100% automatic testing after each operation, only one defective movement could be produced before that operation and hence the line would automatically stop. The cause of the out-of-tolerance condition was then analyzed and the problem corrected.

The Cost Management System

The cost management system at Tanashi was originally installed in 1964, and was continually updated over the next 25 years to adapt to changing conditions in the production areas. A major change was implemented in 1987 when the movement product and completed watch assembly areas were split into separate divisions and treated as independent profit centers. At the same time, the way indirect costs were assigned was changed. Previously these costs were allocated according to headcount; starting in 1987 they were allocated according to the number of units produced.

The cost system identified three major categories of costs: direct and indirect production costs and common indirect costs. *Direct production costs* encompassed three categories: parts production, movement assembly, and royalties. Parts production costs were split into direct material and labor costs. Direct material consisted of raw material and purchased parts. The purchase prices of these two types of material inputs were negotiated every six months. For each product, the cost system computed a material cost equal to the standard quantities of material consumed, after allowing for standard yield, multiplied by the actual material prices specified by contract.

The direct labor expenses associated with parts production were charged to products based upon the standard time they took to be produced. The parts production process was divided into three areas that represented the major subassemblies of a watch movement: gear train, base plate, and printed circuit board. Each of these major areas was further divided into numerous cost centers, each representing an operation required to manufacture the subassembly. For example, the printed circuit board area contained three centers relating to soldering: placement of solder, soldering the chips, and soldering other parts. In total, there were 59 such production cost centers for parts.

These 59 cost centers represented the smallest unit of cost control at the factory. Each center had a group leader who was responsible for that center's labor costs. The typical group leader had a high school education and approximately 25 years of experience. The labor costs for each center were directly charged to that center at the negotiated rate (labor rates were negotiated every three months). The direct labor hour standards for each component represented the average time required to produce the part over the previous three months, adjusted for any expected savings.

Direct material and labor expenses associated with movement assembly were treated virtually the same as they were for parts production. Any part of the movement that was subcontracted was charged directly to the movement at its negotiated price. Like other material contracts, these were negotiated every six months. The labor costs were directly charged to each assembly line and then to the model using standard hours, again based

upon the previous three months' actuals. Royalty expenses were charged directly to the products to which they related.

The *indirect production costs* were also split into four categories: research and development, tooling, quality assurance, and administration. The expected costs for each of these four categories over a six-month period were divided by the number of units produced to give an estimated cost per unit. The number of units varied for the three cost categories because different models were involved. For example, research and development expenses were charged to the type of movement to which they were related and then divided by the expected production volume of that type of movement.

The *common indirect expenses* included a prorated share of both the expenses of corporate headquarters in Tokyo and the firm's technical laboratory at Tokorozawa, the administration expenses of Tanashi, and interest charges. Headquarters and laboratory expenses were prorated between operating divisions based upon their sales volumes. They were then allocated to manufacturing areas responsible for different product lines within Tanashi based upon headcount. These costs were then allocated to individual products based upon the number of units produced. Tanashi administration expenses, which included executive salaries, secretarial, and computer services, were treated similarly, except that the initial proration to the facility was not required. Interest expenses were charged to product lines based upon the level of their inventories and accounts receivable and then to products based upon the number of units produced.

The product costs reported by the cost system were used primarily to support product-related decisions such as product introduction, discontinuance, cost reduction, and redesign. Cost-plus pricing was rarely used at Citizen because most products were sold into competitive markets where the competitors had similar product offerings. Occasionally, Citizen would bring out a watch or movement for which there was no direct competitive offering. In these cases, where there was no market price, the selling price was determined using a "to be accepted" market price. This price was determined by market savings and analysis that consisted of an evaluation of the attractiveness of the product and a comparison with other watches and other consumer products.

Reported product costs played an important part in product introduction because products would be introduced only if they could be sold at a profit. Once a new product had been designed, a market analysis was undertaken. This analysis identified the likely selling price of the new product and its potential sales volumes. The next step was to estimate the full cost of production. This cost estimate used the same definitions of cost as the cost system. If this estimate was accurate it would equal the reported cost of the product after it went into production. This cost estimate included allowances for both production volume and learning curve effects.

The final step was to estimate the profitability of the new watch, which was determined by subtracting the expected costs from the selling price and multiplying the result by the anticipated volume. If the watch was profitable it was introduced and orders accepted from Citizen Trading Company and other customers. If the watch was unprofitable, then the selling price, production cost, and design were reviewed. If there was no way for the product to be made profitable it was never introduced. The only exceptions to this rule were products that were considered strategically important to Citizen's corporate image, such as the perpetual calendar watch.

A similar process was used for established products to determine if they should be subjected to specific cost reduction efforts, redesigned, or discontinued. The firm monitored the rate at which selling prices were falling on all its products. When the selling price of a product was expected to fall below its cost in the near future, the product was subjected to an intense specific cost reduction analysis. This analysis consisted of identifying the major cost components of the product to determine if they could be produced at a lower cost. For example, if the largest costs were associated with machining, then ways to replace the machined parts with stamped or plastic components were explored. If the cost reductions identified by the analysis were insufficient to reduce costs so that the product would remain profitable, then complete product redesign was explored. If even complete redesign was unable to make the product profitable, it was usually discontinued.

The Cost Reduction Program

The cost reduction program at Citizen encompassed the entire production chain, including subsidiaries and outside suppliers. For subsidiaries, the firm knew the material, labor, and overhead content of the purchased parts or subcomponents. The corporate technical staff would provide engineering support to help the subsidiaries find ways to become more efficient. The technical staff

would visit the subsidiaries to observe the production process and make suggestions on how it might be improved. For external suppliers, the process focused on steady cost reduction. Citizen's current target was 3% per annum. All external suppliers were expected to deliver at least this level of annual cost reduction. If a supplier was able to exceed the 3% target, then it retained the surplus. If a supplier was unable to achieve the 3% target, there was no punishment, but Citizen's engineers would assist it in achieving the 3% the following year.

The maturity of quartz watch technology made it very difficult to remove significant costs by improving product designs. Consequently, the firm identified its major cost reduction opportunity as becoming more efficient in the production process. Considerable effort was made to remove the direct labor content of products by increasing the number of machines, on average, run by a single employee.

Labor content was reduced primarily in two ways: either production engineering would change the way the product was produced or the work force would find ways to become more efficient. In the early 1990s, about 80% of all cost reductions were expected to be achieved by production engineering changes. Only 20% was expected from the work force, because it had already spent years becoming more efficient and management believed that any remaining savings opportunities were limited.

The major way to reduce labor was by altering the time it required to operate or support the production machines. There were two major approaches to machine time reduction. First, ways to increase the running speed of the machines were identified; increasing the running speed allowed more parts per hour to be produced. Second, ways to increase the number of machines a single employee could operate were identified.

The success of this program was illustrated by the turning machine department. The 150 turning machines in the department were operated by 15 people during the day shift and only 2 people on the night shift. The high ratio of machines to people had been achieved by paying considerable attention to what events caused downtime and eradicating them. The 15 people on the day shift were primarily involved with setting up the manual machines, troubleshooting, and keeping the machines loaded with wire. Only 2 people were required on the night shift because high volume components that did not require changeovers were produced at night. The only task of the night shift was to keep the machines running. If a machine broke down or drifted out of tolerance, it was left for the day shift to troubleshoot.

Group leaders were responsible for labor content reduction. Each of the 59 group leaders was required to set cost reduction targets every three months. These targets were submitted to the administration department, which consolidated the targeted reductions and, if they were sufficient firm-wide, accepted them. If the overall reductions were not satisfactory, they were sent back to the group leaders for more aggressive targets. This process of adjusting the targeted savings could go several rounds before an acceptable overall target was reached.

Individual group leaders' cost reduction targets were reviewed by the 14 managers to whom they reported. These managers had all previously been group leaders and, because of their prior experience and relationship with the current group leaders, were able to evaluate the appropriateness of the individual target reduction objectives. The final plans were reviewed by two general managers. The emphasis of the review was not on the individual targets but on the division-wide savings level. Citizen felt it was more important to achieve its overall target than worry about whether one center should achieve 6% cost reductions as opposed to 5%.

The target labor reductions for each group were included in the standards every three months. For expected savings that were due to changes in the production process, the savings were not included in the standards until the month after which the change was expected to occur. For example, if a process change was planned to be implemented in the second month of a three-month cycle, the standard would be adjusted for the third month. Therefore, if all went according to plan, there would be no positive or negative variance from the process change. Only if the savings were different from expected would a variance occur.

The success of cost reduction efforts was measured using an achievement ratio, which was obtained by dividing actual labor hours by standard labor hours. Achievement ratios were computed monthly for each group and semiannually for each product. The expected value of the achievement ratio was 100%, reflecting the incorporation of the cost reduction targets into the standards on a monthly basis.

If the achievement ratio for a group was above 101%, then a review was triggered. At this review, the group leader would discuss ways to ensure that the following month's achievement ratio would fall to 100%. The standard was not changed for the first month that the achievement ratio was over 100%. This created additional pressure on the group to achieve its cost reduction targets. If the ratio remained above 100% for a second month in a row, then the standard was adjusted in the third month to reflect the failure to achieve the desired cost reductions. In effect, the cost reduction target for the group was revised downwards. Even though the target was revised, the review continued of why the targeted savings were not achieved and how they could subsequently be achieved. There was no direct reward or punishment associated with over- or underachieving. The reasons behind the failure to reach an achievement ratio of 100% were discussed thoroughly and fully analyzed. If the reason was based on the manager's ability, the results would be reflected in his or her personal evaluation and promotion potential.

To achieve continuous direct labor cost reduction, the involvement of the entire work force was required. Even incremental improvements in efficiency were considered important. To create incentives for the work force to identify savings, picture boards were placed throughout the factory. These boards contained pictures of before and after improvements, and identified the group and individual who identified the savings and the degree of savings. For example, one set of before and after pictures covered a reduction in the time required to read a set of meters. The person reading the meters determined that the time he required to read them could be reduced by shifting them. Prior to moving them, it required 2 minutes and 58 seconds to read each meter. After they were moved, it required only 1 minute and 30 seconds.

Considerable effort had been focused on reducing the indirect costs, both production and common, at Tanashi. The long-term objective was to reduce these costs by 30% and to use the freed-up resources in other functions. Several approaches were used. The first was to identify unnecessary activities. The workload of each indirect person was reviewed to see if the position could be eliminated or the duties reduced. This analysis typically resulted in a new job description, which was prepared by the cost center group to which the indirect person belonged and reviewed by the general managers. At the heart of this cost reduction exercise was the belief that if the work did not go away there would be no long-term savings. The second approach was to identify the necessary indirect activities, and where possible automate them so that they could be performed less expensively.

The result of these labor content reduction programs

was to considerably reduce the number of people involved in watch movement production. In 1972, 2,952 people were required; by 1980 it was down to 2,520, and by 1990 it had fallen to 1,542, which was an overall reduction of almost 50%, though the number of units produced and subcontracting to subsidiaries must be

taken into consideration. The displaced work force had guaranteed lifetime employment, so Citizen was responsible for finding them new positions within the firm. Fortunately, the diversification program was able to absorb all of the displaced work force.

EXHIBIT 1 1988–1990 Revenues by Major Product Lines (in Millions of Yen)

	1988	1989	1990
Watches	161,745	164,186	200,835
Clocks and Jewelry	35,580	38,606	41,940
Information and Fine Mechanics	84,374	112,428	147,166
Other	19,057	19,193	19,215

SUMITOMO ELECTRIC INDUSTRIES, LTD.: THE KAIZEN PROGRAM

Sumitomo Electric Industries, Ltd. (SEI) was founded in 1897 as Sumitomo Copper Rolling Works, a manufacturer of bare copper. Manufacture of insulated wire began in 1900 and trial production of communication cables in 1909. Since its founding, SEI continued to produce electric wires and cables, and was the world's third-largest manufacturer of these products after the French firm Alcatel and the UK firm B.I.C.C. Over the years, the firm expanded the range of wire and cable products it produced to cover a variety of uses, ranging from large ultra-high-voltage power transmission lines to tiny wiring harnesses that were used in automobiles and airplanes.

SEI's top management considered the firm to be one of the most highly diversified in Japan. Sumitomo's diversification program, which began in 1931 when the firm started to manufacture its own extrusion dies, was considered extremely successful. In 1992, wire products only accounted for about 50% of revenues, though this percentage was misleading because wire products included numerous new items, such as flexible circuit boards, that were not part of the firm's original core business. The firm diversified along technological lines

by taking advantage of the distinctive competencies it had developed in the manufacture of electric wires and cables. These competencies included metal drawing, coating and insulation, and general metallurgy. Relying upon these core competencies, the firm had branched out into optoelectronics, new materials, and systems.

Starting in 1974, SEI began to invest heavily in optoelectronics (the fusion of optics and electronics). By 1992, it was producing a wide range of optoelectronics products, including a variety of optical fibers and cables and a range of light-emitting- and photo-diodes. The firm had entered the optoelectronics market when it decided to produce the light-emitting- and photo-diodes that were used at the ends of fiber-optics cables to convert the signals between optical and electrical formats. In 1981, SEI expanded its involvement in the optoelectronics field by commencing production of fiber-optic data links and local area networks for computers.

SEI's second major area of diversification was new materials, including compound semiconductors, first manufactured in 1970; synthetic diamonds, first manufactured in 1985; and new forms of alloys, fine ceramics, and high-performance polymers. Over the years, SEI had developed innovative approaches to the mass production of a number of these products; for example, SEI was the first in the world to successfully mass-produce high-quality, large-diameter gallium arsenide in-

Professor Robin Cooper of the Peter F. Drucker Graduate Management Center at The Claremont Graduate School prepared this case.

Copyright © 1994 by the President and Fellows of Harvard College. Harvard Business School case 195-078.

gots and large-size (1.4 carat) synthetic diamonds. The firm had entered the compound semiconductor market based upon its expertise in manufacturing solid-state diodes. It had developed expertise in the manufacture of synthetic diamonds because they were used to produce extrusion dies.

SEI's third major area of diversification was systems. The firm had entered the systems market in order to manufacture the equipment that used the communications networks the firm was installing. This decision was driven by the observation that the profit generated by the equipment attached to these networks was greater than that generated by installing the networks themselves. The growing need for efficiency and speed in information processing, logistical control, and the management of virtually all areas of society and industry was seen as creating a major new market for SEI. Consequently, the company had developed expertise in designing systems for computer and communication processing, traffic control, medical information, and cable television. Recently, the company had created a showcase capability in artificial intelligence technology.

Adapting to Changing Times

Three major pressures emerged in the early 1970s that forced the firm to modify its cost management systems: the worldwide oil crisis, Japan's discontinuation of the gold standard, and a growing awareness in Japan of the consequences of environmental pollution. These pressures made the management of the firm's product mix both more difficult and more important. Product-mix management became more difficult because the increased awareness of pollution forced the firm to shift away from products and production processes that created polluting by-products. And product-mix management became more important to SEI's ability to sustain its traditional levels of profitability, both because the oil crisis put pressure on prices by slowing the global and domestic economies, and because coming off the gold standard led to greater fluctuations in exchange rates, which made overseas profits more difficult to sustain.

In response to these pressures, SEI enhanced its cost management and divisional profitability systems to enable them to report both divisional and product profitability. The firm had adopted a divisional form in the 1960s and had been refining its cost management system ever since. Major refinements were implemented in the late 1960s and early 1970s. As part of the refine-

ments introduced in the 1970s, the divisional profit and loss system was altered to enable it to support long-term and short-term planning. Long-term planning was enhanced by including resource allocation, capital investment, and human resource planning. Short-term planning enhancements consisted of improving methods for both estimating and achieving profits.

By the late 1980s, SEI had adapted to the effects of the oil crisis and the high value of the yen. However, it faced an additional major challenge, that of becoming a truly global company. The company had set up manufacturing and marketing facilities in the United States, Europe, Australia, Southeast Asia, and Africa. In addition, it had managed the installation of ultra-high-voltage overhead transmission lines in many regions of the world, including Southeast Asia, the Middle East, and South America.

In the early 1990s, the increasing importance of its overseas affiliates had forced SEI's senior management to think of SEI as a global entity and not just a Japanese firm. Adopting a global perspective made it difficult, if not impossible, to ignore the well-being of the overseas affiliates and simply take actions that were most beneficial to SEI in Japan. These constraints were coupled with those imposed by SEI's membership in the Sumitomo keiretsu. The Sumitomo keiretsu contained 21 major companies, including Sumitomo Corporation (the group's trading company), Sumitomo Bank, Sumitomo Chemicals, and NEC. Unlike the major keiretsus, the Sumitomo keiretsu did not place many restrictions on the activities of its members. For example, member companies were free to buy products from outside the keiretsu if their price and quality exceeded those of the equivalent products produced internally.

The Kaizen Program

SEI had developed a sophisticated kaizen program to continuously reduce the cost of its products. A cost-reduction orientation emerged at SEI around 1955 because the union leaders believed that any salary increases they demanded should come out of their own efforts, not out of the pockets of the firm's other stakeholders. Responding to union requests, the firm began to invest heavily in human resource management (HRM). The objective of the new HRM system was to create pressure on the work force to increase its productivity.

At the heart of SEI's HRM approach was a willingness to increase the pay of the work force as it became more efficient. This HRM policy allowed the work force to demand higher pay in exchange for higher productivity. The success of this policy created a work force willing to become more efficient and to change the nature of their jobs as required. This flexibility allowed SEI to very rapidly and effectively introduce mass production despite the dislocations it caused in the workforce.

Under the new HRM policy, salaries consisted of three elements: base salary, bonus, and productivity enhancement bonus. Each year, the pool of funds provided to employees for their productivity efforts was determined for each facility based upon its productivity. Each individual's productivity enhancement bonus was determined by multiplying the individual's base pay (excluding bonus) by the appropriate factory's productivity ratio. This ratio was determined by dividing the total funds in the productivity pool by the total salary base of the participating employees. Thus, the pay scheme was designed to create positive pressure for increased productivity throughout the organization.

As the pay system evolved, the three salary elements were still maintained but the productivity enhancement bonus was not negotiated for all employees by the unions. In 1992, the productivity enhancement was set at just over 71% of base pay. This change in computation reflected the system's success in promoting a mentality of continuous improvement throughout the firm.

For the productivity incentive scheme to work, SEI had to be able to measure productivity improvements accurately. Several systems were developed or modified to support the productivity program, including two accounting systems—the total budget system and the direct cost system—as well as the blue-collar and white-collar cost reduction target programs.

Total Budget System   The productivity of SEI's work force increased significantly during the 1950s, so management adopted the total budget system (TBS). This system was integrated into SEI's existing productivity systems. The TBS remained relatively unchanged until the mid-1960s, when the firm adopted a divisional form.

SEI's divisional structure differed from that adopted by most Japanese firms. In SEI, the divisions were politically weaker and lacked full autonomy. For example, both finance and personnel were centralized functions and were managed at headquarters. The primary purpose of the divisions was to maximize their profits based upon the limited resources at their disposal. Se-

nior management at SEI had decided against divisional autonomy because it believed that such an organizational form would encourage the divisions to maximize their own economic welfare and not that of the overall firm. By keeping certain critical functions centralized, top management believed it was better able to optimize overall firm performance. The cost of this organizational form was a larger head office staff than was usual for a Japanese firm of SEI's size.

The adoption of a divisional structure created a problem for the existing cost and profit control systems because the manufacturing divisions, reflecting their product focus, produced products for a single product line or business segment while the sales divisions, reflecting their geographical and customer focus, sold products that were produced by many manufacturing divisions. For example, SEI's divisions included electric wires and cables, special steel wires, sintered alloy products, and brake products.

The new organizational form made it difficult to establish meaningful profitability statements for the manufacturing divisions because both sales prices and volumes were controlled by the sales divisions. To help overcome this problem, two additional evaluation systems were developed: the division profit and loss system and the sales department system. In both systems, the primary basis for performance evaluation was contribution margin. These systems were used for internal management purposes, not financial reporting purposes.

The research and development (R&D) laboratories were evaluated as cost centers because they did not generate revenues. However, their ability to produce output in the form of commercial products and the willingness of the internal market (i.e., the business divisions) to commercially develop the new products were monitored. SEI had created a three-stage procedure to bring products developed by its R&D laboratories to market. First, new products were released to the development room, which was part of R&D and which manufactured the new products in low volumes so that their long-term market potential could be evaluated. Development divisions were created for products that were thought to have market potential. Development divisions were expected to launch products and prove that they were capable of generating profits for the firm. These divisions were expected to break even; once a development division's revenue exceeded ¥5 million per month, it was either converted into a new operational division or merged with an existing one. Finally, administration departments were evaluated on their ability to reduce costs.

Blue-Collar Cost Reduction Program   Cost management, and cost reduction in particular, was considered critically important at SEI. In 1992, the overall objective of SEI's cost reduction program was to decrease costs by approximately 10% of profits per annum, or about ¥500 million. Cost reduction was considered so critical that it was attended to every day. Daily meetings were held to make everyone in the firm aware of the importance of managing and reducing costs. These daily meetings to set cost reduction targets did not have a name, because everyone in the firm understood their purpose. Daily plans were developed at each facility to determine ways to reduce costs. These plans were based upon the monthly budgets, which reflected the savings anticipated from the kaizen programs. The objectives of the daily meetings were to discuss the savings achieved the previous day and how they compared to the budget, and the savings expected to be achieved that day. The rate of achieving these cost savings was measured against the monthly budgets (see Figure 1). Cost reduction plans were prepared at the facility level and then consolidated at the divisional level to see if they provided an adequate cost reduction objective for the division.

Each facility was broken into a number of distinct manufacturing processes, each run by a self-directed work team. Usually, these groups were treated as cost centers and were responsible for collecting cost information. However, sometimes there were several groups within a cost center, in which case costs were collected at the group level, not at the cost-center level. The average factory had between 20 and 30 groups. Each group would identify its own cost reduction target for a six-month period. The only costs that were included in these targets were those that were directly under the control of the groups. Controllable costs included supplies such as the lubricants for the extrusion dies, machine maintenance, and the amount of labor consumed. Costs considered outside the groups' control were excluded, including wage rates and depreciation of equipment.

All blue-collar workers were very much aware of the cost system. Charts were posted throughout the factory that indicated both the cost of products and processes and the level of cost reduction achieved (the charts consisted of graphs or tables). This sharing of cost information was considered a critical part of the firm's kaizen program. Only by sharing the relevant cost and quality

information could management expect the workers to be able to most effectively achieve cost reduction by setting and committing to sensible targets.

The blue-collar workers were expected to reduce the costs of running their equipment. Given the different abilities and working conditions of the groups, it was not unusual to find that two identical machines cost different amounts to run in different groups. Such a discrepancy was not ignored, however; the group with the higher cost was expected to learn from the group with the lower cost and to bring its performance up to the same level of efficiency. The superior group was expected to create an environment where it continued to improve its efficiency; groups were not expected to rest on their laurels.

Two of the mechanisms used to encourage superior performing groups to keep improving were the awards ceremonies and model zone program. The superior groups' achievements were recognized in award ceremonies that were held in front of all factory personnel. There was great prestige associated with winning these awards more than once, thereby creating considerable pressure on superior-performing groups to keep improving their performance. The model zone program consisted of granting participating groups additional funds to find ways to increase their productivity. Groups volunteered to participate and their achievements were reviewed by a panel of judges that declared annual winners in the competition. Again, considerable prestige was associated with winning the competition.

The kaizen program created strong pressures to innovate. All groups were expected to imitate the innovations of other firms. Several mechanisms existed to help groups identify innovations that might be beneficial; these mechanisms included a special group at SEI head offices, the ready availability of publications that reported on innovations, membership in industrial groups, and attendance at seminars given by SEI's major customers, especially the automobile industry.

When investments in production process improvements were made, the blue-collar targets had to be changed to reflect the new conditions. To ensure that the new blue-collar target costs were appropriately set, the monitoring period was reduced from six months to three months. Once management was convinced that the new targets were appropriately set, the monitoring period returned to six months. The objective of this more frequent monitoring was to ensure that the targets were adjusted to reflect the new conditions and that the maximum target cost reductions were achieved. When the new conditions led to increased cost reduction targets, there was little problem; however, when the new conditions resulted in a decrease in the blue-collar target reductions, then the plant manager was expected to find ways to still achieve the overall cost reduction target for the plant.

The cost reduction targets were set at achievable levels (see Figure 2). The majority of groups achieved their cost reduction targets to within ±2%. Typically, between 10% and 20% of the groups failed to achieve their targets, with a similar percentage achieving higher savings. No statistics were kept on group performance because management considered it more important to monitor how each group performed rather than how close it came to its target.

The level of expected cost reduction depended upon the product. Some products had the potential for high kaizen savings, while the costs of other, more mature products were difficult to reduce. For this reason, no attempt was made to compare cost reduction performance across groups. Such comparisons were not made because management felt that they ignored the relative ease of achieving cost reductions.

For kaizen cost reductions, the trend was to delegate cost reduction to the factory level. In particular, management tried to use accounting data at that level. Previously, cost data had been collected at the factory level and then sent to the accounting department, where it was compiled into accounting information. This information was not subsequently used at the factory level, but rather at the division level to help report on divisional performance. The accounting department collected only the information it required to produce the financial reports; it did not collect information specifically for managerial purposes. To transfer ownership of accounting information from the accounting department to the shop floor, factory personnel began to prepare shop floor cost management information, and subsequently some of it was used by accounting department to produce financial reports.

Negotiation of Cost Reduction Targets

Group leaders were expected to negotiate their group's cost reduction targets. These negotiations were part of a hierarchical negotiations process, which was a mixture of informal and formal communications. Given the informality of some of the process, it is difficult to describe its exact sequence. The division managers were responsible for setting the cost reduction targets at both the division and group levels. The critical player in setting these targets was the plant manager, who had access to detailed information about what was happening on the factory floor and at the division level. The plant manager would act as the conduit between the factory floor and the divisional manager, helping him or her identify realistic stretch targets for each group. Once the informal targets were established, the groups entered formal negotiations to fine-tune the targets and commit to them.

SEI's budgeting procedure was used to formalize these negotiations. Budgets were prepared every six months, and were based upon sales forecasts provided by the marketing division and cost estimates provided by the plant managers. These cost estimates included allowances for the cost reduction targets negotiated by the divisional general manager, plant manager, and group managers. Reflecting its central objective—profit management—the basic budget plan was known as the profit plan.

The six-month profit plan was prepared in two stages. In the first stage, the first three months of the plan were enumerated individually and the second three months were averaged together. In the second stage, at the end of the third month, the remaining three months were estimated individually. Thus, although the profit plan covered a six-month period, it was reviewed quarterly.

Delegation of Cost Management to Workers

The plan to delegate cost management to the workers contained five major elements:

1. Workers were provided with cost information and were expected to manage with it.
2. Accounting was performed in the plants as well as at headquarters.
3. Some investment decisions were made by the blue-collar workers.
4. There were separate financial and management accounting systems.
5. Monthly meetings were held with blue-collar workers to evaluate plant and divisional performance.

The accounting system was used to determine when the division was not achieving its cost reduction targets. It was plant accounting's responsibility to draw attention to any cost reduction shortfalls and obtain an explanation from the division general managers as to why the planned cost reductions were not achieved. Every six months, a more thorough review was undertaken that included analyzing the cost reductions due to investments. Investment-related cost reduction analyses were only performed every six months because, unlike the blue-collar cost reductions, they required off-line calculations.

Direct Costing System   The primary system for the determination of contribution margin at SEI was the direct costing system (DCS). Within the divisional performance reporting system, the DCS played two critical roles: it formed the basis of the divisional profit and loss system, and it acted as the bridge between the financial and managerial accounting systems.

The DCS was first introduced in 1953 and had remained the basis for the firm's cost system ever since. Over the years, the system had been improved by increasing the level of detail it could report; these improvements were achieved primarily through automation. The DCS contained three major elements: a standard costing system, a direct costing system, and an annual standards revision procedure. The primary use of the standard costs reported by the DCS was to compute the split between cost-of-goods-sold and inventory valuation for financial accounting purposes. At year end, the actual results were used to calculate a conversion ratio that was used to convert cost of goods and inventory valuations from standard to actual for the year. This conversion ratio was computed by dividing total actual costs by total standard costs. Conversion ratios were determined for each of the firm's six product groups: electric wires and cables, special steel wires, sintered alloy products, brake products, hybrid products, and other products. Product groups identified SEI's major business areas (see Figure 3).

The design of SEI's cost system reflected the underlying production process. There were four major steps in the production process for insulated electrical wire: drawing the purchased wire to the appropriate gauge, stranding, insulation with PVC, and marking the wire. To determine the final cost of the wire required calculating the cost of the copper purchased from SEI's bare wire division, adjusting it for scrap levels and time to manufacture. The time to manufacture was the time taken to produce one kilometer of wire, plus set-up time. The cost per hour was determined by dividing the group's direct costs, including labor, energy, maintenance, and lubricants costs, by the group's hours of production.

One of the major purposes of the cost system was to determine the price of products. Prices were set in three

steps. First, the annual price for copper was set by the purchasing department, located at the firm's Tokyo head office. (An annual price, not a current price, was established because copper prices fluctuated daily, and since there was no mechanism for SEI to track actual material costs, a standard was required. An annual standard was chosen because it allowed the firm to monitor price changes across the year via the calculation of monthly price variances.) The purchasing department also set the annual price of all of the other metals used in SEI products. Second, the cost of the bare wire was set by the bare wire division, located in the Osaka Works. It was determined by adding the direct and indirect production costs to the scrap-adjusted cost of the copper. And third, the cost of the assembled products was determined by adjusting the material costs by the standard loss ratio to allow for material losses.

The standard loss ratio consisted of three factors: the loss ratio of surplus, the loss ratio of giveaway, and the loss ratio for scrap. The loss ratio of surplus captured the extra length of product that was unavoidably produced in the production process or consumed by inspection. The majority of the surplus loss ratio was caused by the production department running "a little extra" for each customer to ensure that the customer received at least the length of usable wire that was ordered. Obviously, if the customer received less than ordered, it would return the wire, which usually would have to be scrapped. Running a little extra avoided this problem. The loss ratio of giveaway was the difference between the planned and actual diameter of the product. Finally, the loss ratio for scrap captured the amount of PVC and other materials that were wasted at the beginning of a production run. This head loss was unavoidable because of the length of the machine and the way the wire was produced. For example, when polyethylene-coated wires were produced, the first few meters were scrapped because it took a while for the coating process to stabilize.

Standard loss ratios were determined by multiplying the loss ratio of surplus by the loss ratio of giveaway plus the loss ratio for scrap. Standard loss ratios were generated every year for each group of products, not for each product; product groups consisted of products that differed primarily by the gauge of the wire. For such product groups, the loss ratios were essentially identical among products. Any minor variations between products in a group were not considered worth tracking.

The reduction of the standard loss ratio was one of the critical objectives of the firm's kaizen program. Kaizen objectives for materials included getting the difference in the standard and actual gauge of the wire to be within specification but always negative. That is, if the specification was 50mm ± 5mm, the wire was always manufactured with a diameter between 45mm and 50mm. The objective for the loss ratio of giveaway was to reduce the loss ratio as much as possible. The kaizen program had been very successful, and many believed that the giveaway ratio was as low as it could be made without changing the machines.

The three loss ratios were monitored for each production run and the results were plotted in graphical form. These graphs were XY plots, and were displayed around each machine so that the blue-collar workers could see the improvements they were achieving. In the early days of the kaizen program, all investment recommendations were made by the staff engineers. Over time, the blue-collar workers began to make investment recommendations. This shift was driven in part by the kaizen objectives having been achieved for many of the production processes. These mature processes were so efficiently run that the workers could no longer see ways to improve them without investment in new equipment. For example, the rate of production of polyethylene-coated cable could only be increased if new coating equipment was purchased.

Use of Cost Information for Product Decisions

The high capital-intensity of wire manufacture, coupled with the high capacity of the machines, had led SEI to adopt a strategy of trying to sell large quantities of product at the lowest price. Top management believed that it was more important to maintain or gain market share than it was to be profitable. However, products were expected to at least cover their direct costs. The criteria for accepting a bid was that it should at least cover its direct, depreciation, and finance charges. If a product could not cover these charges, and it was a mature product with little opportunity for additional cost reduction, it became a candidate for cost reduction.

Department Unit Price

Department unit prices were determined by dividing the conversion cost by the total standard machine hours for each department at the Osaka Works. The conversion cost for each department was the sum of the wages and salaries, miscellaneous expenses (such as die lubricants), power, repair and maintenance, and other expenses (such as office supplies). The standard machine hours for each product were determined by summing the standard production time for one kilometer of wire plus the set-up time. One kilometer was used to develop the standard transfer price because it represented a consistent metric for all products. No attempt was made to develop a standard based upon more practical lengths because the length of wire produced in a single run depended upon each customer's order, and this varied widely. The advantage of the one-kilometer standard was that it could be applied to all products. The standard machine hours were adjusted by the operating loss ratio, which was given by dividing the manufactured length of the product by the ordered length.

Every month, variances were calculated that determined the difference between the standard and actual amount of each major element of conversion costs. These conversion cost variances were determined for each department. For example, the wage variance was calculated by multiplying the unit labor price by the actual machine hours consumed every month by each department. This estimated amount was compared to actual and the variance calculated. Each month, the conversion cost variances were plotted on the department's variance chart. Because the standards were set each April and based upon the previous year's performance, positive variances were expected to result from the various cost reduction efforts; these variances were expected to increase as the year progressed.

The effect of the blue-collar cost reductions was captured in the unit price variance. The actions taken to create these variances included reducing the number of people required to run a given machine, increasing the speed at which the machine was run, shifting to more expensive diamond dies because they lasted longer and therefore reduced unit cost, and reducing energy costs.

White-Collar Cost Reduction Program The white-collar cost reduction targets included costs that were considered uncontrollable in the blue-collar program. These costs included utilities, purchased parts for maintenance, office supplies, and white- and blue-collar wages. The white-collar program also differed from the blue-collar program in the range of activities that were anticipated. White-collar workers were expected to find ways to change the production processes in order to make them more efficient. In contrast, blue-collar workers were expected to accept the production processes as given and try to make them more efficient. In practice, though, this split in responsibilities was less clear, because it was not unusual for blue-collar workers to identify ways to change the production processes in order to make them more efficient. The range of techniques used to achieve white-collar cost reductions included investing in equipment, changing raw materials, changing production flows, introducing new manufacturing technologies (such as CIM), and redesigning products. For example, a typical white-collar cost reduction project was exploring the use of electricity instead of steam to heat polyethylene. If it could be shown that the switch to electric heating was cost-justified, then a proposal would be made; if accepted, the change would be made.

SEI's head office expected every staff member involved in the white-collar cost reduction program to develop an aggressive quarterly cost reduction plan. These individual plans were then combined into a divisional plan that was submitted to top management. If the total planned reductions did not meet the divisional target, then division management was expected to explain at the monthly director's board meeting why it could not find sufficient cost reduction opportunities. While the white-collar objectives were planned quarterly, their progress was monitored monthly.

Although the blue-collar workers were unaware of the market prices of the products they produced because their cost reduction targets were not sensitive to changes in selling prices, white-collar staff were held responsible for price changes. Therefore, the staff's cost reduction targets were adjusted to reflect any price changes. The objective of including sales price information was to make the staff sensitive to declining prices and hence declining profits. The primary objective of including price information was to ensure that no product became unprofitable. Product profitability was determined by adding indirect costs to the direct product costs reported by the firm's direct cost system. Indirect costs, which included white-collar salaries, equipment depreciation, sales personnel salaries, and engineering costs, were allocated to products based upon their membership in product groups. The ratio of direct to indirect costs for each of the firm's product groups was determined and this ratio was used for all of the products in that group. Thus, six different indirect to direct cost ratios were calculated, one per product group.

When the market price of a product declined and the product was at risk of becoming unprofitable, the staff cost reduction target was adjusted downwards. The extent of this downward shift was determined by the rate of price decline expected in the foreseeable future. The objective was to ensure that the product remained profitable. This new cost reduction target, because it was more aggressive than the previous target, required that white-collar workers go beyond kaizen and find ways to fundamentally change either the design of the product or its production processes. If it was not possible to maintain profitability, the product was at least expected to maintain a positive contribution. Any product that could not achieve a positive contribution was a serious candidate for redesign or discontinuance.

Thus, there were two types of cost reduction activities included in the white-collar program. The first was the ongoing continuous improvement activities; the second was the discontinuous activities that were triggered by products losing profitability. The second type of activity required "breakthroughs" in the way the products were manufactured.

Two groups of engineers supported the blue- and white-collar kaizen programs. The first group was involved in the continuous improvement program. The engineers in this group resided at the plants and were knowledgeable about the production processes. They would occasionally work with R&D personnel to increase the efficiency of existing production processes. The other group of engineers resided in the R&D laboratories; they were involved in the breakthrough projects that were initiated when a product was in danger of becoming unprofitable. For example, the price of optical fibers fell rapidly once the technology matured. The blue-collar program could not reduce costs fast enough to keep up. The engineers were required to find ways to triple the rate of production of the fibers on existing machines. A breakthrough was achieved but required that the glass blocks from which the fiber was drawn be manufactured in larger volumes. This technical problem had to be overcome before the cost of the optical fiber could be reduced sufficiently to make it profitable again.

Managing Indirect Costs   Responsibility centers were established for all indirect costs. Examples of indirect centers included administration-general, process engineering, R&D at the plants, quality control, and equipment analysis. Each indirect cost responsibility center was responsible for developing a six-month budget. Like other budgets, this was prepared with the first three months in detail and the last three averaged. The budget was expected to cover all of the center's expenses, including wages and salaries, overtime charges, travel, and office supplies. Each responsibility center submitted its budget to the division general manager for approval. Any discrepancies between corporate objectives and the center's budget were subject to negotiations before approval was received.

Some of the targets for the reduction of indirect costs were set by the budget section of the accounting department at the head office. This section was responsible for setting the corporate policy on indirect cost reduction. For example, it might set a corporate policy of reducing indirect costs by 3% for the year or reducing travel expenditures by 10%. These policies were communicated to the divisions and were expected to be incorporated into the divisional profit plans. The penalties for not achieving these policies depended upon economic conditions. In a stable economy, if a cost reduction plan was in place, as long as the division was profitable there was little penalty for not achieving the policy. In economic downturns, managers had to explain why they had not achieved the policy.

Indirect expenses were subject to monthly variance control. Every month, the variance for each indirect expense item was determined. If the cumulative variance for a line item was both negative and large, then a meeting was held to discuss the cause of the variance. At this meeting, the managers responsible for any cost overruns had to explain their lack of performance and promise to develop an action plan to bring the line item back under control.

Reducing indirect costs was particularly difficult because the largest portion of indirect costs was labor. Because all SEI labor was subject to lifetime employment, wages and salaries were essentially a fixed cost and could not be easily reduced in the short term. However, they could be reduced by natural attrition and reassignment.

The high proportion of fixed costs made it difficult to apply kaizen techniques to indirect expenses. Instead, the concept of savings dominated when the budgets for indirect costs were prepared. Kaizen suggestions were designed to permanently increase the efficiency of a process. Savings suggestions, in contrast, simply reduced the level of expenditure without changing the underlying efficiency of the process. For example, a savings suggestion might be to reduce the number of people that travel for a given task from two to one. This reduction would save money but it would not fundamentally change the way the task was performed.

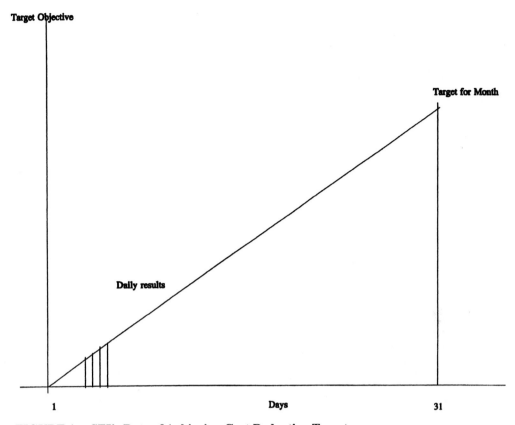

FIGURE 1   SEI's Rate of Achieving Cost Reduction Targets

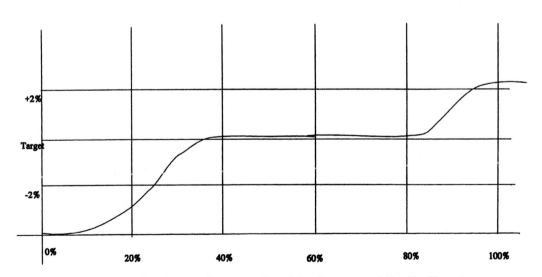

FIGURE 2   Probability Chart of a Group Reaching Between ±2% of its Target

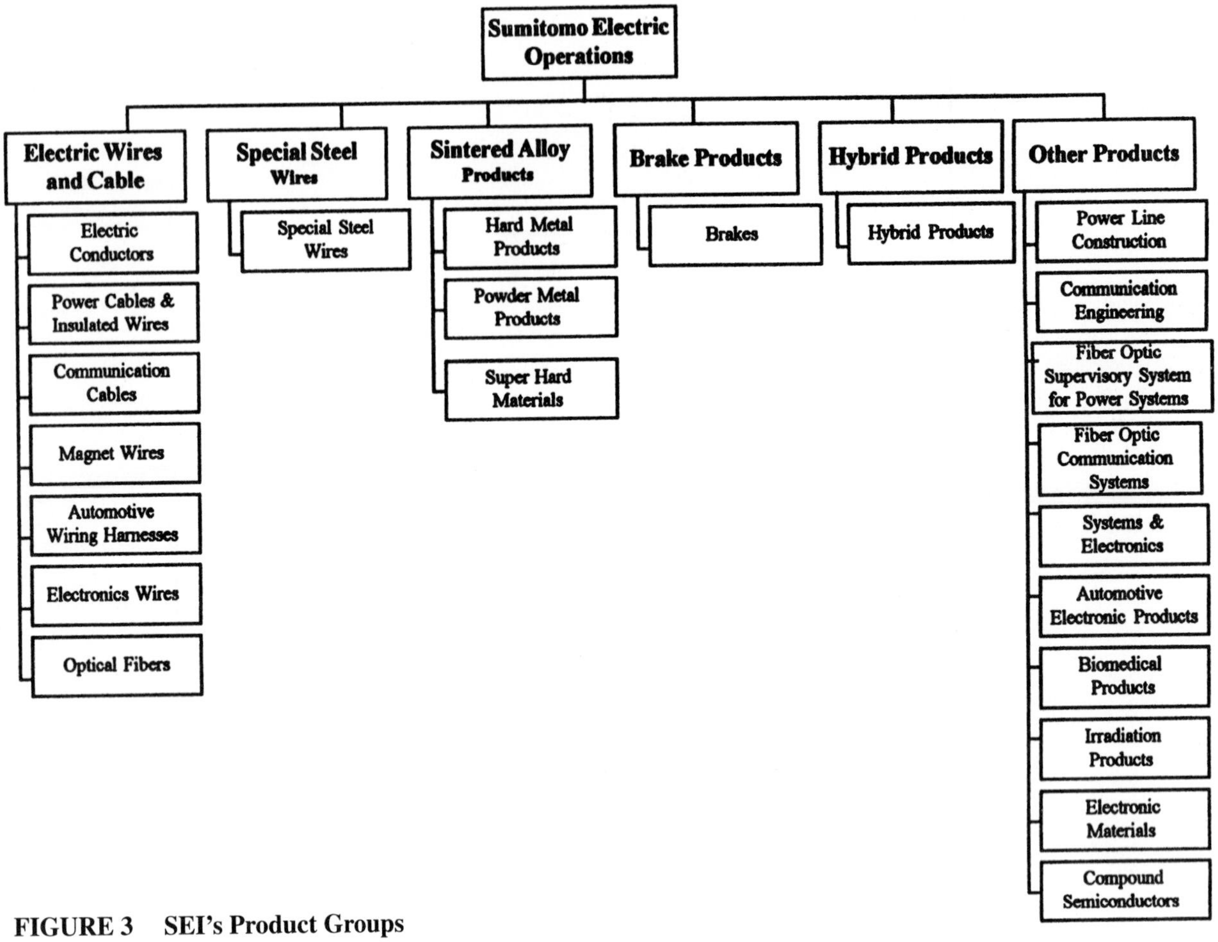

FIGURE 3   SEI's Product Groups

TEXAS EASTMAN COMPANY

Tom Wilson, Company Controller, reflected on the changing role for the Accounting Department in Texas Eastman Company's new operating environment.

Traditionally, Accounting was the recorder of history, but perhaps we were not directly relevant for the operational decisions taken every day by the departmental managers. We see the need to move accountants physically into manufacturing areas so that they can serve as financial advisors to manufacturing managers. But in order for them to function in this capacity, we need information on a real-time basis. Operators can see hundreds of observations on their processes every couple of hours, but we're issuing cost summaries only every four weeks. We need to break our frame of vision in order to develop more timely and useful information for operating employees.

Company Background

A visitor is unprepared for a first visit to the Texas Eastman (TEX) chemicals plant in Longview, Texas. No noxious smells or clouds of smoke hang over the 6,000-acre site, and one can almost imagine people fishing in the man-made ponds used as a source of cooling water for the plant. The TEX plant is one of six companies in the Eastman Chemicals Division of the Eastman Kodak Company. (Summary data on the Division appear in Exhibit 1.)

This case was prepared by Professor Robert S. Kaplan.
Copyright © 1989 by the President and Fellows of Harvard College. Harvard Business School case 190-039.

The Longview plant, established in 1950, produces about 40 chemical and plastic products that are sold to other manufacturers for conversion into construction, industrial, and consumer products. Nearly 9 million pounds of product per day were shipped during 1988. The location in Northeast Texas gives the plant easy access to the East Texas Oil Field for the primary inputs of ethane and propane. Well served by water, rail, and pipeline transportation, the plant consumes weekly the equivalent of 700 railcars of feedstock—propane and ethane—and 50 railcars of bituminous coal. Employment in 1988 was 2,650 persons. Of these, 1,560 were production workers and 760 worked in engineering and managerial positions.

In TEX's chemical processes, feedstock is converted in a cracking plant into ethylene and propylene. These olefin products are then further processed in chemical plants to produce a variety of alcohols, aldehydes, and specialty chemicals, and in polyolefin plants to make various forms of plastics and adhesives. Computerized models are used to optimize inputs and outputs as a function of current feedstock costs and the output prices of the plant's products.

Quality Management Program

The Eastman Chemicals Division made a strong commitment to Total Quality Management in 1983. Because of the strong dollar in the early 1980s, foreign goods were increasing their U.S. market penetration and customers soon discovered that not only were Japanese and European goods lower in price, they also had higher (more consistent) quality. The automotive industry, feeling the brunt from foreign imports, began to take action by developing their own comprehensive quality programs, such as Ford's Q-1 Program. In addition to internal efforts, the manufacturers began requiring that their suppliers produce delivered goods under Statistical Process Control (SPC).

The Eastman Chemicals Division established its quality policy in 1984. The division president articulated the overall quality goal, "to be the leader in quality and value of its products and services," and backed this goal with a statement of the 11 principles by which the quality goal could be achieved (see Exhibit 2). He hoped to instill an intense focus on quality throughout the organization.

The Quality Management Program was built on a Triangle Model of teamwork, performance management, and statistical process control. The teamwork leg, with its roots in the quality of work life, job enrichment, and employee participation literature, was implemented through quality management (QM) teams that permeated the organization. Every person in the plant, from the president to the lowest-skilled employee, served on at least one QM team. The teams were linked hierarchically by having members of each QM team serving on a team at a higher or a lower level of the organization so that ideas and programs developed at one level could be communicated throughout the organization.

The performance management leg was built on B. F. Skinner's behavioral school of psychology and reinforcement. It stressed the need for establishing Key Result Areas (KRA) and developing measures for each KRA. The performance management process used seven specific steps:

1. Define the *mission* in terms of the results the organization is expected to contribute.
2. Identify the *key result areas* critical to success in achieving the mission. Key result areas could be financial, safety, or environmental goals, or SPC implementation.
3. Define *measures* for each key result area that indicate how well the unit is performing its mission.
4. Decide how the measures will be *displayed* for monitoring to signal significant changes in measures.
5. Develop *control strategies* that outline a plan of action when significant changes in processes occur.
6. Develop plans to *reinforce* progress and achievements for each measure.
7. Implement *improvement projects* and *allocate resources* where they have the most impact on the key result areas.

The implementation of Statistical Process Control, the third leg of the quality management process, required an even more drastic change in TEX's operations. Prior to installing SPC procedures, operators were continually monitoring the hundreds of variables, such as temperatures, pressures, humidities, and flow rates, that governed the performance of each chemical process. As any variable moved away from its nominal mean value, operators would tweak the process, attempting to bring the variable back to its standard value. Frequently, this intervention introduced more variation into the final product than if the operators had left the process alone.

The first step along the route of complete SPC was to define upper and lower control limits for each process variable between which operator intervention should not occur. Because no computer capability existed in 1984 for manufacturing operations, the SPC charts had to be plotted by hand and analyzed manually. If an observation were outside the control limit, specific actions were defined to bring the parameter back into control. Runs tests were performed to detect consistent positive or negative biases even while each observation remained within the control limits. Taguchi methods were employed that mathematically modeled operations so that process variation—the distance between the upper and lower control limits—could be reduced even further. But TEX's quality initiatives were limited by the enormous amount of data that had to be collected, analyzed, and stored manually.

Information Systems

TEX operating personnel had, for years, been collecting extensive data on operating processes. Operators were assigned to take readings on 180 routes throughout the plant every two to four hours. The data collection process yielded between 30,000 and 40,000 observations on the plant's process parameters (such as temperatures, pressures, flow rates, and tank levels) every four hours. These data were entered on preprinted, multicolumn worksheets that the operators carried on clipboards as they toured their routes. Clerks entered output data from the worksheets into the daily production report and then sent the process sheets to a nearby warehouse where they were stored in filing cabinets.

Each day, department managers personally reviewed the data collected from operations of the day before. This next-day review, however, conflicted with TEX's current emphasis on quality. The review would frequently detect unfavorable trends in key operating parameters much too late, enabling many pounds of product to be produced with varying product characteristics. Even though only a small fraction of off-spec material might be produced, the variations in product characteristics could create problems for customers' production processes.

When customers complained about variations in product characteristics, or when TEX people themselves detected unusual variations in products or operations, an engineer would go to the warehouse, occasionally spending many hours locating the relevant worksheets for the particular product or operating department. Once the data were located, the engineer performed an extensive analysis, attempting to learn which

parameters might have been outside normal limits. The search and analysis process was tedious, requiring several days or even weeks of work, and occasionally some of the needed process sheets could not be found in the extensive and often cluttered, storage files. Attempts at process improvement were also limited by the availability of operating data only on the paper worksheets in the warehouse storage files.

The first step in providing more accessible information for real-time quality analysis was taken in 1986 with the installation of the Manufacturing and Technical (M&T) system. A stand-alone computer was acquired for manufacturing to accumulate and store operating data and perform the statistical analysis. Exhibit 3 shows the extent of the data collection in the plant by major operating division. About 15% of the observations were updated automatically, about once per minute. The remainder were updated every two to four hours. Because of the SPC analysis, fewer data points were being collected than in 1984.

By 1988, the M&T system had been significantly supplemented by a more general and flexible information system embracing both extensive Digital Equipment Corporation VAX clustered computing and advanced software packages. One package, purchased from an external vendor, monitored those departments equipped with electronic control systems to perform automatic SPC analysis, historic graphs of data, and automatic alarm processing. A second system fed data from daily production reports into the financial control system. The third, using advanced programming techniques, enabled operators to specify which SPC tests should be performed on the operating data, and if an out-of-control situation were detected, generated a recommended course of action to bring the process back into control. By early 1989, 200 such analytic models had been written. A fourth system provided statistical summaries of operations for individual departments and analysts. The reports included information on shipments and production, process improvements, control limits, historical analyses, and incidence and disposition of customer complaints.

Existing Accounting System

TEX prepared fully allocated actual cost reports for its operating departments every four weeks. Direct manufacturing and delivery costs were 90% of total costs, manufacturing supervision and clerical costs were 5%, and general factory overhead and support (including computer expenses) represented the remaining 5% of costs. Almost all costs could be traced to individual plants and departments on an actual consumption basis.

An Annual Operating Plan (AOP) was prepared in October and November for the subsequent year. The AOP incorporated all budgets, standards, and plans for the next year. Sales quantities and prices were provided by Marketing. Each support group provided forecasts of prices for materials, supplies, and utilities. The Accounting Department then prepared forecasts of departmental and product costs based on this information. The departmental and product cost forecasts became the baseline against which plant performance was measured.

At the end of each four-week reporting period, Accounting received information about actual departmental costs and production quantities. It multiplied production quantities by variable standard costs and added AOP fixed-cost items to obtain a plan unit cost for each product and department. Five variances were computed and reported back to department managers.

1. *Usage variance*: The effect on unit cost of using more or less of an item than planned; measured as the change in input quantity consumed for a given level of output, evaluated at standard prices.
2. *Price variance*: The effect on unit cost of a change in the price of an input, based on actual consumption of each input. Only price variances for labor and for materials and supplies purchased from outside vendors were included in the price variance.[1]
3. *Volume variance*: The effect on unit cost of not operating at the planned capacity utilization. The volume variance reconciled differences in unit costs due to spreading fixed costs over varying volumes.
4. *Change in standard variance*: The effect of not implementing a planned change in operations or of implementing an unplanned change. It represented the difference between the current standard and the planned standard. Any capital authorization with a justification based on cost savings or output increase was always translated into a change in future standards.
5. *Mix variance*: The effect, in a multiproduct facility, of producing with an actual product mix different from the planned mix, or of producing a nonstandard ratio of formulas for a given product class.

The sum of the five variances equaled the difference between total departmental costs and total plan cost. Exhibit 4 shows the format for a sample Departmental Cost Sheet. At the bottom of the cost sheet, the five variances were split into controllable and noncontrollable components:

Controllable	Noncontrollable
Volume	Volume
Change in standard	Change in standard
Usage	Price
	Mix

The total volume variance was classified into both controllable and noncontrollable components. Reductions in volume due to shortages of input materials or lack of sales demand were treated as a noncontrollable variance. The manager received a *controllable unfavorable* volume variance when the department produced less than demand and demand was below capacity. The manager received a *controllable favorable* volume variance only when demand was high and he was able to operate his plant beyond rated capacity.

Controllable change in standard variances represented changes in operations under the control of department managers (such as staff levels and material yield changes). In addition to the planned changes in standards resulting from capital expenditures, the standard for any cost element that had experienced a consistently favorable variance during the year would be changed by at least 50% of the annual mean favorable variance.[2] Changes in standards initiated by the Accounting Department, such as labor rates, depreciation adjustments, and changes in accounting methods, were considered department noncontrollable.

The Departmental Cost Sheets were typically issued 12 to 15 days after the close of each four-week reporting period. The Accounting Department performed analytic studies of the information before its people walked the reports over to explain the results to each Departmental Manager.

Variances for all operating departments were summarized on Division Cost Summaries for division superintendents and upper management. These summaries included the plant total cost variance as well as

---

[1]No price variance was generated for materials and supplies produced by other TEX departments since these variances were already incorporated in those departments' cost sheets. These internal price variances, called Prior Department Variances, however, were shown on the consuming department's cost sheets so that the department manager could consider alternative suppliers or materials if the variance was significant.

[2]The 50% factor reflected a compromise between Accounting and Operations. Departmental managers were reluctant to incorporate 100% of the gain since they did not want to risk unfavorable variances in subsequent years.

controllable variances for each department and division. Finally a report was issued each period for the President, Director of Administration, and Comptroller that summarized the manufacturing cost of TEX products and gave explanations for significant variances from the AOP.

Pat Kinsey, Chief Accountant, explained the rationale for the plant's elaborate hierarchy of cost reports as follows:

> The goal of our cost reporting system is to provide to managers on all levels the information they need to manage their areas of responsibility, from the production manager concerned with the efficient operation of the cost centers under his control to the senior members of management who must decide which products to produce and how to allocate company resources. Our system works fine for responsibility accounting and emphasizing controllable variances. But the information is received too late for analyzing the financial consequences from most operating decisions. Our operations personnel must rely on their daily review of key indicators (such as production, yields, and equipment availability) to learn how their operation is performing. To understand more clearly the problem of delayed and aggregate financial information, you could think of the department manager as a bowler, throwing a ball at pins every minute. But we don't let the bowler see how many pins he has knocked down with each throw. At the end of the month we close the books, calculate the total number of pins knocked down during the month, compare this total with a standard, and report the total and the variance back to the bowler. If the total number is below standard, we ask the bowler for an explanation and encourage him to do better next period. We're beginning to understand that we won't turn out many world-class bowlers with this type of reporting system.

The Threebee Company

Steve Briley, Department Manager of Cracking Plant 3B, had recently devised a supplemental departmental financial report for his operating department.

> The diagram of the cracking process is very simple. We have two inputs of natural gas and energy, and we produce two main products, ethylene and propylene, plus several byproducts, such as hydrogen and methane gas. But inside the black box that converts feedstock into propylene and ethylene is an incredibly complex chemical process with thousands of control points, multilevel refrigerants, and recycling intermediate products.

> Operators had little information to help them make decisions about tradeoffs among production output, quality, and cost. For example, we could crack gas at higher temperatures and get more conversion of raw material into main and byproducts. But this is costly both in terms of achieving the higher temperatures and in wear and tear of the equipment. Also, as we push the cracking plant to maximize the rate of production, it becomes much more difficult to keep quality under control. We face constant tradeoffs among cost, production output, and quality but have virtually no information to point us in the right direction in making these tradeoffs.

Briley took an unconventional approach to solving this problem by creating a fictitious company for his employees and developing a simple financial statement for that company. The Threebee Company was formed in September 1987, and each employee in Plant 3B was issued a share of stock (see Exhibit 5). Briley then created an income statement for the Threebee Company (see Exhibit 6).

> In preparing the income statement, the quantities for outputs produced and inputs consumed were readily available from the daily production report. I needed to supply prices. I estimated the prices for ethylene and propylene and several byproducts (hydrogen, methane, and steam) from nominal market values for these products. It wasn't important to get these prices precisely right, as long as I was in the right ballpark for them. I introduced one wrinkle by recognizing different prices for in-spec and off-spec material. Threebee would earn the full price for ethylene and propylene only if the product was within the upper and lower control limits (set initially at 3 sigma). If product was outside the control limits but still within rated specifications, the product price was set at half the normal price. This 50% discount was a little arbitrary, but I tried to approximate the discounts that final producers might face when selling substandard product. No revenues (zero price) would be earned for material produced outside of specifications.

> The basis for the input prices for feedstock and utilities were actual costs, which turned out to be reasonably close to the plant's standard costs. But I would occasionally adjust these costs for additional emphasis. For example, I increased the price of cooling water since the company was starting a conservation drive and I wanted to encourage operators to be even more thrifty with cooling water.

> For equipment costs, I computed a mortgage payment for the capital invested in the department based on a rough estimate of the replacement cost and the company's cost of capital. This figure remained constant in each report, of course, but I wanted the operators to be aware of the cost of the equipment they worked with. I also opened up a loan repayment account to repay any capital expenditures made for product or quality improvements. And I added an additional category, called Other Costs, as a target for some future cost reduction program. My goal was to start

the Threebee Company off in a zero profit condition, after paying the cost of capital, so that even a zero profit would reflect a good return on investment.

Briley encountered some initial skepticism from his colleagues about whether workers would understand or respond to an income statement to evaluate their efforts. He responded as follows:

> In my experience, the operators were able and willing to use a new tool, such as this profit statement, as long as they were given sufficient explanation and enough time to grow accustomed to it. Some operators had never worked with an income statement before, and it took some time to explain the concept to them. Fortunately, several of the operators had small businesses on the side, selling crops or raising livestock, and they were familiar with an income statement format. They helped to explain the concept to the others. More than the details of the income statement, it was the whole change in culture that took some time to get used to. In the past, TEX had never shared financial information with operating people. We just gave the operators specific rules — "Do this, don't do that, watch out for this condition" — but never told them about the economics of the business they were running.

Once the daily income statement had been designed, data such as actual outputs produced, their quality, and the actual quantities of inputs consumed were obtained from the daily production record. With these data, Briley personally prepared the Threebee Company income statement each day.

> The operators' first reaction to the income report was surprise about the cost of raw materials and energy consumed in the plant each day. They had no idea about the financial scale of operation of the 3B plant, or how their actions produced large effects on the costs and revenues of the plant. By varying our feedstock inputs, we can shift the ratio of ethylene to propylene production, but that change may require more inputs, decrease total production, and influence the amount of byproduct produced. On a cost basis this may look bad, but if the sales value of the production is greater, the operators can see that the company is better off even though output is down and costs are up.

As operators made suggestions for improving the format or the calculations, Briley soon found himself working 12 hours a day to keep abreast of his normal supervisory responsibilities plus producing the daily Threebee income statement.

> When I was away on business, one of the first things the operators wanted me to do when I returned was calculate the profits for the days I missed. They would be disap-

pointed if results were bad during that period because it was too late for them to correct any problems.

Briley's initial goal had been to double the current operating profit of the plant.

> Even though I tried to start from a zero profit condition, our September 87 operations were yielding a period (four-week) profit of about $200K, mostly because the plant was producing more than standard. I set a goal of achieving a period profit of $400K. If we could hit that figure, I promised to install a new kitchen in the control room for the operators.

> We kept charts, updated daily, of daily profits and cumulative profits for the period [see Exhibit 7]. It only took the operators four periods to achieve the $400K rate of profit, and along the way we broke five new production records for ethylene and propylene. Operators were posting quality statistics every two hours, and quality measures had improved by 50%. Operators had gotten so good at having all material within the 3-sigma limits, we agreed to set a more challenging target by reducing the upper and lower control limits to 2 sigma.

Briley felt satisfied and suspended the program when the higher outputs and quality enabled the $400K profit goal to be achieved. The operators and supervisors had their new kitchen, but they told Briley that they missed the daily calculations. They had enjoyed seeing the daily income statement and the challenge of achieving profit targets. Briley responded as follows:

> One of our Threebee Company officers is a computer whiz. He decided to write software so that the daily report could be prepared automatically, using data the operators entered into the system. Now when operators come in each day at 7 A.M. to start their shift, they look first at the profit report for the previous day. When I show up, an operator immediately tells me about yesterday's profits, happy when they had had a good day and disappointed when profits had declined.

Operators and supervisors in the 3B plant were using the information from the daily income statement to make decisions that formerly they were forbidden to make or else they had taken to Briley for approval. According to Briley,

> When the company started the Quality Management Program, we had told the operators not to tweak flow rates or change operating conditions without prior approval from their supervisor. They were to hold feed rates and operating conditions constant. Within several periods of operations of the Threebee Company, operators had learned how to tweak the system to *increase* profit; they're taking ac-

tions now that they formerly were not allowed to do. They have also learned to focus on a few key items and really keep an eye on those. For example, they found that if propylene quality is good, everything else was working pretty well, so propylene impurities are monitored continuously. They have also narrowed the control limits for many operating parameters to guarantee that the product is never outside the 100% price limits. In fact, they got so good at this I had to build in a new challenge. I established a top-grade gold quality region and set a 25% price premium for product falling within the gold region. My rationale was that the higher-quality product could be sold to new outside customers at this higher price.

The operators were also more willing to take action when I wasn't around. For example, one night a hydrogen compressor failed. Normally, repair efforts would have been undertaken on a routine, nonexpedited basis. But the shift supervisor on duty had just seen the value of hydrogen gas from the income report. Knowing the value of the lost output of hydrogen gas, he made an immediate decision to authorize overtime to get the compressor repaired and back on line as soon as possible.

Briley was asked how he used the Period Departmental Cost Reports that he received from the Accounting Department:

> Some data are only available from the Period Report. For example, I don't see daily maintenance records, so we're using budgeted numbers in the Daily Income Statement. The Period Report shows me actual maintenance costs and helps me to calibrate and monitor our maintenance activity. The Period Report also forces us to reconcile between meter readings we take locally and plantwide meterings. Because of metering discrepancies, we need to absorb a pro-rata allocation of deviations between local and plantwide meterings.

Gayle English, a production Division Superintendent, provided additional comments about the cost reports he received from Accounting.

> The problem with the Period Report is that the information comes too late—a cost incurred near the start of a period will not be reported until six or seven weeks later—and results from all the events of that period are aggregated together. As a result, production people often pay little attention to the financial reports since they already know about any chronic problems.

> TEX, historically, had shared cost information with departmental managers but was reluctant to disclose information on product profitability. Virtually no financial data had been provided to the operators. With the new report, operators were really surprised about the costs of materials being consumed in the cracking process. Even the costs of small items like filters or half-filled bags of material that

they might have been throwing away or discarding surprised them. They never appreciated the cost consequences of things they were doing.

Jerry Matthews, an Assistant Department Superintendent, offered his observations on how the Daily Income Statement changed the roles of the operators.

> Initially the work teams were not used to selecting and working on projects. They had to be fed ideas from department managers. But as they got more comfortable with the reports and with the freedom they had, they started to take more initiatives. Without having good measures, it would have been difficult to get them interested and involved and to take the ownership for the processes they were controlling. The financial data, on costs and profits, turned out to be a lot more meaningful to them than just trying to control quantities of steam. It helped them set priorities among different projects. Before, they may have been concentrating on controlling one part of the process which cost only $200 per day. Now they can set priorities to focus where their efforts can have the greatest impact.

> For example, before we established different prices for in-spec and out-of-spec material, it was hard to mobilize enthusiasm about quality. Occasionally, the cracking department might ship off-spec material to downstream processing plants. Those plants accepted the material but eventually paid a higher price for doing so. They had to perform more purges to get rid of impurities from their chemicals, they might have more rework, and their catalysts would get fouled up sooner. This really ran up the costs of the processing department, but the costs were attributed to that department, not to the supplying department that created the problem. Now, by putting a lower price on off-spec material from the cracking plant, we have everyone's attention.

> The daily financial reports have also become a tool for my decision making. I need to decide whether to shut down the plant for maintenance for six days or for eight days. The Daily Income Statement helps me decide whether the additional improvements are worth two more days of shutdown. I can trade off overtime and higher rates of spending during the maintenance period in return for getting the plant back on line one or two days earlier. When demand falls, I can ask whether it is better to run at a reduced rate or to keep producing at capacity and then shut down for a few days.

Matthews reflected on the changes brought about by the new systems at TEX.

> There's so much information out there, and we're still learning how to use it effectively. An operator always has more demands for his time than he can deliver. Which problems should he solve to have the greatest impact? Operators can now see the relative priority of raw material costs versus maintenance costs versus other categories.

With the Daily Income Statement, we've empowered the operators, making our mission statements about teamwork and ownership real. Doors are opening up; it's mind boggling. It's like giving someone a car who formerly only had a horse. There are new directions and distances we can now consider traveling.

Accounting Department Reactions

Jess Greer, a cost analyst in the Accounting Department, wondered about the changing role for the finance function in the new operating environment of the TEX plant.

There's certainly been a lot of interest in Threebee's Daily Income Statement, and the people seem very enthusiastic about it. In finance, we have been trying to be responsive. Financial information is being used for more and more things. We introduced statistical control limits on some of the variance analysis reports and adjusted standards rapidly to current operating conditions. We're also doing a lot more analytic work on the numbers to explain deviations between actual and standard. The finance people are working much more closely with operations, giving them information which seems to be helping them to manage. But we can clearly do more to improve the delivery of the existing cost system, to make it more timely and to switch from paper to electronic presentation.

Tom Wilson, Company Controller, concurred with the need for the finance function to go beyond its traditional role.

Continuous improvement requires very rapid, accurate timely feedback. I don't see how we can maintain our continuous improvement efforts without some kind of daily operating report. Our focus of attention has to be to get cost information to the first-level teams, the people on the line turning the valves that operate the plant.

The senior managers in Accounting were highly supportive of the Threebee initiative but wondered about its implications for the overall system of financial reporting at TEX. They were uncertain about the consequences if every department developed its own financial summaries. The businesspeople at the top of the organization were used to making decisions based on the Period Cost Reports, and they expected the financial reports for each department to tie into the results for the plant as a whole. They would not want individual department managers thinking they were doing a terrific job when the plant as a whole was showing poor performance. Among the questions confronting the senior Accounting managers were the following:

Should there be two systems, the official financial one and one for departmental operations? If each department develops its own financial system, how should the local departmental reports be reconciled with the upper management reports?

EXHIBIT 1

TEXAS EASTMAN COMPANY
Eastman Chemicals Division: Summary
of Operating Results
($000,000)

	1988	1987	1986
Sales	$3,033	$2,600	$2,378
Operating earnings	628	388	227
Assets	2,875	2,514	2,266
Capital spending	475	394	314

EXHIBIT 2

TEXAS EASTMAN COMPANY

EASTMAN CHEMICALS DIVISION
QUALITY POLICY

QUALITY GOAL
To be the leader in quality and value of products and services

QUALITY MANAGEMENT PROCESS
- Establish mission, vision, and indicators of performance.
- Understand, standardize, stabilize, and maintain processes.
- Plan, do and reinforce continual improvement and innovation.

OPERATIONAL POLICY
- Achieve process stability and reliability.
- Control every process to the desired target.
- Improve process capability.

PRINCIPLES WHICH SUPPORT AND ENABLE ACHIEVEMENT
OF THE QUALITY GOAL

CUSTOMER FOCUS	Emphasize understanding, meeting, and anticipating customer needs.
CONTINUAL IMPROVEMENT	Current level of performance can be improved.
INNOVATION	Everyone searching for creative process, product, and service alternatives.
PROCESS EMPHASIS	Focus on processes as the means to prevent defects and improve results.
MANAGEMENT LEADERSHIP	Create an inspiring vision, maintain constancy of purpose, and establish a supportive environment.
EMPLOYEE INVOLVEMENT	Every employee participates in decision making and problem solving, along with teamwork among all functional areas and organizational levels.
STATISTICAL METHODS	All employees understand the concept of variation and apply appropriate statistical methods to continual improvement and innovation.
PERFORMANCE MANAGEMENT	Take pride in work through clear accountabilities, feedback, reinforcement, and removing barriers.
EDUCATION AND TRAINING	Encourage learning and personal growth for everyone throughout their career.
CUSTOMER AND SUPPLIER RELATIONS	Build long-term partnerships with customers and suppliers.
ASSESSMENT	Benchmark against world best and assess performance against the Quality Policy for improvement planning and reinforcement.

E.W. Deavenport, Jr.
President

EXHIBIT 3

TEXAS EASTMAN COMPANY
Data Collection Statistics

DIVISION	NUMBER OF ROUTES	NUMBER OF OBSERVATONS
Olefin	27	6,800
Oxo-ethylene products	51	12,100
Polyethylene	28	3,600
Polypropylene-eastobond	30	3,700
Utilities	20	3,100
Supply and distribution	8	600
Totals	164	29,900

EXHIBIT 4

TEXAS EASTMAN COMPANY

RESTRICTED INFORMATION TEX 7112-01	TEXAS EASTMAN COMPANY DEPARTMENTAL COST OF MANUFACTURE CHEMICAL ONE MFG. PLANT 1			SHEET NO. 98 THIRD PERIOD ISSUED 03/31/89		
				ACTUAL	PLANNED	VARIANCE
CHANGE IN STANDARD						
PERIOD BASIS				$1,000*	$2,000	$3,000*
YEAR-TO-DATE BASIS				2,000*	2,000	4,000*

PRODUCTION		DEPARTMENTAL COST THIS PERIOD			DEPARTMENTAL COST THIS YEAR		
PERIOD	80,000						
YEAR	169,000		VARIANCE FROM STANDARD			VARIANCE FROM STANDARD	
		AMOUNT	AMOUNT	UNIT	AMOUNT	AMOUNT	UNIT
Raw materials		$35,000	$2,500	$.0313	$82,000	$8,500*	$.0503*
Recoveries							
Packing materials							
Net materials		35,000	2,500	.0313	82,000	8,500*	.0503*
Labor and benefits		10,000	2,000*	.0250*	26,000	2,700*	.0160*
Manufacturing supplies		1,200	500	.0063	1,900	3,200	.0190
Maintenance and repairs		8,800	1,200	.0150	29,000	1,000	.0060
Plant utilities		5,000	1,200*	.0150*	12,000	3,700*	.0219*
Other expenses							
Laboratory							
Planning and production records							
General plant							
Depreciation, insurance, and taxes		3,000			9,000		
Miscellaneous					700	700*	.0042*
Underground storage							
Work done for/by other							
Materials handling							
Storage and shipping							
Waste treatment							
Total conversion cost		28,000	1,500*	.0188*	78,600	2,900*	.0172*
Total departmental cost		$63,000	$1,000	$.0125	$160,600	$11,400*	$.0675*

			VARIANCES			
COST SUMMARY		DEPARTMENTAL COST	USAGE/ PRICE	VOLUME/ MIX	CHANGE IN STANDARD	AOP
Period—Amount		$63,000	$500*	$12,500	$3,000*	$72,000
Unit		.7875	.0063*	.1563	.0375*	.9000
Year—Amount		160,600	14,200*	15,345	4000*	157,745
Unit		.9503	.0841*	.0908	.0237*	.9223

Variance Analysis

		DEPARTMENT CONTROLLABLE			DEPARTMENT NONCONTROLLABLE		
	CHANGE IN STANDARD	USAGE	PRODUCT VOLUME	PRICE	CHANGE IN STANDARD	DEMAND VOLUME	PRODUCT MIX
Period	2,000*	1,000	1,335*	1,500*	1,000*	8,902*	4,933
Year	3,000*	11,400*	4,750*	2,800*	1,000*	2,228	17,867

EXHIBIT 5
TEXAS EASTMAN COMPANY

INCORPORATED UNDER THE LAWS OF THE STATE OF TEXAS

Threebee Company

NUMBER
47

3

SHARES
1

PAR VALUE:

ONE FULL MEASURE OF DEDICATION

QUALITY, QUANITY, SAFETY

This Certifies that _Paul D. Fokenlogen_ is the
registered holder of _one full_ Shares

THREEBEE COMPANY
A wholly owned subsidiary of the
Olefin Division

In Witness Whereof, the said Corporation has caused this Certificate to be
signed by its duly authorized officers and its Corporate Seal to be hereunto affixed
this _11_ day of _September_ A. D. 19 _87_

SECRETARY James H. Cox, Jr.

Royce Ford
PRESIDENT

EXHIBIT 6

TEXAS EASTMAN COMPANY

Daily Profit Statement for Threebee Company 1988 April 21

			$/day	
Sales				
Steam	+ 600#	87,938 lb/hr	8,416	
	+ 160#	11,972 lb/hr	1,068	
	− pyro	24,516 lb/hr	2,368	
	− 30#	11,624 lb/hr	1,037	
	Net	63,770	$6,079	
Ethylene:	Hi grade	776,042 lb/day	124,167	
	Lo grade	0 lb/day	0	0% out
	Waste	0 lb/day	0	
	Total	776,042	$124,167	
Propylene:	Hi grade	358,280 lb/day	68,073	
	Lo grade	32,429 lb/day	3,081	8.3% out
	Waste	0 lb/day	0	
	Total	390,708	$71,154	
Hydrogen,	capacity	7 lines	$57,708	
Methane,	capacity	9 lines	5,058	
Heavies		(fixed for now)	1,732	
Total sales			$265,898	
Costs				
Feedstock:	Ethane	227,865 lb	6,471	
	Propane	1,595,066 lb	108,305	
	Total	1,822,930 lb	$114,776	
Maintenance and repair (1987 avg.)			$4,168	
Utilities:				
Electricity		1,234 amps	8,359	
Cooling water		4.8 lines	4,109	
Natural gas		3.1 lines	3,442	
Other (typical)			607	
Total utilities			$16,517	
Other costs			$45,714	
Total cost of goods sold			$181,175	
Loan repayment			0	
Mortgage			$54,946	
Total costs			$236,122	
Gross profit			$29,776	
Less taxes @ 35%			$10,422	
Net profit*			$19,354/day*	

*Equivalent to $541,923/period profit.

EXHIBIT 7

TEXAS EASTMAN COMPANY

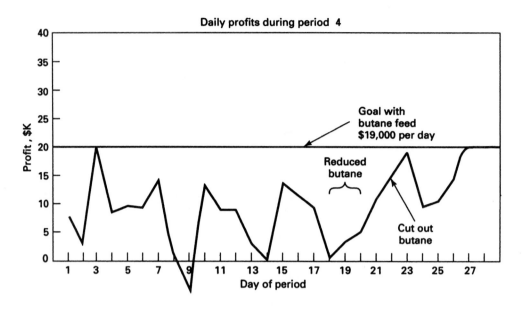

Daily profits during period 4

HIGASHIMARU SHOYU COMPANY, LTD. (A): PRICE CONTROL SYSTEM

The Higashimaru Shoyu Company, Ltd., a manufacturer of soy sauce, was formed in 1942 by the merger of the Kikuichi Shoyu Goshi Gaisha and Asai Shoyu Gomei Gaisha companies. The name of the new firm, Higashimaru, was made up of two Kanji symbols: higashi, which means east, and maru, which means circle. Higashi was chosen because the Asai Gomei warehouse was east of the Tatsuno castle. Maru was chosen because placing the Kanji symbol for east in a circle created the firm's distinctive trademark (see Exhibit 1).

Higashimaru's 1992 sales were approximately ¥21 billion. The firm employed 510 people and was capitalized at ¥545 million. It produced a variety of products, the most important of which was light soy sauce. The firm also produced dark soy sauce, Japanese-style porridge, Japanese-style salad dressings, sweet sake (which was used as a seasoning in cooking), soup stocks, and noodle sauces. In 1992, the firm produced over 200 different products in approximately 650 packaging forms.

There were two major types of soy sauce, dark and light. Dark soy sauce was deep brown in color and was used primarily as "kake joyu," i.e., for pouring over food and as a dipping sauce. Light soy sauce was lighter brown in color and had a saltier, well-balanced, and more refined taste. Light soy sauce was developed in the Kansai area around Kyoto in the seventeenth century. At that time, the cooking style of the Kansai area was devoted to maintaining natural colors. The advantage of the lighter soy sauce was that it hardly changed the color of food.

The salt content of light soy sauce exceeded 18%; for dark soy sauces it was between 16% and 17%. Unlike dark soy sauce, light soy sauce was produced by using higher concentrations of salt, keeping the sterilization temperature about 5° centigrade lower, and reducing the sterilization time by rapidly cooling the sterilized liquid instead of letting it cool naturally. In recent years, two low-salt varieties of soy sauce had been developed in response to concerns over the adverse health effects of high-salt diets. These sauces were Asajio Soy Sauce, or low salt content soy sauce, which had a salt content of about 14%, and Genen Soy

Professor Robin Cooper of the Peter F. Drucker Graduate Management Center at The Claremont Graduate School prepared this case.

Copyright © 1994 by the President and Fellows of Harvard College. Harvard Business School case 195-050.

Sauce, or reduced salt content soy sauce, which had a salt content between 7% and 8%. The only other significant change in industry practice in recent years was the introduction of bulk delivery of soy sauce to prepared food manufacturers.

Higashimaru produced 80 types of soy sauce. These included Premium Light Soy Sauce and Premium Dark Soy Sauce. The market for light soy sauce remained strongly regional. Most light soy sauce was consumed in Kansai and surrounding areas. In Tokyo, which was only about 600 kilometers west of Tatsuno, dark soy sauce was predominantly used.

The Manufacture of Soy Sauce

The production of soy sauce began with the careful selection of the highest quality ingredients to ensure the flavor of the finished product. The major ingredients were soy beans, wheat, salt, and rice. The wheat was parched by heating it indirectly; indirect heat was critical because burned wheat would give the soy sauce a bitter flavor. The wheat was heated in specially designed ovens that were held at the temperature required to parch the wheat without burning it. Once parched, the wheat was crushed into small pieces.

The soy beans were steam-cooked and mixed with the crushed wheat. Seed koji was added, and the resulting mixture was cultured for 48 hours to produce koji. Salt was dissolved in water to produce brine, which was added to the koji. The greater the amount of brine added to the other ingredients, the more vigorous the fermentation process and the lighter the color of the soy sauce. Next, white rice was steam-cooked to degrade its starch into fermentable sugars and was added to the koji-brine mixture to form moromi.

Moromi was fermented using three different organisms. The first organism, aspergillus orgzae, was used to break the starch and protein into sugars and amino acids, respectively. The second organism, yeast, was used to convert the fermentable sugars into alcohol. Finally, lactic bacillus was used to convert the remaining sugars in the mixture into lactic acid. After fermenting for six months, the moromi was separated into two fractions, one solid and the other liquid. The solid fraction, a by-product of the production process, was used for cattle feed. The liquid fraction, the raw soy sauce, was pasteurized and filtered to produce the finished product. After several quality checks were completed, the soy sauce was bottled, packed, and shipped.

The Soy Sauce Industry

Soy sauce had been produced in Japan for almost a thousand years. Traditionally, the industry had been dominated by a large number of very small local producers. Most of these firms were quite old. Kikuichi Shoyu Goshi Gaisha, for example, could trace its origins back to the Edo period in the early nineteenth century, while Asai Gomei Gaisha, a relative newcomer, was formed in 1872.

Since 1955, the industry had been dominated by a small number of large firms. By 1992, this concentration was fairly advanced. Fifty percent of the market was dominated by five firms, with the largest being over three times the size of its nearest rival. The next 25% of the market was dominated by 27 companies, and the remaining 25% by approximately 2,000 small local firms.

The largest firm in the industry was Kikkoman, with just over a 30% market share. The next-largest firm was Yamasa, with a market share of about 9%. Both of these firms were located in the Chiba prefecture about 39 kilometers north of Tokyo. Higashimaru, with 5% market share, was the third-largest firm in the industry. The next-largest firms were Higeta and Marukin, respectively. Higeta, with just under 3% of the market, was also located in the Chiba prefecture; Marukin, with a 2% share, was located in the Kagawa prefecture, which was about 130 kilometers from Osaka.

Historically, supply and demand had remained balanced and prices, after adjusting for inflation, had remained relatively constant. For example, for nearly a hundred years, the price of a two-liter bottle of soy sauce remained equivalent to the price of a man's haircut. Around 1960, demand ceased to rise, while supply continued to increase. By the early 1980s, supply significantly exceeded demand and prices fell drastically.

The low price of soy sauce products made it difficult for firms to achieve their historical levels of profitability. Prior to 1960, a well-managed company could expect its cost structure to be approximately 30% fixed and 60% variable, leaving a profit ratio of 10%. This ratio had been maintained by increasing selling prices to match increased costs. By 1980, the profit ratio had dropped to about 8%, driven primarily by increases in labor costs that could not be passed on to the consumer.

From 1846, when soy sauce was first commercialized, until 1960, only a few varieties of soy sauce were marketed in Japan. For example, during those years, Higashimaru sold only 10 different soy sauce products.

Starting about 1960, the firm, following industry trends, introduced a new product roughly every year. The objective of this strategy was to allow the firm to continue to grow despite the relatively flat demand for soy sauce.

In the early 1980s, as prices fell, Higashimaru adopted a strategy of rapid new product introduction. Over the next ten years, more than 150 new products were developed and introduced. Unfortunately, competition made it impossible to increase the selling prices of products to cover the higher costs associated with a more complex product offering. Consequently, from 1985 to 1991, fixed costs rose another 2.5%, causing the firm's profitability ratio to fall to 5.5%.

Organization Structure

Higashimaru's factory was organized in five sections, which contained a total of 17 groups. The five sections, responsible for the major production processes, were fermentation, production, inspection, machinery maintenance, and distribution. Each section contained one or more groups. The fermentation section contained five groups, the highest number of any section. Of these five groups, two were devoted to koji preparation, two to moromi pressing, and one to wastewater treatment. In contrast, the machinery maintenance section only contained one group, machinery maintenance.

The groups were run by group leaders. The average group leader had been with the firm for over twenty years. These individuals were not highly educated; however, they were very proud of their achievements and were highly motivated. Within the factory they were considered "self-made men." Unfortunately, they were not sufficiently well-educated to help manage the modernization program that was shortly to be introduced. This program included plant automation, increased cost awareness, and the development of more modern production control procedures such as temperature monitoring. Toshio Okuno, who was plant manager, was responsible for managing the modernization program. One of the techniques that he developed to increase the managerial skills of the group leaders was the Price Control System.

Price Control System

The Price Control System (PCS) was introduced in 1980. Under this system, each group was treated as a profit center and was expected to buy its resources from the previous group in the production process and to sell its products to the next group. Each group was expected to make a small profit every month. For example, the koji preparation group, the first in the production process, was expected to buy the resources it consumed from headquarters and sell its output to the moromi management group, the next one in the process.

The objective of the PCS was to instill a profit-making attitude in the groups. Group leaders were expected to act like presidents of small firms. They were not expected to act like entrepreneurs, because as Okuno stated, "It was too difficult to get them to act like entrepreneurs; that was asking too much."

Transfer prices between groups were set by Okuno. There were six groups responsible for the major production steps: koji preparation, fermentation, moromi management, pasteurization and filtration, bottling, and shipping. The budgeted cost per unit of output of each group was increased by 0.5% to give the transfer price. Thus, across the entire production process a 3% profit was generated. This 3% profit did not equal either the actual or expected profits generated by the production process. Okuno decided that it would be too complex to try to tie the profitability figures generated by the PCS into the actual or expected profits of the firm. Instead, Okuno decided that each profit center should have the ability to generate a small profit each month if it operated at expected efficiency.

A similar approach was adopted for raw material prices, which were kept constant over a three-year period. The rationale behind keeping both raw material prices and budgeted profit margins constant was that it allowed the groups to more easily understand the effect of their actions on group profitability. Okuno believed that if raw material and selling prices were allowed to vary, then it would be too difficult for the groups to observe the effects of their improvements. In addition, Okuno did not want the PCS to become an accounting system replete with variances and other forms of reconciliations. Instead, he wanted a very simple system that everyone could understand.

The monthly profit earned by each group was calculated by subtracting the sum of its monthly expenses and purchases from its monthly revenues. Monthly expenses were determined from the group's annual budget. The input purchases were determined by multiplying the volume of inputs consumed by their PCS transfer prices. Monthly revenues were calculated by multiplying the quantity of output sold to the next group in the production process by the appropriate transfer price.

Given the highly coupled nature of the production process, it was virtually impossible for any one group to significantly increase its output. For example, the input provided to the moromi management group by the koji preparation group effectively determined the amount of raw soy sauce that could be produced. Only by increasing yield could the moromi management group increase its output. Current yields were already high and only marginal improvements were expected. However, the groups could improve the quality of their output. To encourage increased quality, they were paid a higher price under the PCS for any output that was above a preset quality level. For example, the mold preparation group was paid ¥500 extra for every ichi shiire (a standard weight) of mold that it produced that ranked above the 0.3 standard measure of enzyme activity set by the R&D department, and ¥500 less if the enzyme activity level measured below the 0.3 standard. The incremental prices for quality were set by the plant manager. The primary objective of these quality rewards was to generate both cost and quality awareness.

Three support groups were covered by the PCS: the inspection, machinery maintenance, and water treatment groups. These groups provided support services for the production groups. The inspection group was responsible for inspecting the bottling and packing processes. The machinery maintenance group was responsible for providing all equipment maintenance. Finally, the water treatment group was responsible for processing all wastewater so that it could be released into a local river.

The three support groups were allowed to charge for their services. The objective in charging for support services was to make the production groups use those services more efficiently. For example, the machinery maintenance group was allowed to charge 50% of the labor cost of any unexpected repair but only 20% of the labor cost of any planned repairs. These percentage figures were chosen to enable the machinery maintenance group to be profitable. It was not necessary for the group to charge 100% of labor costs because it also sold repair services and steam. Therefore, partial charging for labor costs was all that was required to allow the group to report a 0.5% profit. The objective in charging different rates for the two types of maintenance was to

make the production groups think more carefully about how they treated their equipment.

Soy sauce production was seasonal because of Japanese eating habits. In the winter, the Japanese tended to eat more nimono (broiled) and nabemono (pot) dishes than in the summer. Reflecting these habits, approximately twice as much soy sauce was consumed in the peak winter months as in the off-season summer months. However, due to the extended production process, different parts of the plant would experience peak demands at different times of the year. To encourage the efficient use of personnel, the groups were allowed to buy time from other groups. The transfer price for workers' time was set at about ¥14,000 per day, which closely approximated the actual labor cost per worker.

To make the PCS more concrete, Okuno created the Higashimaru Bank. This fictitious bank printed its own money modeled after old Japanese bank notes (see Exhibit 2). Seven denominations were printed: ¥1,000, ¥5,000, ¥10,000, ¥100,000, ¥500,000, ¥1,000,000, and ¥2,000,000. These notes were stamped with the firm's seal in red to validate them.

Every month, the PCS books of account were closed by the group leaders and summarized by the section manager. Each group leader went to the next one in the process and presented a bill for goods rendered; the bills were paid in Higashimaru money. In addition, each group had to pay headquarters for the labor it employed, the depreciation on the equipment it used, and, if it consumed them, raw materials. Okuno had considered making each group pay interest on the money it borrowed but decided that it was too complex and abandoned the idea.

After each group had paid its bills and collected its revenues, its monthly profits or losses were determined by the value of the remaining bank notes. When a group ran out of money, it could borrow more from the production control section, which acted as the Higashimaru Bank. For the first few months that the PCS operated, all of the groups were profitable. However, in one month all of the groups reported losses. The problem was that Okuno had forgotten to include the semiannual employee bonuses in the profit calculations. Because each bonus was equivalent to approximately 2.7 months of pay, they easily dominated the 0.5% profits generated on revenues. Employees joked that, "If only we did not have to pay bonuses, we would be profitable." The system was subsequently modified to allow for the semiannual bonuses.

The PCS was run on an experimental basis for a year. After a year, Okuno met with all participating group leaders to ask them how they felt about the system. All of the participants strongly supported the system and were interested in finding out how their group's profitability compared to others. At the conclusion of this meeting, the system was declared a success and formally introduced.

The PCS operated for ten years, until Okuno was promoted to managing director. During those years, the groups initiated numerous actions that increased their profitability. Some actions were fairly straightforward, while others were more subtle manifestations of the influence of the system.

Some of the actions taken to improve group profitability affected only one group. The objective of these actions was to reduce head count. For example, the bottling group reduced the number of its employees by installing new servo-mechanisms to test each bottle to ensure that it was a 2-liter soy, not a 1.8-liter sake, bottle. Testing was required because the glass soy bottles were returnable and sometimes a sake bottle would get mixed in with the soy ones by accident. The application of servo-mechanisms to make the size tests was suggested by group members when the employee who usually performed that test left the company. Normally, the group would simply have requested a replacement. However, the group wanted to see if it could reduce its head count by introducing the new equipment. The automated equipment was successful, and after a year of operating without the replacement person the group's head count reduction was made permanent and its budget adjusted for both the increased equipment and the reduced labor expense.

Other actions reduced the cost of the services required by the support groups. For example, the koji preparation group, among others, reduced the size of the monthly bill it received from the machinery maintenance group by paying more attention to the way it monitored the temperature of the electric motors used to stir the fermenting koji, operate conveyor belts, and run machinery. By placing temperature sensors on the motors, it was possible to detect when they were overheating. By reducing the speed of rotation or, if necessary, stopping the motor completely, burnout could be avoided. If the motor was undamaged, no service call

was required. If the motor was at the end of its useful life, these preventative actions allowed the machinery maintenance group to make a scheduled, as opposed to unscheduled, visit to replace the motor. Thus, introducing thermal sensors allowed the koji preparation group to reduce the demands it placed on the machinery maintenance group and thereby increase its profitability.

The koji preparation group was the first to reduce its wastewater charge simply by picking up rubbish and brushing the floor clean before it was washed. The reduction in wastewater was significant because this part of the production process required very clean conditions and the floors were washed thoroughly several times a day. While wastewater only represented 1% of the group's budget, the savings were still considered important.

Still other actions were designed to improve the safety of the plant and thereby avoid accidents that led to absenteeism. For example, the bottling group focused on the high cost of employee absenteeism because it had to pay more for an employee it borrowed than one it loaned. The bottling process used many conveyors and workers were forced to either climb over or under the conveyor belts. Occasionally, a worker would be injured by the conveyor equipment. The group decided to monitor these small accidents to see if it could reduce their frequency. To reduce injuries, it placed soft, sponge-like material where people were likely to bump their heads, removed sharp edges that were likely to cause cuts, and placed warning signs where appropriate.

Some of the actions taken to improve profitability affected more than one group. Okuno considered these measures important because they showed how well the PCS encouraged communication between groups. For example, the bottling group noticed that the task of checking and adjusting the acidity of the wastewater created when the returned bottles were washed in a weak solution of caustic soda and detergent did not keep the worker responsible for that task completely occupied. The alkali was neutralized automatically by an acid-dispensing machine, but sometimes too much acid was released. When this occurred, a buzzer would sound and the worker would manually adjust the acidity level. This checking and adjustment process was not particularly time consuming, and thus the employee who performed this process was not particularly busy. Close to the bottling group was a boiler that a member of the machinery maintenance group was to monitor. This individual had to monitor the boiler on an ongoing basis but was also not particularly busy. To increase the profitability of both groups, the bottling group and the machinery maintenance group negotiated to share the two tasks. As a result, the machinery maintenance group agreed to perform the acidity testing and adjustment process for a fee of ¥40,000 per month. This agreement allowed the bottling group to reduce its head count by one, thereby saving ¥150,000 per month. Thus, both groups increased their profitability.

There were no direct rewards for becoming more profitable under the PCS. Okuno had considered tying the system into the firm's incentive scheme but had decided that making the profits too important would adversely affect relationships among the groups. In particular, it might make the groups reluctant to cooperate.

There were benefits to being profitable, however. First, group profitability was taken into account when evaluating individual performance. The leader of a highly profitable group could expect to be promoted faster than the leader of a less profitable one. Second, the two most profitable groups were awarded a ¥30,000 prize for their superior performance. These groups could spend the money at their discretion. The amount of the prize was purposely set low to reinforce the idea that the recognition was important, not the money.

Group Leader Monthly Meetings   Monthly meetings were a critical aspect of PCS. These were attended by Okuno, the group leaders, section managers, and, occasionally, staff from head office. At these meetings, one group leader would present the results of his or her group's activities. For this presentation, the group would prepare a profit and loss statement as the basis for discussion. The profit and loss statement for the fermentation group is shown in Exhibit 3.

During the presentation, the leader of the fermentation group identified the way his group had managed to generate a profit of 0.6% of revenues. In particular, he identified the various actions taken by the group to either increase revenues or reduce costs. In order to increase revenues, the group managed to increase the average quality of the mold it produced during the year. This increase in quality generated ¥27 million of extra revenue for the group.

The major actions taken during the year to reduce costs included reducing the speed of the stirring motors. The mold had to be stirred continuously, and this used a lot of energy. By experimenting with slower rotation speeds during the early phases of koji preparation, the group was able to reduce electricity costs below its historical level of 3.2%. Additional savings were achieved by making moromi at night instead of during the day. Nighttime preparation allowed the refrigerator, a heavy consumer of electricity, to take advantage of cheaper nighttime rates for electricity. The group was also reducing wastewater costs by cleaning the floor before washing it. Finally, it was trying to predict when machinery failures would occur in order to avoid the extra 30% surcharge from the machinery maintenance group for emergency repairs.

The Group Leader Public Subscription System   In 1985, there were two vacancies for group leader, including the mold fermentation group. Normally, group leaders were appointed by the plant manager. This time, Okuno decided to use a different approach to selecting group leaders. He held a competition where anyone that wanted to be a group leader could write reports on two topics chosen by Okuno. The first topic was how to make the mold fermentation group profitable. That group was currently unprofitable because it had proven difficult to automate and still required many workers. The second topic was how to revitalize that group, because its morale was low. Each applicant took the annual profit and loss statement prepared by the group as part of the PCS and developed detailed plans on how to make the group profitable. These plans were accompanied by a second report that addressed the morale issue. Eight applications were received, and their plans analyzed. The two best applicants were promoted to group leader. The best applicant was promoted to run the mold fermentation group.

Reactions to the PCS   Overall, employee reaction to the PCS was positive. One group leader said, "The Price Control System is important because it allows us to identify our own plans and run our own group. The amount of profits we generate each month allows us to see the results of our efforts. Seeing these results gives us an incentive to work even harder."

Another group leader described why making a profit was considered so important to his group even though no significant reward was associated with those profits: "It is not easy to increase group profits. It is a real achievement when we do. More importantly, we are trying to better a target set by ourselves. The company looks positively on the profits we generate. Finally, if we can make enough profits, we can win the ¥30,000 prize."

The success of the PCS, which reduced costs by 7% in its first year alone, drew attention from numerous companies. Executives from several companies, including Matsushita, the giant electronics company, Yuki-jirushi, a manufacturer of dairy products, and Kirin, the country's largest beer manufacturer, visited and studied the system. At least one of these firms, Kirin, implemented its own version of the Price Control System.

EXHIBIT 1   Higashimaru Shoyu Product Labels

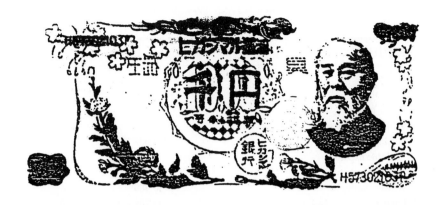

EXHIBIT 2   Examples of Higashimaru Bank Money

EXHIBIT 3 Fermentation Group Profit and Loss Report

Revenues

Sales of mold	¥985,607	97.1%
Bonus for quality	27,000	2.9
Support revenue for lending out personnel	31	0.0
Total revenues	¥922,638	100.0%
Variable expenses		
Material cost	¥687,450	74.7%
Wheat-roasting cost	13,309	1.4
Energy cost	63,791	6.9
Electricity	29,791	3.2
Wastewater charge	8,972	1.0
Support expenses for borrowing personnel	465	0.0
Total variable expenses	¥803,641	87.3%
Fixed expenses		
Personnel	¥51,711	5.6%
Depreciation—machines	41,520	4.5
Machine costs—maintenance	10,231	1.1
Machine costs—repair	7,349	0.8
Machine costs—parts	3,793	0.3
Factory maintenance	847	0.1
Miscellaneous consumables	1,565	0.2
Total fixed expenses	¥117,641	13.7%
Total expenses	¥920,717	100.0%
Summary		
Revenues	¥922,638	100.0%
Variable expenses	803,641	87.1
Contribution	¥118,997	12.9%
Fixed expenses	117,076	12.7
Profit	¥1,921	0.2%
Breakeven point	¥907,875	98.4%

OLYMPUS OPTICAL COMPANY, LTD. (B): FUNCTIONAL GROUP MANAGEMENT

Olympus, which consisted of Olympus Optical Company, Ltd., and its subsidiaries and affiliates, manufactured and sold opto-electronic equipment and other related products. The firm's major product lines included cameras, video camcorders, microscopes, endoscopes, and clinical analyzers. Olympus also produced microcassette tape recorders, laser-optical pickup systems, and industrial lenses. Olympus was founded in 1919 as Takachiho Seisakusho, a producer of microscopes. The brand name Olympus was first used in 1921, and became the firm's name in 1949; the first Olympus camera was developed in 1936. By 1993, Olympus was the world's fourth-largest camera manufacturer. Consolidated net income for 1993 was ¥4 billion and total revenues were ¥268 billion.

Olympus consisted of six divisions plus a headquarters facility. Four of the six divisions—consumer products, scientific equipment, endoscope, and diagnostics—were responsible for generating revenues. The other two divisions were responsible for corporate research and production engineering, respectively. Head-

Professor Robin Cooper of the Peter F. Drucker Graduate Management Center at The Claremont Graduate School prepared this case.

Copyright © 1994 by the President and Fellows of Harvard College. Harvard Business School case 195-073.

quarters was responsible for corporate planning, general affairs, personnel, and accounting and finance.

The consumer products division manufactured and sold 35mm cameras, video camcorders, and microcassette tape recorders. In 1993, the division employed 3,700 people (31% of the total Olympus work force) and generated revenues of ¥87 billion (32% of group revenues). Cameras were by far the firm's most important consumer product, accounting for ¥74 billion in revenues. Camera sales were worldwide, with approximately 77% sold outside of Japan.

The 35mm Camera Market

The world's 35mm camera market was dominated by five Japanese firms: Asahi Pentax, Canon, Minolta, Nikon, and Olympus. Canon and Minolta were the largest of the five firms, each with approximately 17% of the market compared to Olympus' 10%. There were two major types of 35mm cameras: single lens reflex (SLR), and lens shutters (LS) or compact cameras. SLR cameras, first introduced in 1959, used a single optical path to form the images for both the film and the viewfinder, allowing the photographer to see exactly what a picture looked like before it was taken. The ability to see the same image that would expose the film allowed SLR cameras to take advantage of interchangeable lenses. This feature enabled SLR cameras to rapidly gain a dominant share of the professional photographic market. As their price fell, they also came to dominate the high-end amateur market.

The low-end amateur 35mm market continued to be dominated by cameras with two separate optical paths. This market was divided into two segments. One segment contained very inexpensive cameras that were produced primarily by film manufacturers. The economics of this segment were driven predominantly by film, not camera, sales. The cameras in this segment primarily used the disc or 110mm film formats, though film producers had started to sell 35mm cameras that included new single-use versions. The other segment consisted of 35mm cameras that were less expensive than SLR cameras. This segment had undergone a dramatic change in the 1980s with the introduction of compact cameras.

Compact cameras, as suggested by their name, were smaller than SLR cameras. The first compact camera, the "XA," was introduced by Olympus in 1978 when miniaturized electronic shutters allowed the size of non-

SLR cameras to be significantly reduced. The size of SLR cameras could not be equivalently reduced because their single optical path required a retractable mirror. This mirror was positioned between the lens and the film when in the "down" position and reflected the image into the viewfinder. When the shutter was pressed, the mirror retracted "up" into the body of the camera, allowing the image to expose the film. The retractable mirror, which was approximately the same size as the image, required SLR cameras to remain relatively bulky. Cameras with two optical paths, however, did not require a retractable mirror and therefore could be reduced to quite small sizes. For example, the Olympus Stylus, which was ergonomically designed to fit the hand, was only 4.6″ long by 2.5″ wide by 1.5″ deep and weighed 6.3 ounces.

The early compact cameras were relatively unsophisticated and posed little challenge to the SLR market. However, as advances in electronic control systems allowed auto-focusing and automatic exposure features to be added at relatively low prices, the compact camera began to be viewed as a serious alternative to SLR cameras. The introduction of zoom auto-focus compact cameras in the mid-1980s removed the last major advantage of SLR cameras (i.e., variable focal length lenses). Sales of SLR cameras plummeted.

The Tatsuno Facility

Olympus' consumer products division consisted of six departments: division planning, quality assurance, marketing, product development, production, and overseas manufacturing. Responsibility for the division's production facilities was centered at the Tatsuno plant, which opened in 1981 and was the firm's main camera production facility. Tatsuno was responsible for trial production of experimental products, introductory production of new products, and, to a limited degree, camera and lens production. Five other manufacturing facilities reported to Tatsuno. These facilities were all located in Japan and were responsible for the manufacture of plastic molded parts, the assembly of lenses and cameras, and die casting.

Tatsuno was organized around 10 semiautonomous groups (this group structure was in place when the plant was established in the late 1970s). Four of these groups were responsible for production activities; the other six were responsible for support and administrative activities. The four production groups were machining, assembly 1, assembly 2, and assembly 3. Machining was responsible for producing all of the plant's machined parts. Tatsuno produced metallic parts (such as pressed/lathed parts, lens frames, and plated parts) in addition to the other parts required for camera manufacture (such as integrated circuits, motors, flash units, and mold injection parts). These other parts were either produced at the firm's other manufacturing facilities or purchased from suppliers and subcontractors. Approximately 60% of these other parts were purchased outside the firm.

The remaining three production groups were each responsible for a major step in camera assembly. Assembly 1 was responsible for final assembly, assembly 2 for flexible electronic circuit assembly, and assembly 3 for the production of lenses and lens assemblies. Final assembly consisted of taking the components produced by the other three manufacturing groups and other sources and using both manual and automated processes to assemble and test completed cameras. In 1993, Tatsuno assembled 20 different models, including the Infinity Stylus Zoom, the IS-3, and the Infinity Super-zoom 110.

Flexible electronic circuit board assembly consisted of automatic surface mounting of the components onto small flexible circuit boards that were used for the cameras' electronics. After the majority of the components had been automatically mounted, a few were manually attached because they were delicate. The completed boards were used at Tatsuno as well as at other manufacturing facilities inside and outside of Japan.

Lens and lens assembly consisted of manufacturing the lens or taking an externally manufactured lens and building the lens assembly. Lenses were made either out of glass or plastic. Plastic lenses were produced by injection molding and glass lenses by grinding blanks. Plastic lenses were used in cameras that required relatively small diameter optics, such as the Stylus. Glass was used in the IS series, which required larger diameter optics. The lens assembly consisted of the lens, focus, and zoom mechanisms.

Tatsuno's six support and administrative groups were general affairs, administration, material purchasing, technical production, technical manufacturing, and inspection. General affairs was responsible for labor control and facility control. Administration was responsible for production control, parts arrangement, cost administration, and products control. Material purchasing was responsible for all material acquisition activities, including vendor selection, price negotiations, order placement, and warehouse operations. Technical production was responsible for the start-up production of new products. Technical manufacturing was responsible for innovations in production engineering. Finally, inspection was responsible for all major inspection activities; however, line inspections were performed by the workers of the production groups and did not fall under the responsibility of the inspection group.

Cost Management System

Since the early 1970s, Olympus' cost system had undergone three major changes. Prior to 1976, there was only one overhead rate at the Tatsuno plant. The system directly traced some material costs to products, but all other costs were allocated. These allocated costs were divided into two categories, processing and overhead. Processing costs included the indirect material, direct and indirect labor, and direct expenses of the production process. Direct labor was allocated because the direct labor wage rates varied by individual and it was considered too expensive to assign directly to products. The overhead costs contained the indirect material, indirect labor, and indirect expenses associated with support and administration. The processing overhead costs were combined and divided by the number of direct labor hours to give an average allocation rate. The reported cost of a product was given by the sum of the direct material charge and the direct labor hours consumed by the product multiplied by the allocation rate. Such a simple system was considered adequate because there were only small differences in the cost structure of the products. In addition, the level of automation was small, as was depreciation. The stated objective of this system was to differentiate material cost from other expenses and to provide mechanisms for total cost reduction.

In 1976, the cost system was updated. The overhead costs were split into two categories, procurement and other costs. Procurement costs were those costs associated with obtaining raw material and purchased parts. They included the personnel expenses of the procurement section, transportation charges, carfares, and miscellaneous procurement-related expenses. The procurement costs were allocated to products based upon the sum of the direct material charge plus the allocated processing costs. A separate rate was determined for other costs, which were mainly associated with administration and production technical sections. The costs of these two sections were allocated to the production and procurement sections based upon head count. The primary purpose of this change to the cost system was to draw attention to the procurement costs, which had grown substantially over time. This increase was due both to an increase in production capacity (which was accompanied by a corresponding increase in the volume of procured parts) and an increase in the ratio of procured to internally manufactured parts. The other important change in the cost system was its focus on the cost of quality. The cost of defects was isolated from the standard costs to give it more visibility. Separate variances were computed for standard production and defects.

In 1983, Olympus' cost system was again updated. The general structure was maintained, but now multiple allocation rates were computed for processing costs. The production process was divided into 10 cost centers (these were not the same as the functional groups) and different overhead rates were computed for each center. Examples of the cost centers included camera final assembly, electronic flexible board assembly, lens processing, and lens assembly. In addition, the firm had begun to enter into OEM contracts with other firms that would produce components for Olympus. The support and administration costs for OEM production were significantly different from Tatsuno's production. To capture this difference, the two overhead cost allocation rates were computed, one for general suppliers and the other for OEM suppliers. These two rates replaced the single procurement rate computed in the prior system. The treatment of other costs as partially related to processing and partially related to procurement was suspended and all other costs were allocated as part of the support and administration costs. The primary purpose of this system was to provide improved control over production, support, and administration costs.

The 1987 Reconstruction Program

The shift in consumer preference to compact cameras adversely affected Olympus in particular, because the firm had historically relied heavily upon SLR sales and had failed to develop a leadership position in the compact camera arena. In the mid-1980s, Olympus' camera business began to lose money; by 1987, the losses were considerable. Olympus' top management reacted to the losses by introducing an ambitious three-year program to "reconstruct" its camera business. At the core of this program were three objectives: first, to recapture lost market share by the introduction of new products; second, to dramatically improve product quality; and third,

to reduce production costs via an aggressive set of cost reduction programs.

The program to reconstruct Olympus' camera business, which began in 1987, achieved its objectives. The plan to introduce new products was successful, allowing the firm to recapture its lost market share. By 1990, the firm had increased camera sales volume by almost 70% to ¥50 billion from ¥30 billion and almost doubled its market share for compact cameras. The improvements continued over the next three years, and by the end of 1993 camera sales volume was ¥54 billion and market share was 14%.

Unfortunately, the program was not as successful for the SLR product line. The firm continued to lose market share from 1987 through 1990. But with the introduction of a completely new camera line (beginning with the IS-1 in September of 1990, followed by the IS-2 in October of 1992 and the IS-3 in January of 1993), the firm hoped to turn the situation around. The IS-1 was different from other SLR cameras because its lens was not removable. Consumer research had determined that the majority of SLR camera owners only owned a single lens. Therefore, they were not taking advantage of one of the major "advantages" of SLR technology, the ability to change lenses. Creating an SLR camera with a fixed, not a removable, lens allowed Olympus' engineers to remove certain limitations in SLR camera design. They could develop a more ergonomic design by integrating the lens into the camera body, and they could achieve superior optical performance by locating the lens closer to the film. Though the IS series proved to be a success in the market, the results were below the firm's original expectations.

The combined results of the cost reduction program were impressive. By the end of 1990 every measure of productivity at Tatsuno had improved. For example, overall production had increased by 50%; the production cost ratio, determined by dividing cost by sales, had improved by 20%; the production value per employee had risen 70%; and gross added value per person had increased over 125%. Simultaneously, the work-in-process inventory had not increased despite the higher activity levels and a reduction of lead time by almost half.

Despite the success of the 1987 plan, top management determined that additional cost reductions were going to be necessary in the coming years. In particular, they were worried by three trends that together would place significant pressure on the firm's profitability: a proliferation of products required to satisfy consumer demand in the domestic market, an additional shortening of the product life cycle to below a year in Japan, and reduced selling prices. The decision to introduce a new cost reduction program was driven by these considerations, in addition to the observation that savings derived from the 1987 plan decreased over time. The prolonged recession that began in the early 1990s also greatly affected the firm's sales and profits. This accelerated Olympus' plans to shift more manufacturing overseas to achieve further cost reduction.

At the heart of the new cost reduction program were two important concepts: increased automation and functional group management. The drive towards accelerated automation of the production process involved applying new automation technology to all stages of production. Functional group management consisted of treating the 10 autonomous groups at Tatsuno as profit centers, not cost centers. The primary motivation behind the introduction of the functional group management system was to increase the pressure on the work force to improve the production cost ratio by both decreasing costs and increasing output at the group level.

The Functional Group Management Approach

The shift from cost to profit centers was motivated by four perceived benefits. First, it created a change in the mind-set of the factory workers from a passive "wait for instructions" approach to a more proactive approach as they pursued their group's profit target. Second, in order to increase their level of output and hence revenues, the groups were interacting more frequently with the technical production group to increase the capacity of each group. Third, the technical production group was providing improved support to the groups in helping them increase their level of automation. This was achieved, for example, by increasing the processing speed of machines, introducing unmanned operations, and reviewing current processing methods to generate ideas for new methods. Finally, the firm's cost management system had to be modified to support the functional group management system. Tatsuno management believed that many of these modifications greatly improved the cost management system.

Change in Mind-Set The functional group management approach, unlike the cost reduction program, was a bottom-up, not a top-down, approach. In the cost re-

duction program, cost reduction targets were identified for each product produced by the group. These targets were negotiated by division management with the group leaders. The group leaders recommended their cost reduction targets, which were reviewed by divisional management. If the overall reductions were sufficient to achieve the division's cost reduction objectives, the targets were accepted. If the overall savings were insufficient, the targets were renegotiated until the savings were acceptable to divisional management. The critical point was that division management had the final say about the magnitude of the groups' final cost reduction targets.

The procedure for setting group cost reduction targets was part of a hierarchical target-setting process. The process began with the corporatewide cost reduction targets, which were set in the annual planning process. The corporatewide cost reduction targets were allocated to each division in a negotiation process that was virtually identical to the process used to set group cost reduction targets, except that the negotiations were between the corporate planning department and divisional managers. In the next stage in the process, the divisional cost reduction targets were allocated to each production facility in the divisions and then to the groups, utilizing a top-down approach.

Although the cost reduction targets were based upon input from the groups, the underlying top-down nature of the negotiation process reduced the level of commitment that group members felt about achieving their targets. Sometimes, when the group targets were increased due to divisional pressure, group members did not believe that they could achieve them. Over the years, the groups' initial cost reduction targets had become biased downward to create "slack" that could be used to help the groups achieve their negotiated targets. To the extent possible, when divisional management became aware of this practice it would take this into consideration when establishing new targets.

Under the functional group management approach, the groups set their own targets. The targets were set via a budgeting process in which each group set its own revenue and cost objectives. These group objectives had to be coordinated with divisional objectives. The functional group management approach would not be effective if each group went its own way. Consequently, group budgets were established within a set of "unifying themes" that were incorporated into the corporate/divisional objectives. An example of such a theme was setting the cost reduction target for the year for the plant at ¥200 million.

The corporate/divisional objectives identified the sales goal for the factory. These sales goals were divided into output goals for each group. By finding ways to increase their output levels, the groups increased their ability to generate "revenues" and hence profits. As the groups increased their revenues, the capacity of the factory also increased.

One unexpected advantage of the functional group management approach was that the bias to understate cost reduction estimates was removed. One reason for this was that, under the new objective of increasing profits, "padding" the cost estimates led to reduced profits and hence reduced predicted performance. In contrast, under the old objective, "padding" the cost estimates was essentially a neutral act because the groups' performance was measured against the final cost reduction target, not their initial estimate. Another reason that the functional group management system had proven to be so effective was that Tatsuno management had not found it necessary to try to increase the groups' improvement estimates; under the new system, the Tatsuno facility outperformed the cost reduction objectives set by divisional management.

Performance Evaluation   The functional group management approach was considered important because it helped the work force become more flexible. Top management considered this increased flexibility critical for the future because there were clearly major changes coming and any increase in the ability of the work force to adapt to new conditions was viewed as a significant improvement.

Under the functional group management approach, each group leader was given full management responsibility for his or her area of responsibility. Leaders were expected to manage their groups as if they were independent companies. However, there were some significant restrictions on their freedom to act. For example, they were not able to choose which components to buy from outside the firm or to negotiate purchasing prices. Instead, they had to go through the material purchasing group for externally acquired components and through the other production groups for internally produced components. In addition, the degree of changes that the groups could make to their production processes without top management permission was relatively limited. The types of changes the groups could make included

minor improvements in productivity (such as increasing the processing speed of the machines), introducing unmanned operations, and reviewing current processing methods in order to find ways to improve them. The range of actions that each group could take was restricted based upon the level of expenditures they were allowed to make and personnel considerations.

To motivate each group leader to act appropriately, the production groups were evaluated based upon the profits they generated. Each group was treated as a profit center by estimating the revenue it would have generated if it was a separate company that sold its output to Olympus. Top management felt that holding the groups responsible for profitability, as opposed to cost, would increase the motivation to reduce costs while simultaneously generating an increase in outputs.

The "revenue" for the four production groups was estimated by the technical manufacturing group, which used its knowledge of the production processes performed by those groups and costs charged by the firm's external suppliers and subcontractors to estimate the price the firm would have to pay external suppliers for each of the components and assemblies produced by the groups. These estimated prices were then multiplied by the output of each group for the period to produce their estimated total revenues. Great care had to be taken when estimating group revenues; trial production and other activities that were designed to improve future products had to be identified and the revenue computed accordingly. There was no point in identifying a group as unprofitable simply because it performed a lot of experimental production that did not generate revenues or was not immediately cost-justifiable.

Each group's profits were determined by subtracting its total costs from its total revenues. Thus, under the functional group management approach, each group's performance was captured in three numbers: estimated revenues, costs, and profits. Of these three performance measures, profit was considered the most important, followed by costs, and then revenues.

Once the groups had set their own target profits and these had been accepted by plant management, monthly targets were established. If a group did not reach its monthly target, the group's leader was expected to explain at the monthly group leader meeting why his or her group had not met target. At this meeting, other group leaders would often suggest how to achieve the targets and would be generally supportive. In the history of the functional group management approach, no team leader had consistently failed to meet targets (theoretically, if a group consistently failed to achieve its objective, its leader would be replaced). Typically, the groups were outperforming their plans.

Increased Interaction with Engineering Support
To achieve increased profits, several of the groups discovered that they required additional engineering support. To get this help, the groups had to request help from the engineering groups. Because the engineering groups were not treated as profit centers, no charge was made for their services. Under the functional group management system, the changes to the production processes that were envisioned were not expected to be substantial. Only minor changes to the equipment and fixtures were anticipated. The normal objective of these engineering changes was to increase output (i.e., capacity) though some of them did reduce costs. In the first three years of the program, approximately 80% of the profit improvements were from changes that increased output; the remaining 20% of improvements were from cost reduction initiatives, such as increased use of unmanned processing and improvements in shortening processing time. The dominance of the output-related improvements initially surprised Tatsuno management, which expected a more even balance between the two sources of increased profits. Imbalances between the production rates of the various groups were controlled via the product order system, so significant inventory between the two groups did not develop.

Increased Automation   Olympus was dedicated to increasing the level of automation throughout its production processes. For example, it introduced automated testing and unmanned production of plastic lenses. The primary purpose of automation was to reduce labor costs and improve product quality.

Changes to Tatsuno Cost Management System   The cost management system had to be modified in several ways to support the functional group management system. First, the old system did not provide group members with information about how the groups' output contributed to the revenues or profits of the plant. Instead, it simply informed them of the costs of their groups and how those costs compared to budget. For the groups to be treated as profit centers, they had to be provided with revenue information. Consequently, the cost system had to be modified to enable it to report the revenue and hence the profitability of the groups. Using the "selling prices" identified by the engineering department, the system provided each group with its budgeted and actual revenues for each month. Because these selling prices did not reflect reality, the sum of the profits of the 10 groups did not equal the profits of the plant.

Other changes included modifying the way the standards were set. In the old corporate cost system, standards were established every six months at the level of current performance (see Figure 1). Therefore, as the groups improved their performance, positive variances were generated. The functional group management cost system was different. It used standards that were based upon the midpoint of expected efficiency during a three-month period (see Figure 2). Therefore, variances started negative and then became positive as the improvements took effect. The price at which the output of a group sold was also updated every six months. Because the firm's suppliers were getting more efficient, the group management standard or selling price was continuously decreasing (see Figure 3). Thus, only groups that were at least as efficient as the firm's suppliers could remain profitable. If no way could be found to make a group profitable, it would become a candidate for outsourcing. The only exceptions were the experimental production lines that were testing ways to increase the level of automation for new products. These lines were protected because top management felt that they were too strategically important to outsource. Thus, the functional group management approach placed the production groups effectively into competition with the firm's suppliers. It thereby created intense pressure on the groups to improve their performance.

Purchasing Group

The purchasing department's revenue was determined from historical data about the rate of reduction of the selling prices of the components it purchased. These historical price reduction rates were used to predict the future prices of components that the firm purchased. In turn, these future prices were used to determine the purchasing group's revenues for the period. Revenues were defined to be the estimated selling price of the parts purchased multiplied by the volumes purchased. The costs of the department were defined to be the actual selling prices of the parts purchased multiplied by the volumes purchased. Consequently, the purchasing department generated profits only when it could find ways to increase the rate at which the price of the parts it purchased decreased.

To achieve profitability, the purchasing group was forced to change the way it related to both suppliers and the two technical groups. Traditionally, purchasing's role was to explore the market and, subject to quality constraints and long-term vendor relationships, find the cheapest source for each of the parts that it had to purchase. The functional group management approach was designed to change that mission; it required purchasing to work with design, engineering, and production to find innovative ways to reduce the costs of purchased parts.

There were two major benefits to this change in mission. First, the purchasing agents were able to generate more compelling arguments about why the purchase prices should be falling more rapidly. For example, instead of simply using a desired percentage for purchase price reduction, they could now discuss technological changes that affected pricing. This additional knowledge enabled the agents to be more aggressive in the way they interacted with suppliers, thereby increasing the rate at which prices fell. Second, the purchasing agents were able to identify technological solutions that were fundamentally cheaper (e.g., by reducing the specifications of a part or finding new ways to manufacture the part).

Suppliers benefitted from this change in behavior. First, if real technological changes could be identified, then both sides stood to gain. For example, the manufacturing process that was used for light-emitting diodes (LEDs) typically produced products whose light intensity varied. Because of the tight specifications that were necessary for camera applications, only the brightest of the four intensities satisfied Olympus' requirements. Olympus' technical staff found a way to adjust the intensity of the LEDs that allowed the firm to purchase and use all four intensity levels. This technical advance reduced the suppliers' costs and, thus, Olympus' purchase price.

Implementation Process

The functional group management approach was implemented in three phases. The first phase was introduced in October, 1990. It consisted of converting the four production groups and the materials purchasing group

from cost centers into profit centers. The other groups were not included because Tatsuno management could not find ways to estimate meaningful revenues for these groups. During the first phase, the infrastructure to support the functional group management approach and to ensure the necessary change in mind-set was developed. The infrastructure consisted primarily of the monthly group leader meetings, profit reporting, and a group performance evaluation system. Although the technical procedures were put in place fairly rapidly, the change in mind-set that really signalled the success of the approach was gradual, making it difficult to determine precisely when the first phase was completed. Despite this difficulty, Tatsuno management had identified April, 1992 as the date by which it considered the first phase complete.

The second phase consisted of implementing the functional group management approach throughout the factory. The key to this phase was having the groups take the initiative. The change in mind-set was complete and the groups were now acting like profit centers. Each group developed its own plan; included in those plans was the implementation of functional group management. The major problem that faced management in this phase was identifying revenues for the support groups. By late 1993, little progress had been made in this regard. Full functional group management had only been applied to the four production groups and purchasing.

Phase three was the evolution of overseas manufacturing. Olympus was expanding its production capability by opening a new factory in the southern coastal province of Shenzen in the People's Republic of China; the factory was named Olympus (Shenzen) Industrial Limited. The new factory, scheduled to open in February, 1994, was expected to undertake a considerable portion of the firm's production. With the opening of this factory, Olympus expected domestic production to remain stable for the foreseeable future and possibly decline over time. Given the differential costs of production of cameras in Japan and China, the firm accepted that eventually all production might occur in China, with the exception of the firm's advanced products that required special engineering support. If this scenario occurred, it would leave Tatsuno as the firm's design and advanced manufacturing facility.

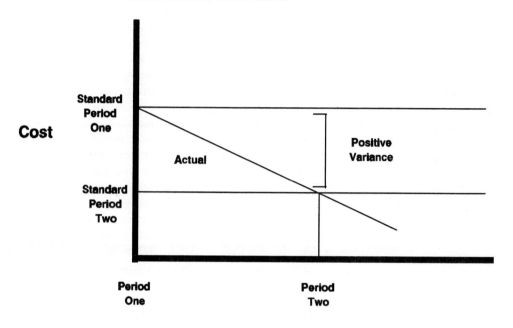

FIGURE 1 **Standard Setting in Olympus' Cost System**

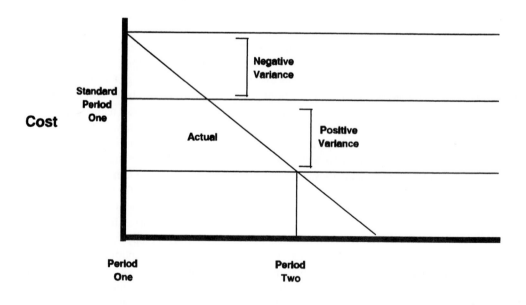

FIGURE 2 **Standard Setting in Olympus' Functional Group Management System**

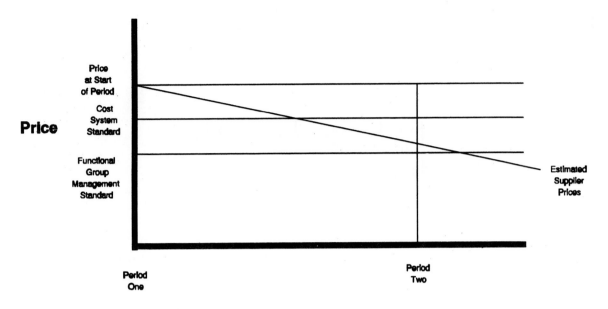

FIGURE 3   Price Setting in Olympus' Functional Group Management System

4

Activity-Based Costing: Introduction

Activity-Based Cost (ABC) systems are the second major new component of Stage III systems. Recall that Stage II costing systems assign indirect and support costs to products with volume-based cost drivers, such as direct labor, machine hours, and material dollars. This practice leads to distortions in the calculation of product costs because many indirect and support costs are not used by products in proportion to their production volumes. ABC systems avoid such distortions by assigning costs through a logical and systematic set of procedures:

1. Identify the activities performed by the organizational resources.
2. Determine the cost of performing these organizational activities and business processes.
3. Determine how much of the output of each activity is required for the organization's products, services, and customers.

A properly constructed ABC model provides an economic model or map of the organization's expenses, based on organizational activities.

WHY ABC SYSTEMS: THE PEN FACTORIES

The motivation for ABC systems is simple to articulate. Think about two hypothetical and almost identical factories.[1] Simple Factory makes one million pens, all the same color: blue. Complex Factory also makes one million pens, but of many different colors, sizes, and varieties. This factory, in a typical year, produces about 2,000 different types (SKUs) of pens, ranging from specialty pens, with annual production volume as low as 50–100 per year, to higher-volume standard pens (blue and black), whose annual production volumes are each about 100,000 per year.

Even though both factories make the same basic product, Complex Factory requires many more resources to support its highly varied mix. Relative to Simple Factory, Complex Factory has a much larger production support staff. It requires more people to schedule machines and production runs, perform setups, inspect items after setup, move materials, ship orders, expedite

---

[1]Example taken from R. Cooper and R. S. Kaplan, "Measure Costs Right: Make the Right Decisions," *Harvard Business Review* (September–October 1988), pp. 97–98.

orders, rework defective items, design new products, improve existing products, negotiate with vendors, schedule materials receipts, order, receive, and inspect incoming materials and parts, and update and maintain the much larger computer-based information system. Complex Factory also operates with considerably higher levels of idle time, setup time, overtime, inventories, rework and scrap. Since both factories have the same physical output, they would both have roughly the same cost of direct materials (ignoring the slightly higher acquisition costs in Complex Factory for smaller orders of specialty colors and other materials). For actual production, if you assume that all pens are of about the same complexity, both Simple and Complex Factory would require the same number of direct labor hours and machine hours for actual production (not counting the higher idle time and setup times in Complex Factory). Complex Factory would likely also have about the same property taxes, security costs, and heating bills as Simple Factory. But Complex Factory would have much higher indirect and support costs (i.e., overhead) because of its more varied product mix and complex production task.

Consider now the operation of a traditional Stage II standard cost system in these two plants. Simple Factory has little need for a cost system to calculate the cost of a blue pen. The financial manager, in any single period, can simply divide total expenses by total production volume to get the cost per blue pen produced. For Complex Factory, the cost system first assigns the indirect and support expenses to its various production cost centers using techniques discussed in chapter 2. Once expenses are accumulated in each production center, they are applied to products based on the volume-based cost driver selected for that cost center; for example, direct labor, machine hours, units produced, or materials quantity processed. On a per-unit basis, high-volume standard blue and black pens require about the same quantity of each of these cost drivers as the very low volume, specialty products. Therefore, Complex Factory's overhead costs would be applied to products proportional to their production volumes. Blue and black pens, each representing about 10% of the plant's output, would have about 10% of the plant's overhead applied to them. A low-volume product, representing only .01 of 1% of the plant's output (100 pens per year) would have about .01 of 1% of the plant's overhead allocated to it. Therefore, the Stage II standard costing system would report essentially identical product costs for all products, standard and specialty, irrespective of their relative production volumes and production complexity.

Clearly, however, considerably more of Complex Factory's indirect and support resources are required (on a per-unit basis) for the low-volume, specialty, newly-designed products than for the mature, high-volume, standard blue and black pens. Stage II cost systems, even those with hundreds or thousands of production cost centers, will systematically and grossly underestimate the cost of resources required for specialty, low-volume products, and will overestimate the resource cost of high-volume, standard products. The distortion in reported costs between standard and specialty products can only be avoided if the standard and specialty pens are manufactured on separate machines in different cost centers.

Abandoning the assignment of support resource costs entirely and moving to direct costing systems does not solve this problem. Under direct or marginal costing, blue and black pens, which have the same materials and direct labor cost as the low-volume, specialty pens, will also have the same variable costs. Direct costing systems cannot explain why the two factories with exactly the same physical units of production (e.g., one million pens) have dramatically different levels of "fixed costs."

Even as they begin to build activity-based cost systems, companies should, however, retain their Stage II traditional cost system to meet the financial reporting requirement to allocate factory overhead costs to production. Companies may find that an even simpler version of such a cost system, with a single cost center for the entire plant and using a single allocation base (such as direct labor), would be adequate for financial reporting purposes and very inexpensive to operate.

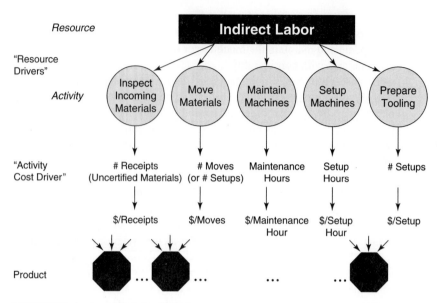

EXHIBIT 4–1   ABC System: Expenses Flow from Resources to Activities to Products

FUNDAMENTALS OF ACTIVITY-BASED COST SYSTEMS

Activity-based cost systems extend traditional Stage II cost systems by linking resource expenses to the variety and complexity of products produced, not just the physical volumes produced. Exhibit 4–1 shows the structure of an ABC system for factory operations.

At first glance the ABC system appears quite similar to the traditional cost systems described in chapter 2. But the underlying structure and concept are very different. At the heart of all ABC systems lie two critical assumptions. First, resources are consumed only by the performance of activities, and second, activities are performed to produce outputs. These are robust assumptions. The first one is violated only by resources that decay over time so that no activity can be traced to the consumption of the depleting resource. However, by including time-based depreciation in the ABC system, this limitation can be overcome. The second assumption is violated when resources are supplied but not used; that is by supplying committed resources in excess of actual demands. This limitation of ABC is overcome by the capacity-adjusted ABC model we will discuss in chapter 5.

We now describe the process of building an organization's first activity-based cost model.

DESIGNING AN ABC SYSTEM

1.   Develop the Activity Dictionary

In the first step of developing an ABC system, the organization identifies the set of activities being performed by its indirect and support resources. Activities are described by verbs and associated objects: schedule production, move materials, purchase materials, inspect items, respond to customers, improve products, introduce new products, and so on. The identification of activities culminates with construction of an activity dictionary that lists and defines all the major activities performed in the production facility.

Initially, when ABC systems were first being introduced in the mid- to late-1980s, ABC project teams had to invent activity dictionaries virtually from scratch. Now, with nearly a decade of implementation experience, companies and consulting organizations have developed standard activity dictionaries that provide a template for selecting the appropriate activities to be used in any particular application. Some organizations, however, like to use their front-line employees in a bottoms-up process to define the activity dictionary. Such a process engages the entire organization in the ABC modeling exercise and helps to build confidence that the model reflects the reality of the organizational setting. This is a longer, more expensive process but it may yield compensating benefits in terms of greater commitment and ownership of the final model.

Activity dictionaries can be relatively brief, say 10–30 activities, especially where the prime focus of the ABC system is to estimate product and customer costs. In other applications, ABC systems continue to be built with hundreds of activities. Typically, such highly detailed systems have been constructed to serve as the foundation for process improvement and process redesign efforts. The number of activities, therefore, is a function of the purpose of the model, and the size and complexity of the organizational unit being studied.

With the set of organizational activities identified, we can now move to the second step.

2. Determine How Much the Organization is Spending on Each of Its Activities

The ABC system now maps from resource expenses to activities, using resource cost drivers (see Exhibit 4–1). The resource cost drivers link spending and expenses, as captured in the organization's financial or general ledger system, to the activities performed.[2] For personnel expenses, most organizations ask individuals to fill in a survey form on which the activity dictionary is listed. The individuals estimate the percentage of time they (or their subordinates) spend on any activity (in excess, say, of 5% of their time) on the list. For nonpersonnel resources, the ABC project team either relies on direct measurement (how much power, computer, or telecommunications time) or estimates the percentage of the resource used by each activity in the dictionary. In fact, this procedure does not really differ substantively from that done by excellent standard cost–flexible budgeting systems described in chapter 2. The main difference is that Stage II standard cost–flexible budgeting systems drive indirect expenses only to other responsibility centers, typically production cost centers. ABC systems, like Stage II systems, can drive expenses to production cost centers where the activity is part of the actual product conversion process, like *fabricate parts*, *mix chemicals*, or *assemble products*. But, in addition, the ABC system drives operating expenses to activities that are not directly involved in converting materials into intermediate and finished products, like *setup machines*, *schedule production runs*, and *perform engineering change notices*.

One does not need extensive time-and-motion studies to link resource spending to activities performed. The goal is to be approximately right, rather than precisely wrong, as is the case with virtually all traditional product costing systems.

[2]See, for example, J. A. Brimson, *Activity Accounting* (New York: John Wiley & Sons, 1991); G. Cokins, A. Stratton, and J. Helbing, *An ABC Manager's Primer* (Chicago: Irwin Professional Publishing, 1993); T. Pryor and J. Sahm, *Using Activity-Based Management for Continuous Improvement* (Arlington, Texas: ICMS, Inc., 1995); D. T. Hicks, *Activity-Based Costing for Small and Mid-Sized Businesses: An Implementation Guide* (New York: John Wiley & Sons, 1992); and G. Cokins, *Activity-Based Cost Management Making It Work: A Manager's Guide to Implementing and Sustaining an Effective ABC System* (Chicago: Irwin Professional Publishing, 1996).

Activity Attributes

Attributes are coding schemes that facilitate reporting of activity costs. Consider an activity dictionary with 125 activities. Activity attributes enable the activity cost information to be reported at higher levels of aggregation than tabulating or charting data for 125 individual activities. ABC systems have used numerous types of activity attributes, but three are most common: cost hierarchy, business process, and value-added–non-value-added.

Cost Hierarchy   Business activities can be classified along an important cost hierarchy dimension. Most common are unit, batch, product-sustaining, and customer-sustaining activities.[3]

Unit-level activities are the activities that have to be performed for every unit of product or service produced. The quantity of unit-level activities performed is proportional to production and sales volumes. Examples include drilling holes in metal parts, grinding metal, and performing 100% inspection.

Batch-level activities are the activities that have to be performed for each batch or setup of work performed. Batch activities include setting up a machine for a new production run, purchasing materials, and processing a customer order.

Product-sustaining activities are performed to enable the production of individual products (or services) to occur. Extending this notion outside the factory leads to *customer-sustaining activities* that enable the company to sell to an individual customer but that are independent of the volume and mix of the products (and services) sold and delivered to the customer. Examples of these product- and customer-sustaining activities include maintaining and updating product specifications, special testing and tooling for individual products and services, and technical support provided for individual products and to service individual customers.

Beyond these activities, other resources supply capabilities that cannot be traced to individual products and customers. Some activities, such as product development and advertising, can be classified as *brand* or *product-line sustaining*, since they support an entire brand or product line. Activities, such as pricing and invoicing, may be *order-related*, specific to a particular order, but independent of the volume or content of the order. Other activities provide general production or sales capabilities (*facility-sustaining* expenses—a plant manager and administrative staff) and *channel-sustaining* expenses—trade shows and advertising, catalogs—that cannot be traced to individual products, services, or customers. The expenses of product line, facility, and channel resources can be assigned directly to the individual product lines, facilities, and channels but should not be allocated down to individual products, services, or customers within these product lines, facilities, and channels.

Business Process   Activities can also be grouped together into higher-level business processes. Some designers have attempted to organize their entire ABC system around a few business processes, ignoring the finer detail available from an activity perspective. The problem is that a business process, like procurement, might be too heterogeneous for costs to be driven to products, services, or customers by a single cost driver. For example, activities within the procurement function could include ordering materials, scheduling delivery of materials, receiving materials, inspecting materials, moving materials, storing materials, negotiating with and selecting vendors, and paying vendor invoices. Each of these activities may require a different cost driver. If all the activities were aggregated together, then only a single cost driver, like the number of purchase orders, would have to be selected for driving all procurement process

---

[3]R. Cooper, "Cost Classifications in Unit-Based and Activity-Based Manufacturing Cost Systems," *Journal of Cost Management* (Fall 1990), pp. 4–14.

costs to materials. Such an aggregation would fail to identify differences in the activities required for ordering different types of materials from different vendors and using different ordering relationships. Activities with unique cost drivers are the basic unit of analysis for ABC systems. They capture the diversity of use by individual products, services, and customers that create the demand for the activities.

Activities, however, can still be aggregated together so that managers can see the total cost of performing a business process by coding each activity, say with the first two digits of its numeric code, to represent the business process associated with each activity. Such a coding scheme enables activity costs to be accumulated and reported by business processes. For example, the activities—ordering materials, scheduling delivery of materials, receiving materials, inspecting materials, moving materials, storing materials, negotiating with and selecting vendors, and paying vendor invoices—would be aggregated into a *procurement* process. Understanding costs at the aggregate business process level facilitates internal and external benchmarking. Managers can compare the cost of performing the same business process (e.g., procurement or customer service) at different plants or across different organizational units to identify where particularly efficient practices should be studied or particularly inefficient processes improved.

Value-Added–Non-Value-Added   Activity-based systems often help to signal where to undertake process improvement by identifying value-added and non-value added activities. The definition of what constitutes a value-added activity varies considerably among firms. Some common definitions for value-added include an activity that adds value in the eyes of the customer or an activity that supports the primary objective of producing outputs. For example, for the finance group, the activities required to produce the firm's annual report might be viewed as value-added.

We are not necessarily advocates of such a coding scheme, but we can identify two potential justifications for attempting to distinguish value-added from non-value-added activities. First, non-value-added activities can be removed without risk to the customer. Managers apparently fear that attempting to reduce costs in value-added activities might risk customer disapproval. The focus on non-value-added activities has some credibility. The virtual elimination of work-in-process through just-in-time production is invisible to the customers (they may even notice an improvement through an accompanying improvement in quality). In contrast, switching from a four-bolt to a three-bolt mounting system will be highly visible.

But eliminating an apparent non-value-added activity can introduce risk; for example, if a company decreases inventory levels too rapidly, stock-outs can occur which will decrease value to customers. Improvements in a value-added activity may enhance value to customers; for example, some customers may prefer the new three-bolt design since changeovers and replacements will be faster. Similarly, setups, viewed by many as a non-value-added activity, enable a company to provide variety and options that customers value. Thus, there is no guarantee that elimination of apparently non-value-added costs will not affect customer performance, and some cost reduction in value-added activities may create additional value to the customer.

Second, proponents of the value-added–non-value-added coding scheme apparently believe it is easier to reduce the cost of non-value-added activities than of value-added ones. Such a belief might be justified since industrial engineering resources, for most of the 20th century, were concentrated on direct labor reduction, automation, and increasing the speed with which machines can operate. All these improvements were aimed at reducing the cost of value-added activities. This focus left many indirect and support activities, those that did not directly or obviously benefit end-use customers, with virtually no industrial engineering–process improvement attention. Consequently, these were likely performed quite inefficiently so that an initial focus on non-value-added activities can undoubtedly pick some low-hanging fruit—identifying and eliminating activities that clearly provide no benefit to customers. But once this initial surge of simple activity redesign and elimination has occurred, opportunities for cost reduction can occur in direct production, product design, and customer service activities as well as in indirect and support activities. We actually prefer an attribute that estimates, say on a 1–5 scale, the opportunities for cost reduction in an activity, where:

1. Highly efficient, little (< 5%) apparent opportunity for improvement.
2. Modestly efficient, some (5–15%) opportunity for improvement.
3. Average efficiency, good opportunities (15–25%) for improvement.
4. Inefficient, major opportunities (25–50%) for improvement.
5. Highly inefficient, perhaps should not be done at all; 50–100% opportunity for improvement.

Other Activity Attributes   There are numerous different types of activity attributes that can be used to increase the explanatory power of an ABC model. These include coding for the variability of the activity cost, the location in which the activity is performed, and the person responsible for the bulk of the resources that perform the activity.

Primary and Secondary Activities

There are two categories of activities—primary and secondary. Primary activities are those performed directly for products, services, and customers. The acid test for primary activities is that individuals performing the activity can identify the cost object that triggers, and hence benefits from, the activity. For example, an individual who is maintaining a bill of materials can identify the product (red pens as opposed to blue pens) that benefits from the activity.

Secondary activities support primary activities; they are the activities that create the environment that enables the primary activities to be performed. For example, the human resources department enables production and sales activities to be performed by helping to hire employees. Without human resources, the workforce that performs the primary activities could not be hired and trained. Notice, however, that people in human resources cannot identify individual products (or customers) as their cost objects. In ABC systems these secondary activities are assigned to the primary activities that they support. From there, the costs are assigned to the cost objects using the activity cost drivers selected for the associated primary activities. The procedure is essentially identical to assigning service department costs to other service departments and production cost centers, as described in chapter 2.

The category to which an activity is assigned depends upon the object being costed. For example, if an ABC system of the human resources department is being developed, then most of the activities in that department will be primary. Whereas, if the cost objects are products, customers, and channels, they will be predominately secondary.

In traditional product costing systems (see section titled "Assigning Costs of Service and Support Departments" in chapter 2), many outputs from support departments, such as scheduling production runs and maintaining product specifications, are assigned to production cost centers. When, in the subsequent step, these costs are allocated to products using volume-based drivers, considerable distortion is introduced. ABC systems, in contrast, treat such activities as primary and assign them directly to specific products. The direct assignment of the costs of primary activities contributes to the much greater accuracy and explanatory power of activity-based costing systems. Furthermore, many of the costs of secondary activities can be assigned to the appropriate unit, batch-level, and product-sustaining activities, and hence to the products. This assignment of secondary activity costs creates a second mechanism to reduce distortion in reported product costs. For example, some of the costs of the human resource department will be assigned to activities such as assemble products, setup and parts administration, and then to products based upon their demand for unit, batch-level, and product-sustaining activities.

Once activities have been identified, resource costs have been linked to activities (including the assignment of secondary activity costs to primary activities), and activities have been coded using attribute fields, the ABC system designer now contemplates how to drive activity costs down to cost objects: products, services, and customers.

3. Activity Cost Drivers: Determine How Much of the Output of Each Activity is Required for the Organization's Products, Services, and Customers

Activity-cost drivers link activity costs to cost objects. An activity-cost driver is a quantitative measure of the output of an activity. The selection of an activity-cost driver reflects a subjective trade-off between accuracy and the cost of measurement. Because of the large number of potential activity-to-output linkages, designers attempt to economize on the number of different activity cost drivers. For example, activities triggered by the same event—prepare production orders, schedule production runs, perform first part inspections, and move materials—all can use the same activity-cost driver: number of production runs or lots produced.

ABC system designers can choose from three different types of activity cost drivers: Transaction, duration, and intensity or direct charging.

Transaction drivers, such as the number of setups, number of receipts, and number of products supported, count how often an activity is performed. Transaction drivers can be used when all outputs make essentially the same demands on the activity. A subset of transaction drivers called *Product Characteristic drivers* use physical measures about the product, such as number of components, to generate driver quantities.

Duration drivers, such as setup hours, inspection hours, and direct labor hours, represent the amount of time required to perform an activity. Duration drivers should be used when significant variation exists in the amount of activity required for different outputs. Duration drivers are more accurate than transaction drivers when activity homogeneity exists but they are also more expensive because they require more information about resource consumption by activity.

For some activities, however, even duration drivers may not be sufficiently accurate. *Intensity drivers* directly charge for the resources used each time an activity is performed. Intensity drivers are the most accurate activity cost drivers but are the most expensive to implement; in effect they require direct charging via a job order costing system to keep track of all the resources used each time an activity is performed. They should be used only when the resources associated with performing an activity are both expensive and vary depending upon the cost object in terms of both the quantity and price of the resources consumed.

The activity cost driver should match the level of the cost hierarchy of its associated activity. For example, the cost of unit-level activities (such as machining surfaces) should be driven to products and customers using unit-level activity drivers (such as machine hours), and the cost of batch-level activities (setup machines) should be driven to products and customers using batch-level activity drivers (number of setups, setup hours). Failure to perform such matching guarantees that product and customer costs will be distorted. For example, using unit-based cost drivers (machine hours) for non-unit-based activities (setup machines) leads to the distortions inherent in traditional cost systems: high-volume and complex products will be overcosted and low-volume, simple products will be undercosted. Driving product-sustaining costs using batch-level drivers will cause products that use more than the average level of batch activities to be overcosted and those with less than average use of batch activities to be undercosted.

Often, ABC analysts, rather than actually recording the time and resources required for an individual product or customer, may simulate a duration or intensity driver with a weighted index approach that utilizes *complexity indexes*. They ask individuals to estimate the relative difficulty of performing the task for one type of product–customer or another. A standard product or customer may get a weight of 1; a medium complexity product–customer can get a weight of 3 to 5, and a particularly complex (demanding) product–customer can get a weight of 10. In this way, the variation in demands for an activity among products and customers can be captured without an overly complex measurement system. Again, the important message is to make an appropriate trade-off between accuracy and the cost of measurement. The goal is to be approximately right; for many purposes, transaction drivers or estimates of relative difficulty may be fine for estimating resource consumption by individual products, services, and customers.

WHERE TO APPLY ACTIVITY-BASED COST SYSTEMS

When will activity-based cost systems have the greatest impact? Or, asking this question another way, where should an organization look initially to demonstrate the potential benefits from building an activity-based cost system? We have found two simple rules to help guide the search for high-potential ABC applications:

1. *The Willie Sutton rule:*[4] Look for areas with large expenses in indirect and support resources, especially where such expenses have been growing over time. Operations whose expenses are almost all direct labor and direct materials may have less need for ABC systems since these expenses can be directly and accurately traced to individual products by traditional costing systems. In effect, if organizational activities are all at the unit level (virtually no batch or product-sustaining activities), then ABC systems and traditional cost systems will likely give very similar economic signals.

2. *The High Diversity rule:* Look for a situation in which large variety exists in products, customers, or processes. For example, facilities that produce both mature and newly introduced products, standard and custom products, high-volume and low-volume products demonstrate high product diversity. Similarly, a firm that has a mixture of customers who order high-volume, standard products with few special demands as well as customers who order in small volumes, special volumes, and require large quantities of pre-sales and post-sales technical support will demonstrate high customer diversity. Facilities with complex, heterogeneous processes (some manual, others completely automated) also have high process diversity.

ABC: THE ACCURACY–COST TRADEOFF

The goal of a properly constructed ABC system is not to have the most accurate cost system. Instead, the goal should be to have the best cost system, one that balances the cost of errors made from inaccurate estimates with the cost of measurement (see Exhibit 4–2). Stage II cost systems may be inexpensive to operate but they lead to large distortions in reporting the cost of activities, processes, products, services, and customers. Consequently, managers may make serious mistakes in decisions taken based on this information; there is a high cost of errors. But attempting to build an ABC system with 1,000 or more activities, and using duration drivers or directly charging actual resource costs to each activity performed for each product, service, and

---

[4]Willie Sutton was a successful bank robber in the U.S. during the 1950s (see W. Sutton, *Where The Money Was: The Memoirs of a Bank Robber* (New York: Viking Press, 1976)). Willie, who was eventually captured at his home not far from a local police station, was asked during his initial interrogation, "Why do you rob banks?" Willie replied, with the wisdom that had made him successful for many years, "That's where the money is!" When developing ABC systems, we should follow Willie's sage advice (but not his particular application of the insight) to focus on high cost areas where improvements in visibility and action could produce major benefits to the organization. Applying an ABC analysis to a set of resource expenses that are below 1% of total spending will not lead to high payoffs to the organization.

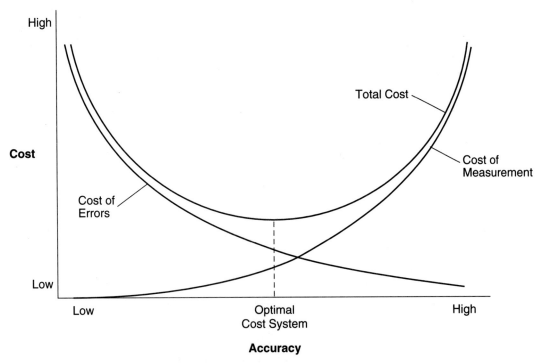

EXHIBIT 4–2   Designing the Optimal ABC System

customer, would lead to an enormously expensive system. The cost of operating such a system would greatly exceed the benefits in terms of improved decisions made with this slightly more accurate information.

SUMMARY

Activity-based cost systems provide more accurate cost information about business activities and processes, and of the products, services, and customers served by these activities. ABC systems focus on organizational activities as the key element for analyzing cost behavior in organizations by linking organizational spending on resources to the activities and business processes performed by these resources. Activity cost drivers, collected from diverse corporate information systems, then drive activity costs to the products, services, and customers that create the demand for (or are benefiting from) the organizational activities. These procedures produce good estimates of the quantities and the unit costs of the activities and resources deployed for individual products, services, and customers. Just how to use and interpret this more accurate information is the subject of the next several chapters.

CASES

The cases in this chapter deal with historical activity-based cost systems. These were the first ABC systems that were encountered and are the type that most firms implement as their first ABC system. As long as there is not significant unused capacity, these systems provide powerful insights into the cost and hence profitability of products.

The first case, *Classic Pen*, applies ABC in a simple manufacturing setting. The *Western Dialysis Clinic* case applies ABC in a simple health care setting. In both situations, the ABC analysis gives very different insights about cost and profitability than had been previously indicated by the organization's existing cost system. *Siemens EMW* case explores how a changing corporate strategy can lead to the obsolescence of even an excellent Stage II cost system, and the role for an ABC system to help a company implement its new strategy. The *John Deere (A)* case illustrates the design of an ABC system in a more complex setting. The *(B)* case demonstrates some of the actions that managers can take with the insights their new ABC system provides about product cost and profitability.

THE CLASSIC PEN COMPANY

Jane Dempsey, controller of the Classic Pen Company, was concerned about the recent financial trends in operating results. Classic Pen had been the low-cost producer of traditional BLUE pens and BLACK pens. Profit margins were over 20% of sales.

Several years earlier Dennis Selmor, the sales manager, had seen opportunities to expand the business by extending the product line into new products that offered premium selling prices over traditional BLUE and BLACK pens. Five years earlier, RED pens had been introduced; they required the same basic production technology but could be sold at a 3% premium. And last year, PURPLE pens had been introduced because of the 10% premium in selling price they could command.

But Dempsey had just seen the financial results (see Exhibit 1) for the most recent fiscal year and was keenly disappointed.

> The new RED and PURPLE pens do seem more profitable than our BLUE and BLACK pens, but overall profitability is down, and even the new products are not earning the margins we used to see from our traditional products. Perhaps this is the tougher global competition I have been reading about. At least the new line, particularly PURPLE pens, is showing much higher margins. Perhaps we should follow Dennis's advice and introduce even more specialty colored pens. Dennis claims that consumers are willing to pay higher prices for these specialty colors.

Jeffrey Donald, the manufacturing manager, was also reflecting on the changed environment at Classic Pen:

> Five years ago, life was a lot simpler. We produced just BLUE and BLACK pens in long production runs, and everything ran smoothly, without much intervention. Difficulties started when the RED pens were introduced and we had to make more changeovers. This required us to stop production, empty the vats, clean out all remnants of the previous color, and then start the production of the red ink. Making black ink was simple; we didn't even have to clean out the residual blue ink from the previous run if we just dumped in enough black ink to cover it up. But for the RED pens, even small traces of the blue or black ink created quality problems. And the ink for the new PURPLE pens also has demanding specifications, but not quite as demanding as for RED pens.

> We seem to be spending a lot more time on purchasing and scheduling activities and just keeping track of where we stand on existing, backlogged, and future orders. The new computer system we got last year helped a lot to reduce the confusion. But I am concerned about rumors I keep hearing that even more new colors may be introduced in the near future. I don't think we have any more capability to handle additional confusion and complexity in our operations.

Operations

Classic produced pens in a single factory. The major task was preparing and mixing the ink for the different-colored pens. The ink was inserted into the pens in a semiautomated process. A final packing and shipping stage was performed manually.

Each product had a bill of materials that identified the quantity and cost of direct materials required for the product. A routing sheet identified the sequence of operations required for each operating step. This information was used to calculate the labor expenses for each of the four products. All of the plant's indirect expenses were aggregated at the plant level and allocated to products on the basis of their direct labor content. Currently, this overhead burden rate was 300% of direct labor cost. Most people in the plant recalled that not too many years ago the overhead rate was only 200%.

Activity-Based Costing

Jane Dempsey had recently attended a seminar of her professional organization in which a professor had talked about a new concept, called activity-based costing (ABC). This concept seemed to address many of the problems she had been seeing at Classic. The speaker had even used an example that seemed to capture Classic's situation exactly.

The professor had argued that overhead should not be viewed as a cost or a burden to be allocated on top of direct labor. Rather, the organization should focus on activities performed by the indirect and support resource of the organization and try to link the cost of performing these activities directly to the products for which they were performed. Dempsey obtained several books and articles on the subject and soon tried to put into practice the message she had heard and read about.

This case was prepared by Professor Robert S. Kaplan.

Copyright © 1997 by the President and Fellows of Harvard College. Harvard Business School case 198-117.

Activity-Based Cost Analysis

Dempsey first identified six categories of support expenses that were currently being allocated to pen production:

EXPENSE CATEGORY	EXPENSE
Indirect labor	$20,000
Fringe benefits	16,000
Computer systems	10,000
Machinery	8,000
Maintenance	4,000
Energy	2,000
Total	$60,000

She determined that the fringe benefits were 40% of labor expenses (both direct and indirect) and would thus represent just a percentage markup to be applied on top of direct and indirect labor charges.

Dempsey interviewed department heads in charge of indirect labor and found that three main activities accounted for their work. About half of indirect labor was involved in scheduling or handling production runs. This proportion included scheduling production orders; purchasing, preparing, and releasing materials for the production run; performing a first-item inspection every time the process was changed over, and some scrap loss at the beginning of each run until the process settled down. Another 40% of indirect labor was required just for the physical changeover from one color pen to another.

The time to change over to BLACK pens was relatively short (about 1 hour) since the previous color did not have to be completely eliminated from the machinery. Other colors required longer changeover times; RED pens required the most extensive changeover to meet the demanding quality specification for this color.

The remaining 10% of the time was spent maintaining records on the four products, including the bill of materials and routing information, monitoring and maintaining a minimum supply of raw materials and finished goods inventory for each product, improving the production processes, and performing engineering changes for the products. Dempsey also collected information on potential activity cost drivers for Classic's activities (see Exhibit 2) and the distribution of the cost drivers for each of the four products. Dempsey next turned her attention to the $10,000 of expenses to operate the company's computer system. She interviewed the managers of the Data Center and the Management Information System departments and found that most of the computer's time (and software expense) was used to schedule production runs in the factory and to order and pay for the materials required in each production run.

Because each production run was made for a particular customer, the computer time required to prepare shipping documents and to invoice and collect from a customer was also included in this activity. In total, about 80% of the computer resource was involved in the production run activity. Almost all of the remaining computer expense (20%) was used to keep records on the four products, including production process and associated engineering change notice information.

The remaining three categories of overhead expense (machine depreciation, machine maintenance, and the energy to operate the machines) were incurred to supply machine capacity to produce the pens. The machines had a practical capacity of 10,000 hours of productive time that could be supplied to pen production.

Dempsey believed that she now had the information she needed to estimate an activity-based cost model for Classic Pen.

Required

1. Estimate the costs for the four pen products using an activity-based approach.
2. What are the managerial implications from the revised cost estimates?

EXHIBIT 1 Traditional Income Statement

	BLUE	BLACK	RED	PURPLE	TOTAL
Sales	$75,000	$60,000	$13,950	$1,650	$150,600
Material costs	25,000	20,000	4,680	550	50,230
Direct labor	10,000	8,000	1,800	200	20,000
Overhead @ 300%	30,000	24,000	5,400	600	60,000
Total operating income	$10,000	$ 8,000	$ 2,070	$ 300	$ 20,370
Return on sales	13.3%	13.3%	14.8%	18.2%	13.5%

EXHIBIT 2 Direct Costs and Activity Cost Drivers

	BLUE	BLACK	RED	PURPLE	TOTAL
Production sales volume (no. of units)	50,000	40,000	9,000	1,000	100,000
Unit selling price	$1.50	$1.50	$1.55	$1.65	
Materials/unit cost	$0.50	$0.50	$0.52	$0.55	
Direct labor hr/unit	0.02	0.02	0.02	0.02	2,000
Machine hour/unit	0.1	0.1	0.1	0.1	10,000
No. of production runs	50	50	38	12	150
Setup time/run (hours)	4	1	6	4	
Total setup time (hours)	200	50	228	48	526
Number of products	1	1	1	1	4

WESTERN DIALYSIS CLINIC (ABC AND HEALTHCARE)

Western Dialysis Clinic is an independent, nonprofit full-service renal dialysis clinic. The clinic provides two types of treatments. Hemodialysis (HD) requires patients to visit a dialysis clinic three times a week,

This case is adapted from T. D. West and D. A. West. "Applying ABC to Healthcare," Management Accounting (February 1997), pp. 22–33.

where they are connected to special, expensive equipment to perform the dialysis. Peritoneal dialysis (PD) allows patients to administer their own treatment daily at home. The clinic monitors PD patients and assists them in ordering supplies consumed during the home treatment. The total and product-line income statement for the clinic is shown below:

CLINIC INCOME STATEMENT	TOTAL	HD	PD
Revenues			
Number of patients	164	102	62
Number of treatments	34,067	14,343	20,624
Total revenue	$3,006,775	$1,860,287	$1,146,488
Supply costs			
Standard supplies (drugs, syringes)	664,900	512,619	152,281
Episodic supplies (for special conditions)	310,695	98,680	212,015
Total supply costs	975,595	611,299	364,296
Service costs			
General overhead (occupancy, administration)	785,825		
Durable equipment (maintenance, depreciation)	137,046		
Nursing services (RNs, LPNs, nursing administrators, equipment technicians)	883,280		
Total service costs	1,806,151	1,117,463	688,688
Total operating expenses	$2,781,746	$1,728,762	$1,052,984
Net income	$ 225,029	$ 131,525	$ 93,504
Treatment Level Profit			
Average charge per treatment		$129.70	$55.59
Average cost per treatment		120.53	51.06
Profit per treatment		$ 9.17	$ 4.53

The existing cost system assigned the traceable supply costs directly to the two types of treatments. The service costs, however, were not analyzed by type of treatment. The total service costs of $1,800,000 were allocated to the treatments using the traditional ratio-of-cost-to-charges (RCC) method developed for government cost-based reimbursement programs. With this procedure, since HD treatments represented about 61% of total revenues, HD received an allocation of 61% of the $1,800,000 service expenses (approximately $1,100,000).

For many years, the clinics such as Western received much of their reimbursement on the basis of reported costs. Starting in the 1980s, however, payment mechanisms shifted, and Western now received most of its reimbursement on the basis of a fixed fee not the cost of service provided. In particular, because HD and PD procedures were categorized by the government as a single category—dialysis treatment—the weekly reimbursement for each patient was the same: $389.10. As a consequence, the three HD treatments per week led to a reported revenue per HD treatment of $129.70, and the seven PD treatments per week led to a reported revenue per PD treatment of $55.59. Both procedures appeared to be profitable, according to the clinic's existing cost and revenue recognition system. David Thomas, the controller of Western Dialysis was concerned, however,

that the procedures currently being used to assign common expenses may not be representative of the underlying use of the common resources by the two different procedures. He wanted to understand their costs better so that Western's managers could make more-informed decisions about extending or contracting products and services and about where to look for process improvements. Thomas decided to explore whether activity-based costing principles could provide a better idea of the underlying cost and profitability of HD and PD treatments.

Phase I

In his initial analysis, Thomas decided to focus on the General Overhead category. But rather than continue to use the RCC method for allocating equipment and nursing costs, he asked the clinic staff for their judgments about how these costs should be allocated. On the basis of the staff's experience and judgment, they felt that HD treatments used about 85% of these resources, and PD about 15%.

Thomas decomposed the General Overhead category into four resource cost pools. Then, for each pool, he chose a cost driver that represented how that resource was used by the two treatments. A summary of his analysis is presented below:

GENERAL OVERHEAD RESOURCE COST POOL	SIZE OF POOL	COST DRIVER
Facility costs (rent, depreciation)	$233,226	Square feet of space
Administration and support staff	354,682	Number of patients
Communications systems and medical records	157,219	Number of treatments
Utilities	40,698	Kilowatt usage (estimated)
Total	$785,825	

Thomas then went to medical records and other sources to identify the quantities of each cost driver for the two treatment types:

GENERAL OVERHEAD COST DRIVER	HD	PD	TOTAL
Square feet	18,900	11,100	30,000
Number of patients	102	62	164
Number of treatments	14,343	20,624	34,967
Estimated kilowatt usage	563,295	99,405	662,700

Required

1. Prepare the revised set of cost estimates and treatment profit and loss statements for HD and PD, using the information gathered during Phase I. What led to any major difference between the RCC method for allocating cost and the Phase I ABC method?

Phase II

Thomas was uncomfortable with the consensus estimate that nursing and equipment costs should be split 85:15 between HD and PD treatments, respectively. In particular, he knew that just the nursing resource category contained a mixture of different types of personnel: registered nurses (RNs), licensed practical nurses (LPNs), nursing administrators, and machine operators. He thought it was unlikely that each of these categories would be used in the same proportion by the two different treatments. In the next phase of analysis, Thomas disaggregated the nursing service category into four resource pools and, as with general overhead, selected an appropriate cost driver for each resource pool (see below):

NURSING SERVICES RESOURCE POOL	SIZE OF POOL	COST DRIVER
Registered nurses	$239,120	Full-time equivalents (FTEs)
Licensed practical nurses	404,064	Full-time equivalents
Nursing administration and support staff	115,168	Number of treatments
Dialysis machine operators	124,928	Number of clinic treatments
Total	$883,280	

NURSING SERVICES COST DRIVER	HD	PD	TOTAL
RNs, FTE	5	2	7
LPNs, FTE	15	4	19
Total number of dialysis treatments	14,343	20,624	34,967
Number of clinic dialysis treatments	14,343	0	14,343

Thomas felt that the 85:15 split was still reasonable for the durable equipment use, and, in any case, the relatively small size of this resource expense category probably did not warrant additional study and data collection.

Required

2. Use the information on the distribution of nursing and machine operator resources to calculate revised product-line income statements and profit and loss for individual treatments.

3. Analyze the newly produced information and assess its implications for managers at Western Dialysis Clinic. What decisions might managers of the clinic make with this new information that might differ from those made using information from the RCC method only?

4. What improvements, if any, would you make in developing an ABC model for Western Dialysis Clinic?

SIEMENS ELECTRIC MOTOR WORKS (A) (ABRIDGED)

Ten years ago our electric motor business was in real trouble. Low labor rates allowed the Eastern Bloc countries to sell standard motors at prices we were unable to match. We had become the high cost producer in the industry. Consequently, we decided to change our strategy and become a specialty motor producer. Once we adopted our new strategy, we discovered that while our existing cost system was adequate for costing standard motors, it gave us inaccurate information when we used it to cost specialty motors.

Mr. Karl-Heinz Lottes, Director of Business Operations, EMW

This case was prepared by Professor Robin Cooper and Professor Karen Hopper Wruck.

Copyright © 1990 by the President and Fellows of Harvard College. Harvard Business School case 191-006.

Siemens Corporation

Headquartered in Munich, Siemens AG, a producer of electrical and electronic products, was one of the world's largest corporations. Revenues totaled 51 billion deutschmarks [DM] in 1987, with roughly half this amount representing sales outside the Federal Republic of Germany. The Siemens organization was split into seven major groups and five corporate divisions. The largest group, Energy and Automation accounted for 24% of total revenues. Low wattage alternating current (A/C) motors were produced at the Electric Motor Works (EMW), which was part of the Manufacturing Industries Division of the Energy and Automation Group. High wattage motors were produced at another facility.

The Electric Motor Works

Located in the small town of Bad Neustadt, the original Siemens EMW plant was built in 1937 to manufacture refrigerator motors for "Volkskuhlschraenke" (people's refrigerators). Less than a year later, Mr. Siemens halted the production of refrigerator motors and began to produce electric motors for other applications. At the end of World War II, the Bad Neustadt plant was the only Siemens factory in West Germany capable of producing electric motors. All the other Siemens production facilities had been completely destroyed or seized by Eastern Bloc countries. After an aggressive rebuilding program, Bad Neustadt emerged as the firm's primary producer of electric motors.

Through the 1970s, EMW produced about 200 different types of standard motors, at a total annual volume around 230,000 motors. Standard motors accounted for 80% of sales volumes—the remaining 20% was customized motors. The production process was characterized by relatively long runs of a single type of motor. Because identical motors were used by a wide range of customers, standard motors were inventoried and shipped as orders were received. The market for standard A/C motors was extremely competitive. The firm was under constant pressure to reduce costs so that it could price aggressively and still make a profit. Despite a major expansion and automation program begun in 1974, by the early 1980s EMW found it could not lower its costs sufficiently to offset the lower labor rates of its Eastern Bloc competitors.

Change in Strategy

An extensive study revealed that EMW could become a profitable producer of low volume, customized A/C motors. To help implement this strategy, the Bad Neustadt plant was enlarged and dedicated to the manufacture of A/C motors with power ratings ranging from 0.06 to 18.5 kilowatts. These motors supported a number of applications including automation engineering, machine tools, plastic processing, and paper and printing machines.

For the new strategy to succeed, EMW needed to be able to manufacture efficiently a large variety of motors in small production runs. Between 1985 and 1988 EMW spent DM50 million a year to replace almost every machine on the shop floor and thereby create a production environment that could support its new strategy.

By 1987 the production process was highly automated with numerically controlled machines, flexible machining centers and robotically fed production processes used throughout the factory. Large volume common components were manufactured using dedicated automated equipment, while very low volume components might be made in manual production processes. Where possible flexible manufacturing was used to produce small volume specialty components. While a normal annual production volume for common components might be 100,000 units, a single component could have up to 10,000 custom variations that might have to be produced one at a time.

To design a custom motor, modifications were made to a standard motor design. The process involved determining where standard components could not be used. These standard components were replaced by custom components that provided the functionality required by the customer.

By 1987, the EMW strategy seemed to be successful (see Exhibit 1). Of a total of 65,625 orders accepted, 90% were for custom motors; 48% for only one motor and 74% for fewer than five motors. But EMW high-volume standard motors still accounted for almost half the total annual output of 630,000 motors.

Change in the Calculation of Product Costs

EMW's product cost system assigned materials and labor costs directly to the products. Overhead costs were divided into three categories: materials related, production related, and support related. Materials-related overhead, containing costs associated with material acquisition, was allocated to products based on their direct materials costs. Production-related overhead was directly traced to the 600 production cost centers. A production cost center had been created for each type of machine. Cost centers with high labor intensity used direct labor hours to allocate costs to products. For centers with au-

tomated machines whose operation required few direct labor hours, machine hours was used as the allocation base. Support-related overhead was allocated to products based on manufacturing costs to date: the sum of direct materials and direct labor costs, materials overhead, and production overhead. The breakdown of each cost category as a percent of total costs was as follows:

	PERCENT OF TOTAL COSTS	BURDEN RATE
Direct materials	29%	
Direct labor	10%	
Materials overhead	2%	6% of materials cost
Production overhead	33%	DM/DLH or DM/MH (600 rates)
Support-related overhead	26%	35% of other manufacturing costs
Total	100%	

Two years after the change in strategy, problems with the traditional cost system became apparent. The traditional cost system seemed unable to capture the relation between the increased support costs and the change in product mix. Management felt that most support costs related more closely to the number of orders received or the number of customized components in a motor rather than to materials expense or to the quantity of labor and machine hours required to build the motor.

An extensive study was undertaken to identify the support costs that management believed were driven by the processing of orders and the processing of special components. The following departments' costs were most affected by the large increases in number of orders and number of special components.

Costs Related to Order Processing
Billing
Order receiving
Product costing and bidding
Shipping and handling
Costs Related to Special Components
Inventory handling
Product costing and bidding
Product development
Purchasing
Receiving
Scheduling and production control
Technical examination of incoming orders

An analysis of the Order Processing costs revealed that the same resources were required to process an order of one custom motor as for an order of 200 standard motors. A similar analysis indicated that the number of different types of special components in each motor design determined the work load for the departments affected by Special Components. The demand for work in these departments was not strongly affected by the total number of special components produced. For example, an order of five custom motors requiring ten special components per unit generated the same amount of work as an order of one custom motor with a design requiring ten special components. In 1987, the factory used 30,000 different special components to customize their motors. The special components were processed 325,000 different times for customized orders.

The costs in each support department associated with these two activities were removed from the support related cost pool and assigned to two new cost pools. Exhibit 2 illustrates, for 1987, the formation of the two new cost pools. The first column presents total costs grouped by traditional costing system definitions. The new cost system removes 6.3 million from engineering support costs, and 27.0 million from administrative support costs. These expenses are then assigned to the new cost pools, 13.8 million to order processing costs, and 19.5 million to special components costs. Over 1 million special components were manufactured during the year.

Exhibit 3 shows the cost buildup for five typical motor orders. The Base Motor cost includes direct materials and labor costs, materials and production overhead, and the portion of support overhead not assigned to the two new cost pools. To this Base Motor cost must be added the cost of processing the order, and the materials, labor, production overhead and support overhead required for the special components.

Effect of the New Cost System

In 1987 EMW received close to DM1 billion in orders, accepted only DM450 million, and ran the factory at 115% of rated capacity. Mr. Karl-Heinz Lottes, Director of Business Operations, EMW commented on the role of the redesigned cost system with the new strategy:

> Without the new cost system, our new strategy would have failed. The information it generated helped us to identify those orders we want to accept. While some orders we lose to competitors, most we turn down because they are not profitable. Anyone who wants to understand the importance of the system, can simply compare some typical orders costed with the traditional system with the costs produced by our new system.

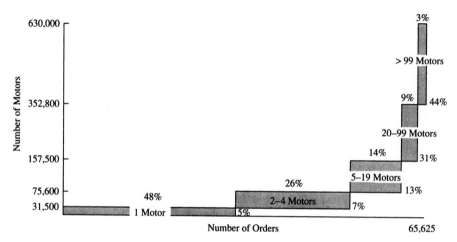

EXHIBIT 1 Distribution of Orders Accepted for Production in 1987

EXHIBIT 2 1987 Reconciliation Transforming the Traditional Cost System (000 DM)

	TRADITIONAL	TRANSFERRED	NEW
Materials	105,000		105,000
Materials overhead	6,000		6,000
Labor	36,000		36,000
Labor or machine overhead	120,000		120,000
Manufacturing cost	267,000 (74%)*		267,000 (74%)
Engineering costs	12,000	6,300	5,700
Tooling costs	22,500	0	22,500
Administrative costs	60,000	27,000	33,000
Support-related cost	94,500 (26%)†	33,300 (9%)	61,200 (17%)
Order processing cost		13,800	13,800
Special components cost		19,500	19,500
Total cost	361,500	0	361,500

Percent of total cost.
†*This figure corresponds to the 26% of support-related overhead discussed in the text.*

EXHIBIT 3 Manufacturing Costs for Five Motor Orders

	A	B	C	D	E
Cost of base motor (without assignment from new cost pools)	304.0	304.0	304.0	304.0	304.0
Cost of all special components* (without assignment from new cost pools)	39.6	79.2	118.8	198.0	396.0
No. of different types of special components per motor	1	2	3	5	10
No. of motors ordered	1	1	1	1	1

	BASE MOTOR COST	SPECIAL COMPONENTS COST
Materials	90	12.0
Materials Overhead	5	0.7
Direct labor	35	4.5
Production-related	117	15.0
Overhead	247	32.2
Support-related overhead[†]	57	7.4
Unit manufacturing costs	304	39.6

*For illustrative purposes, all different types of special components are assumed to cost 39.6 apiece.
[†]Support-related overhead excludes the expenses associated with processing individual customer orders and handling special components.

JOHN DEERE COMPONENTS WORKS (A) (ABRIDGED)

The phone rang in the office of Keith Williams, manager of Cost Accounting Services for Deere & Company. On the line was Bill Maxwell, accounting supervisor for the Gear and Special Products Division in Waterloo, Iowa. The division had recently bid to fabricate component parts for another Deere division. Maxwell summarized the situation:

They're about to award the contracts, and almost all of the work is going to outside suppliers. We're only getting a handful of the parts we quoted, and most of it is low-volume stuff we really don't want. We think we should get some of the business on parts where our direct costs are lower than the outside bid, even if our full costs are not.

Williams asked, "How did your bids stack up against the competition?" Maxwell replied:

Not too well. We're way high on lots of parts. Our machinists and our equipment are as efficient as any in the business, yet our costs on standard, high-volume products appear to be the highest in the industry. Not only are we not competitive with outside suppliers, but our prices are also higher than two other Deere divisions that quoted on the business.

Deere & Company

The company was founded in 1837 by John Deere, a blacksmith who developed the first commercially successful steel plow. One hundred years later, Deere & Company was one of seven full-line farm equipment manufacturers in the world and, in 1963, had displaced International Harvester as the number one producer. During the 1970s, Deere spent over a billion dollars on plant modernization, expansion, and tooling.

This case was prepared by Research Associate Artemis March, under the supervision of Professor Robert S. Kaplan.

Copyright © 1987 by the President and Fellows of Harvard College. Harvard Business School case 187-107.

During the three-decade, post–World War II boom period, Deere expanded its product line, built new plants, ran plants at capacity, and still was unable to keep up with demand. Deere tractors and combines dotted the landscape throughout America.

During this same period, Deere had diversified into off-the-road industrial equipment for use in the construction, forestry, utility, and mining industries. In 1962, it also began building lawn and garden tractors and equipment. By the mid-1980s, Deere had the broadest lawn and garden product line in the world.

The collapse of farmland values and commodity prices in the 1980s, however, led to the worst and most sustained agricultural crisis since the Great Depression. Several factors exacerbated the crisis. The high dollar reduced U.S. exports and thus hurt both American farmers and American farm equipment producers. Farmers had been encouraged to go into heavy debt to expand and buy land, so when land values and farm prices plummeted, the number of farm foreclosures skyrocketed. Few farmers were in a position to buy new equipment, and resale of repossessed equipment further reduced the market for new equipment.

In response, Deere adjusted its level of operations downward, cut costs where possible, increased emphasis on pushing decision making downward, and restructured manufacturing processes. Although outright plant closings were avoided, Deere took floor space out of production, encouraged early retirements, and did not replace most of those employees who left. Employment was reduced from 61,000 at the end of 1980 to about 37,500 at the end of 1986. It implemented new manufacturing approaches such as just-in-time production and manufacturing cells that grouped a number of operations for more efficient flow-through production and placed quality control directly at the point of manufacture. To add production volume, Deere wanted its captive component divisions to supply other companies and industries.

John Deere Component Works

For many years, all the parts for tractors were made and assembled at the tractor works in Waterloo. To generate more production space in the 1970s, Deere successfully split off parts of tractor production. Engine machining and assembly, final tractor assembly, and product engineering each were moved into new plants in the Waterloo area. By the end of the decade, the old tractor works buildings were used only for component production, ranging from small parts to large, complex components such as axles and transmissions. The old tractor works buildings in Waterloo were renamed the John Deere Component Works (JDCW).

In 1983, JDCW was organized into three divisions. The Hydraulics Division, which was soon consolidated into a nearby, refurbished warehouse, fabricated pumps, valves, and pistons. The Drive Trains Division made axles, transmissions, and drive trains. The Gear and Special Products Division made a variety of gears, shafts, and screw machine parts and performed heat treating, cast iron machining, and sheet metal work.

As part of a vertically integrated company, JDCW had been structured to be a captive producer of parts for Deere's equipment divisions, particularly tractors. Thus, it had to produce a great variety of parts whose volume, even in peak tractor production years, was relatively low. During the 1970s, operations and equipment had been arranged to support tractor production of approximately 150 units per day; by the mid-1980s, however, JDCW was producing parts for less than half as many tractors. The lower volume of activity had a particularly adverse effect on JDCW's screw machine and sheet metal businesses, because their machines were most efficient for high-volume production.

Internal Sales and Transfer Pricing   Virtually all of JDCW's sales were internal. Deere equipment-producing factories were required to buy internally major components, such as advanced design transmissions and axles, that gave Deere a competitive advantage. For smaller components, corporate purchasing policy placed JDCW in a favored, but not exclusive, position for securing internal business.

Corporate policy stated that transfers between divisions would take place at full cost (direct materials + direct labor + direct overhead + period overhead). Corporate also had a make-buy policy that when excess capacity was available, buying divisions should compare component divisions' direct costs, rather than full costs, with outside bids. (Direct costs equal full costs less period overhead.) Thus, for example, if JDCW full costs were $10, its direct costs $7, and an outside bid $9, the make-buy decision rule held that the buying division should buy from JDCW. But the transfer pricing policy required the buyer to pay $10 to the component division. Bill Maxwell described the conflict:

The equipment divisions looked only at price and acted like profit centers rather than cost centers. They are starting to act in the interest of their factory rather than the corporation as a whole. The transfer pricing policy wasn't a problem until times got bad and capacity utilization went down. At Component Works, we said to our sister divisions, "You should look at our direct costs and buy from us." They replied, "We don't want to pay more than it would cost us from outside vendors."

In practice, equipment divisions did not always follow the corporate guidelines for internal sourcing, and JDCW lost a portion of the equipment factories' business to outside vendors.

Turning Machine Business

Deere's effort to push decision making down into more manageable units encouraged divisions to view their product lines as stand-alone businesses that sold to external markets. By early 1984, JDCW operations were so far below capacity that managers realized they could not wait for the agricultural market to turn around. In the Gear and Special Products Division, several people thought that turning machine products offered a promising niche.

Turning machines transformed raw materials (primarily steel barstock) into finished components and were the most autonomous of the division's operations. As one manager put it, "We could shut down the turning machine area and not affect the rest of the plant—except that we would then have to buy machined parts from outside suppliers." Only the master schedule connected the area with the activities of the rest of the plant.

The turning machine operations were organized into three departments. These departments were distinguished by the diameter of the barstock its machines could handle and by the number of spindles on each machine. A six-spindle machine could handle six different orientations, for example, and thus make more-complex parts than a four-spindle machine.

Turning Machine Capabilities and Operations
Turning machines automatically fabricated small metal parts. Raw barstock was brought to a staging area near the machines by an overhead crane, the amount depending on the lot size to be run. Barstock (in round, square, or hexagonal sections) was fed horizontally by the operator into the back of the machine. Multiple stations each performed different operations simultaneously on what would become parts; when the longest cycle time (they

ranged from a few seconds to 6 minutes) was completed, a machine indexed to the next position. Small parts, such as pinions, collars, gears, bushings, and connectors continually emerged from the final station. Finished parts were transported in 50-pound baskets stacked in trailers that carried up to 1,500 pounds.

Once set up, automatic turning machines were very fast, had excellent repeatability, and were particularly good at drilling, threading, grooving, and boring out large holes. New, the machines could cost as much as $500,000 each; their replacement value was estimated at about half that amount.

Operators were assigned to a battery of two or three specific machines; they did their own setups and tool changes. Setups, like runs, were timed; operators punched in and out, creating a record of how long setups actually took. Operators were also responsible for quality, machine cleanup, and housekeeping in their areas. After a first-part inspection by an inspector, operators ran the lot. Roving inspectors also checked samples from each lot or basket for conformance to quality standards.

Layout Component Works had 120 automatic turning machines lined up in four long rows in an 80,000-square-foot building (almost the size of two complete football fields). The chip and coolant recovery system was constructed under the floor, running the entire length of the building. It was connected up to each machine, much as houses are connected to a sewer system, to carry off the tremendous amount of chips generated by the machines as well as to cool and lubricate the machines. The layout of the cooling system made it infeasible to redesign the turning machine layout into cellular configurations that would group attendant secondary and finishing operations together.[1] Machines could be shifted around or dedicated to certain parts, but owing to the prohibitive expense of duplicating a chip coolant system, they were forced to remain in rows in S Building.

During the 1970s, secondary operations had been moved off the main floor in S Building to make room for more turning machines; this move increased materials handling distances for most parts. For example, the enormous heat treatment machines were located about one-quarter mile from the main turning machine area.

---

[1]Secondary operations included heat treating, cross-drilling, plating, grinding, and milling: most parts required one or more secondary operations.

Process Engineering To bring a new part into production required extensive process engineering activities. Operations had to be sequenced, and tooling requirements had to be specified for each spindle. If the appropriate specialized tooling did not exist, it had to be either purchased or designed and built (usually outside). Both setups and runs had to be timed and standards established. Process engineers had to make sure that the process they had designed would in fact make the part correctly. Data bases then had to be set up for each machine.

All of these activities had to be conducted whether or not the part number ever ran. John Gordon, head of the process engineering group for turning machines, commented, "We have to do as much work for a part we run once a year—or one we never ever run—as for one we set up every month or that runs every day."

Recently, process engineering and production people had begun to make changes in how they ran turning machine parts. . . . As Andy Edberg, head of process engineering for the division, noted, "Turning machines are extremely high-volume machines, so you want to dedicate them if possible." Process engineers were starting to outsource some low-volume parts or to transfer them to more labor-intensive processes. Edberg pointed to the fundamental nature of the shift:

> We always made all the components for tractors, so we ran lots of part numbers but never really looked at the costs of individual parts. What was important was the efficiency of the whole rather than the efficiency of making the parts.

Competition and Strategy By 1984, Gear and Special Products had roughed out a general strategic thrust toward marketing machine parts to the outside world such as automobile OEMs [original equipment manufacturers]. Initial efforts to gain outside business,

however, soon made it obvious that competing in the external market was going to be harder than anticipated. Competition came in two forms: captive producers of other vertically integrated companies (about whom Deere found it difficult to obtain information) and independent machine shops. The latter had sprung up around geographical clusters of end users. On the East Coast, the independent shops fed the defense industry, particularly shipyards; on the West Coast, they supplied the aircraft industry; and in Michigan and Indiana, they sold to the automotive industry. Dick Sinclair, manufacturing superintendent, observed:

> The key to successful competition in the outside market is price. We found we have a geography problem. We are not in the midst of heavy users, and it is expensive to ship steel both in and out. We also found our range of services to be less useful than we thought they would be.

Bid on 275 Turning Machine Parts

Both excess capacity and its new thrust toward developing stand-alone business motivated Gear and Special Products to bid on 275 of the 635 parts Deere & Company offered for bid in October 1984. All 635 parts had high potential for manufacture on automatic turning machines. Gear and Special Products bid on a subset for which it had the capability, and where the volume was large enough to exploit the efficiencies from its multiple-spindle machines. The buying group consisted of several equipment factories plus a corporate purchasing group; its aims were to consolidate turning machine purchasing by dealing with just a few good vendors and to gain improved service, quality, and price for these parts. Gear and Special Products had one month to prepare its bid.

Results of the bid are summarized below (dollars are in thousands and represent the annual cost for the quantity quoted):

Comparison—JDCW vs. Vendor

	PARTS WITH JDCW LOW TOTAL COST	PARTS WITH JDCW LOW DIRECT COST	TOTAL JDCW DIRECT COST HIGH	TOTAL ALL PARTS
Part numbers	58	103	114	275
JDCW direct cost	$191	$403	$1,103	$1,697
JDCW full cost	272	610	1,711	2,593
Low outside quote	322	491	684	1,507
Percent of $ value	22%	33%	45%	100%
% JDCW of low vendor:				
Direct cost	58	82	161	113
Full cost	82	124	250	172

The purchasing group awarded Gear and Special Products only the 58 parts for which it was the low bidder on a full-cost basis. Most of these were low-volume parts that the division did not especially want to make. Gear and Special Products could be the source for the 103 parts on which its direct costs were below the best outside bid only if it agreed to transfer the parts at the same price as the low outside bidder. The division passed on this "opportunity."

The bidding experience generated a good deal of ferment at Gear and Special Products and confirmed the feeling of many that "we didn't even know our costs." Sinclair recalled:

> Some of us were quite alarmed. We had been saying, "Let's go outside," but we couldn't even succeed inside. Deere manufacturing plants in Dubuque and Des Moines also quoted and came in with lower prices — not across the board, but for enough parts to cause concern. If we weren't even competitive relative to other Deere divisions, how could we think we could be successful externally? And when we looked at the results, we knew we were not costing things right. It was backwards to think we could do better in low-volume than high-volume parts, but that's what the cost system said.

JDCW Standard Cost Accounting System

A standard cost accounting system was used throughout Component Works. . . . The standard or full cost of a part was computed by adding up the following:

- Direct labor (run time only)
- Direct material
- Overhead (direct + period) applied on direct labor
- Overhead (direct + period) applied on material dollars
- Overhead (direct + period) applied on ACTS [actual cycle time standard, see below] machine hours

Establishing Overhead Rates Once a year, the JDCW accounting department reestablished overhead rates on the basis of two studies, the normal study and the process study. The normal study determined the standard number of direct labor and machine hours and total overhead for the following year by establishing a "normal volume." In order to smooth out sharp swings, normal volume was defined as the long term "through the business cycle" volume. One of the measures for setting normal volume was the number of drive trains produced per day.

The process study broke down projected overhead at normal volume among JDCW's 100-plus processes, such as painting, sheet metal, grinding, turning machines, and heat treating. To determine the overhead rate for each process, accounting computed the rate from actual past charges, and then asked, "Do we expect any changes?" (Accumulated charges were collected by charging the specific process code as production took place.) Applying judgment to past rates, next year's normal volume, and any probable changes, accounting established a new overhead rate for each process for the coming year.

Evolution of Bases for Overhead Rates For many years, direct labor run time was the sole basis for establishing overhead rates at Component Works. Thus if $4,000,000 in overhead was generated by $800,000 of direct labor, the overhead rate was 500%. In the 1960s, a separate materials overhead rate had been established. This rate included the costs of purchasing, receiving, inspecting, and storing raw material. These costs were allocated to materials as a percentage markup over materials costs. Over time, separate rates had been established for steel, castings, and purchased parts to reflect the different demands these items placed on the materials handling resources.

Both labor- and materials-based overhead were subdivided into direct and period overhead. Direct (or variable) overhead, such as the costs of setups, scrap, and materials handling, varied with the volume of production activity. Period (or fixed) overhead included accounts, such as taxes, depreciation, interest, heat, light, and salaries, that did not vary with production activity.

In 1984, Component Works introduced machine hours as well as direct labor and materials to allocate overhead. With the increased usage of automated machines, direct labor run time no longer reflected the amount of processing being performed on parts, particularly when one operator was responsible for several machines. Every process was studied and assigned a machine hour or ACTS (actual cycle time standard) rate. Labor hours was retained for processes in which labor time equaled machine time; if these were different, ACTS hours were used to allocate overhead. Total overhead (other than materials overhead) was then split between direct labor overhead and ACTS overhead. As before, each overhead pool was subdivided between direct and period overhead.

Launching a Cost
Study for Turning Machines

Keith Williams had been aware that the existing standard cost system, although satisfactory at an aggregate level, was ineffective for costing and bidding individual parts. He was experimenting with other ways to apply overhead to products. When Maxwell called him in November 1984, Williams realized that the situation at Gear and Special Products provided an opportunity to demonstrate the weaknesses of the current system and to develop a new approach that would be more useful for decision making.

After his phone conversation with Maxwell, Williams quickly put together a proposal to management at Deere & Company, and to the Division Manager of Gear and Special Products. The study would focus on one cost center—the three turning machine departments—because turning machine ACTS hours were the highest chunk of costs in the bid; more than 60% of total machining for the parts occurred on the turning machines. To conduct the study, Williams chose Nick Vintila, who had begun his career at Deere as a manufacturing supervisor at Component Works. During his second year, Vintila had worked in the turning machine area. Not only had he become very familiar with its operation, but he had worked with people such as Gordon, then in methods, and Edberg, then a manufacturing superintendent, who would now also be working on the cost study. Vintila had subsequently served as a liaison between systems development and manufacturing to implement a labor reporting system that tied into Manufacturing Resource Planning System, and then became an accounting supervisor at the Tractor Works.

As a first step, Williams and Vintila studied a sample of 44 of the 275 bid parts (see Exhibit 1). This examination showed: (a) an enormous range of variation among quotes for many parts; (b) a large dispersion between JDCW and vendor quotes, ranging from 50% to 60% on some parts and 200% to 300% on others; (c) that JDCW estimated standard costs exceeded vendor prices by 35%, on average; and (d) that JDCW appeared to be most cost-effective on low-volume and low-value parts. (See Exhibit 2 for summary measures of the characteristics of the 44 sample parts.) These findings raised numerous questions about the validity of the standard cost system for determining costs of individual parts and reaffirmed the need for an alternative costing method.

Vintila spent the first half of 1985 working full-time on what became known as the ABC—activity-based costing—study. After detailed study of the shop process flow, he and Williams learned that use of overhead resources could be explained by seven different types of support activities: direct labor support, machine operation, setup hours, production order activity, materials handling, parts administration, and general and administrative overhead. Vintila then went through each overhead account (e.g., engineering salaries, crib attendant costs), asking others and himself, "Among the seven activities, which cause this account to occur? What creates work for this department?" He began to estimate the percentages of each overhead account that were driven by each of the seven activities. He conducted specific studies to estimate the total volume of each of the seven overhead driving activities (such as number of production orders, total machine hours). This work was circulated among people like Maxwell, Edberg, Gordon, and Sinclair, who, drawing on their experience and judgment, accepted the seven activities as the key overhead drivers and adjusted the final percentages for allocating budgeted items to each activity. (See Appendix A for a description of the seven overhead drivers and how Vintila arrived at the seven overhead rates.) When the ABC method was used to allocate overhead, 41% of the overhead shifted to activity bases 3–7 (see Exhibits 3 and 4). The data needed to estimate the cost of a particular part are shown in Exhibit 5.

The detailed work to design the ABC system had now been completed. The next step for Williams and Vintila was to test and gain acceptance for their new costing approach.

Appendix A:
John Deere Component
Works Activity-Based Costing (A)

ABC Activities for Applying Overhead to Turning Machine Parts The ABC study used the accounting estimate of normal volume and total overhead costs as its starting point. Overhead costs were then allocated to seven rather than just two activities. A separate overhead rate was derived for each activity (see Exhibits 3 and 4 for comparison of the two methods.) Vintila used the following approach to apportion overhead and to develop overhead rates:

CHAPTER 4   ACTIVITY-BASED COSTING: INTRODUCTION   **233**

1. *Direct Labor Support* overhead was generated by incentive employees working on parts. It included allowances for benefits, break periods, and a percentage of supervision, personnel, payroll, and industrial engineering salaries. All direct labor support overhead costs were summed ($1,898,000 in 1985) and divided by the total amount of direct labor dollars ($1,714,000) to derive an overhead rate for this activity (111%).

2. *Machine Operation* overhead was generated by operating the turning machines, plus an allocation of facility and capacity charges. This activity received most of the costs of machine maintenance, small tools, jigs, and dies, as well as smaller proportions of inspection and defective work, engineering and supervision salaries. Allocations were also made for depreciation, taxes, interest, and utilities. The total dollars required to operate the machines ($4,045,000) were divided by the total number of machine hours (242,000) to develop the $16.70 per hour overhead rate for this activity.

   Whereas the standard cost system used the same ACTS rate for all machines, Vintila examined the machines individually and ultimately developed separate rates for four different-sized machines. He gathered data on several factors to create machine-specific estimates of the costs of running them. For example, kilowatt-hours multiplied by the load factor was used to generate utilities cost; replacement costs to estimate the share of insurance, taxes, and depreciation; square footage to calculate a proportion of facilities costs; and the "spindle factor" to allocate tooling and maintenance costs. The spindle factor took into account the number of spindles on a machine; when multiplied by its annual load (or ACTS hours), it provided a basis for allocating tooling and maintenance costs according to size and use of the machine. For all of these factors, Vintila obtained percentages by dividing the total (e.g., replacement costs of all machines) by that for the particular machine. To obtain an overall direct overhead rate for a machine, he divided all its direct overhead by its ACTS hours.

   Once this information had been generated for each of the machines, similar-sized machines were grouped, and a single overhead rate was determined for each group. In this way, machines that happened to have a lower load would not be penalized by a higher rate.

3. *Setup Hours* overhead was generated by changing the job to be run. It included actual setup costs; a small share of machine and small tool maintenance, supervision, and engineering salaries; and a share of depreciation and other facility costs. These costs ($1,111,000) were divided by the estimated number of setup hours (32,900) to arrive at an hourly overhead rate ($33.80).

   The number of setup hours was estimated through an examination of production control data that showed the average setup time to be 4 hours. This figure was multi-

plied by the average number (4) of annual runs per part number and by the 2,050 parts in the system.

4. *Production Order Activity* was generated by shop activity resulting from each production order. The largest cost was material control salaries. Percentages of crib attendant costs, inspection, defective work, and manufacturing costs were also applied. The sum was divided by the total number of annual production orders (7,150) to yield a cost of $114 per production order.

5. *Materials Handling* overhead arose from moving barstock to the machines and then moving the parts to the next operation. The major cost elements were materials handling labor and equipment maintenance. This activity also received a share of inspection and defective materials costs. An overhead rate ($19.42) was derived by dividing the total allocated costs ($303,000) by the number of loads (15,600).

   The number of loads was estimated through a six-step process:

   a. $\dfrac{\text{part weight} \times \text{annual volume}}{\text{runs/year for that part}} = \text{weight/run}$

   b. $\dfrac{\text{weight/run}}{\text{pounds/load}} = \text{loads/run}$
      (average of 2000 lb per transport container)

   c. loads/run + 0.5, then round result to nearest full integer (a calculation to correct for incomplete loads)

   d. multiply result in (c) by number of runs of that part/year = number of loads/year moved away from machines

   e. loads/year × 2 (movement to and from machine) = total number of loads/year for that part

   f. repeat process for all part numbers, and add number of loads/part to obtain total number of loads per year

6. *Parts Administration* overhead was incurred just by having a part number in the department's repertoire. It included the cost of establishing and maintaining records and systems documentation and a share of salaries in process engineering, industrial engineering, supervision, and materials control. The sum of $999,000 in overhead, when distributed among the 2,050 parts in the system, generated a head tax of $487 per part number.

7. *General and Administrative* overhead was attributed to the entire factory, not to a particular manufacturing process or activity. It included a large share of taxes, utilities, and depreciation, as well as smaller shares of salaries such as accounting, reliability, and manufacturing engineering. The $998,000 of general and administrative (G&A) overhead was prorated to products on the basis of their value added: the sum of direct labor plus the other six overhead activity costs for each part. The value-added sum became the denominator for determining the G&A rate to be applied to the part.

EXHIBIT 1 Comparison of JDCW vs. Outside Vendor Bids for Sample of 44 Parts

PART NUMBER	PART DESCRIPTION	QUOTE VOLUME	JDCW EST DIR. COST	JDCW EST MFG. COST	1	2	3	4	5	6	7	% TO JDCW to VDR. 2 DIR. COST.	% TO JDCW to VDR. 2 MFG. Cost.	DIRECT LABOR $ EACH
Component Works Low on Full-Cost Basis:														
F382	Fitting	4,009	$ 2,248	$ 3,153	$ 3,940	$ 9,822	$13,550					23%	32%	$0.05
S209	Spacer	950	183	291	399	522	551	$ 1,244	$ 1,244			35	56	0.03
P594	Pin	692	297	430	692	796	817	1,012	1,509			37	54	0.03
T815	Stud	3,150	719	1,162	1,712	1,859	2,158	2,300	3,131	$ 9,356		39	62	0.03
P675	Pin	3,596	1,703	2,649	3,587	3,740	6,024	7,947				46	55	0.07
H622	Hub	4,450	3,207	4,365	5,687	6,324	6,743	7,518	8,463	12,875	$12,875	51	69	0.05
S245	Spacer	4,912	1,249	1,917	2,210	2,335	2,536	3,276	3,585	4,076		53	82	0.03
R647	Sprocket	5,167	6,792	9,196	11,907	12,142	12,400	13,124	16,116	16,674	17,516	56	76	0.10
T501	Stud	4,879	902	1,492	1,537	1,610	1,625	1,820	2,196	2,976	6,294	56	93	0.03
S071	Spacer	5,661	4,896	6,885	8,378	8,433	10,133					58	82	0.09
C784	Cap	71,200	13,101	19,537	17,088	22,072	22,606	23,332	29,832	41,253		59	89	0.04
P583	Pin	3,402	2,775	4,285	4,380	4,467	4,826	5,233	5,391	17,200		62	96	0.09
R410	Sprocket	792	878	1,226	658	1,349	2,162	2,273	2,866	2,946	3,983	66	91	0.08
Total or Average		112,860	$ 38,949	$ 56,590		$ 75,471						52%	75%	$0.05
Component Works Low on Direct-Cost Basis:														
R918	Rocker	1,091	$ 663	$ 1,063	$ 905	$ 1,036						64%	103%	$0.05
P220	Pin	3,204	6,685	11,754	9,048	10,413	$12,655	$14,642	$18,711			64	113	0.45
P057	Pin	1,281	979	1,675	1,460	1,487	2,306	2,985				66	113	0.09
T566	Stud	2,452	7,925	12,037	9,563	11,843	12,628	13,461	18,568			67	102	0.42
P736	Pin	38,955	6,837	10,475	9,181	10,167	11,492	11,492	13,323	22,983		67	103	0.03
P904	Pin	950	1,170	1,801	1,606	1,729	1,767	1,995	3,420			68	104	0.10
H355	Hub	1,155	1,947	3,090	2,552	2,872	2,979	3,026	4,775	6,846		68	108	0.13
P423	Pin	3,402	2,661	4,157	2,994	3,912	5,137	5,477	11,805			68	106	0.09
B605	Bolt	10,561	2,239	3,373	2,893	3,273	3,485	3,707	3,970	4,718	$ 4,718	68	103	0.03
H346	Hub	1,088	2,223	3,570	3,007	3,122	3,151	3,242	3,438	4,034	4,128	71	114	0.15
H554	Hub	1,490	1,551	2,214	1,967	1,997	2,077	2,216	2,298	2,459	2,459	78	111	0.06
P244	Pin	7,383	7,438	10,948	7,591	8,786	9,498	10,705	11,270	12,677	23,773	85	125	0.11
L209	Lever	5,351	2,480	3,827	1,578	2,745	3,692	4,334	4,486	4,548	4,826	90	139	0.05
R316	Roller	18,058	2,470	4,610	2,257	2,691	3,250	4,050	4,231	4,939	4,984	92	171	0.03
S451	Spacer	2,785	645	1,226	390	697	852	1,104	1,253	1,276	1,306	93	176	0.04
P333	Pin	4,258	6,818	12,088	6,898	7,324	9,197	11,113	12,008			93	165	0.32
P379	Pin	6,807	6,984	10,249	5,037	7,352	7,760	9,394	9,421	21,919		95	139	0.11
P682	Pin	3,402	4,037	5,880	2,824	4,208	5,035	5,817	11,533			96	140	0.08
Total or Average		113,673	$ 65,753	$104,038		$ 85,654						77%	121%	$0.08
Cumulative		226,533	$104,703	$160,629		$161,125						65%	100%	$0.08
Component Works Not Cost Competitive:														
H265	Hub	4,464	$ 15,311	$ 24,341	$13,570	$ 15,236	$17,275	$17,454	$17,901	$20,489		100%	160%	$0.57
A152	Shaft	2,972	7,749	12,841	6,685	7,667	8,470	10,877				101	167	0.38
R717	Sprocket	4,869	6,834	10,003	6,205	6,707	7,421	7,839	7,887	8,868	$ 9,450	102	149	0.16
S771	Spacer	11,092	971	1,689	909	942	1,053	1,275	1,852	2,107	2,203	103	179	0.02
R428	Sprocket	3,180	4,374	6,888	3,637	4,226	4,285	4,293	4,624	4,709	5,599	103	163	0.18
R946	Roller	5,904	6,254	10,727	4,815	6,022	6,199	6,494	7,947	9,269	19,837	104	178	0.14
R157	Roller	3,181	1,651	2,934	1,082	1,565	1,645	1,749	1,890	1,917	2,004	106	188	0.08
B823	Button	18,200	3,296	5,622	2,347	3,094	3,257	3,276	3,314	3,516	6,042	107	182	0.03
T863	Stud	7,120	11,136	17,790	8,231	8,590	9,185	13,243	24,706			130	207	0.37
T237	Stop	4,258	12,719	18,713	7,877	8,516	9,112	9,623	10,228	16,606		149	220	0.35
N281	Nut	8,500	6,350	11,322	3,392	3,789	4,114	6,375	7,548	8,925	15,640	168	299	0.18
T166	Stud	5,645	8,766	16,014	3,912	5,024	5,701	13,209				174	319	0.41
T586	Stud	10,000	15,957	27,273	7,525	8,900	9,540	11,000	11,520	26,700		179	306	$0.40
Total or Average		89,385	$101,367	$166,157		$ 80,278						126%	207%	$0.21
Total/Avg. all Parts		315,918	$206,069	$326,786		$241,403						85%	135%	$0.11

EXHIBIT 2 Characteristics of Sample of 44 Parts

CATEGORY	NUMBER	VOLUME	DIRECT LABOR $	ACTS HOURS PER 100 PARTS	ANNUAL ACTS HOURS	DL $/ MATERIALS $
Low on full-cost basis	13	4,009*	0.05	0.04	19	21%
		[692; 71,200]	[0.03; 0.10]	[0.3; 1.5]	[2; 266]	[9; 51]
Low on direct-cost basis	18	3,402	0.09	1.2	31	23%
		[950; 38,955]	[0.03; 0.45]	[0.3; 2.8]	[10; 159]	[9; 224]
Not cost competitive	13	5,645	0.18	1.5	70	57%
		[2972; 18,200]	[0.02; 0.57]	[0.2; 3.4]	[18; 150]	[22; 480]
Total	44					

Top number is the median value in that category.
The range [minimum; maximum] appears beneath the median.

EXHIBIT 3 1985 Turning Machine Overhead Allocation Using Standard Cost System

	APPLIED BASED ON DIRECT LABOR (DL)		APPLIED BASED ON MACHINE HOURS		TOTAL $000s	% TOTAL
Direct Overhead						
Maintenance	$ 32	0.3%	$1,038	10.2%	$ 1,070	10.5%
Labor allowances	459	4.5	0	0.0	459	4.5
Machine setups	0	0.0	524	5.2	524	5.2
Other OH lab	130	1.3	164	1.6	294	2.9
Scrap & misc.	80	0.8	96	0.9	176	1.7
Employee benefits	1,296	12.7	556	5.5	1,852	18.2
Total direct OH	$1,997	19.6%	$2,378	23.4%	$ 4,375	43.0%
Period Overhead						
Maintenance	$ 127	1.2%	$ 527	5.2%	$ 654	6.4%
Salaries	796	7.8	826	8.1	1,622	15.9
Depreciation	0	0.0	1,790	17.6	1,790	17.6
Gen. & misc.	227	2.2	717	7.0	944	9.3
Employee benefits	354	3.5	432	4.2	786	7.7
Total period OH	$1,504	14.8%	$4,292	42.2%	$ 5,796	57.0%
Total overhead	$3,501	34.4%	$6,670	65.6%	$10,171	100.0%
Overhead base	$1,714 DL$		242,000 ACTS hrs			
Direct overhead rate	117%		$ 9.83 per hr			
Period overhead rate	88%		17.73 per hr			
Total overhead rate	205%		$27.56 per hr			

EXHIBIT 4 1985 Turning Machine Overhead Allocation Using ABC Method

	DIRECT LABOR (DL) SUPPORT OVERHEAD		MACHINE OPERATION OVERHEAD		MACHINE SETUP OVERHEAD		PRODUCTION ORDER OVERHEAD		MATERIAL-HANDLING OVERHEAD		PART ADMIN. OVERHEAD		GENERAL AND ADMINISTRATION OVERHEAD		TOTAL	
	$000s	% TOTAL	$000s	% TOTAL	$000s	% TOTAL	$000s	% TOTAL	$000s	% TOTAL	$000s	% TOTAL	$000s	% TOTAL	$000s	% TOTAL
Direct Overhead																
Maintenance	$ 0	0.0%	$ 899	8.8%	$ 45	0.4%	$ 62	0.6%	$ 63	0.6%	$ 0	0.0%	$ 0	0.0%	$ 1,069	10.5%
Labor allowances	329	3.2%	47	0.5%	61	0.6%	10	0.1%	12	0.1%	0	0.0%	0	0.0%	459	4.5%
Machine setups	0	0.0%	146	1.4%	378	3.7%	0	0.0%	0	0.0%	0	0.0%	0	0.0%	524	5.2%
Other OH lab	0	0.0%	67	0.7%	0	0.0%	106	1.0%	122	1.2%	0	0.0%	0	0.0%	295	2.9%
Scrap & Misc.	0	0.0%	141	1.4%	0	0.0%	30	0.3%	6	0.1%	0	0.0%	0	0.0%	177	1.7%
Employee benefits	1,100	10.8%	339	3.3%	246	2.4%	77	0.8%	90	0.9%	0	0.0%	0	0.0%	1,852	18.2%
Total direct OH	$1,429	14.0%	$1,639	16.1%	$ 730	7.2%	$285	2.8%	$293	2.9%	$ 0	0.0%	$ 0	0.0%	$ 4,376	43.0%
Period Overhead																
Maintenance	$ 10	0.1%	$ 333	3.3%	$ 40	0.4%	$ 9	0.1%	$ 8	0.1%	$238	2.3%	$ 17	0.2%	$ 655	6.4%
Salaries	270	2.7%	179	1.8%	62	0.6%	243	2.4%	0	0.0%	421	4.1%	448	4.4%	1,623	16.0%
Depreciation	27	0.3%	1,424	14.0%	226	2.2%	25	0.2%	0	0.0%	43	0.4%	45	0.4%	1,790	17.6%
Gen. & Misc.	59	0.6%	323	3.2%	19	0.2%	152	1.5%	0	0.0%	90	0.9%	298	2.9%	941	9.3%
Employee benefits	103	1.0%	147	1.4%	34	0.3%	103	1.0%	2	0.0%	207	2.0%	190	1.9%	786	7.7%
Total period OH	469	4.6%	$2,406	23.7%	$ 381	3.7%	$532	5.2%	$ 10	0.1%	$999	9.8%	$998	9.8%	$ 5,795	57.0%
Total overhead	$1,898	18.7%	$4,045	39.8%	$1,111	10.9%	$817	8.0%	$303	3.0%	$999	9.8%	$998	9.8%	$10,171	100.0%
Overhead base	$1,714 DL$		242,000 annual ACTS hours		32,900 annual setup hours		7,150 annual orders		15,600 annual loads		2,050 part nos.		$10,887 value added*			
Direct overhead rate	83.4%		$ 6.77 per hour*		$22.18 per hour		$ 39.86 per order		$18.78 per load		—		—			
Period overhead rate	27.4%		$ 9.94 per hour		$11.58 per hour		$ 74.41 per order		0.64 per load		$487 per part		9.1%			
Total overhead rate	111.0%		$16.71 per hour		$33.76 per hour		$114.27 per order		$19.42 per load		$487 per part		9.1%			

$ 1,714 DL$
1,898 DL$ OH
4,045 Mach. oper. OH
1,111 Setup OH
817 Prod. order OH
303 Mat. h. OH
999 Part. adm. OH
$10,887 Value added

Rates shown are averages across all turning machines. In practice, separate machine overhead rates were calculated for each major class of machines.

EXHIBIT 5 Elements for Costing Part A103 in 1985

$6.44 materials cost/100 parts

Materials Overhead Rates:

2.1%	Direct
7.6%	Period
0.185	Direct labor hours/100 parts
0.310	ACTS hours/100 parts
$12.76	Labor rate for screw machine operation
4.2 hr	Machine setup time
0.176 lb	Part weight

8,000 quote volume (annual volume as specified by user)

2 runs/year

6-spindle machine rates: (under ABC systems)	Direct: $8.99 Period: $7.61

JOHN DEERE COMPONENT WORKS (B)

Frank Stevenson had been appointed division manager of Gear and Special Products in September 1986 after spending 20 years in manufacturing and manufacturing engineering. He summarized his division's response to activity-based costing (ABC):[1]

> Few things have generated more excitement. Even though it's still an allocation, it's such an improvement. Parts we suspected we were undercosting have turned out to be even more expensive than we had thought. It's proven what we suspected about the costs of material handling and transport distances, and triggered our making layout changes. When it showed us the costs added by secondary operations, we brought them back onto the main floor.

ABC Cost Estimating Model

In order to use ABC for costing individual parts, a model was developed that could be run using a Lotus 1-2-3 spreadsheet on an IBM personal computer (separate from the overall accounting and data processing systems). It provided considerably more information than the standard cost model, and some elements of the model were interactive. The ABC model, for example, calculated material costs on the basis of the type of steel, part length, and machine number (which affected tools used and waste). Also, materials that were delivered directly to the machines on the floor, bypassing receiving, inspection, and storage, were not charged for any materials overhead. Therefore, material costs depended on how the material was used, as well as its purchase price. (The standard cost system, by contrast, calculated an average cost for parts of a certain weight based entirely on the purchase price of the barstock.) Materials of different prices could be fed into the ABC system, and the model would make cost trade-offs among them. The model could calculate the number of annual runs that produced the lowest manufacturing costs on an annual basis for a part number; it included inventory holding costs as a factor in making this assessment. It could also compare setups on different machines for their differential cost effects.

Although the ABC method was developed on the basis of normal volume, the model could also calculate

costs at a par (full capacity) level of utilization. Par volume was higher than current normal volume and represented what Gear and Special Products managers considered a more reasonable level of utilization than the currently existing very depressed normal volume. Par overhead rates spread period overhead across higher volumes of parts than did normal rates.

Completing the ABC Study

Keith Williams and Nick Vintila, the authors of activity-based costing, were able to demonstrate the change in estimated costs, from standard to ABC, for the sample of 44 parts examined earlier (see Exhibit 1). They also experimented with changing the lot size from that currently being used in the division's MRP system. In particular, the ABC model recommended that the average lot size be doubled—thereby halving the number of annual runs per part—in order to optimize manufacturing costs (see Exhibit 2). The costs saved in reduced setups, materials handling, and production order processing more than offset the increased inventory holding costs.

A third study showed the impact of shifting the product mix to exploit the efficiencies from running longer jobs on the turning machines. Exhibit 3 shows the current workload on the turning machines based on the annual machine hours (ACTS) for each part. The overhead assignment (using the new ABC model) to each class of parts is shown at the bottom of the exhibit. Exhibit 4 shows a simulated overhead assignment assuming that the more than 1,000 parts with less than 100 annual ACTS hours run time were transferred from the machines, with the freed-up machine time used to produce 30 new parts that each required at least 500 annual ACTS hours. This change would reduce by 77% the number of part numbers being processed on the machines and reduce the number of setup hours and orders processed by about 60%. Williams explained the rationale for this study:

> We wanted to estimate the impact from substituting a few high-volume parts for the large number of low-volume parts we are now running. Overhead is reduced by $2.2 million, or about 21%. The overhead rate declines from 593% to 467% of direct labor. The key question is whether actual overhead reductions of that scale would result from such a change.
>
> Our impression is that at least this amount of overhead reduction should occur. The reduced number of parts should

Research Associate Artemis March prepared this case under the supervision of Professor Robert S. Kaplan.

Copyright © 1987 by the President and Fellows of Harvard College. Harvard Business School case 187-108.

[1]See "John Deere Component Works (A)," HBS No. 9-187-107.

directly reduce the expenses for machine setups and for material management scheduling and coordination. Process and tool and industrial engineering would be supporting only a fifth of the part numbers now being supported. Such a change should make it much easier to standardize raw material, which should reduce coordination in that area. Also, it should be much easier to implement other operational improvements such as sequencing jobs so as to minimize setups, using pick-offs or other attachments to eliminate secondary operations, or possible rearrangements to create a cell environment for the high-volume parts.

Division Changes

Stevenson located activity-based costing in the context of a division trying to reorient itself to a new reality: "We must dramatically increase our competitive position in the worldwide market. That requires a quantum leap in manufacturing quality and in reducing our costs." To this end, the division had, during the 1985–1986 period, formally demarcated its product lines into five businesses: gears and shafts, machined parts, cast iron machining, heat treating, and sheet metal work. Wherever possible, departments were reorganized from processes to manufacturing cells and a just-in-time approach adopted to shorten lead times, improve quality, and thus lower costs. Stevenson stated, "We want 'visual management' to replace routing; we want to stand here at the beginning of the process and see parts being completed right within our view." In addition, a marketing department had been added at the factory level.

Use of ABC

ABC was widely embraced for decision making in the machined parts business and for implementing other changes more effectively.

Bidding   The ABC model was being used to cost machined parts and to prepare bids to both Deere and outside customers. Sinclair commented, "We are more confident now about our quote prices. And because ABC more properly penalizes low-volume products, we now know which business we don't want." Also, the ABC model could generate costs at either normal or par volume, making it easier to prepare par-based quotes for the machining portion of the parts.

The division had also changed its transfer pricing and bidding practices. Attempting to bid and transfer at full cost had lost Gear and Special Products much inter-

nal business. It began to negotiate "market-based prices," which could be below the full costs calculated by the existing cost accounting system. After a period of experimentation, the use of market pricing became official corporatewide policy in April 1986.

Process Planning   John Gordon, head of process engineering for the machining area, was using the model to compare relative machining efficiencies for different types of steel and part numbers in order to decide which parts should be run on which types of machines. Because ABC revealed much higher setup and production order costs than those used in the MRP ordering formula, larger lot sizes and fewer annual runs per part number were indicated. Process engineering was using ABC to cost parts on the basis of optimal runs per year and to negotiate with customers to accept fewer runs at lower prices.

Low Value-Added Parts   Gear and Special Products was already accelerating the movement of low-volume, short-running parts off the turning machines. About one-third (31%) of parts required over 20 hours each of direct labor; collectively these accounted for 97% of all direct labor hours and were likely to all remain on the machines. But parts with less than eight hours of labor were being outsourced or would soon go to the low value-added (LVA) jobshop that was being set up adjacent to the machining area. The fate of the remaining parts was still undetermined, but decision making was now aided by the much more accurate costing under ABC. This would eventually allow the division to determine the breakeven point; Dick Sinclair, the manufacturing superintendent, commented, "We don't yet know where the point is that says, 'Put it on the turning machine.' We've eliminated the clearly LVA parts and are working our way up."

The combination of moving LVA parts off the turning machines and moving toward fewer runs for the remaining parts was expected to increase the average run time, reduce scheduling complexity, and eventually reduce the demands for staff support.

Cell Arrangements   While physical manufacturing infrastructure constrained dramatic rearrangement from rows of machines to cells, certain machines could be clustered together and dedicated to a particular high-run part. For example, twelve adjacent machines were now dedicated to running just two parts for General Motors.

Layout   ABC was helping division managers decide how to arrange the machining departments. Sinclair noted, "We did a lot of things in the 1970s that made a lot of sense then, but now we must undo them." The high cost of secondary operations caused management to move these operations not only back into the division (they had been part of Drive Trains for years), but into a corner of the main floor in S Building where they were now being requalified. To make room for these operations, less-efficient turning machines had been scrapped; relative efficiencies had been revealed by Vintila's detailed machine study. To reduce handling distances, barstock staging had been made more efficient, and packaging and shipping were being relocated closer to final operations.

These layout changes had not yet been tried out during production. They had been made during the August 1986 vacation shutdown, but the factory had been closed until January 1987 by a corporatewide UAW strike.

One layout change implemented in April 1985, however, already had made a considerable impact. Gordon's process engineering group, formerly one-half mile from the shop floor, was now located right in the middle of the machining area. According to Andy Edberg, division head of process engineering. "The effect has been tremendous. The output of our process engineers has tripled, and communication between them and the operators has improved enormously."

Future of ABC

Useful as it was, ABC's impact was still limited. First, it was run on a personal computer and not integrated with the other division data bases; and second, it was being applied only to turning machine operations.

Extending ABC to secondary operations was Sinclair's top ABC priority: "If we are to price the whole business, we need to extend the model to secondary operations." While the model costed machine operations for parts that would eventually be assembled into major parts such as drive trains, the old standard cost system was still being used for inventory valuation and for costing major parts. Stevenson noted:

> We don't want parallel systems; their development and maintenance is too costly. We would like to get rid of the standard system and have just one system—ABC.

EXHIBIT 1   Comparison of Machined Parts Overhead: Standard Costing versus Activity-Based Costing for the 44 Sample Items— Turning Machine Operations Only

PART NUMBER	PART DESCRIPTION	QUOTE VOLUME	PART WEIGHT	ABC RUNS/ YEAR	ACTS HR PER 100	ANNUAL	DIRECT LABOR	JDCW OVERHEAD COST DIRECT OH	PERIOD OH	TOTAL OH	ABC OVERHEAD COST DIRECT OH	PERIOD OH	TOTAL OH	ABC OVERHEAD AS % JDCW DIRECT OH	PERIOD OH	TOTAL OH
The 10 Parts Most Helped by ABC																
H265	Hub	4,464	3.703	4	3.4	150	$1,127	$3,750	$4,905	$8,654	$3,347	$3,104	$6,451	89%	63%	75%
R946	Roller	5,904	0.600	3	2.4	139	695	2,621	3,700	6,321	2,064	2,726	4,792	79	74	76
R428	Sprocket	3,180	1.556	2	2.2	70	527	1,672	2,187	3,859	1,575	1,744	3,319	94	80	86
R717	Sprocket	4,869	1.956	2	2.0	95	713	2,035	2,661	4,696	2,181	2,087	4,266	107	78	91
A152	Shaft	2,972	1.252	3	1.7	51	379	1,359	1,777	3,136	1,363	1,618	2,981	100	91	95
P244	Pin	7,383	1.085	3	1.8	132	706	2,198	3,064	5,262	2,358	2,696	5,054	107	88	96
H355	Hub	1,155	3.052	1	2.3	26	130	677	955	1,632	540	1,028	1,568	80	108	96
R157	Roller	3,181	0.243	1	1.5	46	231	839	1,185	2,024	711	1,274	1,984	85	108	98
C784	Cap	71,200	0.166	4	0.4	266	1,994	4,151	5,425	9,576	4,929	4,472	9,401	119	82	98
P379	Pin	6,807	1.116	3	1.8	133	651	2,039	2,843	4,882	2,238	2,561	4,798	110	90	96
	Total/Average	11,112	1.473	2.6	1.9	110	$7,152	$21,341	$28,702	$50,043	$21,306	$23,310	$44,614	100%	81%	89%
The 10 Parts Most Penalized by ABC																
S771	Spacer	11,092	0.039	1	0.2	20	$100	$329	$466	$795	$411	$934	$1,346	125%	200%	169%
P675	Pin	2,596	0.412	1	0.4	14	69	263	371	634	377	858	1,236	144	231	195
P220	Pin	3,204	0.743	3	0.6	19	139	444	580	1,024	824	1,188	2,011	186	205	196
T815	Stud	3,150	0.281	1	0.4	12	58	237	336	573	317	828	1,144	134	246	200
N281	Nut	8,500	0.222	3	0.2	18	135	411	537	949	817	1,183	2,000	199	220	211
T566	Stud	2,452	1.779	3	1.0	24	178	564	738	1,302	1,228	1,519	2,748	218	206	211
R918	Rocker	1,091	0.703	1	0.9	10	40	193	281	473	262	783	1,047	136	279	221
R410	Sprocket	792	2.786	1	0.7	6	42	172	225	397	339	766	1,105	197	341	278
P594	Pin	692	0.722	1	0.3	2	11	61	87	148	207	702	910	338	811	615
S209	Spacer	950	0.141	1	0.3	3	15	58	82	140	173	688	862	299	842	617
	Total/Average	3,229	0.712	1.5	0.5	12	$788	$2,732	$3,702	$6,434	$4,955	$9,449	$14,409	181%	255%	224%

EXHIBIT 1 *continued* Comparison of Machined Parts Overhead: Standard Costing versus Activity-Based Costing for the 44 Sample Items—Turning Machine Operations Only

PART NUMBER	PART DESCRIPTION	QUOTE VOLUME	PART WEIGHT	ABC RUNS/ YEAR	ACTS HR PER 100	ACTS HR ANNUAL	DIRECT LABOR	JDCW DIRECT OH	JDCW PERIOD OH	JDCW TOTAL OH	ABC DIRECT OH	ABC PERIOD OH	ABC TOTAL OH	%JDCW DIRECT OH	%JDCW PERIOD OH	%JDCW TOTAL OH
Remaining Parts																
H346	Hub	1,088	3.614	2	2.8	31	$151	$823	$1,166	$1,989	$735	$1,225	$1,960	89%	105%	99%
B823	Button	18,200	0.069	2	0.5	84	417	1,305	1,844	3,149	1,317	1,898	3,215	101	103	102
R316	Roller	18,058	0.042	2	0.4	80	401	1,266	1,784	3,050	1,278	1,854	3,132	101	104	103
T237	Stop	4,258	1.818	5	2.7	116	706	2,072	2,924	4,996	2,413	2,753	5,176	116	94	104
P682	Pin	3,402	1.347	2	1.8	61	325	1,131	1,577	2,708	1,253	1,618	2,872	111	103	106
T586	Stud	10,000	0.602	4	0.7	77	573	1,595	2,086	3,681	1,888	2,061	3,947	118	99	107
S071	Spacer	5,661	1.507	2	1.0	54	407	1,167	1,527	2,694	1,449	1,545	2,994	124	101	111
P583	Pin	3,402	1.253	2	1.5	52	258	935	1,320	2,255	1,056	1,479	2,534	113	112	112
P736	Pin	38,955	0.160	2	0.4	159	795	1,944	2,742	4,686	2,480	2,915	5,394	128	106	115
P423	Pin	3,402	1.354	2	1.5	52	258	931	1,314	2,245	1,131	1,489	2,619	121	113	117
P333	Pin	4,258	0.937	3	1.3	56	282	1,021	1,441	2,462	1,232	1,668	2,899	121	116	118
L209	Lever	5,351	0.533	2	0.8	41	204	747	1,054	1,801	858	1,332	2,190	115	126	122
P057	Pin	1,281	0.569	1	1.5	20	97	438	618	1,056	404	926	1,330	92	150	126
T863	Stud	7,120	1.110	4	1.0	74	553	1,396	1,825	3,220	2,217	2,100	4,316	159	115	134
T166	Stud	5,645	0.258	3	0.6	36	232	757	1,023	1,780	1,098	1,415	2,511	145	138	141
B605	Bolt	10,561	0.286	2	0.3	32	242	659	864	1,523	911	1,250	2,161	138	145	142
P904	Pin	950	2.179	1	1.8	17	86	384	542	925	430	894	1,325	112	165	143
R647	Sprocket	5,167	3.522	3	1.4	74	372	1,254	1,769	3,023	2,329	2,054	4,383	186	116	145
H622	Hub	4,450	1.913	2	0.6	26	130	548	773	1,320	756	1,171	1,927	138	152	146
S451	Spacer	2,785	0.120	1	0.6	17	83	347	490	837	370	887	1,257	107	181	150
H554	Hub	1,490	1.582	1	1.1	16	79	361	510	871	423	895	1,319	117	176	152
T501	Stud	4,879	0.151	1	0.3	17	85	322	454	775	376	894	1,269	117	197	164
F382	Fitting	4,009	0.711	2	0.5	20	153	488	636	1,124	738	1,103	1,840	151	173	164
S245	Spacer	4,912	0.281	1	0.4	19	94	336	475	811	433	921	1,355	129	194	167
	Total/Average	7,054	1.080	2.2	1.1	51	$6,983	$22,226	$30,757	$52,982	$27,575	$36,357	$63,925	124%	118%	121%
Total/Avg. All Parts		7,180	1.102	2.1	1.1	56	$14,924	$46,299	$63,161	$109,459	$53,836	$69,116	$122,948	116%	109%	112%

Note: Dollar figures are annual totals for the quote quantity.

EXHIBIT 2 Comparison of Costs: Changing Lot Size

PART DESCRIP-TION	MACHINE SETUP TIME	ANNUAL REQUIRE-MENTS	ACTS HOURS/ C	ANNUAL ACTS	OBESERVED RUN SIZE	ANNUAL RUNS	ANNUAL SETUP HOURS	% ANNUAL SETUP TO ANNUAL ACTS	ABC ANNUAL RUNS PER YEAR	ABC ANNUAL SETUP HOURS	ABC % ANNUAL SETUP TO ANNUAL ACTS	ABC SETUP/ORDER DIRECT	ABC SETUP/ORDER PERIOD	ABC SETUP/ORDER TOTAL	% ABC SETUP HR IMPACT	SAVINGS DIRECT	SAVINGS PERIOD	SAVINGS TOTAL
Valve	2.80	6,566	5.63	370	1,112	6	16.8	5%	3	8.4	2	$326	$300	$626	−50	$326	$300	$626
Pin	5.61	9,330	3.16	295	1,034	10	56.1	19%	4	22.4	8	709	505	1,214	−60	1,064	757	1,821
Bushing	5.61	8,505	2.17	185	1,991	5	28.1	15%	3	16.8	9	532	378	911	−40	355	252	607
Pin	5.61	12,461	1.69	211	2,970	5	28.1	3%	3	16.8	9	532	379	911	−40	355	253	607
Blocker	5.61	2,350	3.02	71	518	5	28.1	40%	2	11.2	16	355	252	607	−60	532	379	911
Sleeve	4.20	16,568	1.02	169	6,904	3	12.6	7%	3	12.6	7	429	340	769	0	0	0	0
Swivel	4.20	20,055	0.31	62	3,750	6	25.2	41%	2	8.4	14	287	227	513	−67	574	453	1,027
Neck	3.27	6,381	1.05	67	1,598	4	13.1	20%	2	6.5	10	240	209	449	−50	240	209	449
Washer	4.20	17,014	0.34	58	7,480	3	12.6	22%	1	4.2	7	145	112	257	−67	289	225	514
Connector	5.61	11,467	1.92	220	1,014	12	67.3	31%	5	28.1	13	886	631	1,517	−58	1,241	883	2,124
Pinion	5.61	642	5.80	37	371	2	11.2	20%	2	11.2	30	355	252	607	0	0	0	0
Pin	2.34	91,629	0.19	174	19,440	5	11.7	7%	3	7.0	4	293	284	577	−40	195	189	385
Plug	4.91	20,825	0.48	100	4,279	5	24.6	25%	4	19.6	20	641	479	1,120	−20	160	120	280
Connector	4.20	11,892	0.32	38	3,370	4	16.8	44%	2	8.4	22	285	226	511	−50	285	226	511
Spacer	3.27	2,154	0.56	12	841	3	9.8	81%	1	3.3	27	120	104	225	−67	240	209	449
Rod	4.20	582	1.22	7	305	2	8.4	118	1	4.2	59	143	113	256	−50	143	113	256
Total/Average				2,075	56,977	80	370	18%	41	189	9%	$6,279	$4,791	$11,070	−49%	$6,000	$4,567	$10,567

EXHIBIT 3 Assignment of Machine Overhead by Activity: Present Distribution of Parts

	PART GROUPING BY ANNUAL ACTS HOURS						
ACTIVITY DATA	0	1–50	50–100	100–500	500–1000	OVER 1000	TOTAL
Direct Labor ($000)	$0	$251	$207	$783	$236	$236	$1,713
% of total	0.0	14.7	12.1	45.7	13.8	13.8	100.0
Machine (ACTS) Hours	0	17,000	14,000	53,000	16,000	16,000	116,000
% of total	0.0	14.7	12.1	45.7	13.8	13.8	100.0
Number of Part Numbers							
Parts with no requirements	1,110						1,110
Parts with requirements		877	208	256	22	8	1,371
% of total		64.0	15.2	18.5	1.6	0.6	100.0
Annual Setup Hours (est.)							
Orders/part (est.)	0	4	6	8	10	12	
Hours/setup (est.)	4	4	5	5	5	3	
Total setup hours	0	14,032	6,240	10,240	1,100	288	31,900
% of total	0.0	44.0	19.6	32.1	3.4	0.9	100.0
Annual Production Orders							
Orders/part numbers (est.)	0	4	6	8	10	12	
Total production orders	0	3,508	1,248	2,048	220	96	7,120
% of total	0.0	49.3	17.5	28.8	3.1	1.3	100.0
Material Handling Data							
Loading factor (est.)	0	0.67	0.8	1.0	1.0	0.8	
Cost weighting	0	25,373	17,500	53,000	16,000	20,000	131,873
% of total	0.0	19.2	13.3	40.2	12.1	15.2	100.0
Overhead Assignments ($000)							
Direct labor support	$0	$278	$229	$867	$262	$262	$1,898
Machine operation	0	593	488	1,848	558	558	4,045
Machine setup	0	498	211	356	37	10	1,112
Production orders	0	401	143	237	25	11	817
Material handling	0	58	40	122	37	46	303
Part administration	5	636	151	186	16	6	1,000
General administration	1	268	137	393	102	97	998
Total overhead	$6	$2,732	$1,399	$4,009	$1,037	$990	$10,173
Total overhead/DL$	NA	1,088%	676%	512%	439%	419%	594%

EXHIBIT 4 Assignment of Machine Overhead by Activity: Assumed Distribution of Parts

| ACTIVITY DATA | 0 | PART GROUPING BY ANNUAL ACTS HOURS | | | TOTAL | INDICATED CHANGE IN ACTIVITY/COST | |
		100–500	500–1,000	OVER 1,000		%	($000)
Direct Labor ($000)	$0	$783	$465	$465	$1,713	0	
% of total	0.0	45.7	27.1	27.1	100.0		
Machine (ACTS) Hours	0	53,000	31,500	31,500	116,000	0	
% of total	0.0	45.7	27.2	27.2	100.0		
Number of Part Numbers							
Parts with no requirements	1,110				1,100	0	
Parts with requirements		256	44	16	316	−77	
% of total		81.0	13.9	5.1	100.0		
Annual Setup Hours (est.)							
Orders/part (est.)	0	8	10	12			
Hours/setup (est.)	4	5	5	3			
Total setup hours	0	10,240	2,200	576	13,016	−59	
% of total	0.0	78.7	16.9	4.4	100.0		
Annual Production Orders							
Orders/part numbers (est.)	0	8	10	12			
Total production orders	0	2,048	440	192	2,680	−62	
% of total	0.0	76.4	16.4	7.2	100.0		
Material Handling Data							
Loading factor (est.)	0	1.0	1.0	0.8			
Cost weighing	0	53,000	31,500	39,375	123,875	−6	
% of total	0.0	42.8	25.4	31.8	100.0		
Overhead Assignments							
Direct labor support	$0	$867	$515	$515	$1,897	0	$0
Machine operation	0	1,848	1,098	1,098	4,044	0	0
Machine setup	0	356	74	19	449	−60	(663)
Production orders	0	237	50	22	309	−62	(508)
Material handling	0	122	72	90	284	−6	(19)
Part administration	5	186	32	12	235	−77	(765)
General administration	1	393	200	191	785	−21	(213)
Total overhead	$6	$4,009	$2,041	$1,947	$8,003	−21	$(2,170)
% Overhead/DL$	na	512%	439%	419%	467%	−21%	

Note: Assumes transfer of parts with less than 100 ACTS and replacing available ACTS hours with parts having more than 500 ACTS.

5

Measuring the Cost of Resource Capacity

Activity cost driver rates should reflect the practical capacity of the resources supplied. Measuring, creating, and managing unused capacity is at the heart of activity-based costing. In fact, one can view the entire ABC approach as giving managers insights about the existence, creation, and deployment of capacity, both used and unused. In this chapter, we show how to incorporate capacity information into ABC models.

Virtually all Stage III activity-based cost systems get started by estimating activity cost driver rates from historical data. As a simple example of the use of historical data in an ABC model, consider an activity *handle customer orders*. The interview and survey procedures described in chapter 4 enable ABC analysts to review historical data for the most recent period (e.g., quarter, half-year, or year) and estimate the quantity of organizational expenses that can be traced to resources (people, systems, facilities) performing this activity. Suppose the traced expenses equal $275,000. In the next step, the analysts select an activity cost driver for this activity, *number of customer orders*, and review historical records to determine the quantity of this activity cost driver in the most recent period. Say this number is 3,500 orders. The analysts then estimate the historical cost driver rate as $78.57 per order ($275,000 in expenses divided by the 3,500 orders). They use this rate to calculate the cost and profitability of individual orders and customers during the estimation (historical) period.

Such a calculation, while much more accurate and revealing than traditional costing systems about the cost of resources required by individual products and customers, is not quite as useful or correct as it should be. Historical cost driver rates have two major limitations. First, the actual cost driver rate is not calculated until after the period is over. Second, the accuracy of the cost driver rate is compromised if the capacity of the resources supplied to perform the activity was not fully used during the period. If the organization had the capacity to handle, say, 5,000 customer orders during the period, not just the 3,500 that actually presented themselves, then the correct cost driver rate of about $55 per order is considerably less than the $78.57 calculated from historical data. The $78.57 rate includes both the cost of resources used to handle each customer order as well as the cost of resources that were supplied *but not used* during the period. Both these limitations need to be overcome if ABC systems are to be used proactively, not reactively. Ideally, managers should use the ABC information to make better decisions about current and future processes, products, and customers, not just to reflect on the past.

The first limitation is easy to overcome. Once the basic structure of an ABC model has been determined, it need not be restricted to driving actual historical expenses to activities, products, and customers. The analyst can use, as inputs to an ABC model, the budgeted expenses for resources in the upcoming period. The analyst can also estimate next period's forecast of activity cost driver quantities so that the cost driver rates are a function of anticipated, not historical, expenses. The analyst calculates cost driver rates at the beginning of a period and managers can use this information in real time when making decisions about products and customers.

Continuing our numerical example, assume that for an upcoming period the budgeted resource expenses for performing the *handle customer order* activity is $280,000. Then suppose the expected number of customer orders during the period is 4,000 orders. The ABC model uses the budgeted data to calculate a cost driver rate of $70 per order based on budgeted expenses and activity levels. This amount ($70) will be charged to every customer order received during the period. Managers can use this information to establish reference points for pricing and order acceptance during the period, and decisions about minimum order size. They do not have to wait until the end of the period to learn how much it cost to handle an individual order.

Working with budgeted rather than historical expenses overcomes one of the objections expressed by many managers. They can now have a cost model to forecast the future, not just explain the past. We must still cope, however, with the second limitation. Even working with budgeted data, the forecasted activity volume may be well below the quantity that could be handled by the resources supplied to perform this activity. With our numerical example, the $70 activity cost driver rate includes the expenses of both used and unused resources, at a forecasted activity level of 4,000 customer orders.

MEASURING THE COST OF CAPACITY RESOURCES

If managers use historical or forecasted activity levels to calculate cost driver rates, they risk launching a death spiral in their organization. Suppose, as we have assumed, that the resources supplied to perform most indirect and support activities are fixed in the short run. If activity levels decline—perhaps because of a general slowdown in economic activity or loss of a major customer—then the activity cost driver rate will increase (a simple arithmetic calculation since expenses, the numerator of the calculation, remain the same, while the cost driver quantity, the denominator, declines). If the now higher cost driver rate is used for decisions about pricing, discounting, and order acceptance, the company may set a higher reference price for taking business to offset the higher cost driver rate. But such an action could lead to even lower activity levels if customers balk at the attempt to recover excess capacity at their expense. If these lower activity levels are then fed back into the cost driver rate calculation, an even higher cost driver rate gets calculated the next period, reinforcing the vicious death cycle of losing more business and recalculating higher cost driver rates.

The use of historical or forecasted activity levels not only risks such a death spiral; the calculation is conceptually incorrect. If the resources supplied to perform an activity, such as *handle customer orders*, are essentially fixed in the short run, we need to attempt to obtain an additional and very important new piece of information: how many customer orders could be handled during the period by the resources supplied. In other words, what is the practical capacity of the resources supplied for this activity?[1]

Suppose, for purposes of illustration, that the practical capacity for this activity is 5,000 customer orders per period.[2] In this case, the correct cost driver rate is $56 per order, not the $70 per order calculated using the forecasted activity volume. Why is $56 "more correct" than the $70?

Managers, through past or recent budgeting decisions, have authorized a supply of $280,000 worth of resources to perform the activity, *handle customer orders*. What have they received from this authorization? They have obtained a *capacity* to handle 5,000 customer orders. Assuming that each customer order requires approximately the same resources to handle (if not, the ABC model should use a duration or intensity driver, or a weighted index of order complexity as discussed in chapter 4), then about $56 of resources are used each time a customer order is handled. This number represents the basic efficiency of the order handling process. If, in a period, only 4,000 orders are received, the efficiency of the activity should remain about the same. The process does not suddenly get less efficient (requiring $70 of resources per order handled) just because fewer orders are received in a period. The lower number of orders received means that not all the resources supplied during the period are fully used. Because of the contracts and commitments (explicit and implicit) made to the resources performing this activity, the supply of resources *cannot* be lowered in the short run in response to the expected lower activity level (that is what we mean by a "fixed" cost). Alternatively, managers may want to retain the current level of supplied resources in order to handle higher expected order volumes in the future.

In either case, the cost driver rate should reflect the underlying efficiency of the process—the cost of resources to handle each customer order—and this efficiency is measured better by using the capacity of the resources supplied as the denominator when calculating activity cost driver rates. The numerator in an activity cost driver rate calculation represents the costs of supplying resource capacity to do work. The denominator should match the numerator by representing the quantity of work the resources can perform.

THE FUNDAMENTAL EQUATION OF ACTIVITY-BASED COSTING

When resources' practical capacity is used to calculate activity cost driver rates, the organization has an additional line item in its periodic financial reports—the budgeted cost of unused capacity. These calculations are based on the following fundamental equation:

Cost of Resources Supplied = Cost of Resources Used + Cost of Unused Capacity

Financial systems—whether general ledger systems that measure expenses actually being incurred or budgeting systems that measure expenses expected to be incurred—measure the

---

[1]A further refinement would distinguish, for equipment resources, how much the practical capacity could be increased through improvements in maintenance and repair activities. For example, the rates could be calculated assuming minimal downtime. Then the cost of capacity that could not be accessed, because of unscheduled stops, downtime, and extensive maintenance and repair activities, would be charged to operations but not to products or customers. Such an assignment would provide incentives for manufacturing operations to adopt effective Total Preventive Maintenance (TPM) programs. For extensive discussion of capacity measurement, see T. Klammer (ed.), *Capacity Measurement & Improvement*: *A Manager's Guide to Evaluating and Optimizing Capacity Productivity* (Chicago: Irwin Professional Publishing, 1996); C. J. McNair and R. Vangermeersch, *Measuring the Cost of Capacity*, Management Accounting Guideline # 42 (Hamilton, Ontario: Society of Management Accountants of Canada 1997).

[2]It is not important that such a practical capacity be estimated exactly. Whether the capacity is actually 4,800 or 5,200 is less important than choosing a particular number to approximate the practical capacity, and to continue to use this number each time the cost driver rate is calculated, until the organization has adequate evidence to obtain a better estimate. Distinguishing between practical capacity and normal volume only becomes an issue when normal volume is substantially below practical capacity. As in many cost measurement issues, it is more important to be approximately correct rather than precisely wrong.

left-hand side of this equation. They measure the amount of organizational expenses incurred to make resources available for productive use. This is an important measurement and one that needs to continue to be made for any current or future system. Typically the financial reporting system and the operational control system measure the actual expenses and spending of the organization (see discussion in chapters 2 and 3). But such a measurement, by itself, is inadequate for measuring the costs of resources required to actually perform work.

ABC systems rectify this limitation by measuring the first term on the right-hand side of the equation. ABC systems measure the cost of resources used (or, alternatively, the resource costs of activities performed) for individual products, services and customers. The difference between the resources supplied and the resources actually used during a period represents the unused capacity of resources for the period.

COMMITTED AND FLEXIBLE RESOURCES

Organizations contract to supply most of their resources, especially those other than materials, energy, and other services purchased from external vendors, before they are actually used. The organization makes a commitment or actual cash outlay to acquire such resources that will be used for current and future activities. We refer to these resources as *committed resources*. As examples of committed resources, the organization acquires buildings and equipment that will supply a capacity for work for several periods into the future. Such a transaction leads to an expense being recognized in each period during the useful life of the resource. The expense of supplying this resource is incurred each period, independent of how much of the resource is used. As another example, the organization can enter into an explicit contract to obtain the services from a resource for several periods in the future. It can lease buildings and equipment, and guarantee access to energy or key materials through take-or-pay contracts. Again, the amount of the cash payment and associated expenses are independent of the actual quantity of usage of the resource in any period.

Perhaps the most important example occurs when an organization enters into implicit contracts (and occasionally explicit contracts, especially with top executives or a unionized work force) to maintain employment levels despite short-term downturns in activity levels. Engineers, purchasing managers, production supervisors, sales and marketing managers, and the salaried work force remain on the payroll even when the short-term demand for their services declines. The spending and accrued expenses for such employees remains constant, independent of the quantity of work performed by these employees.

For most resources, therefore, the organization acquires units of service capacity before the actual demands for the service are realized. Consequently, the expenses of supplying the service capacity from these resources are incurred whether the resources are used or not. This independence in the short-run supply and expenses of these resources has led many to label these as *fixed costs*.[3]

From this perspective, variable costs represent only those resources, typically from outside suppliers, that the organization acquires as needed. We refer to such resources as *flexible resources*; they include materials, energy, telecommunications services, temporary workers hired on a daily basis, employees paid on a piecework basis, and overtime that is authorized as

---

[3]Economists attribute the existence of these fixed costs as arising from economies-of-scale in contracting for the resources. Some service units, like machine capacity, come in lump amounts and it is cheaper to acquire them in the quantities that the suppliers prefer to offer than to get the exact quantity the company thinks it will actually use. Managers also find it less expensive and more reliable to acquire many resources (such as engineers and managers) on a long-term commitment basis rather than to contract continually in spot markets to acquire resource capacity as needed.

needed. For these resources, the organization acquires only what it needs to meet short-term demands, so the cost of acquiring these resources equals the cost of using the resources. Such resources have no unused capacity; whatever is supplied is used; or conversely, whatever is needed is supplied.

Activity-based systems differ from traditional cost systems by estimating the costs of all resources, both flexible and committed, used by activities and products. ABC systems recognize that almost all organizational costs (other than those of flexible resources) are not variable in the short-run just because demand fluctuates up and down. Rather, committed costs become variable costs over longer time periods via a two-step procedure. First, demands for the resources supplied change because of changes in activity levels. For batch and product-sustaining resources, the activity levels change because of changes in variety and complexity. Second, the organization changes the supply of committed resources, either up or down, to meet the new level in demand for the activities performed by these resources.

When the capacity of existing resources is exceeded, the pain is obvious through bottlenecks, shortages, increased pace of activity, delays, or poor quality work. Such shortages can occur on machines, the usual case that people think about, but the ABC approach makes clear that such shortages can occur for resources performing support activities, such as designing, scheduling, ordering, maintaining, and handling products and customers. Companies, facing such shortages, implement the second step to make committed costs variable: they relieve the pain by spending more to increase the supply of resources and relieve the bottleneck.

Demands for resources can also decline. Should the demands for batch and product-sustaining resources decrease from managers' actions, little immediate spending improvement will be noticed. Even for many unit-level resources, like machine and labor capacity, a reduced demand for work from these resources will not lead to spending decreases. The reduced demand for organizational resources will *lower the cost of resources used* (by products, services, and customers) but this decrease will be offset by an equivalent *increase in the cost of unused capacity*.

For committed costs to become variable in the downward direction—after the demand for the supplied resources has decreased and created unused capacity—the organization must manage the unused capacity of these resources out of the system. Only at that time will the costs of resources supplied start to decrease. Thus, what makes a resource cost "variable" in a downward direction is not inherent in the nature of the resource; it is a function of management decisions—first to reduce the demands for the resource, and second, to lower the spending on the resource.[4]

ABC systems can signal those resources that are currently at or expected to soon reach capacity constraints. Improvement initiatives can then be focused on the activities performed by these constraining resources. Alternatively, the ABC systems will signal where unused capacity already exists in the organization, or where it will be created after improvement activities or decisions about products, services, and customers. Such a signal directs managers' attention to formulating plans for eliminating the unused capacity. Unused capacity can be eliminated in only two ways:

1. *Revenue increases*, by increasing the quantity of activities demanded for the resources to perform.
2. *Spending reductions*, by reducing the supply of resources for performing the activity.

Often, however, organizations create unused capacity but do nothing about it. They keep existing resources in place, even though the demands for the activities performed by the re-

---

[4]Managers do not seem to have any problem recognizing that costs are "variable" in an upward direction. Examination of past history will usually reveal how organizational spending has increased to cope with increased variety and complexity of operations. It is the mechanism for costs to head in the downward direction that has eluded many economists, accountants, and managers.

sources have diminished substantially. And they fail to find new activities that could be handled, without incremental expenses, by the resources already in place. In this case, and only in this case, the organization receives no benefits from its decisions. The failure to capture benefits from operational or strategic decisions, however, is not due to costs being intrinsically "fixed." Rather, the failure occurs because managers are unwilling or unable to exploit the unused capacity they have created. The costs of these resources is only "fixed" if managers cannot or do not exploit the opportunities from the unused capacity they helped to create.

Generally, the cheapest source of new capacity is that freed up by reducing the production of unprofitable products or the sales to unprofitable customers. In a capacity-constrained situation, ABC gives companies the information to outsource or eliminate unprofitable products and customers and replace these with profitable ones. The capacity made available through operational and strategic decisions based on activity-based costing information is likely a much cheaper source of new supply than the capacity created by hiring additional employees, purchasing additional equipment, or building additional facilities. ABC should be used to identify, measure, create, and manage capacity. Understanding the subtle interplay between the actions taken with ABC information and capacity management is the central message from the approach.

FROM AN ABC RESOURCE USAGE MODEL TO DECISIONS ABOUT RESOURCE SUPPLY

As a model of resource usage (not spending), activity-based cost systems are not designed for automatic decision making. ABC identifies the relationship between revenues generated and resources consumed. However, ABC does not identify the relationship between changes in resources used and changes in resources supplied.

Making decisions based solely upon resource usage (the ABC system) is problematic as there is no guarantee that the spending to supply resources will be aligned with the levels of resources demanded in the near future. For example, if an action causes the number of inspections to decrease by 10%, no economic benefit will be achieved unless the resources supplied to perform inspection, which are no longer needed, are eliminated or redeployed to generate additional revenue. Consequently, before making decisions based on an ABC model, managers should perform special studies to determine the resource supply implications of their contemplated decisions.

For example, managers can perform special studies to determine when the reduction in resource demands from dropping the right mix of products enables enough resources to be redeployed so that the cost savings exceed the revenue losses. Managers will then have the confidence to drop products, eliminate the resources currently supplied, and have the resulting cost savings produce a profit increase for the company.

The ABC resource usage model produces, at relatively low cost, an economic map of the enterprise. Performing special studies between decisions about products (or customers) and spending changes (due to changes in resources supplied) without the initial ABC model is a difficult and expensive search. There are too many possibilities to consider. For example, consider managers at a company that produces a narrow range of products, say only 100. The managers are contemplating whether to eliminate a subset of these products (a simple, binary, go−no go decision for each product). In an exhaustive and unguided search through all the possible combinations of products that could be dropped, the managers would have to evaluate 2^{100} possible decisions, a calculation beyond the collective computational power of all existing computers. The ABC model reduces the dimensionality of managers' search problems. It guides managers to the special studies that will have the most promising opportunities for profit improvement.

ASSIGNMENT OF UNUSED CAPACITY COSTS

When activity cost driver rates are based on practical capacity, the cost of unused capacity is not assigned down to individual products or customers. But the cost of unused capacity should not be ignored; it remains someone's or some department's responsibility. Usually you can assign unused capacity after analyzing the decision that led to creation of the unused capacity.

You can think about the assignment of unused capacity costs using the *rational customer rule*. This rule states that unused capacity costs should only be assigned to a customer if that customer, acting rationally under a cost plus contract, would accept that cost. For example, a customer who orders on a predictable, regular basis, without making any changes, would not accept the cost of any unused capacity. Nothing in the way the customer acts requires its supplier to maintain unused capacity. But consider a customer who demands perfect service, whose demands are difficult to forecast, or who continually modifies the volume and timing of orders. The supplier, in order to maintain service to this customer, requires some degree of reserve capacity to meet the unpredictable demands from this customer. In this situation, a rational customer should recognize that its behavior leads to some unused capacity for its supplier and, therefore, an assignment of the unused capacity costs.

If a rational customer does not accept the cost of the unused capacity, then one can look back to the individual who authorized the acquisition of the capacity. For example, if the capacity was acquired to meet anticipated demands from a particular customer or a particular market segment, then the costs of unused capacity due to lower than expected demands can be assigned to the person or organizational unit responsible for that customer or segment. Such an assignment should be done on a lump-sum basis (e.g., a sustaining, not a unit-level expense).

If the unused capacity relates to a product line, say when certain production resources are dedicated to individual product lines, then the cost of unused capacity is assigned to the individual in charge of the product line where demand failed to materialize. It should not be treated as a general cost, to be shared across all product lines. Nor should the product line's unused capacity be allocated down to individual products. That could cause some products to appear unprofitable, risking the launch of a death spiral by repricing or dropping products within the product line.

As another situation, suppose division management knew in advance that resource supply would exceed resource demand, but wanted to retain existing resources for future growth and expansion. Then the cost of unused capacity could be division-sustaining, assigned to the division making the decision to retain unused capacity. In making such an assignment of unused capacity costs, we want to trace the costs at the level in the organization where decisions are made that could affect the supply of capacity resources and the demand for those resources. The lump-sum assignment of unused capacity costs provides feedback to managers on their supply and demand decisions.

SUMMARY

An organization's initial ABC system almost always calculates historical activity cost driver rates, based on last period's expenses for resources actually supplied and the realized (actual) quantities of cost drivers. But ABC should not be thought of as an historical accounting or general ledger system. It can and should be used proactively to estimate the costs of activities that will be performed in current and future periods. Decisions can then be made that will influence future cost incurrence, not just better assign past costs. For this purpose, activity cost driver rates should be calculated using budgeted expense data for the forthcoming period.

In addition to using budgeted expense information, the rates should be calculated using the practical capacity of the resources supplied. This enables the activity cost driver rates to represent the underlying efficiency of the activity, as measured by the cost of resources required to perform one unit of the activity. In addition to having a more accurate estimate of the activity cost driver rate, the use of practical capacity enables ABC to distinguish between the cost of resources used during the period versus the cost of unused resources. This distinction provides a powerful signal for management as it contemplates decisions about process improvement, products, customers, and investments in new capacity. We turn to such decisions in the next four chapters.

CASES

The *Micro Devices Division* case demonstrates how ignoring the role of capacity leads to distorted product costs in traditional systems. It explores several different definitions of capacity and illustrates how issues of unused capacity can arise in subtle ways. The numerical exercise, *Hogan Containers*, explores how seasonality can be incorporated into the capacity-costing model. The *Insteel* case illustrates the important role for capacity in an ABC model. The *Lehigh Steel* case integrates the theory of constraints into an ABC model.

MICRO DEVICES DIVISION

When we built our new wafer fab facility, we thought we would have to expand within a few years. But our yields have been so high we can meet demand for our current products operating at 60% capacity. The dilemma I now face is whether I should bring more product in from the outside. With our huge fixed costs it seems to make sense. But which costs should I use to make that decision?

Jeri Batina, Division Manager

Division Background

Micro Devices Division (MDD) was a captive supplier of integrated circuits (ICs). Located in California's Silicon Valley, the division employed approximately 3,200 hourly and salaried personnel. Its 1989 operating budget exceeded $200 million.

The IC market was extremely price sensitive. MDD had elected not to compete on a price basis with high-volume integrated circuit producers to leverage its resources and technologies. Consequently, it stayed away from the commodity chip business and concentrated on designing and manufacturing proprietary designs that gave its parent company a competitive advantage in the marketplace.

To obtain state-of-the-art semiconductor technology, MDD gave other chip suppliers a substantial share of the parent company's IC volume in return for access to the latest technical knowledge. The division then used the acquired technology to develop unique applications for its parent. In total, outside manufacturers supplied 60% of the parent's semiconductor requirements.

Each product manufactured by MDD was given a number based on criticality:

1 — Proprietary

2 — Can consider second supplier

3 — Can buy from anyone

New business was typically won because it was proprietary. As the proprietary technology became public, the

This case was prepared by research associate Chris Ittner under the supervision of Professor Robin Cooper.

Copyright © 1990 by the President and Fellows of Harvard College. Harvard Business School case 191-073.

unit was frequently faced with severe competitive pressures as lower cost suppliers entered the market.

Production Process

IC manufacturing encompassed four distinct operations: raw wafer production, wafer fabrication, assembly, and test. In wafer production, purchased wafers were prepped, precleaned, and put into the production process.

In wafer fabrication, the building blocks (e.g., diodes and transistors) of an integrated circuit were made by selectively introducing impurities (dopants) into the pure silicon. This created areas (features) with dissimilar electrical characteristics. The patterns of dopant introductions were contained on a set of glass plates called masks. Since ICs were constructed in layers, several masks were required, one for each layer. A typical IC might require 10 masks, and a highly complex state-of-the-art device might have as many as 16.

In the assembly operation, the integrated circuits were packaged in their final form. Since each wafer contained from 100 to 2,000 identical ICs, the wafers were first "diced" into individual chips. Each chip was then mounted, using a die-bonding machine, onto a metal frame. Next, tiny gold wires were bonded from leads on the metal frame to aluminum pads on the silicon chip using an ultrasonic wire-bonding machine. Finally, an epoxy plastic lid was cemented or molded on top of the base leadframe to complete the integrated circuit package.

In the final test operation, the completed device was subjected to extensive electrical testing to determine its electrical characteristics. Because the number and complexity of tests was large and the required precision high, MDD utilized sophisticated computers to control the test sequence.

Several weeks were required to complete the production process, a time period typical in the semiconductor industry. MDD produced 203 different part numbers, using 82 different die. Many part numbers varied only with respect to packaging, customer, and test parameters. Products were grouped into process families, each of which contained a dozen or so devices. The only difference between devices in a family was the masks; the processing was nearly identical.

Cost System

MDD's cost system employed "yield" accounting. Direct labor, direct material, and scrap costs were traced directly to wafer lots. Overhead rates were developed for each department and subsequently allocated to wafer lots based on the actual direct labor dollars expended in producing each lot. The cost of a wafer lot was then divided by the actual number of good die in the lot to calculate individual unit costs. Packaging and test costs were developed in the same manner. The allocated cost totals were roughly evenly divided among die, package, and test costs.

MDD typically transferred products to its parent at full cost. However, the unit had some leeway in determining which costs to include in the transfer price. For example, to win a bid against an outside competitor, the division would sometimes include in the transfer price only the depreciation associated with the additional equipment acquired to provide capacity for the proposed work.

Available Capacity

For the past several years, MDD had been operating far below capacity. The problem was most acute in wafer fab, where a facility designed to process 650 wafers per day was only processing 350. Several factors had contributed to this condition:

1. *Long-term yields.* The success of the IC manufacturing process was measured by yields—the percentage of initial product started into production that, after the last step of the process, tested out as acceptable. Final yields had several components. *Line yields* referred to the ratio of good wafers to wafer starts. *Multiples* represented the number of good dies per wafer. *Packaging yields* denoted the ratio of good packaged dies to the number of dies entered into the packaging process. As yields improved, fewer wafer starts were required to achieve the same number of good dies at the end of the manufacturing process (see Exhibit 1 for an example). As a result, yield improvements increased the amount of available capacity.

To meet increased demands, MDD had constructed a new state-of-the-art wafer fab facility. Management had originally estimated near-term capacity utilization at 80% given projected yields and demand; volume increases were expected to fill capacity by the early 1990s. Actual yields turned out to be much higher than expected, however. Within a year, the facility was meeting demand while operating at 60% capacity. Noted one engineer, "When we built the new facility we estimated yields for products we had never built before. We never knew we would be this good." Yields continued to improve as engineers identified and eliminated the sources of defects (see Exhibits 2 and 3). Because of these improvements, the number of wafer starts needed to meet demand fell far below the initial forecasts (see Exhibit 4). The reduced wafer starts created more available capacity than anticipated.

2. *Short-term yields.* In determining the number of required wafer starts, manufacturing planners utilized average yields. Actual yields, however, could vary by as much as $\pm$ 15% from the average yields being used by the planners. Because of these statistical fluctuations, a downstream process could at times have less input than was required to produce the necessary output, while at other times it could have more than enough. Statistical fluctuations were compounded as the number of sequential operations increased.

Statistical fluctuations made it desirable to hold extra capacity. For example, MDD might need to produce 100 wafers each day for a month. Five sequential operations might be required to manufacture the wafers. Assume that on average, each operation had the capacity to produce 100 wafers per day (i.e., no excess capacity). On any production run, actual output per operation would vary between 85 and 115. The next operation would then receive either too much or too little input, even though on average the correct amount of material would be received. If too little was received, any downstream bottleneck operations would be starved for input, and output would fall below requirements. If more than 100 were received, the downstream bottleneck operation would still only have the capacity to produce 100 units on average and would be unable to make up for shortages earlier in the month. Because bottleneck operations lacked the capacity to compensate for shortfalls in earlier stages, the eventual outcome would be throughput less than the required number of wafers and a buildup in inventory. Consequently, it was useful to hold extra capacity to make up for statistical fluctuations in earlier operations.

3. *Product mix changes.* A third source of available capacity was changes in the division's product mix. Due to technological changes and competition from outside competitors, as much as one-third of the division's vol-

ume from existing products could go away in a three-year period. This created the continual need for new products to fill capacity.

Because much of the equipment was dedicated to particular process families, however, the introduction of new products did not guarantee that existing capacity would be filled. Unless new products belonged to process families with available capacity, additional equipment had to be purchased, and equipment designed for process families with declining demand would remain underutilized. As a result, utilization of certain process family equipment was falling at the same time the division's overall volumes were rising.

4. *"Lumpy" capacity.* MDD would sometimes purchase more capacity than was required to meet current demand. In some cases, it was more economical in the long run to provide for future needs at the time the assets were acquired. In others, the required equipment was only available in large-capacity increments. To add even a small amount of capacity, the division would need to purchase equipment capable of accommodating substantial volume increases.

Each of these factors contributed to imbalances between capacity and demand. Imbalances were found both within and between operations. For example, the wafer fabrication process consisted of numerous steps carried out in a circular flow. Individual pieces of equipment in the process flow differed with respect to the capacity they could accommodate. An equipment imbalance in this case involved differences in the capacity of one machine in contrast with the output of other machines with which it had to be synchronized. Similarly, capacity imbalances also occurred between the wafer fab, assembly, and test functions; current capacity utilization ranged from 55% in wafer fab to 75% in IC assembly.

The In-Sourcing Decision

The availability of capacity prompted Jeri Batina, MDD's division manager, to explore the possibility of in-sourcing some of the ICs currently being produced by outside suppliers. In-sourcing seemed desirable for a number of reasons. First, the additional volume would allow the division's substantial fixed costs to be spread over a larger number of units. This, in turn, would reduce unit product costs. Second, wafer fabrication yields were highest when the equipment ran continuously. Wafer cleanliness, one of the primary determi-

nants of wafer yields, was inversely related to the amount of time the wafer spent in the fabrication process. When demand fell below the capacity of the wafer fabrication equipment, the production process shifted from continuous to batch production. Consequently, until a full batch accumulated, partially completed wafers were stored in racks waiting to be processed. Additional volume would allow the equipment to run uninterrupted for longer periods of time, thus increasing yields by reducing time in the process. Finally, the credible threat of in-sourcing provided an incentive for suppliers to reduce prices.

Batina was not sure which costs to use in analyzing the feasibility of in-sourcing. The IC market was extremely price sensitive, with price swings as low as 5% determining the competitiveness of suppliers' bids. Because of the competitiveness issue, MDD struggled with which cost elements to include in the cost-estimating process. Moreover, Batina wondered whether it even made sense to consider sunk costs in her pricing decision. If new products could be produced on available equipment, no additional equipment investment would be necessary.

Strategic considerations also played an important part in the in-sourcing decision. MDD relied on outside suppliers for technology. Taking work away from them jeopardized the strategic relationships that had been developed. One engineering manager noted the following:

> A strategic issue is the key partnerships we have with some of our semiconductor suppliers. We rely on partners for technology. Because our parent is a big user, we can trade volume for technology. This allows us to keep a smaller advanced development group. We try to acquire and tweak technology for unique applications. Our strength lies in our ability to develop unique designs that give our customer strategic advantage. If we lose access to new technology because of in-sourcing, we threaten our competitive edge.

Capacity Costing Alternatives

While Batina's current concern was with in-sourcing, she realized that the capacity cost allocation method also had potential implications for outsourcing of current products, future make/buy analyses, transfer pricing policy, investment decisions, and performance evaluation of the division's managers. Recognizing the importance of this decision, Batina called a meeting with representatives from engineering, manufacturing, finance, and cost estimating to discuss capacity costing options.

The initial discussion centered on the definition of capacity. Four potential alternatives emerged:

1. *Theoretical capacity* assumed that the facility would operate at 100% of its rated capacity. It assumed that the equipment would run continuously with no downtime for maintenance, holidays, setups, etc.
2. *Practical capacity* adjusted the theoretical capacity definition to account for the number of shifts worked or unavoidable delays due to holidays, vacations, time off for weekends, machine breakdown, etc. This yielded a measure of available capacity given current operating conditions.
3. *Normal capacity* represented the average actual utilization over a time period long enough to level out capacity highs and lows.
4. *Expected actual capacity* was based on the expected actual output for the next year.

The meeting participants agreed that theoretical capacity was not a viable alternative for costing decisions, but could not agree on which of the other definitions was most appropriate. (Exhibit 5 provides various capacity measures for the equipment families in wafer fabrication.)

A member of the engineering staff noted that a further distinction needed to be made between idle capacity and excess capacity. According to the engineer, idle capacity was the result of volume fluctuations; equipment idled by temporary sales declines would be restored to full use when demand increased. This was in contrast to excess capacity which resulted from greater productive capacity than the division could hope to use, or from an imbalance in equipment.

There was some resistance to allocating less than 100% of capacity costs. A representative from cost estimating argued as follows: "You have to do something with the cost of excess capacity. There's no free ride. You can't say that you have a $2 million investment but you're only going to allocate $1 million. The costs have to go somewhere."

As the meeting progressed, however, several alternatives to full cost were presented. The division's controller proposed new bidding rates based on an allocation of 80% of capacity costs. The 80% figure represented the long-term capacity utilization goal for the division; maintaining a 20% "capacity cushion" would allow the division to remain responsive to demand fluctuations by its parent.

A second proposed alternative was the allocation of capacity costs based on actual utilization within the departments. For example, a department operating at 60% capacity would only have 60% of its capacity costs allocated to products.

A third option was allocating capacity costs based on actual utilization in the bottleneck department. For example, wafer fab might be operating at 60% capacity, assembly at 75%, and test at 90%. Without additional investment in test, all of the available capacity in wafer fab and assembly could not be exploited. Consequently, under this alternative, 90% of the capacity costs in each department would be allocated to products.

Finally, the division could bid on the work at variable cost. However, Batina was not sure that the division had a good grasp of what its variable costs actually were and suspected that the only true fixed costs were building occupancy, insurance, and taxes.

As the meeting came to a close, Batina concluded that the capacity costing issue required additional study. She instructed the cost estimating group to develop a full cost estimate for a product the division was considering in-sourcing (see Exhibit 6), as well as revised estimates using each of the proposed alternatives (see Exhibit 7 for details on cost structure and capacity utilization by department). When the results were ready, the meeting would reconvene and the representatives would present their recommendations. As the participants prepared to leave, Batina made the following statement:

> I think we've come up with a number of good options, but I'm sure that there are others we haven't considered. We need to keep thinking about other alternatives. I'm concerned that the capacity cost allocation method we choose for our current in-sourcing decisions may not be appropriate for product costing, transfer pricing, bidding for new business, and other purposes such as forecasting and performance evaluation of departmental managers. Should the same method be used for each of these purposes? I'm not sure. When we get together again, we need to address these issues.

EXHIBIT 1

MICRO DEVICES DIVISION

Effect of Yield Changes on Number of Wafer Starts

Good output = wafer starts × line yield × multiple × package yield

	1986	1989
Line yield (% good wafers)	55%	85%
Multiple (Good dies per wafer)	200	400
Packaging yield (% good packaged dies)	85%	95%

Example—20,000 good dies required

1986

20,000 good dies = wafer starts × .55 × 200 × .85

Required wafer starts = 214

1989

20,000 good dies = wafer starts × .85 × 400 × .95

Required wafer starts = 62

Therefore, because of yield improvements, production of 20,000 good dies in 1989 required only 62 wafer starts as opposed to the 214 wafer starts required in 1986.

EXHIBIT 2

MICRO DEVICES DIVISION

Line Yield

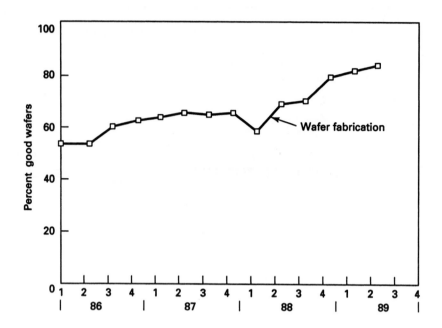

EXHIBIT 3

MICRO DEVICES DIVISION

Multiple History for a Representative Part

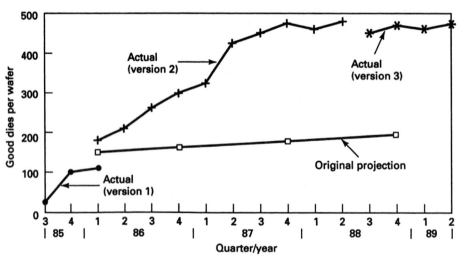

Three generations of this part were produced. Version number refers to the part generation each trend line represents.

EXHIBIT 4

MICRO DEVICES DIVISION

Shipment History for a Representative Part

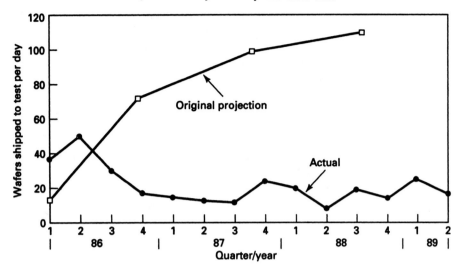

EXHIBIT 5

MICRO DEVICES DIVISION

Wafer Fabrication

Equipment Family Capacities

(Wafers per Day)

EQUIPMENT FAMILY	CAPACITY DEFINITION		PLANNED LONG-TERM UTILIZATION	CURRENT UTILIZATION (AVERAGE)
	THEORETICAL	PRACTICAL		
Oxidation	950	750	520	350
Photolithography	1,000	800	520	350
Diffusion	900	650	520	350
Ion implantation	1,000	900	520	350

Wafer fabrication had approximately 40% empty floor space that could be utilized with an additional investment of $30 million to increase practical capacity to 1,100 wafers per day.

EXHIBIT 6

MICRO DEVICES DIVISION

Fully Absorbed Cost Estimate

($ per Die)

DEPARTMENT	MATERIALS	LABOR	OVERHEAD	TOTAL
IC assembly—die and wire bond	.1830	.0820	.3314	.5964
IC assembly—mold, trim, form	.0118	.1190	.4126	.5434
Final IC test	.0000	.1483	.6506	.7989
Wafer fabrication	.6760	.0860	.9364	1.0900
Wafer test, saw, load, visual	.0000	.0153	.0947	.1100
	.2629	.4586	2.4722	3.1937

EXHIBIT 7

MICRO DEVICES DIVISION

Budgeted Departmental Cost Structures and Current Capacity Utilization

---

IC Assembly—Die and Wire Bond

Direct labor	$2,341,970

Overhead:

Variable	4,023,729

Fixed

Depreciation—equipment	698,374
Building depreciation, insurance, and taxes	120,077
Other facility costs[1]	95,381
Other fixed[2]	4,526,340

Current practical capacity utilization—75%

IC Assembly—Mold, Trim, Form

Direct labor	$4,189,427

Overhead:

Variable	6,322,543

Fixed

Depreciation—equipment	600,719
Building depreciation, insurance, and taxes	142,785
Other facility costs	960,042
Other fixed	6,542,842

Current Practical Capacity Utilization—75%

Final IC Test

Direct labor	$4,039,746

Overhead:

Variable	7,150,508

Fixed

Depreciation—equipment	2,287,558
Building depreciation, insurance, and taxes	312,382
Other facility costs	9,60,042
Other fixed	6,498,655

Current practical capacity utilization—70%

Wafer Fabrication

Direct labor	$2,348,377

Overhead:

Variable	6,790,974

Fixed

Depreciation—equipment	2,355,003
Building depreciation, insurance, and taxes	776,394
Other facility costs	2,866,907
Other fixed	12,779,854

Current practical capacity utilization—55%

(continued)

Exhibit 7 (cont.)

Wafer Test, Saw, Load, and Visual	
Direct labor	$2,608,917
Overhead:	
Variable	6,496,947
Fixed	
Depreciation—equipment	2,515,422
Building depreciation, insurance, and taxes	360,251
Other facility costs	1,032,156
Other fixed	6,664,027
Current practical capacity utilization—60%	

[1]Other facility costs include general facility maintenance, plant security, and house-keeping.
[2]Other fixed costs include plant management and support departments.

HOGAN CONTAINERS

Hogan Containers manufactures waxed paper containers for ice cream. Demand is highly seasonal. For one of its most important product lines, 16 oz. round containers, Hogan produces 36,000 units per month for the five months of April through August. During the rest of the year, it produces 24,000 per month. Demand has been stable for the past several years and Hogan has been able to acquire capacity that is fully utilized during the busy season. The total capacity from the machines used to produce the 16 oz. containers is 36,000 per month. The annual cost associated with operating the machine is $1,044K or $87K/month. What is the cost per unit as calculated by:

1. Dividing monthly costs by monthly production volumes.
2. Dividing annual costs by annual production volume.

3. Dividing annual costs by annual *potential* production volume.

4. The approach recommended by advocates of theory of constraints to charge operating expenses to production volumes only when operating at peak capacity.

5. Assume (somewhat heroically) that acquisition costs and operating costs are linear in the capacity provided; that is the monthly cost of providing 24,000 of capacity would be (2/3) * $87,000 = $58,000. Assign the cost of supplying only the capacity *used* during the slack months to the production of those months; and add the costs of supplying the unused capacity in these slack months to the production costs of the peak months. (Why (or why not) is this a plausible procedure to consider?)

6. What are the strengths and weaknesses of these five approaches? Which, if any, do you prefer? Can you suggest any other alternatives that Hogan should consider?

INSTEEL WIRE PRODUCTS: ABM AT ANDREWS

It was 5 p.m. and the management team at Insteel's Andrews, SC plant were preparing for a presentation to senior Insteel managers, scheduled for 10 am the next morning. The first item on the meeting's agenda was a summary of the results of a year-long ABM project at the Andrews plant. The managers from the Mt. Airy headquarters would be particularly interested in the profitability projections and actual profitability of various products and customers. Sales managers would also be flying in from Mt. Airy in order to explain sales figures and to provide projections for the coming year. Bill Sronce, the plant manager, knew that attention would be focused on the figures for galvanized pallet nails. This product line had been targeted for expansion and growth based on profitability figures from a 1996 ABC study, but a similar ABC analysis in 1997 indicated that galvanized pallet nails were now losing a lot of money.

Assistant Professors V.G. Narayanan and Ratna G. Sarkar prepared this case.

Insteel Wire Products: Background

Insteel Wire Products (IWP) a division of Insteel Industries, Inc., manufactures and markets a broad range of wire products including concrete reinforcing products, industrial wire, bulk nails, collated fasteners and agricultural fencing. The company's primary markets are the construction, home furnishings, appliance and agricultural industries. Insteel Industries is headquartered in Mt. Airy, North Carolina. The company currently operates eight manufacturing facilities serving markets nationwide. Annual sales revenues are about $300 million.

In 1996, the company decided to undertake an ABC analysis of the operations of one of its Andrews, SC plants, and to implement process and pricing changes as indicated by the study. Four product lines are produced at the Andrews plant steel wire of different gauges, galvanized wire of different gauges, wire mesh and nails. Spread across these four product lines are 477 individual products. However, 20% of the products account for 85% of Andrews' annual revenues of about $60 million. Likewise, 20% of Andrews' customers account for 95% of all sales. Raw material costs represent 70% of all costs. Raw material prices and prices of Andrew's finished products had remained fairly constant over the last twenty-five years and this trend was expected to continue. Wages and salaries, however, had been growing at the inflation rate. Thus there was tremendous pressure to control overhead and labor costs by boosting productivity.

Production Process at Andrews

The bright and galvanized wire product lines are produced to order, the other two product lines are produced to stock (about 20 days inventory). All of Insteel's nail products are manufactured at Andrews, in Nail Mill A (commodity nails and sinkers, a large-volume, non-differentiated product line) and Nail Mill B (pallet nails, manufactured to tight tolerances on diameter, heading and threading specifications).

The main raw material is hot-rolled steel rod purchased in large rolls of about 4000 pounds, chiefly from Georgetown Steel's nearby facility in Georgetown, and some foreign suppliers at about $300–320/ton. There is concern that the lower quality steel of foreign-sourced-rod can significantly impact wire-drawing throughput, which is the first common stage for all of Andrews' production and is operating at capacity. See Exhibit 1 for a graphical representation of Insteel's production process.

The ABC/ABM Initiative at Insteel

In the 1950s, Insteel had started business as a provider of wire mesh products for concrete reinforcing applications. Over the years, it had broadened its product offering, and indeed, largely moved beyond the mesh business, expanding into higher-value-added products. But it had retained its sales strategy to be primarily volume-oriented. Before the introduction of ABC, Insteel did not have a sophisticated cost system. The price per ton of steel rod, the basic raw material, was closely monitored. This price was used to estimate the material costs of all of Insteel's products—by multiplying the weight of the product by the price of steel rod. Freight was tracked as a separate cost, identifiable at the customer level, as each truck or box car was shipped. Price quotations were based on the weight of the product and estimated freight costs.

Bill Sronce described the 'old days:'

> "Before the ABM study we did not have any specific product or customer costing information. . . . Our sales people were instructed to chase tons without any information about costs, available capabilities or profit."

With increasing pricing pressure and capacity constraints at various locations, Insteel's management recognized the need for a cost system which would guide managerial decisions about various choices and tradeoffs facing the firm. They decided to adopt an activity-based cost system that would potentially provide a better understanding of resource consumption by products and by customers than a traditional volume-based cost system.

Wishing to limit the upheaval caused by a change in the status quo, and also to maximize the possibility of enthusiastic adoption, Insteel's management selected the Andrews plant as its first ABC site. The plant had had a history of good communications between plant management and workers and supervisors, it was independent, with little operational overlap with other plants and was run by Bill Sronce, a willing and enthusiastic champion of the process. Dave Conrad, the director of cost management, was also assigned full-time to the project.

ABC at the Andrews Plant

Insteel engaged a big-six accounting firm to help them with their ABC effort. The ABC team analyzed Andrews' business and identified 12 business processes. Within each business process a number of activities were identified—a total of 146 activities. Next, 426

TABLE 1 (All Figures in $ Millions)

PRODUCT GROUP	SALES	MATERIAL COST	PRODUCTION COST	CUSTOMER COST	BUSINESS/FACILITY SUSTAINING COST	TOTAL COST	PROFIT
Bright Wire	10.462	6.763	1.235	1.499	0.416	9.913	0.549
Galv Wire	12.866	8.816	2.057	1.567	0.545	12.985	− 0.119
Nails	30.613	19.902	6.585	1.327	1.219	29.033	1.58
Mesh	5.07	4.277	0.708	0.504	0.24	5.729	− 0.659
Total	59.011	39.758	10.585	4.897	2.42	57.66	1.351

employees were surveyed to estimate how they allocated their time to different activities. All overhead costs were then collected in 80 cost pools and a cost driver was associated with each cost pool to assign the overhead costs to cost objects such as products and customers (some cost pools included multiple activities that had the same cost driver). The cumulative product and customer profitability charts are in Exhibit 2 and Exhibit 3 respectively.

Major Findings of the ABC Study

The product group profitability analysis at Andrews for the period July 1995 through June 1996 revealed the information in Table 1.

The ABC team discovered that galvanized wire products (previously thought to be very profitable) and mesh products (thought to be break-even) were losing money. Another surprise was the discovery that many small wire customers were more profitable than larger customers. About 45% of the plant's customers and 45% of its products were unprofitable. Finally, the nail business, previously thought to be moderately profitable, was actually their most profitable business. Within nails, galvanized pallet nails turned out to be the plant's most profitable product.

Activity Based Management (ABM) at Insteel

Based on this intensive investigation of activities and resource consumption patterns, a number of process improvements were initiated in quality, preventive maintenance, and freight handling. Product and customer mix were changed. For example, pallet nails were being manufactured in two cells running at capacity. Insteel decided to expand the number of cells to four: first, they would add a third cell and if the product continued to perform well, a fourth cell would be added. In July

1996 itself, Insteel spent $900,000 on an additional heading and threading machine for the third cell. This machine was expected to have a zero salvage value at the end of its 10-year life. $200,000 was spent on labor during the period September 1996 to June 1997 to staff the third cell. However, the third cell did not go into production until June 1997 because of problems in getting the equipment installed, up, and running.

Insteel did a follow-up ABC study in 1997 for the period July 1996 to June 1997. This study showed that total sales had increased by $5.9 million, total operating costs by $5.4 million and thus total operating profits were up by more than half a million dollars. Directly attributable to the ABC effort was a reduction in quality costs of $1.8 million and a reduction in freight costs by $555,000. Raw material prices, however, had increased during this period relative to the year earlier.

Overall, while ABC had improved profitability and efficiency, galvanized pallet nails were now losing money and in fact, that product group had become one of Insteel's most unprofitable products. The change in profitability of this product line is summarized in Table 2 where conversion costs include all production, customer, and facility sustaining costs. Exhibit 4 provides detailed information regarding galvanized pallet nails' overhead costs for the two years. Exhibits 5 and 6 pro-

TABLE 2

	1995–96	1996–97
Sales ($M)	1.950	2.100
Sales in Tons	2600	2817
Material Costs ($M)	0.900	1.100
Conversion Costs ($M)	0.859	1.271
Net Profits ($M)	0.191	(.271)

vide information on cost-driver units consumed by galvanized pallet nails and other costs assigned to galvanized pallet nails, repectively. Note that Exhibit 4 contains representative data on cost drivers and cost pools at plant level, while data in Exhibits 5 and 6 pertain to pallet nails only.

The ABC team, and the plant and sales managers were trying to understand what had gone wrong. The sales manager felt that there was enough demand for galvanized pallet nails at the current price and if production could be ramped up, the line could be very profitable. The plant manager agreed that there had been some initial problems in getting the third cell up to speed but felt that the third cell would reach full volume production in the near future. In hindsight, was their decision to add a third cell justified?

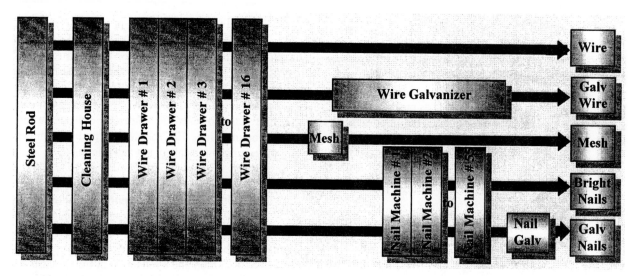

EXHIBIT 1   The manufacturing process at Andrews.

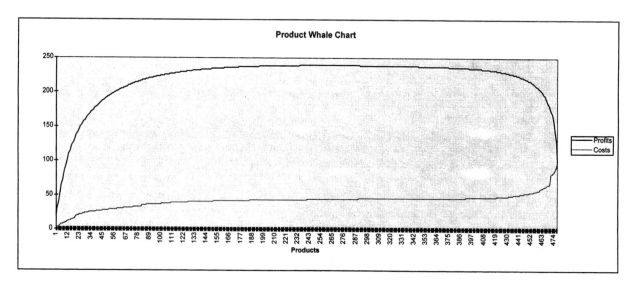

EXHIBIT 2   Product profitability whale curve.

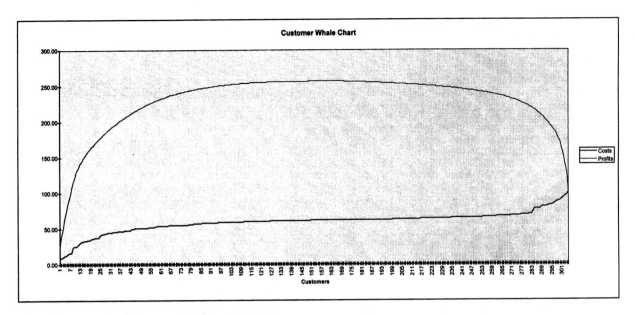

EXHIBIT 3   Customer profitability whale curve.

EXHIBIT 4 Galvanized Pallet Nail-Related Overhead Cost Information, 1995–96 and 1996–97.

Cost Pool	Cost Hierarchy	Cost Driver	1995-96 Driver Volume	1995-96 Spending	1996-97 Driver Volume	1996-97 Spending
Cleaning House	Unit	Tons Cleaned	100,000	$210,000	110,000	$222,000
Depreciation-Wire Drawing Machine	Unit	Tons Drawn	100,000	$420,000	110,000	$420,000
Depreciation - Nail Galvanizer	Unit	Tons Galvanized	40,000	$623,000	45,000	$623,000
Depreciation- Heading and Threading Machine[1]	Unit	Tons headed/threaded	2,600	$50,000	2,817	$140,000
Material Handling	Batch	Number of Moves	4,000	$305,000	4,500	$350,000
Dies Retooling	Batch	Toolshop Hours	3,000	$352,000	3,300	$382,000
Wire Drawing Changeovers	Batch	No of Changeovers	700	$267,000	700	$272,000
Quality Inspection	Batch	No of inspections	1,000	$407,000	1000	$420,000
Pricing and Advertising	Product	Traced to Products		$300,000		$287,000
Order Processing	Customer	Number of Orders	3,000	$163,000	3000	$143,000
Invoicing	Customer	Invoices Issued	3,000	$87,000	3000	$92,000
Freight	Customer	Traced to customers		$1,110,000		$1,290,000
Information Systems	Facility	Tons Produced	100,000	$1,287,000	110,000	$1,330,000
EVA on Wire Drawing Equipment[2]	Unit	Tons Produced	100,000	$1,800,000	110,000	$1,724,000
EVA on Nail Galvanizer[2]	Unit	Tons Galvanized	40,000	$1,800,000	45,000	$1,688,000
EVA on Heading/Threading Machine[1,2]	Unit	Tons headed/threaded	2,600	$90,000	2,817	$227,000
Inventory EVA[2]	Unit	Tons Produced	100,000	$692,000	110,000	$703,000

[1] Each nail type had dedicated heading and threading equipment. This data pertains to heading and threading equipment used exclusively for galvanized pallet nails.

[2] EVA™ costs at 18% of ending net book value of each type of equipment and inventory were collected in cost pools and assigned to cost objects based on pounds produced.

EXHIBIT 5 Cost-Driver Units Consumed by Galvanized Pallet Nails, 1995–96 and 1996–97.

Cost Pool	Units of driver consumed in 1995-96	Units of driver consumed in 1996-97
Cleaning House	2600	2817
Depreciation-Wire Drawing	2600	2817
Depreciation - Galvanizer	2600	2817
Depreciation- Heading and threading[3]	2600	2817
Material Handling	20	21
Dies Retooling	15	13
Wire Drawing Changeovers	2	2
Quality Inspection	4	4
Order Processing	10	9
Invoicing	10	9
Information Systems	2600	2817

[3] This data pertains to heading and threading equipment used exclusively for galvanized pallet nails.

EXHIBIT 6 Other Costs Assigned to Galvanized Pallet Nails; 1995–96 and 1996–97.

Cost Pool	Spending in 1995-96	Spending in 1996-97
Pricing and Advertising	$10,000	$9,000
Labor	$400,000	$600,000
Freight	$30,000	$31,000
Inventory EVA™ @ 18%	$18,000	$18,000
Equipment EVA™ @ 18%	$253,800	$376,800

LEHIGH STEEL

Lehigh had gone from record profits to record losses in less than 3 years.

—*Bob Hall, ABC Project Manager*

Bob Hall studied the product profit report prior to the 1993 First Quarter Financial Review. The report was the culmination of a year's effort calculating and analyzing customer and product profitability using Activity-Based Costing (ABC). Hall had been hired to implement ABC to restore profitability at Lehigh Steel, which had reported record losses in 1991 after posting record profits in 1988. Not uncommon in an industry characterized by cyclic demand and large capital investment, such losses could not be long sustained. Lehigh was under pressure to return to profitability.

The goal of this Quarterly Financial Review—and the ABC program itself—was to rationalize Lehigh's product mix. Management felt that the decline from record profits to record losses was only partially explained by the traditional profit driver, volume. Another factor was the product mix running through the cost base. The recession of 1991 had presented a very different demand profile offering limited contributions to profit. With demand recovering in 1993, the ABC profit reports would enable marketing managers to identify profitable products, and select the 'right' mix.

Although the ABC model was running smoothly, the results were puzzling. Not only were product profits significantly different from those under standard costing, but they were counterintuitive to operations staff, who believed that products that tied up critical resources in the production process should reflect higher costs, and lower profitability. They were advocating a different approach called Theory of Constraints (TOC) to enhance profitability. Quickly Hall ran through the ABC model in his head. Which approach was right?

Lehigh and Specialty Steel

The Palmer Company, Lehigh's parent, was a global manufacturer of bearings and alloy steels with 1992 revenues of $1.6 billion. Palmer took pride in its long-

Professor V. G. Narayanan and Research Associate Laura E. Donohue prepared this case.

term decision-making that concentrated corporate resources on delivering superior performance for specific products and markets. Palmer believed that long-term specialization developed knowledge and innovation, the true source of competitive advantage. Palmer's corporate objective was to "increase penetration in markets providing long-term profit opportunities" by taking "a long-term view in decision making by strategically managing [the] business," and "emphasizing the fundamental operating principles of quality, cost, investment usage and timeliness."

Founded in 1913, Lehigh Steel enjoyed a niche position as a manufacturer of specialty steels for high strength, high use applications. Products included high-speed, tool and die, structural, high temperature, corrosion-resistant and bearing steels, available in a wide range of grades in a variety of shapes and finishes. Markets included aerospace, tooling, medical, energy and other performance industries. Lehigh enjoyed a premium market position because of its superior ability to integrate clean materials with precision processing to produce high quality products, which were often customized for specific applications, and bundled with metallurgy and other technical services. Primarily a manufacturer, Lehigh also operated a small distribution division which served certain market segments by offering a broad product line comprising products from multiple manufacturers.

Palmer had acquired Lehigh in 1975 not for synergies with its own specialty steel businesses, but for the Continuous Rolling Mill (CRM), specialized equipment that could convert steel intermediate shapes to wire for Palmer's bearing rollers. Only 6 such mills existed in the US.

Lehigh's financial performance trended with but generally outperformed the industry as a whole, driven by the superior quality that had earned it numerous awards from customers. The years 1988 and 1989 had been banner ones for Lehigh, which posted record profits during a period of general industry strength as reflected in shipments, operating rates and prices. But, broad recessionary business conditions drove a severe industry decline in 1991, reducing shipments, operating rates and prices. Lehigh posted record losses in 1991.

Lehigh operated under a matrix organization structure. Reporting to the company president were General

Managers of Primary Operations, Finishing Operations, and Marketing and Technology; Vice President of Sales; Director of Operations Planning and MIS; and CFO. Marketing managers assumed product line responsibilities that crossed functional boundaries. They developed marketing strategies, determined product offerings, established minimum order quantities, selected orders and set price, all with the goal of building volume at strong prices. Their performance was measured by product contribution margin calculated using standard costs: revenue less materials, direct labor, and direct manufacturing costs such as utilities and maintenance; other overhead was considered beyond their control. Manufacturing staff executed the orders brought in by the marketing managers, and were measured on variances from standard cost for the output mix produced. Their goal was to deliver quality product within the specified lead time at the lowest cost.

Industry Structure Specialty steel comprised roughly 10% of the total US steel industry, and like other high-tech, specialty industries, offered growth and profit opportunities to firms who targeted specific applications and developed unique technical competencies. Specialty steel was characterized by variations in the metallic composition and manufacturing processing which enhanced the properties of basic carbon steel. For example, adding nickel and chromium to carbon steel created 'stainless' steel, which resisted corrosion. Tungsten and molybdenum combined to strengthen, harden and temper carbon steel for cutting applications. Several industry segments evolved reflecting basic metallic combinations, which required different equipment and knowledge bases for manufacture.

Steel products were defined by several attributes which determined the product application and defined quality. Grade described the metallic (chemical) composition of the steel, or the elements added to the basic recipe of iron and carbon to create the desired properties. Product described the shape of the product, including semi-finished shapes, such as blooms, billets and bars; and finished shapes, such as wires and coils. Surface finish described the smoothness and polish that could be applied to the material's surface to enhance presentation. Size described the latitudinal and longitudinal dimensions of the product. Structural quality described the absence of breaks in the inner metallic structure. Surface quality described the absence of cracks or seams on the surface. Because specific applications

called for specific attributes, many products were customized along one or more attributes for the customer. However, of all attributes, customers valued most the grade, which determined primary product performance.

Producers typically focused on a selected portfolio of product shapes within a single segment, carving niches out of the broad industry. The focus strategy helped to protect volume and capital investments. The industry was capital intense in several areas. First, capacity additions were 'lumpy' and expensive, with equipment scaled in 100,000 tons of annual production, costing $10–$100 million, and requiring 18–24 months to install. Second, the cost structure was significantly changed only by new technologies, such as Lehigh's Precision Forging Facility (PFF), which were expensive, risky, generational ventures. Finally, knowledge work performed by metallurgists and other technical specialists was a significant portion of the cost structure. Hall summarized the 'focus' strategy: "You choose to make product which you can make better than the competition."

Economics and 'focus' also divided producers into manufacturers, who melted, refined, molded and rolled steel into basic shapes; and finisher/distributors, who broke semi-finished steel orders and shapes down to specific products for metalworking shops and original equipment manufacturers (OEMs). Manufacturers and distributors worked closely together, often as separate divisions within a firm. The manufacturing process focused largely on the materials science, in which metallurgists supervised the careful blending of alloy additives with carbon steel to create the precise properties required in a product application. Formerly mere warehousing, distribution had assumed the industry marketing role, creating product lines across material segments and shapes, enabling a firm to serve a diverse metalworking market while maintaining focused manufacturing processes. Both manufacturers and distributors provided technical services for everything from material composition to design to installation of the finished product.

Industry Conduct and Performance Maintaining high standards of product quality while keeping costs competitive were essential to compete in the specialty steel industry. Quality differences among manufacturers meant that products were not perfectly substitutable. Considerable value differentiation across producers within product classes had actually been confirmed and quantified by the International Trade

Commission during trade case investigations. Intended to protect suppliers, differentiation also benefited buyers, who enjoyed a range of choices within a product category, and could pay for the precise level of quality required. Technical services also differentiated suppliers while benefiting buyers, and were becoming increasingly important. Over time, customers had become sophisticated about the value of the product, and the price they would pay for it.

Not a commodity like carbon steel, which was sold primarily on a price and delivery basis, specialty steel was nonetheless highly price competitive. Producers were small, fragmented price takers in a market dominated by powerful, sophisticated customers. Market share could be bought or sold by pricing slightly below or above market price. Niches provided some protection for producers. Reputation for exceptional quality and technical services also earned producers some price premium. However, when cost and price were noticeably out of alignment, manufacturers exited, pricing themselves quietly out of non-profitable products, sourcing those critical to their product line from other firms. Cost, therefore, was a significant competitive weapon in determining share and profits.

To manage utilization rates and unit costs, producers sought volume and long production runs. When demand was strong, producers could select high volume orders which allowed continuous operation at high-setup time workstations. In low demand, firms chased low-volume niche business to fill plants, rationalizing the poor margins as volume that would contribute against fixed-cost while adding little variable cost. Unfortunately, this business required short production runs if Lehigh were to avoid inventory buildup of customized products.

Steel performance trended with the economy. Industry profitability fluctuated widely, ranging from −16.7% to 5.0% in the late 1980s. Industry capacity utilization peaked in 1988 at 89.2%, plummeted to 74.1% in 1991, and recovered partially to 82.2% in 1992.

Markets and Products   Customers ranged from large forge shops to original equipment manufacturers (OEMs), from distributors to tiny metalworkers, many of whom added further value by cutting down the product or the order size. Lehigh classified its customers into 33 market segments whose requirements for grade specificity, technical support and shipping varied. See Exhibit 1 for a market summary.

During the recession, Lehigh pursued marginal business to fill the plant, attracting many new customers in 1991–2. Under standard costing this business looked potentially profitable. However, specialized products required specialized processing and were ordered in smaller quantities. The average order size declined from 1600 pounds in 1988 to less than 1200 pounds in 1991. Accordingly, Lehigh's sales distribution broadened: customer sales ranged from $5.9 million for 2.7 million pounds of steel, to $84 for 8 pounds, with the average customer buying 36,635 pounds of steel for $63,407. Only 18 customers spent more than $1.0 million, and only 130 spent more than $100,000; over 420 customers spent less than $1,000.

Lehigh had 7 product lines—Alloy, Bearing, Conversion, Corrosion, Die Steel, High Speed and High Temp—of which three—Alloy, Die Steel and High Speed—comprised 70% of sales. Die Steel was steel hardened and strengthened for use in machine dies and molds. The Die Steel market was broad, ranging from ingots to semi-finished and finished parts, and market participants felt the need to offer a full product line to maintain share. High Speed products served endurance applications, such as metal cutting and punching, and were narrower in focus. Production of High Speed and Die Steel products was relatively simple, requiring little technical or process support. By contrast, Alloy products were complex. Their applications in aerospace frames, landing gears, missile cases and fasteners required steel precisely graded by metallurgists within tighter-than-standard ranges, super-cleaned by a double melt, and precisely rolled to narrow tolerances. By virtue of its superior product performance, Lehigh was able to command a small price premium for its alloys.

Lehigh also carried niche product lines—Bearing, Corrosion and High Temp—whose volume fluctuated with market conditions. Bearing steels were designed for a broad range of aircraft bearings and similar highly stressed parts whose grade precision required a triple melt. Corrosion-resistant steels were designed to operate in challenging environments in markets such as oil and gas exploration and medical implants. High Temperature steels were designed to withstand sustained exposure to temperatures from 800F to 1300F, such as in jet engines. These product lines were highly complex, requiring significantly higher levels of support from metallurgy, for making very clean steel, and process engineering, for testing and certification. For example, steel for artificial limbs had to pass stringent requirements for purity, for which each part had to be certified.

Almost 80% of metallurgists' time was spent on the niche product lines.

Conversion involved the processing of non-Lehigh owned material on equipment such as the PFF or the CRM that was not economical for some producers to own. The primary 'product' was the conversion of billet to roller wire for Palmer. Conversion was subtly complex, as the breadth of the end customer's product line translated into multiple rolling specifications, and multiple setups.

Lehigh's product hierarchy was structured as follows: product lines were broken down into grades, which were subdivided into product shapes, and further into skus, which reflected variations in size and finish. In any one year, Lehigh produced over 100 grades of steel, 500 individual products, and over 7,000 individual stock-keeping units (skus). Over multiple years, actual production could span over 10,000 skus. See Exhibit 2 for a product line summary.

Production Operations Specialty steel producers used steel scrap as the primary raw material, and essentially recycled rather than manufactured steel. Production involved six steps, whose complexity varied by product. See Exhibit 3 for a summary of the production process.

Hauled in with magnets and cranes, scrap purchased for $114.20 per ton was pre-processed, or combined with iron-based compounds to achieve the low composite residual (contaminant) levels required by Lehigh's high-grade products. The scrap compound was *Melted* in the Electric Arc Furnace, where high-powered (80 megawatts) electrical charges heated the solid metal by zapping it with arcs of electricity emanating from carbon electrodes. Synthesized fluxes containing limes refined the hot metal by binding with phosphorus and other impure elements, which were skimmed off.

The steel was further *Refined* by Argon Oxygen Decarbeurization (AOD), in which oxygen or argon was bubbled through the molten metal to further burn off impurities. Alloys were then added to achieve the special properties. The Melting and Refining processes constituted chemical reactions between various elements which created the desired material. As temperature was an essential factor in generating the appropriate chemical reaction, the hot metal processes were carefully monitored and controlled by metallurgists to achieve the precise grade.

The molten steel was teemed from ladles into octagonal *Molds*, forming ingots. Once solidified, ingots were stripped and left to soak in a storage furnace to maintain malleability and prevent damage. Molding was a relatively laborious process, as each 2500-pound ingot had to be handled and moved manually. Some ingots were then remelted to meet stringent purity requirements at either the Vacuum Arc Remelt Furnace or the Electro Slag Remelt Furnace, which cleansed the steel in solid form. Ingots were then *Broken down* into semi-finished (rectangular) shapes such as billets and bars. The Mesta press hot-worked bars over 12″ in diameter, a small percentage of overall output. Most ingots were routed to the PFF. The PFF was $40 million of relatively new technology in which an ingot was heated and forged by 4 hammers programmed to produce intermediate billets or bars. After being worked, the solid steel underwent a thermal treat called annealing, or slow cooling, to prevent shrinking and cracking caused by air cooling.

Rolling transformed intermediate billets and bars into finished shapes. A hot rolling mill had a soaking furnace to heat the steel, followed by a series of stands with progressively narrower rollers that pressed the hot steel into progressively thinner sizes until it achieved its final shape, such as a wire. A mill contained several sets of stands to roll different shapes; however, only one shape could be rolled at a time. Unique product shapes were rolled manually on the Hand Mill. 95% of intermediates were rolled on the CRM into one of 4 products: rods, flats, coils and bars. Shape changeovers were time-consuming events which dictated continuous 3 shift production, as well as a set production schedule with dedicated windows rotating within a 4 week cycle. One out of four weeks was dedicated to the conversion of billet to coil for Palmer. At $50 million, the CRM represented a capital investment that could not be duplicated in less than five years. Labeling it the plant bottleneck, Hall described the CRM as "the one manufacturing process that has the most impact on Lehigh . . . in terms of the resources used and the schedule it drove."

The final step was Finishing, which included a variety of treatments. Most products were annealed a final time to improve formability and make the surface more durable, and rough turned, or straightened. Other treatments included pickling (dipping in acid to clean off scaling) and polishing (grinding to produce a shiny, buffed finish). Pieces were tested or inspected if customer requested special tolerances in grade or shape. Finished product was shipped directly to customers.

Support activities were also critical to production. Maintenance, depreciation and utilities were basic costs required to run the plant, and comprised 21% of revenues. Production support activities such as material handling/setup, production planning and order processing ebbed and flowed with order volume. Technical support—metallurgy and engineering—was considered the lifeblood of Lehigh's reputation. Around the industry it was rumored that Lehigh had more metallurgists per ton of steel than anyone in the world. General & administrative included company-wide activities such as management, finance and research and development (R&D). R&D combined raw research in materials science with applied research in production technologies.

The Case for Change

Industry wisdom stated that steel profits were a simple function of prices, costs and volume. However, 1991 presented challenges in all three fundamental profit drivers. Market prices declined sharply to near or below product cost, lower in real terms than 1982 levels. Volume was available at market price, though in the form of niche specialties and small orders, but virtually disappeared at premium prices. Costs failed to decline with price or volume: shrinking operating rates drove up unit costs, and broader customer bases and product lines bred complexity and increased labor resources, particularly in scheduling. Profit could not be generated simply by working the tradition levers of price, cost or volume.

Particularly pressing were the simultaneous decline of the average order size and shortening of lead times, which had left volume-driven Lehigh flush with inventories and cost. In an effort to meet these demands and eliminate inventory 'waste', Mark Edwards, Director of Operations Planning and MIS, drove the 1991 move to synchronous flow manufacturing. Edwards believed that Toyota's lean, pull-based manufacturing concepts were key to reducing inventory cost, and pushed for their adoption at Lehigh. The new approach appealed to the marketing managers, who could broaden their customer base by offering smaller orders. However, under the current technology, it proved difficult to eliminate the steps in setups and changeovers critical to efficient small order throughput, and production staff observed a dramatic decline in efficiency.

In late 1992, Lehigh was reprieved somewhat by a slow but steady market recovery. Facing an increase in demand, Lehigh now had to choose which products to emphasize to convert sales into profits. Following its market strategy, Lehigh targeted a high value product mix that would lever profits in strong demand, and cushion it in downturns with greater contributions to fixed costs per unit volume. CFO Jack Clark suggested a firm-wide product profitability analysis, which would enable market managers to rationalize unprofitable products and focus resources on high value ones.

Clark reviewed the products' standard costs, which were used for both inventory valuation and decision-making. Product weight (pounds) was the primary unit of measure for standard cost, which included materials, labor, direct manufacturing expense and overhead cost categories. Standards for materials and direct labor were based on the bill of materials and routings, and included yield factors for scrap and rework. Scrap preprocessing was handled as a material burden rather than a routing step. Direct manufacturing costs such as maintenance and utilities were allocated to products based on machine hours. Indirect manufacturing and administrative costs were allocated to products based on pounds produced, since weight was assumed to be the primary driver of resource consumption.

The results were not news: the most profitable products—alloys—were already heavily promoted by marketing and sales. If these products were truly profitable, where were profits?

The Case for ABC In 1992, Clark attended a seminar on Activity-Based Costing. He realized that Lehigh was a perfect application for ABC as a discrete manufacturer of thousands of skus that shared the same production processes, serving a diverse customer base with a wide range of support needs. They knew that individual customers and products made different demands for resources, and that their standard cost system was likely averaging the diverse resource use by products and customers. Resources were heavy on his mind: support resources had increased through the recession. The number of production planners alone had increased by 25% to handle the increased scheduling complexity of the extra business.

Believing that ABC presented an opportunity to understand the drivers of profitability, Clark hired Bob Hall from Armco Steel. A steel industry accountant, with undergraduate and MBA degrees in Accounting & Finance, Hall had spent a year developing an activity-based product costing application at Armco. As Manager for Operations Accounting, Hall was assigned to implement ABC at Lehigh, with the goal of arriving at a clearer sense of the product and customer channels that were profitable to the company.

Hall investigated the issue by performing a regression analysis between the various product mixes and overall company profitability over time. The results were curious: company profitability was highly correlated with high volumes of High Speed and Die Steel sales. Under standard costing, the marketing managers had only tolerated these products, since they contributed against fixed costs, but believed that the real generators of profits were Alloys. Familiar with the theory of ABC as well as the specialty steel business, Hall agreed with Clark that standard costing was probably averaging uneven resource consumption across products, and that resources thought to be benefiting the whole business were in fact only benefiting a subset. The full ABC analysis would highlight the resource consumption of individual products.

The ABC model encompassed all customers, products and operations. Hall followed the two stage methodology of assigning general ledger account balances ('resource costs') to activities, using the resource driver 'percentage of time or effort expended', and allocating activities to products and customers using cost drivers appropriate to that activity. The activity pools and cost drivers reflected a 4 level ABC cost hierarchy of unit, batch, product and facility costs. The model included 50 business processes and 270 activities. Activity pools ranged from $5,017 for secretarial support to $1,096,952 for direct sales, with most covering $50,000 to $200,000.

As with standard costing, material costs were based on the bill of materials structure (i.e. 14″ ingot to 4 5/16″ billet to 0.71″ rod product), and included a burden rate for material pre-processing, as well as a scrap yield factor. Labor costs were based on the routing and standard labor rates, and included a rework yield factor. Overhead activities were driven to products using cost drivers that defined the causal relationship between the product and the activity, such as number of orders, machine hours, or number of skus per product (a measure of product complexity). For activities that were environmentally required, such as administrative activities, costs were allocated by the generic driver, 'pounds produced'.

The results were as Hall expected, and he was pleased with the study. However, responses by the rest of the organization were understandably mixed. Anticipating small changes in profits, managers were not prepared for the magnitude of the shift. Hall argued that the ABC model was correcting distortions created by standard costing, and that the ABC data was a true reflection of resource consumption. To facilitate acceptance, the project team refined some allocations to more accurately reflect the consumption of certain activities and resources. The refinements did not substantively change the results.

Support for the ABC model began to grow. In particular, production operations staff felt that the model confirmed some of their intuitions about profitable and unprofitable products, which were based on how smoothly material flowed through the plant. Certainly, it was felt that ABC was an improvement over standard costing. However, some results remained counter-intuitive. For example, high temps showed a similar ABC profitability to high speeds, even though high speeds could be processed across the CRM at a rate 6 times faster. Surely product profitability should reflect such vast differences in resource consumption.

The Case for TOC Edwards thought he understood why the ABC profit figures did not make sense. He had thoroughly researched recent manufacturing theories in his effort to reduce order planning and inventory costs, and had become a convert to lean manufacturing. He had read all of Eli Goldratt's books on synchronous manufacturing, summarized as the Theory of Constraints (TOC). TOC advocated proactive management of the constraint in a business system, and vilified absorption accounting as the driver of unprofitable decision-making. It was intriguing that a theory of production and operations management incorporated a theory of management accounting. Perhaps the key to the profit puzzle would be found in TOC.

Edwards reread his notes on the principles of TOC accounting, which proposed a simple operational measure to guide an organization toward the goal of making money. *Throughput* was defined as the quantity of money which the (business) system generated through sales over a specified period of time. Generalized as sales less direct variable cost, it was most commonly calculated as sales less material cost, and was roughly comparable to contribution margin. Profit for the system was increased by maximizing throughput per unit of the constrained resource. Interestingly, product costs played no part in TOC accounting. In fact, TOC proponents argued that product costing of any kind led to suboptimal decision-making because it ignored the constraint of time in a process. Edwards focused on a phrase he had underlined several times that contradicted every thing he had ever been taught about cost accounting:

> Throughput is not measured in terms of units produced, but in gross profit realized from units produced that are sold. Emphasis is placed on getting products through the manufacturing process and sold in the least time possible.

Edwards often walked through the plant as he ruminated. The ABC figures were not the only seemingly contradictory results at that time. Despite a decrease in demand during the recession, Lehigh's lead times had not decreased comparably. Excess material could easily be found on the shop floor despite the reduced process batches, which were supposed to facilitate the rapid flow of material through the plant, and the reduction of inventories. Had the reality of Lehigh's synchronous manufacturing fallen short of the vision? Or was the traditional accounting system contradicting the concepts of synchronous flow, impeding its full implementation and the realization of results? He decided to investigate one batch of steel as it traveled through the plant. He paused with his batch at rolling, where it would wait several days for its scheduled run, and reviewed what he had seen.

He observed that some WIP piles were larger than others, and his batch had waited longer at some workstations than at others. He considered the possibility of a constraint in the process. TOC advocated that management attention be focused exclusively on the constraint, which acted as the drum that set the pace for the entire operation. The capacity of the constraint determined the capacity of the entire system. To increase throughput through the constraint was to increase throughput for the entire system. Alternatively, to ignore the constraint was to lose control of the process. He also noted that products had moved at vastly different rates across workstations. Thinking of throughput,

he imagined the 'faster' products flowing smoothly through the plant, out the door to a customer. Other products seemed to crawl through the plant, requiring slower machine speeds, and routing promptly to inventory. He began to visualize the slowpokes at the bottleneck, tying up that critical resource, constraining throughput and profits. Time was the only resource that mattered in TOC, but time was not typically a factor used in Lehigh's decision-making.

The key to profitability was to send only the most profitable products through the constraint. Operations staff would unequivocally identify the CRM as the constraint in the plant. Edwards abandoned his production batch and returned to his desk to calculate Throughput for Lehigh's products. The results were almost as shocking as the ABC results, though for different reasons.

Accounting for Change Edwards called Clark before the next Quarterly Financial Review, eager to share his results. Concerned by the contradictions between the three accounting theories—standard costing, ABC and TOC—Clark asked Hall and Edwards to present their theories in the meeting. The managers would agree on one and use it to target products. To simplify the accounting for the other managers, Hall and Edwards agreed to model five products that were representative of the major product lines. Exhibit 4 contains product data for the sample products. Exhibit 5 contains their standard costs used in the initial analysis. Exhibit 6 contains activity cost pools prior to Stage 2 cost allocation.

The managers were equally confused by the different results. Surely calculating profits was a straightforward exercise. They preferred to focus on the decision at hand: which products to rationalize. Following either set of recommendations would likely have significant impact on Lehigh's product portfolio, not to mention profits.

EXHIBIT 1 Lehigh Market Summary

Market Segment	No. of Customers	1992 Sales (lbs)	1992 Sales ($)
Auto Die	2	9,394	$30,595
Bar	16	966,896	$1,631,655
Bearing	8	130,714	$600,398
Billet	2	1,598,041	$556,615
Coil	7	981,341	$2,044,536
Cold Head	25	332,631	$876,704
Core Pin	7	1,044,121	$2,688,430
Die Cast	13	1,026,699	$1,487,216
Distributor	154	10,533,749	$16,585,553
Extrusion	28	5,667,407	$5,042,492
Fastener	10	148,345	$2,259,677
Forge Billet	9	396,945	$395,515
Forge Die	6	323,131	$357,229
Forge Shop	34	7,416,347	$10,716,024
Gauge	3	10,274	$34,687
Ingot / Electrode	2	251,897	$56,269
Intercompany	1	431,672	$433,369
Knife	18	2,637,048	$2,893,755
Label Die	11	108,665	$153,991
Large OEM	92	7,576,997	$19,995,673
Mandrel Bar	19	19,452	$263,544
New	841	6,373,893	$12,811,325
Other	5	16,922	$39,651
Plastic Mold	6	51,906	$105,433
Punch	23	952,428	$1,967,775
Rock Bit	1	35,192	$33,784
Roll Form	8	291,928	$406,876
Special Machinery	11	3,725	$149,986
Spring	3	3,609	$118,992
Thread	3	614,882	$1,681,541
Wheel Mold	1	6,074	$8,204
Wire	1	5,074	$10,758
Z-Mill	3	332,021	$619,269
Total	**1373**	**50,299,420**	**$87,057,521**

EXHIBIT 2 Lehigh Product Summary

Product Line	No. of Grades	No. of Products	1992 Sales (lbs)	1992 Sales ($)
Alloy	21	153	11,836,227	$17,494,283
Bearing	7	24	329,816	$1,541,070
Conversion	16	16	5,516,107	$6,878,068
Corrosion	4	20	762,448	$1,327,111
Die Steel	49	156	22,336,768	$29,046,569
High Speed	24	97	9,375,129	$26,298,139
High Temp	3	16	142,925	$4,472,281
Total	124	482	50,299,420	$87,057,521

Process Flow

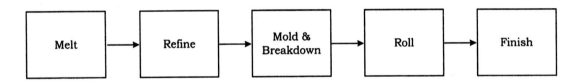

Workstations

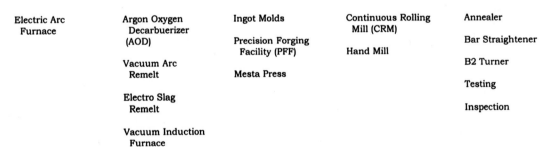

Melt	Refine	Mold & Breakdown	Roll	Finish
Electric Arc Furnace	Argon Oxygen Decarbuerizer (AOD)	Ingot Molds	Continuous Rolling Mill (CRM)	Annealer
	Vacuum Arc Remelt	Precision Forging Facility (PFF)	Hand Mill	Bar Straightener
	Electro Slag Remelt	Mesta Press		B2 Turner
	Vacuum Induction Furnace			Testing
				Inspection

EXHIBIT 3 Lehigh Production Processes

EXHIBIT 4   Sample Product Data

	Alloy: Condition Round	Conversion: Roller Wire	Die Steel: Chipper Knife	Die Steel: Round Bar	High Speed: Machine Coil
Production (lbs)	478,679	2,081,543	2,413,299	6,697,682	2,530,552
Number of skus	311	473	418	172	102
Number of orders	957	4,163	3,218	3,349	1,012
Bill of Materials (lbs / lb of output)					
Steel scrap	1.00	0.00	1.00	1.00	1.00
Alloys	0.01	0.00	0.01	0.01	0.01
	(@ $48.29 / lb)		(@ $6.29 / lb)	(@ $15.29 / lb)	(@ $152.29 / lb)
Machine Time (min / lb; crew = 1)					
Melting (Electric Arc Furnace)	0.20	0.00	0.09	0.09	0.09
Refining (VOD)	0.21	0.00	0.10	0.10	0.10
Molding / Breakdown (Ingot / PFF)	0.12	0.00	0.07	0.08	0.07
Rolling (CRM)	0.10	0.15	0.33	0.09	0.03
Finishing (multiple)	0.06	0.02	0.07	0.08	0.05
Total time	0.69	0.17	0.66	0.44	0.34

EXHIBIT 5   Standard Cost Results

Standard Cost ($ / lb)	Alloy: Condition Round	Conversion: Roller Wire	Die Steel: Chipper Knife	Die Steel: Round Bar	High Speed: Machine Coil
Price	$2.31	$0.77	$1.02	$0.93	$2.33
Materials	$0.54	$0.00	$0.12	$0.21	$1.58
Direct labor	$0.29	$0.07	$0.28	$0.18	$0.14
Direct manufacturing expense	$0.24	$0.06	$0.23	$0.16	$0.12
Contribution margin	$1.24	$0.64	$0.39	$0.38	$0.49
Contribution margin (%)	53.7%	83.1%	38.2%	40.9%	21.0%
Total contribution	$593,562	$1,332,188	$941,187	$2,545,119	$1,239,970
Manufacturing & administrative overhead	$0.64	$0.64	$0.64	$0.64	$0.64
Operating profit	$0.60	$0.00	($0.25)	($0.26)	($0.15)
Operating profit (%)	26.0%	0.0%	-24.5%	-28.0%	-6.4%
Total operating profit	$287,207	$0	($603,325)	($1,741,397)	($379,583)

EXHIBIT 6   Lehigh Activity Cost Pools

Activity	Driver	Driver Volume	Amount
Melting: Depreciation	melt machine minutes	5,145,632	$2,139,865
Melting: Maintenance	melt machine minutes	5,145,632	$975,130
Melting: Utilities	melt machine minutes	5,145,632	$2,036,477
Refining: Depreciation	refine machine minutes	5,691,042	$1,711,892
Refining: Maintenance	refine machine minutes	5,691,042	$780,104
Refining: Utilities	refine machine minutes	5,691,042	$1,745,551
Molding: Depreciation	mold machine minutes	4,226,965	$427,973
Molding: Maintenance	mold machine minutes	4,226,965	$390,052
Molding: Utilities	mold machine minutes	4,226,965	$290,925
Rolling: Depreciation	roll machine minutes	8,258,382	$2,995,811
Rolling: Maintenance	roll machine minutes	8,258,382	$975,130
Rolling: Utilities	roll machine minutes	8,258,382	$872,776
Finishing: Depreciation	finish machine minutes	4,057,311	$1,283,919
Finishing: Maintenance	finish machine minutes	4,057,311	$780,104
Finishing: Utilities	finish machine minutes	4,057,311	$872,776
General & Administrative	pounds	50,299,420	$5,400,955
Material Handling & Setup*	orders	57,147	$4,936,068
Order Processing	orders	57,147	$3,953,709
Production Planning	orders	57,147	$3,339,500
Technical Support	skus	6,642	$5,766,579
Total			$41,675,296

*Material Handling & Setup includes Depreciation for setup hours

6

Operational and Strategic Activity-Based Management in Manufacturing Companies

Activity-Based Management, or ABM, refers to the entire set of actions that can be taken, on a better informed basis, with activity-based cost information. With ABM, the organization accomplishes its outcomes with fewer demands on organizational resources; that is, the organization achieves the same outcomes (e.g., revenues) at a lower total cost (lower spending on organizational resources). ABM accomplishes this objective through two complementary applications, which we call *operational* and *strategic* ABM.

Operational activity-based management encompasses the actions that increase efficiency, lower costs, and enhance asset utilization; that is, to do things right. Operational ABM takes the demand for organizational activities as given, and attempts to meet this demand with fewer organizational resources. In other words, operational ABM attempts either to increase capacity or to lower the spending (i.e., reduce the cost driver rates of activities), so that fewer physical, human, and working capital resources are required to generate the revenues. The benefits from operational ABM can be measured by reduced costs (through lower spending on resources), higher revenues (through better resource utilization), and cost avoidance (because the expanded capacity of existing resources obviated the need for additional investments in capital and people).

Strategic ABM—doing the right things—attempts to alter the demand for activities as a way to increase profitability while assuming, as a first approximation, that activity efficiency remains constant. For example, the organization may be operating at a point where the revenues being earned from a particular product, service, or customer are less than the cost of generating those revenues. Strategic ABM encompasses actions that shift the mix of activities away from such unprofitable applications by reducing the cost driver quantities demanded by unprofitable activities. The ABC model also signals where individual products, services, and customers appear to be highly profitable. This information can be used by marketing and sales managers to explore whether demand for those highly profitable products, services, and customers can be expanded to generate new revenues that exceed their incremental costs. Thus, with strategic ABM, managers can take actions that shift the activity mix towards more profitable uses. Strategic ABM also encompasses decisions about product design, product development, and supplier relationships that reduce the demand for organizational activities.

Obviously, operational and strategic decisions are not mutually exclusive. Organizations

277

will get the greatest impact when they both reduce the resources required to perform a given quantity of activities and, simultaneously, shift the activity mix to more profitable processes, products, services, and customers. But before launching an ABC analysis, managers should attempt to forecast where they expect to obtain their near term benefits. The design of an ABC system can differ, depending on the intended application. Strategic systems may require relatively few activities (typically 20–60) while operational ABM systems often require several hundred activities to provide a finer view of the processes that underlie production and customer service.

ABC: THE ORGANIZATIONAL COST FUNCTION

It is important to recognize the limitations of activity-based management as well as the opportunities. To make many decisions, an organization needs a broader information base than just knowledge of its cost structure. As a cost model, ABC does not really provide insight in how to grow revenues. For this, organizations need models of what drives customer demand. Marketing people estimate how multiple factors, such as price, functionality, features, and convenience create demand for the organization's products and services.

One should think of ABC as providing the organization with information about the cost of supplying quantities of demanded products and services to customers. To get maximum benefits from the strategic component of ABM, managers must combine the cost driver knowledge available from their ABC model with information obtained from their marketing and sales organizations on customer and market demand—that is, the organization's demand or revenue curve.

In this chapter, we present various aspects of both operational ABM—improving the efficiency and reducing the resources required to perform activities—and strategic ABM—focusing the organization on the most profitable uses of its resources.

OPERATIONAL ABM

Organizations today are currently deploying many performance improvement programs. The initial impetus for these programs arose from the shock of learning about the efficient practices used by many leading Japanese manufacturing companies, especially those in the automotive, heavy transportation, electronic, and semiconductor industries. Total Quality Management programs of one kind or another have, by now, been adopted by most Western companies.[1] In the 1980s, companies also adopted Time-Based Competition ideas.[2] In general, these initiatives have been referred to as continuous improvement programs. Employees are directed to study the processes they are managing and to suggest and implement methods to continually improve the performance of these processes.

Reengineering launched another wave of improvement programs.[3] We characterize reengineering and transformation programs as discontinuous improvement. These programs are deployed when existing processes are so badly designed that improvement by a sequence of incremental (continuous) steps will not lead to the dramatic breakthroughs in process performance that often becomes possible when a completely new approach is taken. Reengineering

---

[1]David Garvin, *Managing Quality* (New York: Free Press, 1988); and Jeremy Main, *Quality Wars: The Triumphs and Defeats of American Business* (New York: Free Press, 1994).

[2]J. L. Bower and T. M. Hout, "Fast-Cycle Capability for Competitive Power," *Harvard Business Review* (November–December 1988); and G. Stalk and T. M. Hout, *Competing Against Time* (New York: Free Press, 1990).

[3]M. Hammer, "Reengineering: Don't Automate, Obliterate," *Harvard Business Review* (July-August 1990) 104-112. J. Champy and M. Hammer, *Reengineering the Corporation* (New York: Harper Business, 1993). Also, F. J. Gouillart and J. N. Kelly, *Transforming The Organization* (New York: McGraw-Hill, 1995).

also yields substantial benefits even when operating processes have been optimized within existing functions and departments. Such a reengineering initiative enables a process to be optimized across multiple functions and multiple departments; an opportunity that becomes highly visible with an operational ABM approach. Reengineering in its purest and most radical form urges employees and managers to start with a completely clean piece of paper and redesign important business processes from the ground up, with a view to achieving large multiples of (discontinuous) performance improvement; not the continuous, incremental improvements pursued in TQM programs.

Even though the actual practice of total quality (continuous) improvement differs considerably from reengineering (discontinuous) improvement, we have seen activity-based cost information used in a very similar fashion for both types of efforts. Therefore, we will present the role for operational ABM for both continuous and discontinuous improvement programs. In general, operational ABM is used in conjunction with TQM and reengineering using a five step approach.

1. Develop the Business Case

The first benefit from an activity analysis occurs from classifying activity expenses by opportunities for cost improvement. The improvements arise either by designing entirely new processes or by improving the quality and performance of existing processes. The activity classification enables managers to see how much of their current operating expenses occur in inefficient and low-quality processes. Used in this way, the ABC information provides the front-end insight and motivation for launching continuous and discontinuous improvement programs.

This initial effort to develop costs at the activity and business process level also provides an invaluable educational experience for the organization. The building of a cross-functional, cross-departmental map of activities brings together, usually for the first time, employees from different organizational units who are involved in the same process. This experience enables the employees to understand the linkages between their functions and departments, and facilitates the subsequent reengineering and business process improvement initiatives.

2. Establish Priorities

The scarcest resource in an organization is a manager's time. Managers, to conserve this resource, must follow the Willie Sutton rule and go where the money is. Rather than disperse employees' improvement initiatives across isolated and low-impact processes, managers can direct employees' efforts to improving activities and processes where the opportunity for substantial cost reduction is highest. The ABC model identifies where the largest opportunities for cost reduction exist. Managers can then use this information to set priorities for TQM and reengineering programs that, if successful, will deliver substantial and quantifiable financial benefits to the organization. The ABC information is not the ongoing operational tool for such improvement activities. For that, employees need direct feedback on quality, yield, and cycle time improvements, as well as information on cost reduction received through the kaizen costing and pseudo-profit centers discussed in chapter 3. The ABC model provides the front-end guidance for deciding where initiatives like kaizen costing, pseudo-profit centers, TQM, and reengineering should be launched.

3. Provide Cost Justification

To accomplish either TQM or reengineering, organizations will often have to incur some front-end investment costs. Reengineering programs in particular are not inexpensive. They usually involve heavy commitments to external and–or internal consultants to identify and facilitate the reengineering program; employee involvement to design and implement new processes; and spending on new technology, particularly the information technology required to provide the infrastructure for the new processes. Many organizations may be understandably reluctant to launch such major and expensive initiatives on faith alone. They will want to see a benefits case to justify the heavy commitments of time, energy, and financial resources required for a successful reengineering effort. The ABC economic map enables managers to identify the costs currently being incurred for inefficient and fragmented processes. Once the real costs of inefficiencies are understood, then the programs to remove them become much easier to justify.

4. Track the Benefits

The ABC model provides information about resource elements (general ledger expense code, assets, and full-time equivalent (FTE) personnel) assigned to an activity. By periodically refreshing and updating the basic ABC model, the organization can reestimate the resources (expenses, assets, and FTEs) deployed for performing activities and business processes. In this way it can verify whether the operational improvements are yielding actual benefits in terms of reducing resource capacity: fewer assets, less people, and lower spending required for the activity. The periodic ABC models provide tangible, documented feedback on whether benefits have been achieved from prior operational improvements, and signal when anticipated benefits have yet to be realized.

5. Measure Performance for Ongoing Improvement

The Cost Management Systems Program of an industry group, CAM-I, developed a genetic illustration of an activity-based costing model that added a dimension for performance improvement.[4] The CAM-I model introduced a process view as a horizontal axis at the activity level (see Exhibit 6–1). The process view introduces a different type of cost driver, which we shall call a process driver. Process drivers help to explain the quantity of resources, and hence the cost, required to perform an activity. Recall that activity cost drivers (the cost drivers used in the vertical dimension to assign activity costs to products) measure the quantity of activities demanded by individual products. Process drivers relate to the efficiency of performing the activity. Any activity could have several process drivers associated with it. For example, an activity such as processing materials through a machine might have, as a process driver, the quality of incoming materials. If incoming materials are out of specifications, or just inside specifications, more time and rework may be required to convert them to finished goods. So the quality of incoming materials is one process driver. Another process driver might be the training and skill levels of employees operating the process.

Focusing ABC systems on process drivers and continuous improvement of local activities and processes is certainly an element of operational ABM. This focus can lead to gradual improvements in cost, quality, and cycle time of individual activities and processes. But it is not clear that such incremental, local improvement is where employees' energies are best applied.

Setting priorities for improvement of local processes is performed better within the framework of the Balanced Scorecard (BSC).[5] The BSC approach to performance improvement identifies and highlights processes that are most critical for strategic success. It identifies critical processes not just for their potential for cost reduction, but for their ability to meet targeted customer expectations. With the Balanced Scorecard, managers usually see that excelling at entirely new processes may be much more important for successful strategy implementation than

---

[4]See "The CAM-I ABC Basic Model," Appendix B, pp. 17–19, in M. Raffish and P. B. B. Turney (eds.), *The CAM-I Glossary of Activity-Based Management* (Arlington, Texas: CAM-I, 1991).

[5]R. S. Kaplan and D. P. Norton, *The Balanced Scorecard: Translating Strategy into Action* (Boston: HBS Press, 1996).

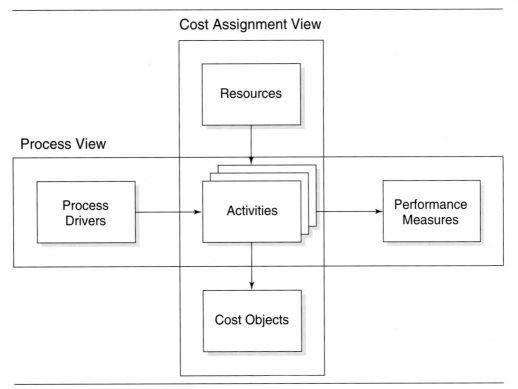

Source: Adapted from The CAM-I Glossary of Activity-Based Management, edited by Norm Raffish and Peter B.B. Turney (Arlington, Texas: CAM-I, 1991).

EXHIBIT 6–1   CAM-I Basic ABC Model

making gradual cost improvements in existing processes. Perhaps the best use of ABC information for local process improvement occurs after those processes have been identified by a high-level strategic implementation process, such as constructing the organizational Balanced Score-card, to be most critical for organizational success.

Alternatively, the strategic ABM approach, to be described later in this chapter, will highlight the quantity and cost of activity cost drivers used by products and customers. Strategic ABM will often identify where process improvements will be most critical for lowering the cost of producing important products or serving valued customers. Defining process drivers for those processes will focus employees' efforts on improvements most critical for these vital products and customers.

In summary, managers can define process drivers for activities that will signal to employees where they should direct their attention to improve the efficiency, quality, and responsiveness of existing, local processes. Using process drivers as performance measures directs employees' efforts toward continuous improvement of existing processes. Whether such information is superior to allowing employees to identify for themselves where the most promising opportunities are for process improvement depends on who has better insights about where these opportunities are likely to be: managers or front-line employees. Also, the managers need to determine, before defining process drivers as performance measures, whether they want lots of local process improvement, or radical process improvement of a limited set of processes that have been identified as being the most critical for the organization's long-term success.

OPERATIONAL ABM: A SUMMARY

Operational activity-based management enables managers to get highly visible successes from their Stage III activity-based costing system. Opportunities for transformation, reengineering, and continuous process improvements get quickly identified and quantified (though, depending on the magnitude of the projects undertaken, the benefit stream may take some time to get realized). Often such improvement initiatives can be quite costly undertakings. The partial ABC model provides the benefits case for launching the initiatives by revealing how much is spent each period by continuing to operate inefficiently. Many improvement projects turn out to be self-funding, with even substantial front-end costs being rapidly repaid through much more efficient and responsive processes. Subsequent ABC models can track whether anticipated benefits have been achieved in the transformed processes. And process drivers can be defined to direct employees' attention for ongoing, continuous improvement of the transformed–reengineered process.

We now turn to strategic activity-based management where companies can reap the benefits of a full activity-based cost model by driving costs to and making decisions about individual products, services, and customers.

STRATEGIC ACTIVITY-BASED MANAGEMENT: PRODUCT MIX AND PRICING

Strategic ABM works by shifting the mix of activities away from costly and unprofitable applications to more profitable ones, those where the revenues earned exceed the cost of activities required to generate the activities. Strategic ABM encompasses decisions made about:

- Product mix and pricing
- Customer relationships
- Supplier selection and relationships
- Product design and development

Many ABM practitioners focus only on operational ABM, attempting to improve the efficiency of existing activities. Such practitioners are leaving an important weapon unfired when they ignore strategic ABM. The demand for activities and business processes is not homogeneous. Often, individual products, services, and customers demand a complex mix of expensive activities for which the business unit is not adequately compensated under current pricing and volume arrangements. Managers must understand the incidence and frequency of such unprofitable products, services, and customers. With such knowledge, they can take actions so that they are more adequately compensated for the complex set of activities demanded. Alternatively, managers can shift the mix to less costly activities. The demand for activities ultimately arises from individual products, services, and customers. Managers need to understand how decisions taken at this level affect the quantity and the cost of organizational activities. In this chapter, we will discuss decisions made about existing products. In subsequent chapters, we will discuss the customer, supplier, and product design components of strategic ABM.

ABC PRODUCT PROFITABILITY: THE WHALE CURVE

Product costing was the first application of strategic activity-based costing. Distortions from using traditional costing systems, particularly those that relied on direct labor to allocate indirect and support costs to products, led several companies in the early- to mid-1980s to use activity-

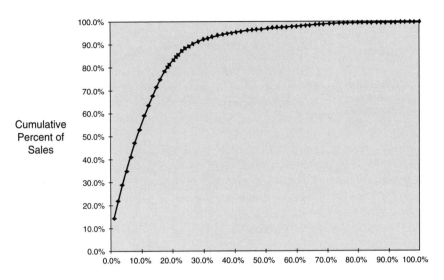

EXHIBIT 6–2   Cumulative Sales Distribution: The 20–80 Rule or 40–1?

based costing to assign their overhead costs more accurately to products. The new ABC systems defined and used a broader set of activities and cost drivers, particularly batch and product-sustaining activities (see chapter 4). The output from the ABC approach gave a very different picture of product cost from that derived either from traditional full-costing, direct-labor based systems, or direct (or marginal) costing systems. Both full cost and direct costing systems assumed that no relationship existed between product mix and volume and the demand for indirect and support resources. For example, Exhibit 6–2 shows the cumulative sales volume versus cumulative number of products for a typical full-line producer.

Exhibit 6–2 shows the normal 20–80 rule associated with business activities; the highest volume 20% of products generated about 80% of sales. More revealing, however, is the 60–99 rule: the highest volume 60% of products generated 99% of sales. Or, looking at the curve from the other direction, the lowest volume 40% of products generated a cumulative total of 1% of sales. Companies' traditional direct labor costing systems generally report, however, that all of these low-volume products are profitable since pricing is based on a normal markup over standard costs.[6]

In contrast, an activity-based cost analysis will generally show that, after assigning accurately the cost of activities such as setup, purchasing, quality assurance, inventory management, and product support, many products are extremely unprofitable. For example, Exhibit 6–3 shows a typical ABC finding: cumulative profitability is plotted against products, where the products are ranked on the horizontal axis from the most profitable to the least profitable. The most profitable 20% of products can generate about 300% of profits. The remaining 80% of products either are break-even or loss items, and collectively lose 200% of profits, leaving the division with its 100% of profits. The curve shown in Exhibit 6–3 happens so frequently in ABC analysis that it has been given a name. ABC analysts refer to the graph of cumulative

---

[6]A direct costing or marginal costing approach, of course, would show much higher margins for these low-volume products since no "fixed" overhead would be assigned to them.

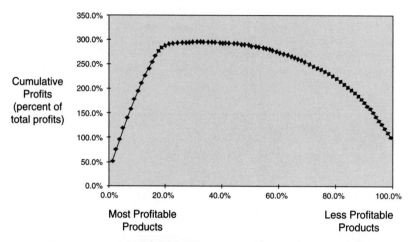

FIGURE 6–3   The ABC Whale Curve of Cumulative Profitability.

profits as the "whale curve." The height or hump of the whale indicates the profits earned by the business unit's most profitable products. The remaining products, break-even and loss, bring total profits down to sea level.

Typically, the costs of high-volume products are relatively unchanged by the shift from traditional to activity based costing (the ABC-assigned costs for these products will decrease, but usually by less than 10%). Therefore, their traditional and activity-based profit margins are not grossly different.

Low-volume products, in contrast, tend to be unique, customized products. Companies often rely on their traditional standard costing system to set prices for these products since often no competitive product exists. The company may even set the apparent profit margin somewhat higher on these unique products to reflect the lack of competitive forces. But because the company's standard cost system severely underestimates the cost of designing, producing, sustaining, and delivering these low-volume, custom products, the higher margins fail by substantial amounts to cover the cost of resources used for these products. The ABC costs are often more than 100% higher than the costs assigned to these products by the existing Stage II cost system.

The whale curve in Figure 6–3 gets reproduced in virtually every activity-based cost system built for business units that meet the two rules introduced in chapter 4:

1. *Willie Sutton rule*: large expenses in indirect and support resources.
2. *High diversity rule*: large differences in products, customers, and processes.

Companies, operating for decades with signals from either traditional standard cost systems or direct (marginal) costing systems, overproliferate their product lines and overcustomize their product offerings. They fail to see how decisions on product variety and complexity inevitably lead to much higher expenses in the indirect and support resources required to implement this full-line product strategy.

Even great Japanese manufacturers have not been immune to the adverse consequences from excessive variety. For example, there is evidence that the Japanese automobile manufacturers have excessive product line complexity.[7] Similarly, Japanese electronics companies and other consumer product manufacturers also suffer from excess part and product proliferation.[8]

---

[7]"A Lower Gear for Japanese Auto Makers," *New York Times* (Sunday, August 30, 1992), Section 3, p. 1.
[8]G. Stalk and A. Webber, "Japan's Dark Side of Time," *Harvard Business Review* (July–August 1993) 93–102.

Lacking activity-based cost models that identify the high costs of product variety and proliferation, even excellent companies can introduce and sustain far more products than are economically warranted. The whale curve of product profitability provides a signal and a discipline for companies to address whether customers truly value all the variety of products currently being provided.

PRODUCT-RELATED ACTIONS

Managers or students, when they first encounter the whale curve of total profitability, often suggest that the company can work less hard by producing only a small fraction of existing products. Apparently the business unit, by retaining the profitable 80–85% of existing sales, can see profits double or triple by eliminating the loss products. On subsequent reflection, the respondents soon see several fallacies with this line of reasoning. First, many existing customers may want to buy from a full-line producer. While the business unit may earn the bulk of its profits from selling higher-volume standard products, like vanilla and chocolate, they must also offer their customers the occasional small quantity of specialty flavors, like butter-pecan fudge swirl, that are much more expensive to design and produce.

Second, many of the expenses assigned to products by the ABC analysis will remain in the short run, even were the products to be dropped. In this case, the revenues will disappear immediately, but most of the costs (other than materials) will likely still be incurred. If no further actions are taken, the remaining expenses could be (incorrectly) spread back to the remaining products, causing many of them to now look unprofitable.[9] Should these be dropped, the business unit is now well along in a death spiral that will soon lead to the unit contracting itself out of existence.

Clearly, for strategic ABM to be effective, it must cope with these legitimate concerns. In fact, managers have a great array of actions that they can deploy to modify their whale curves, and increase the profitability of their product lines. These actions, illustrated in many of the cases at the end of this chapter, include:

- Reprice products
- Substitute products
- Redesign products
- Improve production processes
- Change operating policies and strategy
- Invest in flexible technology
- Eliminate products

As suggested in the ordering of this list of potential actions, dropping unprofitable products is, perhaps, the last possible action to be contemplated.

The product-related actions listed above, if implemented successfully, will reduce the resources required to produce products. Pricing and explicit product substitution will shift the product mix from difficult-to-produce products to simple-to-produce products. Redesign, process improvement, focused manufacturing facilities, and new technology will enable the same products to be produced with fewer organizational resources. Also, eliminating products clearly implies that fewer resources are required for the remaining products. In order for the organization to capture the benefits from these actions, however, managers must eliminate the spending associated with the resources no longer needed.

---

[9]Of course, as we discussed in chapter 5, such a death spiral should not occur in a properly designed ABC system. Activity cost driver rates should be set based on practical capacity of resources supplied, so unused capacity costs will not be driven to existing products.

Most if not all of the batch and product-sustaining expenses are associated with committed resources (recall the discussion in chapter 5), whose supply is determined in advance of demand. Therefore they will not be variable costs, as conventionally defined. Performing one less setup, ordering one less batch of materials, moving one less load of materials, and performing one fewer engineering changes will not result in any automatic reduction in spending. The totality of product-related actions discussed in this chapter will create additional unused capacity. Benefits will accrue only when managers take action to eliminate the unused capacity created (as discussed in chapter 5).

SUMMARY

ABM, either operational or strategic, identifies opportunities for creating unused capacity. Operational ABM creates unused capacity by making existing processes more efficient and productive. Strategic ABM either generates more revenues from repricing actions or creates unused capacity by reducing the demand for high-cost activities. To capitalize on any unused capacity created, managers must be prepared to either reduce spending on resources no longer needed or redeploy the unused capacity to more profitable uses. Thus activity-based management and capacity management are intimately intertwined.

CASES

The cases for this chapter illustrate how companies use activity-based management to support the firm's existing strategy or help identify a new one. The *Schrader Bellows* case series provides a hands-on ABC design experience with computer software. It enables students to design an ABC system, interpret the output from the system, and critique a strategic ABM plan derived from the insights provided by the ABC system. *Stream International* provides a good example of the opportunities for operational ABM. The *Maxwell Appliance Controls* case combines both operational and strategic ABM possibilities. All the cases in this chapter give ample opportunity to discuss not only the technical aspects of an ABC model but also the important issues that arise in managing an ABC project and implementing an ABM action plan.

SCHRADER BELLOWS (A)

Introduction

In a diversified company, a few great businesses often sustain a whole kennel of dogs. Within divisions, one or two fabulously profitable product lines frequently support a slew of miserable money-losers. And within product lines, it is common for a small portion of the range to subsidize an astonishing number of unimportant products whose true ROI can easily be worse than −100%. Our traditional cost accounting systems systematically mask the damage caused by the losing divisions, product lines, and products. Sorting out the true profitability of business units, product lines, and of individual products is at the heart of strategic analysis.

This sentiment was expressed by William F. Boone, Vice-President of Planning and Development at Scovill, Inc. In 1983, Boone, a 1977 Harvard MBA, was analyzing the product profitability of the Schrader Bellows Automation Group, one of six Scovill divisions. Prior to accepting his current position at Scovill, Boone had worked for Bain & Company and for The Strategic Planning Institute.

Scovill, a diversified group of manufacturing companies, had 1983 sales of $743 million, operating income of $71 million, and net earnings of $27 million (Exhibit 1). In addition to Schrader Bellows, Scovill owned Schrader Automotive, the world leader in tire valve manufacturing; the Apparel Fasteners Group, producers of fasteners for the clothing industry; Yale Security Group, whose product line included Yale locks; Hamilton Beach, a leading full-line producer of electric housewares; and Nu-Tone, a producer of built-in products for the home such as radio-intercoms, exhaust fans, and door chimes.

Schrader Bellows Automation Group was created in 1979, the year after Scovill purchased Bellows International and amalgamated it with Schrader Fluid Power operations. The new group was viewed by Scovill as a world leader in pneumatic controls. Its strategic advantages were a broad line of quality products, the largest direct salesforce and distributor network in the industry, and a strong market position in emerging industrial countries.

In 1983 Schrader Bellows accounted for 13% of group sales but only 6% of operating income. In 1979, in contrast, it had accounted for 15% of sales and 21% of operating income. In the last five years, Schrader Bellows had lost profitability almost continually (Exhibit 2) and was viewed as a problem division by Scovill senior management. Management of the division attributed the declining profitability to sales decreases caused by a dramatic drop in demand for capital goods.

The Fluid Power Industry

Schrader Bellows competed solely in the pneumatic segment of the fluid power market. This segment contained numerous competitors, each with its own specialized niche, producing a set of nonstandard products that could not be replaced by a competitor's equipment without major circuit redesign. This practice resulted in each firm having a captive customer base.

In recent years, foreign competitors, especially from the United Kingdom and Japan, had introduced many well-received standardized components. Industry experts were predicting that standardized parts would gradually dominate the fluid power market.

Schrader Bellows had analyzed the competitive markets in which it operated and had identified 13 major and numerous minor competitors. While each product line could be analyzed as a separate competitive market, management had found it productive to treat the product groups as the unit of analysis and had estimated the market share of each major competitor in its four product groups (Exhibit 3).

Products

Schrader Bellows produced over 2,700 pneumatic control products in its Wake Forest, North Carolina plant. These were grouped into four major product groups and a number of other minor products that were either experimental in nature (e.g., robots) or supplemented the productive output of other Scovill divisions (e.g., automotive tire valves). Total 1983 revenue from Wake Forest was just over $20 million. The plant was expanded in 1978 when the Bellows manufacturing facilities had

This case was prepared by Professor Robin Cooper and Lawrence A. Weiss, research assistant.

Copyright © 1985 by the President and Fellows of Harvard College. Harvard Business School case 186-050.

been integrated into Wake Forest. There were several other Schrader Bellows plants throughout the world, but Boone had identified Wake Forest as the focus for the initial investigation because of the large number of different products manufactured at that plant.

The air preparation and accessories manager since 1966 was Joe Hinton, a 25-year Schrader Bellows veteran. Air preparation and accessories consisted of two main product groups: the filter, regulator and lubrication (FRL) group, and the maintenance, repair, and overhaul parts (MRO) product group.

The FRLs were used to prepare the air passing from a compressor into a compressed air system. Preparation was necessary to lengthen the life of the valves and tools used in the system. Air preparation required three distinct and separate steps: filtration, regulation, and lubrication. Filtration removed the majority of the moisture in the system and particulate matter with a diameter over 5 microns. Regulation maintained a constant downstream pressure even if the compressor was surging. Lubrication prolonged the life of the air valves, cylinders, and rotary tools by reducing friction between moving parts.

While available separately, FRLs were typically sold as a single, integrated unit placed between the compressor and the rest of the air system.

The MRO product group consisted of a hodgepodge of air preparation accessories including blow guns, mufflers, and quick connect couplers. Blow guns are small, hand-held compressed air guns used to direct a blast of compressed air at a recently machined part or at the work area to remove metal and wood chips. Blow guns are relatively simple and inexpensive devices used in almost all metal cutting and woodworking shops. Mufflers, or more properly air exhaust mufflers, are used to silence blasts of compressed air at the exhaust port of valves. They are required by OSHA to reduce air noise below a specified level. Quick connect couplers allow tools to be quickly connected and disconnected from the air line. They are used throughout the typical factory compressed air system.

Hubie Jenks, the product manager for the directional and flow control groups, was a 20-year veteran with Schrader Bellows. Since 1980, he had been the manager of the directional control and flow control valve product groups; previously he had been the assistant product manager. The valve products were used in numerous applications in many industries; a typical use was to control the movement of a part that was being machined.

The directional control valve product line consisted of six major families, all providing the same general service, direction control, but varying in operating conditions permitted, complexity of service provided, and pressure ranges accommodated.

The flow control valve line contained three major product lines all providing the same general service, flow control, but varying in the accuracy of flow control, the ease of adjustment, and the direction of flow control (one or both directions).

The division marketed a complete range of valves, a policy Jenks viewed as fundamental to the firm's marketing strategy. In a recent meeting Jenks remarked, "A full line allows you the opportunity to service the ultimate number of accounts. Many accounts buy a number of products at once and will not multisource; the amount of sales represented by that type of customer is a substantial fraction of the total valve market." Jenks's belief in the value of offering a full product line was strongly shared by the marketing and sales department.

The other product groups included production machine components, pneumatic cylinders, two small robots, and automotive tire valves. The tire valves were being made at Schrader Bellows for the first time; previously, they had been manufactured in the Schrader Automotive plant. Scovill management felt that Schrader Bellows could introduce new production techniques and reduce the cost of manufacture. These tire valves were significantly smaller than the typical Schrader Bellows product and were causing manufacturing a lot of headaches.

The various product groups were sold directly by the firm's salesforce and via distribution houses to the end user. The direct salesforce produced 40% of the domestic revenues through sales to machinery and equipment manufacturers. Schrader Bellows was proud of its direct salesforce and felt it was both the largest and the best in the industry.

Salesforce compensation consisted of two major components, base salary and commissions. In 1985 the salary base averaged $22,000 per year. This varied by $2,000 to $3,000 depending on seniority. Sales representatives on average earned commissions equal to 60% of their base salary. The commission structure was entirely based on planned sales. Up to 75% of planned sales, the salesperson earned a maintenance fee of only 1/2% of sales. Above that level, the commission rose rapidly to its maximum of 7% for sales above plan.

For FRL and MRO products, OEM sales were not

common because Schrader Bellows was generally seen as a high-price producer with little quality advantage (though their FRL line was viewed as the Cadillac of the industry, having several advanced easy-to-maintain features that were only matched by one other competitor). This price disadvantage was less serious in the end-user market because end users typically only buy one or two units and are more interested in delivery and ease of ordering than price.

In comparison to the FRL and MRO products, valves were special-application items that required a salesforce with considerable technical skills. Schrader Bellows valve prices were in the top 25% of the market and typically were about 20% above the market average. In the valve lines, the technical demands of the marketplace, coupled with a perceived quality advantage, allowed the firm to recover its higher than average production costs.

Over the years, the firm's strategy of providing a full product line had resulted in a considerable proliferation of variations for each product. The plant now produced over 2,700 different final products and stocked up to 20,000 parts. Some of these variations were quite simple and required minimal change to the production process. Others, however, required a substantially changed production process. Many of these variations and some of the less popular sized items had relatively small demand and tended to disrupt the smooth flow of production in the plant. For example, it was quite common for a long-run production process to be interrupted because a special variation small-volume product was wanted in a hurry. The existing setup would have to be broken down and set up for the new part. Once the special part had been manufactured, the machine would be broken down and then set up again for the original part. The production personnel at the plant felt that the sales, marketing, and senior management people, who were all located in Akron, Ohio, were not aware of the nuisance these constant interruptions caused.

Production Process

There were five manufacturing departments: automatic machining, plating, general machining, assembly, and packing.

Production began in the automatic machining department where bar stock, castings, and forgings were machined. Parts manufactured from bar stock were produced on screw machines, and those from castings and forgings on chucking machines. Both types of machines

were automated, designed to produce high-volume parts, and were capable of performing several operations sequentially without human intervention. The two main tasks of the operators were keeping the machines loaded and undertaking in-process inspection.

In the plating department, parts were immersed in large chemical baths and electrochemically plated. Once plated, the completed parts were stored in work in process.

Parts manufactured from purchased parts or subassemblies were produced in the general machining department. This department contained relatively simple machines: drills, lathes, and grinding machines. These machines performed drilling, tapping, shaping, deburring, and finishing operations. Most of the machines were manually loaded and operated, but recently some numerically controlled and automatic loading machines had been purchased.

Finished products and subassemblies were produced in the assembly department. This was a labor-intensive process that used relatively simple machines to assemble the products from the manufactured, purchased, and subassembled parts stored in work in process.

In the packing department, finished products, associated documentation, and spare parts were put in a cardboard box and the box sealed.

Product Costing

Product costs were calculated by the firm's computerized standard cost system as the sum of material, direct labor, and overhead costs (Exhibit 4).

The standard material cost of the product was the sum of all the raw material and purchased parts included in the finished product.

The standard direct labor cost of the product was determined by identifying all the direct labor required to produce the manufactured parts and to assemble the product. Direct labor costs were tracked by labor class. In all, there were 15 labor classes with rates varying from $6.50 to $10.00 per hour. The appropriate labor class required by each operation was specified by manufacturing engineering. The wage rate for each class was supplied by the personnel department.

Overhead was allocated based on the number of direct labor hours required to manufacture and assemble the product in each of the five manufacturing departments. Each department had its own overhead allocation rate (Exhibit 5) which represented the total overhead costs associated with the department divided by the expected number of direct labor hours in that department.

The overhead associated with each department consisted of two elements. The first was the overhead directly traceable to that department (e.g., factory space and indirect personnel). The second overhead element was the support department and fixed plant expenses allocated to the manufacturing department (Exhibit 6). This allocation was achieved using a number of different bases.

The total costs of four of the eight support departments (finished goods inventory, purchasing, raw materials inventory, and manufacturing engineering) were allocated to the manufacturing departments on the basis of the number of direct labor hours expected to be charged in each of the manufacturing departments. For example, if the total direct labor hours of the five manufacturing departments was budgeted at 100,000 hours, of which the assembly department accounted for 20,000 hours, assembly would be allocated 20% (20,000/ 100,000) of the total cost of these four support departments.

The total cost of the work-in-process inventory department was allocated to the manufacturing departments on the basis of the percentage of direct labor hours expected to be charged in the automatic manufacturing, plating, packing, and general machining departments (assembly was excluded because it was not responsible for any significant work-in-process costs).

The production control department cost was allocated to the manufacturing departments on the basis of the ratio of total labor hours (direct and indirect) expected to be charged in each of the five manufacturing departments.

The total costs of the setup and quality control departments were allocated to the manufacturing departments based on the estimates of the workloads associated with each manufacturing department provided by the managers of each department.

The allocated costs from each of the support departments were then added to the overhead costs of the manufacturing departments, creating a separate overhead pool for each manufacturing department. Departmental burden rates were determined by dividing each overhead pool by the direct labor hours worked in that department. To illustrate, assume the assembly department had an overhead cost pool of $480,000 ($120,000 of its own and $360,000 allocated from the support departments) and that 20,000 direct labor hours were expected to be worked in that department. The burden rate for the assembly department would then be calculated at $24.00 per direct labor hour ($480,000/20,000).

Product Pricing

Schrader Bellows generally priced its products based on cost, but market considerations came into play at both the beginning and the end of the price-setting process. A target price was set when a new product was first sent to engineering. This target price was based on the anticipated costs and potential market for that particular product. After engineering was complete, the cost to manufacture the product was determined. A standard formula was used to arrive at the selling price. Generally, the objective was to obtain a standard margin of 40% to 45%.[1] This price was evaluated against the target price and any relevant information regarding the market. If the price was too high, either the product would be reengineered in an effort to lower the cost, or the margin would be decreased.

Once a product was in production, its price was reviewed annually when new standard costs were published. If a product's cost was too high, the price was raised, the product was reengineered, or it was dropped (the industry norm was to support a product for five years, after which it was dropped). If none of these options were feasible, the product was left in the line at the old price.

---

[1]For example, if a valve cost $3.52 and a 40% margin was required, the cost was multiplied by 1.67 to give the discounted price of $5.88. If the average discount was expected to be 35%, the discounted price was divided by 0.65 to give the list price of $9.05.

EXHIBIT 1

SCHRADER BELLOWS (A)

Scovill Five-Year Financial Review

SELECTED FINANCIAL DATA (IN MILLIONS OF DOLLARS, EXCEPT PER SHARE DATA)	1983	1982	1981	1980	1979
Net sales	$742.6	$691.4	$817.9	$793.0	$788.1
Cost of sales	513.9	470.2	572.4	561.3	554.2
Interest on borrowed money	19.8	26.3	26.7	27.4	24.9
Pretax earnings from continuing operations	51.6	23.2	59.8	54.0	65.9
Federal, foreign, and state income taxes	23.6	8.3	27.5	24.4	29.5
Minority interest in net earnings (loss) of consolidated subsidiaries	3.1	(.3)	2.3	2.2	1.1
Earnings (loss):					
From continuing operations	24.9	15.2	30.0	27.4	35.3
From discontinued operations		4.7	(34.5)	(3.4)	(3.3)
Extraordinary credit	2.5				
Net earnings (loss)	27.4	19.9	(4.5)	24.0	32.0
Earnings (loss) per share of common stock:					
Primary:					
From continuing operations	2.30	1.60	3.18	2.92	3.81
From discontinued operations		.50	(3.68)	(.36)	(.34)
Extraordinary credit	.23				
Net earnings (loss)	2.53	2.10	(.50)	2.56	3.46
Fully diluted:					
From continuing operations	2.25	1.56	3.13	2.87	3.69
From discontinued operations		.49	—	(.36)	(.35)
Extraordinary credit	.22				
Net earnings (loss)	2.47	2.05	—	2.51	3.35
Total assets	490.4	460.5	557.8	554.1	573.3
Long-term obligations	86.6	110.0	113.2	129.3	163.1
Cash dividends per share of common stock	1.52	1.52	1.52	1.52	1.43

EXHIBIT 2

SCHRADER BELLOWS (A)

Financial Statistics:

Schrader Bellows Automation Group

1979–1983

($ million)

	1983	1982	1981	1980	1979
Sales	$99.7	$102.5	$123.2	$123.1	$120.2
Operating income	6.0	4.7	12.0	16.9	19.5
Identified assets	92.8	87.5	96.1	97.4	97.2
Capital expenditures	4.0	4.7	5.0	5.8	5.0

EXHIBIT 3

SCHRADER BELLOWS (A)
Market Analysis by Product Group

PRODUCT GROUP (1983 MARKET SHARE AND SALES VOLUME)							
MAINTENANCE, REPAIR, OVERHAUL		FILTRATION, REGULATION, LUBRICATION		DIRECTIONAL CONTROL VALVES		FLOW CONTROL VALVES	
Parker Hannifin	(20%)	Norgren	(30%)	Numatics	(20%)	Deltral	(35%)
U.S. Gauge	(15%)	Watts	(20%)	MAC	(15%)	Schrader	(20%)
Deublin	(10%)	Wilkerson	(15%)	Schrader	(10%)	ARO	(15%)
Hansen	(10%)	Schrader	(10%)	Others	(45%)	REGO	(10%)
Schrader Bellows	(10%)	Others	(25%)			Others	(20%)
Others	(35%)						

Sales Volume (Wake Forest)

$4.5 million	$5 million	$6 million	$4 million

EXHIBIT 4

SCHRADER BELLOWS (A)
Standard Cost Report: Valve 60073

	MATERIAL COST	LABOR COST	OVERHEAD COST	TOTAL COST
Purchased part	$1.1980			$1.1980
Operation				
Drill, face, tap (2)		$0.0438	$0.2404	0.2842
Degrease		0.0031	0.0337	0.0368
Remove burrs		0.0577	0.3241	0.3818
Total cost, this item	1.1980	0.1046	0.5982	1.9008
Other subassemblies	0.3253	0.2994	1.8519	2.4766
Total cost, subassemblies	1.5233	0.4040	2.4501	4.3773
Assemble and test		0.1469	0.4987	0.6456
Pack without paper		0.0234	0.1349	0.1583
Total cost, this item	$1.5233	$0.5743	$3.0837	$5.1813
Cost component	29%	11%	60%	100%

EXHIBIT 5

SCHRADER BELLOWS (A)
Overhead Burden Rates per Direct Labor Hour

DEPARTMENT	ACTIVITY	OVERHEAD BURDEN RATE PER DIRECT LABOR HOUR
201	Assembly	$24.21
203	Automatic manufacturing	67.65
205	Plating	84.16
213	Packing	40.51
214	General machining	40.07

EXHIBIT 6

SCHRADER BELLOWS (A)

Overhead Budget by Department

($ thousands)

Manufacturing

201	Assembly	$ 337	
203	Automatic manufacturing	671	
205	Plating	290	
213	Packing	352	
214	General machining	955	
			2,605

Support

230	Work-in-process inventory	253	
231	Finished goods inventory	404	
234	Production control	748	
235	Purchasing	102	
239	Raw materials inventory	206	
240	Setup	640	
250	Quality control	855	
260	Manufacturing engineering	1,484	
			4,692
	Fixed plant expenses*		2,054
	Total overhead		$9,351

*Includes property taxes, product liability insurance, general
maintenance labor, and plant management.

SCHRADER BELLOWS (B)

Support department activities are expensive; in a plant such as Wake Forest about 50% of all overhead representing 25% of total manufacturing costs occur in support departments. Conventional cost systems do a poor job of allocating these costs to the products. Our major task at Schrader Bellows was to identify appropriate allocation bases for support department costs so that we could calculate accurate product costs.

Pierre Guillaume, Manager of Strategic Planning

Introduction

In early 1983, William F. Boone, Vice-President of Planning and Development at Scovill, Inc., decided to send two of his people, Paul Bauer, Director of Strategic Planning, and Pierre Guillaume, Manager of Strategic Planning, into Schrader Bellows to determine the

profitability of the products manufactured at the Wake Forest Plant. This action was triggered by the continued decline in Schrader Bellows's sales and profits. "We are probably the largest producer of pneumatic products in the world," declared Boone. "So why aren't we making an adequate profit?"

The Planning and Development department often acted as internal consultant to Scovill's various divisions. The department's assistance could be requested by division management, but, if the department felt a problem was serious enough, it could initiate its own review. In the case of Schrader Bellows, the initiative came from Planning and Development. Boone explained this decision.

I was convinced that we needed to reexamine the fundamental principles on which Schrader's cost accounting system was based. While at Bain I was involved in a number of studies designed to determine product line profitability, but we never got down to costing individual products. At the Strategic Planning Institute, I developed interviewing techniques for obtaining from line people

This case was prepared by Professor Robin Cooper.
Copyright © 1985 by the President and Fellows of Harvard College. Harvard Business School case 186-051.

fairly accurate allocations of assets and expenses to product lines. These techniques were more efficient than those we had used at Bain.

When you are dealing with high-level strategic issues, you are making binary decisions (stay in business or get out of it). At this level of decision making, determining ballpark figures for profitability is quite sufficient; it's not important whether ROI is −30% or −40%: In either case, you are in bad trouble. Spending lots of time and money to be precise does not improve the accuracy of your analysis, nor does it change your recommendations.

For product costing work, however, we could not be quite so cavalier about the accuracy of our estimates. Nevertheless, I was convinced that the same "soft" analytical techniques I had employed when studying product line profitability to circumvent the vices of average costing could be used to improve the accuracy of individual product costing. I needed an approach that was not concerned as much with precision as with overall accuracy. The typical cost accounting system produces product costs that are very precise and totally inaccurate. I wanted relatively accurate product costs and was not overly concerned with precision.

This is why I chose Paul Bauer and Pierre Guillaume for the job. Paul is a PhD aeronautical engineer with an MBA in finance from Chicago. Pierre combined degrees in economics and law with an MIT MBA. He had also taught accounting to students majoring in data processing. Both had a lot of experience in the trenches gathering data for the Scovill strategic data base, which was organized around 200 individual competitive arenas rather than around the existing accounting system. This meant that we almost always ended up developing P&Ls and balance sheets for pieces of the business which had never been reported separately.

In February 1983, Bauer and Guillaume visited the Wake Forest plant. Bauer commented as follows:

We started by touring the plant, talking to people, and trying to get a feel for the production process. We both agreed that thoroughly understanding the production process was critical to our ability to identify product profitability.

The most striking aspect of the production process was the great discrepancy between lot sizes. For successful products, large lots of several hundred pieces are manufactured. For the less successful products, lots are typically less than 10 pieces.

Once we understood the production process and related economics, we were able to consider what was required to cost the firm's products properly. The costs of the support departments greatly exceeded the overhead costs of the production departments, and yet the procedures used to allocate support department costs to the products were simplistic and, in our opinion, bore little relationship to the underlying economic reality.

As a matter of practicality, we decided to live with the costing system for the five manufacturing departments.[1] It adequately captured the material and direct labor costs and, for the overhead costs that were directly associated with those departments, allocated them to the products reasonably well. The same could not be said of the allocation of the overhead costs for the eight support departments,[2] and we decided to focus on their assignment to the five manufacturing departments.

We interviewed the heads of each support department to learn what events triggered activities in their departments. Our goal was to identify appropriate allocation bases to distribute support department costs on the frequency of activity-triggering events.

Support Departments

The eight support departments had a total budget of $4.7 million (Exhibit 1). The three inventory departments and the production control department were managed by the same person; each of the other four had its own department head. The Scovill team interviewed all five department heads extensively.

The first person interviewed was Nancy Massey. Massey, a 20-year Schrader Bellows employee, was responsible for four departments: raw materials inventory (number 239), work-in-process inventory (230), finished goods inventory (231), and production control (234).

Guillaume first asked Massey to describe the activities of the Production Control and Inventory Department personnel.[3]

PG   How many people do you have in the Production Control and Inventory Department?

NM   Well, I've got five people involved with inventory control plus the supervisor, that's six. And there are another eight including a supervisor in the production scheduling function. That's a total of 14. Oh, and I spend most of my time, say 80%, in this department supervising the people here.

PG   How are the schedulers assigned to production departments?

NM   Out of the seven, three spend all of their time in 203 and 214. A fourth did some 201 scheduling very early this year but now spends most of his time in 203 and

---

[1]Assembly, automatic manufacturing, plating, packing, and general machining.

[2]Raw material inventory, work-in-process inventory, finished goods inventory, production and inventory control, purchasing, setup, quality control, and manufacturing engineering.

[3]These interviews have been edited. All unnecessary passages have been removed. The actual interviews were considerably longer.

214 as well. The remaining three schedule setups throughout the plant.

PG   What determines the amount of work, the number of hours, that your people spend on scheduling?

NM   It's essentially a function of the number of production runs.

PG   The number, not the size? In other words, if production runs were twice as big but there were the same number, then your work would still be the same?

NM   Yes, that's essentially correct.

PG   Good. You mentioned a supervisor. Does he do scheduling as well?

NM   Occasionally, when the schedulers are overloaded. The rest of the time he supervises the others. He is there when there is a problem, a production crunch, for example; his responsibility is to get the products out when they are required. He tries to make sure that the right products are assembled, even to the extent of modifying the shop orders so that products can be shipped in time.

PG   Let's move on. What generates the work for the inventory control people?

NM   Out of the six people involved in inventory control, three are directly responsible for inventory control. They decide how much and when we have to order raw materials and purchased parts. The fourth edits the inventory transactions, and the fifth prepares the paperwork for the shop. The sixth is a supervisor who is responsible for the inventory control people. Also, one of the three responsible for inventory control spends some time running the office.

PG   What I need to know is what causes the work for those three people so that we can allocate their costs to the products in a sensible manner. In your opinion, what is the best way to allocate these costs, one that really does a reasonably good job of reflecting the work done here?

SB   I don't know if you have talked to the accounting people, but they allocate everything based on direct labor hours.

PG   Yes, we have talked to them, and we're trying to look at allocating costs in other ways. Do you believe that direct labor hours is the right way to allocate costs? Is the work in this department directly proportional to direct labor hours?

NM   No, not really. In fact, if we only had one product in this plant, we wouldn't need any of the people that we have, even for the same volume of output.

PG   Even if there were lots of the product being produced?

NM   Yes, because if there were only one product, inventory control would be simple and production scheduling would be nonexistent. We only need inventory control people because we have a complicated production process, and the more production runs we make, the more people we require.

Guillaume and Massey next discussed the Finished Goods Inventory Department.

PG   How many people do you have working in the Finished Goods Inventory Department?

NM   There are eight people working there.

PG   Do they all do the same thing?

NM   No, come to think of it, there are nine people working there—the ninth is the supervisor. Let me think about what they do. . . . One is in charge of receiving goods from the assembly department.

PG   How is the quantity of his work generated? What's it related to?

NM   Well, every time a production run is made in the assembly department, the product is moved into the finished goods department, generally in one batch unless it's a very long run. There is some paperwork involved, but essentially the task is material handling, taking the products to the shelves.

PG   He doesn't do any inspection or anything like that?

NM   No.

PG   OK, so that's one of the eight people. What about the others, what do they do?

NM   Let's see, three handle customer orders, and the remaining four handle shipments.

PG   For the three who are dealing with customer orders, is the work they do generated by each order? For example, if they handled twice as many orders, would they have twice as much work?

NM   Not necessarily. The work also depends on the size of the orders, the number of different items ordered, and the quantities involved.

PG   Could you be more explicit?

NM   Every time a customer order comes in, it generates some work, and depending on the number of items that are requested, the amount of work is going to be different. In fact, even though there is a fixed amount of work required every time a customer order is received, what actually generates most of the work is the number of items on each order. Also, the work depends on how large the order is in terms of dollars.

PG   Why is that?

NM   First of all, when the order is extremely large, it might have to be shipped in more than one shipment, and that creates additional work for the finished goods people. So, for very large dollar orders, the amount of work required for the three people is higher. The amount of work also depends on the size of the product. When we get an order for flow-control valves, the amount of physical work and handling that's required is not as high as when we get an order for a robot.

PG   Let me see if I understand. It sounds like there are two things affecting the workload. First, incoming orders generate a certain amount of paperwork. Then there is the work related to the mass of the products that will be shipped.

NM   That's right.

PG   What do you estimate is the percentage of time that is spent dealing with the paperwork generated by a customer order?

NM   Paperwork is generated at two stages, first by the three people who receive the orders, and second by the four people who ship it.

PG   Let's just focus on the three in receiving for the time being. What percentage of their work is standing at a desk?

NM   Well, let me think about that. It's definitely more than half.

PG   Is it more than 70%?

NM   No, it's less than 70%.

PG   You're confident that it is between 50% and 70%?

NM   Yes, that sounds about right.

PG   You mentioned four other people, what are they doing?

NM   Well, they are handling shipments, and there the bulkiness of the items is a greater factor than for customer orders.

PG   Is it the majority of the work?

NM   No, it's more like 50% to 60%.

It took all morning to complete two departments. After lunch, Guillaume and Massey started on the raw material inventory control department.

PG   How many people do you have working for you in the raw material inventory department?

NM   I have four people working in that department.

PG   What do they do?

NM   Two of them spend most of their time dealing with the shipments of purchased parts. They handle everything; they handle the receiving documents and transfer the incoming purchased parts to the work-in-process stockroom. The third person works in the raw material area. After the material clears inspection, he moves it into inventory and takes care of the paperwork.

PG   What causes the amount of time required to process an incoming shipment to be different? Is there a big difference if the shipment is a large one compared to a small one?

NM   No, not for the purchased items because they go directly to the work-in-process stockroom, and unless it's a very large shipment, extremely large, it can be dealt with in one trip, so volume is not a real problem. The raw material is a different question because volume can play a major role in the amount of effort required to move it.

PG   So, what you're saying is that, for most of the things coming in, whether it's a large quantity or small, it takes the same amount of time to process. But for

some of the heavier raw materials, the sheer volume does in fact necessitate taking several trips to move it into the stockroom.

NM   That's right, but there are only on a few large raw material shipments. I would say that the amount of time required really depends on the number of times a product is received rather than the size of the shipment.

PG   OK, any other factors that impact the amount of work?

NM   Well, there is the fourth individual; I haven't had a chance to talk about him yet. He disperses raw material to the shop floor and again the volume required is really not an issue. It's more the number of times raw material has to be dispersed to the shop floor, either to department 203 or 214.

PG   Do you usually disperse the total amount of material required for a production run all at once, or does it go out in smaller quantities?

NM   It varies with the size of the run. On a very long run we don't disperse it all at once because the amount of raw material on the shop floor would be too large. On smaller runs, and I would say that's 80% of all production runs, we send it there in a single trip once the setup is completed.

While Guillaume was interviewing Massey, Bauer was talking to Larry Leblanc, head of setup. Leblanc had spent 10 years with Bellows International, joining them directly from high school, and continued with the division after its acquisition by Schrader.

PB   How many people do you have in your department?

LL   I had 14 people in January and then Joe Peak left, so we are now down to 13 people.

PB   OK, are all of your people setting up or do they have other tasks as well?

LL   That's a good question. Two of my staff have recently been spending most of their time in the automotive, cylinder, and robotic departments.

PB   What's being set up there?

LL   It's not really a setup; they have been helping out in those departments.

PB   Are they setting up new equipment?

LL   Not really setting up new equipment, but making sure that the runs are going properly so that things can be completed and so on.

PB   How about the people who really are setting up then?

LL   Five work exclusively in the 203 and 214 departments where they spend 100% of their time doing setups on non-NC (numerically controlled) machines. Another two spend, well, in the first quarter one of them did spend a little bit of time in 203 on other machines, but now they spend most of their time setting up the NC machines in departments 203 and 214.

PB   When you say setting up, is that what they really do all day long? Because it sounds like you've got more people than one would expect given the number of setups to be done and the average setup time.

LL   That's an important observation; first of all, we're doing more setups than we're supposed to.

PB   Why is that?

LL   Because many times we have to stop long production runs to produce 10 or 20 parts for a special product that needs to be shipped out at the end of the month. We then reset the machines, again, for the long running item. Toward the end of the month our people spend a good deal of time on these setups for short jobs. In fact, in the last week of the month, it may be as much as 20% to 30% of their time. Now, another problem is that you probably looked at the standard setup time, and they're not always very reliable. Some machines take a lot more time to set up than standard.

PB   What percentage of the standard setup times do you think are off by at least 50%?

LL   That's a difficult question. . . . I wouldn't be able to give you an answer.

PB   Is it a lot, or just a limited number? Is it more than 50% of them?

LL   No, probably not.

PB   Is it more than 10% of them?

LL   Certainly more than 10%, somewhere in between; it's hard for me to say.

PB   Are there any other activities that these people are doing which is really not setup as such, but they end up doing anyway?

LL   Well, I didn't mention the remaining four persons working in assembly. They are setting up, but here there are no heavy machines to set up. Setting up means making sure that all the necessary parts are available when the assembly person starts working. This doesn't take a lot of time, 15 to 30 minutes per setup.

PB   OK, so other than that, the rest of the time they really have their hands in the grease?

LL   Yes, they do, but in many cases, especially when we have a rush order and we need only produce a very small number of parts for a special product, they end up doing the production themselves because it's not worth turning it over to the regular operator.

PB   Can you estimate roughly, take a whole month altgether, what percentage of the setup person's time is really used in doing the direct operator's job? Is it greater than 20%?

LL   No, it's less than that.

PB   Less than 10%?

LL   It varies a lot, maybe a little more than 10% for the five people working in 214. This type of situation happens almost exclusively in that department.

After interviewing Leblanc, Bauer talked to Paul Finks, head of quality control. Like his counterparts, Finks was a Schrader Bellows veteran with many years of service with the firm.

PB   How many people are in quality control?

PF   I have 13 area inspectors who do quality inspection. I have two senior technicians who have a lot more experience and work as the technical experts on the team. Also, there is one statistical clerk and myself.

PB   Where are these people working?

PF   For the area inspectors, that's fairly simple. Well, not really. Three of them work exclusively in the 203 and 214 departments. You know we just introduced the automotive department last year; one inspector has been working full time on the quality problems of the automotive department.

PB   Now, do you expect his services to be required indefinitely there or is that going to . . .

PF   Let's hope not. That's not a normal way of operating, to spend that much time on a single product, but maybe automotive products are different. Even the tolerances required of the machines are different, and we did have more than our share of problems when we first started. I hope that next year we'll be able to spend a lot less time doing automotive inspection. Going back to your original question, there are two more inspectors who do both the receiving inspections and the assembly inspections, and seven others who work in the whole plant. They work in any department that needs them.

PB   What creates the work of the inspectors?

PF   The inspectors do first-piece inspection, so every time we set up the machines, they are there to check the quality of the first piece produced. Two also check the quality of the parts that we receive. Every time we receive a shipment, we get one of our people there to check the quality.

PB   When you check on the incoming purchase orders, does the size of the sample or the effort required vary, or is it always the same?

PF   Good point. It does vary slightly, but we tend to do more random checking on large shipments than on small ones, so essentially it takes about the same amount of time.

PB   Which is more time consuming, assembly or receiving inspection?

PF   Oh, it's clearly receiving inspection. There is very little quality inspection in assembly.

PB   10% or less?

PF   Maybe more than that.

PB   As much as 50%?

PF   No, less than 30%, between 10% and 30%. Let me try to think. . . . Last week we worked about two days in the assembly area.

PB Two out of five?

PF No, out of 10, there are two people involved. Last week was probably representative of what normally occurs.

PB OK, let's talk about the two people, the technicians. On what activities do they spend the most time?

PF This year they spent a good deal of their time on the automotive products.

PB Other than that, what's the most important time consumer?

PF They probably spend a lot more time in the assembly department than any other.

PB What are the other things that they do? You've got automotive products the most important time consumer, then assembly. . . .

PF Yeah, they are about the same; it's hard to tell.

PB Assembly and automotive require about the same amount of time?

PF This year, yes. I don't expect it to be that way next year.

PB Those two combined, how much of the total time of these two individuals is absorbed in automotive and in the assembly department?

PF Maybe two-thirds of their time.

PB What are the other things that they do?

PF They do have to intervene occasionally in the 203 and 214 department when there is a problem. That's the rest of the . . . not really, because they also spend time on new product development and improving the production process. That's not insignificant.

PB If we say 70% of the time goes to the two activities you discussed, then you've got 30% to allocate. You said they work in 203 and in 214, and then there were these new products. Anything else they do, is there any other activity that they do?

PF They do some administrative tasks, but that's about it.

PB Let's just take those three things, the administrative and the 203 and the 214; how would you divide this 30% that I've got? Is it 10, 10, and 10?

PF No, when I think about it, they probably spend about as much time in 203 and 214 combined as they do in 201 assembly.

PB So, maybe we should change it. Maybe it's not 70%; maybe we can go to 60%.

PF Make it something like 30, 30, 30.

PB OK, we're going to put 30% in automotive, 30% in assembly, 30% in 203 and 214 combined, and then there's 10% in process improvement and product development. Now, for the manufacturing departments, what is the split between 203 and 214?

PF I would say half and half.

PB We've allocated the time of the two technicians to the departments; now what we've got to do is trace that back to the individual products. What's the right way to do that?

PF It's really hard to tell because they don't. . . . Well, let's see. They are called on when there is a problem in the inspection area, but they aren't really there every time an inspection is made. They are only there when there is a problem.

PB Are these problems predictable; are they attributable to an individual product line that's problem prone?

PF Well, if that's the case, I'll put them on it until it's straightened out.

PB Other than that, would you say that. . . .

PF No, we know that certain machines give us more problems than others.

PB OK, there are certain machines that give you problems, but you can't put your finger on a particular problem product?

PF Not really. That would be an interesting study.

PB You don't keep any records?

PF No.

PB You don't have a list of troublesome products?

PF No, but we do keep a list by machine.

PB You mentioned that 10% of the technicians' time was spent on process improvements and product development. Can that be attributed to individual products?

PF It varies quite a bit from year to year. We've been working on process improvement in most of our product lines, so it's really hard to trace it back to specific products.

PB If I understand correctly, in addition to the people we have discussed, there's yourself and one statistical clerk. What do you two do?

PF I supervise the department. I tend to spend more time on administrative tasks, people problems, and so on. The statistical clerk keeps records of the data we are collecting, such as problems by machine, the inspection problems on the automotive products, and so on. It's hard to break his time down into specific product lines or departments.

At the end of the day, Bauer and Guillaume met to discuss their findings. They first reviewed their notes on the interviews they had carried out the previous days and discussed their writeups (Exhibit 2). Once satisfied that they had captured the details for those departments, they focused on today's interviews.

EXHIBIT 1

SCHRADER BELLOWS (B)

Overhead Budget by Department

($ thousands)

Manufacturing			
201	Assembly	$ 337	
203	Automatic manufacturing	671	
205	Plating	290	
213	Packing	352	
214	General machining	955	
			2,605
Support			
230	Work-in-process inventory	253	
231	Finished goods inventory	404	
234	Production and inventory control	748	
235	Purchasing	102	
239	Raw materials inventory	206	
240	Setup	640	
250	Quality control	855	
260	Manufacturing engineering	1,484	
			4,692
Fixed plant expenses*			2,054
Total overhead			$9,351

* Includes property taxes, product liability insurance, general maintenance labor, and plant management.

EXHIBIT 2

SCHRADER BELLOWS (B)

Interview Analysis of the Work-in-Process, Purchasing,
and Manufacturing Engineering Departments
at Wake Forest

WORK-IN-PROCESS

The work-in-process inventory area (230) contained six people. One was a group leader who supervised the other five and helped out when bottlenecks occurred. One of the others was responsible for receipts into WIP from the production plant, while the other four split their time between monitoring inventory in WIP and disbursements to assembly (the split was 40% and 60%, respectively).

PURCHASING

Joe Gahagan was responsible for purchasing (235) and was assisted by a secretary. Orders of raw material and parts for production were made in conjunction with the production control department. This occupied approximately 80% of the department's time. Inventory levels were controlled using the OPT system. Supplies, on the other hand, were ordered as people informed Gahagan or his secretary that stock was low.

EXHIBIT 2 *(Continued)*

SCHRADER BELLOWS (B)

Interview Analysis of the Work-in-Process, Purchasing,
and Manufacturing Engineering Departments
at Wake Forest

MANUFACTURING ENGINEERING

The manufacturing engineering department (260) contained 29 individuals who oversaw the development and determination of the processes required to make parts. These included designing necessary tools and having them made, as well as establishing time standards for the required operations. The department was also responsible for evaluating equipment to verify adequate utilization, improving its efficiency and utilization (i.e., cost reductions), procuring and justifying new equipment, and disposing of unnecessary equipment.

The manufacturing services manager, Hank Eide, had a wide range of duties. He not only supervised his department personnel but often was directly involved in the various activities. He was responsible for the departmental budget, labor grievances, hiring and firing (done in conjunction with the personnel department), and reviewing performance of the personnel in his department.

The six industrial engineers solved problems on the production floor and continually reviewed the manufacturing process for improvements. For example, a particular part was being damaged as it fell from a machine into a basket. The solution was to put tennis balls into the basket. This effectively stopped the parts from damaging themselves. These engineers also made suggestions for new machinery and to improve the plant layout. They handled the coordination with quality control and design. They processed new engineering releases to ensure that the product would be properly produced. Finally, they prepared cost estimates for new or changed products.

There were two numeric control programmers who were responsible for the 10 numerical control machines (lathes and screw machines). The programs specified the sequence of milling, drilling, tapping, which tool to use, what speed to operate at, etc.

Three tool engineers designed all the tools necessary to make the products. The range of tools went from cutting tools to jigs and fixtures. Approximately half of the tools were made in the tool room, and half were subcontracted out. The tool room had 13 people making these parts.

Manufacturing developments operated in an advisory capacity, working with other departments to introduce new techniques and processes. In one dramatic case, the setup time on a machine was reduced from three hours and 56 minutes to 19 minutes with the help of this department. There were four people working in the department.

SCHRADER BELLOWS (D-1)

In early 1983, William Boone, Vice-President for Planning and Development at Scovill, Inc., initiated a product costing study at Schrader Bellows, a Scovill subsidiary. The Scovill team, consisting of Paul Bauer, director of strategic planning, and Pierre Guillaume, manager of strategic planning, had visited the Wake Forest plant and interviewed the heads of the support departments. The interviews were completed and the Scovill team had identified the appropriate cost allocation bases. Bauer and Guillaume were reviewing their progress on the product costing study.

Guillaume described the product costing procedure:

Our first step was to explode the sales data. We took the quantity sold of each end product, determined the individual components contained in the end products, and then estimated the quantity of each component required in 1982.

The second step, costing the components according to the selected allocation bases, was the most challenging. A great deal of judgment was required to allocate the support department costs down to individual components. We also spent a considerable amount of time insuring that the factory and sales, general, and administration costs were appropriately allocated. In our opinion, very few of these costs were truly fixed.

After we completed the allocation of costs to the components, we imploded these costs back to the product level by summing the costs of all components in a given product.

Estimating product costs required an enormous number of calculations. Paul Bauer and Pierre Guillaume had to develop a special computer program. While developing the program, they realized that the processing time would exceed the available daytime capacity of the Wake Forest computer. Fortunately, the Wake Forest IBM 4341 was not being used at night, and this time slot was dedicated to the project. Pierre Guillaume described its use.

We kept the IBM busy all night all by ourselves. We knew we would use a lot of computer time, but actual use far exceeded our expectations. It was a long, time-consuming process. You take the output of a run, analyze it, make corrections, run the program, and start again. Each run took about 10 hours. Six hours were required to allocate the costs into their components, and it took another four to implode the costs back to the product level. Fortunately, we did not have to run the explosion routine, which takes another three hours, more than once or twice. The number of things that could go wrong was massive. For example, if a product was sold but not manufactured in 1982, there was no 1982 manufacturing data for that product and, consequently, it was not assigned any setup-related costs. The small-lot-size products interrupting the large-lot-size products caused the number of actual set-ups per large-lot-size product to be much higher than we had expected.

Bauer and Guillaume spent several months debugging the program and resolving problems like the ones just described. Eventually a satisfactory run was achieved. The program produced a list containing the product cost data for about 2,000[1] separate products. Initially, Bauer and Guillaume tried to analyze the data for the entire 1982 production. It rapidly became apparent that a structured analytic approach was required. Guillaume elaborated as follows:

We needed to analyze the data in a way that made sense to the company. We decided to focus our analysis on one product group at a time. We selected valves for initial analysis because valves are the flagship product of Schrader Bellows. To further limit our analysis, we selected flow control valves for particular attention because they are a small but representative product group. There are only a few major types of flow control valves; 77 distinct items were manufactured in 1982 [Exhibit 1].

The product profitability data for the flow control valve line were transferred to a floppy diskette so that they could be analyzed on an IBM PC.

This case was prepared by Jane Montgomery, research assistant (under the supervision of Professor Robin Cooper).

Copyright © 1985 by the President and Fellows of Harvard College. Harvard Business School case 186-053.

---

[1]Seven hundred products produced at Wake Forest were not included in this analysis.

EXHIBIT 1

SCHRADER BELLOWS (D-1)

Flow Control Valve Group

The flow control valve group accounted for sales of $4 million in 1982 and contained three major product lines: micrometer flow control valves, flow control valves, and needle valves.

1. Micrometer flow control valves: Used to control the flow of air in a pneumatic circuit. The micrometer line provided full flow in one direction and adjustable flow in the other. They were typically used in applications where flow settings needed to be changed regularly. The micrometer control knob provided accurate, calibrated flow.

2. Flow control valves: Provided the same function as the micrometer valves but were more precise in their operation. They used a fine screw thread adjustment to allow precise settings which could be secured by a sturdy lock nut. Due to their design, they provided the most effective adjustment and highest flow rate of any control valve in their class. They were typically used in applications where exact flow settings were necessary and where changes were rarely required.

3. Needle valves: Similar to the micrometer valves but provided infinite flow adjustment in both directions.

Flow control valves were manufactured in eight different sizes ranging from ⅛″ to 1½″ in diameter. For each of the eight sizes, up to four different variations were manufactured.

- *Standard valve:* These valves contained seals made of polyurethane, were the least expensive of the various seals, and were applicable to a wide range of different conditions.
- *Viton:* These valves contained Viton 0 rings and poppet seals. Viton had a higher life expectancy than polyurethane in high-temperature settings and was impervious to a wider range of chemicals than polyurethane.
- *Nitrile seal:* These valves contained seals that were better suited to low-pressure applications or where a definite positive seal was required.

The eight different sizes, four different variations, and three product lines produced a possible 96 different products, of which 77 were in the 1982 Schrader Bellows catalog.

SCHRADER BELLOWS (E)

Introduction

The Schrader Bellows strategic cost analysis had demonstrated that a large percentage of the products produced at the Wake Forest facility had negative operating profits and residual incomes (see Schrader Bellows (D-1).

The Scovill team was now faced with the problem of developing an action plan that would allow the firm to take advantage of the findings of the study.

Attacking the Problem

Bauer described the approach they adopted.

Our first step was to approach the product managers to obtain their reactions to the cost analysis. We created a list of

This case was prepared by Jane E. Montgomery, research assistant (under the supervision of Professor Robin Cooper).

action codes representing a set of mutually exclusive actions which could be taken with respect to the unprofitable products. This ensured that the product managers would review and select a course of action for every product with a negative residual income. The possible actions included the following:

a. Drop the product.

b. Raise the unit price enough to bring the residual income up to zero.

c. Add a setup charge to the price of any order. The setup charge would be the same whether the order was for 10, 50, or 100 units.

d. No change.

e. Take no action because the validity of the data was questionable. The profitability of this product should be analyzed further.

f. Attempt to reduce the cost of the product.

g. Buy the item outside.

We sent a memo to the product managers [Exhibit 1], asking them to recommend a course of action for all products for which they were responsible. The product managers recommended that action be taken with respect to 1,355 items [Exhibit 2]. They proposed dropping 794 products, repricing 471 to bring residual income to zero, adding a setup charge to 51, reengineering three, and buying 36 outside.

With the results of the product manager survey in hand, Bauer and Guillaume initiated a series of meetings with management of the Wake Forest plant. Key players were Thomas White, group vice-president for Schrader Bellows world-wide, Jack Couchois, manager of the Wake Forest plant, and Joe Reardon, production manager at Wake Forest.

These meetings focused on what products should be dropped. While the product managers had lowered the number of products being considered for elimination, everyone agreed that dropping close to 800 products would be a drastic move. Many believed that Schrader Bellows could not afford to do much pruning of its product offerings because the company's major competitive advantage was its broad product line. The management team was also unwilling to drop a large number of products because they were not adequately convinced that the data were accurate enough to feel confident about such a dramatic paring of the product lines. With these concerns in mind, plant management tried to determine what could be done to rationalize the product line while minimizing the associated risk of lost sales.

After much debate, management developed a list of five characteristics required for products to be identified as safe to drop; the safe products could presumably be eliminated without negative consequences.

1. Low sales volume. If a product had more than $100,000 in sales, it would not be eliminated.
2. Easily substituted with another Schrader Bellows product. If there was no functional difference between the product to be dropped and another product which would continue to be offered, the customer could be sold the alternative product.
3. Known to be a "dog" before the study. There were products which were known to be considerably more difficult to make than the standard cost would suggest. Common sense already indicated that these products were losing money, and this intuition was supported by the cost study.
4. Variation on a main product. Schrader Bellows made many products which had various combinations of additional features beyond those offered on the standard products. These were manufactured in response to the preferences of certain customers. However, in most cases a simpler substitute would be adequate to meet customer needs.
5. No major customer involved. No product would be dropped if there were a risk of losing significant sales of other products to the same customer.

Once these criteria were established, further meetings with the product managers were held to determine which products were to be dropped. Eventually 250 such products were identified.

Determining Potential Savings

Having identified 250 safe products to drop, Bauer and Guillaume estimated the impact on residual income from eliminating these products (Exhibits 3 and 4). The 250 products represented planned 1984 sales of $1,178,000. Bauer described their approach.

> Initially, we estimated that if all of the 1984 safe product planned revenue was lost and all of the associated costs were avoided, the improvement in residual income would be $845,000. In actual fact, we expected, based on our knowledge of the affected product lines, that a significant amount of the revenue would be transferred to remaining product lines which would increase profitability beyond that predicted in my analysis. We believed that our analysis provided a good first approximation of the lower bounds of the potential impact on residual income, although we knew that it was not exact.

After management reviewed the estimate of the increase in residual income, they expressed two concerns. First, because the list of safe products had been developed under the assumption that a limited amount of sales would actually be lost by dropping those products, management wanted to see an estimate based on the assumption that sales of other Schrader Bellows products would replace the eliminated products. Second, they wanted to know what the impact would be on the measures of income generated by the existing cost accounting system. They asked the plant controller, Preston Smith, to write a memo documenting the increase in planned 1984 net income if the 250 products were dropped. The controller predicted 1983 savings of $516,000 and ongoing savings of $761,000 (Exhibit 5).

The Scovill team reviewed the controller's estimate with satisfaction, because both their estimate and the controller's showed savings of around three quarters of a million dollars. They both felt that, although the estimates were not exact, it was clear that there was a large benefit to be derived from dropping the safe products.

After listening to the reactions of plant management and reviewing the plant controller's report, Bauer and Guillaume attempted to gain commitment from the support department managers so that the planned cost savings could actually be realized. They took the list of safe products to the managers of the various support departments and asked them to analyze the potential savings in their departments if the 250 products were dropped. The managers were also asked to commit to making these cuts if the products were in fact dropped.

Obtaining the Savings

Finally, an implementation strategy had to be determined. As Bauer described it, "You can't just drop products in this business, a few you can, but most you have to phase out." Thus, there were two possible courses of action: phase out a product in the near future or drop it immediately. A detailed strategy for each course of action was outlined.

If plans were made to drop a product sometime in the near future, three initial steps were necessary. First, a plan for scaling down production and reducing inventory levels was necessary. Second, the date of the announcement of discontinuance of the product had to be coordinated with the balancing of production. Third, a deadline for accepting orders had to be announced.

There were seven additional steps to be taken when it came time to actually drop the product. These seven steps were also required for products that were to be dropped immediately. First, the catalog had to be modified. Second, the product had to be eliminated from the price sheet (the price sheet lists the prices of all products within a particular line, by product number). This second step was very important because customers usually order from price sheets (prices were not listed in the catalog). Therefore, customers might continue to order products which had been dropped if the products were still listed on the price sheets. Bauer recognized that the natural reluctance within the organization to turn down orders made it critical to delete dropped products from the price sheets.

The third step was to educate the sales force. Each sales representative and each distributor had to be informed of the products which were eliminated so that they would not take any further orders for those products. They would also encourage customers to substitute other Schrader Bellows products for the dropped products.

The fourth step was to change the computer data base. Two levels of change were required. First, the pricing information had to be eliminated. But this alone did not preclude sales of the product. Production could still continue, and orders could be taken because price information could be entered manually. A greater barrier could be erected by eliminating the bill of materials and routing information from the data base because production would become more difficult without this information.

The fifth step was to determine the level of spare parts necessary to support the products already in the hands of customers. Warranties and service agreements generally dictated that Schrader Bellows be able to support these products for three to five years. This was a sensitive issue, requiring a thorough understanding of customers.

The sixth step was to analyze the inventory requirements and eliminate items which would no longer be necessary. It would, in most cases, be necessary to scrap any finished goods, work in process, or purchased parts (usually castings) which were associated with the dropped products and which were not required to support existing customers. The raw materials for these products could be sold or put to an alternative use and were not seen as a significant problem.

Once management was convinced that a product had been permanently removed from the product line, it was still necessary to take one final step to prevent the product from being made. Guillaume explained why this step was necessary.

> When it comes down to it, there is really only one way to get rid of a product, and that is to burn the engineering drawings and destroy any special tooling. Otherwise, the temptation is too great to let products creep back into the line. If the engineering drawings are available and a customer request for the discontinued product comes in, it becomes too easy to pull out the drawings and put the product back into production. The only effective barrier to production is to make it necessary to start all over as though it were a new product.

Presentation to Division Management

In late 1983, in Akron, Ohio, the team presented their analysis to division management: Bill Cavanaugh, CEO, Brayton Campbell, Director of Marketing, and Chuck Dombrowski, Controller. Bauer described the presentation.

> We had kept division management apprised of our progress as we were working on the study through a series of interim presentations and meetings. We saw the final presentation as a way to really impress on division management the magnitude of the problem.

Everyone seemed to agree that some rationalization of the product line was necessary. Someone reminded the group that duplicate products from the merger of Schrader and Bellows still existed. However, management had difficulty embracing the idea of dropping 250 products. Marketing issues seemed to be their main concern. They said that Schrader Bellows's full product line was a strategic advantage and an important factor in the company's ability to charge premium prices. Thus they were reluctant to make any immediate moves to drop products without first studying the problem themselves. When we concluded the presentation, I was not sure what the eventual outcome would be.

EXHIBIT 1
SCHRADER BELLOWS (E)

TO: Hubie Jenks, Joe Hinton
FROM: Paul Bauer and Pierre Guillaume
DATE: August 28, 1983
SUBJECT: Product profitability analysis

As we have discussed, we need your input on the actions to take with respect to the products which my study predicts have negative residual income. Attached is a form which lists all the products with negative residual income in your product lines. Across the top of each form are seven possible actions, coded A through G. In our previous discussions of the possible steps to be taken, you have expressed certain reservations and concerns about particular courses of action. We have summarized these concerns below and identified by code the action to which they relate. Please use your best judgment as to the appropriate course of action taking these concerns into account. We would appreciate your response as soon as possible.

A. Drop the product: Self-explanatory.

B. Raise unit price: The unit price should be raised to bring residual income up to zero.

C. Add a setup charge: This action would be appropriate for products which were ordered in small volumes by only one or two customers. The setup charge would be set to cover the additional costs associated with a short production run.

D. No change: This course of action might be chosen when it is feared that dropping the product might cause customers to take all of their business elsewhere because they would no longer be able to obtain all of their requirements through Schrader Bellows.

E. Questionable data: This category should be chosen when you honestly do not believe the data produced by the cost study. However, this is only a temporary category. We will need to meet to discuss how to resolve the questions about these items.

   To our knowledge, there are three reasons why you may find the data questionable. First, for some products you have expressed your belief that the estimates used contained errors large enough to cause the resulting measure of residual income to have the wrong sign. Second, we relied on the cost accounting system to allocate the overhead costs of the direct departments, and there is some evidence that these costs are not always sufficiently accurate. Third, there will be cases where you reject the data not on the basis of any specific problems but rather on gut feelings developed over the course of many years spent dealing with the products.

F. Cost reduce: This action may be recommended for some products which are known to be poorly designed. In most cases, reengineering of the product may be called for, but in some cases redesign of the production process may be suggested.

G. Buy from outside vendor: In some cases, Schrader Bellows produces items for which we have only a very small share in a market dominated by two or three major competitors. Usually these items are made on equipment which had overcapacity (screw machines, for example). The reason for keeping the products in the past was to provide for greater absorption of costs, which, as my study points out, is not a valid reason. Therefore, these products would be good candidates for buying outside.

(continued)

EXHIBIT 1 (*cont.*)

PRODUCT LINE: MICROMETER FLOW CONTROL	PROPOSED CHANGE						
	DROP	REPRICE	SETUP CHARGE	NO CHANGE	QUESTIONABLE DATA	COST REDUCE	BUY OUT
	A	B	C	D	E	F	G
10 200							
10 300							
10 400							
10 500							
10 600							
10 700							
10 900							
11 300							
11 400							
11 500							
11 600							
11 700							
11 800							
11 900							
12 000							

EXHIBIT 2

SCHRADER BELLOWS (E)

PRODUCT LINE	NUMBER IN PRODUCT LINE	NUMBER WITH NEGATIVE RESIDUAL INCOME	DROP	REPRICE	SETUP CHARGE	NO CHANGE	QUESTION DATA	COST REDUCE	BUY OUT
Directional control valves	869	704	401	268	28	—	7	—	—
Flow control valves	140	68	18	36	—	—	13	1	—
FRL	470	373	175	—	—	198	—	—	—
MRO									
Solenoids	270	257	123	95	23	—	16	—	—
Couplers	172	118	35	35	—	—	10	2	36
Hydraulic gauges	51	35	—	8	—	21	6	—	—
Blow guns	53	34	12	17	—	1	4	—	—
Fittings	259	144	30	12	—	101	1	—	—
	2,284	1,733	794	471	51	321	57	3	36

EXHIBIT 3

SCHRADER BELLOWS (E)

Direct and Factory Indirect Costs for Products to be Eliminated ($000)

PRODUCT LINE	DIRECT COSTS			FACTORY INDIRECT COSTS				
	MATERIAL	LABOR	TOTAL DIRECT	SETUP	GROUP LEADER	MATERIAL HANDLERS	OTHER INDIRECT LABOR	TOTAL INDIRECT
Directional control valves	$139	$154	$293	$70	$23	$24	$14	$131
Flow control valves	15	4	19	3	1	1	1	6
FRL	239	49	288	10	6	7	3	26
MRO								
Solenoids	12	9	21	10	3	3	1	17
Couplers	5	1	6	2	0	0	0	2
Blow guns	2	10	12	3	1	1	1	6
Fittings	2	4	6	1	0	0	0	1
Total	$414	$231	$645	$99	$34	$36	$20	$189

EXHIBIT 4

SCHRADER BELLOWS (E)

Summary Costs and Profit Loses for Products to be Eliminated ($000)

PRODUCT LINE	SALES	DIRECT COSTS	FACTORY INDIRECT COSTS	FACTORY OVERHEAD	PERIOD EXPENSES	FIXED COST	OPERATING PROFIT	WORKING CAPITAL COST OF CAPITAL	FIXED ASSET COST OF CAPITAL	RESIDUAL PROFIT
Directional control valves	$589	$293	$131	$370	$197	$43	$(445)	$54	$45	$(544)
Flow control valves	35	19	6	13	10	2	(15)	2	2	(19)
FRL	480	288	26	95	144	14	(87)	26	10	(123)
MRO										
Solenoids	42	21	17	35	35	2	(68)	3	2	(73)
Couplers	18	6	2	9	10	1	(10)	2	1	(13)
Blow guns	9	12	6	13	16	3	(41)	1	3	(45)
Fittings	5	6	1	11	14	2	(29)	2	1	(32)
Total	$1,178	$645	$189	$546	$426	$67	$(695)	$90	$64	$(849)

EXHIBIT 5
SCHRADER BELLOWS (E)

TO: Wake Forest Management
FROM: Preston Smith
DATE: September 10, 1983
SUBJECT: Impact of dropping safe products on 1986 production

I received from Paul Bauer and Pierre Guillaume a list of 250 products being considered for elimination. These products were identified as being safe to drop because they met certain criteria established by management. Attached is my calculation of the impact which dropping these 250 products will have on planned 1984 net income.

There are three components of my estimate of the change in net income. These are an increase in operating profit, a decrease in carrying charges due to lower inventory levels, and an after-tax charge to income from writing off the inventory.

The change in operating profit is further broken down into two components: changes in product costs (which will result in lowered costs of goods sold and thus higher net gross profit) and changes in period costs.

The changes in product costs reflect the reduction in direct labor and support department costs made possible by eliminating the safe products. For the sake of clarity, I decided to report these changes as variances in exactly the way the cost system would report them if the products were dropped but the standards were not changed. This approach produces what at first appears to be a contradictory result (i.e., there is no change in standard margin). This is a direct result of our standard cost system, which does not accurately account for the higher unit costs of short production runs. Consequently, if the sales of a short production run product (i.e., a safe product) are replaced by those of a similar but long production run product (i.e., the main product), the cost accounting system will show no apparent change in standard margin.

If we use the 1984 plan standard costs and account for the impact of dropping the safe products, four variances will be generated.

1. Labor variance: We can expect to save some labor by dropping the safe products because the number of short production runs will fall. This will reduce the amount of time spent waiting for setups to be completed, checking the early production parts to ensure they are in tolerance, and, finally, getting up to speed on a new production process. The total savings I have estimated at about $40,000.

2. Burden variance: The reduced number of labor hours required to produce the budgeted output will result in a reduction in burden costs. This variance captures this saving. It is calculated by multiplying the burden rate by the number of direct labor hours saved by dropping the 250 products.

3. Lost absorption variance: The burden variance includes some fixed costs that will not be avoided. This variance corrects for the unavoided fixed costs.

4. Spending improvement variance: The net of the burden and cost absorption variances accounts for the decrease in burden costs due to a reduction in direct labor hours. In fact, we expect even greater savings because the short production runs that will be avoided require relatively high levels of support department activities. Dropping the 250 safe products should produce an additional $120,000 reduction in support department costs.

Many of the period costs can also be reduced by simplifying the product offering. The manufacturing costs, division marketing and sales, and general and administrative expenses are all increased by having a large product offering. The small production run products are responsible for more than their fair share of these costs, and these period adjustments reflect my estimates of the potential savings.

Overall inventory levels can be reduced if we drop the safe products which account for almost $500,000 of current inventory. While we can eliminate all of this inventory, we will have to increase the inventory of the substitute products to support their additional sales activity. I estimate the reduction in inventory carrying charges at $31,000.

Dropping products generally results in obsolete inventory which has to be written off. I have reviewed the current inventory levels of the safe products and estimate the after-tax adjustment to be $245,000. This will be a one-time charge to income.

(continued)

EXHIBIT 5 *(continued)*

Impact of Writing Off Inventory in 1983
with No Production and Sales in 1984 of
Products to be Eliminated
($ thousands)

CHANGES TO 1984 PLAN	
Standard margin	$0
Less costs:	
Labor variance	(42)
Burden effect	(224)
Lost absorption	40
Spending improvement	(120)
Increase in net gross profit	346
Period expenses	
Manufacturing	(146)
Marketing	(208)
SG&A	(30)
Increase in operating profit	730
Carrying cost avoided	31
After-tax loss due to writeoff	(245)
Increase in profit after tax	$516

ACTIVITY-BASED MANAGEMENT AT STREAM INTERNATIONAL*

All these proposals for cost reduction seem worthwhile. But we don't have the managerial resources to do them all at the same time. How shall we choose among them?

Michael Michalski, Division Director

Stream International was a new company, created in April of 1995, when the Global Software Services group of RR Donnelley was merged with a previously independent company, Corporate Software. In July of 1995, the six senior managers of Stream's Crawfordsville, Indiana facility were about to meet with Division

Director Mike Michalski. (See Exhibit 1 for the senior organization chart at Stream's Crawfordsville plant.) The plant had just completed the first three months of an activity-based management (ABM) project. The data collected to date revealed unexpectedly high costs for administrative and support processes such as materials management, quality, billing, and shipping. Michalski had asked the six managers to prepare recommendations for process changes at the plant based on the ABM data. The managers had spent two weeks poring over the activity cost data as they prepared their recommendations for the meeting (see summaries of the five proposals in the Appendix). During the meeting, the senior management team would listen to presentations about the proposals and make a decision about which to implement. The stakes were high for Crawfordsville. The

*Norman Klein and Professor Robert Kaplan prepared this case.
Copyright © 1996 by the President and Fellows of Harvard College. Harvard Business School case 196-134.

business and operations at the plant had changed dramatically during the past ten years. In addition, the Crawfordsville facility was one of the first in an RR Donnelley-owned company to perform an ABM study, and the results could be pivotal for the success of ABM in Stream and the larger world of RR Donnelley.

Background

In the early 1970s, the Crawfordsville plant was part of RR Donnelley's Book Division. It was the leading printer of religious books, texts, encyclopedias, and other reference books. The huge web presses and extensive storage in the Crawfordsville plant were well suited to this market niche. In the mid-1970s, the Book Division installed several smaller "narrow web" presses in the Crawfordsville plant so that it could enter the trade book market. With the flexibility from the new machines, Donnelley soon became the largest trade book publisher in the United States.

Short response time and a flexible production environment enabled the Book Division to evolve in a new direction in the early 1980s when it became the leading supplier of manuals and documentation for IBM personal computers. In 1987, the division installed a diskette duplication facility in the Crawfordsville plant so that the Book Division could be a full-line supplier to IBM and also attract additional work from other personal computer companies. Two years later, the software documentation business had grown sufficiently that Donnelley created a new business unit called "Documentation Services." By 1993, the growing demand for diskette duplication services was helping to offset declines in traditional printing services. That year the name of the business unit was changed to Global Software Services (GSS). The name change reflected the division's much broader mix of customers, which now included, in addition to personal computer manufacturers, many software companies that supplied operating systems and application programs, and companies developing computer-based games and educational programs. GSS also expanded its packaging capabilities and moved into the order fulfillment business. When consumers called to order software products, GSS was often at the other end of the "1-800" phone line. This business quickly grew to include phone representatives who received calls to register and license software products. In 1994, the phone licensing group celebrated its millionth call, and in 1995, it logged over 2 million calls.

Corporate Software, the other half of the newly formed Stream company, had been founded in Norwood, Massachusetts in 1983, with an initial focus on providing information and consulting services to software companies. First-year sales were $1.7 million. Internal growth and new services, such as reselling software to corporations, enabled sales to reach almost $60 million in 1987, when the company went public. Corporate Software launched a U.K. subsidiary in 1986, and in 1991 introduced consulting services to provide assistance to companies when they encountered problems with new software packages and hardware configurations, especially as companies migrated to Microsoft Windows. In 1993, the company expanded its support services to include call-in help desks and call-in technical support services for major business software products. With two acquisitions in 1994, Corporate Software had become the largest reseller of microcomputer software to businesses and institutions. Its approximately 1,000 worldwide technical support specialists handled nearly 3.5 million support calls annually on more than 1,000 products. In 1994, a group of investors, led by Bain Capital, took the company private again.

Stream was created in April 1995 by a merger between Donnelley's GSS division and Corporate Software. Each of the new partners had revenues of approximately $650 million in 1994, and thus Stream anticipated sales of more than $1.3 billion in 1995. Stream offered software companies a complete set of fulfillment services. It could produce, package, and distribute a product, license or register it, provide customer support to retail customers, and offer a broad range of support services to businesses and institutions. The range and power of Stream's business model was illustrated when Microsoft released its Windows 95 product by sending the product code to nine Stream locations around the world. Stream first translated the program into foreign languages and then manufactured and packaged the product. Stream also sold and distributed Windows 95 to corporations and provided consulting, call-in support services, and product registration.

Crawfordsville Plant

In the mid-1980s, printing documentation for IBM personal computers at the Crawfordsville plant meant large orders for hefty manuals that required long press runs.

But the business of printing documentation changed dramatically in the 1990s. More information was being provided within the software itself so that documentation manuals became shorter and less substantial. Also, as software makers shortened the time between versions and upgrades, they placed more frequent orders for smaller quantities. Because smaller press runs reduced the demand for printing services, Michalski had recently accepted printing work from the Donnelley book division that lived on the other side of the huge plant they shared. This work fully occupied three of Stream's six large web presses.

Fortunately, as income from printing diminished, the demand for diskette duplication, customized packaging of software and documentation, and distribution and licensing services increased. In 1994, the demand for diskette duplication peaked at 46 million. Technology for delivering software was continuing to evolve as software and personal computer companies began to use a single compact disc (CD-ROM) to replace multiple magnetic diskette packages for newly purchased software. To keep abreast of these developments, Stream arranged for a partnership with another company to replicate CD-ROMs.

Crawfordsville's commitment to the fulfillment business seemed to be working. Software companies increasingly wanted to focus on their core business of software design and marketing, and were willing to outsource to suppliers, like Crawfordsville, the production, distribution, and support services for their products. This trend, however, was leading Crawfordsville to serve many more customers, most of whom placed small, customized orders, and were expecting response times of less than two weeks, down from the 1980s expected turnaround of two months.

Stream was now doing short runs of several hundred items on expensive machines, specifically designed for customized runs, as well as runs of more than 10,000 items on efficient, high-volume machines. But even more than putting ink on paper, Stream was also involved in customer administration and technical support, diskette and CD-ROM replication, and customized packaging. As Michalski recalled: "The new opportunities forced us to confront what business were we in. Was our business putting ink on paper or content on media?"

Michalski loved the challenge of keeping Crawfordsville ahead of the curve of a rapidly evolving industry, and was well aware that getting in and out of technology at the right time was part of the game. But

given the many variables that were so tough to manage, and the rapidly evolving technology and customer base of the business, he needed knowledge and control of his cost structure. For example, administrative expenses had been rising steadily, from 2.9% of sales in 1992 to an estimated 3.4% of sales in 1995. Also, inventory, which in 1990 used just under 100,000 square feet of storage, was projected to require nearly 250,000 square feet in 1995. Some of this inventory was diskettes held on consignment for specific customers, and work-in-process more than one-year old.

Implementing Activity-Based Management

Michalski's introduction to activity-based management came in early 1995, when RR Donnelley executives told him of an initial project undertaken in an Ohio plant with the help of consultants from KPMG Peat Marwick LLP (KPMG). When the ABM concept was explained, Michalski agreed that Crawfordsville was an ideal candidate to be the next ABM project at Donnelley.

Stream was using a traditional job cost accounting system. All machines were in a separate cost center. The cost of the 2- to 15-person crews to operate the machines, the traceable machine costs, plus an allocated share of period plant expense were added together and divided by budgeted machine hours to compute a machine burden rate per hour. All other expenses were applied to jobs based on a per-person crew burden rate per hour, which included direct wages, fringe benefit costs, shift and overtime premiums, plus an allocated share of plant salaried expense. A work ticket system assigned direct materials, direct labor, and crew and machine time burden rates to individual jobs.

Michalski expressed his frustration with the existing costing system:

> The system couldn't report on the costs of individual businesses. The dollars were spread out across everything. In addition to not knowing the costs of doing business with external customers or with the Book Division next door, we were throwing resources at problems relying on our instincts to tell us what was worth doing. I needed to know what kinds of process changes mattered most, and how much should I be willing to spend.

Activity-based management promised a more accurate way of understanding and assigning costs to jobs and customers. With ABM, Stream could link the range and extent of services required by each customer, and then estimate how much it was costing to serve the customer. When the project was complete, Stream would also be able to do predictive costing and develop new pricing guidelines. Equally important, ABM would allow Stream to see early profit trends, or better predict the cost of new business activity.

Michalski knew that he had to balance the interests of Stream's various constituencies as he embarked on the ABM project. The new shareholders wanted cost reduction, higher return on net assets, and business growth. Customers valued faster time-to-market, lower prices, and better value for their money. Software companies, like Microsoft and Lotus, were now offering suites containing word processors, spreadsheets, database managers, and graphics presentation packages that had previously been sold separately. These companies received much lower prices from software sold within suites, causing them to place great pressure on suppliers to reduce the costs of documentation, media, and support services.

The employees were especially important. Michalski viewed the ABM effort as an alternative to the brute force approach to solving problems, asking employees to work harder and for extended hours. He brought workers into the picture by explaining the ABM project to worker committees, communicating to them through the biweekly newsletter, and asking for the help of supervisors. He understood the delicate paradox of management wanting to solicit information from employees to learn what process changes should be made, but at the same time having to assure workers that they would not lose their jobs. Fortunately, Michalski knew that the Book Division, with whom he shared the facility, was growing its business through expanded production of trade books, especially those related to personal computers, such as Que's highly popular ". . . for Dummies" series written for the myriad newly released and continually updated software programs and operating systems. Michalski felt that the Book Division could likely absorb any employees that were no longer needed as a result of process improvements in Stream.

Michalski appointed a three-person team for the initial ABM project. Denise Seeman, a five-year veteran at Crawfordsville, was the project manager. Seeman, initially a supervisor on the floor was now manager of the information technology department, manager of distribution, and of two customer service teams. Kathy Reik, also in the information technology organization, supervised technical services and formerly supervised areas

such as production scheduling and materials handling. Karen Session, an accounting supervisor from the controller's division, completed the team.

The project started with the team getting training and project planning from the KPMG consultants. The team, after talking to supervisors and managers, agreed to collect activity information for 12 basic business and support processes. Then, the team and consultants began to create an all-inclusive activity dictionary that listed every kind of work activity done in the plant (other than that performed by direct labor). Eventually, the team identified 161 different activities. (See Exhibit 2 for a summary of the activity dictionary, organized by the 12 basic processes.) Session and Reik then conducted surveys over the next two weeks, asking a sample of approximately 250 workers how much time they spent on the 161 activities. While the surveys were under way, Michalski spent extra time on the floor to make sure the workers understood and were comfortable with the process.

Session reflected on the complexity of this initial effort:

> Management really liked seeing costs grouped by activities. But maybe we went into too much detail when we created the dictionary. The activity dollars showed that some of these activities were pretty inconsequential and could have been combined into a higher-level definition.

During the next project phase, Session prepared data files for import. She had to format the general ledger files and personnel data into import files that were downloaded into the personal computer containing the ABC software. The ABC software processed the data into activity costs and provided a variety of reports and graphic presentations of the results.

Early Results

By June 1995, the ABM team had calculated costs for the 161 activities, and the 12 aggregate business processes. (See Exhibit 3 for the expenses and personnel assignments to the 12 business processes, and Exhibit 4 for a list of the 20 activities with the highest personnel costs.) Bill Newcomb, manager of administrative and support activities, recalled the initial surprise from the numbers.

> The costs of some of the activities seemed surprisingly high. But as people delved into the numbers, they came to

agree that if that's what I said, it's probably true. The data forced people to think in a new way. The big insight was that we have lots of small volumes of cost involved with an activity, a little here, a little there, and all these little pockets added up to a big number.[1]

The team shared selected parts of the analysis with about 100 people to get their opinions on what to do with this information. Some of the results made a strong and immediate impression on Stream managers. For example, there were large lots of old product that was not turning. Many of the orders placed by IBM in 1992 and 1993 were still sitting in storage in the Crawfordsville facility. Additional storage space had been added to the plant in December 1993 to handle the growing supply of mostly IBM-specific inventory.

Newcomb explained that existing practices had led to a similar problem with work in progress (WIP):

> It's standard publishing practice to print 11,000 items to fill an order for 10,000. Then you will bind 10,500 and store the extra 500 believing it will be useful. But once you store that as WIP, its on your books as an asset, and you can't just throw it away.

The division had acquired additional warehouse space at the Elmore St. facility three miles away to provide storage for the manuals and documentation produced for newer customers like Microsoft, Intuit, and

---

[1]Newcomb was pointing to Exhibit 5, which showed the costs of the activity "Response to Customer Requests" being incurred in seven departments.

Macromedia. While large lots of IBM work-in-process and finished goods inventory sat inactive in the main (South St.) Crawfordsville facility, products finished for newer customers had to be shipped immediately to the Elmore St. warehouse, where it was stored, prior to shipment to customers. By December 1994, 80% of the output from the South St. plant was being trucked over to Elmore St. This output was often shipped one week later to the customer.

Diane Chastain, manager of planning and order fulfillment, commented on this practice:

> Some costs of this arrangement were obvious, like the $150,000 spent annually on trucking. But lots of other costs were hidden until they were revealed through the ABM activity analysis. To address this problem, we had to overcome a major psychological hurdle. This business started with IBM in 1983, and it was a big deal to acknowledge how much our business model had changed in recent years.

Selecting the Winning Proposal

As Michalski thumbed through the five proposals that had been presented, he stopped for a moment when he saw the half-million-dollar price tag accompanying Chastain's proposal. At Donnelley, a manager did not request that kind of money without compelling financials. He was curious to see just how his managers would respond to the ABM data as they helped him to select the winning proposal. He wondered what kind of criteria his management team would bring to the table to help them make their choice.

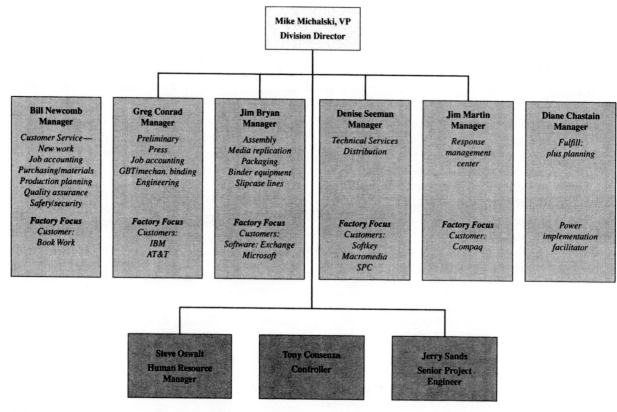

EXHIBIT 1 **Organizational Chart for Crawsfordsville Facilities**

EXHIBIT 2 Summary of ABM Project Dictionary for Crawsforrdsville

1. **Understand Markets and Customers**
   1.1 Determine customer needs and wants
   1.2 Measure customer satisfaction
   1.3 Monitor changes in market or customer expectations

2. **Develop Vision and Strategy**
   2.1 Monitor the external environment
   2.2 Define the business concept and organizational strategy
   2.3 Design the structure, goals, incentives, and relationships between organizations

3. **Design Products and Services**
   3.1 Develop new product/service concepts and plans
   3.2 Design, build, and evaluate prototype products/services
   3.3 Refine and test existing products/services
   3.4 Prepare for production

4. **Market and Sell**
   4.1 Market products or services
   4.2 Sell products or services
   4.3 Accept and enter customer orders

5. **Produce and Deliver**
   5.1 Plan for and acquire necessary resources or inputs
   5.2 Convert resources or inputs into products
   5.3 Make delivery of manufactured product (bulk shipment)

EXHIBIT 2 *(continued)*

      5.4 Fulfill orders (variable quantity fulfilled shipments)
          Includes any fulfilled orders in all buildings
          Includes D.R.O.P.P.
      5.5 Deliver revenue-generating service to customer
      5.6 Manage production and delivery

6. Invoice and Service Customers
      6.1 Bill the customer
      6.2 Provide after-sales support
      6.3 Respond to customer inquiries

7. Develop and Manage Human Resources
      7.1 Create human resource strategy
      7.2 Hire employees
      7.3 Train and educate employees
      7.4 Recognize and reward employee performance
      7.5 Ensure employee well-being and morale
      7.6 Plan employee compensation and benefits

8. Manage Information (excludes prelim computer manufacturing equipment: Scitex, etc.—see 5.6.4)
      8.1 Plan for information resources management
      8.2 Develop and deploy information systems
      8.3 Manage and maintain existing information systems
      8.4 Manage and maintain other communication systems

9. Manage Financial and Physical Resources
      9.1 Manage financial resources
      9.2 Process finance and accounting transactions
      9.3 Report information
      9.4 Conduct internal audits
      9.5 Manage the tax function
      9.6 Manage physical resources (building, property, and nonmanufacturing equipment)

10. Execute Environmental Management Program
      10.1 Execute environmental management program

11. Manage External Relationships
      11.1 Manage external relationships

12. Manage Improvement and Change
      12.1 Measure and monitor overall organizational performance
      12.2 Conduct quality assessments
      12.3 Benchmark performance
      12.4 Make process improvements
      12.5 Implement TQM and employee involvement

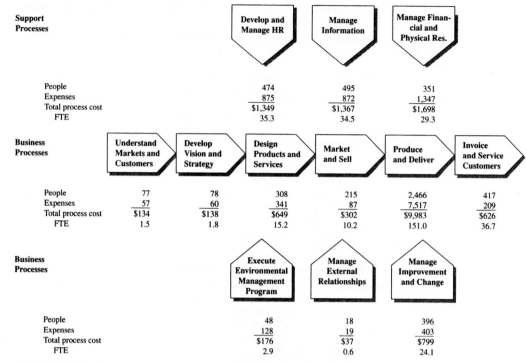

Support Processes	Develop and Manage HR	Manage Information	Manage Financial and Physical Res.
People	474	495	351
Expenses	875	872	1,347
Total process cost	$1,349	$1,367	$1,698
FTE	35.3	34.5	29.3

Business Processes	Understand Markets and Customers	Develop Vision and Strategy	Design Products and Services	Market and Sell	Produce and Deliver	Invoice and Service Customers
People	77	78	308	215	2,466	417
Expenses	57	60	341	87	7,517	209
Total process cost	$134	$138	$649	$302	$9,983	$626
FTE	1.5	1.8	15.2	10.2	151.0	36.7

Business Processes	Execute Environmental Management Program	Manage External Relationships	Manage Improvement and Change
People	48	18	396
Expenses	128	19	403
Total process cost	$176	$37	$799
FTE	2.9	0.6	24.1

EXHIBIT 3   **Process Costs for Crawfordsville Facilities**

EXHIBIT 4   Top 20 ABM Activities for Crawsfordsville Facilities

TOP 20 ACTIVITIES	SIX-MONTH SALARY AND WAGE DOLLARS (IN THOUSANDS)
Prepare and issue job specifications	$198
Train and educate employees	159
Develop and deploy information systems	156
Make process improvements	146
Track job status and expedite jobs	135
Perform application maintenance	132
Prepare/make-ready equipment/process for production	131
Respond to customer information requests	118
Develop new product/service concepts and plans	117
Provide consulting and technical support	117
Evaluate employee performance	109
Find material to be moved	106
Schedule production lines/equipment and crewing	100
Ensure ISO 9000 compliance	97
Prepare for production	94
Compile and maintain billing information	94
Obtain customer intellectual property	89
Maintain job file and enter transactions for completed jobs	86
Plan for information resources/management	83
Monitor line performance	82
Total	$2,349,000, or 44% of all people activities

Source: Stream ABM model; KPMG analysis.
Note: Stream employee costs for period 7/1/95 to 12/31/95.

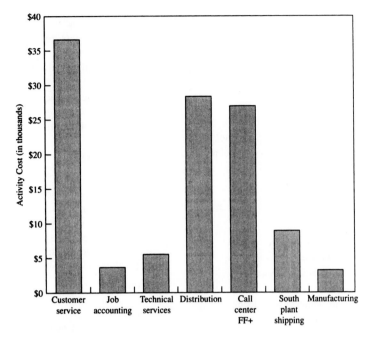

EXHIBIT 5   Costs of the Activity "Response to Customer Requests"—by Department

Appendix: Five Proposals

Presentation 1: ABM Process Improvement Proposal: Responding to Customer Information Requests, Presented by Bill Newcomb

Problems:

1. Seven Stream departments respond to information requests from customers, with no policy or directives to guide the gathering or reporting of information.
2. Customers frequently request the same information from two different departments.
3. Customers refused a request for a special report by department A will go to department B and get a positive response.

[See Exhibits A1 and A2.]

Action Steps:

1. Standardize/reduce ad hoc reporting.
2. Eliminate redundant reporting.
3. Clarify roles/reduce redundant follow-up.
4. Adjust price levels and structure.
5. Generate revenue for select "information services."
6. Create process to share/consolidate client information.

Presentation 2: Price of Quality, Presented by Denise Seeman

Although Stream pays $838,586 annually in quality costs, most of this money is spent gathering information that is never analyzed and never used to drive process improvements.

Problems:

1. Line workers assigned to do quality assurance have never been trained.
2. Inspection methods and sampling protocols have never been reviewed.
3. ISO 9000 documentation is never analyzed. There is no assumption that data will be used for continuous improvement.

[See Exhibit A3.]

Action Steps:

1. Redefine what the Division and our customers need from our Quality Services.
2. Provide the training and direction required.

The analysis will consider:

Pull/Inspect Samples
Improved methods to collect data
Definition of customer reporting requirements
Ensure ISO 9000 Compliance
Isolate and improve hard dollars associated with ISO
Ensure Compliance with Other Requirements (Blue Book)
Measurement definition—related to customer reports and process capabilities
Duplication of effort
What do we do with this information?
Benchmark Performance
Where should we focus?
Currently low dollars; potentially large savings
Make Process Improvements—Fragmented
What are we currently doing with quality information?
Who is doing this, and are they the right people?
What is the return on what we are doing, or have done?
Are we prioritizing by need or potential?
Identify potential
Ensure Process Capabilities
Established operation vs. start-ups
Estimated Results of Project: $257,000
(30% savings of wage dollars)
Plus additional saving from intangibles: benchmarking, process improvements, and best practices

---

Presentation 3: Manage Work in Progress and Finished Goods Inventory Space: ABM Project—July 13, 1995, Presented by Diane Chastain

Problems:
1. We currently have too much inactive inventory stored in the South Street plant, and too much active inventory being shipped to Elmore Street, stored for a week or two, and then shipped to the customer, or end user.
2. We haven't known true cost of storage.
3. The vast majority of WIP inventory is never shipped or used. Storage costs outweigh potential for use.

[See Exhibits A4, A5, A6, and A7.]

Action Steps:
1. Eliminate WIP inventory:
   • Define process to store inventory
   • Kill all parts with no known use
2. Exchange warehouses:
   • Install Mitrak-FG in South Street plant
   • Move active loads to South Plant

• Keep all inactive loads at Elmore
• Press clients to remove inventory or pay higher storage costs
• Redesign South Street for minimum movement layout
• Eliminate outside warehouse (1,001 loads)

Presentation 4: Billing Costs, Presented by Michael Michalski
[See Exhibit A8]

Problems:
1. It costs Stream $492,000 annually to compile and maintain billing information, to bill the final invoice, and to respond to billing inquiries.
2. Eight different Stream departments are involved in compiling and maintaining billing information, and later responding to billing inquiries.

Action Steps:
1. We need to first understand the process better; to determine which departments are doing what and detect any obvious redundancies.
2. We then want to determine what kinds of information are worthwhile for the division—what data are tied to customer complaints, profitability analysis, etc.
3. We want to centralize the function, simplify the process, and reduce the number of people involved.

See Exhibit A9 for costs and required FTEs by activity.

Presentation 5: Human Resource Management in FF+, Presented by Jim Martin and Molly Day
Problems:

1. HR activities are conducted by 34 different people in FF+* and amount to 10 FTEs.
2. Many activities are duplicated by HR department, payroll, and others in FF+.
3. Phone service reps work under three levels of supervision, at a ratio of less than five reps for every supervisor. (See diagram below for current reporting structure.)
4. Roles of the 14 team leaders, 5 team coordinators, 4 assistant account administrators, 10 account administrators, and 7 supervisors are not clear.

Action Steps:
1. Reduce number of supervisors and number of kinds of supervisory positions.

---

*FF+ is short for fulfillment plus all other phone activity, which includes product registration, licensing, password listing, and "upselling" related to these actibities.

Current Information Flow

2. Clarify roles.

3. Reduce fragmentation of employee activities.

4. Realize cost savings in salary and wage.

5. Create a model that improves communication with clients as it eliminates redundant supervision.

EXHIBIT A1 Cost Reduction Opportunities Could Provide Substantial Savings

ACTIVITY	FTES	HEAD- COUNT	FRAGMEN- TATION	SIX-MONTH ABM COSTS	ANNUAL PEOPLE COSTS	TARGET SAVINGS (25%)
Respond to customer information requests	8.2	66	12%	$118,000	$236,000	$ 59,000
Manage customer complaints	4.9	57	9%	$ 73,000	$146,000	$365,000
Track/expedite jobs	8.5	67	13%	$135,000	$270,000	$675,000
Maintain job files	4.5	34	13%	86,000	$172,000	$ 43,000
Total				$412,000	$824,000	$206,000

A 25% cost reduction would yield approximately $200,000 in annual savings.

EXHIBIT A2 Workplan and Resources

TEN-WEEK SCHEDULE	RESOURCES	WEEKLY UPDATE AND FEEDBACK
2–3 weeks—Where are we today?	1 Director/sponsor	
8–10 weeks—Redesign and implementation	1 Project manager	
	1 Systems analyst	
	3 Managers (part time)	
	3 Researchers (full time)	
	KPMG support/involvement	

EXHIBIT A3 Employee Involvement and Cost

		FTE	HEADCOUNT	ANNUAL COST
5.6.3.2.1	Pull samples	1.35	12	$ 43,462
5.6.3.2.2	Inspect samples	4.0	16	155,735
5.6.3.3	Ensure process capabilities	1.95	20	70,307
12.2.1	Ensure ISO 9000 compliance	7.17	48	194,738
12.2.2	Ensure compliance—other	2.55	31.6	59,711
12.3	Benchmark performance	0.45	5.6	23,410
12.4	Make process improvements	7.19	56.3	291,223
		+ all direct labor employees		$838,586

EXHIBIT A4 What Do We Know Today?

Load movement indirect expense	=	$1,412,048 annually	
Managing inventory expense	=	$ 447,660 annually	
Physical facility expense	=	$ 614,758 annually	
(see below for breakdown by activity)			

RELATED ANNUAL EXPENSE—MANAGING INVENTORY
LOAD MOVEMENT INDIRECT EXPENSE SUMMARY

ITEM NO.	DESCRIPTION	PEOPLE	EXPENSE	TOTAL	FTES	HEAD-COUNT
5.2.3.1	Find material to be moved	$212,542	$227,103	$439,645	6.80	29
5.2.3.3	Move WIP	58,754	68,473	127,227	2.15	17
5.2.3.4	Move FG within plant	111,552	193,092	304,644	4.25	24
	Move to/from Elmore Street	81,174	77,077	158,251	2.70	13
5.2.3.5.4	Move material to/from outside	24,594	88,017	112,611	0.60	5
5.2.3.8	Material equipment cost/ (depreciation/rent)		269,670	269,670		
	Total	$488,616	$923,432	$1,412,048	16.50	88
Managing inventory expense						
5.6.2.2	Managing WIP	$110,621	65,023	$ 175,824	3.10	36
5.6.2.3	Managing finished goods	108,699	163,136	271,836	3.85	32
	Total	$219,320	$228,159	$ 447,660	6.95	68
Physical facility expense						

	SQUARE FEET	$/SQUARE FOOT	TOTAL
Elmore Street warehouse rent	80,630	$3.00	$ 241,890
Elmore Street energy, insurance, taxes			76,400
WIP rent—all areas	45,630	2.53	115,287
FG rent—rack aisles only	50,512	2.54	128,381
Outside warehouse			52,800
Total			$ 614,758
Total Annualized Expense			$2,474,466

FTES total: 23.45

EXHIBIT A5

POTENTIAL BENEFIT $—LOAD STORAGE

1. **Store all active loads in CSS**

$318,290	Annual savings in finished goods rent at Elmore Street
(115,000)	Rent 35,000 square feet for long-term storage
(75,000)	Moving expense admin./Mitrak/loads
$128,290	

2. **Load movement improvement**

$158,251	Load movement to Elmore
112,611	Move to/from outside storage
91,393	Move FG within plant—30%
38,135	Move WIP within plant—30%
87,929	Find material—20%
26,967	Equipment savings of 10%
$515,286	

3. **Manage WIP improvement**

$ 43,956	25% improvement
⋮	

4. **Manage FG improvement**

$ 67,959	
	25% improvement

5. **Eliminate outside warehouses**

$ 52,800

Total Annualized Potential Benefit—$808,291

EXHIBIT A6 Associated Costs of Implementation Provide Direct and Immediate Payback

Demolition and rack erection	$ 25,000
Build production office	150,000
Electric, air and data connections	65,000
Equipment for parcel and pick/pack	230,900
Consultant fees	72,400
System hardware (M.A.U., controller, and token rings)	25,000
Pallet flow racks for freight staging	15,000
Total	$583,300

EXHIBIT A7 Resources/Timeline

- Define guidelines and process for keeping WIP material by KPMG and CSRs. Goal to complete by 8/15
- WIP inventory reconciliation by 8/31/95
- Analysis and detailed plan to switch active versus inactive inventory to South Plant as outlined by KPMG, Engineering, and fulfillment staff. Goal to move before heavy activity of fourth quarter.

EXHIBIT A8 Extended Billing Process—$246,000 per Six-Month Period and 20.6 Full-Time Equivalents

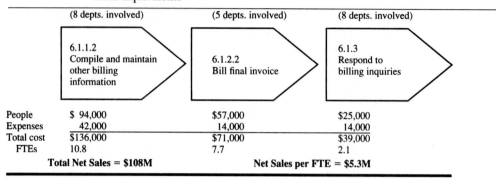

	(8 depts. involved)	(5 depts. involved)	(8 depts. involved)
	6.1.1.2 Compile and maintain other billing information	6.1.2.2 Bill final invoice	6.1.3 Respond to billing inquiries
People	$ 94,000	$57,000	$25,000
Expenses	42,000	14,000	14,000
Total cost	$136,000	$71,000	$39,000
FTEs	10.8	7.7	2.1

Total Net Sales = $108M   Net Sales per FTE = $5.3M

EXHIBIT A9

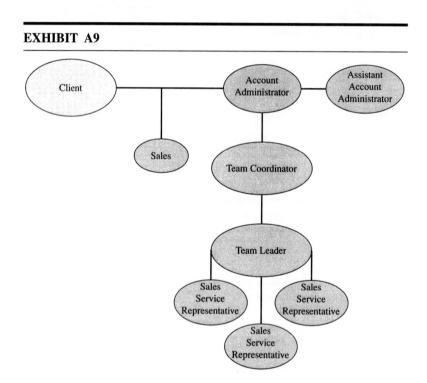

MAXWELL APPLIANCE CONTROLS

The company's goal was for all operating divisions to achieve five to six percent annual productivity gains. During the past ten years, we achieved this by automating many production processes and transferring labor-intensive products to our Singapore plants. By 1988, however, the opportunities for further productivity gains through automation or moving products offshore were limited. And sales forecasts for the next five-year period looked flat to declining. If we were to continue to enjoy productivity gains, we needed to make fundamental changes in the way we did business.

—Roy Green, *General Manager of Maxwell Appliance Controls*

Robert S. Kaplan prepared this case.

Maxwell Appliance Controls (MAC) was a small but highly profitable division of a large diversified company (Exhibit 1 shows a 10-year financial summary). It produced electro-mechanical control devices, such as relays, timers, thermostats, and switches that were installed in automobiles, kitchen and laundry appliances, and heating and air conditioning systems. The devices changed between "on" and "off" conditions in response to signals of changes in temperature, pressure, time, electrical current, or voltage. More than 7,000 different products could be produced; 2,500 were active models, a product customized for a particular application for an individual customer. The top 10 customers accounted for 75% of MAC's sales.

The company produced 129 classes of devices in 16 different product lines. About 40% of production was done in two overseas plants: the first Singapore plant, built in 1971, and the second plant, built in 1982. Domestic production was split between the headquarters plant in Springfield, Illinois and a satellite plant in Anderson, Indiana built in 1972. The work flow in both domestic plants had been designed to maximize individual worker efficiency. All the tools and materials the workers needed were stored around their workstations. Processes were not linked, leading to long materials flow paths. The plants, designed for high-volume production for a few customers, were now encountering problems as the product mix shifted to small-volume customized batch jobs.

A financial review performed in mid-1988 forecasted flat sales for the next five years, and inflation in materials costs and operating expenses that would outstrip historic productivity gains, leading to a $6 million decline in operating income. Roy Green recalled:

> As a mature business, we had gotten as much savings as we could from direct materials and direct labor. We needed to look elsewhere for future productivity gains. Initially I thought revenue growth would do the job but the 1988 forecast forced us to look more realistically at our internal business processes.

> We needed some way to rally the whole organization to a central theme. Stopping Spending Power Erosion would have to do the job. We had to look at what we were doing in the central stockroom, materials handling, inventory and transactions processing, procurement processes and factory layout. If there were gains from just-in-time and reduced cycle time, we should exploit them. We also needed to look at the complexity in our business caused by parts proliferation and the sheer number of different models demanded by our customers.

The Role for Finance

Bill Leonard, manager of Finance and Information Systems, had joined MAC on January 1, 1988 following a job assignment on the Corporate Audit Staff. Roy Green asked Leonard for assistance in achieving the 6% annual productivity gains and in supporting the plant's teamwork and empowerment initiatives. Green also wanted more accurate calculations of product costs, especially for products that had been outsourced to the two Singapore plants. As an old-line manufacturing business, product costs were the primary focus of management attention. Leonard recalled that senior managers used to spend two hours at every management meeting arguing about product costs; each area had its own estimating procedure.

Leonard wanted the finance and accounting function to play an important role in the campaign to Stop Spending Power Erosion. He circulated a memo to his staff in December 1988:

> Finance can help this process but we need to eliminate global financially-based internal measurements. The information needed by Corporate and Business management is different from that needed by Operational management. We confuse people when we try to push financial reporting measurements downward into the organization. This might explain why operations people create, develop, and monitor their own measurements . . . and why we are put in the critic's role rather than in the helper/team player role.

> We need to become a part of Operations to deprogram them from an intense concern for financial measurements and help them focus on waste elimination. This can be achieved through activity-based performance measurements. In order to truly influence operations, we must establish methods to highlight and communicate wasteful (nonvalue-added) activities. This is a critical point because people influence activities, not dollars. Dollars are the result of good and bad activities. Once we see costs, it is too late — the activity or need has already happened.

> We must understand cost drivers and waste generators so that business opportunities and investment need can be realistically evaluated. Management needs accurate, full product cost information to effectively manage a product portfolio, beat competitors, and evaluate/determine business needs.

> The barrier to effectively maintain this information today, appears to be our cost system. The required level of system upkeep is astronomical. This is because it not only costs out inventory, but also serves as a labor reporting, line planning, cost improvement, and market opportunity evaluation system. This makes for one complicated system whose cost may outweigh its benefits.

The existing cost system at MAC used two different definitions of "product cost." **Full standard costs** were used only to calculate inventory values and the cost of sales for financial statements. Full standard costs included materials, labor, factory overhead that was applied as a percentage of direct labor, and materials overhead (including transportation cost), applied at 9% of direct material costs. **Variable cost** was used to determine product contribution margin and as a basis for assessing the impact of product and process design changes. It included materials, labor, and materials overhead, plus a separate variable overhead rate calculated for each of the 31 cost centers in Springfield and Anderson. Profits at each plant were calculated by subtracting plant overhead expenses from the contributions of product lines produced at each plant. Operating expenses were allocated to product lines to determine product-line profitability. No system existed to determine customer profitability.

Under the old system, cost improvement activities were managed separately from day-to-day spending control. A cost improvement budget was specified for each department but improvement activities were localized and segmented. Spending was monitored by detailed examination of line items (such as travel and living expenses, outside engineering) in each manager's functional budget. Key performance measures included labor efficiency, absenteeism, and cost improvement.

The Cost Management System (CMS) Approach

Bill Leonard initiated an effort in late 1988 to develop a new cost management system (CMS) for MAC. The finance group surveyed all salaried personnel and interviewed foremen, asking them to estimate the percentages of their time spent on 88 different activities. The activity survey identified 75 activities that accounted for more than $9 million of salaried expenses. Leonard commented:

> The study showed that, of the top ten most time-consuming activities, only the ninth—product design—contributed to customer-perceived value. And by the time we reached the ninth activity, 34% of the payroll resources had already been used up [see Exhibit 2].

The survey also asked supervisors about the measurements they were using on a routine basis. About 65 measures were reported. Absenteeism was on every-

one's list; only 2% of the measures related to cycle time or quality.

The Finance Staff performed a rough assignment of the division's factory overhead costs to the major product lines, based on the survey results. But the survey only revealed profitability at the major product line level; expenses could not be driven down to the level of individual products, models, and variants, and the overhead assignments still seemed arbitrary and inaccurate.

The team attempted to get management's attention by classifying the activity survey results into value-added and nonvalue-added activities.[1] They estimated that up to $28 million of expenses in MAC were associated with nonvalue-added activities, and, therefore, targets for the division's improvement efforts (see Exhibit 3). The analysis generated considerable controversy within MAC, especially the $28 million estimate of nonvalue-added activities. Leonard attempted to get the organization to take immediate action to attack the $28 million "buckets of opportunity." He recommended that the organization reduce the existing fragmentation and segmentation of activities, and eliminate excessive layers of management. His initial efforts were met with indifference or skepticism:

> In retrospect, I probably tried to move the business too far, too fast. I thought the key was to change the organization structure from its traditional functional orientation to one that aligned better with underlying business processes. I did not spend enough time upfront educating people about the activity analysis and, more important, getting a consensus about the root causes of our nonvalue added activities. Although we all agreed to the magnitude of the waste, we had little agreement about the generators of waste.

> The people in the organization were certainly not prepared for a radical reorganization and the more we talked about costs, the more we turned people off. Operating people, like Frank Jackson [MAC manufacturing manager], felt that costing was just a finance issue and didn't help him to run the factory better.

Organizing the Factory For Action

In March 1989, Roy Green shut down all operations for several hours, assembled all the employees in the middle of the factory, and announced that MAC had to learn how to conduct business differently. He identified

---

[1] A "nonvalue-added" activity can be eliminated with no deterioration of product attributes; examples include moving materials, waiting while a set-up is being performed, and expediting materials. A "value-added" activity changes the physical form of a product to improve its functionality for the customer; examples would include machining a part, assembling components, and ordering materials.

six big problem areas and requested volunteers to work on task forces that would help to inform management about the steps required to solve these problems and to define new ways of doing business in the six areas:

- Standardization
- Inventory Reduction
- Elimination of Nonessential (Waste) Work
- Communication
- Cycle-time Reductions
- Quality

About 65% of the employees volunteered to work on the six task forces. The task forces worked for six to eight weeks and then made presentations to senior management. Several task forces recommended eliminating piecework pay, a suggestion that was rapidly adopted (60% of the work force was eligible for incentive pay but only 20%–30% of these were earning anything significant from the program). Under the piecework plan, people were overproducing, frequently the wrong products, and quality considerations were secondary to exceeding production targets. When piecework was eliminated, attention shifted from keeping workers and machines busy to producing good products in accordance with a just-in-time schedule.

A second recommendation was to eliminate manual vouchering for labor and inventory records. This produced an annualized savings of $1.8 million in direct labor time formerly spent on record-keeping activities, and in the reduced demands for bookkeeping personnel, computer time, and vouchering cards.

Roy Green recalled:

The task forces told us about a lot of problems. Top management struggled for a while with how to incorporate their ideas. We did adopt team gain-share programs and established, in both Springfield and Anderson, more than 100 families of between 5 to 15 people who shared a common work area to do training on the line and cross-training within the family. The families started to communicate across shifts and families to encourage self-sufficiency and continuous improvement.

The process was working but then revenue forecasts, starting in mid-1989, showed that our market predictions were not going to be met. We could not just sit here and watch the business go downhill. Finance's CMS initiative became more important to us by making our wasteful activities more visible. With the increased visibility, we could start to attack the problems.

Green formed a group of 35 senior operating and functional managers at Springfield. The group, which came to be known as the Gang of 35, met two days each month at Focus on the Future (FOF) workshops that attempted to establish new methods for doing business. Leonard kept presenting his initial finance study at the FOF workshops, asking the group how it should proceed with this information, how could the Gang of 35 use the information from the activity analysis?

Implementing Activity-Based Costing

By Summer 1989, the various plant efforts started to come together. Leonard noted that people had stopped arguing about concepts and definitions. They had begun to focus on the $28 million buckets of opportunity and the flows of activities to perform business processes. Frank Jackson, manufacturing manager, while not endorsing completely the Finance study, acknowledged that $18–$20 million was a possible target for cost improvements. People accepted that savings would have to come, not by having employees work faster, but by adopting fundamentally new ways of doing business. Leonard trashed his reorganization vision and set out to formalize his activity-costing study. "We had a mission and we knew that the activity analysis was a sound approach. But we were getting buried in complexity and detail."

In Fall 1989, a consulting group was brought in to restructure the activity analysis performed by the Finance Group and to recommend the next steps. MAC decided to work with the consultants to develop a complete activity-based cost model of the organization. To gain credibility and expand ownership for the CMS project, a one day training session, covering activity-based cost concepts and actual case studies, was held for the Gang of 35 in November 1989. Leonard recognized the contribution from the outside viewpoint:

The consultants provided structure to everything we had been doing. They moved us away from thinking about the details of actual materials and labor usage by products and manufacturing cells, and helped us to use the information we had already collected. Their software, organized around activities and business processes, enabled us to illustrate our business process concept. We collected expenses into activities and then, through cost drivers, were able to assign the expenses accumulated in activities to products and customers. The approach succeeded in mechanizing and translating our thoughts into a workable model.

The expenses of the business units were assigned to the activities and aggregated into business processes based on the survey and expense analysis of nonpayroll costs conducted by the Finance Group in early 1989. Exhibit 4 describes the activities used in the initial model. The activities could be linked to improvement activities such as supplier certification, just-in-time processes, total quality management, and integrated product and process development.

Each of the 12 business processes (see Exhibit 5) represented a group of activities with a similar objective or related to a similar output. The business process presentation shifted the focus from functional expense analysis to understanding the costs of performing activities and business processes.

Leonard was enthusiastic about the new presentation:

> For the first time, we could see how much we were spending on processes like quality control, customer administration, and procurement. We could understand how resources were consumed by business processes. Previously, the expenses of these processes had been scattered across numerous general ledger accounts in different functional responsibility centers.
>
> The presentation led to confusion and organizational resistance, however, because the business was not organized by the activities and business processes we had defined. People would say, "How can I control customer administration? Who would I write a note to: I don't have a manager of customer administration, and besides, some of the costs showing up in customer administration are incurred in other functional groups." We had to explain that the activity and business process analysis was a model to show how we do business, not on how we are organized. Some people expected the model to help them in day-to-day process control or for performance measurement and were disappointed when we produced something that didn't meet those expectations.

One of the impacts from the activity analysis was a consolidation of routine processes. Secretarial and business analysis functions were made a central support function. This consolidation produced a savings of 10 to 12 people.

The next stage of analysis was to drive the activity expenses down to product lines and products. For this purpose, activity cost drivers were defined for each activity. Exhibit 6 describes and defines the most important cost drivers used in the study. Information on the quantities of the cost drivers came from a variety of sources: the existing cost system, the MRP history file, the bill of materials file, and the sales file; some data, such as on internal and customer-generated ECNs, were collected manually.

In March 1990, the CMS Task Force performed a sample run to obtain revised costs for all Springfield products. The analysis for a single product, a defrost control device (see Exhibit 7), was presented at a dinner meeting of the Gang of 35, who got excited about finally seeing product cost information, rather than just business process costs. The defrost control device was a high-volume product, and the analysis showed that its domestic production costs exceeded the current selling price. Active discussion pursued; production people asked marketing why a higher price could not be obtained for the device, and marketing people questioned why production costs couldn't be lowered, and what would the effect be of increased volume on product costs.

Leonard recalled the subsequent discussions:

> The activity analysis presentation shifted us away from materials and labor costs to a focus on how we could reduce or eliminate some of the nonvalue added activities in business processes—such as Procurement or Production Management (see Exhibit 8). People started to ask about the efficiency of internal processes versus outsourcing.

Roy Green endorsed the approach being presented:

> The activity-based information developed a common language and understanding of where waste existed in the business. It became a focusing tool for management attention.

Performance Measurement

After obtaining the preliminary results, the CMS Task Force formulated a set of drivers to improve production processes and eliminate the waste that had been revealed. For the major activities, the team attempted to identify the principal causes of that activity and derive behavior-based measures that could be used to focus employees' continuous improvement activities (see Exhibit 9). These measures helped the employees to understand the linkages between measures they could influence and the overall company goals on quality, innovation, rapid response time, and total cost leadership that senior management kept talking to them about.

Leonard said:

> The 16 metrics that constitute the playbook [see Exhibit 10] helped employees know specifically what behaviors of theirs would favorably affect the quarterly scoreboard. Employees had gotten confused about all the programs that were going on. We needed to tell them that if they improved the playbook measures, the scoreboard measures would then take care of themselves.

The measures were displayed on greaseboards in each department throughout the facility, providing daily updates on the workers' achievements. Process Attack Teams were formed to work on improving business processes: Supplier Teams, Assembly Teams, and Business Process Teams for Customer Administration and New Product/Model Introductions. Roy Green recalled:

> The new measurements enabled the Gang of 35 to communicate to the families in Springfield and Anderson what they should be attempting to improve: reduce the distance between stop points, reduce the number of areas with more than four hours of inventory, reduce the number of parts we need to stock to produce our products, and increase the number of people with SPC training and problem-solving techniques. The families could now focus on the drivers of waste activity the ABC study had helped us to identify. I wanted to print on a card, for all employees, these drivers so that two times a day they could look at that card and ask "Am I doing something that's not on this card?" If I am, I should either stop doing it or go to my manager and ask him or her why I am doing this.

Leonard:

> We wanted to highlight the choices that create costs. These measures became simple feedback mechanisms to help everyone understand what triggers an activity so that they could minimize the resources consumed to perform that activity. Communicating the 16 metrics is much more effective than measuring and communicating results, like cycle time or quality costs, and having people guess at how they can influence the input activity to get the desired results. Everyone—from engineers to line workers—could get better at reducing costs without focusing on the cost itself. Talking about "costs" always seemed to make operations people squirm, but the activity-based cost information was invaluable in getting senior-level managers to agree that the playbook metrics would be effective motivators. ABC allowed us to quantify the cost that could be saved by reducing the number of parts, the number of operations, or the number of production stop points.

Product Costing and Product-line Profitability

In addition to the focus on process improvements, the ABC Task Force completed the data collection and analysis and was able by June 1990 to produce detailed product and product-line profitability reports. Exhibit 11 shows the cost summaries of two devices within an important product line. The D28X3 product was a mature, high-volume product produced in an automated production process. The D28Y4 product was a newly introduced product requiring several new parts for a particular customer-based application. Roy Green commented on the impact of the new information:

One of the biggest surprises occurred for devices supplied to two appliance manufacturers. One manufacturer used a basic system for all its models and the cost of supplying the product for this single system turned out lower than we had thought. The other manufacturer, however, had proliferated its designs, requiring us to offer more products for them. I now see that this led to much more engineering and support costs. If I had understood this better, we probably would have cut the price of our basic product and also raised the price for the newly designed variants to discourage the customer from switching to the new devices. It's probably too late now; we're locked into the current pricing structure and we've already added the support and engineering staff to handle the different devices.

Compared to what I had thought before, based on our standard cost system and my experience with the business, I was surprised more on the upside than on the downside. One product that I thought was a dog, or breakeven at best, turned out to have a better that 10% return on sales. It was being produced in an area with few other products, and therefore did not required much support resources.

Exhibit 12 shows the cumulative profitability across 101 product families produced in the United States. The most profitable 15 of the product families produced 115% of total profits, the top 25 produced 131% of total profits. The next 65 to 70 families about broke even and the least profitable 6 product families lost 26% of the profits.

The analysis of the different types of cost drivers revealed that only 57% of expenses were driven by volume: the number of units made. The remaining expenses (see Exhibit 13) were driven by the number of batches or customer orders made, by the variety of different products, or were general plant expenses, unrelated to the number or variety of products produced.

Bob Tucker, vice president of Marketing, commented on the implications of the ABC study for marketing:

> I had been exposed to product-line profitability analysis at a training seminar so I was sold before I came here [in December 1989]. One of our best customers builds room air conditioners and has one-third of the market. We produce one defrost controller for all this customer's models; it's produced in high volume, introduces no complexity to the factory or sales staff, and we offer it at a low price. But our refrigeration customers have models from A to Z. The defrost controller is only a $2 item and we have customized the device for each model.

> We have some small OEMs and distributors that want many small-lot shipments. We have taken on much of this business because it has a high markup based on our traditional contribution margin measurements. ABC will change that

thinking, forcing us to reassess those customers and their pricing. The ABC analysis beats doing lots of special studies, each time we deal with a different customer.

Increasingly, as customers come under competitive pressures, they are sharing savings with their suppliers. We all have an interest now in driving down model count where it doesn't affect product performance, and sharing the savings from lowering proliferation and raising production volumes. If some loss items have to be kept to offer a full product line, then we should focus on how to reduce their production costs.

When questioned about the process of developing the ABC costs, Tucker commented:

Bill Leonard kept stressing that the system was flexible; that the business processes or the data input could be changed easily. This was very important to me. I want the system to give us some insights to guide our business decisions. If the system has some problems, I have confidence that we can fix these and improve the system in the next round. I didn't want to nitpick and second-guess each business process definition and activity cost driver. The numbers coming out seemed sensible; my feeling was "let's get on with it," not argue about names of business processes.

Mike Carroll, MAC engineering manager, described the impact of the ABC study on the engineering and design function:

We have two different mechanisms for design activities. New products are handled by a Design Engineer who needs to make tradeoffs among alternative considerations. He could probably make good tradeoffs intuitively, if he didn't have to explain his decisions. But the design engineer has to interact with an Advanced Manufacturing Engineer [AME] who designs the process that will build the new product. The product designer and AME need an arbitrator for all the tradeoffs that need to be made; how many parts, how to keep commonality as long as possible through the assembly process, common versus unique parts, etc. The ABC data have only recently become available at an individual product level; and the data are only for existing products, not for new products. An additional complication is that the design engineer works for me, and the AME works for Frank Jackson. Each of us has his own "body language" about the ABC approach and our people are reading our reactions.

The other ongoing design mechanism operates for existing products. These products are the responsibility of Device Teams, consisting of an applications engineer who talks directly to the customer, a production engineer who coordinates between the design and the process, a process engineer who understands the limits of equipment capability and the impact of the TQM efforts, and a foreman and planner from the fabrication and assembly areas. This team deals with day-to-day problems, how to fix problems on the line, introduce new models and variants of existing products, and implement cost improvements. The members of the team argue about where to spend their time and capital resources for cost improvements and new models. For example, when a new model is proposed, should you buy a tool that works only for this one model or should you get a more expensive, flexible tool that can do five different models? In the cost improvement projects, should you just focus on touch labor or should you work on cycle time and product flow also? The team wants a cost model that will enable them to choose projects to work on and to rank alternative courses of action.

The existing ABC model is OK but it tells us about the cost of what we are doing now, or last period. The team wants a model with what-if capabilities. So the Design Team has the tool now, but is not yet using it in its deliberations. They're arguing about whether the numbers are exactly right; they're not comfortable with what they feel are the ballpark estimates used to derive the numbers. I'm still waiting to see an Authorization Request for a new project based on data from the ABC model rather than on touch labor savings.

Right now, we seem to be depending on a diffusion process for the tool to be adopted; waiting for an opinion leader to do it, while others watch and eventually copy if it is successful. We're using the new numbers as a basis of discussion, not as absolute truth. They've become an additional factor to be talking about when comparing alternatives.

When asked about the next steps, Carroll recommended:

We should probably bring each design team together for common education and definition of terms. I will try to force my people to use ABC-like terms (beyond materials and touch labor) when making authorization requests. We should also redo the salary survey to identify all the causal drivers. The initial survey identified what I call the "primary drivers," the triggering event for activities. We need to understand also the "secondary drivers," all the steps required to accomplish the task.

In my mind, however, the present ABC model mainly optimizes existing operations. It would be more useful if it could help us change the trajectory in our business. How can ABC be used in an environment of constant change with increased proliferation of technologies and customers demanding new products?

Frank Jackson, manufacturing manager of MAC, had spent 30 years in manufacturing at nine different plants. Jackson had been manufacturing manager at Maxwell for 10 years.

In the last 10 years, higher production volumes from automotive business, and reductions of about 500 people from automation, and off-shore production moved this division from an 7% ROS to an 11% ROS. We now face the problem of how to keep people focused on improvement activities when we're earning greater than 10% ROS.

The business has historically been overcontrolled by the green eyeshade types. They controlled spending by monthly budget authorizations. The new system has eliminated monthly budgetary spending control and we've yet to replace it with anything.

The CMS effort is too new for me to conclude that it has done anything significant for us. Its only application has been in a few make-versus-buy decisions, and then only in a cursory fashion. I had some high expectations that the new system would put day-to-day information in the hands of responsible managers that would enable them to drive the business. For example, yesterday I had a discussion with maintenance on how much they're spending on red rags. The cleaning service told us that they're delivering 1,000 red rags and they're picking up only 800. MAC is getting charged with the 200 missing red rags. Our spending on red rags is apparently way out of line. The maintenance people are now studying whether we should use white paper towels. We needed, however, a system that would have given the red rag problem visibility, as a separate expense item, so that a responsible manager could have taken action earlier.

Jackson articulated that the need for a new cost management system came from several factors:

We needed to have something to reduce our emphasis on direct cost reduction and to maintain our recent employee involvement commitments. We need to look at overhead implications, in the toolroom and stockroom, from our decisions. So far, the ABC study has not played much of a role in our continuous improvement program. Certainly, we need a whole new education effort for the Device Teams to get them to understand the new cost information that is now available. Even before CMS, we were doing special studies for make/buy decisions but we didn't look at the implications on stockroom or change costs. We used to think that a purchase order cost $25, but the CMS study showed it to be about $150. We had casual estimates of the savings from reduced part numbers; the new estimates should have more credibility.

The biggest hurdle is likely to be organizational. I'm not convinced yet that the organization is geared to making difficult decisions based on information. It took us five years to drop a product line that we knew was not making money for us. If we're not prepared to take tough decisions, we don't need a fancy new information system. We get lots of information that is nice to have and see but we don't take real action. It may take two to three years to understand how to use the tool and to take advantage of the benefits.

This whole effort would have gone nowhere without Bill Leonard and now he is leaving MAC to go to another division. Bill had the vision and drove it to a conclusion. He didn't know the meaning of "No," even when it was said to

him five different ways. The new finance manager better have a sense of urgency about the new system, since I don't think that Mike Carroll or I is going to lead the charge. My priorities are to keep nurturing the Family Process and Employee Involvement. This is a big transformation, not dictating to people but getting them to share goals, give them discretionary spending at lower levels for improvements, and make sure they have the confidence that they can take actions. We're starting to bring in the hourly employees from our suppliers to talk with our hourly employees about products and processes.

World Defrost Control Device

In the summer of 1990, a high-priority project for MAC was to expand the sales of a defrost control device to European refrigerator manufacturers. MAC already enjoyed a substantial share of the North American market, but saw excellent opportunities for penetrating the large European market. The device was currently being manufactured in both Singapore and Springfield. The Singapore plants were already operating at full capacity. Springfield had available capacity but its production costs were presently above the price required to obtain additional European business.

Larry Morrissey, a manufacturing engineer and recently designated program manager for the World Defrost Control Product, anticipated that a massive change in the production process would be required for Springfield to be competitive in the $40 million world market for the device.

Defrost control devices are priced on a commodity basis. With our standard cost system, high-volume devices seem to be breakeven or unprofitable, and low-volume specialty products appear to have high margins. Our gut feeling, however, is that the low-volume specialty products are probably grossly undercosted.

Expectations seem too high for the new CMS system. We all understood the fallacy of the old standard cost system; we reduced direct labor but we still had all the indirect labor. But people are waiting for a new system in which we plug in the same inputs—direct labor and direct materials—and get out accurate predictions of future costs.

The number we have started to see do confirm our intuition. But where do we go with this? It may be too late to change pricing decisions for existing products; I suppose it will discourage small lot orders and guide us in further mechanization decisions, especially to think about the implications for indirect labor like materials handlers. The visibility of resource consumption has been good but the real benefits will come in forecasting. Forecasting will require lots of inputs from people like me, but many people are expecting the model to pump out accurate predictions of the future based on the old inputs.

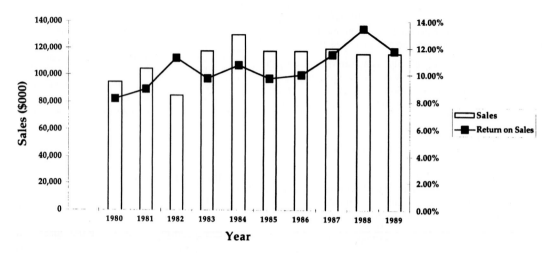

EXHIBIT 1 **Sales and Return on Sales: 1980–1989**

EXHIBIT 2 Activity Survey: Top Ten Most Time-Consuming Activities

Rank	Activity Name	Equivalent # of People	Dollars	% of Total	Cumulative %
1	Personnel Management	11.9	$ 596,253	6.5	6.5
2	Information Systems	14.6	493,480	5.4	11.9
3	Administrative Assistance	18.3	436,808	4.8	16.7
4	Decision Support Data & Forecast	8.9	424,382	4.6	21.3
5	General Accounting	11.4	335,766	3.7	24.9
6	Product Service	7.1	294,704	3.2	28.2
7	Human Relations	7.5	292,036	3.2	31.4
8	Shop Floor Control	7.5	272,036	3.0	34.3
9	CM Product Design	8.1	264,595	2.9	37.2
10	Strategic Planning	4.0	259,553	2.8	40.0
-	---	-	-	-	-
-	---	-	-	-	-
Total		244.0	$9,165,490		100.0

EXHIBIT 3 Activity Analysis of Materials and Operating Expenses ($000,000)

	Value-Added		Nonvalue Added	
I.	**MATERIALS-RELATED EXPENSES**			
	Direct materials	$30	Scrap	$ 2
			Stockkeeping	1
			Carrying costs	2
			Tariff	1
			Logistics	2
			Total	$ 9
II.	**LABOR-RELATED EXPENSES**			
	A. HOURLY EMPLOYEES			
	Direct labor	$22	Maintenance	$ 1
			Test & inspection	2
			Set-up	3
			Materials handling	1
			Leaders	1
			Toolroom	2
			Other	3
			Total	$13
	B. SALARIED EMPLOYEES			
	Production related	$2	Reporting paperwork	$ 1
	New products and processes	3	Personnel management	2
	Support	3	Administrative assistance	3
	Total	$ 8	Total	$ 6
	TOTAL	$60	TOTAL	$28

EXHIBIT 4 Activity Dictionary

CUSTOMER ADMINISTRATION

1. **Price Regular Orders** Price existing models for existing customers.

2. **Price New models** Price new models.

3. **Price Adjustments** Written confirmation to customers (per negotiation: update records).

4. **Price Negotiations** Customer contact to device new price (existing models).

5. **Generate Sales Orders** Dealings with the customer that produce orders.

6. **Process Customer Orders** Receiving, keypunching, entry to open order register, etc.

7. **Process Accounts Receivables— Exceptions** Monitor status of disputed inventories, contact customer and shipping in order to resolve disputes over billing, provide proof of shipments to verify receipt of goods.

8. **Process Customer Inventories & Accounts Receivable—Normal** All activity (other than pricing) to complete, process, and collect customer invoices.

PROCUREMENT

9. **Purchase Order (P.O.) Processing** Routine activities involved in P.O. administration. Includes such tasks as determining order quantities, timing issues, completing the P.O., and all "normal" processing of the P.O.

10. **Selecting New Vendors** Change vendors for a material once the product is in production.

11. **Resolution of Purchased Material Quality Issues:** Settle incoming quality problems.

12. **Contract Negotiations:** Negotiate, develop, and sign vendor contacts.

13. **Inventory Material—Receiving** Record the receipt of material; verify incoming quantities

14. **Incoming Material Inspection:** Assess the quality of incoming material

15. **Processing Accounts Payables:** Accumulate necessary documents, provide authorization to pay where documentation is missing, provide related reports, check status of payables.

16. **Expense Material Purchasing:** Purchase material such as office supplies, nondurable tools, etc.

PRODUCTION CENTERS

17. **Equipment, Maintenance, and Repair** Maintain, repair, and replace existing production equipment.

18. **Shop Floor Control:** Supervise production and production personnel.

19. **Facility Maintenance** Plant construction and facility maintenance.

(continued)

EXHIBIT 4 (*continued*)

PRODUCTION MANAGEMENT

20.	**Sales Forecast:**	Obtain a regular short-term sales forecast.
21.	**Production Scheduling—Normal:**	All time spent to schedule orders excluding reschedules per customer request.
22.	**Producing Scheduling—Rescheduling**	Change production due to customer request.
23.	**Production Monitoring:**	Collect production data (e.g., labor usage, output, material usage) at the shop floor level.
24.	**Expediting**	Speed up the process of production and material procurement to meet production schedules.
25.	**Inventory Material—Raw and In Process Material:**	Track material available within the factory premises; including physical counts to verify MRP records.
26.	**In Process Material:**	Manage in-process inventories regarding their storage distribution and evaluation, etc.
27.	**Capacity Planning:**	Determine the capacity of areas on the production floor and the procedures to expand or contact capacities. These decisions reflect medium- to long-term strategies.
28.	**Analysis of Labor & Material Variances**	Pull files from systems; run edit listings; disposition variances (e.g., explanation by purchasing personnel); update current costs in standard cost system; write journal entries.

QUALITY CONTROL

29.	**Product Service/Handling Customer Complaints:**	Customer contact regarding complaints about quality, shipping, etc.
30.	**Product Service/Lab Testing:**	Lab testing resulting from customer complaint.
31.	**Shop Floor Process Control:**	Monitor shop floor processes to ensure quality output. Includes SPC data gathering.
32	**Quality Complaint Analysis:**	Determine the "root cause" of quality problems. Complaints can be generated by production personnel or customers.
33.	**Lab Testing for Quality Evaluation:**	Perform lab tests when needed to fully analyze a quality problem.
34.	**Q.C. Support:**	Quality cost reductions, write quality plans, work with families to correct problems, support tolerance analysis.
35.	**Final Inspection:**	Final inspection of finished product including issues such as customers' specific requirements.

PRODUCTION TOOLING

36.	**Tool Maintenance and Repair:**	Maintain and repair existing production tooling; includes tool condition survey.

WAREHOUSING

37.	**Outgoing Material Control:**	Handle and distribute finished goods.

EXHIBIT 5 Business Process Definitions

Business Processes

Business Processes are groups of activities that accomplish a business objective. All resources consumed by the individual activities are included in the cost of a business process.

PRINCIPAL BUSINESS PROCESSES

Production

There are 25 Springfield Production Processes. They are based on the current cost centers for shop floor measurement. These business processes receive all indirect labor and materials, supplies, and other overhead costs that can be directly attributed to the activities within the cost center.

Customer Administration

Activities related to dealings with customers. Generating sales, pricing activity, contract negotiations, bill collection, and order processing are examples.

Procurement

Activity required to provide the business with all the materials needed for operation. This includes vendor relations, negotiating, ordering, and receiving production and expense materials, in bound transportation, and accounts payable activity.

Production Management

Plant-wide activities of scheduling, monitoring, and control of all production areas. This includes expediting, inventory tracking, MRP processing, product costing, inventory management including imputed interest on inventory.

Quality Control

All quality related activities dealing with production processes, in-coming material, and product service. This includes quality issues arising from internal processes, customer complaints and vendor dealings.

Production Tooling

Maintenance, repair, or replacement of existing tooling.

Maintenance

Maintain, repair, or replace existing equipment and facilities.

Warehousing and Shipping

All the activity involved in the handling and distribution of finished goods are included from the time products are transferred from the production area.

(continued)

EXHIBIT 5 *(continued)*

CHANGE RELATED BUSINESS PROCESSES

Internally Generated Modifications

Activity for dealing with product or process changes due to an internal (MAC) decision. This would include process development work, planning changes, documentation work, product design, and customer interaction regarding changes MAC has initiated.

Customer Driven Changes

Activity for dealing with product or process changes due to customer request or requirement. This would include process development work, planning changes, and documentation work, product design, and customer interaction regarding changes a customer has initiated.

R&D—New Product, Process, Market

Development of products or processes to enter a previously untapped market or use a new technology. This includes all activity and costs from concept through pilot run.

SUPPORT RELATED BUSINESS PROCESSES

Business Information Systems

All activity related to development of new information systems and computer systems. This includes researching new technology, programming, training, etc. to put system into production.

General Administration & Finance

Activity for external financial reporting, general accounting, special studies, and reserves.

Human Resources

Administration of employee & community services and programs, and workforce maintenance.

Environment & Safety

Activities to ensure a safe, secure work environment including costs to comply with OSHA, EPA, Underwriters Laboratory specifications, workman's compensation, waste disposal, etc.

EXHIBIT 6 Definition of Activity Cost Drivers

ACTIVITY COST DRIVER

The basis for assigning activity costs to products or product families. This generally is a quantification of what triggers or causes an activity to be performed.

ABC uses the quantities entered to develop ratios as a basis to apply the activity costs to products.

EXTERNAL ECN's

Number of alteration notices per product line that were generated by a customer request or change. This ties activity related to making changes to the products being affected.

INTERNAL ECN's

Number of alteration notices per product line that were generated for internal reasons. This ties activity related to making changes to the products being affected.

UNITS PRODUCED

Device/component volume by production activity center. Production quantity of finished devices in assembly area and quantity by part in the fabrication areas. This makes the assumption that each unit passing through the activity center consumes an equal amount of the resource.

P.O. LINE ITEMS

Number of receipts for each raw material and purchased part. This is taken from an MRP history file. This ties the activity which occurs for each material order and receipt to the product receiving that material. Purchase order administration, incoming inspection, and accounts payable activity are primary examples.

STOCKROOM TRANSFERS

Number of stock-to-stock transfers per part number. Taken from MRP history file. This is an indication of the number of batches run. It gives added weight to devices with a large number of parts.

DIRECT LABOR

Hours of direct (standard) labor per device/component per activity center. Where the resource consumption is proportional to hours worked or number of employees, direct labor is the driver used.

TOOL ROOM HOURS

Hours of toolroom labor per part number. This is taken from the tool room vouchering database. This associates fabrication tooling activity with the parts being worked on.

(continued)

EXHIBIT 6 *(continued)*

SALES PER DEVICE

Dollar sales by device. For costs proportional to sales and many general administration activities.

WAREHOUSE WITHDRAWALS

Number of finished goods warehouse withdrawal transactions per product. This is from MRP history. This is used to mirror number of customer invoice line items and number of orders.

SCRAP

Dollars of reported scrap per product line. This drives activity and costs due to scrap to the products producing scrap.

NUMBER OF COMPLAINTS

Customer complaints per product line. This links externally influenced activity such as service request activity to the product lines affected.

NUMBER OF PLATED PARTS

Volume per part number processed through the plating activity center. There are unique issues with plating which should be tied to the products using plating. This driver makes that connection.

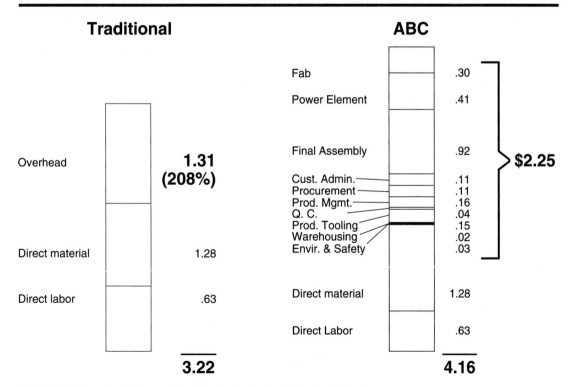

EXHIBIT 7   Preliminary Cost Output: Defrost Control Device

EXHIBIT 8 Preliminary Cost Output—Defrost Control Device

$2.25 . . . in overhead costs

Business Processes		Activity Cost Driver
• Procurement (11¢)		
- Purchase order processing	1.8¢	P.O. line item
- Inventory material	1.3¢	P.O. line item
- Receiving inspection	.8¢	P.O. line item
⋮		
• Production Management (16¢)		
- Production scheduling	1.5¢	Stockroom transfers
- Production monitoring	2.0¢	Stockroom transfers
- Stockroom . . . delivery to line	1.4¢	Stockroom transfers
⋮		
• Final Assembly (92¢)		
- Depreciation	9.0¢	Unit produced
- Set-up	7.0¢	Direct labor/device
- Test and inspection	4.5¢	Direct labor/device
- Quality Institute Lab	1.0¢	Unit produced
⋮		

EXHIBIT 9 Performance Measurements

Activity	Process Drivers	Measurements
Materials handling	Product line lengths	Assembly line feet/line
	Noncontinuous operations	Number of stop points/line
		No. of areas containing > 4 hours of material or parts
Set-ups	Difficult set-ups	Average set-up time
		No. set-ups > 10 minutes
	Inflexible machinery	No. of different dies
Parts administration	Stockkeeping practices	No. of parts/product line
		No. of Purchase Orders issued and received
Product redesign	New parts; new processes	No. of new parts introduced
		No. of unique parts

The playbook...

Process

⇓ No. of stop pts./line
⇓ Ave. distance between operations
⇓ Ave. set-up time
⇑ % of schedule attainment
⇓ ECN process time
⇓ ECN by type
⇓ No. of operations/product line

Material/Vendor

⇓ No. of areas containing > 4 hrs. of
　material or parts
⇓ No. of parts/product line
⇓ No. of deliveries requiring inspection
⇓ No. of vendor invoices received

People/Skills

⇑ % of employees certified in SPC
⇑ % of employees graduated from
　problem solving
⇑ % of employees knowing name of:
　customer, competitor, Teamshare
　pools

Customer

⇓ No. of schedule changes w/i
　established lead times
⇓ No. of days in excess of terms

The scoreboard...

• **By product line**

　- cycle time

　- total quality costs to sales

　- quality rating by key customers

　- funds flow

• **Suggestions per employee**

The mission...
world champs

External

• Worldwide choice for control solutions

• Innovation & teamwork

• Quality

• Rapid response time

• Total cost leadership

Internal

• Close P & I Gap

EXHIBIT 10　The Playbook

EXHIBIT 11　Revised Product Costs: Two Sample Products

	D28X3	$/Unit	D28Y4	$/Unit
Units	4,256,027		799,262	
Revenues	10,029,796	$2.36	1,220,626	$1.53
Direct materials	1,508,455	0.35	265,955	0.33
Direct labor	1,047,043	0.25	188,689	0.24
Contribution margin	7,474,298	1.76	765,982	0.96
Principal Processes				
Production	1,994,694	0.47	540,849	0.68
Nonproduction				
Customer administration	83,774	0.02	24,835	0.03
Procurement	98,630	0.02	19,514	0.02
Production management	193,585	0.05	45,838	0.06
Quality control	157,898	0.04	49,078	0.06
Production tooling	99,090	0.02	62,279	0.08
Maintenance	739	0.00	93	0.00
Warehousing	23,914	0.01	4,121	0.01
Total nonproduction	657,630	0.15	205,758	0.26
Total principal	2,652,324	0.62	746,607	0.93
Change Processes				
Internal changes	2,889	0.00	4,626	0.01
External changes	177	0.00	2,444	0.00
Total change processes	3,066	0.00	7,070	0.01
Support Processes				
G&A and finance	-134,122	-0.03	-14,273	-0.02
Human resources	111,315	0.03	14,952	0.02
Environmental and safety	81,436	0.02	17,016	0.02
Total support processes	58,629	0.01	17,695	0.02
Total indirect expenses	2,714,019	0.64	771,372	0.97
Production income before taxes	$ 4,760,279	$ 1.12	$ (5,390)	$ (0.01)

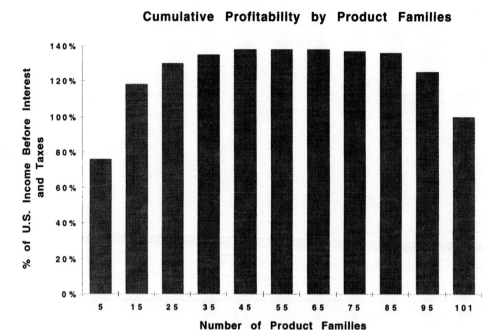

EXHIBIT 12   Cumulative Income Before Interest and Taxes: U.S. Products

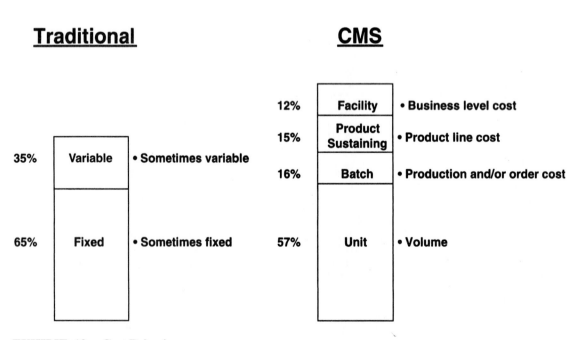

EXHIBIT 13   Cost Behavior

7

Strategic Activity-Based Management for Customers and Suppliers

Organizations can perform more comprehensive activity-based cost analyses by extending the domain of analysis beyond manufacturing and factory costs. Managers who analyze expenses that appear below the gross margin line on the income statement—marketing and selling expenses, procurement expenses, and many administrative expenses—learn that many demands for organizational resources arise not only from products but also from customers, distribution and delivery channels, and suppliers.

Managers, with a more accurate understanding of the costs to serve different customers, can take a variety of actions, including:

- Protecting and expanding business with highly profitable customers,
- Repricing expensive services, based on cost-to-serve,
- Discounting, if necessary to gain business with low cost-to-serve customers,
- Negotiating win-win relationships that lower cost-to-serve with cooperative customers,
- Conceding permanent loss customers to competitors, and
- Attempting to capture high-profit customers from competitors.

These actions should enable managers with good (ABC) instrumentation to dramatically improve their profitability, especially in industries where their competitors do not understand the economics of their customer relationships.

SELLING, MARKETING, DISTRIBUTION, AND ADMINISTRATIVE EXPENSES: FIXED, VARIABLE, OR "SUPER-VARIABLE"

Some people have argued against attempting to assign selling, marketing, distribution, and administrative (SMDA) expenses to cost objects like customers or marketing channels. These people claim that such expenses are fixed costs; therefore any assignment to individual customers would be arbitrary and misleading.

For many companies, however, their SMDA expenses are a significantly higher percentage of sales today than they were 30 years ago. Think about the situation of most companies today. Suppose that their SMDA expenses today are, for example, 22% of sales. What would the SMDA expenses have been 30 years ago as a percentage of sales? Most managers, extrapolating from the experience of their own organizations, would think that SMDA expenses were lower decades ago, say 15–20% of sales. They also would recognize that over the past three decades real sales volumes, if they have been tracking general worldwide economic growth, have likely increased at least threefold. But if SMDA expenses were truly a "fixed" cost, and sales volumes have tripled, then SMDA expenses should be only one-third as high a percentage of sales—say 5–7%—as they were 30 years ago. That is the definition of a fixed cost, one that stays constant even as sales volume increases or decreases. If SMDA expenses were just a "variable" cost, one that increases in proportion with sales volume, then they should remain as a constant percentage of sales; that is, they would still be 15–20% of sales. In most company's situations, however, SMDA expenses have become an *increasing* percentage of sales. They are not fixed costs. They are not even variable costs. These are *super-variable* costs. The costs are rising faster than sales volume.

For an expense category to be treated as fixed it should remain constant, independent of production and sales levels. So organizations have a simple test: track whether, as production and sales volume expands, the expense category stays constant (in absolute amount). If the absolute value of the expense does not stay constant as volume increases, it makes little sense to treat the expense category as a fixed cost. An alternative and complementary approach is to look across the industry. If an expense is fixed, then every company in the industry should have the same absolute expense level. For the smallest company, the expense will be a high percentage of total costs; for the largest company, the expense will be an extremely small percentage of total costs. If, however, the expense category represents about the same percentage of total costs, independent of size, then the expense is much more accurately described as variable, rather than fixed.

A final test on this fixed versus variable cost issue is the "Rule of One." Skeptics, when confronted with the evidence of costs increasing proportionally with or faster than sales, often resort to questioning, "How are you going to allocate the cost of the CEO to all the products and customers. Don't you need one CEO regardless of production and sales volume?" The response to this question is, of course, to admit that any allocation of the CEO's expense to individual products or customers would indeed be arbitrary. Such an expense is an excellent example of a *corporate-sustaining expense*; one that is required for each corporation, independent of production and sales activity.[1] Also, sustaining expenses should not be allocated to individual units supported by the resource. But most departments, other than the CEO's office, have more than one unit of a resource: they consist of more than one salesperson, accounts receivable clerk, human resource person, security guard, market researcher, economist, or financial analyst. The Rule of One states that departments or resource categories (e.g., a collection of similar machines) that have more than one resource unit must have a demand for work that requires more than a single resource unit to perform. And this demand for work—leading to multiple resource units in a department—provides a clear and logical basis for cost assignment.

Having now established that SMDA expenses are neither fixed nor likely subject to the Rule of One, we can now proceed to see how the assignment of these expenses can reveal dramatic opportunities for profit improvement.

---

[1] Strictly speaking, if the compensation of the CEO is a function of sales volume (as done in many compensation schemes), then one could argue that even though the quantity of the resource (one CEO) is fixed, independent of sales volume, the price of this resource is affected by sales volume. Such a relationship could be used to assign the variable portion of the CEO's compensation to production or sales volume.

CUSTOMER COSTING

The assignment of SMDA expenses to customers is valuable because not all customers consume resources at the same rate. Activity-based costing enables managers to identify the characteristics that cause some customers to be more expensive or less expensive to serve. Previously, such differences in cost-to-serve were hidden because either no attempt was made to assign marketing, selling, technical, and administrative costs to individual customers, or else the assignment was done arbitrarily using sales dollars rather than the actual cost drivers.[2] Exhibit 7–1 shows the characteristics of high cost-to-serve and low cost-to-serve customers.

All companies can generally recognize customers that exhibit some or all of the high cost-to-serve characteristics. Occasionally companies are fortunate to enjoy low cost-to-serve customers as well. The only downside from having a low cost-to-serve customer arises when the customer itself realizes that its behavior reduces costs to its supplier, and demands low prices (high discounts from list price) in exchange. Wal-Mart, in particular, has from its inception leveraged its unique purchasing characteristics to negotiate exceptionally favorable terms with suppliers.

Managing High and Low Cost-to-Serve Customers

Companies can view their customers through the lens of a simple 2×2 diagram (see (Exhibit 7–2). The vertical axis shows the net margin earned from sales to the customer. The net margin equals net price, after all sales discounts and allowances, less manufacturing cost (as measured by an ABC product costing model, of course). The horizontal axis shows the cost of serving the customer, including order-related costs, plus the specific customer-sustaining marketing, technical, selling, and administrative expenses associated with serving each individual customer, as measured by an ABC customer costing model of these expenses.

This diagram shows that companies can enjoy profitable customers in different ways. A customer such as Wal-Mart would be at the lower left hand corner of the curve: demanding low prices, so net margins will be low, but also working with its suppliers so that the cost-to-serve is

---

EXHIBIT 7–1: Characteristics of High and Low Cost-to-Serve Customers

HIGH COST-TO-SERVE CUSTOMERS	LOW COST-TO-SERVE CUSTOMERS
Order custom products	Order standard products
Small order quantities	High order quantities
Unpredictable order arrivals	Predictable order arrivals
Customized delivery	Standard delivery
Change delivery requirements	No changes in delivery requirements
Manual processing	Electronic processing (EDI)
Large amounts of pre-sales support (marketing, technical, and sales resources)	Little to no pre-sales support (standard pricing and ordering)
Large amounts of post-sales support (installation, training, warranty, field service)	No post-sales support
Require company to hold inventory	Replenish as produced
Pay slowly (high accounts receivable)	Pay on time

---

[2]See B. P. Shapiro, V. K. Rangan, R. T. Moriarty, and E. B. Ross, "Manage Customers for Profits (Not Just for Sales)," *Harvard Business Review* (September–October 1987), pp. 101–108.

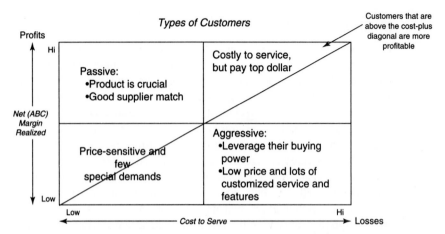

EXHIBIT 7–2 **Measuring and Managing Customer Profitability**

Source: Shapiro, Rangan, Moriarty and Ross, "Manage Customers for Profits (Not Just Sales)," *Harvard Business Review* (Sept–Oct 1987).

also low. High cost-to-serve (hidden cost) customers, exhibiting characteristics in the left-hand column of Exhibit 7–1, can also be profitable (these would be located in the upper right hand corner of Exhibit 7–2) if the net margins earned on sales to these customers more than compensate the company for the cost of all the resources deployed for these customers.

Occasionally, a company may count its blessings by observing that several of its customers are in the upper left hand quadrant: high margins and low cost-to-serve. These customers should be cherished and protected. They could be vulnerable to competitive inroads. Managers should be prepared to offer modest discounts and incentives, or special services to retain the loyalty of these "hidden profit" customers if a competitor threatens.

The most challenging set of customers is found in the lower right-hand corner: low margins and high cost-to-serve. The first action should be to improve the performance of the processes now revealed to be critical; that is, reduce the cost of activities associated with serving these customers (in effect, switching to operational ABM). Second, the bill of activities may show that the high cost-to-serve is caused by customer ordering patters: unpredictability, changes, excessive frequency, customized products, nonstandard logistics and delivery requirements, and large demands on technical and sales personnel. The company can share this information with the customer, indicate the costs associated with such actions, and encourage the customer to work with the company in a less costly manner; that is, reduce the number of activities demanded by the customer. Both improvement of internal activities and business processes and better coordination between the company and its customers will have the effect of lowering the cost-to-serve, thereby moving the customer in a westerly, more-profitable, direction on Exhibit 7–2.

Alternatively, if the customer is not able or is unwilling to shift its buying and delivery patterns to lower cost-to-serve, the company can take actions to augment its revenues. For example, it can consider modifying its pricing arrangements; for example, lowering the discounts it grants, or adding price surcharges for special services and features.

Managing Unprofitable Customers

Pricing initiatives and process improvements, either by the company or jointly with its customers, are often successful in transforming customers from unprofitable to profitable, moving them out of the lower-right hand quadrant of Exhibit 7–2. These will be discussed in cases at

the end of the chapter. What about customers that remain in this lower-right
Should the company consider firing these unprofitable customers?

Not yet!

Some of the currently unprofitable customers in the lower right-hand qu⸱⸱⸱⸱⸱ ⸱
7–2 may be relatively new to the company. Considerable expenses (now accurately traced to
these new customers) may have been incurred to attract them as customers. And the customers
may be testing its new supplier by giving it only a small portion of its total business, and that in
relatively demanding applications, so that it can assess how well the new supplier can perform.
The company (the new supplier) hopes to grow these customers into long-term, profitable relationships. For these new customers, the initial losses revealed by the cost-to-serve ABC model
can be considered part of the investment in obtaining new customers. This initial investment
will, the company hopes, be repaid in higher volume and a more profitable mix of business in
subsequent years leading to substantial lifetime customer profitability.[3] So companies will certainly not seek to fire new but unprofitable customers. Instead, they will track them to ensure
that such customers migrate in a northwesterly direction on Exhibit 7–2 in subsequent periods.
They will hope that such customers will soon reach profitability through some combination of
higher volumes, higher margins, and lower cost-to-serve once the initial courtship leading to the
new customer acquisition has been fully consummated.

Other unprofitable customers in the lower right-hand quadrant of Exhibit 7–2 may give
the company benefits that can not be quantified by the ABC cost-to-serve model. For example,
some companies are prestigious to have as customers because they are known to be demanding
on their suppliers for quality and performance. In effect, as an on-going supplier to such prestigious customers, the company has gained benefits that it can leverage with other customers.
The losses reported on Exhibit 7–2 by the ABC model then become interpreted as an element
in the company's advertising or promotion costs. They represent the price of establishing the
company's reputation and credibility. As in any discretionary expense, of course, such losses
should be monitored and managed. It would be even more desirable to establish reputation and
credibility at a negative cost by finding ways to transform the currently unprofitable relationship
with the prestigious customer into a profitable one.

Another difficult-to-quantify benefit from certain customers is the opportunity for learning. Japanese companies like Toyota, Nissan, and Honda, that established manufacturing pres-
ences in the U.S., have demanded performance from U.S.-based suppliers that is comparable to
what they enjoy from their Japanese-owned suppliers. Many U.S. suppliers found it quite costly
to meet the stringent requirements for quality, delivery times, and flexibility from their new
Japanese customers. If they were to understand the full costs they are incurring to provide such
stringent performance to these customers, they likely would find these customers to be unprofitable, especially initially. The company could rationalize some of these losses because these
customers are currently using capacity that otherwise would go unused. A much more compelling justification, however, is that the working relationships with such customers provide a
learning opportunity. The demanding customers are prepared to work with their new suppliers
and show them how new management processes, equipment, and technology will enable them
to satisfy the customers' demands without incurring excessive cost penalties. Thus, the initial
losses incurred in satisfying these customers demands can be viewed as the cost of education
about new manufacturing and logistics processes that can be beneficially deployed to all of its
customers in the future.

---

[3]See F. F. Reichheld, "The Right Measures," chapter 8 (pp. 217–253) of *The Loyalty Effect* (Boston: HBS Press, 1996).

Firing Customers

Suppose, however, that a customer resists all the company's attempts to transform the unprofitable relationship into a profitable one. This is not a new customer, and the only thing it has learned from 10–15 years of working with this customer is that it does not want another 10–15 years like the ones just experienced. Now the company can contemplate firing the customer. Or, perhaps, let the customer fire itself, by refusing to grant discounts and reducing or eliminating marketing and technical support. The company can reassign its technical and marketing resources formerly deployed for the unprofitable customers to search for new, profitable customers; those with characteristics similar to the customers in the upper left-hand quadrant of Exhibit 7–2.

SUPPLIER RELATIONSHIPS

Moving back in the value chain to supplier–company relationships, historically, relationships with suppliers have been conducted in an arms-length adversarial mode. Purchasing managers were directed to search for and negotiate with potential suppliers with a view towards obtaining the lowest possible purchase price. For example, the major U.S. automobile companies would not enter into long-term relationships with their suppliers. Every six months, their demand for steel would be put up for bid and all the steel companies would compete to win the business by offering the lowest price for the next six month period.

Such continual spot-market contracting based on price was entirely consistent with a traditional standard costing view of the world. In this perspective, managers and industrial engineers established standards for materials prices and materials usage. Production managers and workers were held accountable for meeting the quantity or usage standards and purchasing managers were held accountable for meeting or improving upon the price standards. The performance of purchasing managers was evaluated by *purchase price variances*. Such variances were unfavorable when the actual purchase price exceeded the standard price and favorable when the actual price was less than the standard price. Purchasing managers soon figured out how to reduce the risk of unfavorable variances. They could identify lower-priced supply sources by purchasing:

- In bulk quantities, earning volume discounts from suppliers;
- From marginal suppliers, whose quality, reliability, and delivery performance were less than outstanding;
- From distant domestic suppliers, especially if freight costs were not traced to individual shipments, who offered slightly lower prices;
- From suppliers in low-wage countries;
- From suppliers with low overhead because of their underinvestment in technology and systems; and
- From suppliers with limited engineering and technical resources.

Such actions would lower purchase prices, the metric used to evaluate purchasing performance, but lead to much higher costs in the organization to perform the activities listed in Exhibit 7–3. The cost of all the activities listed in Exhibit 7–3 can be appropriately identified in a Stage III ABC system. In Stage II systems, however, the cost of resources performing these activities are buried in large overhead pools, and allocated to products using unit-level drivers (such as material dollars, direct labor, and machine hours). Consequently, companies with Stage II systems cannot distinguish between suppliers and components that create a high demand for internal procurement activities versus those that make minimal demands on the organization's procurement resources.

EXHIBIT 7–3 Procurement Activities

Receive materials
Inspect materials
Return materials
Move materials
Store materials
Scrap obsolete materials
Scrap and rework products because of (undetected) defective incoming materials
Order materials
Delay production because of late deliveries
Expedite materials to avoid shutdowns because of late-arriving materials
Design, engineer, and determine materials specifications (using internal engineering resources, not suppliers' engineers)
Pay for materials

Choosing Low-Cost Not Low-price Suppliers

All these developments indicate why suppliers cannot be chosen solely on the basis of low price. Purchasing managers cannot be evaluated by their ability to avoid unfavorable purchase price variances. The best suppliers are the ones who can deliver at the lowest total cost, not the lowest price. Does purchase price remain important? Of course, but purchase price is only one component of the total cost of acquiring materials. The total cost of acquiring materials, referred to by many companies as the *total cost of ownership*, includes the purchase price plus the cost of all the procurement-related activities, such as those listed in Exhibit 7–3.

How can companies choose and evaluate suppliers based on low total cost, not low price? A traditional standard cost system will, at best, report net purchase price from a supplier. Only an ABC system enables a company to understand the total costs of working with an individual supplier, including ordering, receiving, inspecting, expediting, storing, and the rest of purchasing-related activities. Items purchased from an "ideal supplier" may have a somewhat higher purchase price but will be assigned no other purchasing costs. Conversely, a low-price supplier that cannot meet any of the requirements associated with the "ideal supplier" will have many other costs assigned to its purchased items. The activity-based costs of supplier-related activities enables a company to engage in fact-based discussions on how it wishes to work with suppliers and how cost savings from efficient supply can be shared between supplier and customer.[4]

VENDOR-SUSTAINING COSTS

To complete this discussion, we can link the ABC cost hierarchy (see discussion in chapter 4) to the costing of supplier relationships. Other than the purchase price itself, only a very limited number of purchasing costs are unit-related. Some costs are batch-related, such as the costs associated with ordering, receiving, inspecting, moving, and paying for materials. Other costs are product-sustaining; the costs of designing and maintaining specifications on individual materials and components. Also, the supplier perspective gives us a new category, *vendor-sustaining*

---

[4]See P. Bennett, "ABM and the Procurement Cost Model," *Management Accounting* (March 1996), pp. 28–32; and L. M. Ellram, "Activity-Based Costing and Total Cost of Ownership: A Critical Linkage," *Journal of Cost Management* (Winter 1995), pp. 22–30 for applications of ABC for managing supplier relationships.

costs. These are the costs associated with a given vendor that are independent of the quantity and variety of items ordered. Such costs include ongoing discussions between vendor and company about the company's product plans, delivery requirements, and production plans; maintaining files on vendor identity, characteristics, and performance; and periodic evaluations of vendor performance. Companies have discovered that because of vendor-sustaining costs, they may have too many vendors. With this information, they can attempt to consolidate their vendor base so they can work more effectively and more efficiently with fewer vendors.

ASSIGNING BUSINESS AND CORPORATE-LEVEL EXPENSES

Now that expenses for operations and service, direct customer administration and support, and purchasing have been analyzed, managers question whether the approach can be applied to the remaining organizational expenses. The basic insight for assigning corporate or division-level expenses is the same as for using activity cost drivers for assigning factory level expenses to activities and to products, or marketing and selling expenses to customers. Look for a quantitative measure or measures representing the output of the staff department. In effect, such corporate and division-level expenses should be treated as support departments and assigned based on a quantitative measure that represents the output provided from these departments. This approach has already been discussed in chapter 2, under the topic of assigning support department costs to primary and secondary activities.

If a quantity measure for the output of the department cannot be identified, so that the only method for allocation is to use percentages of operating departments, say of sales, expenses, or assets, then any assignment would be an arbitrary allocation, not an attribution based on a cause-and-effect relationship. Rather than do an arbitrary allocation using percentages, the ABC cost model should treat the expense at the sustaining level, and not attempt to drive it further down the organization.

ASSIGNING BRAND, PRODUCT-LINE, AND CHANNEL SUPPORT EXPENSES

The analysis of corporate staff level expenses can also be applied to brand, product-line, and channel expenses. Take the cost of managing a brand, such as Procter & Gamble's well-known detergent, Tide. P&G spends considerable resources on a brand management team for Tide, for ongoing enhancements of the products that carry the Tide label, and for promotions and advertising the brand name. Suppose that the company has 100 different stock-keeping units (SKUs) that carry the Tide name, representing different package sizes, variations in color, and different formulations (such as powder or liquid). How can the cost of brand management, product improvement, and brand advertising be assigned to each of the 100 different SKUs that carry the brand name? The answer, of course, is that the cost cannot be assigned, unless a cause-and-effect relationship can be estimated between the quantity of brand management, support, and advertising expenses and some characteristics of individual SKUs. If most such expenses would be incurred, even if only one SKU carrying the Tide name existed, then the expenses should be considered *brand sustaining* and not allocated down to individual SKUs.

And continuing up the organizational hierarchy, Procter & Gamble markets several brands of detergent; some represent alternative laundry detergent brands, some represent detergents for dishwashers and other cleaning applications. Suppose that some expenses are incurred for a manager and support staff of the detergent sector. Also, some expenses are incurred to improve the performance of all detergent brands, not just Tide. For example, product development

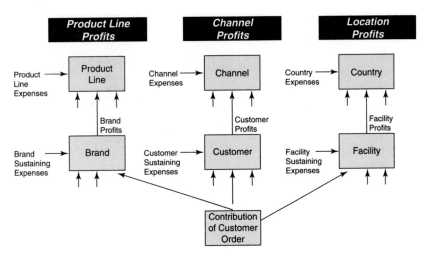

EXHIBIT 7–4   Activity-Based Profitability Branches

may be done to improve the environmental characteristics of all detergent products, or to improve their cleaning effectiveness. Such expenses can be unambiguously attributed to the detergent product line—they are detergent *product-line sustaining*, and certainly not the costs of being in the toothpaste, potato chip, or paper diaper business—but any allocation to individual detergent brands within the product line would be arbitrary. Exhibit 7–4 gives a pictorial representation of measuring profitability from different perspectives and hierarchical levels.

A similar line of reasoning would reveal that some marketing expenses cannot be attributed to individual customers. For example, the costs of advertising in trade journals, attendance and promotions at trade conferences, and the administrative infrastructure dedicated to particular distribution channels, such as retail, wholesale, or electronic commerce, support the sales activity for all customers who purchase through that channel. Rather than arbitrarily allocating such *channel-sustaining* expenses down to individual customers within the channel, these expenses can be attributed to a higher level of the marketing hierarchy (the channel level, sitting above the customer level; see Exhibit 7–4), and used to determine channel profitability, but not individual customer profitability within that channel.

An alternative way of representing the organizational cost hierarchy is with spreadsheets. Exhibit 7–5 shows a spreadsheet for product and product-line profitability. Unit, batch, and product-sustaining expenses are traced to individual products, and enable product profitability to be calculated. From the sum of all the products in a product line, we subtract the cost of any unused capacity that can be traced to an individual product line (such as excess capacity on equipment dedicated to that product line) plus the product-line sustaining expenses. Summing across all the product-line profitabilities yields total product and product-line profitability in the last column of this report. From this we subtract non-product and non-product-line expenses—customer-related costs, unused organizational capacity costs, and facility and business unit-sustaining expenses—ending up with the total profitability of the enterprise.

Similarly, Exhibit 7–6 shows the spreadsheet for customer and channel profitability. The unit, batch, and order-related expenses associated with customer purchases are traced directly to each customer. Then we subtract customer-sustaining expenses (traced to individual customers) and calculate individual customer profitability. Add the profitability of all customers within a channel to obtain channel contribution margin, and subtract channel-sustaining expenses to obtain channel profitability. Adding across all customers and channels yields total customer prof-

EXHIBIT 7–5 Product and Product-Line Profitability

	PRODUCT 1	PRODUCT 2	PRODUCT 3	PRODUCT LINE P1
Sales	XXX	XXX	XXX	XXX
Unit-Level Expenses				
Materials	XXX	XXX	XXX	XXX
Direct Labor	XXX	XXX	XXX	XXX
Machine Time	XXX	XXX	XXX	XXX
Other Unit-Level	XXX	XXX	XXX	XXX
Batch-Level Expenses				
Setups	XXX	XXX	XXX	XXX
Material Movement	XXX	XXX	XXX	XXX
Purchases	XXX	XXX	XXX	XXX
Order Handling	XXX	XXX	XXX	XXX
Other Batch-Level	XXX	XXX	XXX	XXX
Product-Sustaining				
Design & Development	XXX	XXX	XXX	XXX
Engineering Changes	XXX	XXX	XXX	XXX
Product Maintenance	XXX	XXX	XXX	XXX
Total Product Costs	XXX	XXX	XXX	XXX
Product Profits	XXX	XXX	XXX	XXX
Unused Capacity				XXX
Product-Line Expenses				XXX
Product-Line Profitability				XXX
Other Expenses				
Customer-Related				
Unused Capacity				
Facility Expenses				
Region–Business Unit				
Total Profits				

itability in the last column of the spreadsheet. Then we subtract non-customer and non-channel related expenses—product and product-line sustaining expenses, unused capacity costs, and facility and business-unit sustaining expenses—to reconcile back to total enterprise profitability.

With these methodologies, all expenses traced to a cost object—whether a product, brand, product line, customer, facility, channel, or business unit—are, in principle, controllable or influenced by decisions taken about that cost object. Cost traceability and cause-and-effect relationships are maintained since no arbitrary allocations, using percentages, have been made. This representation, however, is only a first-order approximation since it does suppress second and higher-order interactions across cost objects.

Hierarchies: A General Perspective

Exhibit 7–4 (and Exhibits 7–5 and 7–6) identifies three groups of hierarchies; for product lines, marketing and distribution channels, and location or business units. We refer to costs incurred at any hierarchical level as sustaining costs at that level. Hierarchies identify the lowest level to which certain costs can meaningfully be assigned. The identification of hierarchies al-

EXHIBIT 7–5 (*continued*)

PRODUCT 4	PRODUCT 5	PRODUCT 6	PRODUCT LINE P2	. . .	TOTAL
XXX	XXX	XXX	XXX		XXX
XXX	XXX	XXX	XXX	XXX	XXX
XXX	XXX	XXX	XXX	XXX	XXX
XXX	XXX	XXX	XXX	XXX	XXX
XXX	XXX	XXX	XXX	XXX	XXX
XXX	XXX	XXX	XXX	XXX	XXX
XXX	XXX	XXX	XXX	XXX	XXX
XXX	XXX	XXX	XXX	XXX	XXX
XXX	XXX	XXX	XXX	XXX	XXX
XXX	XXX	XXX	XXX	XXX	XXX
XXX	XXX	XXX	XXX	XXX	XXX
XXX	XXX	XXX	XXX	XXX	XXX
XXX	XXX	XXX	XXX	XXX	XXX
XXX	XXX	XXX	XXX	XXX	XXX
XXX	XXX	XXX	XXX	XXX	XXX
			XXX		XXX
			XXX		XXX
			XXX		XXX
					XXX
					XXX
					XXX
					XXX
					XXX

lows managers to forecast the effect of decisions to add or drop objects such as products, brands, customers, and facilities.

Such a scheme assumes that no interactions occur across different groups of hierarchies. Such an assumption may be violated; for example, returning to the manufacturing cost hierarchy, if a product is dropped then all batch activities related to unique components for that product will automatically disappear. But activities related to components that are also used in other products may not disappear. If a common component is used in other products, and only one batch of that component is produced in the period, then the batch-level activities for that common component will remain. In this case, only the dropped product's share of the unit-level activities are eliminated.

The existence of common elements, whether they are components, products, customers, or facilities introduces another layer of complexity into estimating the effect of changing the object mix produced or served by the firm.[5] For example, in Exhibit 7–4, if a company drops a

---

[5]The first layer of complexity is mapping between decisions taken to change resource usage (based on the ABC model) and the subsequent impact on spending (or resource supply); see discussion in chapter 5.

EXHIBIT 7-6 Customer and Channel Profitability

	CUSTOMER 1-1	. . .	CUSTOMER 1-N	CHANNEL 1
Sales	xxx	xxx	xxx	xxx
Unit-Level Expenses	xxx	xxx	xxx	xxx
Batch-Level Expenses	xxx	xxx	xxx	xxx
Order Expenses	xxx	xxx	xxx	xxx
Contribution Margin	xxx	xxx	xxx	xxx
Customer-Sustaining Exp.	xxx	xxx	xxx	xxx
Customer Profitability	xxx	xxx	xxx	xxx
Channel Expenses				xxx
Channel Profitability				xxx
Other Expenses				
Product Related				
Unused Capacity				
Facility Expenses				
Region–Business Unit				
Total Profits				

brand, how will that affect customers? Presumably, revenues (and unit and some batch-level expenses) will decrease to the extent that the customers do not switch their purchases to alternative brands made by the company. But the customer-sustaining expenses should remain the same since, by assumption, those expenses are independent of the volume and mix purchased by the customer. Only if a customer were buying that single brand from the company, and could not be switched to another brand, would the customer-sustaining expenses be affected by the decision to drop the brand. Similarly, dropping a single customer or group of customers will affect the sales of products and brands (and their unit and batch-level expenses), but should not affect the product and brand-sustaining expenses, unless these were the only customers purchasing those products and brands.

These conditions for interactions across different categories of sustaining expenses (brand vs. customer-sustaining) are sufficiently rare in most settings, that the profitability branches captured by Exhibit 7–4 seem to represent useful ways for viewing the underlying profitability structure of the organization. Managers can use the profitability map in Exhibit 7–4 to make decisions at individual hierarchical levels (product, brand, product line, customer, distribution channel, facility, business unit, and region) with minimal impact on other portions of the profitability map.

Of course, second-order effects can still occur. Dropping a product or brand could cause a currently profitable customer to become unprofitable, because of lower volume of sales to that customer; and dropping a group of customers could cause currently profitable products or brands to become unprofitable. Exhibit 7–4 gives a first-order approximation of where the company is making or losing money. Managers can review the objects (such as products, customers, brands facilities, and business units) that are highly profitable or unprofitable and explore opportunities to increase the profitable objects and decrease the unprofitable ones. But, as in the resource usage–resource supply decisions discussed in chapter 5, special studies should

EXHIBIT 7–6 (*continued*)

CUSTOMER 2-1	. . .	CUSTOMER 2-M	CHANNEL 2	. . .	TOTAL
XXX	XXX	XXX	XXX		XXX
XXX	XXX	XXX	XXX		
XXX	XXX	XXX	XXX		
XXX	XXX	XXX	XXX		XXX
XXX	XXX	XXX	XXX	. . .	XXX
XXX	XXX	XXX	XXX	. . .	XXX
XXX	XXX	XXX	XXX	. . .	XXX
			XXX		XXX
			XXX		XXX
					XXX
					XXX
					XXX
					XXX
					XXX

be done to explore the impact of such decisions on the profitability of other objects and on overall resource supply. The ABC profitability map (Exhibit 7–4) focuses managers' attention on profit and loss opportunities, but still requires that special studies be performed to assess interactive effects and potential impact on resource supply.

SUMMARY

We have shown in this chapter the wide variety of actions managers can take to transform unprofitable customers into profitable ones:

- Protecting existing highly profitable customers;
- Repricing expensive services, based on cost-to-serve;
- Discounting, if necessary, to gain business with low cost-to-serve customers;
- Negotiating win-win relationships that lower cost-to-serve with cooperative customers;
- Conceding permanent loss customers to competitors; and
- Attempting to capture high profit customers from competitors.

A company with a Stage III ABC system geared to customer profitability can target discounts and value-added services based on actual cost-to-serve. These actions should provide such companies with significant competitive advantages, especially when their competitors continue to follow the signals from their Stage II cost systems, which makes them vulnerable to the targeted actions taken by informed companies.

In addition to major profit enhancements through better management of customer relationships, strategic ABM also offers large cost savings opportunities from improved upstream operations. By understanding the costs associated with ordering, receiving, inspecting, moving,

storing, and paying for materials, companies can make better decisions to choose the lowest total cost suppliers, not just the lowest price suppliers. An ABC model of the supplier relationship
enables managers to work with their best suppliers to search for ways to lower inventory levels
and total supply chain costs; benefits that will benefit both them and their suppliers. The ABC
model of the "as-is" supply chain cost provides the insights and justification for exploring such
opportunities, and an ABC model constructed for the streamlined supply chain will identify the
cost savings that can be shared across supplier and customer. The ABM actions from such supplier models will enable companies to lower their costs of acquiring and using purchased materials and services.

We have proposed the use of a hierarchical profitability map to capture all organizational
expenses at the lowest possible activity level. The profitability map provides managers with
guidance about where special attention should be devoted to brands, product lines, customers,
distribution channels, facilities, and regions.

CASES

The cases for this chapter extend ABC to customers and suppliers. The value of understanding
customer profitability is highlighted in several of the cases by the decisions taken to either improve either the firm's customer mix or to modify the behavior of existing customers so that
their costs are lower. The role of customers in determining several aspects of the production
process is illustrated in some of the cases.

The *Kanthal (A)* case explores an environment in which customers influence both manufacturing and SMDA expenses. The case demonstrates a relatively simple procedure to assign
some SMDA costs to customers. The *Pillsbury* case illustrates the role for extending strategic
cost analysis outside the factory to customers and suppliers. The *Seneca Foods* case is a disguised case of how an entrepreneurial private-label food manufacturer could use a variety of
ABC models as it attempts to reach a broader and more diverse customer base. Finally, the
Winchell Lighting case illustrates the extension of ABC to product-line and channel levels, with
emphasis on cost hierarchies and sustaining costs.

KANTHAL (A)*

Carl-Erik Ridderstråle, president of Kanthal, was describing his motivation for developing a system to measure customer profitability.

> Before, when we got an order from a big, important customer, we didn't ask questions. We were glad to get the business. But a small company, competing around the world, has to concentrate its sales and marketing resources. We needed an account management system if we were to achieve our strategy for higher growth and profitability. An account management system as part of the Kanthal 90 Strategy will enable us to get sales managers to accept responsibility for promoting high-margin products to high-profit customers.

History

Kanthal, the largest of six divisions in the Kanthal-Hoganas group of Sweden, was headquartered in Hallstahammar a town of 17,000 persons about 150 km northwest of Stockholm. The company's history can be traced back to an ironworks founded in the seventeenth century to exploit the water power available from the stream running through the town. Kanthal specialized in the production and sales of electrical resistance heating elements. "We work for a warmer world," was its motto.

Kanthal had about 10,000 customers and 15,000 items that it produced. Sales during 1985 through 1987 had been level at about SEK 850 million.[1] Export sales, outside of Sweden, accounted for 95% of the total. Summary statistics for the past two years appear in Exhibit 1.

Kanthal consisted of three divisions:

> Kanthal Heating Technology supplied manufacturers of electrical appliances and heating systems with wire that generated heat through electrical resistance. Products included heating wire and ribbon, foil elements, machinery and precision wire. Kanthal's 25% market share made it a world leader in supplying heating alloys. Sales growth was sluggish in Europe and the United States but rapid growth was occurring in the Far East and Latin America.

> Kanthal Furnace Products produced a wide range of heating elements for electric industrial furnaces. Its 40% market share gave it a dominant position in the large markets of the United States, Japan, West Germany, and the

United Kingdom. A new product, Kanthal Super, was generating substantial growth because of its substantially improved performance over conventional materials, including longer service life, lower service costs, and higher operating temperatures.

Kanthal Bimetals was one of the few companies in the world with fully integrated manufacturing of thermo-bimetals for temperature control devices used in the manufacture of thermostats, circuit breakers, and household appliances.

Kanthal's manufacturing facilities were located in Hallstahammar, Brazil, the United Kingdom, West Germany, the United States, and Italy.

Kanthal 90

Ridderstråle, upon becoming president in 1985, saw the need for a strategic plan for Kanthal.

> The company had been successful in the past. We needed to use this base of experience to influence the future. We had to have a consolidated view to ensure that we did not sub-optimize in narrow markets or with a narrow functional view. Resources were to be allocated so that we could increase profits while maintaining a return on employed capital in excess of 20%.

The Kanthal 90 plan specified overall profit objectives by division, by product line, and by market. Currently, however, salespersons were compensated mostly on gross sales volume. Higher commissions were being paid for selling obviously higher-margin products, such as Super, and higher bonuses were being awarded for achieving sales targets in the high-margin products. But Ridderstråle wanted to achieve the additional growth planned under Kanthal 90 without adding sales and administrative resources to handle the increased volume anticipated.

> We needed to know where in the organization the resources could be taken from and redeployed into more profitable uses. We did not want to eliminate resources in a steady-state environment. We wanted to reallocate people to generate future growth.

> With our historically good profitability, and lacking any current or imminent crisis, we could not realistically consider laying off people at the Hallstahammar plant. But we wanted to be able to redeploy people so that they could earn more profit for us; to move people from corporate staff to divisions, from the parent company to operating subsidiaries, and from staff functions into sales, R&D, and production. Ideally, if we could transform an accounting

---

*Professor Robert S. Kaplan prepared this case. Copyright © 1989 by the President and Fellows of Harvard College. Harvard Business School Case 190-002.
[1]In 1988, the Swedish kroner (SEK) was worth about US$0.16.

clerk at Hallstahammar into a salesman of Kanthal-Super in Japan, we could generate a substantial profit increase.

Exhibit 2 shows the distribution of Kanthal's incurred costs. The existing cost system treated most sales, marketing, and administrative costs as a percentage of sales revenue. Therefore, customers whose selling price exceeded the standard full cost of manufacturing plus the percentage mark-up for general, selling, and administrative expenses appeared to be profitable, while a customer order whose selling price was below standard manufacturing cost plus the percentage mark-up appeared unprofitable. Ridderstråle knew, however, that individual customers made quite different demands on Kanthal's administrative and sales staff.

> Low profit customers place high demands on technical and commercial service. They buy low-margin products in small orders. Frequently they order nonstandard products that have to be specially produced for them. And we have to supply special selling discounts in order to get the business.
>
> High profit customers buy high-margin, standard products in large orders. They make no demands for technical or commercial service, and accurately forecast for us their annual demands.

He felt that a new system was needed to determine how much profit was earned each time a customer placed a particular order. The system should attempt to measure the costs that individual customer orders placed on the production, sales, and administrative resources of the company. The goal was to find both "hidden profit" orders, those whose demands on the company were quite low, and the "hidden loss" orders, those customer orders that under the existing system looked profitable but which in fact demanded a disproportionate share of the company's resources to fulfill.

Ridderstråle pointed out the weaknesses with the present method of profitability measurement.

> We distribute resources equally across all products and customers. We do not measure individual customer's profitability or the real costs of individual orders. In this environment, our sales and marketing efforts emphasize volume, more than profits. In the future, we want Kanthal to handle significantly increased sales volume without any corresponding increase in support resources, and to gain the share in our most profitable products.
>
> Our current method of calculating product costs may show two customers to be equally profitable on a gross margin basis. But there could be hidden profits and hidden costs associated with these customers that we are not seeing (see Exhibit 3). If we could get more accurate information about our own manufacturing cost structure, as well as the

costs of supplying individual customers and orders, we could direct our resources to customers with hidden profits, and reduce our efforts to customers with the hidden losses. We might end up with the same market share, so that our competitors would not even see this shift in our strategy, but our profitability would be much higher. To execute such a strategy, however, we need better information about the profitability of each order, each product, and each customer.

> The biggest barrier we have to overcome is the notion that production overhead, selling, and administrative costs are "fixed." The definition of strategy is to recognize that all costs are variable. Our sales people must learn how to deploy resources to their most profitable use.

The New Account Management System

Per O. Ehrling, Financial Manager of Kanthal, worked with SAM, a Swedish management advisory group, to develop a system to analyze production, sales, and administrative costs at the Hallstahammar facility. Over a period of several months, finance managers and the consultants conducted extensive interviews with all department heads and key personnel. The interviews were designed to elicit information about the nature of the activities being performed by support department personnel and the events that triggered the demands for these organizational activities. Ehrling described the philosophy of the new approach:

> In our previous system, indirect costs were either manufacturing costs that were allocated to products based on direct labor, or they were Selling & Administrative Costs, that were treated as period expenses and were unanalyzed. This treatment may have been correct 100 years ago when we had one bookkeeper for every 10 blacksmiths, but today we have eight bookkeepers for every three blacksmiths. This means that most of our costs today are indirect and our previous system didn't know how to allocate them.
>
> We wanted to move away from our traditional financial accounting categories. We found that most of our organizational costs could be classified either as Order-related or Volume Costs. Actually, we did investigate three additional cost drivers—product range, technical support, and new products. But the total costs assigned to these three categories ended up being less than 5% of total costs so we eliminated them.

Using the interview information, the project team determined how much of the expenses of each support department related to the volume of sales and production and how much related to handling individual production and sales orders (see Exhibit 4). The manufacturing volume costs, in addition to material, direct labor, and variable overhead, also included the costs of production orders to replenish inventory stocks. Only 20% of Kanthal's products were stocked in inventory, but these products represented 80% of sales orders so the cost of continually replenishing these products was assumed to be related to the volume of production. Manufacturing order costs therefore included only the cost of set-up and other activities that were triggered when a customer ordered a product not normally stocked. Manufacturing order costs were calculated separately for each major product group. The sales order costs represented the selling and administrative costs that could be traced to processing an individual customer's order. The S&A costs that remained after subtracting sales order costs were treated as sales volume costs and were allocated proportionately to the manufacturing volume costs.

For example, the Sales Department activities (see Exhibit 4) relating to preparing a bid for an order, negotiating with the customer about the order, and following-up with the customer after the order was delivered were classified as "order-related." All remaining activities, such as public relations and sales management, that could not be traced to individual orders were classified as "volume-related."

Follow-up interviews were conducted to corroborate the split of effort in each department between volume- and order-related activities. Sample calculations are shown in Exhibit 5. Bo Martin Tell, controller of the Furnace Products Division, recalled the amount of tedious work required to collect all the numbers.

> It took almost a year to develop a system to collect the data in the proper form. Even in production, we had problems identifying the costs that related to stocked and non-stocked orders.

Initial Output
from the Account Management System

Exhibit 6 shows a profitability report for a sample of individual orders from Swedish customers. Profit margins on these individual orders ranged from −179% to +65%. Previously, almost all of these orders would have appeared profitable. Similar reports were prepared to show total profitability by customer, by product group, or by all the orders received from customers in a country. For example, Exhibit 7 shows, for a given product group—Finished Wire N, the sales volume and profitability of a sample of Swedish customers.

Leif Rick, general manager of Heating Technology remembered the initial reactions to the account management reports:

> The study was a real eye-opener. We saw how the traditional cost accounting system had been unable to truly report costs and profits by market, product, and customer.

> At first, the new approach seemed strange. We had to explain it three or four times before people started to understand and accept it. People did not want to believe that order costs could be so high; that order costs had to be treated as an explicit cost of selling. Most surprising was finding that customers thought to be very profitable were actually break-even or even loss customers. Salesmen initially thought the approach was part of a master plan to get rid of small customers. But people who have been working with the system now are convinced of its value and are beginning to take sensible actions based on the information.

Exhibit 8 shows the profits from Swedish customers, ranked by customer profitability. The results surprised even Ridderstråle. Only 40% of Kanthal's Swedish customers were profitable and these generated 250% of realized profits. In fact the most profitable 5% of the customers generated 150% of the country's profits. The least profitable 10% of customers lost 120% of the profits (see cumulative profitability chart in Exhibit 9).

Even more surprising, two of the most unprofitable customers turned out to be among the top three in total sales volume. These two customers had gone to just-in-time (JIT) delivery for its suppliers. They had pushed inventory back onto Kanthal which had not recognized the new demands being placed on its production and order-handling processes by the JIT approach. Moreover, further investigation revealed that one of these customers was using Kanthal as a backup supplier, to handle small special orders of a low-priced item when its main supplier could not deliver. Because of the size and prestige of the two customers, Kanthal people had always welcomed and encouraged their orders. Ridderstråle now realized how expensive it had become to satisfy them.

The immediate problem was to devise a strategy for the large number of nonprofitable customers, particularly the very high volume ones. Corporate management had started a series of meetings with the general and sales managers of the operating divisions in Sweden to discuss how to handle these customers.

Also, while the account management system had been developed for the Swedish operating divisions, some overseas divisions remained skeptical about the value of the exercise. The account management system was seen as yet another intrusion of the headquarters staff into their operations. Ridderstråle knew he faced an uphill battle gaining acceptance for the account management system around the world.

EXHIBIT 1 Summary of Operations

	1986	1987
Invoiced sales (MSEK)*	839	849
Profit after financial items	87	107
Return on capital	20%	21%
Number of employees	1,606	1,591

*MSEK, million Swedish kroner.

EXHIBIT 2 Cost Structure

COST COMPONENT	PERCENTAGE
Materials	23
Production salaries and wages	19
Variable processing costs	5
Fixed processing costs	16
Subcontracted services	3
Selling and administrative	34
Total costs	100

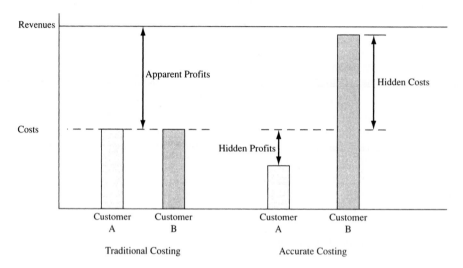

EXHIBIT 3   Hidden Profit and Hidden Cost Customers

EXHIBIT 4 Order and Volume Costs

TYPE OF PERSONNEL	ORDER-RELATED WORK	VOLUME-RELATED WORK
Production		
Stock replenishment	None	All activities
Production planning	Order planning Order follow-up	Inventory management
Operators	Set-up Start-up expense	Direct hours
Foremen	Order planning Order support	Machine problems
Stock	Order input Order output	Order handling
Transportation	Order planning Order handling	
Selling and Administrative		
Management	Offer discussion Offer negotiation	General management
Sales	Offer work Order negotiation Delivery follow-up	Sales unrelated to orders General public relations Sales management
Secretarial	Offer typing	
Administration	Order booking Order adjustment Invoice typing Customer ledger Supervision	Accounting

EXHIBIT 5 Sample Calculation of Order and Volume Costs, by Product Group

Step 1. Calculate Selling & Administrative (S&A) Order Costs

Total selling & administrative order costs		SEK2,000,000
Total number of orders	2,000	
Stocked products	1,500	
Non-stocked products	500	
S&A order costs per order		SEK 1,000

Step 2. Calculate Manufacturing Order Cost for Non-stocked Products

Total manufacturing order costs (for non-stocked products)		SEK1,000,000
Number of orders for non-stocked products		500
Manufacturing order costs per non-stocked order		SEK 2,000

Step 3. Calculate Allocation Factor for S&A Volume Costs

Compute total manufacturing and S&A costs		SEK7,000,000
Subtract order costs		
Non-stocked products	1,000,000	
Selling & administrative order costs	2,000,000	3,000,000
Total volume costs		SEK4,000,000
Manufacturing volume costs of goods sold (CGS)	3,200,000	
Selling & administrative volume-related costs	800,000	
S&A volume allocation factor: S&A volume costs/mfg. volume CGS (800/3,200)		25%

Step 4. Calculate Operating Profit on Individual Orders for Non-stocked Products

Sales value		SEK 10,000
Less: Volume costs: Manufacturing cost of goods sold (@ 40% of sales value)		4,000
Volume costs: Selling & administrative (@ 25% of mfg. CGS)		1,000
Margin on volume-related costs		5,000
Less: Mfg. order cost for non-stocked product		2,000
Selling & administrative order cost		1,000
Operating profit for order		SEK 2,000

*SEK, Swedish kroner.

EXHIBIT 6 Customer Order Analysis

Standard order cost: SEK 572
Manufacturing order cost for non-stocked products: Foil Elements: SEK1508
  Finished Wire: SEK2340

COUNTRY CUSTOMER	ORDER LINES	INVOICED VALUE (SEK)	VOLUME COST (SEK)	ORDER COST (SEK)	NON-STOCKED (SEK)	OPERATING PROFIT (SEK)	PROFIT MARGIN %
Sweden							
S001	1	1,210	543	572	0	95	8
S002	3	46,184	10,080	1,716	4,524	29,864	65
S003	8	51,102	50,567	4,576	12,064	(16,105)	−32
S004	9	98,880	60,785	5,148	13,572	19,375	20
S005	1	3,150	1,557	572	2,340	(1,319)	−42
S006	5	24,104	14,889	2,860	4,680	1,675	7
S007	2	4,860	2,657	1,144	4,680	(3,621)	−75
S008	1	2,705	1,194	572	0	939	35
S009	1	518	233	572	0	(287)	−55
S010	8	67,958	51,953	4,576	12,064	(635)	−1
S011	2	4,105	1,471	1,144	0	1,490	36
S012	8	87,865	57,581	4,576	12,064	13,644	16
S013	1	1,274	641	572	2,340	(2,279)	−179
S014	2	1,813	784	1,144	0	(115)	−6
S015	2	37,060	15,974	1,144	3,016	16,926	46
S016	2	6,500	6,432	1,144	3,016	(4,092)	−63

Note: All financial data reported in Swedish kroner (SEK).

EXHIBIT 7   Finished Wire N Customer List

CUSTOMER NO.	INVOICED SALES (SEK)	VOLUME COSTS (SEK)	ORDER COST (SEK)	NON-STOCKED COST (SEK)	OPERATING PROFIT (SEK)	PROFIT MARGIN (%)
33507	3,969	1,440	750	0	1,779	45
33508	4,165	1,692	750	2,150	(427)	−10
33509	601	139	750	2,150	(2,438)	−406
33510	13,655	6,014	750	2,150	4,741	35
33511	2,088	350	750	2,150	(1,162)	−56
33512	1,742	637	750	0	355	20
33513	4,177	932	750	2,150	345	8
33514	7,361	3,134	750	0	3,477	47
33515	1,045	318	750	0	(23)	−2
33516	429,205	198,277	9,000	0	221,928	52
33517	31,696	13,128	3,750	0	14,818	47
33518	159,612	58,036	2,250	6,450	92,876	58
33519	48,648	17,872	9,750	12,900	8,126	17
33520	5,012	1,119	750	2,150	993	20
33521	4,933	2,170	1,500	4,300	(3,037)	−62
33522	17,277	7,278	1,500	0	8,499	49
33523	134	120	1,500	4,300	(5,786)	−4,318
33524	1,825	523	1,500	0	(198)	−11
33525	13,874	4,914	3,750	6,450	(1,240)	−9
33526	3,762	1,452	750	0	1,560	41
33527	64,875	18,559	3,750	8,600	33,966	52
33528	13,052	5,542	3,000	6,450	(1,940)	−15
33529	39,175	12,683	3,750	8,600	14,142	36
33530	383	87	750	0	(454)	−119
33531	6,962	1,865	750	2,150	2,197	32
33532	1,072	314	1,500	0	(742)	−69
33533	14,050	6,333	1,500	2,150	4,067	29
33534	820	244	750	0	(174)	−21
33535	809	181	750	2,150	(2,272)	−281
33536	1,366	316	750	2,150	(1,850)	−135
33537	155,793	65,718	21,750	49,450	18,875	12
33538	7,593	2,772	2,250	2,150	421	6
Total	1,060,731	434,159	84,000	131,150	411,422	39%

Note: All financial data reported in Swedish kroner (SEK).

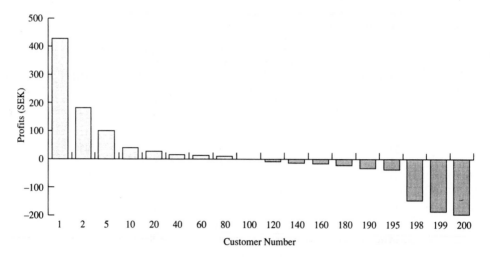

EXHIBIT 8 **Customer Profitability: Ranked from Most to Least Profitable Customers**

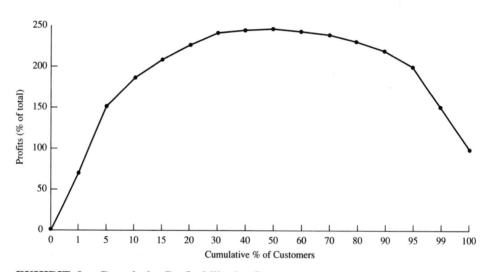

EXHIBIT 9 **Cumulative Profitability by Customers**

PILLSBURY: CUSTOMER DRIVEN REENGINEERING

We entered our Customer Driven Reengineering intiative expecting to achieve significant levels of cost reduction and efficiency. To our delight, we also discovered a new way to compete.

Paul S Walsh
CEO, The Pillsbury Company

Company

The Pillsbury Company was founded in 1869 as a flour milling firm in Minnesota. Its milling operations soon extended into branded bakery goods products, and, during the next century, the company expanded to become one of the leading branded food product companies. In 1989, Grand Metropolitan (GrandMet), a diversified UK-based consumer goods and retailing corporation, purchased The Pillsbury Company for $5.8 billion (see Exhibit 1 for a summary of Pillsbury's financial information prior to its acquisition in 1989). The acquisition was part of GrandMet's new strategy to become a world leader in branded food and drinks businesses.

In 1994, the annual sales of GrandMet's North American Food operations, now called the Pillsbury - North America sector, were $4.0 billion. Included in the sector, of course, was the Pillsbury brand of prepared dough products, baking mixes and flour, a leader in the U.S. market, with refrigerated dough products achieving a 75 percent market share of the refrigerated dough category. The Green Giant division was the number one branded vegetable producer in the U.S. and Canada, producing canned, jarred, frozen and fresh vegetables such as corn, peas, and beans. The frozen pizza business, with Totino's, Jeno's and Pappalo's brands, held the number one position in its market segments. Häagen-Dazs was the world's leading maker of superpremium ice cream and frozen yogurt products. GrandMet Foodservice was a leading provider of flour, dry baking mixes and frozen unbaked and pre-baked products to in-store, foodservice and wholesale bakery markets. Pillsbury products were perhaps most identified with two well-known characters—the Jolly Green Giant and Poppin' Fresh the Pills-

bury Doughboy. Pillsbury's strongest competitors included Dean Foods (Bird's Eye Brands), Del Monte, General Mills and Nestle food companies.

GrandMet, with its origins in hotel operations had acquired over the years a diversified collection of food, beverage, and retailing companies. In the late 1980s, GrandMet began the sale of billions of dollars of assets, including its original hotel operations, so that it could concentrate on becoming a leader in the branded food, and drink businesses. Exhibit 2 presents a summary of GrandMet's recent financial information.

Consistent with Paul Walsh's strategy of focusing on core businesses, Pillsbury itself had recently sold all of its flour mills, some of whose ownership dated back more than a century. In 1991, four mills were sold to Cargill with Pillsbury continuing to receive the processed flour output from these plants through supplier contracts. Two years later, Pillsbury sold its four remaining mills to Archer-Daniels Midland (ADM), a large grain producer. Pillsbury retained access to the output from these ADM mills through a long term supply agreement. Tom Debrowski, Senior Vice President of Operations, explained the rationale for the flour mill sales:

> It became apparent that we were not the low cost producer of flour. In a rapidly consolidating and highly competitive market, we wanted to focus our assets on the more value-added parts of the bakery business, our branded food products. The sale of the flour mills enabled us to get large amounts of aging, under-utilized assets off our balance sheet, while gaining guaranteed access to a long-term supply of low-cost, high-quality flour, produced to our specifications.

Pillsbury Capabilities

Competitive pressures, technology advances, and demanding consumer preferences were causing all companies in the food industry to reexamine their operations and attempt to eliminate waste and inefficiency throughout the food chain. The Efficient Consumer Response (ECR) effort was a multi-industry project, involving food processors, manufacturers, distributors, wholesalers, brokers, and retailers. ECR's goals were to reduce costs and drive inventory levels down throughout the system, while simultaneously enhancing capabilities to meet the needs of diverse consumer market segments. Pillsbury executives were unsure whether their company was prepared for the new ECR environment. Larry McWilliams, Vice President, Frozen Sales, identified the current challenge for Pillsbury:

> When I came to the company 18 months ago, I encountered a company with strong brands but with little prospect for volume growth. Customers perceived us as an average company, not the best, not the worst, and without much innovation.

John Mann, Senior Vice President and General Sales Manager, and another newcomer to the Pillsbury senior management team, concurred with McWilliams' assessment:

> "We were viewed as a laid-back Midwestern company, one that found it difficult to create a sense of urgency."

McWilliams felt that Pillsbury had to become a different company if it was to change the perception of customers.

> The company's strategy has been to create strong brands that could be marketed directly to the consumer and it was very successful with this strategy. By attracting consumers to purchase the products, the company didn't have to be overly concerned with its relationships with the retailers who bought and stocked the branded products.

The new food marketing environment, however, was much more fragmented. Network television ads were reaching a smaller share of consumers, and marketing methods—using cable TV, direct mail, and billboards—could be targeted to much more specific market segments. Even more important, brand images were becoming less important in consumers' purchasing decisions. Current market research indicated that more than 50% of consumers' purchasing decisions were made in the store, where shelf availability and price could outweigh brand image in the consumer's choice. McWilliams anticipated how Pillsbury must react to this new environment:

> We must learn to market to the consumer in alliance with our customers. Competitive success will come from fact-based marketing, exploiting our information systems that tell us about the demographics of the consumers around an individual store, including what and how they purchase. If we can forge alliances with our customers, we can micro-market at the individual store level.

Mann concurred by pointing out that retailers were facing their own competitive pressures:

> Food retailing had also been a sleepy industry. Competition from new formats [such as warehouse and discount stores] has forced the industry to recognize that it must change. The change must include help from manufacturers to develop effective collaborative strategies.

This pressure on food retailers offered manufacturers the potential to transform what had been an arms-length adversarial relationship into a competitive advantage. Mann believed that those companies who could demonstrate their value to retailers would earn the right to manage a product category in partnership with the retailer.

The executives perceived that Pillsbury lacked several critical capabilities to win in this new environment. First, the company was still organized according to traditional functional lines: purchasing, operations, distribution, finance, and marketing and sales. This organization led to local excellence and optimization of the individual functions but not necessarily to the optimization of the entire value chain. Second, the company's financial measurements and performance measurement system reinforced local optimization. The measures encouraged, for example, cost minimization at an individual plant but not across the entire value chain, or, as another example, sales expansion and SKU proliferation but without regard to the profitability of the incremental sales and SKU introductions to either Pillsbury or its customers (see Exhibit 3).

Activity-Based Costing at Pillsbury

In 1991, Dan Crowley as Controller of Green Giant, had launched an activity-based cost (ABC) initiative to examine the group's high cost structure. This initiative eventually led to ABC models being developed for 20 Green Giant plants in the U.S. and Mexico. The study revealed startling plant-to-plant variations in costs for essentially the same process, large dispersion of actual costs from the company's standard cost per case across different vegetable groups and between canned and frozen products, and large amounts of excess capacity, particularly in the plants that processed vegetables in the peak period during and immediately after harvesting crops. For example, Exhibit 4 shows how volume and complexity affected unit case costs for bean products. The traditional cost system had indicated the same cost per case for the five bean products shown in Exhibit 4.

Based on the insights from the ABC analysis, Green Giant management closed about a half-dozen plants and consolidated operations more efficiently in the remaining plants. Crowley then took on a broader finance role within Pillsbury as Operations Controller and extended the ABC analysis to many of the dough manufacturing plants. The traditional cost system in these plants (like in the Green Giant plants) had been reporting a constant labor and overhead cost per case across all the cake mixes produced in a plant. The ABC analysis (see Exhibit 5) indicated a more than 3:1 cost variation in the various cake mixes. At the high end were the low-volume complex cake mixes, some of which required hand-insertion of a pouch of special ingredients. At the low cost end were the high-volume standard cake mixes that could be produced efficiently on the plant's machinery (see Exhibit 6).

Jerry Young, ABC director at Pillsbury, saw an immediate impact from the analysis:

> The ABC information really seemed to energize people. They could now look at the relationship between gross margin and volume by individual product lines. Particularly surprising was one type of cake mix that was high volume but was unprofitable even after the ABC analysis because it required special colors and package inserts.

The project team prepared the classic ABC "whale curve" (see Exhibit 7) which showed a few product lines producing all the profits, with the remaining SKUs either breaking-even or losing money. The message from the ABC analysis was reinforced when Young lined up consumer complaints with the profitability analysis (see Exhibit 8). Few complaints had been received for the high-volume profitable products. Most of the complaints were concentrated in the breakeven or loss product-lines. These products were both more complex to produce and produced in standard batch sizes that greatly exceeded near-term demand. As a consequence, the low-volume products stayed in inventory for a long time and their shelf aging led to a poor-tasting final product. Thus many of the product lines were not only losing money, they were also hurting the brand image.

The ABC approach received even greater visibility when Debrowski was handed, from Marketing, a directive to add more than 100 new SKUs to the production line-up at a time when Debrowski was under pressure from corporate management to reduce significantly his production costs. The sales mentality in the company was that new items generated additional sales without adding to operating expenses. Debrowski requested and received from the ABC team, an estimate of the large increase in the so-called fixed costs that would be caused by the introduction of the more than 100 new products. A much greater awareness in the company had now been created on the cost impact of volume, product complexity (such as color, and special pouches and inserts), and SKU proliferation. As a result of this work, an SKU rationalization program was initiated, which eventually became part of the reengineering effort.

Dan Crowley's responsibility, however, remained within the manufacturing organization:

> We now had good insights about the cost drivers for our cost of goods sold. The weak link was developing comparable information for our warehouse, sales, marketing, and promotion expenses. We had no ability to trace these expenses to our customers so that we could produce individual customer P&L's.

Marketing and Sales Performance Measurement

During the 1980s, Robert Slocumb, then Director, Technical Services, had been a leading advocate for applying Total Quality Management principles in the company. TQM at Pillsbury during the 1980s had, as its principal accomplishment, the establishment of Statistical Quality Control programs in manufacturing.

In April 1992, Rob Hawthorne, President of Pillsbury's Baked Goods Division, appointed Slocumb to a corporate position as Vice President of Continuous Improvement. Slocumb was tasked with developing measures for marketing and sales that would drive improvement efforts. Hawthorne had been a proponent of TQM/continuous improvement in his previous position as President of the ALPO pet food division and he wanted to disseminate these ideas more broadly within Pillsbury.

Executive management, however, remained skeptical that TQM was delivering its promised benefits to the P&L bottom line within a reasonable time frame. For example, an internal study compared companies known to have adopted TQM principles with a control sample of "non-TQM" companies. The study found no discernible difference in financial performance between the two sets of companies. If TQM was to become part of Pillsbury's culture, it would have to be positioned as an effective management strategy, capable of significantly impacting the P&L. He quoted Gandhi as he described his approach:

> "If you want to change a culture, you must first adopt its value system."

Slocumb realized that he would have to:

1. Develop a sound business case for the initiatives using the values of the organization.
2. Document the benefits that would flow from the initiatives.

Slocumb and Crowley soon discovered that even though they came from different parts of the organization (Crowley from Operations, Slocumb from Marketing & Sales), they shared common values and had a common mission. Slocumb reflected:

> Dan brought a process mind-set from his work with activity-based costing. My process mind-set was imbedded from more than a decade of total quality management initiatives. Dan had already imbedded ABC thinking into much of the manufacturing organization but could not get past the organizational wall to incorporate the marketing, sales, and distribution organizations. I had responsibility for improving marketing and sales performance, but the TQM lesson was that significant P&L benefit could only come from optimizing the broader customer value chain. We decided to combine, as a two-person team, to see if we could launch an effort that would bring substantial bottom-line benefits to the entire organization.

Launching the Reengineering Program

In August 1993, Crowley and Slocumb took a proposal to CEO, Paul Walsh's, Strategy and Policy Group, which comprised the division presidents of Pillsbury's major business units and the top functional department heads.

The proposal identified a process which would complement Pillsbury's existing strategic plan to achieve top quartile financial performance amongst its strategic peers. The vision was contained in a diagram from a McKinsey study that would soon be published in the *Harvard Business Review*.[1] Based on an analysis of 20 reengineering projects, this study claimed that most of the companies used only narrow TQM-type process improvements. For these companies, the effort produced substantial cost savings in isolated processes, but negligible benefits relative to total business-unit operating expenses. For six of the 20 companies, however, the reengineering effort had produced dramatic, 13–22%, cost savings for the entire business-unit. Those companies that had produced these remarkable success stories had two features in common:

1. the projects encompassed one or more processes that contained most of the critical activities in the business unit; and,

[1]Gene Hall, Jim Rosenthal, and Judy Wade, "How to Make Reengineering *Really* Work," *Harvard Business Review* (November–December 1993), pp. 120.

2. the projects restructured not just one but several of the key drivers of individual and organizational behavior: roles and responsibilities, measurements and incentives, organizational structure, information technology, shared values, and skills.

Crowley and Slocumb's vision of a potential for 15% cost improvement (about $300 million) in a staid and mature food processing company was met with some understandable skepticism and disbelief. Despite that, Walsh and his management team provided to Crowley and Slocumb a modest budget and 90 days to develop a business case to determine whether a $300 million cost reduction was possible. Crowley was appointed to a new position, Vice President for Customer Driven Reengineering, and Slocumb became Vice President for Business Process Reengineering. The business case was to focus on cost and margin improvements in three major divisions: Pillsbury branded products, the Green Giant products, and the frozen pizza businesses. These businesses had $2.5 billion of sales in Fiscal Year 1994.

Reengineering: Phase I

The Pillsbury team selected a consulting firm to work with them to help build the business case. Three months of analysis led to identifying three core business processes that offered targets for improvement:

- Customer Supply Chain
- Brand Management
- New Product Commercialization

This list represented the cross-functional organizational processes, from suppliers through customers and consumers, where reengineering offered the opportunity for substantial cost reduction and margin improvement. The study soon focused on the first item in the list, the Customer Supply Chain since this process accounted for more than 85% of operating expenses (see Exhibit 9). The Customer Supply Chain (CSC) was decomposed into three sub-processes:

TOTAL CUSTOMER DEVELOPMENT INITIATIVES	GROSS MARGIN IMPROVEMENT ($ MILLION).	
	REVENUE	COST
Reengineer trade planning and analysis; Target promotional spending to eliminate trade spending inefficiencies.	—	$24–30

continued

Develop planned customer segmentation strategies to define capability requirements and drive cross-functional resource deployment	—	—
Reengineer customer relationships: fact-based selling, better focus of resource teams across customers, deliver value to key strategic customers to build stronger trade relationships	$11–19	$ 6–11
TOTAL	**$11–19**	**$30–41**

- Total Customer Development
- Fast Flow Demand Replenishment
- Value Based Sourcing and Supply

The team then proceeded to identify the opportunities for process improvement within each of the three CSC sub-processes.

Total Customer Development   Three improvement initiatives were identified within the Total Customer Development process (see table below).

Fast Flow Demand Replenishment   The analysis of the Fast Flow Demand Replenishment sub-process identified the savings that could be realized by better matching Pillsbury's purchasing, manufacturing, and distribution operations to consumers' purchases. The cost of not having a synchronized supply chain were readily apparent. Exhibit 10 shows enormous bulges and fluctuations in Pillsbury's inventory to supply a relatively constant rate of consumer purchases. The inventory bulges were especially severe in low volume SKUs. The inventory accumulation could be causally related to excessive costs in manufacturing, warehousing, and financing, plus the risk of stale products when they were eventually purchased and (even later) consumed. The team identified more than $30 million of potential savings from reengineering the physical supply chain:

FAST FLOW DEMAND REPLENISHMENT INITIATIVES	MARGIN IMPROVEMENT	INVENTORY
Inbound/Outbound Transportation: Manage the transportation of purchased materials as part of the total logistics network	$ 8.0	

continued

General & Administrative: Reduced transactions processing in a reengineered supply chain will reduce demands for G&A resources	7.0	
Finished Goods Inventory: Increase flexibility of manufacturing processes and effectiveness of production planning process	1.0	$10
Unsaleables: Expand continuous replenishment to reduce obsolescence and stale product	10.6	
Distribution Center: Streamline warehouse and distribution management; flexible operations to serve a wide variety of customer types	2.0	
Other miscellaneous initiatives (including revenue enhancements)	$ 6.4	
TOTAL SAVINGS	**$37.0**	**$10.0**

Value Based Sourcing and Supply

The third CSC sub-process, Value Based Sourcing and Supply, focused on Pillsbury's extremely complex system of vendors and sourcing arrangements for its more than $500 million of raw material purchases. The system encompassed:

- 1200+ different material specifications (recently reduced from more than 1900)
- 260 vendors (recently reduced from more than 400)
- Complex recipes and ingredient specifications
- Arm's-length, price-sensitive relationships with vendors; virtually no technology or information integration with vendors

Historically, Pillsbury had reduced its material costs by exerting price pressure on its suppliers. Further gains from such price pressure were considered limited. The project team believed that more flexible and robust ingredient specification would allow them to select more efficient vendors, and that additional gains could be realized by leveraging vendor resources and knowledge. To gain these benefits, however, vendors would have to become partners with Pillsbury in a total cost reduction process. Cost savings from Value Based Sourcing and Supply were estimated at about $40 million (around 8% of purchases), plus savings in working capital reduction of about $14 million.

By the end of the 90 day Phase I effort, the Pillsbury project team and consultants had developed a business plan that promised margin improvements through cost reductions and revenue enhancements of more than $100 million, plus reductions in working capital of about $25 million.

Reengineering: Phase II

Phase II was launched in January 1994 to determine whether the business case developed in Phase I was feasible and realistic. About 25 Pillsbury employees, supported by the external consultants, spent four months analyzing customer data bases on more than 100 top accounts, conducting in-depth interviews with key customers and suppliers, and mapping and assessing the state of all existing internal business processes in the customer supply chain. The study of internal processes revealed highly complex, time-consuming processes with dozens of handoffs, and multiple recycling of requests for decisions and resource authorizations. The customer interviews revealed that important food retailers, wholesalers, and brokers were moving aggressively forward with plans for category management. Category management promised to give retailers far more effective management capabilities over their store shelf space allocations, SKU rationalization, and demographic marketing plans.[2]

The Phase II studies confirmed the vision established at the end of Phase I (see Exhibit 11) that reengineering the customer supply chain could provide upwards of $100 million in benefits. About half would come from working more closely with customers—adopting a more focused customer segmentation strategy, targeted marketing using local demographic information on consumer purchasing behavior, and exploiting store-specific cost and profitability information to promote the most profitable mix of brands and SKUs for both Pillsbury and the local store. The other half would come from better managing Pillsbury's entire supply chain—from growers and other key vendors, through manufacturing, transportation and distribution to warehouses and individual stores.

The first half of the savings, improving the customer development stream, would clearly require the capability for much more accurate cost and profitability measurement. Dan Crowley envisioned developing these measurements in cooperation with retailers:

> We will need to take activity-based costing (ABC) down to retail store level P&Ls. We want to be able to understand the costs of work that the trade does and what Pillsbury does if we are to end up with a highly efficient system that lowers costs and raises profits to all the parties. The cost measurement process must move forward to the point-of-sale and encompass all costs in the process to reach that point. We can not be satisfied just by measuring Pillsbury's costs up to the loading dock. The cost measurement process must move backwards, as well, to our raw material suppliers.
>
> This will require a big change in our thinking of how Pillsbury works with its trade customers, and how retailers will work with their consumers. The old financial model calculated standard costs per case and produced product line P&Ls. The new model will measure activity-based costs of entire processes and give us customer P&Ls.

McWilliams concurred with Crowley's new vision for using activity-based cost information to redefine customer relationships:

> We should be shifting our pricing focus so that we can charge more for special services that some of our customers may desire but that others do not want. We can define a base level of service that everyone receives, with an explicit statement of what that includes. Then we can develop service-based pricing for special customer-desired initiatives like category management, modular pallets for promotions, direct store delivery, cross-docking, one-way pallets, and other delivery options all of which save the retailer money. Alternatively, when Pillsbury does all these services, we can negotiate with the retailer to pass on the savings by lowering the prices of our products to their consumers and by special merchandising and promotion of our products.
>
> Or a retailer may come back to us and say, look, we're not doing any coupon redemption and we're stocking only 30 SKUs. This saves Pillsbury some money, and we want some price breaks in exchange. To make these partnerships work, both companies will require activity-based cost systems to keep track of cost incurrence and cost savings. It won't work if retailers continue to peanut-butter their operating expenses across all suppliers, brands, and SKUs. We should be capturing the cost from the point-of-sale, not just from the loading dock.

The second half of the proposed savings, achieved by reengineering the supply chain, would also require a major change in measurement. Steve Gartner, Vice President of Logistics, saw the need for new performance measurements for the organization:

---

[2]Category Management was a key component in the Efficient Consumer Response program. It was a process by which retailers would achieve their marketing, merchandising, sales, margin and profit objectives by managing product groups as strategic business units, focused on delivering consumer value (see "A user's guide to Efficient Consumer Response," *Grocery Marketing* (August 1993), pp. 14–15.

Our performance measurements will need to be driven by customers' and consumers' expectations. In the past, we forecasted what we thought the customer wanted in terms of service. We considered a 95% fill rate of customers' orders to be OK. But this still led to a lot of out-of-stock of our products on store shelves. New systems should enable us to achieve 100% on-shelf availability. We will need to tighten our parameters of what acceptable on-time-delivery means, perhaps from days to minutes. Cycle time, from receipt of order for delivery to actual delivery to customer will be critical. This will increase our expectations of performance from our raw material suppliers and our distribution companies.

Reengineering: Meeting the Challenge

In June 1994, the Pillsbury team had completed the customer analysis and was ready to move into redesign. Before the meeting to present the findings and recommendations to the Integration Committee, Slocumb expressed some concern about the current set of recommendations.

The business case to achieve $100 million in cost savings and margin enhancements is now credible. But the target may be too reachable. People may obtain the $100 million in cost savings from local process improvements, not from the complete redesign of our high-level business processes that we described in Phase I. Our present target of $100 million has come to be the objective rather than the fundamental redesign of our Customer Supply Chain.

Slocumb emphasized:

We initiated this project with a vision of achieving the 13–22% gains, $300 million, based on the benchmarks reported in the HBR article. We won't be able to achieve such a dramatic improvement just by making local processes more efficient. We are going to challenge the committee to question what our objectives should be from the project: a definite commitment to realize $100 million in cost savings, or a commitment to completely redesign our core business processes with an expectation that in several years we should be realizing $300 million in annual margin improvement.

Post-Meeting Discussion

Slocumb commented after the meeting:

Initially, the Integration Committee felt betrayed by our proposal for a $300 million target. They had signed up for a $100 million project and now we were saying that was not enough. We pointed out, however, that $100 million represented about 5% of our Customer Supply Chain cost base—well short of our initial objectives and our Reengineering benchmarks. The issue is not what we're going to do, but the degree to which we'll do it. For example, our

Fast Flow Demand Replenishment initiative is all about moving from a "push" (forecast-driven) system to a "pull" (demand-driven) system. Supporting a $100 million objective might mean increasing inventory turns somewhat whereas a $300 million objective might require a true point-of-sale driven replenishment cycle. Same headlines—very different outcomes.

Tom Debrowski, Senior Vice President of Operations and Chairman of the Integration Committee, supported expanding the project's scope to the (apparently) more ambitious target:

If we get $100 million in benefits, that's certainly a worthy goal, but it will not redefine the organization. We have a choice whether to be a company with a $25 stock price, or take the actions that will take us to a $50 stock price.

Larry McWilliams, who had led the Customer-Driven Analysis, had also bought into the more ambitious target:

We're at a cross-roads. Are we in a continuous improvement mode or in a radical re-design mode? I now believe that we can get the $100 million by "skinnying-up" today's organization, exploiting continuous improvement and best practices. But what will we do after that?

We should be re-designing the organization around customer and consumer values to create a new and sustainable competitive advantage. We should strive to be the best in providing the freshest product at the lowest cost to retailers along with unique consumer insights from our superior information systems.

John Mann concurred with adopting a much more aggressive target:

We can achieve the $100 million without redefining the way we do business. But to achieve the $300 million, we will have to become a very different supply organization. We will have to get the supply chain to a high level of competitive fitness by getting cost savings that will make us more efficient than our competitors, and, then generating growth through our value-added consumer insights, getting the right product to the shelf at the right time at low cost to the retailers.

The largest barrier for achieving this level of competitive fitness is introducing and managing change. Having a single sales-person calling on a customer will cease. Why should we be sending a $60,000 per year MBA to stock shelves? Multi-skilled, multi-functional teams, including finance, need to be working with our customers.

Steve Gartner reinforced stretching for the more ambitious goal:

Many companies view reengineering as just a cost cutting exercise. They cut people first and then attempt to redesign their processes. We should start with a clean slate. We need to start by understanding our existing processes, but then we must re-design them so that they are more effective, more timely and much less costly.

To achieve the $300 million improvements, we'll need to approach the organization with a completely open mind, to think the unthinkable. It will force us to think completely out of the box if we are going to achieve benefits of that magnitude. We need to stop managing individual functional departments, and begin to manage core operating processes.

We always talked about flowing our products through pipelines, but we operated with functional silos that optimized their own processes. And not just us but our suppliers and customers as well—with the old model, the manufacturer, the distributor, and the retailer each attempts to optimize its own operations. The new way, through reengineering, should enable us to optimally source raw materials, convert to finished goods, distribute to trade customers, and sell to consumers in ways that minimize total system cost. By determining who can do each process in the chain most efficiently, we can let that process get done only once, at the most efficient site. That way we can eliminate waste from the system. In the best scenario, the redesigned processes will generate growth that creates new opportunities for personnel, such as in customer-focused teams.

Crowley felt this initiative would extend the cultural change now occurring in the organization:

During the last three years, the entire strategic direction of the company has changed. Selling off the flour mills was an epochal event. It was a major cultural shock to many people inside and outside the organization who thought of us as a vertically-integrated flour manufacturing company. We have demonstrated that we can become a consumer-based company that is prepared to get out of operations that do not add value.

Tom Debrowski concluded:

The last three months of effort have demonstrated that what once seemed possible, less than a year ago, now seems likely, maybe too likely. So why not set the target higher, and attempt to achieve it through competitive fitness and growth, not just cost savings.

This is the most exciting thing we've seen in the food industry in 25 years. Selling our flour milling business has given us confidence that we can change our historical strategy and mindset. We have lots of local enthusiasm and support from our GrandMet parent who is looking for us to show the way for the entire corporation. Our customers are enthusiastic about shifting from changing the way we do business together and are willing to endorse new relationships, such as service-based pricing.

Our group now needs to go back to the drawing board and develop the business case for how to achieve $300 million in improvement. We will meet in about three months to assess whether we're ready to go ahead for the big deal.

EXHIBIT 1 Pillsbury's Financial Summary*

	FY 1981	FY 1982	FY 1983	FY 1984	FY 1985	FY 1986**	FY 1987
Net Sales	$3,302	$3,385	$3,686	$4,172	$4,671	$5,848	$6,128
Cost of Sales	2,388	2,390	2,590	2,953	3,293	4,103	4,292
Sales & General Expenses	647	728	827	872	985	1,271	1,388
Net Income	$ 120	$ 136	$ 139	$ 170	$ 192	$ 208	$ 182

*Million dollars
**Reflects change in accounting for pensions

EXHIBIT 2 Grandmet's Financial Summary*

GRAND METROPOLITAN	FY 1989	FY 1990	FY 1991	FY 1992	FY 1993
Sales	£ 9,298	£ 9,394	£ 8,748	£ 7,913	£ 8,120
Operating Profit	911	1,013	1,020	937	1,035
Net Income	1,219	963	441	913	630

*Million pounds

Historic Supply Chain Design Characterized by "Functional Silos"

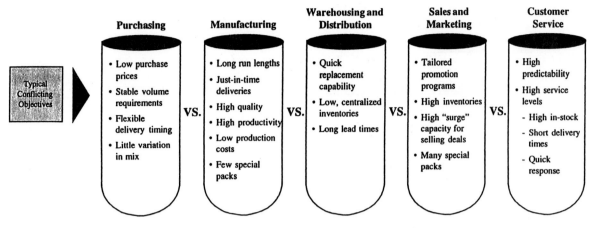

EXHIBIT 3

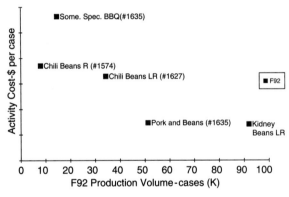

EXHIBIT 4   Plant ABC Analysis

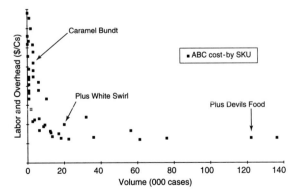

**EXHIBIT 5   ABC Conversion Cost—Cakes
(Includes Plus, Bundt, Strudel)**

Cakes - Production Cost Drivers

Volume		

Cases / month	Typical Conversion cost	Additional Cost per case
> 10,000	100 %	
5,000	118%	+ 15%
1,000	142%	+ 30%
500	182%	+ 45%

Why: - Changeover costs become significant
- QA costs do not decrease linearly with volume
- Tracking, scheduling, accounting, and reporting of SKU is batch-oriented
  (lower volumes=smaller run size)
- Lines not effectively utilized

EXHIBIT 6

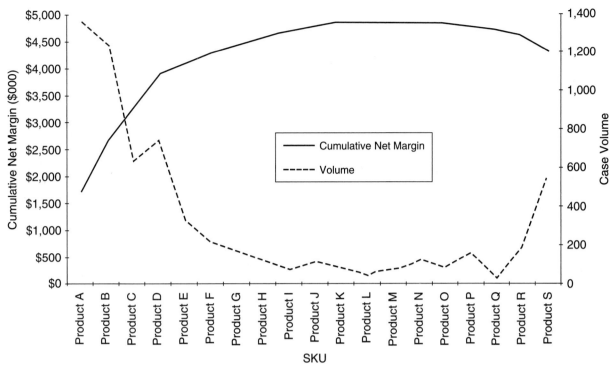

Note: Volumes are annualized from F93 production actuals Oct-Feb; product costs based on ABC data for period. All other costs based on F93 QF3 averages for group.

EXHIBIT 7   Cumulative Net Margin by SKU vs. Volume

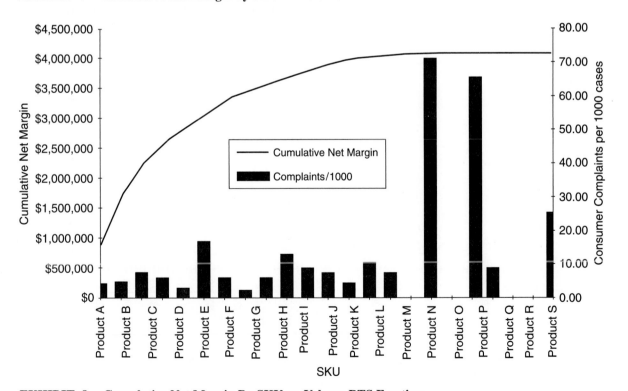

EXHIBIT 8   Cumulative Net Margin By SKU vs. Volume RTS Frosting

The scope of this initiative was the Customer Supply Chain. As defined, this supply chain represents 85% of the GMFAX total cost base.

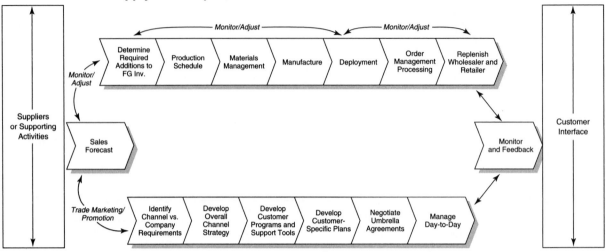

EXHIBIT 9

Functional excellence alone will not eliminate the cross-functional impacts of independent decisions. For example, trade promotions send ripples throughout the supply chain.

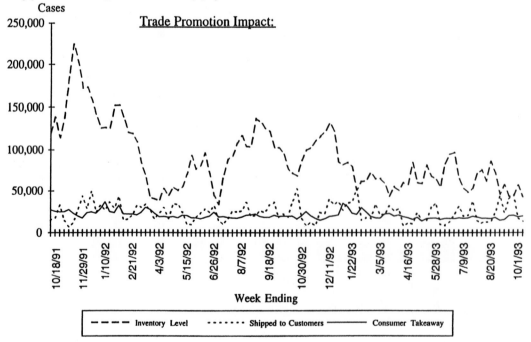

EXHIBIT 10

Customer Driven Reengineering   Learnings to Date

Developing "Make to Consumer Take Away" and "Consumer Focused Trade Alliance" capabilities will significantly improve the bottom line.

Customer Supply Chain Key Capabilities

CONSUMERS

| V E N D O R S | MAKE TO CONSUMER TAKE AWAY
Synchronized Business Flow
Flow Through Planning
Need Based Capabilities
Direct Response
Vendor Alignment | CONSUMER FOCUSED TRADE ALLIANCES
Consumer Based Planning
Service Based Pricing
Front-Line Decision Making
Fact Based Selling/Category Management |

CUSTOMERS

ONE HUNDRED MILLION DOLLAR BENEFIT

•Significant Business Opportunity Exists
•Business Case is Fundamentally Sound
•Early Implementation Opportunities are Under Way

EXHIBIT 11

SENECA FOODS

Seneca Foods is a regional producer of low-priced private-label snack foods. Seneca contracts with local supermarkets to supply good-tasting packaged snack foods that the retailers sell at significantly lower prices to price-sensitive consumers. Because Seneca's production costs are low, and it spends no money on advertising and promotion, it can sell its products to retailers at much lower prices than can national-brand snack food companies, such as Frito-Lay. The low purchase prices often allow the retailer to mark this product up and earn a gross margin well above what it earns from brand products, while still keeping the selling price to the consumer well below the price of the brand products.

Seneca has recently been approached by several large discount food chains who wish to offer their consumers a high-quality but much lower-priced alternative to the heavily advertised and high-priced national brands. But each discount retailer wants the recipe for the snack foods to be customized to its own tastes. Also, each retailer wants its own name and label on the snack foods it sells. Thus, the retailer, not the manufacturer, would be providing the branding for the private-label product. In addition, the retail chains want their own retailer-branded product to offer a full snack product line, just as the national brands do.

Seneca's managers are intrigued with the potential for quantum growth by becoming the prime producer of retailer-brand snack foods to large, national discount chains. As they contemplated this new opportunity, Dale Williams, the senior marketing manager, proposed that if Seneca enters this business, it can think of even higher growth opportunities. Seneca does not have to sell just to the discount chains that have approached it. Local supermarket chains may also be attracted to the idea of having their own brand of high-quality but lower-priced snack products that could compete with the national brands, not just be a low-priced alternative for highly price-sensitive consumers. Perhaps Seneca could launch a marketing effort to regional supermarket chains around the country for a retail-brand snack food product line. Williams noted, however, that the local supermarket chains were not as sophisticated as the national discounters in promoting products under their own brand name. Each supermarket chain likely would need extensive assistance and support to learn how to advertise, merchandise, and promote the store-brand products to be competitive with the national-brand products.

John Thompson, director of logistics for Seneca Foods, noted another issue. The national-brand producers used their own salespeople to deliver their products directly to the retailer's store and even stocked their products on the retailer's shelves. Seneca, in contrast, delivered to the retailer's warehouse or distribution center, leaving the retailer to move the product to the shelves of its various retail outlets. The national producers were trying to dissuade the large discount chains from following their proposed private-label (retailer-brand) strategy by showing them studies that the apparently higher margins they would earn on the private label would be eaten away by much higher warehousing, distribution, and stocking costs for these products.

Heather Gerald, the controller of Seneca, was concerned with the new initiatives. She felt that Seneca's current success was due to its focus. It currently offered a relatively narrow range of products aimed at the high-volume snack food segments to supermarket chains in its local region. Seneca got good terms from its relatively few suppliers because of the high volume of business it did with each of them. Also, the existing produc-

tion processes were efficient for the products and product range currently produced. She feared that customizing products for each discount or supermarket retailer, plus adding additional products so that they could offer a full product line, would cause problems with both suppliers and the production process. She also wondered about the cost of providing new services, such as consulting and promotions, to the supermarket chains and of developing some of the new items required for the proposed full product line strategy. Heather was attracted to the growth prospects offered by becoming the preferred supplier to major discount and supermarket chains. But she was not as optimistic as Dale Williams that these retailers truly believed that selling their own private-label foods would be more profitable than selling the national brands. Perhaps they were only using Seneca as a negotiating ploy, threatening to turn to private labels to increase their power in setting terms with the national manufacturers. Once production geared up, how much volume would these retailers provide to Seneca? How could Seneca convince the large retailers about the profitability associated with the new private-label strategy?

Gerald knew that Seneca's existing cost systems were adequate for their current strategy. Most expenses were related to materials and machine processing, and these costs were well assigned to products with their conventional standard costing system. But the new strategy would seem to involve a lot more spending in areas other than purchasing materials and running machines. She wished she knew how to provide input into the strategic deliberations now under way at Seneca, but she didn't know how to quantify all the effects of the proposed strategy.

WINCHELL LIGHTING, INC. (A)

Introduction

In January 1986, Ken Johnson, Vice-President and General Manager of Winchell Lighting, Inc. (WLI), assigned Pamela Wright, Marketing Analyst, and Elizabeth Conrad, Division Controller, to undertake the 1985 WLI Strategic Marketing Analysis. The Strategic Marketing Analysis effort arose from a collaboration, starting in 1982, between WLI management and the members of the planning group of WLI's parent, Hawkes. The goal was to trace marketing costs to individual product lines and channels so that the overall profitability of each line and channel could be determined.

Company Background

Winchell Lighting, Inc. manufactured and sold lighting fixtures. Consumer lines were sold through mass merchandisers and wholesale suppliers. Commercial products were sold through contract distributors and industrial suppliers. In 1985, WLI had total revenues of $128 million, generating an operating profit before taxes of $11 million (Exhibit 1).

Product Lines

The company manufactured thousands of different products, segmented into eight distinct product lines.

1. Consumer Incandescent Fixtures contained a broad range of fixtures designed specifically for easy installation in the residential market. They were all surface mounted, requiring no carpentry work. The products included pendants, close-to-ceiling fixtures, and chandeliers. Residential units were manufactured to less demanding standards than commercial fixtures and were considerably cheaper.
2. Consumer Fluorescent Fixtures contained a small range of surface-mounted fixtures designed specifically for the residential market.
3. Commercial Recessed Fixtures contained fixtures for incandescent bulbs designed to be recessed into the ceiling.
4. Commercial Fluorescent Fixtures contained fixtures for fluorescent lighting designed to be recessed into the ceiling.
5. Commercial Track contained both tracks and the fixtures designed to be attached to the tracks. Tracks were lengths of plastic tubing into which the fixtures could be snapped. Track lighting used conventional incandescent, tungsten-halogen and, recently, compact fluorescent lighting.

6. Commercial Ceiling Fixtures contained high-quality ceiling-mounted fixtures that had a high artistic content.
7. Commercial Wall Fixtures contained a diverse set of fixtures that were wall mounted. Many of these fixtures used the new compact, energy-efficient fluorescent light sources.
8. Commercial External Fixtures contained fixtures specifically designed for external use. These fixtures were of heavy construction to withstand weather conditions that required waterproof electrical connections.

Competitive Environment

Sales to the consumer markets generated about 15% of Winchell's total dollar volume (see Exhibit 2). WLI was the only company in the two almost independent consumer segments: fluorescent and incandescent. The fluorescent segment was dominated by three U.S.-based competitors—Gold, Conway, and Englehart—who together controlled about 70% of the market. The incandescent segment was more competitive, with three U.S. companies controlling about 70% and imports the other 30% of the market. Most of the U.S. companies used offshore sourcing to match the low cost of imported products.

The commercial market, accounting for the other 85% of Winchell's revenues, had three other full-line producers—Haddon, Conway, and Hobart—plus two companies, Somerset and King, that had gained a respectable percentage of the track and external fixture markets, respectively (see Exhibit 3).

Marketing Channels

The marketing department was organized along functional lines with separate departments for the three major business segments: Commercial Incandescent, Commercial Fluorescent, and Consumer Products. The Commercial Incandescent department was further split into two administrative areas—contract and industrial sales. The Fluorescent department supported a full line of fluorescent lighting fixtures and sold them to the commercial market through a separate sales force. The Consumer department had its own sales force, which sold consumer products to mass merchandisers and wholesale suppliers.

WLI sold its products through six distinct distribution channels. Two of these channels, mass merchandisers and wholesale suppliers, served the consumer market, and the other four served the commercial market.

This case was prepared by Professors Robin Cooper and Robert S. Kaplan. Copyright © 1987 by the President and Fellows of Harvard College. Harvard Business School case 187-074.

The channels differed considerably in the amount and method of selling effort required. The six channels were as follows:

1. **Mass merchandisers**—Mass merchandisers were the large-volume consumer outlets, such as K-Mart, Caldor, and Zayre, that sold directly to the public. They typically carried a small range of lighting fixtures. The mass merchandisers often promoted these products heavily, and WLI provided support for this activity. WLI favored these companies with a liberal returns policy and deep cash discounts. In 1985, mass merchandiser sales amounted to approximately $11 million.

2. **Wholesale suppliers**—Retail hardware chains (such as True Value and Ace) had formed cooperative associations to obtain bulk discounts based on their combined purchasing power. The associations used central warehouses to store their bulk-purchased merchandise that would be shipped, in small lots, to members on request. In 1985, WLI's sales to wholesale suppliers were $3 million.

3. **Contract distributors**—WLI provided complete lighting systems for commercial buildings. To compete in this market, WLI employed highly skilled marketing personnel who worked closely with architects. High-quality products and timely delivery were critical for this market segment.

   When an architect asked for a bid, the salesperson examined the architect's building plans and generated a complete list of lighting fixtures for the project. This activity required considerable knowledge of WLI's product lines and of local fire, building, and electrical codes. The end document provided a detailed specification for every fixture in a building. Contract sales were nearly $80 million in 1985.

   The recessed and fluorescent product lines' sales were not independent in the contract channel. Architects selected the types of fixtures that were to be used, usually a mixture of recessed and fluorescent lights. WLI had little real influence on the type of fixture selected.

4. **Industrial suppliers**—A large portion of the industrial supplier business was replacement of lighting fixtures. Building owners and operators purchased their lighting fixtures from two types of wholesalers. Master wholesalers, such as Mass Gas and Electric and Standard Electrical Supply, specialized in supplying lighting fixtures to smaller distributors, such as Mass Hardware, who carried a broad range of products for the building trade. Independent stores, such as Commonwealth Light in Boston, carried a large variety of fixtures sold directly to the end users. The independent stores demanded high-quality products and timely delivery but did not require specialized or customized products.

   Salespersons to industrial suppliers had to be well informed about the company's products. They regularly called on suppliers to take inventory, assist in the preparation of orders to keep the suppliers adequately stocked, and alert the suppliers about building code changes that would affect WLI products. Intermediary agents and distributors, if applicable, were also involved in this process.

In 1985, sales to suppliers totaled $25 million.

5. **Government**—The United States government occasionally requested a bid for very large volumes of fixtures. Over the years, WLI had not placed much effort into getting listed on the government's acceptable vendor lists. Sales in 1985 amounted to just over $400,000.

6. **Original equipment manufacturers (OEMs)**—Certain equipment manufacturers required special light fixtures for their products. For example, Sampson Furniture needed recessed fixtures for glass cabinets, and Lamb Cabinets required fluorescent fixtures for its aluminum and glass display cabinets. Since this kind of company was difficult to identify, WLI responded to bid requests but did not actively seek out the business. Once a contract was awarded, the OEMs typically sent in large orders at regular intervals. Sales in 1985 amounted to just over $9 million.

The Strategic Marketing Analysis

In 1982, WLI had adopted a product-channel perspective following a cost study performed with the assistance of the Hawkes Strategic Planning Group. Douglas Farish, Vice-President of Strategic Planning at Hawkes, commented on the process of developing the new product-channel perspective at WLI.

> In 1981, the Hawkes planning department initiated the development of a strategic data base by business segment. Each Hawkes business was partitioned into much finer segments than were reported by the existing accounting system. Only by disaggregating could we focus on economic units that were reasonably coherent—that is, units within which we had roughly the same share, perceived quality, and profitability.
>
> The existing accounting system, which broke the business into about 150 product groupings, failed to reflect the different costs of doing business in each distribution channel. With marketing expenses exceeding 15% of sales revenue, management wanted to know how each product line was performing in total and by channel. Thus, the product-channel perspective was developed.
>
> As we began the initial marketing cost analysis, we quickly learned that tracing period expenses was more difficult than allocating factory overhead. While in the factory, proxies for cost drivers can often be found where actual data do not exist, the same cannot be said of many selling, general, and administrative activities. To understand the economics of how work was generated in the SG&A departments, we relied heavily on the qualitative information stored in the heads of managers who were most familiar with the activity of each department. The art of this sort of analysis is to be able to quantify the qualitative, that is, to convert the qualitative insights of managers into a quantitative model.
>
> We organized a series of meetings to bring together a number of managers from a given function so that different

perspectives on the same issue could be represented. My primary function as moderator of these sessions was to pose the right questions so that we could discover the principal drivers of cost. I also synthesized the estimates given me and fed them back to the managers so that they could judge their reasonableness.

In addition to debriefing knowledgeable managers, we sampled the experience of the sales force to gather qualitative data for the model-building effort. Ultimately, I wanted WLI management to acquire the skill we had developed through experience in reducing soft data to a reasonably reliable model. This was important because the system needs to be revised periodically to reflect changes in the relative importance of the cost drivers and of our expenditure of effort among channels. The system therefore must not be rigid, but rather capable of evolving with the business.

By 1986, the company had developed specific procedures to facilitate the marketing cost study. The analysts started from a channel profitability report in which SG&A expenses were treated as a common or below-the-line cost and not allocated to individual product lines (see Exhibit 4). The difference in gross margins across the six channels reflected the margins earned over manufacturing costs on the products sold through each channel. In the past, if management wanted to know operating profit after fully allocating all costs, the cost analysts had allocated SG&A costs based on sales revenue. Since SG&A expenses were about 25% of sales revenue, the operating profit for each channel equalled the gross margin percentage less 25%.

Description of Marketing Expenses

The strategic marketing analysis attempted to trace more accurately the selling and marketing expenses to individual channels and product lines. The analysis started from detailed descriptions of each marketing expense category reported in the income statement (see Exhibit 5).

Commissions   WLI products were sold on a commission basis by independent manufacturers' representatives. These representatives often carried a complementary line of products manufactured by other firms, but they were not allowed to carry directly competitive products.

Representatives did not maintain an inventory. They sold to customers, and then WLI shipped the products directly to the customers. The manufacturing representatives received a 5% commission for incandescent products and up to 12 1/2 for fluorescent products. The

higher rate for fluorescent sales reflected an historical attempt to increase sales in certain fixture lines.

WLI commercial products were also sold by company personnel who received a flat 5% commission but no base salary. WLI paid benefits such as health, pension, and FICA. Sales personnel absorbed all travel expenses, including any automobile costs. In some instances, a ± 1/2% commission adjustment was made to compensate for the size of the salesperson's territory.

Catalog   The company published three catalogs: fluorescent commercial, incandescent commercial, and consumer. The commercial catalogs were published as three-ring binders to facilitate easy updating and insertion of new product descriptions. Because the product descriptions did not contain price data, the binder arrangement also allowed for price list supplements as required. WLI products were endorsed by *Sweet's Catalog*, the architect's reference manual for all building materials. WLI paid Sweet's to prepare and include separate subsections in the *Sweet's Catalog*.

WLI's contract sales business used the latest lighting technology and, therefore, required up-to-date commercial catalog information. Industrial suppliers also used the catalog, but since they concentrated more on the replacement business and only stocked bestsellers, they could use out-of-date catalogs with little risk. In both instances, products were ordered just as specified in the catalogs; unique designs could not be obtained. All WLI representatives kept copies of the catalogs and passed order requests through to WLI headquarters. Because of the large number of requests for the catalogs, no records were kept at headquarters or by representatives on where the catalogs were sent.

The WLI consumer catalog contained 8 to 10 pages listing all products sold in the mass merchandiser and wholesale supplier channels.

Advertising   Advertising expenditures were primarily the cost of advertisements in trade and industry publications, attendance at trade shows, and the costs of displays and exhibits. The firm placed advertisements in publications such as *Lighting Institute Magazine, Light Fixture Digest* (used by the supplier channel), *Discount News, Do It Yourself,* and the *Hardware Retailer*. Peripheral journals, such as *Architectural Record*, were not generally used.

Two of the most noteworthy trade shows attended were the Lighting Fixture Institute Show and the

National Hardware Show. The advertising expenses for these shows included registration fees and the costs of creating and installing the booths, exhibits, and displays.

Cooperative Advertising Cooperative advertising was directed to the consumer market. Mass merchandisers placed color pull-outs in Sunday newspapers. Local hardware stores placed smaller advertisements in local papers. Radio advertisements were used to announce promotions and special prices.

The Advertising Checking Bureau monitored advertising copy for WLI. It received a supply of slicks, a copy of the advertising bill, and a proof of the advertising. WLI then paid the advertisers for their costs up to a cap set at 5% of last year's sales.

Sales Promotion Sales promotions were used to increase sales in both the commercial and consumer markets. Some commercial promotions offered incentives to distributors to purchase WLI products by awarding points based on the number of specified product items ordered. These points were then exchangeable for gift certificates or merchandise at a major department store. Others offered baker's dozen sales, in which the distributor received, say, 12 products for the price of 10. The costs of such promotion schemes included developing, printing, and distributing brochures, mailings, and order forms.

Consumer promotions were product specific. They typically consisted of bakers' dozen or special discount offers to mass merchandisers and wholesale suppliers.

Warranty Warranty expenses were incurred on major contracts to overcome problems that could only be resolved in the field. Sales returns were not included in warranty expenses but were treated as a direct deduction from sales.

Sales Administration Sales administration expenses included costs that were too small to be treated as separate line items (see Exhibit 6).

Cash Discounts If WLI shipped before the twenty-fifth of the month and payment was received before the tenth of the following month, the customer could take a 2% discount. If WLI shipped after the twenty-fifth of the month, the discount could be taken if payment was received before the tenth of the second month. About 60% of goods were shipped during the first 25 days of each month.

Tracing Marketing Expenses

Wright and Conrad described the procedures they used for assigning marketing costs to the product lines and distribution channels.

PW The distribution of marketing expenses starts with the document describing each component of expense. It formed the basis for our analysis. After we were sure we understood how each expense behaved, we began to develop allocation routines. Obviously, we relied heavily on the procedures used in prior years.

EC Commissions were the simplest to handle. We traced commission payments to the various product lines and then allocated them to channels on the basis of the sales volume of product lines in each channel.

PW Catalog expense was slightly more difficult. We publish three catalogs, one for each of the three business segments. It is easier to talk about the commercial and consumer segments separately.

The WLI commercial catalogs are really a collection of mini product line catalogs that we combine together in a three-ring binder. This approach is economical because it allows us to change one product line catalog without replacing the others. Unfortunately, we do not keep development costs for each product line catalog separately, so we could not break it down any further than the catalog level. This forced us to estimate the relative share of catalog costs by product line and channel.

EC We used our knowledge of the business to guide us. For example, we knew that the incandescent commercial catalog is used in the contract and industrial supply channels. However, the contract business is always into new products, and it requires the most up-to-date catalogs; we are continuously sending them catalogs. The industrial supply channel is exactly the opposite. In the replacement business, the suppliers usually only stock a limited range of the bestsellers. These tend not to change from year to year, and consequently industrial suppliers are not bothered if their catalogs are not up to date.

PW In contrast, the *Sweets Catalog* is used only in the contract business. We simply took all of the associated costs for this catalog and assigned them to the contract channel.

For catalogs that covered several channels, we split catalog costs using the number of different outlets in each channel as the allocation base. We assigned catalog costs to the product lines on the basis of sales dollars in each channel.

We assigned the cost of consumer catalogs in the same way. The mass merchandisers only stock a limited range of products and do not need a large catalog. But the wholesalers, who stock our entire line, need full-line catalogs. Again, we used our knowledge of the number of outlets and the intensity of use in each channel to estimate their relative share of catalog costs.

EC Our catalogs do not contain price information because prices change more frequently than the contents of the catalogs. We issue a new price list whenever we want to change prices. The expense of printing and distributing these lists was assigned using the same ratios as we had identified for the catalogs themselves.

PW Commission and catalog expenses were relatively easy. Advertising, on the other hand, was more difficult because of the range of different activities we undertake. We broke advertising into two sections, trade and cooperative. These two types of advertising are quite different from each other.

EC Trade advertising in the industry magazines could be easily traced to the three business segments. First, we have project control over all advertising-related costs. Second, we advertise incandescent and fluorescent products separately. Third, the consumer market is reached by different magazines. The real problem was how to allocate the costs among the channels served by each magazine. We felt that some magazines really only served one channel. For example, *The Lighting Ledger* served industrial suppliers and *Discount Store News* reached mass merchandisers. Other magazines, for example, *Electrical Supplies*, covered several channels, in which case we estimated the relative benefit by channel and allocated the costs accordingly.

PW Cooperative advertising was completely different. First, it predominantly occurs in the two consumer channels, mass merchandising and wholesale suppliers. Second, the Advertising Checking Bureau invoices could be traced to each channel, which gave us an accurate measure of the advertising expenses in each channel.

Tracing channel advertising costs to product lines was more difficult. An advertisement often contained pictures of products from several product lines, and there was no easy way to determine how much benefit was attributable to each line. It was simply not practical to count square inches; in any case, in many ads, the largest image was the company name. The local radio spots suffered from the same problem. We were not going to count seconds, and anyway the company name was often the most prominent part of the ad.

EC In the end, we opted to use sales within the channel to allocate advertising costs to the product lines.

PW Sales promotions occur at the product and product line level, so we ended up adopting exactly the opposite ap-

proach than we had taken for advertising. Instead of tracing costs to the segments or channels, and then to product lines, we traced promotion costs first to products or product lines and then summed up the costs for each product line in a channel. This was relatively straightforward because we record promotion expenses by product code.

EC We used the same approach with warranty expenses. These occur when we have to go into the field and correct a problem that has developed in a large commercial contract. If the expenditure is above $10,000, then we open a special project. These expenses are easily traced to the channels in which they occurred. However, if the expenditure is below $10,000, then the costs are captured only by product line. These can be allocated to the channels on the basis of the sales of each product line in that channel.

PW Sales administration is a collection of nine relatively small expense categories. We had to deal with each one separately [Exhibit 7]. We were surprised by how much resources were required by some channels and not by others. The allocations all made sense after we looked at them; it was the magnitude of the effect that was unexpected.

EC Cash discounts were allocated to channels by selecting large representative accounts within each of the channels and determining their accounts-receivable-to-sales ratio. From these ratios, we computed the day's-sales outstanding (DSO). We used the DSOs to estimate the cash discounts in each channel.

EC After performing all the analysis, we produced two sets of reports. The first reported the marketing costs as a percentage of sales for each major product line [see Exhibit 8 for an example of the new report for the Commercial Track Lighting product line]. The second added up all the marketing costs in each of our six distribution channels to obtain a new Channel Profitability Report [Exhibit 9]. For the channel report, we also traced the utilization of net invested capital, including working capital items such as inventory and accounts receivable, to individual channels so that we could measure the return on capital for each channel.

PW The Channel Profitability Report is the most important. It demonstrates how significant the marketing cost analysis really is. The resulting channel profitabilities, returns on investment, and residual incomes are very different from what we used to think they were.

EXHIBIT 1

WINCHELL LIGHTING, INC. (A)

1985 Income Statement ($000)

Sales		$127,960	100%
Cost of sales			
Material	45,529		
Labor	7,082		
Overhead	32,393		
		85,004	67
Gross profit		42,956	33%
Sales and general administrative expenses			
Marketing expenses	20,953		
General/administrative	10,861		
		31,814	25%
Operating income		$11,142	8%

EXHIBIT 2

WINCHELL LIGHTING, INC. (A)

Market Share Analysis—Consumer Products

FLUORESCENT

	SHARE BY CHANNEL OF DISTRIBUTION					
COMPETITORS	MASS MERCHANDISERS	COMMERCIAL SUPPLIERS	CONTRACT	INDUSTRIAL SUPPLIERS	GOVERNMENT	OEM
WLI	15	25	10	10	25	15
Gold	30	25	30	25	20	25
Conway	20	20	10	20	20	30
Englehart	25	10	40	20	30	30
Gellis	10	20	10	25	5	0
% of WLI total product line sales	25	50	5	10	5	5

INCANDESCENT

	SHARE BY CHANNEL OF DISTRIBUTION		
COMPETITORS	MASS MERCHANDISERS	WHOLESALE SUPPLIERS	INDUSTRIAL SUPPLIER
WLI	20	20	20
Commonwealth	25	25	25
Celebrity	25	25	25
Imports	30	30	30
Percent of WLI total product line sales	30	50	20

EXHIBIT 3

WINCHELL LIGHTING, INC. (A)

Market Share Analysis—Commercial Products

RECESSED

COMPETITORS	SHARE BY CHANNEL OF DISTRIBUTION		
	MASS MERCHANDISERS	WHOLESALE SUPPLIERS	INDUSTRIAL SUPPLIER
WLI	15	15	15
Haddon	20	25	25
Hobart	20	10	10
Conway	20	30	30
Others	25	20	20
% of total product line sales	70	20	10

FLUORESCENT

COMPETITORS	SHARE BY CHANNEL OF DISTRIBUTION			
	CONTRACT	INDUSTRIAL SUPPLIER	GOVERNMENT	OEM
WLI	10	15	20	10
Haddon	45	45	35	75
Hobart	20	5	5	5
Conway	20	25	25	0
Others	5	10	15	10
% of total product line sales	40	25	15	20

TRACK

COMPETITORS	SHARE BY CHANNEL OF DISTRIBUTION			
	CONTRACT	INDUSTRIAL SUPPLIER	GOVERNMENT	OEM
WLI	20	20	20	
Haddon	20	20	20	
Hobart	20	20	20	
Conway	20	20	20	
Somerset	20	20	20	
% of total product line sales	60	25	15	

CEILING

COMPETITORS	SHARE BY CHANNEL OF DISTRIBUTION			
	CONTRACT	INDUSTRIAL SUPPLIER	GOVERNMENT	OEM
WLI	30	30	20	30
Somerset	50	50	50	50
Haddon	15	15	25	10
Other	5	5	5	5
% of total product line sales	30	20	20	30

WALL

	SHARE BY CHANNEL OF DISTRIBUTION		
	CONTRACT	INDUSTRIAL SUPPLIER	OEM
WLI	10	20	10
Conway	50	10	25
Haddon	25	40	50
Hobart	15	20	5
King	0	10	10
% of total product line sales	20	20	60

EXTERNAL

COMPETITORS	SHARE BY CHANNEL OF DISTRIBUTION			
	CONTRACT	INDUSTRIAL SUPPLIER	GOVERNMENT	OEM
WLI	50	50	60	50
Conway	30	30	5	30
Haddon	10	10	25	10
Other	10	10	10	10
% of total product line sales	20	20	45	15

EXHIBIT 4

WINCHELL LIGHTING, INC. (A)

Channel Profitability Report

(Existing System $000)

| | CONSUMER | | | COMMERCIAL | | | |
	MASS MERCHANDISING	WHOLESALE SUPPLIERS	CONTRACT	INDUSTRIAL SUPPLIERS	GOVERN- MENT	OEM	TOTAL
Net sales	10,694	3,120	79,434	25,110	402	9,200	127,960
Material	8,503	2,083	25,089	6,886	99	2,869	45,529
Labor	29	62	4,798	1,437	33	724	7,082
Overhead	150	268	22,172	6,503	154	3,146	32,393
Total	8,681	2,413	52,059	14,826	286	6,739	85,004
Gross profit	2,013	707	27,375	10,284	116	2,461	42,956
Gross margin	19%	23%	34%	41%	29%	27%	34%
SG&A							31,814
Operating profit							11,142
Profit margin							9%
Net invested capital							54,141
Return on investment							21%

EXHIBIT 5

WINCHELL LIGHTING, INC. (A)

Marketing Expenses by Category (000)

CATEGORY	1985 EXPENSES	%
Commission	$7,376	35
Advertising	230	1
Catalog	714	3
Co-op advertising	1,006	5
Sales promotion	1,132	5
Warranty	94	1
Sales administration	8,957	43
Cash discount	1,444	7
Total	$20,953	100

EXHIBIT 6

WINCHELL LIGHTING, INC.

Allocation of Sales Administration Expenses

Customer service. Customer service involved order entry and editing using an on-line system. The largest users were the industrial suppliers, who placed many small orders, thereby creating a lot of paperwork, and contractors, who, while only placing a small number of orders, required much telephoning back and forth to establish the correct mixture of products. Other users, such as the OEMs, mass merchandisers, and the government, required little attention.

Customer service expenses were allocated on the basis of management estimates. Contractor and industrial suppliers received the highest amounts because most of the customer service activity was concentrated in those two channels.

Marketing management. Marketing management expenses were the salaries of all of the managers in the marketing department.

Marketing management expenses were allocated proportionally to the time spent by the managers. For functional managers this was relatively easy because they were assigned to particular segments (e.g., a marketing manager and a sales manager). It was more difficult for support function managers because their activities were firm-wide (e.g., research manager and pricing manager). Where possible, the costs of these activities were traced to the channels. Otherwise, they were allocated on the basis of sales dollars.

Sales policy. Sales policy expenses arose from settling disputed claims. Mass merchandisers had the largest numbers of disputed orders, typically complaining about short shipments and other shipment mistakes. They used their large outstanding receivables balances as leverage against the firm and would withhold payment until all issues relating to the shipment were settled. The firm used a commonsense approach on whether to fight. Contractors similarly disputed pricing, shrinkage, and any shortages of the trivial accessories, such as screws, that accompanied their orders. Other channels, such as the industrial suppliers, raised similar issues but to a lesser extent.

Sales policy expenses were first traced to the three business segments and then allocated to the channels using managerial estimates. Within the channels, they were allocated to the product lines using relative sales dollars.

Marketing travel and entertainment. Marketing travel and entertainment expenses consisted of the travel expenditures of the marketing managers. The contract business required extensive travel because there were no regional managers; large individual contracters, the competitiveness of the business, and the technical complexity required a lot of handholding and entertainment by management. The other channels required relatively little travel, typically only for shows and other events.

Marketing travel and entertainment expenses were traced to the person that filed the expense report and hence to the business segment. Certain channels required more traveling than others—for example, the contractor channel, because there are no regional managers. These costs were allocated using a mixture of managerial estimates and sales lars.

Postage. The majority of postage expenditures were related to catalog mailings. They were allocated on the basis of the catalog expenses in each channel.

Administrative travel and entertainment. Administrative travel and entertainment expenses are the costs incurred when the director of marketing, the pricing manager, or marketing analyst traveled to meet contractors, mass merchandisers, and industrial suppliers. The three individuals that charge to this line item were asked to estimate the percentage of their share of these costs by channel.

Warehousing. Warehousing expenses were the costs of keeping finished goods inventory in the warehouse ready for shipment. These costs were allocated to the product lines based on the inventory level of each product line and to the channels by relative sales level.

Meetings. Meeting expenses were incurred for the firm's regular national sales meetings. The costs of national sales meetings were tracked to the three business segments and then allocated to the channels on the basis of managerial estimates.

Fixed expenses. Fixed expenses consisted of a number of different items such as depreciation; heat, light, and power; telephone; building maintenance; supplies and equipment rental charges.

The expenses were allocated to each segment by department using a number of different allocation routines and then to the channels using managerial judgment.

EXHIBIT 7

WINCHELL LIGHTING, INC. (A)

Allocation of Sales Administration Expenses to Channel

	CONSUMER (%)		COMMERCIAL (%)			
	MASS MERCHANDISING	WHOLESALE SUPPLIERS	CONTRACT	INDUSTRIAL SUPPLIERS	GOVERNMENT	OEM
Customer service	1	16	38	43	1	1
Marketing management	20	10	60	10	0	0
Sales policy	34	28	30	8	0	3
Marketing travel and entertainment	8	44	43	5	0	5
Postage	8	35	35	23	0	0
Administrative travel and entertainment	21	15	42	21	0	0
Warehousing	5	21	60	14	0	0
Meetings	12	12	42	35	0	0
Fixed expenses	13	18	50	20	0	0

EXHIBIT 8

WINCHELL LIGHTING, INC. (A)

Production and Marketing Costs as a Percent of Sales
Commercial Track Lighting

	DISTRIBUTION CHANNEL COMMERCIAL			
	CONTRACT (%)	INDUSTRIAL SUPPLIERS (%)	GOVERNMENT (%)	OEM (%)
Sales	100.0	100.0	100.0	100.0
Material	29.5	28.6	34.4	35.3
Labor	15.3	6.5	8.6	8.5
Overhead	25.1	22.0	33.0	28.2
Total	69.9	57.1	76.0	72.0
Gross margin	30.1	42.9	24.0	28.0
Commission	5.9	5.4	2.8	4.0
Advertising	0.2	0.2	0.0	0.0
Catalog	0.6	0.6	0.0	0.0
Co-op advertising	0.5	0.5	0.0	0.0
Sales promotion	0.5	0.5	0.0	0.0
Warranty	0.1	0.1	0.0	0.0
Sales administration	7.2	6.8	4.7	3.8
Cash discount	1.1	1.0	2.8	1.2
Total	16.1	14.7	10.3	9.1
General and administration	8.5	8.5	8.5	8.5
Profit margin	5.5	19.7	5.2	10.4

EXHIBIT 9
WINCHELL LIGHTING, INC. (A)
1985 Channel Profitability Report
(Marketing Cost Analysis)
($000)

	CONSUMER		COMMERCIAL				
	MASS MERCHANDISING	WHOLESALE SUPPLIERS	CONTRACT	INDUSTRIAL SUPPLIERS	GOVERNMENT	OEM	TOTAL
Net sales	10,694	3,120	79,434	25,110	402	9,200	127,960
Material	8,503	2,083	25,089	6,886	99	2,869	45,529
Labor	29	62	4,798	1,437	33	724	7,082
Overhead	150	268	22,172	6,503	154	3,146	32,393
Total	8,681	2,413	52,059	14,826	266	6,739	85,004
Gross profit	2,013	707	27,375	10,284	116	2,461	42,956
Gross margin	19%	23%	34%	41%	29%	27%	34%
Marketing Expenses							
Commission	696	270	4,682	1,344	12	372	7,376
Advertising	46	12	132	38	0	2	230
Catalog	36	14	504	160	0	0	714
Co-op advertising	380	90	416	120	0	0	1,006
Sales promotion	494	128	394	114	0	2	1,132
Warranty	2	2	64	22	0	4	94
Sales administration	908	268	5,696	1,714	20	351	8,957
Cash discount	118	56	892	252	12	114	1,444
Total	2,680	840	12,780	3,764	44	845	20,953
General and administration	907	265	6,740	2,131	36	781	10,860
Operating profit	(1,574)	(398)	7,855	4,389	36	835	11,143
Profit margin	−15%	−13%	10%	17%	9%	9%	9%
Net invested capital[1]	5,447	1,643	33,154	10,974	184	2,748	54,149
Return on investment	−29%	−24%	24%	40%	30%	30%	21%
Residual income	(2,936)	(809)	(433)	1,646	10	149	(2,374)

[1]Allocated on the basis of equipment utilized and working capital levels.

WINCHELL LIGHTING, INC. (B)

In spring of 1986, Ken Johnson, Vice-President of Winchell Lighting, Inc., Ted Phillips, Director of Marketing, Pamela Wright, Marketing Analyst, and Elizabeth Conrad, Division Controller, dicussed the overall value of the strategic marketing cost analysis.

KJ   We sell in several markets, using many distribution channels, each requiring different intensities and methods of selling. Prior to the marketing cost analysis, we virtually ignored the differential costs of marketing our products. We simply added all of the marketing expenses together and treated them as a below-the-line period cost. Our main focus was on gross margin, not on profit margin.

PW   The product line distribution channel perspective coupled to the marketing cost analysis provided a better way for us to analyze our business. The study influenced our strategic emphasis. We are now interested in distribution channels, such as government, that we previously ignored and are expending less effort in other channels, such as mass merchandising, that we no longer view as attractive.

TP   The study was important in helping us redirect our attention. It is now much easier for management to see things clearly at the divisional level without getting bogged down in the data. The greatest breakthrough is our ability to develop marketing strategies that take advantage of our knowledge of the business. For example, the study helped direct us to a new product, the budget recessed fixture line, and to a new distribution channel, the 100 top builders.

    The budget recessed fixture line is aimed at the low-cost end of the market. Our old perspective could have kept us out of the market because the gross margins there are lower than average. The new perspective shows, however, that these fixtures also have low period cost[1] and hence are attractive products.

    Similarly, we have aggressively approached the top 100 big residential builders. If we can break into that market by selling to them directly, we will have created a new commercial distribution channel.

    The additional insight provided by the study, that the channel costs would be low once the channel was established, enabled us to see this opportunity.

PW   We can now identify low-margin niches that we can service economically. We can also identify which product-channel combinations have high or low returns so that we can better manage the competitive environment to increase our long-term profitability. Take our reaction to the external fixture results. We knew we were making good profits but not to the extent we now believe.

KJ   Since the study, we have taken several strong actions in the marketplace to protect those products. We have increased the discount structure so that it is more difficult for our competitors to underprice us. We have added technical support so that we are providing a better service than our competitors and, finally, we have increased advertising. By this concerted set of actions, we aim to create entry barriers that keep our competitors out, while still allowing us to earn high profits. If we hadn't undertaken the analysis, we would not have acted so quickly or thoroughly, and we might have lost the advantage.

PW   We have also instituted some other pricing and discounting activities aimed at making certain products more attractive to our customers or reducing the loss on others. For example, we increased the discounts on the recessed lighting fixtures for insulated ceilings and reduced discounts on standard recessed. This made insulated ceiling models more competitive while increasing the margin on the standard units.

EC   I never really understood that action. I thought the sales of those products were so interconnected that it really doesn't make any difference if we move the discounts around. Each building needs a certain number of insulated and standard recessed fixtures, and the increased discounts on insulated tend to be balanced out by the decreased discounts on the standard line. The new discount structure is not going to change the mix of products sold. So why bother?

TP   There is some truth to that. But we want each product to stand on its own, and moving the discount around helps achieve that objective. Also, there are some independent sales of the various product lines, and we definitely do not want to sell those at a loss. It makes good sense to maintain a reasonable profit margin on as many products as possible.

PW   We have also increased profits by identifying products that are performing poorly and reviewing what actions we can take regarding them. For example, we discontinued the entire chandelier line and many of the less profitable products we manufacture for original equipment manufacturers (OEM). We also reengineered the fluorescent fixture lines, and they are now considerably cheaper to manufacture. They used to be poor performers; now they are very attractive products.

KJ   We should be careful not to overemphasize the effect of the study. We already had the fluorescent project in the pipeline. We knew that fluorescent fixtures were not making adequate profits and had begun to think about reengineering them. The analysis simply confirmed our fears and made us act that much quicker.

    This case was prepared by Professors Robin Cooper and Robert S. Kaplan. Copyright © 1987 by the President and Fellows of Harvard College. Harvard Business School case 187-075.

    [1]Period costs include marketing, sales, and general administration.

TP Also, while we got rid of the chandeliers, we still sell many other products that are not making an adequate profit. We can't drop them because they are a necessary part of our product offering. Take, for example, standard recessed fixtures. According to the study, we don't make money on them, but, given who we are, we have to continue to sell them. Our entire commercial market strategy is based on being a full-line producer.[2] We sell to customers who are undertaking large construction jobs that require a mixture of fixtures. If we dropped one of these fixture types, we would not be perceived as a full-line producer. If we cherry-pick our lines, we would no longer be competitive with the other full-line vendors.

KJ That is a more important point than it might at first seem. The strategy we have adopted, of being a full-line producer, is ingrained into the way we do business. It is reflected in our organizational structure, the way the sales force perceives the business, the channels we serve, and the customers we attract. Changing strategy requires that all of these elements be rethought and, if needed, changed. That is not an overnight process.

TP There are other factors that make it difficult to take advantage of the insights provided by the study. Take government sales, for example. We learned from the analysis that government business was attractive, and we started to promote it a couple of years back. But, if you look at the results, you would never guess we have changed our approach. First, in 1984, the business began to disappear. Then, in 1985, the government substantially decreased the number of bids it requested. This caused a lot of low-ball pricing, and we were not aggressive enough. Consequently, we only gained a small sales increase from the prior year. However, this year we are going to be really aggressive and expect to gain a major share of the market.

PW The biggest problem was the defense department. We used to have a 50% share in that market, but in 1985 this dropped to 25%. We expect to achieve about a 75% penetration in 1986.

TP The way the government channel reacted raises an important issue. You simply cannot use the information provided by the analysis without taking into account competitive forces. If our competitors decide to become more active and increase the level of advertising, discounting, or special offers, then we are often forced to do the same even if we have decided on a different strategy. You just cannot turn your back on a product because it is not super-profitable. Most of our products are part of an integrated marketing strategy, and we cannot afford to lose them.

KJ Remember, our competition is entrenched in the way they do business, and this makes it difficult for us to change our strategy. We keep having to compete with them in ways that are now fundamentally different from where we would want to go. It is just not possible, given our market position, to withdraw from many product markets.

TP You cannot overemphasize that point. The analysis has shown retail margins to be even worse than we had originally thought. On the surface, our best strategy would be to leave that market. But it is not that easy. A large amount of goodwill for the commercial business is generated by having the WLI name in the consumer market. You cannot put a dollar sign on it, but it's there. You simply cannot turn your back on history.

KJ When we reentered the consumer market, we effectively committed ourselves to it. You cannot afford to be seen as capricious in the marketplace. Our task is to find ways of making that business profitable.

PW We are not helpless, though. We have reduced the cooperative advertising cap from 5% to 3%, and this significantly reduces our expenditures on such advertising. We have also decided to put less effort into the wholesale supplier channel. It is by far the least profitable, and we intend to reduce the relative size of that channel.

KJ The practicalities of business stop us from reacting immediately to the insights provided by the marketing cost analysis. We cannot just drop products, change their prices, or close distribution channels without incurring a substantial penalty in the market as a whole. We are forced to be more subtle: We reduce activity in one market and increase it in another, or we shift discounts to make one product look more attractive and another less so. It would be naive to expect us to drop all poorly performing products. We drop what we can and try to improve the rest. It is a long, slow process, but I am convinced it is the right approach.

KJ That raises an important point. Demonstrating that the strategic marketing analysis has benefited the group is a difficult proposition. We have never really attempted to prove that the analysis made a difference. We simply reacted to it and, I think, in ways that make sense.

TP It is probably too soon to tell if it's had a beneficial effect. We have only been using this approach for two to three years, and we are still learning to take advantage of it. We have only just begun to alter our behavior. Two to three years may seem like a long time to implement a new approach, but it really isn't. First, it took us several years to create a reliable data base; in fact, we are still refining it. It's taken time to modify our data collection procedures to be able to measure accurately, maintain, and store the data required by the new strategic marketing analysis. Second, in the past, we have tended to act too quickly, and, with a project like this, that's dangerous. You rush to use the information provided by the study before you really understand it. This leads to poor decisions and a loss in commitment to the approach. This time, we have been very cautious in the way we have used the data.

---

[2] In this industry a full-line producer sells recessed, fluorescent, and track ceiling and wall fixtures.

PW   It is important to remember that the analysis is only part of what is going on at WLI. We are continuously reacting to changes in the competitive environment and, while the marketing analysis has had an effect, it is difficult to untangle that effect against the background of changing conditions.

KJ   We don't have special strategic marketing analysis meetings where we discuss the findings of the study each year, but that doesn't mean we don't pay attention to the study findings.

EC   One way you might detect the effect of the study across time is to look at the first marketing cost analysis that was completed. It restated the 1982 financials into approximately the same format [Exhibit 1]. Market conditions were different then, and it's not a case of simply comparing results, but it might provide you with some insights if you compare it to the latest analysis [Exhibit 2].

KJ   That might work, but the 1982 market was inherently more profitable. The previous four years had been very busy, and prices had risen correspondingly. The same isn't true of 1985. It is a better year than 1983 or 84 but not as good as 82.

EC   I agree it is difficult to show the effects, but I think it's worth the effort. Another place to look is those new low ROI products quarterly reports. They help us to focus our efforts on the low ROI products. They are designed to highlight the effect of our actions on the low performer product lines such as commercial fluorescent fixtures [Exhibit 3], wall fixtures [Exhibit 4], and residential incandescent [Exhibit 5].

TP   Those reports are a good way to make sure that we do not lose our impetus on the project. I expect to see some real changes in the profitability of the poor performers in the next few years. However, I think it may be too soon to detect anything yet.

PW   If I wanted to demonstrate the effect of the analysis, I would probably look at the sales of recessed fixtures [Exhibit 6]. As we discussed earlier, we have changed the discount structure of the insulated and standard cylindrical products. So there might be something there.

EC   It is possible you might detect something. However, you have to take into account the nonresidential starts for the previous year. We generally use that as a planning guide to sales volume. I have the Dodge's numbers[3] for the same time period, and that should help analyze the sales numbers [Exhibit 7].

TP   The analysis will not be that easy. Architects frequently change the type of fixtures they choose to incorporate in their designs, and that dramatically affects sales. At the moment, recessed fixtures are in, but in the next few years it could easily change back to fluorescent. If you look at the comparison of the two lines, you will see the ratio changes over the years [Exhibit 8].

KJ   Our business is too complex and it changes too rapidly for the effects of any single action to be detectable. The commercial and consumer markets are cyclical, and that dominates anything we have discussed today. We are forced to manage our business on faith. I believe, thanks to the strategic marketing analysis, we are doing the right things and are improving our performance. I cannot prove it, but that doesn't stop me from believing it.

---

[3]Dodge Construction Potentials, Construction Information Group: McGraw-Hill Information System Company.

EXHIBIT 1

WINCHELL LIGHTING, INC. (B)
1982 Channel Profitability Report
(Marketing Cost Analysis)
($000)

	CONSUMER		COMMERCIAL				
	MASS MERCHANDISING	WHOLESALE SUPPLIERS	CONTRACT	INDUSTRIAL SUPPLIERS	GOVERNMENT	OEM	TOTAL
Net sales	9,948	6,982	57,616	19,438	266	9,070	103,340
Material	5,168	2,064	16,683	4,908	74	2,946	31,843
Labor	693	721	3,760	1,276	18	904	7,372
Overhead	2,537	2,750	14,203	4,807	97	3,221	27,615
Total	8,398	5,534	34,646	10,991	189	7,071	66,829
Gross profit	1,550	1,448	22,970	8,447	77	2,019	36,511
Gross margin	16%	21%	40%	43%	39%	22%	35%
Marketing expenses	2,498	1,601	7,470	2,366	22	61	14,018
General and administration	901	689	5,692	1,785	28	808	9,904
Operating profit	(1,849)	(843)	9,808	4,296	27	1,150	12,589
Profit margin (%)	−19%	−12%	17%	22%	10%	13%	12%

EXHIBIT 2

WINCHELL LIGHTING, INC. (B)
1985 Channel Profitability Report
(Marketing Cost Analysis)
($000)

	CONSUMER		COMMERCIAL				
	MASS MERCHANDISING	WHOLESALE SUPPLIERS	CONTRACT	INDUSTRIAL SUPPLIERS	GOVERNMENT	OEM	TOTAL
Net sales	10,694	3,120	79,434	25,110	402	9,200	127,960
Material	8,503	2,083	25,089	6,886	99	2,869	45,529
Labor	29	62	4,798	1,437	33	724	7,082
Overhead	150	268	22,172	6,503	154	3,146	32,393
Total	8,681	2,413	52,059	14,826	266	6,739	85,004
Gross profit	2,013	707	27,375	10,284	116	2,461	42,956
Gross margin	19%	23%	34%	41%	29%	27%	34%

(continued)

(continued)

Marketing Expenses

Commission	696	270	4,682	1,344	12	372	7,376
Advertising	46	12	132	38	0	2	230
Catalog	36	14	504	160	0	0	714
Co-op advertising	380	90	416	120	0	0	1,006
Sales promotion	494	128	394	114	0	2	1,132
Warranty	2	2	64	22	0	4	94
Sales administration	908	268	5,696	1,714	20	351	8,957
Cash discount	118	56	892	252	12	114	1,444
Total	2,680	840	12,780	3,764	44	845	20,953
General and administration	907	265	6,740	2,131	36	781	10,860
Operating profit	(1,574)	(398)	7,855	4,389	36	835	11,143
Profit margin	−15%	−13%	10%	17%	9%	9%	9%
Net invested capital	5,447	1,643	33,154	10,974	184	2,748	54,149
Return on investment	−29%	−24%	24%	40%	20%	30%	21%
Residual income	(2,936)	(809)	(433)	1,646	(10)	149	(2,394)

EXHIBIT 3

WINCHELL LIGHTING, INC. (B)
Low ROI Products Quarterly Reports
Commercial Fluorescent Fixtures
($ million)

	1984		1985			
			TRADITIONAL ACCOUNTING			FULL
	STRATEGIC ACCOUNTING	TRADITIONAL ACCOUNTING	Q1–Q2	Q3	Q4	YEAR
Sales	$13.2	$13.2	$13.4	$13.4	$13.4	$13.4
Gross profit	5.0	5.0	5.2	5.6	7.8	6.2
Period expenses	3.6	4.4	4.2	4.0	5.0	4.4
Operating profit	1.4	0.6	1.0	1.6	2.8	1.8
Accounts receivable	2.6	3.0	2.8	3.0	2.8	2.8
Inventory	9.6	8.6	6.4	5.2	5.6	6.0
Property, plant, and equipment (PPE)	2.4	2.4	2.6	2.4	2.6	2.4
Current liabilities	1.8	2.0	1.8	1.8	2.2	2.0
Net invested capital	12.8	12.0	10.0	8.8	8.8	9.2
Gross margin (%)	26.3%	26.3%	31.2%	31.7%	44.7%	36.5%
Return on sales (%)	7.4	3.2	5.3	9.1	15.6	10.6
Return on investment (%)	10.9	5.0	8.7	18.2	30.6	19.2

Notes:
1. All quarterly sales profit period expense and operating profit has been annualized for comparison purposes.
2. All accounts receivable, inventory, PPE, current liability, and net invested capital are at period end levels.

EXHIBIT 4

WINCHELL LIGHTING, INC. (B)
Low ROI Products Quarterly Reports
Commercial Wall Fixtures
($ million)

| | 1984 | | 1985 | | | |
| | STRATEGIC ACCOUNTING | TRADITIONAL ACCOUNTING | TRADITIONAL ACCOUNTING | | | FULL YEAR |
			Q1–Q2	Q3	Q4	
Sales	$ 8.1	$ 8.1	$ 8.7	$ 9.9	$10.5	$ 9.3
Gross profit	2.7	2.7	2.7	2.7	3.6	3.0
Period expenses	2.1	1.8	2.1	2.1	3.0	2.4
Operating profit	0.6	0.9	0.6	0.6	0.6	0.6
Accounts receivable	1.2	1.2	1.5	1.5	1.8	1.5
Inventory	4.5	3.9	3.0	2.7	3.3	3.0
Property, plant, and equipment (PPE)	0.6	1.2	1.2	1.5	1.5	1.5
Current liabilities	0.9	0.9	0.9	1.2	1.8	1.2
Net invested capital	5.4	5.4	4.8	4.5	4.8	4.8
Gross margin (%)	33.3%	33.3%	32.2%	28.3%	35.9%	32.2
Return on sales	7.4	11.1	6.3	5.7	6.8	6.4
Return on investment	11.1	16.7	11.4	12.0	14.5	12.7

Notes:

1. All quarterly sales profit period expense and operating profit has been annualized for comparison purposes.
2. All accounts receivable, inventory, PPE, current liability, and net invested capital are at period end levels.

EXHIBIT 5

WINCHELL LIGHTING, INC. (B)
Low ROI Products Quarterly Reports
Residential Incandescent
($ million)

| | 1984 | | 1985 | | | |
| | STRATEGIC ACCOUNTING | TRADITIONAL ACCOUNTING | TRADITIONAL ACCOUNTING | | | FULL YEAR |
			Q1–Q2	Q3	Q4	
Sales	$13.8	$13.8	$ 9.8*	$13.8*	$ 8.2	$10.4
Gross profit	3.4	3.4	2.6	3.4	2.4	2.8
Period expenses	3.0	4.8	2.6	3.2	2.4	2.8
Operating profit	0.4	0.3	—	—	—	—
Accounts payable	2.2	2.2	1.6	2.2	1.2	1.6
Inventory	6.6	7.0	6.2	4.6	3.6	5.2
Property, plant, and equipment (PPE)	1.4	1.4	1.2	1.0	0.8	1.0
Current liabilities	1.4	1.6	1.2	1.6	1.4	1.4
Net invested capital	8.8	9.0	7.8	6.2	4.2	6.4
Gross margin (%)	24.6%	24.6%	26.0%	24.7%	28.8%	26.1%
Return on sales	2.9	1.4	—	2.1	—	—
Return on investment	4.5	2.2	—	4.8	—	—

Notes:

1. All quarterly sales profit period expense and operating profit has been annualized for comparison purposes.
2. All accounts receivable, inventory, PPE, current liability, and net invested capital are at period end levels.

EXHIBIT 6

WINCHELL LIGHTING, INC. (B)
Sales of Commercial Recessed Fixtures 1977–1985
(million)

PRODUCT LINE	1977	1978	1979	1980	1981	1982	1983	1984	1985
Standard	3.6	4.4	5.5	5.4	7.2	7.2	6.8	9.4	9.6
Insulated	4.2	6.2	6.6	6.6	9.0	8.4	8.8	9.4	10.2
Total	7.8	10.6	12.1	12.0	16.2	15.6	15.6	18.8	19.8

EXHIBIT 7

WINCHELL LIGHTING, INC. (B)
Nonresidential Construction Starts 1977–1985
(million square feet)

1977	1978	1979	1980	1981	1982	1983	1984	1985
1,050	1,150	1,369	1,195	1,166	915	989	1,210	1,195

Source: Dodge Construction Potential, Construction Information Group: McGraw-Hill Information System Company.

EXHIBIT 8

WINCHELL LIGHTING, INC. (B)
Sales of Commercial Recessed and Fluorescent Fixtures 1977–1985
(million)

PRODUCT LINE	1977	1978	1979	1980	1981	1982	1983	1984	1985
Recessed	7.8	10.6	12.1	12.0	16.2	15.6	15.6	18.8	19.8
Fluorescent	6.1	7.2	6.8	9.4	11.3	11.8	12.9	13.2	13.4

8

Strategic Activity-Based Management: Product Development

Perhaps the biggest opportunity for cost reduction arises when products are first designed. Most operational and strategic ABM actions work to reduce the costs and improve the profitability of existing products, customers, and supplier relationships. The potential for cost reduction for new products may be even more dramatic. Some scholars have documented that 80% or more of manufacturing costs get determined during the product design and development stages[1] (see Exhibit 8–1). The challenge is to give excellent predictive cost information to product designers at a time when they have the greatest opportunity to influence costs.

Traditional Stage II cost systems (see chapter 2) focus on the costs of direct materials, direct labor, and machine processing time. Such systems underestimate the costs of using unique versus common parts, new versus existing vendors, and simple versus complex production processes. Stage II cost systems also overestimate the cost of using any cost factor that has been used to allocate overhead costs to products. Such cost distortions provide signals for designers to overinvest in reducing new products' consumption of direct labor, machine hours, or any other cost allocation base. Also, when product designers and engineers had only the distorted cost signals from Stage II cost systems, they often made decisions that led to unexpectedly high indirect and support costs. For example, they would select components with low purchase prices but ignored high procurement costs and usage costs. Many companies are now using their Stage III ABC systems primarily to provide better information to help their product engineers and designers lower the total manufacturing costs of new products.

CHOOSING ACTIVITY COST DRIVERS FOR PRODUCT DESIGN: ACCURACY VERSUS INFLUENCING BEHAVIOR

Using ABC to influence product design decisions requires a balance between two important objectives. First is the normal ABC objective: provide relatively accurate information about the economics of a product's manufacturing and service costs. The second objective is to provide information that product engineers can understand and use in their design decisions.

---

[1]See B. S. Blanchard, *Design and Manage to Life-Cycle Cost* (Portland, OR: M/A Press, 1978); and J. E. Michaels and W. P. Wood, *Design to Cost* (New York: John Wiley & Sons, 1989).

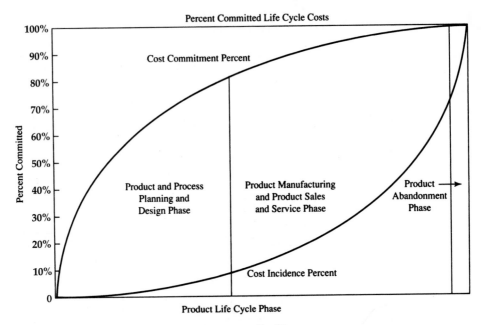

EXHIBIT 8-1   Cost Commitment versus Incidence

For this second objective, consider a choice between two alternative activity cost drivers used in electronic printed circuit manufacture: *insertion hours* and *number of insertions*. If each insertion process of a certain type (say through-hole insertion, or surface mount) takes the same amount of time for all components, then the two drivers will report identical product costs. But most engineers will understand number of insertions a lot easier than insertion hours, since number of insertions is identical to the number of components in their circuit design. Therefore, the driver *number of insertions* will send a clear message that every additional component adds manufacturing cost, whereas the driver, *insertion hours*, will likely require that engineers convert back to number of insertions and of which type to get a clear message about how they can reduce product costs.

Because the choice of an activity cost driver sends such a powerful message to product designers, managers must consider the behavior they could be inducing. For example, a traditional standard cost system, focusing on direct materials and direct labor cost, sends a message to engineers that they should reduce the cost of purchased materials. This led product designers to proliferate the number of components, to find the most cost-effective solution for each decision, and for purchasing people to search among a large number of vendors to find the cheapest source. To counter this trend towards proliferating part counts and vendors, the electronics companies chose a new cost driver, *number of different part numbers*. This cost driver sent a clear message to engineers to attempt to increase the use of common components. Further, if the cost per part number is assigned to individual products and models by dividing this component-sustaining expense by the volume of the part used, engineers are encouraged to use the common parts that are already purchased and used in high volumes. Thus, the driver *number of part numbers* encourages engineers to reduce part proliferation and to increase part commonality.

Some electronics companies, in their early applications of ABC to product design, implemented extremely simple systems with only a few activity cost drivers. The explicit objective of these systems was to load most expenses on those drivers, such as *number of part numbers*, and thus place extreme pressure on engineers to design products using already existing components and to avoid adding new components. As product engineers developed new designs, however, that had very low reported costs according to the simplistic ABC system, more experienced designers could tell that the new designs would actually be quite high in cost. The outcome of these poor "low-cost" designs was either a loss of faith in the system on the part of the engineers and eventual demise of the system, or a redesign of the system to make it more accurate by adding additional drivers. This increased accuracy restored the engineers' faith in the system.

The explicit behavior modification approach may be called for when managers already know what the best near-term solution is; for example, reduce part count or decrease the number of vendors. In this case, the managers are using the ABC system to reinforce decisions already taken, not to inform the decisions. Soon engineers and purchasing personnel will shift away from their previous extremely inefficient behavior, which was driven by the inadequacies of the previous Stage II cost system, not their own errors. At that time, we advocate that managers opt for accuracy over their perceived need to influence engineers' and purchasing department's behavior in a particular way. The desire for accuracy, however, must still be balanced by having a system in which engineers can readily understand the impact of their decisions on the required quantity of activity cost drivers.

Many firms resolve this trade-off by starting with a relatively simple system that the engineers readily understand, and is sufficiently accurate that the engineers will believe in it. As they gain experience with using the system and begin to understand its limitations, more activity cost drivers are added to reflect their increased understanding. This iterative design process continues until the system has reached sufficient sophistication that there are diminishing returns to accuracy from adding new drivers, and increasing risks that engineers will have problems using a more complex system.[2]

TARGET COSTING[3]

Japanese manufacturers noticed early the powerful leverage on manufacturing costs from excellent product designs. Many Japanese companies use target costing to motivate product engineers to select designs that can be produced at low cost.[4] At the heart of target costing is a very simple syllogism:

1. Let the marketplace determine the selling price of the future product.
2. Subtract from this selling price the profit margin the company want to achieve.
3. This yields the target cost at which the product must be manufactured.

In the target costing approach, the cost of a new product is no longer an *outcome from* the product design process; it becomes an *input into* the process. The multifunctional product design team has the mission to design a product with the functionality and quality that the customer demands, and which can be manufactured at a target cost that enables the company to earn a desired profit.

---

[2]For examples of this process in action, see G. Foster and M. Gupta, "Activity Accounting: An Electronics Industry Implementation," chapter 8, pp. 225–268, in R. S. Kaplan (ed.), *Measures for Manufacturing Excellence* (Boston: HBS Press, 1990); and D. Berlant, R. Browning, and G. Foster, "How Hewlett-Packard Gets Numbers It Can Trust," *Harvard Business Review* (January–February 1990).

[3]This section is taken from R. Cooper and R. Slagmulder, "Target Costing and Value Engineering" (Portland, OR: Productivity Press, 1997).

[4]M. Sakurai, "Target Costing and How to Use It," *Journal of Cost Management* (Summer 1989), pp. 39–50; T. Hiromoto, "Another Hidden Edge—Japanese Management Accounting," *Harvard Business Review* (July–August 1988), pp. 22–26; Y. Monden and K. Hamada, "Target Costing and Kaizen Costing," *Journal of Management Accounting Research* (Fall 1991), pp. 16–34; and R. Cooper, *When Lean Enterprises Collide: Competing Through Confrontation* (Boston: Harvard Business School Press, 1995).

We describe contemporary practice by decomposing the target costing process into four major steps: market driven costing; product-level target costing; component-level target costing; and chained target costing.

Market-Driven Costing

The market driven costing process starts by identifying the target selling price—the product's anticipated price when launched. This price must reflect the perceived value of the product in the eyes of the customer, the anticipated relative functionality and selling price of competitive offerings, and the firm's strategic objectives for the product.

Firms that undertake target costing typically have extensive market analysis procedures to identify what their customers want and how much they are willing to pay for it. Occasionally, however, a new product may not come from surveying potential customers. For example, the initial Xerox machine or Sony Walkman was not a product that customers were asking for. Once customers saw the implications of dry paper copying and how the Walkman could improve the quality of their commutes and exercise routines, however, the companies had extremely successful products. So there is a real skill to listening to the customer but also allowing for creativity in anticipating consumer preferences.

Managers, in setting the target market price, must also be cognizant of the prices of competitive products. If competitive products have higher functionality and quality then the target selling price will have to be lower than the competitor's selling price. If the functionality and quality are higher, then selling prices can either be equal to competitors' prices (thus increasing market share) or above these prices (thus increasing profits).

Finally, the firm's strategy for the future product helps influence its initial selling price. The firm might want to set a lower price to gain market share rapidly, or a higher price to increase overall long-term profitability and create an image of technical excellence.

After setting a target price, the market-driven costing process continues by establishing the target profit margin. For products that replace earlier generations, the margin will typically be the historical profit margins earned by the existing products. This historical margin is adjusted for two additional factors; any unusual costs at the front-end (e.g., research and development) or back-end (e.g., salvage or disposal) of the life cycle, plus revised profit objectives for the product line.

In the final step, managers calculate an allowable cost by subtracting the target profit margin from the target selling price. The allowable cost is the cost at which the product must be manufactured if it is to earn the target profit margin at the target selling price. The allowable cost is different from the target cost because the market-driven costing process has yet to take into account the capabilities of the firm and its suppliers. Therefore, the firm may not be able to design the product so that it can be manufactured at its allowable cost. The objective of the product-level target costing process is to set target costs that are achievable.

Product-Level Target Costing

The product-level target costing process starts with the current cost of the proposed product. This is the cost at which the firm could launch the new product today without undertaking any design changes or introducing any process improvements in existing manufacturing processes. The initial discrepancy between the current cost and the allowable cost gives the project team an estimate of the magnitude of the cost reduction opportunities it must identify to achieve the allowable cost.

The cost reduction objective is split into two portions, achievable and unachievable. The achievable portion, the target cost reduction objective, captures the level of cost reduction that the design teams believe they can achieve by expending considerable effort during the design process. Three engineering techniques typically play a critical role in achieving the target cost reduction objective: value engineering, quality function deployment, and design for manufacture and assembly. If product-level target costs are set properly, and the three engineering techniques are effectively deployed, the target should be achieved about 80% of the time.

The unachievable portion of the cost reduction objective is called the strategic cost reduction challenge. Strategic cost reduction challenges identify how far the firm is from being competitive. Splitting the cost reduction objective between the achievable and unachievable portions takes considerable skill. Setting product-level target costs that are too aggressive will result in unachievable target costs and eventual failure of the discipline from target costing. Setting too high a strategic cost reduction challenge leads to easily achieved target costs but a loss of competitive position.

The cardinal rule for target costing is that the target cost can never be violated. Applying the cardinal rule rigorously implies that even if engineers find a way to improve the functionality of a product, they can incorporate the improvement only if they can also identify how to offset any additional costs. The only exception occurs if the improved functionality allows the target selling price to be increased by an appropriate amount. If the design team cannot achieve the product-level target cost, then the application of the cardinal rule requires the project to be scrapped. It is the rigorous application of the cardinal rule that differentiates firms that truly apply target costing versus those that just perform the calculation of an allowable or target cost.

Component-Level Target Costing

In the component-level target costing process, the design team establishes the target cost for every component contained within the future product. These component-level target costs establish the supplier's selling prices. Therefore component-level target cost transmits the competitive pressure faced by the firm to its suppliers.

In the establishment of component-level target costs, products are typically broken down into the major functions they contain. Major functions represent important performance capabilities that the product must have in order for it to perform its primary function. For example, the primary function of an automobile is to transport passengers from point A to point B. Some of the major functions, such as the engine and transmission system, are required to achieve the basic objective; others are required to augment the basic function, such as the air conditioner and audio system. These major functions enable the passengers to be transported in comfort.

The chief engineer sets the target cost for the major functions. The engineer decides the theme of the product and decides that certain functions should be emphasized. For example, for a car to have a sportier ride, the chief engineer might specify a larger high-performance engine. This decision requires that a greater percentage of the total cost of the product will be spent on the engine than in the previous generation. However, under the cardinal rule, if the chief engineer spends more money on the engine, less can be spent on the other major functions. The sum of the costs of all the major functions has to remain equal to the product-level target cost of the product (after taking into account the assembly and indirect manufacturing costs).

Once the major function target costs are established, then the design team for each major function must find ways to design that function so that it can be produced at its target cost. The team breaks the major function down into its components and then distributes the major function-level target costs to component-level costs. Under the cardinal rule, the sum of the component-level target costs must equal that of the major function that contains them.

The component-level target costs establish the allowable selling prices of suppliers. The assembly companies do not want to squeeze the profits of their component suppliers to zero.

They want to ensure that the entire supply chain is earning sufficient profits to remain viable while delivering low-cost products demanded by the customers. Therefore, they bring their major suppliers into the product design process as early on as possible. The suppliers provide and receive inputs into the design process on how to reduce costs. The suppliers also provide cost estimates for each component. These estimates are imputed into the component-level target costing process subject to the constraint of the cardinal rule.

Chained Target Costing

In today's highly competitive environments it is not good enough to the most efficient player; it is also necessary to be part of the most efficient supply chain. One of the major ways to achieve increased supply chain efficiency is through the use of chained target costing systems. Target costing systems are chained when the output of the buyer's target costing system becomes the input to the supplier's target costing system. The buyer's component-level target costs becoming the supplier's target selling prices. The supplier's target costing system develops both product-level and component-level target costs, thus transmitting the competitive pressure faced by the buyer to the supplier's product designers. If the supplier's suppliers also use target costing then the chaining continues down the supply chain. In this way, chained target costing systems transmit the competitive pressure for cost reduction from the buyer down the supply chain, making the entire chain more efficient.

ABC and Target Costing

Japanese target costing processes focus on savings in materials, labor, assembly, and machining costs; the unit-level cost drivers prominently featured in traditional Stage II cost systems. Therefore, target costing can function effectively even with Stage II cost systems, an observation consistent with Japanese companies being slow adopters of activity-based costing. But as the focus of target costing extends beyond direct manufacturing costs to include supplier relationships, distribution relationships, and customer relationships, the benefits from a total or ABC cost model should enable an integration between ABC and target costing.

By integrating activity-based costing and target costing, designers can make trade-offs between direct costs and indirect costs that are impossible with target costing alone or using a combination of target costing and traditional costing. With such integration, companies have their best chance to develop products that can be produced at low cost, while still offering the functionality and quality that customers demand. The target costing system enables product designers to reduce the direct unit-level costs by focusing attention on new products' material, labor, and assembly costs. At the same time, the designers manage indirect and support costs with an ABC system that reports activity cost driver rates they can use to make cost-benefit trade-offs between indirect and direct costs. For example, to maintain a component in the firm's bill of material might cost $500 a year. Reducing component count by 30 components will therefore save $15,000 per year. These savings might allow unit costs to increase to enhance functionality while keeping total costs unchanged (so that the target cost is still achieved) by obtaining offsetting savings in batch and product-sustaining expenses.

The actions stimulated by ABC costs to, for example, increase part commonality and reduce component count, will result in lower reported product costs. But the apparent savings will only be realized if the resources previously required to support components are reduced. This may require that a significant number of components be reduced before managers can eliminate or redeploy such resources. If only one product is designed with fewer components, then support costs will remain the same despite what the activity-based cost system reports. The seeming contradiction arises because, as discussed in chapter 5, ABC measures the costs of resources used, not the cost of resources supplied. For the savings to be realized, the reductions in resources required to support the manufacture of existing and new products must be translated into a reduced resource supply.

Activity-based product design highlights the interplay between the cost assignment (strategic) and process (operational) views of ABC. The cost assignment view identifies products (current and future) that require aggressive cost reduction in their design stage. During the product design phase, process drivers, such as number and type of components, can get changed relatively easily. The process view identifies the drivers that have the most impact upon future activity costs. With ABC information, product designers can make decisions so that new products will consume fewer of the process drivers, thereby enabling products to be manufactured with low indirect and support costs.

In general, activity-based costing works very compatibly with a target costing approach. The ABC model gives product designers and developers a model of manufacturing support costs that enables them to balance the functionality and quality of the final product with economically-based decisions about component selection and design characteristics.

MEASURING LIFE-CYCLE COSTS AND PROFITABILITY

Many products and customers in their early years will appear unprofitable, particularly if heavy front-end expenses accompany their introduction. Also, initial production and sales volumes are likely to be low for such new products and customers, so that revenues earned will not be sufficient to cover initial year batch, product, and customer-specific expenses. In fact, the profitability of new products is actually even lower than reported in their initial years. In addition to any operating losses, many product-specific expenses, such as the costs of product design and development discussed in this chapter, may have been incurred even before the initial year of production. In Stage II systems, the costs of launching new products and acquiring new customers are spread across all existing products and customers. In ABC systems, these front-end expenses are assigned to the new products and customers that are the specific beneficiaries of launch and acquisition activities.

When product development, product launch, and customer acquisition costs are high, rather than looking at product and customer profitability on a year by year basis, managers should look at a report of lifetime profitability of individual products and customers. Ex post, it is easy to prepare lifetime product and customer profitability reports. They require only two spreadsheets; one for products, one for customers. The rows on the spreadsheet represent individual products, the columns represent individual years. Each year the ABC product and customer profit or loss is entered into the appropriate spreadsheet cell. Such a report makes it easy to calculate break-even times, a key measure for new product launches.[5] The break-even time measures how long it takes a new product (or a new customer) to repay its front-end expenditures and initial operating period losses. Such a presentation also highlights when products have reached the end of their profitable life cycle. At that point, declining sales volume and prices that have been lowered to meet competition or stimulate demand for the mature product are no longer sufficient to repay annual product-sustaining expenses and the batch costs associated with small lot production.

The ABC customer profitability analysis could also be used prospectively. Before launching major marketing campaigns, managers could assess how much they are willing to spend to

---

[5]Charles H. House and Raymond L. Price, "The Return Map: Tracking Product Teams," *Harvard Business Review* (January–February 1991), pp. 92–100; also Marvin L. Patterson, "Designing Metrics," chapter 3 in *Accelerating Innovation: Improving the Process of Product Development* (New York: Van Nostrand Reinhold, 1993).

acquire customers with certain characteristics, based on the volume of business expected to be done with these newly acquired customers and—the ABC part—the specific ongoing costs of serving those customers.[6]

Activity-based costing also applies to the end of a product's life cycle. Environmental laws in North American and European countries are or will soon enforce responsibility for product take-back costs; companies that produce products will be responsible for the recycling or disposal of the product after customers are finished using it.[7] Similarly, companies dismantling or abandoning large production facilities are responsible for any environmental cleanup costs at the site. Companies that wish to minimize such costs will want to recognize and attempt to influence environmental costs during product and process design stages. As with manufacturing costs, the greatest influence on environmental costs occurs during product and process development stages.

SUMMARY

Large opportunities for cost reduction occur during product design and development. When design engineers have an accurate cost model, including the cost of unique components, and of batch and product-sustaining activities, and they work within a disciplined target costing process, they will be able to achieve desired functionality requirements at much lower total manufacturing costs. Understanding the cost of design and development activities enables the costs of these activities themselves to be managed and reduced.

Life-cycle costing enables product and customer profitability to be measured across their expected lifetimes, not just period by period. The lifetime perspective enables managers to make better decisions about product introduction, product design and development, customer acquisition, and, as we have discussed in the final section, the costs incurred after a product has been used. Environmental costs are growing in magnitude and importance for many organizations. Managers can benefit from better understanding the linkage between their total environmental expenses and decisions made about individual products and processes.

CASES

The first two cases in this chapter deal with using activity-based costing to help guide product development. Product designers make trade-offs between competing designs using activity cost driver rates. The next two cases explore the target costing systems at Japanese firms. These target costing systems are used to reduce the direct costs of products under development. The final case applies ABC principles to a U.S. company's product design and development process.

The *Hewlett-Packard: Roseville Networks Division* case documents the innovative work that was undertaken at HP in using cost systems to help product engineers design cost effective

---

[6]For measuring the lifetime profitability of customers see "The Economics of Customer Loyalty," Chapter 2 in Frederick F. Reichheld, *The Loyalty Effect: The Hidden Force Behind Growth, Profits, and Lasting Value* (Boston: Harvard Business School Press, 1996); and "Rethinking Marketing: Building Customer Loyalty," Chapter 4, in James L. Heskett, W. Earl Sasser, Jr., and Leonard A. Schlesinger, *The Service Profit Chain: How Leading Companies Link Profit and Growth to Loyalty, Satifaction, and Value* (New York: Free Press, 1997).

[7]Marc J. Epstein, "Accounting for Product Take-Back," *Management Accounting* (August 1996), pp. 29–33; also, M. J. Epstein, *Measuring Corporate Environmental Performance: Best Practices for Costing and Managing an Effective Environmental Strategy* (Montvale, NJ: Institute of Management Accountants, 1996).

products. The importance of user ownership of the system is also highlighted. The *Tektronix (A)* case illustrates how a cost system can be used to specifically modify designer behavior.

The two target costing cases are chosen to illustrate the different processes used for complex consumer products with long development times *(Nissan)*, and simple consumer products with short development cycles *(Olympus Optical (A))*. *Euclid Engineering* shows how an ABC system was initially used to reduce manufacturing costs by influencing decisions made in the product design and development stage. Subsequently, an activity-based model was used to influence the cost of the design and development process itself.

HEWLETT-PACKARD: ROSEVILLE NETWORKS DIVISION

We want our designers to use as many common parts as possible and we want those parts to come from the minimum number of vendors. In addition, we want the designers to design printed circuit boards so that as many components as possible can be auto-inserted. This means they must not put parts either too close together or too close to the edges of the board.

However, to maintain competitiveness we must allow the designers to take advantage of new technologies. For example, four or five conventional common parts might be replaced by a single integrated circuit (IC) that costs less and is more reliable. Sometimes, we want the designers to use new technologies even when they are unique parts that cannot be autoinserted.

We want our cost system to provide the designer with the appropriate economic information to make the necessary tradeoff between common/autoinsertable parts and new technologies.

Tim Hastrup, Engineering Project Manager

Introduction

Hewlett-Packard (HP) produced computing and electronic measurement equipment for the electronics, telecommunications, aerospace, aircraft, automotive, and scientific research industries. In 1988 the company had sales of approximately $10 billion and employed 86,000 people worldwide.

The Roseville Networks Division (RND) was one of four Hewlett-Packard divisions that designed and marketed networking products and one of two divisions that also manufactured these products. In 1988, networking products accounted for several hundred million in sales, about two-thirds of which were produced by RND.

Products

RND's products were actually a combination of boards and connector cables—circuit boards and connector cables that networked or connected computers to each other and to peripheral devices such as terminals. Boards were used, for example, to connect a terminal to a minicomputer, to connect a personal computer such as

Hewlett-Packard's Vectra to a local area network (LAN), or to connect a LAN to a data center or to a global communications network. Networking boards were also used to connect noncomputer devices, such as medical instruments, to a computer. In total, RND produced several hundred boards for different end products. Many of these boards were produced in low volumes. On average, there were two end products for every board. A typical end product consisted of a board, a cable, and a manual. Networking products had very short lives, and these lives were getting shorter every year. By 1988 the average RND product was under two years old. In addition, the number of different products produced was proliferating as the need for communications increased. Consequently, in 1987, to maintain an up-to-date product offering, RND introduced a new product, on average, every month and implemented a production change to existing products on average every day.

Production Process

The production process consisted of attaching electronic components to the circuit boards. The main production steps to produce a board were as follows:

* *Start station.* Boards were loaded manually into titanium fixtures in the starter station according to the production schedule. A bar code identifying each board was attached to the carrier, and the carrier was forwarded to the automatic insertion machines.

* *Automatic insertion.* Automatic insertion required three different types of machines each designed to insert a different class of component. DIP inserters were used for Dual Inline Package integrated circuits, (i.e., the leads were in two parallel lines), axial insertion for axial (i.e., the leads and the component were in a straight line), and radial insertion for radial (i.e., the leads formed a circle below the component) components.

* There were four DIP inserters. These were used in serial fashion, each board moving from one machine to the next. The serial layout had been adopted to eliminate the setup costs associated with changing the components in the DIP magazines. To allow this layout to function given the very high number of automatically insertable components in the products, the engineers had designed special high-volume carousels to increase the number of slots (feeder tubes to hold magazines of distinct components). This in-line layout coupled to the additional slots in the carousel enabled 588 different components to be inserted without a part setup.

This case was prepared by Professor Robin Cooper and Professor Peter B. B. Turney, Portland State University.

Copyright© 1989 by the President and Fellows of Harvard College. Harvard Business School case 189-117.

- There was one axial inserter which was used to insert axial components. These were supplied to the axial inserter in the form of a tape created by a sequencer. Again, due to the high number of automatically insertable axial components, the engineers had extended the sequencer so that it could create tapes containing most of the required axial components. The sequencer tape was fed directly to the axial inserter.

- The radial inserter was a recent acquisition. This machine inserted radial components from magazines. Prior to its purchase, few radial components were used in the division's products, and these were manually inserted. Currently, the number of different radial components automatically inserted was sufficiently small that they could all be loaded into the machine at once.

- *Manual insertion.* Components that could not be inserted using insertion machines, or whose volume was too low to justify using automatic insertion, were inserted using semiautomatic Royonics machines. The titanium carrier was placed on the Royonics machine, and the bar code on the carrier was scanned using a wand. Software in the Royonics machine presented and identified the appropriate components for insertion and illuminated the holes where the components were to be inserted. The Royonics machine was connected to an automatic storage unit, called a Paternoster, which contained about 1,000 bins of components. The bins were rotated automatically until the bin containing the required components was accessible.

- *Wave solder.* After manual insertion, the boards were placed in a wave solder machine. The wave solder machine automatically fluxed, heated, soldered, and then cooled the boards. The boards moved directly into a washing machine where they were washed to remove any residual flux and dried. Once soldered and washed, the boards were placed on an automatic conveyer that delivered them to the Final Assembly area.

- *Final assembly.* Parts that would be damaged by the soldering or washing process, were too large for the automatic insertion equipment, or required field replacement were manually inserted in Final Assembly.

- *Board test.* The boards were functionally tested using a number of standard tests in the Performance Verification and Defect Analysis departments. The amount of time required for testing varied considerably from board to board, with the total testing time varying from one hour to 10 hours. Boards that failed the functional tests were repaired prior to forwarding to the packaging department.

- *Packaging.* In the Kitting and Shipping department, boards were combined with required cables and manuals and packed in boxes for shipment. About 1,000 boxes were shipped each work day.

Cost Driver Accounting

In 1984, the cost accounting system at RND was a facility-wide direct-labor-dollar-based system. The move to automation over the years had significantly reduced the direct labor content of the products. For example, in the three-year period from 1978 to 1981, the direct labor content alone had fallen from 6% to 3% of total production costs, and by 1988 the ratio had fallen below 1%. This low labor content created overhead burden rates that were over 400%. As the rate climbed, management began to question the validity of the product costs reported by their cost system and the behavioral effects that the cost system was having on the design process.

As an augmentation to the standard cost system, product engineering had developed the MAKE (manufacturing knowledge expert) model. This model had the ability to identify alternative components and make recommendations about how to reduce the cost of the design. Embedded in the MAKE model was a cost estimation model that differed significantly from the division's traditional cost system. It was this model that triggered the design of the new cost system. As Debbie Berlant, Manager of Cost Accounting, said,

> When we discovered that the engineers were using a different definition of product costs to make their design decisions, we knew we were in trouble and had to change our existing cost system. Finance decided that whatever the designers needed we would give them. The MAKE model was actually an off-line cost system. It came in useful in the design process because we could model the effect of the changes we were making without changing the official cost system. Consequently, the MAKE model tended to be one generation ahead of the cost system.

The new cost system that was developed from the MAKE model was known as cost driver accounting (CDA) at RND. John DeLury, Controller, commented on the objective of CDA.

> The purpose of cost driver accounting was not to prevent the engineers from introducing new costly technology. Rather it was to get the engineers to think about cost, and not to go for elegance every time. Cost driver accounting put product costs on the backs of the engineers. It encouraged them to design for manufacturability as well as functionality.

Cost System Redesign

The first modification to the official cost system was implemented in the first half of 1985. The factory was broken into five cost centers—automatic insertion, manual insertion, final assembly, product verification, and defect analysis. In the two insertion and final assembly departments, direct labor costs were traced to the products using the number of insertions. The direct labor cost per insertion was calculated by dividing the budgeted direct labor dollars for the coming six months by the budgeted number of insertions for the period. The number of tests performed was the basis used to trace costs in the other two departments. The direct labor cost per test was calculated for the next six months by dividing the budgeted direct labor dollars by the budgeted number of tests.

The facility-wide overhead was then allocated on the basis of budgeted direct labor dollars to give a full cost of each insertion or test. The overhead rate was about 400%, so the full cost of each insertion and test was about five times the direct labor cost.

The second modification was implemented six months later in the second half of 1985. The overhead was split into two parts, one relating to production and the other to procurement. Procurement costs included the cost of purchasing, storage, product logistics, document specifications, planning, and material engineering. All other costs were viewed as production costs. The procurement overhead costs were traced to the products using the number of parts that the product contained. The production overhead costs were traced as before.

In the first half of 1986, the system was again modified. Production overhead was traced to each major production area. This allowed five production department overhead rates to be calculated—one for each cost center. In addition, direct labor was now treated as an overhead item. Labor vouchering was discontinued except for nonproductive activities such as building prototypes and performing rework.

Production overhead costs were traced to the product using the number of insertions and the number of test hours. The number of insertions was used in the two insertion and the final assembly departments. The number of test hours was used in the product verification and defect analysis departments.

The move to test hours reflected the design team's discomfort with the original choice of number of tests. This was because some boards required tests that were a lot longer than the tests on other boards and consumed more resources. Consequently, number of test hours was considered to be more accurate.

In the second half of 1986 the automatic insertion department was split into three separate centers—start station (this is where the boards were placed in the titanium carriers and their bar code identification attached), axial insertion (where the axial components were in-

serted), and DIP insertion (where the dual in-line package integrated circuits were inserted).[1]

These changes were made at the insistence of engineering. One of the engineers had designed a board that contained a lot of axial components but few DIPs. The cost system generated a product cost that the engineer felt was out of line with reality. His analysis of the situation suggested that it was much cheaper to undertake axial insertion than DIP insertion. The accounting department's analysis supported this contention, and the system was correspondingly modified.

The cost of the start station was traced to the products using the number of assemblies (boards), as the activities in this area were driven by the number of boards. Each board had to be inserted in the carrier and bar coded. The costs of the axial and DIP insertion operations were then traced to the products using the number of insertions in each area.

A second modification was also introduced at this time. The final assembly department was split into two centers—wave soldering and final assembly. The cost of the wave soldering area was traced using the number of assemblies, since each assembly had to be wave soldered and the number of solder joints required (i.e., number of components) did not change the time or cost of soldering.

Finally, the cost of kitting and shipping (the packaging department) had historically been treated as a period cost. The cost driver approach suggested that these costs could be traced to the products using the number of assemblies. The number of assemblies was chosen because each assembly had to be kitted and packed and the size of the assembly did not have much effect on the resources required to kit and ship the product.

In the first half of 1987, the division changed the way the procurement costs were traced to the products. The procurement costs were split into two pools; one related to the number of assemblies and the other to the number of parts. The costs traced using the number of assemblies included production planning, product logistics, product specification, and marketing services (which was responsible for the scheduling activity). The costs traced using the number of parts included purchasing costs, parts storage costs, parts specification, and material planning.

---

[1]The radial inserter had not been acquired at this time.

In the first half of 1988, the costs of the final assembly area were split in two. The first area related to manual insertion. Here the parts that could not be wave soldered were inserted. These parts included large VLSI chips, sockets, edge connectors, and any heat-sensitive or bulky components. These costs were traced to the products using number of insertions.

The second area was manual solder, where hand-inserted components and jumper wires were hand soldered. Not all of the hand-inserted components had to be soldered. EPROMS, for example, were socketed so that they could be replaced in the field. Jumper wires were used to connect printed circuits together. They were viewed by most engineers as necessary evils that should be removed by redesigning the boards as quickly as possible. The costs of this area were traced to the products using the number of solder joints.

The final change made in the first half of 1988 was the introduction of a radial insertion area. This was required by the purchase of a large radial inserter. The costs of this area were traced to the product using a cost-per-radial insertion.

In mid-1988 some potentially critical limitations in the design of the cost system were becoming apparent. In particular, the current system ignored the volume of usage of each component. Since some costs were incurred because the component was used irrespective of the volume used, the existing cost system overcosted high-volume products and undercosted low-volume ones.

The solution proposed for this problem was a volume-sensitive model. The proposed volume-sensitive model included changes in the costing of each production process. The cost of each process, including labor costs, would now be broken into three pools, each with a different cost driver. The first cost pool contained the costs of getting a board to the process. These costs were divided by the number of assemblies handled in each process to obtain a cost per assembly for each process. The second cost pool included the costs of inserting components into the board in each process. These costs were divided by the number of insertions to obtain a cost per insertion. The third cost pool contained the costs related to setting up the machines. These were the slot costs. This pool was divided by the number of different part numbers inserted to give a per-part-number cost. This part-number cost was divided by the number of components of each part number inserted to give a per-insertion charge. Under this approach, a low-volume component had a higher per-insertion cost than a high-volume one.

In the DIP insertion area, this new three-cost-pool approach significantly changed reported product costs. The part-number cost pool in this area contained the labor, equipment, and support costs associated with the carousels that had been installed on the DIP machines. This pool was divided by the number of slots available on the carousel to obtain a cost per slot. Each slot was dedicated to one part number, so the cost of a slot was assigned to each unique part carried in the carousel. The cost per slot was then divided by the semiannual volume of each part number to obtain the cost per part for that part number.

Fred Huang described why he recommended slot costing.

> Slot costing has evolved as a joint project of engineering, manufacturing, and accounting, but I was the one who first suggested charging a rental fee for the use of a slot on the DIP machines. I was concerned that the overhead in the plant might go up because we were setting up new part numbers during the design of the boards. I felt that the slots had a special economic value, and I wanted the cost system to reflect this value.

Debbie Berlant described the likely impact of slot costing.

> I believe that slot costing will have a major impact on decision making because it will tell us what it really costs to occupy a slot. In particular, I see slot costs affecting new product decisions such as making or buying a board and phase-out decisions to obsolete or continue making a board.

Tim Hastrup explained the relationship between the number of part numbers and the use of DIP machine capacity.

> If we had fewer low-volume parts we would not need so many slots. This is important because our capacity is not limited by insertion capacity but by the number of part numbers we can handle. When we buy a machine today we buy it to increase the number of part numbers we can handle, not to increase the number of insertions we can perform.

> Currently we have four DIP machines arranged sequentially. The purpose of this sequential arrangement is to increase the number of part numbers that are available for insertion into a particular board. If each machine has 200 slots, then our total part number capacity per board is 800.

> If we halved the number of part numbers, we could convert from a single four-DIP machine line to two parallel two-machine lines. This would significantly increase our

insertion capacity. Currently all boards must go through all four machines even if a particular machine contains no components for that board, so converting to two parallel lines would permit us to keep the machines busier. Idle time would also be less because boards would no longer be sitting in queues waiting for machines they do not use. Setup time would also be somewhat reduced.

The Designers

The way the designers interacted with the cost accounting and the MAKE model was to develop a series of heuristic design rules that allowed them to make design tradeoffs. The experienced engineer had developed many such rules. Fred Huang, Product Developer, described the type of rules that he used.

1. Manual insertion was three times as expensive as automatic insertion.
2. Introducing a new part into the HP parts list cost the firm $25,000.
3. Introducing a new part to RND that was already on the HP parts list cost the division about $5,000.
4. Connectors that could not go through the wave solder machine and had to be manually inserted, or needed special presolder treatment, added $2 to $3 to the overhead cost of the board.
5. Reliability was critical, and selecting components that had high reliability was better than selecting components that did not. This rule favored using preferred vendors and parts whose breakdown rates and safety margins were known. Each breakdown in the field cost at least $1,000.
6. Time to market was critical, and selecting components that were still under development was risky. If a component was selected that was very new and the production capacity was yet to be established, there was a risk that the component would not be ready when it was required. Using a new component cost between $1,000 and $100,000 per component depending on the risk of nonavailability.
7. Ease of availability was similarly critical. Selecting a component that had excess production capacity in the industry and could be supplied by multiple vendors reduced the risk of component shortages. The rule of thumb used to adjust for availability was that a low-availability component had an additional cost of 10 times its material cost.
8. Using existing designs was sensible. If an existing function or circuit could be used, this was better than starting afresh. Designing a new function or circuit cost from $10,000 (one month of engineering time) for a small project to $30,000 (three months of engineering time) for a large project. In addition, the delay in time to market added 10 times the out-of-pocket cost. The additional cost for a large project was therefore $300,000.

Once designers had developed these heuristics, they did not have to keep going back to the cost system for cost information. However, every time a new cost driver was implemented, the designers would study the effect on the economics of production and adjust their design rules accordingly.

For example, if the cost system said a product cost $100 before the new driver was introduced and $150 afterwards, the designers would ensure that they knew why the change in reported product costs had occurred. The engineers considered understanding the reasons behind the shift in product costs important because the complex mix of products meant that every time a new cost driver was introduced reported product costs of at least some products changed dramatically.

Huang described his use of reported product costs in the design process.

> I do not design to minimize the reported cost of the product, as this will change across time with the introduction of new cost drivers. Instead, I design what I think is the lowest cost product for a given level of reliability and functionality. It is important not to design to minimize the MAKE model cost because the model does not capture all of the relevant costs.
>
> We could improve the model to capture more costs, but we would risk it becoming too complex to understand and hence use. This is especially true for new college hires. They have never been taught to design with cost in mind. If we give them the MAKE model and say, "go for it", they cannot cope. It is better to give them a few rules at a time and slowly bring them up to speed.

The risk of designing to minimize reported product costs surfaced early on in the development of the cost system. An engineer designed a product to minimize reported product costs and was considered by some a hero. That was until the next change in the MAKE model was introduced. That change caused the reported product cost to go through the roof. The old model showed that automatic insertion cost one-tenth of manual insertion, whereas the new model showed it cost one-third.

The engineers saw both benefits and drawbacks to the MAKE model and hence cost driver cost system. In particular, they saw four major benefits and three major drawbacks. The benefits identified were as follows:

1. All engineers could use the same numbers to justify their designs. With the MAKE model supplying the cost information, everyone used the same heuristic rules to assess design tradeoffs.
2. The MAKE model provided a useful training tool to help establish the economic design heuristics and to sensitize the engineers to the cost of their design choices.

3. The MAKE model gave the engineers a good idea of what was really being spent on the products and helped them understand trends in the economics of design.

4. Even though the MAKE model did not capture all of the design costs, it helped identify areas where redesign either of existing products or potential products was called for. For example, one product that contained a very high number of components was redesigned, and the annual savings on the redesign were estimated at $1 million, leading to a payback of under one month.

The drawbacks identified were as follows:

1. There was a tendency on the part of some engineers to use MAKE model data in ways that a broader perspective would not support. This tended to occur when some of the issues that needed to be taken into account were outside the MAKE model. For example, recently a new product was introduced based on the product costs reported by the MAKE model. These costs assumed a sales volume that more careful analysis would have suggested was unrealizable.

2. The cost system and the MAKE model were heavily reliant on accounting rules. The engineer did not believe that these rules were always appropriate.

Huang commented as follows:

You need to understand the limitations of the MAKE model before you use it. I have learned to use it properly now, but it took time. If you do not realize that it is an accounting, not a design, model you can make serious mistakes. It is designed to spread costs the best way possible, but that may not be the best way to report costs for design purposes and other important decisions.

Overall, the engineers were pleased with the cost driver accounting cost system and MAKE model. However, they had mixed feelings about the way the two were implemented. Kyle Black, Engineering Project Manager and Huang's boss, commented as follows:

My initial reaction to the continuous changes in the cost system was anger. I felt it was unacceptable to have cost changes all the time. I wanted one set of numbers that I could rely on. My next reaction was frustration about how little anyone understood the economics of production. My next reaction was to accept the challenge and put it straight. We created a lot of tighter relationships between accounting, research and development, manufacturing, and marketing. We were all learning about the business. Now we are in the training mode. We have broken the back of the cost system design problem and are now refining it and our intuitions on the economics of product design. Overall, the whole experience forced us [the engineers] to understand our design process. We lost the "not invented here" syndrome and started understanding the benefits of leverage—using existing designs.

I would have preferred one transition, but I do not believe it could have been done that way. Accounting simply did not understand enough about the production and design process. If we had attempted one transition, we would have risked freezing the firm on the first system we designed; we would not have changed it to reflect the new insights we gained from it.

TEKTRONIX: PORTABLE INSTRUMENTS DIVISION (A)

The existing cost system did not reflect the realities of our assembly-based production process. We only required about 4% labor to build the product, and yet the cost accounting system was burdening on direct labor. This required an enormous number of transactions to track each stage of production. There was a widespread belief that material usage was a cost driver and that the current system did not reflect that cost driver. Management was quite concerned that we did not have adequate product costs and did not know where to place our strategic emphasis.

Bruce Anderson, Division Controller

This case was prepared by Professor Robin Cooper, Harvard University, and Professor Peter B. B. Turney, Portland State University.
Copyright © 1988 by the President and Fellows of Harvard College. Harvard Business School case 188-142.

Tektronix (Tek), headquartered in Beaverton, Oregon, produced a wide range of electronic equipment systems and software. The company's sales were divided into three product classes; instrument products, design automation and display products, and communication products. Sales in fiscal year 1987 were about $1.4 billion and net income before taxes was $103 million.

Tek's principal product since its founding in 1946 was the oscilloscope (scope), an instrument for measuring and displaying graphically the timing and magnitude of electrical phenomena. Over the years, Tek had developed a reputation as an engineers' company. Engineers were expected to design instruments from the ground up. Tek products were typically the reference for products in the marketplace (i.e., the products that other companies tried to emulate).

Tek had sold portable oscilloscopes since the 1950s, but a portable version did not exist prior to the introduction of the first battery-powered transistorized oscilloscope in 1961. Portables was created as a separate division in 1983 and split into two divisions in 1984. One of these divisions, Portable Instruments, handled high- and medium-performance oscilloscopes, and the other handled lower-priced models.

The Portable Instruments Division

The Portable Instruments Division (PID) viewed itself as a product differentiator, not a low-cost producer. Its strategy was to set the standards that the rest of the industry would try to emulate. Its competitors would analyze each new generation of Portable's products and then try to produce them less expensively. Competitors often achieved this objective because they could study the Portable's design and simplify it by taking advantage of the introduction of new lower-priced technology in the time lag between when Tek's engineers had designed the product and when the product was introduced in the marketplace. To survive, PID had to keep moving the reference, their products, toward more functionality and performance for the dollar. Reflecting this strategy, only one of the products PID sold in 1987 had been produced in 1983.

In 1983, PID sales were less than $100 million with a return on operating assets of −20%, down from its historical norm of 20% to 25%. The negative return reflected the severe price war that had started when Japanese competitors entered the market in 1981 and set prices 25% below PID's prevailing prices. To protect market share, PID had matched the Japanese prices even though these prices were often below the reported cost of their products. The resulting losses were acceptable to the parent corporation in the short run. But PID's management knew that large losses would not be acceptable in the long run.

To match the Japanese prices and make a profit, PID embarked on an ambitious program of continuous improvement. Many of the existing management teams were replaced with new managers whose sole objective was to turn the business around. The new team began to introduce just-in-time (JIT) production processes, total quality control (TQC), and new management styles, such as people involvement (PI), in which the labor force was allowed to become highly involved in making decisions.

In early 1983, Joe Burger was on assignment, from another Tektronix division, to study how to reduce the cost of the 2400 Series of oscilloscopes. He observed a number of managerial, technical, and process-oriented problems with the product line. For example, inventory levels were high and cycle time was over 30 days.

In late 1983, Joe Conrad, the PID group manufacturing manager, asked Joe Burger to head a special task force charged with solving these problems. Following the successful completion of this project in February 1984, Burger was appointed manufacturing manager of the 2400 Series product line and was promoted to PID manufacturing manager when the division was formed in August 1984.

The 2400 line of analog real-time oscilloscopes (ART) was designed to display the time and magnitude of electrical phenomena in real time (i.e., as they occurred). The 2400 line contained two lines, the 2445 and 2465, which comprised five different models. Each model was available with custom options to tailor the scope for specific applications such as communications, avionics, and the design, manufacture, and service of raster scan devices. The total number of different scopes available was about 15.

Burger described the 2400 line production process and the changes and events that had occurred through early 1987.

> The production process consisted of many functional islands: Etched Circuit Board (ECB) insertion, ECB assembly, kit prepping, ECB testing, ECB repair, final assembly, test, thermal cycle, test/QC, fitting the cabinet, finishing, boxing for shipment, and shipment. In addition, master and final assembly scheduling, modification control, order processing, and manufacturing engineering were service groups, not integrated into the production process.
>
> Due to the structure of the production process, each activity required a sequence number and inventory location, a large number of transactions, supporting paperwork and people to support it. A significant amount of work-in-process inventory was always on hand. Several large computer-controlled carousels were employed to handle this inventory.
>
> Realizing the need to change the original 2400 Series manufacturing process, management had implemented a pilot JIT line to begin a learning process that would result in improvements to the production process. This effort had mixed results—the output was low and not predictable—the problem was that management had reduced the work-in-process inventory prior to solving enough of the problems in the process. Consequently, the "excess" inventory was still needed as a buffer between each functional area, and its absence disrupted production.

Burger then described the actions taken.

My first objective was to consolidate the functionally oriented production activities into an integrated system. Initially, we were able to move just about everything but the wave solder system and ECB testers. We created an open work area, one that allowed eye contact and a visual overview of the entire production area. People, WIP, and problems were all out in the open. By bringing the areas together and eliminating the excessive WIP, we were able to reduce the floor space to 5,500 square feet, down from 10,000. We were now prepared to begin our JIT "journey."

We defined JIT as the continuous elimination of all waste. We did not limit this to activities on the production floor. We included functions such as new product introduction, procurement, stockroom, and the vendors, as well as production. Though we did not initially control many of these service activities, we did treat them as members of the team. This allowed us to create the integrated system we knew would be necessary.

The implementation of JIT in these activities was coordinated but did not occur simultaneously. In particular, JIT was implemented in production on a different schedule from that in the materials function. I controlled all the activities in production, so I could make changes rapidly. It was more difficult to make changes in the materials function, however, because this required working with vendors, changing component specifications, and solving product design problems. Many of the people and organizations involved were outside my span of control, and change took a lot longer to implement.

I gave the materials function one immediate goal: to provide the production group with JIT deliveries of fit-for-use material. Initially, this required additional people to work with vendors, to screen materials for defective units, and to ensure that production's need for materials was covered 100% of the time with nondefective units. Our costs and inventory of raw material went up, initially, but the goal of JIT delivery of fit-for-use material was met. Once this goal was met and sustained, a lot of effort was put into solving vendor specification and design problems. Eventually, we saw a significant reduction in material-related costs and raw material inventory levels.

The immediate advantage for production was an assured flow of quality components to meet their production needs. Production was able to focus on their own problems, including technical problems, poorly trained people, and inadequate equipment and tools. Production worked rapidly to solve these problems, first on an interim basis, and then on a permanent basis. Cycle time fell as a result, placing pressure on production to increase the first-pass rate. This drive to reduce cycle time and increase first-pass rates became the ongoing focus for all production personnel.

Following the consolidation, it became obvious that a significant amount of time was being wasted doing labor reporting, a carryover from the functionally structured past.

When we requested the elimination of this reporting, the Finance Group offered a challenge: "Reduce the cycle time to less than 10 days and you can stop tracking (value added) through labor reporting."

In March, the cycle time was approximately 30 days. At the time of the challenge, the cycle time had already been reduced to approximately 12 days. The 10-day cycle time was achieved in a very short time and many benefits resulted: Labor reporting was simplified, WIP was significantly reduced, and the need to closely track material at each work station was eliminated.

Within the next six months, we had integrated many of the previously functional services. The automatic board test system was removed from its climatized, isolated room and put into the ECB build area. Operators were trained to test their own boards and correct and learn from their mistakes. Incoming inspection provided a person to resolve reject material issues—this person "lived" on the line; vendors were immediately contacted when we encountered problems.

Production Process

By 1985, the production process had undergone its first major transition toward a fully integrated JIT process. At this time, production was organized into two areas: machine insertion on the lower floor of the facility, and assembly on the upper floor. Machine insertion had not been moved in line with assembly on the upper floor because it used super machines which serviced multiple products, and divisions and were not suited to in-line manufacturing.

Machine Insertion   The machine insertion area (MI) inserted various components into flats (large boards that contained up to eight separate circuit boards) which were supplied by Tek's Forest Grove plant. The flats were silkscreened and then inserted with integrated circuits (ICs), axial and radial components, and hardware.

Assembly   Flats arrived in assembly from Machine Insertion on kanban carts.[1] The flats were pulled from the carts as required. When all the flats had been removed from a cart, the cart was taken downstairs and exchanged for a full one. The arrival of the empty cart triggered the production of a new batch of flats in MI.

---

[1] A kanban provided a physical limit on the number of parts, subassemblies, and finished items that could be stored. PID used carts, baskets, and square areas of tables to store work-in-process inventory. These storage points were called kanbans.

A pull system was used throughout the assembly process. If there were fewer than the specified maximum number of flats in a kanban, this was the signal to the immediately preceding work station to build more flats. The actual number of boards built was determined by the shortfall in the kanban and the daily production goal.

The assembly process could be split into five distinct operations:

- Manual insertion (Prewave soldering)
- Wave solder
- Manual insertion (Postwave soldering)
- Final assembly
- Testing

The oscilloscopes were then moved to the finishing area where the cabinet was put on, a final functional and safety test was completed, and the soft options (e.g., power cords, additional or special probes, service manuals) were packaged with the scope. The scope then moved to a small finished goods area before being shipped to the customer. It took about five days from entry to the assembly area to this point. The finished goods inventory area was designed to hold up to 300 units.

Cost Accounting System

There were over 100 cost centers in the entire Portable Instruments Plant including about 25 production cost centers. The 2400 line was produced in seven of these production cost centers, although some of these produced products other than the 2400.

The existing system allocated overhead based on direct labor hours, with a separate rate calculated for each manufacturing cost center. Determining the burden rates required calculating frozen standard hours (FSH) and current standard hours (CSH) for each product in each production cost center. Per-unit FSH was the average of the actual number of direct labor hours consumed by a product over a period of a week or more. It was calculated once a year at the end of the fiscal year and was set equal to the most recent CSH at that time. CSH differed from FSH in that it was updated frequently, often weekly, to reflect reported labor efficiencies.

Production cost center overhead consisted of direct and indirect cost. Direct cost was incurred within or directly traceable to the cost center. Total indirect manufacturing costs were allocated among the cost centers based on budgeted FSH.

The system costed products by determining the cost of a single FSH hour in each production cost center. This was calculated by dividing a quarter's actual direct and indirect overhead in the cost center by the total number of FSH earned in that center during the previous quarter. FSH earned was the number of products manufactured, multiplied by the FSH per unit of the product to get the product cost. The rate was updated each quarter.

The CSH system was designed to report on the efficiency of the direct labor force. The labor efficiency reports were very detailed and were prepared on a daily or monthly basis. Efficiency was measured at the cost center level for each major step in the production process and for each individual employee.

Three types of efficiency variance were calculated at the cost center level each month: the method change variance, the volume variance, and the efficiency variance. The method change variance reflected the over- or underabsorption of labor and overhead resulting from changes in the production process (standard labor and overhead rate multiplied by the difference between the center's frozen earned standard hours and the current earned standard hours). The volume variance reflected over- or underabsorption of labor and overhead resulting from differences between planned and actual production (standard labor and overhead rate multiplied by the difference between planned and actual FSH). The efficiency variance measured the over- and underabsorbed labor and overhead resulting from differences between current standard hours and the actual hours paid (standard labor and overhead rate multiplied by the difference between CSH and the actual hours paid). These three variances were calculated for each of the seven cost centers, generating 21 different variances per month. Efficiency variances were not broken down by product.

An efficiency rating was calculated for each major step in the production process. Efficiency was calculated for a large number of operations including sequencing, IC insertion, axial component insertion, radial component insertion in the machine insertion department and hand insertion, flow soldering, additional hand insertion, testing (several tests were separately measured), assembly (several steps were separately measured), burn in, and final testing.

In addition to these functional efficiency measures, the cost system also reported on the efficiency of each individual employee daily. In departments where the operations were of short duration, such as hand insertion, it was not unusual for the employee to make over 50 entries a day. In such departments, it often required about 20 minutes a day for the employee to complete the reports. Most employees chose to complete these reports at the end of the day rather than on an ongoing basis.

Each employee was expected to fill in the quantity produced and the amount of time required to produce it. These data were then used to compute an efficiency measure that formed the basis for the employees' performance evaluation. While these production numbers were policed, employees tended to overestimate the number produced. These optimistic estimates could snowball because, to show improved efficiency against a standard that was updated weekly, an employee would have to report even higher output to compensate for the overestimation in the previous reports.

The quantity of data collected and its poor quality produced many problems. Employees complained about the amount of reporting they had to undertake, and the first-line managers grumbled about the amount they had to review. The inventory group was unhappy about the accuracy of the records and the impact the optimistic reporting had on inventory valuation. In particular, they cited the shop floor misreporting output as the major cause of the semiannual writedowns that were required when the physical-to-book comparisons were made. Accountants and line managers had similar complaints because they were expected to reconcile the reported hours to paid hours, and these rarely agreed. The accounting staff was displeased about the burden of correcting the numerous errors as well as having to process over 35,000 labor transactions and 25,000 inventory transactions per month.

There were many symptoms that suggested that this system was already obsolete and would be unable to adapt to the new changes in the production process. In particular, the emergence of a private engineering cost system, distinct from the financial system, indicated that many managers distrusted the product costs reported by the financial system. This engineering cost system used CSH rather than FSH and treated certain manufacturing support costs that were expressed as period costs in the standard cost systems as product costs.

Another reason to replace the existing system was its complexity and unwieldiness. About 18 months were needed to train a new individual to use the system; moreover, it was not clear that anyone fully understood it.

Changing the Cost System

In 1985, satisfied with their progress on the manufacturing process, management turned its attention to the design of a new cost accounting system. Their first step was to assess the need for cost information. Management identified three distinct uses of cost: special, management, and legal. Special costs were costs derived for special situations, such as make-versus-buy decisions, where the average costs reported by the cost system were inadequate. Management costs were the costs reported by the product costing system. These were used in designing products and guiding cost reduction efforts. Legal costs were the costs used to value inventory for financial accounting purposes.

After these uses for cost information had been identified, the firm embarked on a three-year program to replace the existing accounting systems. The first change was the implementation of an integrated business system that tied together the information used by manufacturing, accounting, and all other areas of the firm.

The second change was to simplify the accounting procedures. Reporting labor performance for each operation was abandoned, reducing the number of monthly labor transactions from 35,000 to less than 100. The number of inventory transactions was reduced by a similar extent, and the number of variances was reduced to three. This simplification freed up the time for a considerable portion of the accounting staff to work on the management cost system and special costing exercises.

The third change was the design of a new cost accounting system for the 2400 Series line of scopes. Management believed that the existing cost system did not reflect the realities of the new production process. Direct labor accounted for only 4% of the manufacturing cost, yet the accounting system used direct labor as the exclusive basis for allocating overhead. The direct labor content of PID's products had been constantly decreasing over recent years, while overhead costs were increasing. The result was that labor-based overhead rates were rising and had become absurdly high.

High overhead rates convinced engineers that the way to reduce overhead costs in products was to reduce labor. As a result, the focus of cost reduction programs had been the elimination of direct labor. Inevitably, since much of overhead was not driven by direct labor, this reduction did not have the desired effect, and overhead rates had continued to spiral upwards.

Given these facts, management was concerned that the product costs reported by the existing system were inaccurate and were not helping them guide the strategic emphasis of the divisions. In 1985, it decided to create a special project team to redesign the cost system. The team initially consisted of Mike Wright, financial systems application manager, and Jeff Taylor, summer student intern. They were later joined by John Jonez, manager of cost accounting.

Phase 1: Material Burdening

Bruce Anderson, division controller, stated the following:

> The problem of the existing system was its inability to recognize the "true" cost of purchased parts. Therefore, it did not allow the engineer to understand the tradeoff between parts proliferation and direct labor content. For example, we had hundreds of different resistors when a dozen would have sufficed. It was costing us money to maintain more and more active parts. Our objective was to reduce the number of vendors so that we could achieve JIT delivery and 100% quality. We believed this would increase our flexibility and reduce our overall costs. We were very worried about part number proliferation and felt that the material burdening system would help reduce it and keep it under control.

Jonez described his assignment to develop a new overhead allocation method.

> As a first step, we established a set of characteristics to guide the new allocation for the new method. We decided that the method must be intuitively logical and easily understandable by management. In addition, it should allow a more accurate correlation of cost to products, thus providing better support for management decisions such as make-versus-buy decisions, product design decisions, product phase-out and start-up decisions, and strategic pricing decisions. Most important, it must support the just-in-time manufacturing strategy of the division. Finally, it needed to provide information that was accessible by decision makers.

The team recognized that the chosen allocation method had to be accepted and supported by management. The time was right for change because almost everybody believed that the current method of burdening was inequitable and because accounting was convinced that the division's burdening method could be improved.

Initially, the team assumed that the new burdening method would be used for inventory valuation as well as for management purposes. This view was abandoned,

however, when it was realized that the new burdening method might change the reported valuation of inventory. One concern was that this change might conflict with reporting consistency. PID also wanted to maintain the option of changing the burdening method for management purposes in the future without having to seek corporate accounting, auditing, and IRS approval. Another reason to keep legal costing separate from management costing was the desire to report full product costs. PID therefore adopted the idea of management costs, which would use the new burdening method and would coexist with the financial costs for inventory valuation. One difference between the two systems was that more elements of costs were included in the new system. Purchasing costs, for example, were treated as a period cost in the old system, whereas the team preferred to include them in the product cost.

In its study, the team discovered that about 50% of overhead costs were related to materials (material overhead costs, or MOH). These costs included the costs of planning, procuring, inspecting, storing, and distributing materials. It was felt that an allocation base should be selected that was relevant to these activities. The remaining 50% of overhead would, for the moment, continue to be allocated using direct labor.

After some preliminary analysis, the following alternative allocation bases were identified:

1. Material dollars
2. Number of parts
3. Number of part numbers.

Material dollars burdening calculated an MOH cost per dollar of material cost. For example, if the budgeted annual MOH was $8,200,000 and budgeted total material purchases was $70,000,000, the material dollar overhead rate would be $.0117 of MOH per material dollar.

The second method calculated a single burden rate that was applied to each part specified in the bill of materials. If a bill specified 100 discrete parts and the number used was five times each, the material overhead for the assembled item would be 500 multiplied by the rate per part.

The third method determined a different rate for each part depending on the volume of usage. If there were 6,000 part numbers, there would be 6,000 rates. Each rate was calculated using a two-step procedure. The first step determined the standard burden cost for each part number. The second step divided the standard burden cost by the volume of each part number to obtain the cost per part for that part number. This calculation produced lower rates for high-volume parts and higher rates for low-volume parts (Exhibit 1).

Step 1:

$$\frac{\text{material overhead}}{\text{number of active}} = \frac{\text{annual cost to}}{\text{carry a part number}}$$
$$\text{part numbers}$$

Step 2:

$$\frac{\text{annual cost to carry}}{\text{annual usage of}} = \frac{\text{MOH rate}}{\text{for each part}}$$
$$\text{the part number}$$

To make a choice from among these three methods, the team had to understand what costs should be included in MOH, to identify the factors that caused those costs, and to determine their relative materiality. After consultation with management, the team broke MOH into the following distinct components:

1. Costs due to the value of parts
2. Costs due to the absolute number of parts
3. Costs due to the maintenance and handling of each different part number
4. Costs due to each use of a different part number.

This breakdown showed that the costs incurred due to the frequency of the use of parts categories (2 and 4) were secondary to the cost of carrying each different part number (3). The costs due to the value of parts were similarly quite small.

The cost of carrying each different part number resulted from a number of activities that had to be carried out for each part number. These activities included planning, scheduling, negotiating with vendors, purchasing, receiving, handling, delivering, storing, and paying for each part number. The more part numbers there were, the more these activities had to be performed.

Given these findings, the team concluded that the total MOH cost of the parts could reasonably be expected to decrease with the use of a smaller number of different part numbers. This cost reduction was the result of two factors. First, higher volume discounts could be achieved by replacing low-volume unique parts with high-volume common parts. As the number of part numbers was reduced, it was also likely that the number

of vendors would be reduced. This would, in turn, reduce the demand for vendor-related activities. Second, the total manufacturing overhead needed to support an operation with fewer unique part numbers would be less than the current amount. While overall cost reduction would not be immediate, management believed that the part number allocation method would increase the awareness of the costs associated with part number proliferation. This awareness would influence engineering decisions and result in real cost savings over time.

On reviewing these facts, management decided that the chosen allocation measure for MOH should focus on the second factor—the reduction of overhead through the reduction of part numbers. They felt that the third method, an allocation measure based on part numbers with a specific rate for each part number, best captured the relationship between material overhead and part numbers. Consequently, after the team made a series of presentations to management, the method received general acceptance.

Under this method, the MOH cost for each instrument was computed from the part numbers in the instrument's bill of materials. The rate for each part number was multiplied by the number of times that part was used in the instrument. The resulting cost was aggregated for all part numbers in the bill (Exhibit 2). Instruments with larger numbers of parts and/or a higher percent of unique parts carried a higher MOH cost.

During these presentations, the following advantages were identified for adopting the part number method:

1. The part number method was the most accurate of the three because it reflected the differential consumption of materials-related activities by the products. An instrument designed with many unique components, for example, would be correctly given a cost penalty. The method would also avoid penalizing high-volume products which, while they might contain a number of different parts, consumed relatively few material related activities per material number.
2. The method would provide engineers with a listing of all parts and the material overhead cost associated with each part. This information would be helpful in determining the value of a new part versus an existing common part and encourage reducing the number of part numbers and increasing the proportion of common parts used in the instruments. Such a listing did not currently exist, and engineers relied on their own judgment in making such evaluations.

The disadvantages of using the part number method were identified as follows:

1. Certain products might be allocated an excessive amount of overhead. The cost allocated to products with infrequent options, for example, might exceed the true cost of adding the options. Products that were being phased out, where little effort was being expended, might also be overcosted.

2. It was the most difficult of the three methods to implement and would require the most computer resources to maintain.

3. It was the most complex method and probably the most difficult for management to understand. For example, management might draw the erroneous conclusion that the material overhead costs of $687.50 were variable with each part number because eliminating one part number in the data base would not reduce total material overhead costs by this amount. Nor would the division save $2.00 in out-of-pocket costs using one fewer low-volume part. Over time, however, and with a sufficient reduction in part numbers, the consumption of materials-related activities and overhead cost would go down.

Given this long-term variability of part-number–related costs, management had difficulty attaching any specific meaning to the $687.50 rate. It was merely an average calculation based on the current overhead cost structure and the current set of part numbers used by the division.

EXHIBIT 1

TEKTRONIX: PORTABLE INSTRUMENTS DIVISION (A)

Number of Part Numbers
Overhead Cost Computation
(Example)

$$\text{Expenses in the MOH pool} = \$5,500,000$$
$$\text{Number of active part numbers} = 8,000$$
$$\text{Annual cost to carry each part number} = \frac{\$5,500,000}{8,000} = \$687.50$$

– High usage part
$$\text{Annual usage of example part number} = 35,000 \text{ units}$$
$$\text{MOH rate for example part number} = \frac{\$687.50}{35,000} = \$.02$$

– Low usage part
$$\text{Annual usage of example part number} = 350 \text{ units}$$
$$\text{MOH rate for example part number} = \frac{\$687.50}{350} = \$2.00$$

EXHIBIT 2

TEKTRONIX: PORTABLE INSTRUMENTS DIVISION (A)

Product Cost Information Using
Material Burdening Approach

Model	A	B	C	D	E	TOTAL
Volume	3,000	3,000	750	400	300	7,450
Selling price	$3,590	$5,550	$7,150	$8,400	$9,200	$38,902,500
Costs:						
Material	$2,000	$2,400	$3,350	$4,100	$4,200	$18,612,500
Labor	250	260	320	380	390	2,039,000
LOH	300	360	250	500	540	2,529,500
MOH	150	160	320	650	700	1,640,000
Other	200	250	350	450	460	1,930,500
Total cost	$2,900	$3,430	$4,590	$6,080	$6,290	$26,751,500
Gross margin	$690	$2,120	$2,560	$2,320	$2,910	$12,151,000
Percent	19.22%	38.20%	35.80%	27.62%	31.63%	31.23%

LOH = Labor Overhead
MOH = Materials Overhead

NISSAN MOTOR COMPANY, LTD.: TARGET COSTING SYSTEM

Nissan Motor Company, Ltd. (Nissan) was by 1990 the world's fourth-largest automobile manufacturer. In 1990, Nissan produced just over 3 million vehicles, supplying approximately 10% of the world's demand for cars and trucks. Of these vehicles, slightly over two million were passenger cars. Nissan, founded in 1933, considered itself the most highly globalized of the Japanese automobile companies, producing vehicles at 36 plants in 22 countries and marketing in 150 countries through 390 distributorships and over 10,000 dealerships.

Nissan had a stated policy of increasing its globalization through a five-step process: first, by increasing local production; second, by raising the local content of its products through expanded use of locally sourced parts and components; third, by strengthening local research and development capabilities; fourth, by localizing management functions; and finally, by localizing decision-making processes. As a result, four out of the five major overseas manufacturing plants were managed by local chief executive officers, and in 1990 regional headquarters were opened in Europe and North America.

The domestic Japanese passenger automobile market was intensely competitive. The largest manufacturer was Toyota, with approximately 45% of the domestic market. Nissan was second with approximately 25%, followed by Honda and Mazda, who together represented about another 20%. In an attempt to increase its market share in the expanding but fiercely contested domestic market, Nissan implemented a plan to achieve annual domestic sales of 1.5 million cars by 1992 and to obtain the number-one rating in terms of customer satisfaction. This strategy depended on designing products that were engineered around clearly defined concepts chosen to offer customers automobiles that matched their lifestyles.

Automobile firms had been steadily increasing their range of products since the 1950s. This increase was driven primarily by changes in consumer preferences. For example, US consumers in the 1950s viewed the automobile as a status symbol, using the make of automobile they owned to signal the level of their economic success. Nissan executives characterized the consumer in this era as "keeping up with the Joneses." As automobile ownership became more widespread, consumers began to view their automobiles as making a statement about *who* they were. Nissan executives characterized the consumer of this era as "doing his or her own thing." Consumer demand of the 1960s required more variations and a broader range of model types than in the 1950s. As the 1960s closed and individualism became less important, consumers came to view their automobiles as making statements about *what* they were. Nissan executives characterized this era as being dominated by a desire for a "consistency of lifestyle," i.e., bankers wanted automobiles that were appropriate for bankers. This shift required that more models and variations be produced to satisfy consumer demand. During the 1980s, consumers started to demand automobiles that suited multiple lifestyles. As one executive summed up the transition, "the old segmentation that assumed a single lifestyle no longer worked; we now have to design cars that allow people to be bankers by day and punk rockers at night." This transition in consumer preference placed additional pressure on the firm to increase its range of product offerings.

Despite this pressure, Nissan had chosen to systematically reduce the number of distinct models it would introduce in the 1990s. This decision reflected two additional trends. First, the differences between consumers in the three major markets—Japan, North America, and Europe—were decreasing, and second, the costs associated with introducing new models were increasing. The decrease in differences among consumers in the three major markets reduced the need to develop models specific to a single market. The increased costs associated with launching new models made it difficult to make acceptable profits if the number of new models introduced each year was too large. These trends suggested to Nissan top management that overall profitability would be increased by reducing the number of distinct models supported, while maintaining the same level of effort to design and market the remaining models.

Introducing New Products

Over the years, Nissan had developed a formal procedure to introduce new products. One of the major elements of this procedure was a sophisticated target cost-

Professor Robin Cooper of The Peter F. Drucker Graduate Management Center at The Claremont Graduate School prepared this case.

Copyright © 1994 by the President and Fellows of Harvard College. Harvard Business School case 194-040.

ing system. In this system, a target selling price for each new model was first established; then, a target margin was determined based upon corporate profitability objectives; finally, the model's target cost was identified as the difference between the target selling price and the target margin. Once the target cost of the new model was established, value engineering was used to ensure that the new model, when it entered production, could be manufactured at the desired target cost.

The procedure to introduce new models was divided into three distinct stages: in the conceptual design stage, projects to introduce new product models were initiated; in the product development stage, the new models were readied for production; and in the production stage, they were manufactured. Taken together, these three stages lasted about 10 years, the average life cycle of a modern passenger automobile. The conceptual design stage required about two years to complete, the product development stage required about four years, and the production stage typically lasted about another four years. Thus, it was not unusual for Nissan to be simultaneously producing the current model, preparing its replacement for introduction, and conceptualizing the next model's replacement.

The Conceptual Design Stage New product models were designed in the conceptual design stage. First, the designers identified the mixture of models that Nissan expected to sell over the next ten years. This mix was described in a matrix of vehicles by major market and body type (e.g., coupe or sedan). The matrix contained qualitative information about each model, such as its price range, target customers and their income levels, and the range of body types supported. This information was maintained for both current and future models and effectively described each model's market position. The primary purpose of the product matrix was to ensure that Nissan achieved the desired level of market coverage.

New entries in the matrix were identified using consumer analysis. This analysis was undertaken by market consulting firms using a number of different techniques, including general economic, psychological, and anthropological surveys as well as direct observation. In recent years, this analysis had identified over 50 potential models that theoretically could be successfully introduced by Nissan. However, top management had identified the optimum number of models that Nissan could successfully support at under 30. This number was limited by

several factors, including the cost of differentiating each model in the minds of consumers, research and development, and the cash flow associated with maintaining dealer floor inventory. Thus, the challenge that Nissan management faced was to select the approximately 30 models that would maximize market coverage.

New models were conceptualized by identifying consumer "mind-sets." Mind-sets captured characteristics of the way consumers viewed themselves in relation to their cars. These mind-sets could be used to identify design attributes that consumers took into account when purchasing a new car. Typical mind-sets included value seeker, confident and sophisticated, aggressive enthusiast, and budget/speed star. By identifying clusters of these mind-sets, Nissan could identify niches that contained a sufficient percentage of the automobile-purchasing public to warrant introducing a model specifically tailored for that niche. For example, the Sentra (a mid-price family sedan) was designed to satisfy the confident/sophisticated and value seeker mind-sets, while the ZX (a high-performance sports car) was designed to satisfy the budget/speed star and aggressive enthusiast mind-sets. As a Nissan marketing executive commented, "If we believe that a sufficient market will exist in four to five years, then we will develop a model to fit it." Thus, each model and its body shape variations, such as sedan, coupe, hatchback, and wagon, was specifically designed to satisfy a different group of consumers.

As a final check on the appropriateness of the proposed model line-up, each model was categorized using three primary attributes: performance, aesthetics, and comfort. For example, comfort was considered the most important attribute for the Sentra model and performance the least important, while for the ZX model, performance was considered the most important and comfort the least. A plot of the attribute characteristics of both current, future, and competitive models allowed top management to determine that the proposed product mix covered an adequate percentage of the market.

At this stage of the product introduction process, the conceptual design was sufficiently developed to allow a rough estimate of the number of vehicles to be sold and the costs associated with its development. These estimates were used in a life cycle contribution study to estimate the overall profitability of the proposed model. The purpose of this study was to ensure that the new model was likely to generate a positive contribution over its life. The life cycle contribution study consisted of comparing the estimated revenues generated by the new model to the expected cost of the product across its life (see Exhibit 1). The model's revenue was estimated by using a rough estimate of the selling price and the anticipated volume of sales. From this estimate the anticipated direct material cost, which included raw material, paint, and purchased parts, was subtracted. The difference between these two quantities was the estimated direct material marginal profit of the new model.

From this profit, four additional sets of expenses were subtracted. The first set contained the direct manufacturing and sales expenses. These were expenses that were predominantly driven by the number of units produced and sold. The direct manufacturing expenses included elements such as the cost of the energy, cutting tools, and indirect materials consumed. The direct sales expenses included logistics costs such as the costs of shipping and delivery. The second set contained the estimated direct labor costs. The third set contained the depreciation charges for machining, die casting, and other major production steps. Finally, the estimated research and development expenses were subtracted to give the life cycle contribution of the particular model under development.

The depreciation charges used in the life cycle contribution analysis were estimated by taking the total depreciation for each machine or process and dividing that by the number of units expected to be produced on that equipment over its life. If the equipment was dedicated to the new model, as was typically the case with stamping dies, then the number of units was the estimated volume of production for that model; if the equipment was common to several models, as was often the case with conveyors, then the number of units was the total of all units expected to be produced of all models using that equipment. The depreciation charge used for the life cycle contribution analysis was not the one used for financial reporting purposes. Nissan reported depreciation using a declining balance approach for both tax and financial reporting purposes. However, for the life cycle contribution calculation it used a straight-line approach. Management modified the depreciation calculation because it felt that the straight-line approach better captured the relationship between asset use and models produced than the declining balance approach. If the life cycle contribution was deemed satisfactory, the conceptual design process was allowed to continue.

As the conceptual design of the new model progressed, additional consumer analysis and financial analysis was undertaken. Consumer analysis was used

to obtain a better idea of the price range over which the model would sell and the level of functionality that the consumer expected. The financial analysis consisted of a rough profitability study in which the profitability of the highest volume variant of the new model was estimated using historical cost estimates and the latest estimate of that variant's target price. This target price was determined by taking into account a number of internal and external factors. The internal factors included the position of the model in the matrix and the strategic and profitability objectives of top management for that model. The external factors considered included the corporation's image and level of customer loyalty in the model's niche, the expected quality level and functionality of the model compared to competitive offerings, the model's expected market share, and finally, the expected price of competitive models.

The first stage of value engineering was designed to determine whether the new model could be manufactured at an acceptable profit (see Exhibit 2). The process began by developing an order sheet detailing the characteristics of the 20 to 30 major functions of the proposed model. Examples of the major functions included the engine, air conditioner, transmission, and sound system. The characteristics of each major function were chosen to satisfy the collection of consumer mind-sets for which the model was designed. For example, the engine specified for a ZX would be a high-performance one, while for the Sentra it would be smaller, less powerful, and less expensive. The current cost of the model was determined by summing the current manufacturing cost of each major function of the new model. This current cost was compared with the model's allowable cost to determine the level of cost reduction required to achieve the desired level of profitability.

The allowable cost of the new model was determined by subtracting its target profit margin from its target price. The target margin was determined by careful consideration of available information on the consumer, the firm's anticipated future product mix, and its long-term profit objective. Each new model's target margin was established by running simulations of the firm's overall profitability for the next 10 years if it was selling the models identified in the product matrix at expected sales volumes. The simulations started by plotting the actual profit margins of existing products (see existing product curve in Exhibit 3). The desired profitability of planned models was then added (see Exhibit 4) and the firm's overall profitability determined over the years at various sales levels. This predicted overall profitability was compared to the firm's long-term profitability objectives set by senior management (see Exhibit 5). Once a satisfactory future product matrix was established that achieved the firm's profit objective, the target margins for each new model were set.

To help minimize the risk that Nissan would not achieve its overall profitability targets, the simulations explored the impact on overall profitability of different price/margin curves for different product mixes. For example, historically higher margins had been earned on higher priced vehicles (see existing product curve in Exhibit 3). However, with the reduced product offering and the increased profitability expected, the future curve might be higher. Alternatively, because there was no guarantee that the existing relationship between price and margin would remain unchanged, simulations were also run to explore the impact of fundamentally different relationships between selling price and margins.

The first stage of value engineering and the identification of target price was an interactive process. When the allowable costs were considered to be too far below the estimated cost, the appropriate price range and functionality were reviewed until an allowable cost that was considered achievable was identified (see Exhibit 6).

The excess of the current manufacturing cost over the allowable cost determined the level of cost reduction that had to be identified by value engineering. For example, the current manufacturing cost of the model might be ¥3,000,000 and the allowed cost ¥2,700,000, which identified a required cost reduction of 10%. The next step in the value engineering process was to identify the allowable cost of each major function. This cost was set by teams derived from almost every functional area of the firm, including product design, engineering, purchasing, production engineering, manufacturing, and parts supply. Although the allowable cost was usually lower than the current cost, sometimes the allowable cost was higher because the new product specifications demanded higher performance and functionality than existing designs. In total, the sum of the cost reduction for each major component was meant to equal the required level of cost reduction to achieve the model's allowable cost (see Exhibit 7).

Several critical decisions about the model were made during this stage of the conceptual design process, including the number of body variations, the number of engine types, and the basic technology used in the vehicle. For example, the original concept for the model might include a five-door variant. However, if during this stage of the analysis it was determined that developing such a variant would be too costly or take an excessive amount of time, plans for a five-door variant would be postponed to the next version of that automobile. Once the projected cost of each major component had been identified, the expected cost of manufacture could be computed.

After the first value engineering stage was completed, a major review of the new model was conducted. This review included an updated profitability study and an analysis of the performance characteristics of the model. In the profitability study, the expected profitability of the model given by the target price minus the target cost was compared to the latest estimates of the capital investment and remaining research and development expenditures required to complete the design of the product and allow production to commence. In the performance analysis, factors such as the quality of the hardware, engine capacity, exhaust emissions, and safety were considered. If both the financial and performance analyses were considered acceptable, the project to introduce the new vehicle was authorized and the model shifted from the conceptual design to the product development stage.

The Product Development Stage The first step in the product development stage was to prepare a detailed order sheet for the new model. This order sheet listed all of the components required in the new model and was analyzed to see which components would likely be sourced internally versus externally. Suppliers, both internal and external, were provided with a description of each component and their potential production volumes. Suppliers were expected to provide price and delivery timing estimates for each component.

The next step in the development of a new model was to produce the engineering drawings for trial production. Value engineering was used at this stage of product development to determine allowable costs for each of the components in every major function of the automobile. This estimate was achieved by identifying a cost reduction objective for each component (see Exhibit 8). There were several ways that cost reduction objectives for components were identified. First, competitors' products were purchased, disassembled, and analyzed. From this analysis, ideas for cost reduction were sometimes generated.

Second, parts suppliers were asked to generate cost

reduction ideas. An incentive plan was used to motivate the suppliers. For example, if an idea was accepted, the supplier that suggested the cost reduction idea would be awarded a significant percentage of the contract for that component for a specified time period, say 50% for 12 months. This incentive scheme was viewed as particularly important because even if a cost reduction could not be achieved for this model, it signalled to the suppliers that when the next model was developed this component would be subject to cost reduction pressures.

Third, ways to increase the commonality of parts across variations and models were identified (e.g., the same seats might be used in two different models). Fourth, ways to reduce the number of components in each model were identified. For example, originally the kick plates used to protect the door were held in place by plastic nuts. However, a way to mold the plastic interior of the door so that no nuts were required had been developed.

To avoid having to develop target costs for all 20,000 components in a typical new model line, the engineers only performed detailed target costing on two or three representative variations. Each variation contained approximately 3,500 components, and typically 80% of the components were common across variations. Therefore, about 5,000 components were subjected to detailed target costing. The target costs of the other 15,000 components were estimated by comparing them to similar components in the 5,000 already target-costed. The completion of this target costing exercise provided cost reduction objectives for all of the components in the new model. The comparison of the allowable cost of each function and the sum of the expected cost of the components in that function after cost reduction indicated whether the major function could be produced at about the allowable cost. When the sum of the component costs was too high, additional cost reductions were identified until the total target cost of the representative variation was acceptable. The target costs for each component were compared to the prices quoted by the suppliers. If the quoted prices were acceptable, the quote was accepted. If the initial quote was too high, then further negotiations were undertaken until an agreement could be reached.

The next phase in product development was to construct two or three prototype vehicles. Several important lessons were learned from the construction of these prototypes. First, any components that were difficult to assemble were identified. Typically, these components or the assemblies into which they fitted were redesigned to improve the ease of assembly. Second, assembly times could now be estimated quite accurately. In the third stage of value engineering, the effect of these redesigns on the target costs of the components was determined and assembly target costs were identified. The output of this stage of value engineering was called the final target cost (see Exhibit 9). It differed from the draft target cost in two ways. First, it included assembly costs and second, the indirect manufacturing costs. The indirect manufacturing costs were assigned to products using the same procedures as the firm's cost system. Thus, the final target cost for a model variant was expected to be equal to its reported product cost during manufacture.

A comparison of the final target costs for each model variant and its expected selling price allowed the anticipated profit on the vehicle to be determined. The expected selling price was reviewed by marketing in light of recent competitive products and market conditions, and a final selling price recommended. Accounting was responsible for authorizing the actual selling price of each variation. It took into account marketing's review of existing conditions, the final target cost of the vehicle, and the target margin for the vehicle. Once set, accounting notified marketing of the recommended selling price. In Japan, this was the price at which the car would be sold across its life. In other markets, such as North America, incentive plans and other marketing techniques could cause the effective price to change across the life of the product.

Accounting was not involved in the value engineering process, which was the responsibility of the cost design and engineering department. The primary function of accounting was to set the final target cost for each model variant and ensure that the vehicles were manufactured for that amount. As the vehicle entered production, accounting would monitor all component and assembly costs and if these were not in line with the final target costs, accounting would notify cost design and engineering that the final target costs were not being met. When the target costs were exceeded, additional value engineering was performed to reduce costs back to the target levels. Thus, the fourth and final value engineering stage ensured that the actual component and assembly costs were equal to their final target costs.

Unless the production cost exceeded the target cost, no cost reduction efforts were undertaken during the production stage. Management had determined that the incremental savings from such efforts were more than offset by disturbances they created to the production process. When inflation or other factors caused costs to rise, pressure was exerted upon the suppliers to find ways to keep component costs at their final target levels. Similarly, pressure was exerted on the assembly plants to achieve the assembly target costs.

The Production Stage The Zama facility, located a few miles from Tokyo, was one of Nissan's five major domestic manufacturing facilities. Built in 1964, it was 852,000 square meters in area and contained two complete stamping and assembly facilities. In addition, the facility housed a car delivery area and the firm's machinery design center. No production parts were produced at Zama. The plant was only involved in producing pressed metal parts, welding them together, assembling the body, painting it, and then assembling the finished automobile.

The Zama plant was designed to produce 90 cars per hour, operating on a two-shift basis with production occurring for 15 hours and 20 minutes per day. A two-shift operation enabled the plant to produce between 1,300 to 1,400 cars per day at full capacity. While preventative maintenance was carried on throughout the day, primary maintenance was performed during the 8 hours and 40 minutes in which no production was scheduled.

Zama was a highly automated plant. Of the approximately 3,000 spot welds per car, over 97% were performed automatically. This high level of automation had been achieved over a number of years. The current high level of automatic spot welding was achieved around 1980. To sustain this high level of automation, Zama contained nearly 300 robots. All of these robots were designed by Nissan but only about 40% were actually manufactured by the firm.

In 1990, the facility was dedicated to the production of two models and three body types. The Sunny, or Sentra as it was called in the North American market, was produced in two body types: the four-door and two-door coupe configurations and the Presea in a single four-door configuration. Each body type could be produced in numerous variations of key components, such as engine, air conditioning, and transmission. When all possible option variations were included, Zama produced approximately 20,000 different variations of each of the three distinct body types.

The large number of variations forced the facility to produce cars to customer order. This production strategy fit well with Nissan's corporate strategy of providing customer satisfaction, high quality, short delivery times, and high functionality. In fact, fast delivery was considered so important that the production strategy was called by a name that translated to "deliver the car with the paint still wet." In 1990, a car ordered from a Japanese dealer and produced in the Zama plant could be delivered to the customer within 2 weeks. Because in Tokyo it required at least a week to get the certificate of space required to enable a car to be purchased, the effective wait for a new Nissan was negligible. This short delivery time despite high product diversity was achieved via aggressive use of just-in-time production.

The Product Cost System The same cost system was used throughout Nissan's assembly plants. It reported full product costs that included both direct and indirect expenses. The indirect expenses were traced to the products in two different ways. Direct and indirect manufacturing expenses were directly charged to the production cost center in which they were consumed, and then allocated to the products. Service and administrative expenses and corporate expenses were allocated to the product without first being allocated to a production center. Corporate expenses were equal to about 15% of the sales revenue. They consisted of three major types of expenses: product-related expenses that included advertisements, warranty, and delivery expenses; geographic-related expenses, such as the costs associated with the sales division in Tokyo that supported sales in all three major markets; and finally, there were the expenses associated with corporate administration, legal, and accounting. The product-related portion of corporate expenses was approximately 30%, the geographic-related portion 50%, and the other expenses about 20%.

Three different product profitabilities were calculated (see Exhibit 10). The first was the direct material marginal profit. This was calculated by subtracting the cost of the raw materials and purchased parts from the selling price. The second was the product contribution, determined by subtracting direct manufacturing costs, research and development expenses, and corporate expenses directly related to the product from the direct material marginal profit.

Direct manufacturing expenses included manufacturing supplies such as cutting tools and machine depreciation. The procedures used to assign these expenses to products varied depending upon the nature of the expenses and how they were consumed. For example, the costs of manufacturing supplies were assigned to the products based upon the number of direct labor hours the product consumed in the center if the department produced several different models, and number of units if only one model was produced; machine depreciation was assigned to products based upon the number of units irrespective of model. Research and development expenses included the cost of the labor, facilities, and supplies consumed in the research and development facility. They were allocated to products based upon the labor hours consumed in research and development on that product. The corporate expenses directly related to the product included items such as product advertisements, product incentives, warranty costs, and delivery expenses.

The third product profitability, operating profit, was calculated by subtracting indirect manufacturing, service, administrative, and the remaining corporate expenses from the product contributions. Indirect manufacturing expenses were directly charged to the production cost center in which they were incurred. Examples of indirect manufacturing expenses included transportation, maintenance, and facility depreciation. These expenses were assigned to the products based on the total direct cost of the products produced in that center. Service and administrative expenses were assigned to the products without first being assigned to the production centers. These expenses were assigned based on the total direct cost of the product. Corporate

expenses were first assigned to the facility and then to the products based on their total direct costs in the same way as were service and administrative expenses. The breakdown of product profitability and cost is shown in Exhibit 11.

The Nissan cost system was continuously undergoing modification. In particular, a program had been initiated to trace as many costs as possible directly to the production departments. Thus, over time the service and administrative categories were dropping in relationship to the direct and indirect manufacturing costs. The success of this program and the heavy reliance upon external parts and service suppliers were visible from the relative importance of the three major cost categories. The direct costs, i.e., those costs that were traced directly to the products, represented 85% of total manufacturing costs; the direct and indirect manufacturing costs that were charged to the production departments and then assigned to the products represented about 10% of total manufacturing costs; while service and administrative costs amounted to only 5% of total costs.

The product costs reported by the cost system had four primary uses. First, they were used in the long-range strategic plan as a basis for estimating future profitability. Second, they were used for cost-control purposes, in particular to ensure that across the production life of a product its target cost was maintained. Third, they were used to help select the product mix, in particular with respect to the variations of a given model. Finally, they were used to identify unprofitable variants that were candidates for discontinuance.

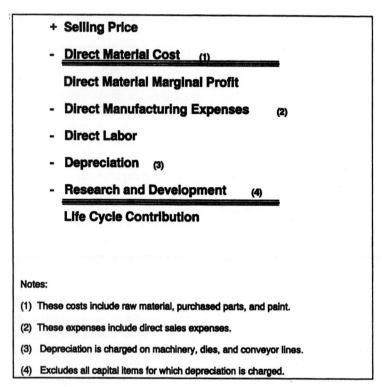

+ **Selling Price**

- **Direct Material Cost**   (1)

   Direct Material Marginal Profit

- **Direct Manufacturing Expenses**   (2)

- **Direct Labor**

- **Depreciation**   (3)

- **Research and Development**   (4)

   Life Cycle Contribution

Notes:

(1) These costs include raw material, purchased parts, and paint.

(2) These expenses include direct sales expenses.

(3) Depreciation is charged on machinery, dies, and conveyor lines.

(4) Excludes all capital items for which depreciation is charged.

EXHIBIT 1   Life Cycle Contribution Study

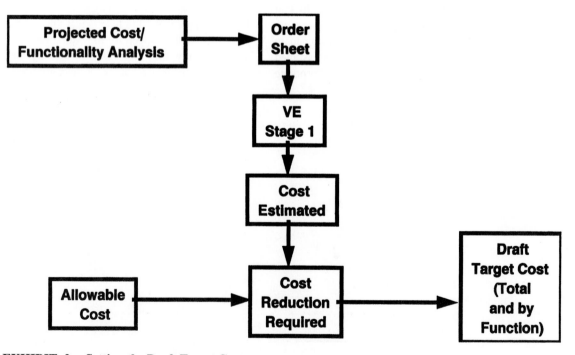

EXHIBIT 2   Setting the Draft Target Cost

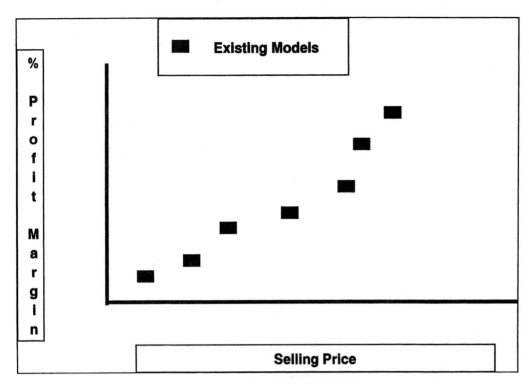

EXHIBIT 3 Identifying the Target Margin (Existing Models)

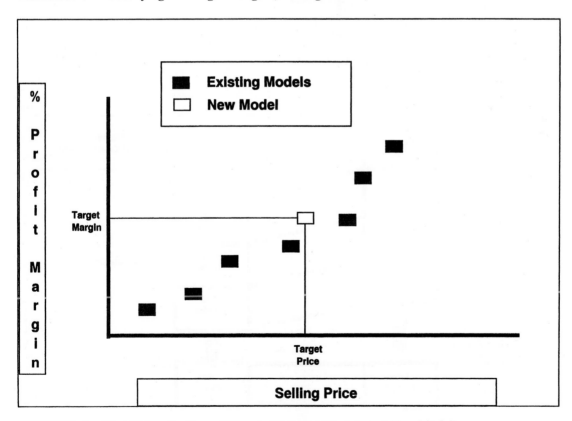

EXHIBIT 4 Identifying the Target Margin (Existing Models and New Model)

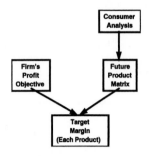

EXHIBIT 5
Setting the Target
Margin

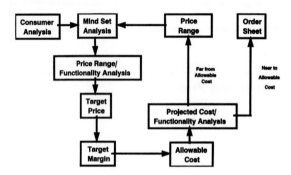

EXHIBIT 6   Identifying an Achievable
Allowable Cost

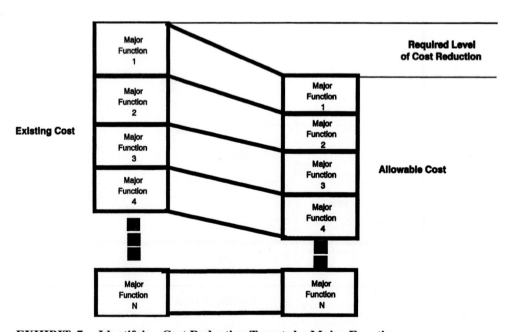

EXHIBIT 7   Identifying Cost Reduction Targets by Major Function

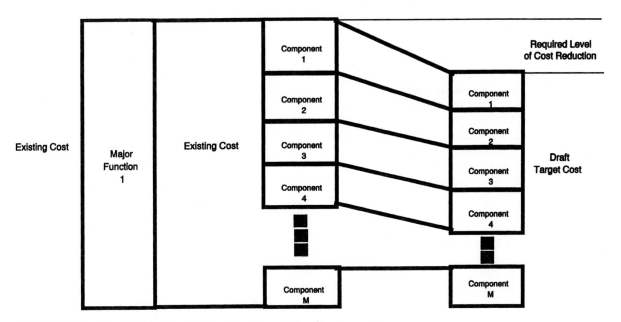

EXHIBIT 8   Identifying Cost Reduction Targets by Component

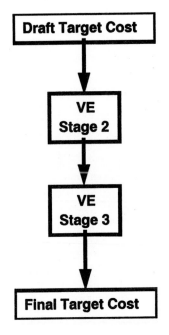

EXHIBIT 9   Setting the Final Target Cost

EXHIBIT 10 Breakdown of Product Profitability

	Revenue			****
	Direct Material Cost			
	1) Purchased parts		****	
	2) Raw materials		****	(****)
Direct Cost &	**Direct Material Marginal Profit**			****
Expenses	Direct Manufacturing Cost			
	1) Direct labor cost		****	
	2) Manufacturing expenses directly variable to		****	
(Directly	the number of units produced		****	
Characterized	(e.g. cutting tools)			
to Products)	3) Tools & machinery	Depreciation charge	****	
		Maintenance cost	****	
		Energy cost	****	
				(****)
	R&D Expense (labor, expenses, facilities)			(****)
	Corporate Expenses Directly Related to Product			
	1) Product advertisements		****	
	2) Product incentives		****	
	3) Warranty		****	
	4) Delivery expenses		****	
				(****)
	Product Contribution			*****
	Indirect Manufacturing Cost Consumed by Manufacturing Shop Floors			
	1) Indirect materials (e.g. monkey wrench, sand paper)		****	
Indirect Cost	2) Indirect labor cost		****	
	3) Shop floor facilities.	Depreciation charge	****	
		Maintenance cost	****	
		Energy cost	****	
				(****)
	Services			
	1) Quality inspection (labor, expenses, facilities)		****	
(Irrespective	2) Logistics (labor, expenses, facilities)		****	
of Product	3) Energy consumed in service department		****	
Characteristics)	4) Maintenance consumed in service department		****	
				(****)
	Administration			
	1) Labor cost		****	
	2) General expenses		****	
	3) Facilities	Depreciation charge	****	
		Maintenance cost	****	
		Energy cost	****	
				(****)
	Corporate Expense (exluding "directly related to product")			
Corporate	1) Expense consumed by geographic sales division			
Expenses	a) Maintenance costs of sales netowrk		****	
	b) Labor cost consumed in the divisions		****	
	c) General expenses consumed in the divisions		****	
	2) General Administration		****	
				(****)
	Operating Profit			****

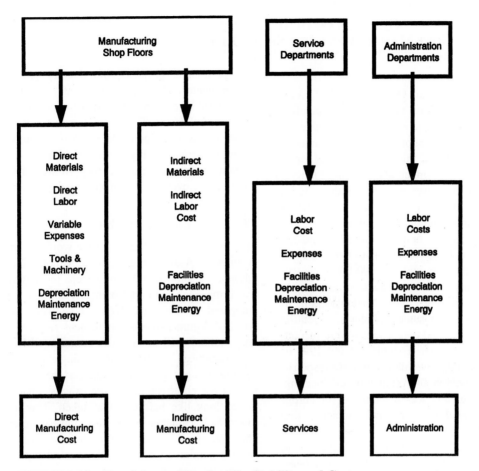

EXHIBIT 11   Breakdown of Product Profitability and Cost

OLYMPUS OPTICAL COMPANY, LTD. (A):
COST MANAGEMENT FOR SHORT LIFE-CYCLE PRODUCTS

Introduction

Olympus, which consisted of Olympus Optical Company, Ltd. and its subsidiaries and affiliates, manufactured and sold opto-electronic equipment and other related products. The firm's major product lines included cameras, video camcorders, microscopes, endoscopes, and clinical analyzers. Olympus also produced microcassette tape recorders, laser-optical pickup systems, and industrial lenses. Olympus was founded in 1919 as Takachiho Seisakusho, a producer of microscopes. The brand name Olympus was first used in 1921 and became the firm's name in 1949. The first Olympus camera was developed in 1936, and by 1990 Olympus was the world's fourth-largest camera manufacturer.

Olympus had six divisions plus a headquarters facility. Four divisions - consumer products, scientific equipment, endoscopes, and diagnostics - were responsible for generating revenues (Exhibit 1 shows 1995 financial results). The other two divisions were responsible for corporate research and production engineering, respectively. Headquarters was responsible for corporate planning, general affairs, personnel, and accounting and finance.

The consumer products division manufactured and sold 35mm cameras, video camcorders, and microcassette tape recorders. In 1995, the division employed 3,900 people (29% of the total Olympus work force) and generated revenues of ¥73 billion (29% of group revenues). Cameras were by far the firm's most important consumer product, accounting for ¥62.8 billion in revenues. Cameras were sold worldwide, with approximately 70% sold outside of Japan.

The consumer products division consisted of six departments: division planning, quality assurance, marketing, product development, production, and overseas manufacturing. Responsibility for the division's production facilities was centered at the Tatsuno plant, which opened in 1981 and was the firm's main camera production facility. Tatsuno was responsible for trial production

of experimental products, introductory production of new products, and, to a limited degree, camera and lens production. Five other domestic manufacturing facilities reported to Tatsuno. These facilities were all located in Japan and were responsible for plastic molded parts, lenses, camera assembly, and die casting. Overseas production facilities located in Hong Kong and China reported to the overseas manufacturing department.

The 35mm Camera Market

Five Japanese firms dominated the world's 35mm camera market: Asahi Pentax, Canon, Minolta, Nikon, and Olympus. Canon and Minolta were the largest of the five firms, each with approximately 17% of the market compared to Olympus' 10%. There were two major types of 35mm cameras: single lens reflex (SLR) and lens shutters (LS) or compact cameras. SLR cameras, first introduced in 1959, used a single optical path to form the images for both the film and the viewfinder, allowing the photographer to see exactly what a picture would look like before it was taken. This ability allowed SLR cameras to take advantage of interchangeable lenses. Because of this feature SLR cameras rapidly gained a dominant share of the professional photographic market. As their price fell, they also came to dominate the high-end amateur market.

The low-end amateur 35mm market continued to be dominated by cameras with two separate optical paths. This market was divided into two segments. One segment contained very inexpensive cameras produced primarily by film manufacturers. The economics of this segment were driven predominantly by film, not camera, sales. The cameras in this segment primarily used the disc or 110mm film formats, though film producers had started to sell 35mm cameras that included new single-use versions. The other segment consisted of 35mm cameras that were less expensive than SLR cameras. This segment had undergone a dramatic change in the 1980s with the introduction of compact cameras.

Compact cameras, as suggested by their name, were smaller than SLR cameras. The first compact camera, the "XA," was introduced by Olympus in 1978 when miniaturized electronic shutters allowed the size of non-SLR cameras to be significantly reduced. The size of SLR cameras could not be equivalently reduced be-

This case was prepared by Professor Robin Cooper of the Peter F. Drucker School of Management at the Claremont Graduate School. The assistance of Professor Regine Slagmulder of the University of Ghent and of Ms. May Mukuda, KPMG Peat Marwick, is gratefully acknowledged.

cause their single optical path required a retractable mirror. This mirror was positioned between the lens and the film when in the down position and reflected the image into the viewfinder. When the shutter was pressed, the mirror retracted up into the body of the camera, allowing the image to expose the film. The retractable mirror, which was approximately the same size as the image, required SLR cameras to remain relatively bulky. Cameras with two optical paths, however, did not require a retractable mirror and therefore could be reduced to quite small sizes. For example, the Olympus Stylus, which was ergonomically designed to fit the hand, was only 4.6″ long by 2.5″ wide by 1.5″ deep and weighed 6.3 ounces.

The early compact cameras were relatively unsophisticated and posed little challenge to the SLR market. However, as advances in electronic control systems allowed auto-focusing and automatic exposure features to be added at relatively low prices, the compact camera began to be viewed as a serious alternative to SLR cameras. The introduction of zoom auto-focus compact cameras in the mid-1980s removed the last major advantage of SLR cameras, that is, variable focal length lenses. Sales of SLR cameras plummeted.

The shift in consumer preference to compact cameras adversely affected Olympus in particular, because the firm historically had relied heavily on SLR sales and had failed to develop a leadership position in the compact camera arena. In the mid-1980s, Olympus' camera business began to lose money and by 1987 its losses were considerable. Top management ascribed these losses to a number of internal and external causes. The major internal causes were poor product planning, a lack of "hit" products, and some quality problems. While Olympus' overall quality levels were above average for the industry, certain products that relied on completely new technologies had rather high defect rates. These quality problems had caused Olympus' reputation to suffer. Externally, two factors were identified as primary contributors to losses: the appreciation of the yen from over 200 to the dollar in 1985 to around 130 in 1990 and an extended low-growth period for the industry that had caused prices (hence profits) to drop.

Strategic Change at Olympus

In 1987, Olympus' top management reacted to the losses by introducing an ambitious three-year program to "reconstruct" the camera business. At the core of this program were three objectives: first, to recapture lost market share by introducing new products; second, to dramatically improve product quality; and third, to reduce production costs via an aggressive set of cost-reduction programs.

Recapturing Market Share   To recapture market share, Olympus developed a new strategy of rapidly introducing, producing, and marketing new 35mm SLR and compact cameras. The firm's strategy in the SLR market was to differentiate its products from competitors' by the innovative use of technology. For compact cameras, Olympus' strategy was to develop a full line of low-cost cameras with particular emphasis on zoom lens models. Rapid introduction was considered important because it would allow the firm to react in a timely fashion to changes in the competitive environment. One of the key elements in improving the firm's ability to react rapidly was a plan to reduce to 18 months the time required to bring new compact cameras to market. The equivalent benchmark when the OM10 SLR camera was developed in 1980 was 10 years.

New products were introduced via the firm's extensive product planning process. At the heart of this process was the product plan, which identified the mix of cameras that the firm expected to sell over the next five years. The information required to develop this plan came from six sources: Olympus' corporate plan, a technology review, an analysis of the general business environment, quantitative information about camera sales, qualitative information about consumer trends, and an analysis of the competitive environment. As part of the three-year reconstruction program, the information collected to support the product plan was extended considerably from pre-1987 levels. In particular, the amount of qualitative data captured was increased. To ensure that all this new information was appropriately incorporated into the product plan, more extensive reviews of the plan were introduced.

The *corporate plan*, which was developed by Olympus' senior management, identified the future mix of business by major product line, the desired profitability of the corporation and each division, and the role of each major product line in establishing the overall image of the firm. It provided division management with a charter by which to operate.

The *technology review* had two sections. The first consisted of a survey of how current and future technological developments were likely to affect the camera business. For example, digital image processing was reaching the stage where electronic still cameras were rapidly becoming both technically and economically feasible replacements for conventional cameras that relied on chemical film for image capture. Olympus was in the forefront of electronic still image capture and in 1990 had introduced its first electronic camera. The second part of the review sought to determine whether Olympus had developed any proprietary technology that could be used for competitive advantage. For instance, Olympus had developed an advanced electronic shutter unit that combined auto-focus control and the lens system, which allowed the size of the camera to be smaller. This shutter unit allowed the firm to develop "small in size" as a distinctive feature of its cameras.

The *analysis of the general business environment* consisted of estimates of how changes in the environment would affect camera sales and the profitability of the business. Factors included foreign exchange rates, how cameras were sold, and the role of other consumer products. How cameras were sold was especially critical, because during the 1980s the percentage of the firm's cameras sold via specialty stores had decreased steadily from 70% to 40%. This change in retail distribution demographics had reduced the average wholesale prices of cameras because the bulk of cameras was now sold through discount houses and mass merchandisers, where profit margins were lower. The role of other consumer products was important because some of them competed for the same segment of the consumer's disposable income. For example, consumer research had shown that many consumers were trying to choose between buying a compact disc player or a compact camera. Therefore, Olympus viewed compact disc players as competitive products.

Quantitative information about the world's 35mm camera market was collected from three primary sources. The first was export and domestic market statistics for cameras published by Japan's Ministry of International Trade and Industry. These statistics included the number of units and dollar sales for each type of camera (e.g., zoom, SLR, and compact) for the entire Japanese camera industry. The second, published by the Japan Camera Industry Association, was statistics on camera industry shipments, which captured the number of units and dollar value of each type of camera shipped from the manufacturers to each major overseas market (e.g., the United States and Europe). The third source

consisted of third-party surveys, commissioned by Olympus, of retail sales by type of camera in each major market.

Olympus collected *qualitative information* from seven major sources. First, the company collected questionnaires from recent purchasers of Olympus cameras. These questionnaires, included with every camera sold, captured information about the purchaser's age, income range, lifestyle demographics, and the other cameras the consumer considered before making the purchase. Second, group interviews were conducted by survey firms two to three times a year in each of the major markets to spot changes in consumer preferences for cameras. Third, surveys were conducted in Roppongi, the trendy fashion center of Tokyo; historically, these interviews had proven to be good predictors of future changes in the lifestyle of the Japanese population as a whole.

Fourth, professional photographers were interviewed to provide insights into both the leading edge of camera design and ways to improve the ease-of-use of compact cameras. Fifth, the Olympus sales force interviewed camera dealers. In addition, Olympus helped pay the salaries of "special salespeople" who worked behind the counters at very large camera stores. These individuals supplied Olympus with feedback about how their cameras were being received by consumers compared to competitive offerings. Sixth, members of the product planning staff would spend some part of the year behind the counter selling cameras, thus becoming familiar with the reactions of both consumers and dealers. Finally, members of the planning staff would attend industry fairs and conventions to obtain additional feedback on industry trends.

The *competitive analysis* was based on any information Olympus could gather about its competitors' current and future product plans. Sources of competitive information included press and competitor announcements, patent filings, and articles in patent publications. This information was used to predict what types of products competitors would introduce in the short and long terms and what their marketing plans were.

The information collected from all these sources was integrated into the preliminary product plan. This plan was the responsibility of a manager in the product planning section. Olympus differed from most other Japanese camera companies in the way it developed its product plan.

First, the product planning function was part of sales and marketing, not research and development, as it had been prior to 1987. Second, the purpose of the product plan review was to balance the demands of a consumer-oriented market with the realities of research and development and production. Third, the firm had a stated objective of trying to design global products. Twice a year, the persons in the firm responsible for worldwide marketing met with the product planners to ensure that proposed products could be sold successfully in all the world's major markets.

Once the preliminary plan was completed, it was subjected to an exhaustive review to ensure its practicality. The review covered issues such as the expected sales volume and profit for each camera model and the load such sales would place on the division's production and research and development resources. A team composed initially of research and development and product planning personnel conducted the review. Subsequently, as the product plan approached acceptance, production personnel were added to the review team. Once the review was completed, a general meeting was held to formally accept the plan. This meeting was attended by division management, by the heads of the marketing, research and development, and production functions, and by the managers of the product planning section. If the product plan was accepted at this meeting, it was then implemented.

Improving Product Quality   Olympus' quality improvement program focused on two areas: the introduction of new products and the manufacturing process in general. The aim of the quality improvement program was to enable the firm to produce the highest-quality products in the industry. Olympus cameras were historically above average in quality, but management felt that it was important to be the best. Highest quality was considered important because it would help the firm recapture its lost market share by improving the reliability of the firm's products from the customer's perspective. In addition, improved product quality was expected to reduce production costs through decreased disruptions to the production flow.

Reducing Production Costs   To bring its high production costs into line, Olympus developed an aggressive cost-reduction program that focused on five objectives: to design products that could be manufactured at low cost, to reduce unnecessary expenditures, to improve production engineering, to adopt innovative manufacturing processes, and to shift a significant percentage of production overseas.

Designing High-Quality Products at Low Cost

At the heart of the program to design low-cost products was the firm's target costing system. The first step in setting target costs was to identify the price point at which a new camera model would sell. For most new products, the price point was already established. For example, in 1995 the simplest compact cameras were sold in the United States at the $80 price point, down from $100 in 1991. The actual selling prices for a given camera varied depending on the distribution channel (e.g., mass merchandiser versus specialty store). Thus, cameras at the $80 price point would sell for between approximately $70 and $100. The appropriate price point for a camera was determined by its distinctive feature (e.g., it might be magnification capability of the camera's zoom lens or the camera's small size). The relationship between distinctive features and price points was determined from the competitive analysis and technology review used in the development of the product plan. The product plan thus described cameras only in terms of their distinctive features. Other features were added as the camera design neared completion.

The price point at which a camera with given functionality was sold tended to decrease over time with improvements in technology. Price points were typically held constant for as long as possible by adding functionality to the cameras offered. Typically, a given type of camera would be introduced at one price point, stay at that price point for several years but with increasing functionality, and then as the functionality of the next higher price point was reached, drop to the next lower price point. The natural outcome of this process was to generate new price points at the low end. For example, the price point for the simplest compact camera was $150 in 1987 and $80 in 1995. At the high end, technology also generated new price points. As the functional gap between the capabilities of compact and SLR cameras closed, it became possible to introduce compact cameras at higher prices. For example, Olympus created a new price point of $300 when it introduced the first compact camera with 3X zoom capability in 1988.

The growing number of price points required camera manufacturers to expand their product offerings to maintain a full line. The decision to be full-line producers was based on two strongly held beliefs: that Japanese consumers trade up over time and that only by offering a full line could a firm obtain a balanced position in the entire market. A firm trying to compete in only the low end of the market would not have access to the high-end technology that would rapidly come to define the low-end market, and a firm selling only at the high end would not have the loyalty of consumers who were trading up.

The proliferation of products due to the increase in the number of price points was further aggravated by Olympus' decision to introduce multiple models for some price points. This change in strategy was prompted by the observation that market share associated with some price points was considerably larger than others. For high-volume price points, it was possible to identify different clusters of consumer preferences and profitably produce and market cameras designed specifically for those clusters. Under the new strategy, the number of models introduced at each price point was roughly proportional to the size of the market. Thus, the expected market share of each camera model offered was approximately the same unless it was designed to satisfy a low-volume strategic price point.

Once the price point of a new camera was identified, the free on board (FOB) price was calculated by subtracting the appropriate margin of the dealers and the U.S. subsidiary plus any import costs, such as freight and import duty. Target costs were established by subtracting the product's target margin from its FOB price. The product's target cost ratio was calculated by dividing the target cost by the FOB price. Every six months, the divisional manager set guidelines for acceptable cost ratios. These guidelines were developed in tandem with the division's six-month profit plans. In 1996, the divisional manager had identified the acceptable cost ratios as 85% for Tatsuno manufactured products and 60% for products manufactured overseas.

The target ratio for a given camera was set based on the historical cost ratios of similar cameras, the anticipated relative strength of competitive products, and the overall market conditions anticipated when the product was launched. Once the target cost ratio was established, it was converted into yen by multiplying it by the target FOB price. This yen-denominated target cost was used in all future comparisons with the estimated cost of production to ensure achievement of the target cost.

As part of the program to design low-cost products, target costs were set assuming aggressive cost reduction

and high quality levels. A target cost system existed prior to 1987, but it was not considered effective. As part of the three-year program to reduce costs, the target cost system was improved and more attention was paid to achieving the targets. Aggressive cost reduction was achieved by applying three rationalization objectives. First, the number of parts in each unit was targeted for reduction. For example, the shutter unit for one class of compact camera was reduced from 105 to 56 pieces, a 47% reduction that led to a 58% decrease in production costs. Second, expensive, labor-intensive, and mechanical adjustment processes were eliminated wherever possible. Finally, metal and glass components were replaced with cheaper plastic ones. For instance, replacing metal components that required milling in an SLR body with plastic ones that could be molded reduced the SLR body costs by 28%. Similarly, replacing three of the glass elements with plastic ones in an eight-element compact camera lens reduced the lens cost by 29%.

During the design phase, the anticipated cost ratio of new products was monitored on a frequent basis, typically two to three times before launch. The FOB price of a new product was sensitive to both market conditions and fluctuations in foreign exchange rates. Olympus sold 70% of its cameras overseas, and the FOB price of a product was the weighted average yen price. Since the FOB price for cameras sold overseas was designated in the appropriate foreign currency, fluctuations in the exchange rates caused the FOB price to change when measured in yen.

If the FOB price changed sufficiently during the design phase to cause the anticipated cost ratio for the camera to fall outside the acceptable range by about 10%, then the target cost of the camera was reviewed and usually revised to bring the anticipated cost ratio back into the acceptable range. If the FOB price was falling, the result was a lower target cost that was harder to achieve. If it was rising, the result was higher profits, which were used to increase promotions and advertising fees as well as reduce prices to overseas subsidiaries.

The target cost was based on the price point for the distinctive feature of the camera. Research and development was responsible for identifying the other features of the camera (e.g., the type of flash and shutter units). Feature identification was an iterative process in which the cost of each new design was estimated and compared to the product's target cost. Production engineering developed estimated costs of production in collaboration with production. Research and development reviewed these estimates and revised them as deemed appropriate. Most revisions resulted in lower estimated costs. The research and development group identified additional ways to reduce the cost of the product either through minor product redesign or a more efficient production process.

Approximately 20% of the time, the estimated cost was equal to or less than the target cost, and the product design could be released for further analysis by the production group at Tatsuno. The other 80% of the time, further analysis was required by the research and development group. First, marketing was asked if the price point could be increased sufficiently so that the target cost was equal to the estimated cost. If the price could be increased, the product was released to the production group. If the market price could not be increased sufficiently, then the effect of reducing the functionality of the product was explored. Reducing the product's functionality decreased its estimated cost to produce. If these reductions were sufficient, the product was released to production.

If it was not possible to raise the price or reduce the production cost enough to reduce the estimated cost below the target cost, then a life-cycle profitability analysis was performed. In this analysis, the effect of potential cost reductions over the production life of the product was included in the financial analysis of the product's profitability. In 1990, Olympus expected to reduce production costs by about 35% across the production lifetime of its products. The product was released if these life-cycle savings were sufficient to make the product's overall profitability acceptable. If the estimated costs were still too high, even with these additional cost savings included, the product was abandoned unless some strategic reason for keeping the product could be identified. Such considerations typically focused on maintaining a full product line or creating a "flagship" product that demonstrated technological leadership.

Once a new product had passed the research and development design review it was released to Tatsuno production for evaluation. The Tatsuno design review consisted of evaluating the research and development design to determine where and how the new product would be produced. To make these decisions, a detailed production blueprint was developed. This blueprint identified both the technology required to produce the

camera and the components it contained. Using this blueprint and cost estimates from suppliers and subsidiary plants, the production cost of the product was re-estimated. If this cost was less than or equal to the target cost, the product was submitted to the division manager for approval for release to production.

If the estimated production cost was too high, then the design was subjected to additional analysis. Frequently, relatively minor changes in the product's design were all that were required to reduce the cost estimate to the target cost level. As long as these changes did not change the product's price point, then the functionality was changed and the product was submitted for approval. If the design changes would change the price point, the product was returned to the research and development group for redesign.

The estimated production cost used in the evaluation of the product was the expected cost of production three months after it went into production. The initial cost of production was higher than this target cost due to the work force's lack of experience with producing the new camera. As the work force gained experience, production costs would fall below target costs. Thus, the cost system would report negative variances for the first three months. In subsequent months the variances were expected to be positive. After the product was in production for six months, the target cost was changed to reflect any expected savings in the next six months due to the firm's cost-reduction programs.

Reducing Unnecessary Expenditures

The program to reduce unnecessary expenditures contained four components:

- It analyzed fixed expenses and curtailed any unnecessary expenditures.
- It analyzed and improved the procedures surrounding new product launching to reduce launch costs.
- It lowered the cost of purchased parts by implementing strict controls to ensure that target costs were met, widening the sources of procurement to obtain lower costs, and identifying multiple suppliers for each component to create competitive pressures.
- It strengthened and integrated its existing cost-reduction programs.

The first program focused on production costs, the second on the costs of defects, the third on capacity utilization costs, and the fourth on overhead expenses. The *production cost control and reduction program* focused primarily on removing material, labor, and some overhead costs from products; the division's profit plan identified cost-reduction targets for these costs for each product. These targets were considered challenging though achievable. The standards were set every six months and included the anticipated reductions that would be achieved in the next six months. Progress toward achieving these cost-reduction targets was monitored using variance analysis. Material price, work improvement, and "budgetary other" cost variances were computed weekly and accumulated monthly.

The material price variance was computed for each product by comparing the actual material cost to the standard material monthly target. This target was the average of the material costs for the previous six months adjusted for any anticipated changes in material costs in the upcoming month. The work improvement variances were the difference between the actual labor hours and the standard labor hour monthly target and between actual machine-hours and the standard machine-hour monthly target. Their target was calculated by assuming that labor cost reductions would occur evenly over time. To these linear cost reductions were added any specific reductions due to planned changes in the production process. The actual "budgetary other" costs, which included general expenses of the factory, were compared to budgeted costs to determine the other budgetary variance.

The second cost control and reduction program focused on the *costs of defective production*. To give these costs high visibility, they were not included in the standard costs and hence were not covered by the production cost control and reduction program. The cost of defects program consisted of setting cost of defects targets for each production group every six months. Groups were responsible for segments of the production process (at Tatsuno there were 10 groups).

Cost-reduction targets were identified for each product the group produced. Division management negotiated with the group leaders to set cost-reduction targets for each product the group produced. The group leaders recommended their cost-reduction targets, then divisional management reviewed these recommendations. If the overall reductions were sufficient to achieve the division's cost-reduction objectives, divisional management accepted the targets. If the overall savings were insufficient, the targets were renegotiated until the savings were acceptable.

The team leader and foreman in each group met daily to discuss their progress at achieving their reduction targets. Group and team leaders held weekly meetings to report on progress. If a group did not meet its weekly objectives, the group leader was expected to explain why the group had failed and what corrective actions would be taken. A request to engineering for assistance might be included in these actions. Occasionally, if a group consistently failed to meet its objectives, management would send in engineering—a serious blow to the group's reputation.

The third program focused on managing the costs associated with *capacity utilization*. The division's long-range management plan included estimates on the amount of overtime, actual working hours, operation days, and attendance rates. These estimates and the expected workload for each cost center were combined to give a capacity utilization cost budget for each center. This budget, which consisted of overall attendance rates and direct labor hours by cost center, was set every six months and updated each month. The updated monthly budget was used to compute a daily variance, which was reported to management weekly and accumulated monthly. The variance captured the over- or under-utilization of direct labor capacity at the standard distribution rate of processing costs.

The final program focused on *overhead expenses*. These expenses included items such as the personnel expenses of support and administration, depreciation of factory buildings, and computer costs. The long-term management plan contained targeted levels for these expenses. Monthly budgets for these expenses were prepared taking into account the production volume for the six-month period, the introduction of new products, and any planned cost-reduction actions by the groups. Division management approved the resulting budget after any necessary adjustments were made. Each month, the budget was compared to actual and multiple cost center variances. Costs subjected to separate variance analysis included machine repair costs, machine maintenance costs, expenses of repair and maintenance personnel, and miscellaneous expenses. These variances were computed monthly because management felt that these expenses could not be controlled in a shorter time frame.

The four cost control and reduction programs each generated variances, which were combined in a monthly cost report. This report provided division management with important insights into the success of the cost control and reduction programs.

Improving Production Engineering

Olympus achieved the desired improvements to production engineering through a three-phase approach. This approach shortened production lead times by decreasing batch sizes. In the production area, for example, batches were halved and moved to a zero inventory system. Improving communications between sales and manufacturing reduced introduction times for new products and production lead times in general. For example, the MRP system was used to check inventory levels twice a day as opposed to once a week. Finally, office automation improved the level of general administrative support provided to both marketing and sales.

Adopting Innovative Manufacturing Processes

The program to introduce innovative production technologies focused on increasing the level of automation in manufacturing, particularly in the assembly, lens production, electronics parts mounting, and molding processes. In all these processes, the level of automation was significantly increased. For example, in assembly four major processes were automated in the three-year period after the new strategy began: the assembly of the film winding and shutter units, the adjustment and inspection processes for the focusing unit, the alignment and related inspection processes, and the transportation system for assembled parts.

Similarly, the molding, lens processing, and IC mounting stages of production underwent complex changes. All told, the program initiated some 23 different automation projects.

Shifting to Overseas Production

The cost reductions that the aggressive application of target costing and production cost reduction achieved were further augmented by shifting some of the manufacturing processes to lower-cost areas of the world. Olympus was the last of the camera firms to open such overseas facilities. Other manufacturers had opened such facilities in the late 1970s and early 1980s. Cost analyses at Olympus had indicated that the potential savings from shifting production offshore was about 15%. In 1988, the firm opened production facilities in Taiwan, Hong Kong, and Korea, and in China in 1989. The firm anticipated offshore production to reach ¥10 billion by 1991 and to expand rapidly thereafter.

The New Cost-Reduction Effort   The 1987 program to reconstruct Olympus' camera business achieved most of its objectives. The program to introduce new products was relatively successful at recapturing lost market share. The firm increased camera sales volume by almost 70% to ¥50 billion from ¥30 billion and almost doubled its market share for compact cameras. Unfortunately, the program was not as successful for the SLR product line. The firm continued to lose market share from 1987 through 1990, but with the introduction of a completely new camera, the IS-1, the firm hoped to turn the situation around.

The combined results of the cost-reduction program were impressive. By the end of 1990 every measure of productivity at Tatsuno had improved. For example, overall production had increased by 50%, the production cost ratio had fallen by 20%, the production value per employee had risen 70%, and gross added value per person had increased over 125%. Simultaneously, the work-in-process inventory had not increased despite the higher activity level and the fact that lead time had almost halved.

Despite the success of the 1987 plan, top management at Olympus determined that additional cost reductions would be necessary in the coming years. In particular, they were worried by three trends that together would place significant pressure on the firm's profitability. These trends were an increased proliferation in products required to satisfy consumer demand in the domestic market, an additional shortening of the product life cycle to less than a year, and reduced selling prices. The decision to introduce a new program was driven in part by the observation that the savings from the 1987 plan had gone down in recent months.

At the heart of the new plan were two important concepts. The first was innovations in technology, and the second was functional group management. Innovations in technology consisted of applying new production technology—primarily automation—to all stages of production. Separate automation projects were initiated for camera assembly, lens processing, molding, and electrical components. The most ambitious of these projects was a fully automated robotic assembly line designed to assemble cameras. This line was undergoing evaluation at Tatsuno before being released to other assembly facilities.

Functional group management consisted of dividing the production process into a number of autonomous groups. Ten such groups were identified at the Tatsuno plant. These groups were given full management responsibility for their area of responsibility or cost center and were expected to manage it as if it were a separate company. Thus each group would effectively become a separate profit center. Top management felt that holding the groups responsible for their profitability would promote greater pressure to reduce costs and hence increase profitability than would any conventional cost-reduction program. By 1990, senior management had yet to operationalize the function group management concept but believed that it was going to play a critical role in the firm's future.

Appendix

The Evolution of the Cost System From 1970 to 1990, the firm's cost system had undergone three major changes. Prior to 1976, there was only one overhead rate at the Tatsuno plant. The system directly traced some material costs to products, but all other costs were allocated. These allocated costs were divided into two categories: processing and overhead. Processing costs included the indirect material, direct and indirect labor, and direct expenses of the production process. Direct labor was allocated because the direct labor wage rates varied by individual, and it was considered too expensive to assign the cost directly to products. The overhead costs contained the indirect material, indirect labor, and indirect expenses associated with support and administration. The processing overhead costs were combined and divided by the number of direct labor hours to give an average allocation rate. The reported cost of a product was given by the sum of the direct material charge and the direct labor hours that the product consumed multiplied by the allocation rate. Such a simple system was considered adequate because there were only small differences in the cost structure of the products. In addition, the level of automation was small, as was depreciation. The stated objective of this system was to differentiate material cost from other expenses and provide mechanisms for total cost reduction.

In 1977, the cost system was updated. The overhead costs were split into two categories: procurement costs and other costs. Procurement costs were those costs associated with obtaining raw material and purchased

parts. They included the personnel expenses of the procurement section, transportation charges, car fares, and other miscellaneous expenses. A single allocation rate was determined for processing costs and some of the other costs. A separate rate was determined for procurement costs and the allocated expenses of the administration and production technical sections. The costs of these two sections were allocated to the production and procurement sections based on head count. The procurement costs were allocated to products based on the sum of the direct material charge plus the allocated processing costs. The primary purpose of this system was to draw attention to the procurement costs, which had grown substantially over time. This increase was due both to an increase in production capacity, which was accompanied by a corresponding increase in the volume of procured parts, and by an increase in the ratio of procured to internally manufactured parts. The other important change in the system was its focus on the cost of quality. The cost of defects was isolated from the standard costs to give it more visibility. Separate variances were computed for standard production and defects.

In 1983, the cost system was again updated. The general structure was maintained, but now multiple allocation rates were computed for processing costs. The production process was split into 10 different cost centers and different overhead rates were computed for each center. Examples of the cost centers included camera final assembly, electronic flexible board assembly, lens processing, and lens assembly. In addition, the firm had begun to enter into OEM contracts with other firms that would produce components for Olympus. The support and administration costs for the OEM production were significantly different from Tatsuno production. To capture this difference, the two overhead cost allocation rates were computed, one for general suppliers and the other for OEM suppliers. These two rates replaced the single procurement rate computed in the prior system. The treatment of other costs as partially related to processing and partially related to procurement was suspended, and all other costs were allocated as part of the support and administration costs. The primary purpose of this system was to provide improved control over production and support and administration costs.

	Millions	of	Yen	Thousands of US dollars
	1995	1994	1993	1995
Net sales	252,097	239,551	267,718	2,801,078
Net income	3,101	556	3,805	34,456
Net income per share:				
Total assets	442,367	434,704	439,716	4,915,189
Working capital	205,256	202,070	164,712	2,280,622
Shareholders' investment	182,418	183,039	145,775	2,026,287

Notes:

1. Net income per share is shown in yen and US dollars.

2. For the reader's convenience, US dollar amounts were translated from yen at the rate of ¥90 = $1.

3. Fully diluted net income per share assuming full dilution is not presented because it is not significant.

4. The above figures were based on accounting principles generally accepted in Japan.

EXHIBIT 1   Olympus Optical 1995 Financial Results

EUCLID ENGINEERING

We've made many improvements in manufacturing and assembly processes. Our goal now is to generate benefits by reducing engineering, design, and purchasing expenses.

Bill Anderson: Vice President, Finance

Euclid Engineering, a closely-owned company in Kokomo, Indiana, provided design, engineering, and manufacturing services, primarily to automotive original equipment manufacturers (OEMs). Euclid's current product line included a wide variety of automotive components and pre-assembled sub-systems. The company also supplied auto companies with "one-offs" of advanced prototypes that could be displayed in futuristic cars shown at auto shows.

Euclid felt that its distinctive competency was high-quality design and engineering work that would be fol-

lowed by a high-volume production contract. Euclid offered complete design and manufacturing services to its customers, from developing the initial concept, through clay modeling, prototypes, and, finally, efficient mass production. As automobile companies attempted to downsize their permanent employment base, specialized firms like Euclid were taking on much more of the front-end design, engineering, and validation work. Its Computer-Aided-Design terminals could be connected to the engineering systems in each of the U.S. Big-3 automakers so that engineers and designers could easily access and share technical drawings. Exhibits 1a and 1b show the upward trends in Euclid's engineering and design costs during the past several years. Customers paid for a portion of the up-front work. The remaining unrecovered front-end expenses were subsequently recovered through a unit charge added to the piece-part cost paid by the customers.

The automobile companies monitored their supplier's costs and prices with dedicated Supplier Cost

Professor Robert S. Kaplan wrote this case.

Copyright © 1992 by the President and Fellows of Harvard College. Harvard Business School case 194-031.

Engineering groups. These groups looked at a supplier's piece-part cost using the traditional cost accounting categories of Materials, Labor, and Manufacturing Overhead. Suppliers competed for the auto companies' business through bids on piece part purchase price. As sales and profit margins of the U.S. automakers eroded, the companies were placing extreme pressure on their suppliers to continually lower quoted prices. Gary Conrad, Euclid's Controller, commented:

> As suppliers took on more of the up-front work, we not only had more out-of-pocket expenses to recover in the piece part price, we also needed to be sure that we recovered our financing costs for these up-front expenses. But our customers were starting to complain about escalating piece part prices.

Bill Anderson voiced his frustration with this procedure:

> The automobile companies sometimes spend too much time with their suppliers worrying about reducing piece-part costs rather than how to sell more cars. For highly engineered parts, volume has such a dramatic impact on piece-part costs that we all would be better off if we concentrated on selling more cars, not just reducing unit costs.

Manufacturing Initiatives

Euclid had implemented several programs to develop a "lean manufacturing" capability that produced higher quality and better service to customers. The lean manufacturing capability also limited the need for Euclid to seek future price increases. The company had a goal for each plant to achieve annual reductions in labor and materials costs of 10% and 5%, respectively. Materials cost savings came from suggestions generated by working cooperatively with suppliers, developing new packaging concepts, and substituting new materials that reduced total costs.

Labor savings were realized by empowering employee teams that were dedicated to produce a particular product for a designated customer. The employee product teams were almost self-contained so little shared overhead was required. Each team performed its own customer scheduling, inspection, job assignments and rotation, training, recruiting, and supplier scheduling.

Just-in-time procedures led to zero finished goods inventory at the end of the day. Flexible platforms and manufacturing cells made changeovers in product mix almost instantaneous, facilitating continuous in-line production with no work-in-process inventory or special materials handling required. The production lines built each day what would be installed in the car, at the customer's location, the following day. The team could perform other responsibilities once its daily production schedule was achieved; if the team fell behind schedule, it stayed late to complete the daily output.

Further operating improvements were being realized by the success of Euclid's Total Quality Management program. To measure performance improvements, employees were provided with the unit costs of key resources so that they could calculate a weekly profit index. For example, the profit index for one team included the measured cost of:

Inventory	
Equipment	(Weekly $ cost for each piece of equipment)
Floor Space	($55 per square foot)
Efficiency	(minutes per piece)
Materials Savings	(through substitution of less expensive materials)
Scrap	

Monthly, the Profit Index champions of each work team met to compare improvements and share ideas that had improved the profitability of their teams.

Stage I: The Existing Cost System Prior to 1987, Euclid used a traditional labor-based manufacturing cost system. Its expenses, by category, were:

Direct Materials	48%
Direct Labor	9
Manufacturing Overhead	23
General & Administrative	20
Total	100%

Brent Alexander, Financial Analyst, recalled:

> Our efficiency improvements in production operations coincided with an increase in the up-front engineering work we were doing for our customers. This led to rapidly escalating overhead rates. We probably had too much focus on automation and other attempts to reduce direct labor spending, and too little on forecasting and controlling launch costs. Our customers were complaining about high overhead rates and high G&A percentages, and we had a "gut" feeling that we were under-costing both low volume jobs and highly automated jobs.

Gary Conrad provided an example of an over-costed job:

> Formerly, we were making complex products that built upon our design and engineering skills, like a complete dashboard panel, with all instruments and electronics installed. But now we occasionally bid for high-volume commodity type products, like a blank dashboard panel. Our bid costs assigned to such high-volume simple products ended up much too high.

The Product Life Cycle   Euclid managers were attempting to develop improved systems for managing costs during the entire life cycle of a product. The company managers viewed the life cycle in three phases (see Exhibit 2). In the initial Concept Phase, designers formulated a new product concept, determined customer interest, and performed a feasibility study. The Concept Phase concluded by generating a quote to manufacture the product for a customer. During the Concept Phase, designers had total control over product cost, but had virtually no product cost information.

The Launch Phase was initiated once the customer approved Euclid's proposal. The Launch Phase included initiating the development effort, and developing the engineering drawings, prototypes, production processes, and tooling for the new product. During the Launch Phase, designers and engineers still had considerable ability to affect product cost, but product cost information was tentative and preliminary.

Large-scale manufacturing of the product occurred during the Production Phase. In this phase, engineers had only a limited ability to affect product costs, but a great deal of product cost information was readily available. Exhibit 3 shows the diagram, familiar to all Euclid engineers: 85% of a product's costs became committed during the Concept Phase, when no production has occurred. The accounting system, however, focused on cost measurement only at the Production Phase when virtually all costs had become locked in.

Euclid managers wanted the product designers to understand better the production cost consequences of their decisions. And, new cost systems were also needed to monitor and make visible the costs incurred during the expensive Design and Launch phases. With greater cost visibility during the design phases, engineers and managers could focus on managing the cost drivers associated with developing and launching new products.

Stage II: Developing the Delphi Model for Production Costs   Several members of the finance staff had attended conferences where the advantages of activity-based cost (ABC) systems had been presented. The finance people recognized that Euclid had the problem described by the conference speakers: distorted cost information arising from using a direct labor cost allocation system in a lean and highly automated manufacturing environment. The finance group gained approval to apply ABC concepts to Euclid's manufacturing operations. They developed "Delphi," a new analytic cost system, which they hoped would help the company forecast cost and profit improvements.

The Delphi task force, after interviewing functional managers and analyzing the general ledger chart of accounts, selected 11 new cost drivers:

Minutes per piece	(the machine hour rate)
Engineering hours	(for product launch)
Part proliferation	
Raw Material $	(raw materials were easy-to-buy)
Purchased Part $	(purchased parts required more engineering and supplier development)
Outside Processing	
Overseas Purchasing	
Equipment Value	(a percentage of equipment replacement cost; equipment cost included training and installation expenses)
Tool Value	
Square Footage	
Sales $	

The finance team decided to limit the number of cost drivers to no more than a dozen since the system had to remain simple and understandable enough to be used for quoting on new jobs. Exhibit 4 shows the assignment of labor and overhead expenses to the 11 cost drivers.

The new Delphi system helped to focus manufacturing on the opportunities for cost reduction. For example, the resources required for a production line could be reduced by shrinking the required floor space and by using lower-valued equipment. Also, the analysis showed that automation was not always the preferred solution to reduce manufacturing costs. Previously, the product engineers emphasized Design-for-Assembly concepts because fast assembly greatly reduced the direct labor hours required for each part. Engineers would strive to design a single, highly complex part to accomplish a particular function. Such a complex part, however, would consume numerous engineering design hours and could require the purchase of specialized tooling. It also might prove difficult to manufacture, thereby requiring extensive (and expensive) additional resources for setup and quality activities. When such a part was produced to specifications, however, it snapped into place easily and therefore consumed very little direct labor time.

With the more accurate ABC information, engineers could spend more time at the early stage of the design process assessing the impact on manufacturing costs of their design decisions. In addition to estimating direct labor assembly hours, design engineers now estimated the amount required to be spent on equipment and tooling for the new product. By shifting to dies with single rather than multiple cavities, the production machines could be smaller and simpler. Designers also saw that replacing a few complex parts with a larger number of simpler parts for a particular application might increase direct labor assembly hours but decrease total costs substantially, especially if purchase of expensive special-purpose machinery could be avoided. The engineering designers began to assess the economics of flexible fixturing that would be shared across different models and product types.

Bill Anderson noted: "The new cost system contributed to our understanding the value of simplicity and flexibility."

Brent Alexander reinforced this point:

> For a new product, like a door panel, we could assemble two pieces with only $500 thousand worth of equipment. Or we can do the door panel as a single piece with new equipment costing over $1 million. The Delphi cost system reduced the direct labor rate from $45/hour to about $22/hour. This reduction made us realize that for low-volume products, direct labor may be less expensive and is certainly more flexible than investing in capital equipment.

The Delphi system revealed that production volumes had a massive impact on unit costs, and that product development costs were everywhere. Product launch costs of 10% of total expenses could now be seen as larger than the entire direct labor expense (of 9%). Some product development costs were incurred for projects that would never be sold to customers. These expenses were subjected to a careful benefit/cost analysis by

business teams and authorized based on their long-term benefit to the company. The product development costs that ended up in a Sold Program were recovered either by customer-supplied upfront payments or in the piece-costs of the manufactured parts.

When bidding for the manufacturing business from a designed product, Euclid divided the unrecovered launch costs by the automobile company's estimate of production volume over the life of the car model. This calculation yielded a standard unit price that would cover manufacturing costs and also repay the up-front design cost. If the production volume of the car model was below expectations (a not infrequent occurrence in recent years), Euclid suffered losses on the contract; if the production volume were unexpectedly higher, Euclid earned more profits than expected.

Stage III: Extending Delphi to Design and Product Engineering   The Delphi activity-based cost system developed in Stage II gave visibility to product launch costs as a separate cost category. Only one component of launch costs, however, the project engineering hours, could be specifically identified with individual programs. Most product launch costs could not be traced to individual programs, and had to be allocated to programs based on engineering hours. These allocated costs included the costs of:

Manufacturing Support
Product Development
Industrial Design
Sales & Marketing
Advanced Manufacturing
Program Management
General & Administrative Support
Electronics Engineering
Validation

Applying the expenses of these activities to engineering hours produced an additional $86/hour cost which, when combined with the direct cost of $45/hour, led to a $131 per engineering hour cost for program launch expenses. In effect, engineering hours had now become the "direct labor" of the launch process. Business managers started to ask why they could no longer make money on low-volume jobs, and why bids for producing simple products had become unrealistically high. New product development teams attempted to lower launch costs by hiding engineers, minimizing their presence and billing in the launch process.

To remedy these problems, the next stage of the cost system design process attempted to reduce the amount of launch expenses that would have to be allocated based on engineering hours. The team succeeded in identifying and segregating the expenses of all design and validation activities. These expense categories could now be charged directly to programs:

Launch Expense Category	Hourly Rate
Project Engineering Hours	$50
Manual Design Hours	45
CAD Design Hours (Designer & Eqpmt.)	70
Electronics Engineering Hours	38
Industrial Design Hours	**
Validation Cost	**

By tracing a much larger fraction of launch costs to individual programs, the percentage of costs that still had to be allocated dropped to 37%; the allocated expense rate dropped to just under $50 per hour.

The Stage III cost system also gave product planners a much more detailed statement of work. This information enabled Euclid managers to negotiate directly with the customer about which type of engineering design and test work Euclid was to perform. The procedure allowed the customer to reduce or eliminate its own engineering resources that were no longer needed for the design and engineering activity. This explicit contracting also helped to assure that Euclid would get paid for the up-front engineering work. Euclid took the position that it just wanted to get reimbursed for these efforts, and would look to make its profits on piece-part manufacturing.

The 1995 Decatur Dashboard Panel System   The Stage III system had recently been used to forecast and track the expenses associated with developing the dashboard panel system for a new car model, the 1995 Decatur. Exhibit 5 shows the analysis of the Product Launch costs for this system. The Delphi system estimated that launch expenses exceeded costs reimbursed from the customer by just over $4,000,000. Most of this

---

**Industrial design and validation costs were calculated based on detailed product specifications.

excess represented the costs of activities not directly chargeable to design and engineering hours, but which had been built into the hourly burden rates (see Exhibit 6). The $4,000,000 of unrecovered expenses were expected to be reimbursed through the piece-part price for the dashboard panel. Given anticipated production volumes of 250,000 annually for 4 years, the amortized launch costs equaled $4.06 per unit.

Euclid had estimated and controlled costs for the reimbursable portion of the launch expenses by adding identifying project numbers for all major sub-systems and tracking actual versus forecast expenses for each sub-system (see Exhibit 7). A report was sent to the department managers in:

Advanced Manufacturing
Design
Engineering
Product Development
Validation Lab

that summarized, for each program, the Delphi plan versus actual monthly costs and hours used. Program managers also received a monthly report summarizing hours used and expenses in each department that was being used for their programs. Exhibit 8 shows a monthly summary report for the program. The top panel indicates the reimbursable charges plus the budgeted launch costs to be amortized in piece parts. The remaining panels show expenses incurred to date, by department, and the amount remaining to be spent before production begins. A more detailed report decomposed the total dollars remaining to be spent on the dashboard panel system into its major sub-systems.

Impact of Stage III System on Design and Engineering Activities   The new reports provided much more information to department and program managers than they had ever seen before. The new accountability for launch expenses led the managers to develop, on their own, even more detailed expense reporting. The engineering group agreed to fill out daily time summaries of their efforts classified into five different categories (see Exhibit 9):

Unsold Development Time
Engineering Aids/Models
Customer Requested Changes
Validation
PC [internally initiated] Changes

The group felt that this classification would give even more visibility to how they spent their time.

Even more surprising, and not to be outdone by the engineers, the industrial design people developed 19 different categories for identifying their time spent (see Exhibit 10). The designers felt that detailed reporting of effort was required if they were to be able to influence the time and cost of the design phase. The industrial designers were now deciding on their own whether they needed the extensive work to prepare armatures[1] and build engineering clay models. Previously, when the cost of these activities were not visible, complete armatures and clay models were developed on a routine basis.

Gary Conrad commented on the impact of the Stage III cost system to Euclid's people:

> We have given ownership of the financial information to the operating people so that they can make decisions with it. Both the customer and the manager now fully understand the activities that we plan to perform and the cost of performing each activity.
>
> The system helps all the people who must interface with a program to identify the cost and technical implications of a design decision well before the design becomes embedded into a technical drawing. This information provides better visibility for trade-offs in design decisions, and helps the product manager assign people to activities and to manage the individual activities. The launch teams now make trade-offs to lower total launch costs, such as by building prototypes without full tooling.

Martin Allen the finance team member on the Decatur dashboard panel project reinforced Conrad's remarks. "People can finally see where projects are spending money. This visibility gave them the opportunity to vary the mix of skill resources to particular tasks, as appropriate."

Allen also identified another key advantage for the new system:

> The activity-based costing approach built into Delphi promotes communication and cooperation with the customer. For example, for one product, the auto company now supplies us with a fully packed armature so we don't have to perform or charge them for this function.

The more detailed breakdown of design and engineering activities enabled customers to see all the activities that were being performed for them. They could determine whether all the activities were really necessary. In some instances, customers were requesting that some proposed activities not be performed (e.g., sweetening the clay model), with the savings used to reduce the quote price.

The system also enabled Euclid to show the customer, in advance, the cost of any customer-requested changes. Previously, when the customer's engineering group requested changes during the product launch phase, Euclid would perform the requested changes and bill the customer at the end of the development phase. The customer's purchasing department, however, frequently balked at the added cost from all the requested changes. With the expanded Delphi system, Euclid engineers could estimate the cost of each customer-requested change and request that the customer's engineering and purchasing groups agree and authorize the change.

The finance staff was now planning to develop the next generation, Stage IV, system. In Stage IV, they would explode the $50/hour allocated expense rate even further by developing budgets for the actual resources in each common function so that these expenses could be tracked and managed down to individual programs.

---

[1]Armatures were the base on which a clay model was constructed.

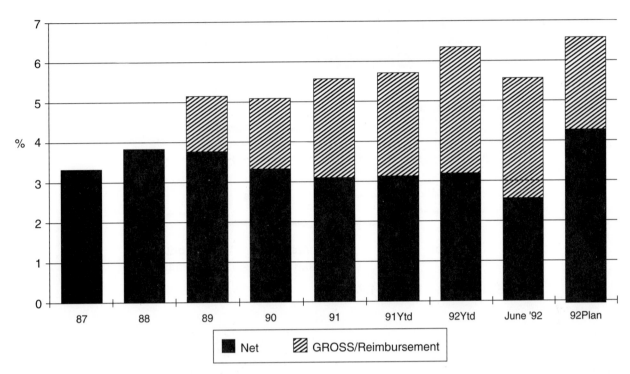

EXHIBIT 1A   Total Engineering Percent of Sales

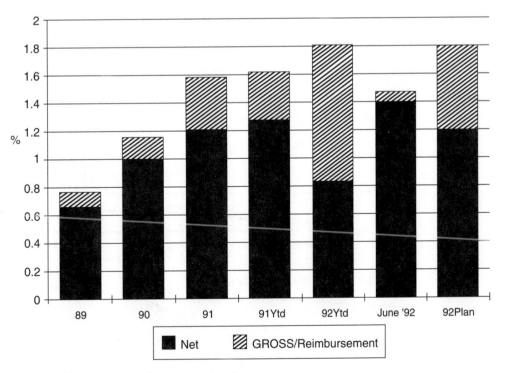

EXHIBIT 1B   Total Design Percent of Sales

Product Life Cycle
Cost Control Phases

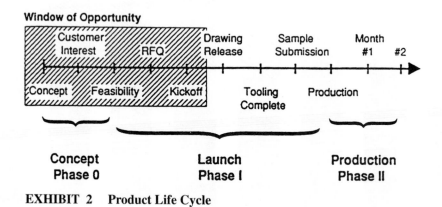

EXHIBIT 2   Product Life Cycle

Cost Generator

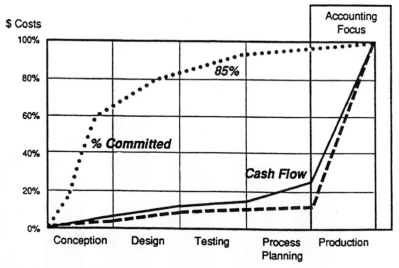

EXHIBIT 3   Product Life Cycle

EXHIBIT 4 Cost Assignment Percentages

	ENG. HOURS	MIN/PCS ACTIVITY	PART PROLIF.	RAW MATERIAL
Labor and Overhead				
Direct Labor		100%		
Indirect Labor Hourly				
Foreman	18%	82%		
Development	100%			
Material Handling			10%	10%
Maintenance	25%			
Employee Training	80%			
Custodial		40%		
Indirect Labor Exempt				
Quality Control	32%	20%	12%	2%
Production Control	5%		35%	10%
Plant Engineering	54%		11%	
Management	25%	75%		
Office	3%	97%		
Administrative	1%	99%		
Other		100%		
Employee Related	9%	91%		
Purchasing Department	20%			33%
MIS Department	8%			84%
Building Expenses				
Equipment Expenses				
Repairs and Maintenance		20%		%
Shop Supplies	10%	70%		
Tooling Maintenance	50%	5%	5%	
Electricity				
Insurance				
Property Taxes				
Depreciation				
Transportation Expenses	20%	40%		
Misc. Expenses	10%	80%		
Freight In	2%		2%	10%
Freight Out	5%			
Shipping Supplies				
Product Launch Expenses				
Advanced Manufacturing	65%			
Advanced Validation	65%			
Design	90%			
Clay Modeling	100%			
Program Management	100%			
Project Development	60%			
Electronics	75%			
Product Engineering	90%		5%	
Selling Expenses	65%			
General & Administrative	27%			

(continued)

EXHIBIT 4 *(Continued)*

	PURCH. PARTS	OUTSIDE PROCESS	OVERSEAS PURCH.	EQUIP. VALUE	TOOL VALUE	SQUARE FOOTAGE	SALES
Labor and Overhead							
Direct Labor							
Indirect Labor Hourly							
Foreman							
Development							
Material Handling	15%	45%					
Maintenance				75%			
Employee Training				20%			
Custodial						60%	
Indirect Labor Exempt							
Quality Control	13%	13%	8%				
Production Control	25%	25%					
Plant Engineering				35%			
Management							
Office							
Administrative							
Other							
Employee Related							
Purchasing Department	12%	15%	12%	8%			
MIS Department	1%	3%	4%				
Building Expenses						100%	
Equipment Expenses							
Repairs and Maintenance				50%	30%		
Shop Supplies				20%			
Tooling Maintenance					40%		
Electricity				50%		50%	
Insurance			100%				
Property Taxes			100%				
Depreciation			100%				
Transportation Expenses		40%					
Misc. Expenses		10%					
Freight In	60%	19%	7%				
Freight Out							95%
Shipping Supplies							100%
Product Launch Expenses							
Advanced Manufacturing							35%
Advanced Validation							35%
Design							10%
Clay Modeling							
Program Management							
Project Development							40%
Electronics							25%
Product Engineering							5%
Selling Expenses							35%
General & Administrative							73%

Planned Project Expenses	Hours	Rate	Total
Actual Expenses			
Project Engineering	4,680	$50.00	$ 234,000
Manual Design	32,432	45.00	1,459,440
CAD Design {Tube & Designer}	39,864	70.00	2,790,457
Electronics Engineering	0	38.00	0
Launch Support Costs (see **Exhibit 6**)	76,976	49.56	3,814,931
Validation Costs - Quoted			645,576
Industrial Design & Clay Models-Quoted			453,601
Product Development-Quoted			396,754
Budgeted Launch Costs			**$ 9,794,759**
Actual less Planned Launch Costs (see below)			226,125
Total Launch Costs			**$10,020,884**
Reimbursements			
Project Engineering	4,680	$45.00	$ 210,600
Manual Design	32,432	45.00	1,459,440
CAD Design	39,864	70.00	2,790,457
Subtotal - Engineering Time			$ 4,460,497
Validation			645,576
Industrial Design - Clay Models			453,601
Product Development - Prototype Parts			396,754
Total Reimbursed Costs			**$ 5,956,427**
Unrecovered Launch Costs			**$ 4,064,456**

Annual Forecasted Volume	250,000 units
Estimated Model Life	4 years
Launch Costs Amortized in Piece Costs	$4.06 per unit

Prototype Phase: Actual vs. Planned Costs

	Actual Costs	Planned Costs	Unrecovered Costs
Project Engineering: 7,020 hours @ $50	$351,000	$210,600	$140,400
Industrial Design	539,326	453,601	85,725
Total	**$890,326**	**$664,201**	**$226,125**

EXHIBIT 5   Launch Analysis: 1995 Decatur Dashboard Panel

	Rate per Engineering Hour	Total
Manufacturing Support		
Indirect Labor Hourly		
Foremen	$ 3,786	
Materials Handling	70,977	
Maintenance	59,383	
Meetings & Training	27,697	
Direct Labor Exempt		
Quality Control	131,605	
Production Control	7,043	
Plant Engineering	163,250	
Management	126,653	
Office Support	4,006	
Administrative	626	
Employee-Related	85,706	
Purchasing	54,236	
Computing Services	29,933	
Shop Supplies	160,222	
Tooling Maintenance, Outside	182,578	
Tooling Maintenance, Inside	25,703	
Transportation	49,064	
Freight In	12,439	
Freight Out	14,387	
Total Manufacturing Support	$15.71	$1,209,294
Advanced Mfg/Validation	3.44	264,797
Program Management	3.34	257,100
Product/Process Development	8.99	692,014
Selling Expenses	13.97	1,075,355
General & Administrative	4.11	316,371
Planned Launch Support Costs	$49.56	$3,814,931
Project Eng. Rate Variance		
4,680 hours @ $5.00	$ 0.30	23,400
Cost Overruns: Prototype Phase	$ 2.94	226.125
Total Unreimbursed Launch Costs	$52.80	$4,064,456

Note: Launch Support Costs:
         Rate per Engineering Hour was calculated using 76,796 Engineering Hours

EXHIBIT 6   Launch Support Costs: 1995 Decatur Dashboard Panel

Production Subsystem	Advance Manufacturing	Clay Models	Engineering & Surfacing	Product Development	Validation	Manufacturing Prog. Management; Sales & Administration	Totals
6700	$257,657		$ 325,910	$475,800	$434,102		$1,493,469
6710			202,123				202,123
6721			77,460				77,460
6730			139,420				139,420
6740			92,995				92,995
6750			22,600				22,600
6760			84,200				84,200
6770			68,420				68,420
6780			168,422				168,422
6790			27,070				27,070
Other Expenses						$916,246	$ 916,246
Prodn. Phases: Budgeted Amts.	**$257,657**		**$1,208,620**	**$475,800**	**$434,102**	**$916,246**	**$3,292,425**
# Months Until Start of Production	25		25	25	25	25	25
Monthly Run Rate	$ 10,306		$ 48,345	$ 19,032	$ 17,364	$ 36,650	$ 131,697

EXHIBIT 7   Launch Cost Budgets: Production Phase, 1995 Decatur Dashboard Panel

Reimbursements and Amortized Launch Costs	Advance Manufacturing	Clay Models	Engineering & Surfacing	Product Development	Validation	Manufacturing Prog. Management; Sales and Administration	Totals
Clay Models		$453,601					$ 453,601
Pre-prototype Parts				$ 174,624			174,624
Component Mockups				39,271			39,271
Prototype Parts - Sedan				77,755			77,755
Prototype Parts - Coupe							0
Prototype Parts - LS Sedan				54,574			54,574
Prototype Parts - LS Coupe				50,531			50,531
Engineering Design			$4,460,518				4,460,518
Validation/Testing					$453,601		453,601
Total Reimbursement		**$453,601**	**$4,460,518**	**$396,755**	**453,601**		**$5,764,474**
Amortized Launch Costs	$264,798			692,016		$2,858,124	3,814,937
Project Eng'g Rate Variance			23,400				23,400
Budgeted Total Launch Costs	**$264,798**	**$453,601**	**$4,483,918**	**$1,088,771**	**$453,601**	**$2,858,124**	**$9,579,412**
Expenses: What we have spent							
Prototype: Actual, 6/30/91	$ 7,141	$1,112,364	$2,645,088	$612,971	$ 19,499		$4,397,063
Design Support of Engineering		-644,486	644,486				
Estimated Support Expenses						$1,941,878	$1,941,878
Total Expenses through Prototype Phase ...	**$ 7,141**	**$ 467,878**	**$3,289,575**	**$612,971**	**$ 19,499**	**$1,941,878**	**$6,338,941**
Balance for Product Phase	**$257,657**	**($14,277)**	**$1,194,343**	**$475,800**	**$434,102**	**$ 916,246**	**$3,292,425**
Months Until Start of Production	25	25	24	25	25	25	25
Monthly Run Rate until Aug. 93	$ 10,306	n/a	$ 47,774	$ 19,032	$ 17,364	$ 36,650	$ 131,697

EXHIBIT 8   Launch—Summary Analysis, 1995 Decatur Dashboard Panel

Name _____ Social Security # _____ Week Ending _____

Project	Func	Mon	Tue	Wed	Thur	Fri	Sat	Total
99								
99								
99								
Sub-Total								
9907 Holiday								
9906 Sick								
9905 Vacation								
9918 Funeral								
9948 Jury Duty								
9943 Other Excused								
GRAND TOTAL								

Dept. _____

Function Code Description

D =   Unsold Development
E =   Engineering Aids/Models
C =   Customer Requested
V =   Validation
P =   PC Changes

Function Code Suffix

2 = CAD-related activity

Minutes--Decimal

:06=.1   :36=.6
:12=.2   :42=.7
:18=.3   :48=.8
:24=.4   :54=.9
:30=.5   :60=1.0

EMPLOYEE SIGNATURE   SUPERVISOR SIGNATURE

EXHIBIT 9   **Time Card: Product Development**

NAME _____ Social Security # _____ Week Ending _____

Description	Project	Func.	Orig/ Chng	Area Code	Mon	Tues	Wed	Thurs	Fri	Sat	Total
99											
99											
99											
99											
Sub-Total											
9907 Holiday											
9906 Sick											
9905 Vacation											
9918 Funeral											
9948 Jury Duty											
9943 Other Excused											
GRAND TOTAL											

Dept. _____

1 = Non-Cad Tim
2 = CAD Time

A-Theme Molding
B-Engineering Clay Modeling
C-Prove-out Clay Mode
D-Templating
E-Armature Prep
F-Layout
G-Communication
H-Mock-up Fabrication
I-Studio Show Prep
J-Casting/Lay-up
K-Modeling: Other ma
(foam,foamcore,cardboard
L-Shipping & Handling
P-Programming NC
Q-Milling
S-Surfacing
T-Studio Eng-Sold
U-Studio Eng-Unsold
V-Studio Eng-Proactive Design
Z-Digitizing

1-CAD Original intent
2-Manual original inten
3-CAD customer change
4-Manual customer cha:
5-CAD Prince change

EMPLOYEE SIGNATURE   SUPERVISOR SIGNATURE

EXHIBIT 10   Time Card: Design Department

453

9

Applying ABC
to Service Industries

So far, we have articulated the development of activity-based costing and activity-based management in manufacturing settings. While ABC had its origins in manufacturing companies, many service organizations today are obtaining great benefits for this approach as well.

In practice, the actual construction of an ABC model is virtually identical for both types of companies. This should not be surprising since even in manufacturing companies, the ABC system focuses on the "service" component of the factory and company as a whole. As a general rule, the ABC system in a manufacturing company retains the direct labor and direct materials elements of the company's Stage II manufacturing cost system and, if it has been well designed, the unit-level activities and drivers.[1] The changes from introducing ABC arise when factory indirect and support expenses are analyzed. These expenses represent the cost of providing *services* to manufacturing operations; that is, ordering, scheduling, moving, setting up, designing, inspecting, training, and supporting are all service activities that facilitate but are not directly involved in actual production.

In chapter 7, we extended the ABC model outside the factory, to include activities performed by marketing, sales, logistics, purchasing, and corporate staff. These activities make the service orientation of ABC even more obvious. In effect, ABC, from its origins, has been service rather than production-oriented. Thus, its extension to organizations that do no production, and instead provide service alone, does not require any new principles.

Also, service companies have exactly the same managerial issues as manufacturing companies. They need activity-based costing to link the costs of the resources they supply to the revenues earned by the individual products and customers serviced by these resources. Only by understanding such linkage, and the interplay among pricing, features, customer usage, and process improvement, can managers make good decisions about:

- The customer segments it wishes to serve,
- The products it will offer to customers in those segments,

---

[1] In the best designed traditional systems, the production cost pools are related to machine types, such as turning machines and lathes. Such systems are essentially activity-based since each machine class usually performs a single class of activity.

- The method of delivering the products and services to those customers, and
- The quantity and mix of resources it will supply,

to enable all this to happen. Because virtually all their operating expenses are fixed once resource supply has been committed, service organizations need the costing insights from ABC even more than manufacturing organizations.

Why then did ABC originate in manufacturing companies and not service organizations? One explanation is that manufacturing companies already had product costing systems to satisfy the inventory valuation requirements of financial reporting. Therefore, when the costing systems used for financial reporting became disconnected from changes in products, customers, and business processes, managers could easily see the problems from making decisions with the distorted signals from these systems.

Most service companies, in contrast, had no statutory requirement to measure the costs of their products or customers. They operated for decades without cost systems. They did not, of course, operate without financial systems. Service companies managed operations through budgetary control of responsibility centers. The companies were organized by functional departments, budgets were established for each department or responsibility center, and financial performance was measured and managed by comparing actual with budgeted results. In effect, service companies had their own version of Stage II cost controlling systems (as described in chapter 2). Service companies, of course, would not have much use for flexible budgeting since almost all of a service company's costs arise from resources committed in advance of use; that is, they are "fixed" costs in the short run. Thus, even though service companies were frequently as complex and diversified as manufacturing companies, managers knew neither the costs of the services they produced and delivered nor the cost of serving their different types of customers. And certainly they had no knowledge of the cost of their business processes that cut across departmental boundaries.

For example, the manager of a supermarket may know how much is spent, by type of expenditure (personnel, building and fixtures, merchandise, energy), at each retail store and at each warehouse. But the manager would not know the cost of receiving a case of canned vegetables from a supplier, storing it in a distribution center, transporting it to the retail outlet, and moving it to a shelf for the consumer to buy. Similarly, a bank president would know revenues and expenses by line item (interest revenue, fee income, retail bank expenses, data processing costs), but would not know the cost of different types of checking accounts or the costs to serve individual customers.

Such a lack of accurate information about the products and customers was not a concern for many decades because most service companies operated in benign, noncompetitive markets. Many service companies have, until recently, been highly regulated, or in the case of Canada and Europe, were government-owned and operated monopolies providing rail and air transport, and telecommunication services. In these noncompetitive environments, managers of service companies were not under great pressure to lower costs, improve the quality and efficiency of operations, introduce new products that made profits, or eliminate products and services that were incurring losses. Regulators set prices to cover the operating costs of inefficient companies. Laws and regulations prevented more efficient competitors from entering the markets in which regulated or government-owned service companies operated; and taxpayers subsidized any losses in government-operated companies.

Lacking strong competitive pressures, managers of service organizations had little demand for cost information about products, customers, and processes. Consequently, the financial systems in most service organizations were simple. They allowed managers to budget expenses by operating department, and to measure and monitor actual spending against these functional departmental budgets.

CHANGING COMPETITIVE ENVIRONMENT

During the last two decades of the 20th century, however, the competitive environment for most service companies became as challenging and demanding as for manufacturing companies. The deregulation movement since the 1970s completely changed the ground rules under which many service companies operated. Pricing, product mix, and geographic and competitive restrictions have been virtually eliminated in the financial services industry. Transportation companies can now enter and leave markets and determine the prices at which they offer services to customers. Telecommunications companies now compete aggressively on price, quality, and service. Health care reimbursement is shifting away from pure cost recovery schemes. Utility companies are crossing previously impermeable borders to compete across geographic regions. Even government monopolies, such as the postal service, are today experiencing competition from private companies. For example, Federal Express and UPS offer overnight delivery of letters and packages; telecommunication companies allow documents to be sent via facsimile transmission; and the Internet and World Wide Web permit the transmission of mail, messages, and documents on international electronic networks. And the trend to privatization that is now sweeping through the world completely changes the rules of the game for former government-operated companies. They must transform themselves into private, competitive companies. Even local retail outlets, historically sheltered from national or global competition, are facing vigorous competition from new entrants of efficient mass merchandisers, whether of food, toys, office supplies, home furnishings, or pet supplies.

Thus, managers of service companies now require information to improve the quality, timeliness, and efficiency of the activities they perform, and to understand accurately the cost and profitability of their individual products, services, and customers.

A COMPLEX ENVIRONMENT FOR COSTING PRODUCTS AND SERVICES

Service companies in general are ideal candidates for activity-based costing, even more than manufacturing companies. First, virtually all their costs are indirect and appear to be "fixed." Manufacturing companies could at least trace important components of costs, such as direct materials and direct labor, to individual products. Service companies have minimal to no direct materials and much of their personnel provide indirect support to products and customers.[2] Probably because of their insulation from strong competitive forces, most service companies did not deploy large numbers of industrial engineers to study and standardize direct labor operations for those employees who did provide direct service for products and customers.[3] Consequently, service companies did not have a platform established for measurement of direct costs on which to erect systems for assigning indirect costs to individual products and customers.

The large component of apparently "fixed" costs in service organizations arises because, unlike manufacturing companies, they have virtually no material costs, the prime source of short-term variable costs. Service companies must supply virtually all their resources in advance. The resources provide the capacity to perform work for customers during each period. Fluctuations during the period in the demand by individual products and customers for the activities performed by these resources do not influence short-term spending to supply the resources.

[2] Or the direct contact that a service employee had with a customer was so brief that detailed measurement of the time elapsed was not considered to be cost-effective.

[3] This is an overly broad indictment. Many individual service companies, like United Parcel Service, McDonald's, AT&T, and large retail banks did use industrial engineers extensively to study and monitor labor times and efficiencies for their repetitive work processes.

Consequently, the marginal cost (as conventionally defined—the increase in spending resulting from an incremental transaction or customer) for many service industries is essentially zero. For example, a transaction at a bank's ATM machine requires an additional consumption of a small piece of paper to print the receipt, but no additional outlay. For a bank to add an additional customer may require a monthly statement to be mailed, involving the cost of the paper, an envelope, and a stamp, but little more. Carrying an extra passenger on an airplane requires an extra can of soda pop, two bags of peanuts (for most coach class U.S. flights these days), and a very minor increase in fuel consumption, but nothing else. Similarly, treating one more patient in a hospital or health care facility may involve an incremental expenditure on pharmaceuticals and bandages, but these are tiny compared to revenues. For a telecommunications company, handling one more phone call from a customer, or one more data transfer, involves no incremental spending. Therefore, if service companies were to make decisions about products and customers based on short-term marginal costs, they would provide a full range of all products and services to all customers at prices that could range down to near zero. But then, of course, the companies would get limited to no recovery of the costs of all the ("fixed") resources they supplied that enabled the service to be delivered to the customer. Only by fully incorporating the capacity-based costing ideas articulated in chapter 5 can service companies be able to measure and manage their cost structure, service offerings, and customer relationships.

For service companies, almost a complete separation exists between decisions to incur costs, and the decisions by customers that generate revenues. Decisions to incur, or subtract, costs involve adding or contracting the supply of resources to provide service, for example:

- Adding a new city to an airline's route schedule,
- Building another rail line or acquiring additional locomotives and freight cars by a railroad,
- Hiring additional physicians or adding operating room capacity for a hospital,
- Expanding the network for a telecommunications company, and
- Building additional branch or retail outlets for a bank or retailer.

Decisions by consumers that generate revenues include:

- The size of their monthly balances in checking accounts,
- Elapsed time of long distance phone calls,
- Number of passenger miles flown, and
- Number and type of health care procedures requested.

In manufacturing companies, the costs associated with meeting customer demands and the revenues associated with selling products to customers are at least linked by the direct costs of materials in a product and the direct labor and energy costs to produce the product. Service companies have no such direct connection. All linkages between the costs of resources supplied and their use by individual products and customers must be inferred and estimated; a process identical to how ABC links indirect manufacturing resources to products. Also, a revenue-generating event—taking an airline flight, shipping a container by rail, obtaining treatment for a disease or injury, completing a long-distance phone call, receiving a kilowatt of energy, and using a checking account for a month—makes demands on and requires the service output from many different organizational units in a service company.

Service companies provide an ideal setting for understanding why companies need different systems for operational control and for measuring the costs and profitability of products and customers (as discussed in chapter 1). For short-term (daily, weekly, monthly) monitoring and control, service companies need an operational control system that provides feedback on expenses incurred in each of its organizational units, as well as other measures of performance, such as quality and response times. Some service organizations have highly detailed systems for measuring expenses, line item by line item, in every one of thousands of different responsibility and cost centers. But knowing how much is being spent in individual cost and responsibility centers in a service organization, by detailed type of expenditure, communicates nothing about how much it costs to process a single customer transaction that benefits from the resources provided in dozens of different organizational units.

For example, take a simple example of a telecommunications company responding to a customer request for a new connection. The process involves people from many different departments: customer call desk, credit check, planning, dispatching, engineering, billing, and customer service, plus several others. The cost of performing this basic service differs dramatically if the customer changes the order specification, complains about the outcome, fails the credit check, or requires additions to capacity. One cannot view this process from the perspective of cost control in responsibility centers. A Stage III ABC system can measure the cost of resources used in diverse responsibility centers by individual products and customers, and by the activities and business processes that deliver the products to customers. Only the end-to-end process look from an ABC perspective reveals the cost of performing basic services for individual customers.

Service Department Activity-Based Cost Systems

While the basic principles of building ABC systems are the same for service and manufacturing companies, some differences do show up in practice. Many service organizations transact directly with customers. Therefore, we can expect more use of duration drivers since the transaction with the customer may differ in complexity. For example, the time to perform open-heart surgery may depend upon the age and health of the patient, and whether the patient has other complications. Or the time to resolve a customer request may vary depending upon the complexity of the situation being handled. In general, professional services, such as legal and consulting services and investment banking relationships, have strong discretionary components that cannot be accurately captured with transaction drivers. The use of duration drivers acknowledges that producing many services is not as standard as producing a standard widget.

Related to the nonstandard nature of many outputs from service organizations, the cost measurement should be accompanied by independent measures of quality. In manufacturing companies, quality can be monitored by inspecting products before they are shipped to customers. While it is preferable to design in rather than inspect in quality, manufacturing companies have the option to place an inspection process between the production process and customer shipment. In service companies, however, the production process is generally delivered directly to the customer. Pressure to reduce costs can lead to compromises in quality; for example, when physicians are told to process patients in 12 minutes instead of 20 minutes, orchestras are encouraged to play Beethoven's Ninth Symphony in 48 minutes instead of 72, and customer service representatives are instructed to reduce the length of phone calls. In these cases, the cost of the service is not being reduced; rather the customer is receiving a different, lower-quality output that can be produced at lower cost. As service companies install better cost systems, they should also be enhancing their measurements of service quality so that customers do not receive a different product from what had been designed and intended to be delivered.

DEMAND FOR PRODUCT AND CUSTOMER COSTS BY SERVICE COMPANIES

Why do service companies find it useful to understand the cost of activities, business processes, products, and customers? The demand for such cost information arises from three broad classes of managerial decisions:

- Managing products and customers,
- Configuring the customer service delivery chain, and
- Budgeting the organization's supply of resources.

We will discuss each of these applications in turn.

Managing Products and Customers

Service companies typically offer a highly diverse set of offerings. Each product, with its unique characteristics, makes different demands on the organization's resources. Service organizations must continually assess the economics of their product line variety, making decisions on pricing, quality, responsiveness, introduction, and discontinuance of individual products. The cost and profitability of individual products is a vital input into such decisions.

But beyond product economics, service companies must be even more focused on customer economics than manufacturing companies. Consider a manufacturing company producing a standard product, let us call it a widget. Manufacturers can calculate the cost of producing the widget without regard to how their customers use the widget; the manufacturing costs are "customer independent." Only the costs of marketing, selling, order handling, delivery, and service of the widget might be customer specific. For service companies, in contrast, even the basic operating costs of a standard product are determined by customer behavior.

Consider a standard product like a checking account. It is relatively straight-forward—using ABC methods—to calculate all the costs associated with such a checking account. The revenues, including interest earned on monthly balances and fees charged to customers for services, are also simple to attribute to this product. The analysis will reveal whether such a product is profitable or unprofitable. But such a total or average look at the product will hide the enormous variation in profitability of this product across customers.

One customer may maintain a high cash balance in his checking account and make very few deposits or withdrawals. A second customer may manage her checking account balance very closely, keeping only the minimum amount on hand, and use her account heavily by making many withdrawals and deposits. Service companies need to identify the differential profitability of individual customers, even of those using standard products. The variation in demand for organizational resources is much more customer-driven in service organizations than in manufacturing organizations. A service company can determine and control the efficiency of its internal activities, but customers determine the quantity of demands for these operating activities.

As another example, customers of a telecommunications company can order a basic service unit in several different ways—through a phone call, a letter, or appearing in a local retail outlet. The customer may order two phone lines at once or just one; engineers may have to appear to install the new line, or perhaps just make a change in the local switching center. The customer may make only one request or several, and can pay either by direct debit, by a mailed check, or in person. The cost of each option is quite different. Therefore, measuring revenues and costs at the customer level provides the company with far more relevant and useful information than at the product level.

Also, a customer may not just have a single relationship with the service (telecommunications) company. In addition to the basic phone line, the customer may have a high-speed data line, a long-distance account, a service contract, and equipment rentals. Therefore, before taking drastic action with a customer with an unprofitable basic phone line, the company's managers should understand all the relationships it has with the customer, and act based on total relationship profitability, not just the profitability with a single product.

Other customers may appear unprofitable because they have been recently acquired. Many service companies invest considerable resources in marketing campaigns to attract new customers. Because of the high cost of acquiring new customers, and the time required to establish a broad and deep relationship (such as across multiple product offerings), new customers may appear to be unprofitable. Service companies need to distinguish the economics of newly-acquired customers from those who have been customers for many years.[4] Thus, in addition to recognizing cross-sectional variation of demands by customers, they must also forecast the longitudinal variation of customers over time to obtain total life-cycle profitability. ABC systems provide service companies with the fine granularity of detail required for intelligent management of customers, individually and over time.

Companies may find it difficult to target their offerings and modify the behavior at the individual customer level. Since many service companies have millions or tens of millions of customers, they must group customers into manageable market segments. Companies may have as few as 3–5 segments or, with sophisticated databases and consumer information, up to 100–200 segments. Rather than report and manage profitability at the individual customer level, service companies may prefer to have their ABC systems calculate cost and profitability information at the segment level. As companies understand the characteristics and the preferences of these segments, they can decide which segments will be most profitable to target and retain, and which should be de-emphasized. It may be impossible to serve profitably all customer segments. Companies, knowing their internal capabilities (or core competencies), can select the value propositions they wish to deliver to targeted segments that enable them to attract significant business from customers in these segments, and also be highly profitable in all targeted segments. Unprofitable customers in untargeted segments are prime candidates to be "de-marketed." The ABC system provides the cost insight for executives following a segmentation strategy.

Configuring the Customer Service Delivery Chain

If service companies understand the preferences of customers in different segments, they can tailor their service offering and the method of delivery to satisfy these diverse preferences. Because service organizations are so close to their customers, any decisions made about product offerings, features, price, and delivery must involve an interplay between customer preferences and the cost of satisfying those preferences. Service companies will make the best decisions when they can combine their activity-based cost analysis with excellent information about the attributes and features valued by customers in different market segments. In this way, companies can select the segments they wish to target for growth and profitability, and customize their service offerings to these different segments so that each targeted segment is individually profitable.

Budgeting the Organization's Supply of Resources

Finally, an accurate activity-based cost model, linking organizational spending that supplies resource capabilities to the activities performed and then to the demands by individual products or customers, will facilitate decisions on the appropriate supply of resources. As described earlier in the chapter, service companies typically budget and manage their costs by responsibility centers. Without an ABC model, service company managers have no way of linking budgeting decisions that authorize the supply of resources for individual responsibility centers to the demands, from products and customers, for the activities and services provided by these responsibility centers. They must set budgets in an annual negotiating process between responsibility center heads and the senior executive team. An ABC model, as we will discuss in chapter 11, can be

---

[4]The interplay among customer acquisition, retention, and lifetime profitability is at the heart of the comprehensive measurement system proposed in F. F. Reichheld, "The Right Measures," chapter 8, pp. 217–253, in *The Loyalty Effect*, Boston: HBS Press, 1996).

used as the foundation of an organization's budgeting process. In this way, decisions to authorize spending in responsibility centers become linked to the outputs demanded from these units by an anticipated volume and mix of products and customers. It enables the service company to supply resources for products and customers that contribute to long-run profitability and to identify where cost reduction may be required for critical processes in the service delivery chain.

SUMMARY

Applying ABC to service organizations requires a keen appreciation of costing for committed resources. Naive observers could look at service organizations and believe that all their costs were fixed, independent of quantity and mix of usage. Such a view would leave little motivation for developing activity-based cost systems in such settings. But once one realizes, using the framework established in chapter 5, that managers determine the supply of committed resources in anticipation of demands for services by products and customers, the rationale for linking resource usage to such demands becomes far more compelling. Companies need the information from an ABC model to make decisions about the products and services they wish to offer, the customer segments they wish to serve, the method of delivering the products and services to those customers, and the supply of resources they require for their products, services, and customers. Managers will use the ABC information to develop products and services that can be delivered to customers at prices that cover the costs of resources used, thereby enabling them to serve customers in profitable relationships.

CASES

The cases in this chapter focus on the application of activity-based costing to service settings. The first objective is to demonstrate how easily the concepts developed in manufacturing settings transfer to service ones. The second objective is to highlight the important role that customer behavior has on the economics of service delivery and how ABC systems have to be designed to take this fact into account.

The *St. Catherine of Alexandria Medical Center* case provides an introduction to relative value unit (RVU) costing. This is the approach that many hospitals are using to upgrade their cost systems from the highly primitive cost-to-charge ratio systems that were introduced by Medicare. The next two cases illustrate ABC in the banking industry. The *Co-operative Bank* illustrates how a retail bank developed its first ABC model for estimating the cost and profitability of its products and customers. The second case, *Manufacturers Hanover*, illustrates the measurement and management of customer profitability in a commercial bank setting.

St. Catherine of Alexandria Medical Center

In the new highly competitive environment in which we find ourselves, we are forced to bid on specialty contracts such as angioplasties. We are no longer in control of directing care of patients, we now compete with other hospitals for specific procedures and have to bid on them. This change in environment requires that we have a much more sophisticated grasp on what our "products" cost.

Judith Mariner, CFO

St. Catherine of Alexandria Medical Center (SCAM), was a 347 licensed bed hospital, who's primary market was in Tulsa, Arizona. The Medical Center had a long tradition of excellence in patient care offering a full range of tertiary services. Every year, there were about 14,000 hospital inpatient admissions, over 7,500 outpatient surgical procedures performed, and more than 163,000 ambulatory visits. SCAM's annual operating budget was close to $293 million. The hospital's occupancy rate in 1995 was 57.9% based on licensed beds and 75% on staffed beds. Total patient days that year were 69,995.

In addition to general acute services, the Medical Center offered services in the specialty areas of Cardiovascular Services; Diabetes; Oncology; Neonatal Intensive Care; Orthopaedics; Women's Services/Obstetrics and Mental Health Services. Its nationally recognized Rehabilitation Center offered specialty programs for injuries such as Brain, Spinal Cord and Stroke Rehabilitation Injuries.

The Medical Center was staffed for 247 beds. Licensed beds were classified as follows: Medical/Surgical; Telemetry; Intensive Care; Cardiac Care; Orthopaedics; Obstetrics; Neonatal Intensive Care; Rehabilitation; Diabetic Metabolic; Oncology and Skilled nursing beds. Nursing was assigned to each level of care based on established nursing ratios.

SCAM's Cardiovascular Program offered a wide range of cardiovascular procedures. Its major product lines include Open Heart Surgery which comprised valve replacement and coronary by-pass surgery. Additional services included Angioplasty, and Cardiac Catheterization. There were 295 open heart surgeries,

240 angioplasties and 320 cardiac catheterizations performed in 1995. SCAM staffed three state of the art heart catheterization labs. Open Heart Surgeries represented 22% of the hospitals total admissions. Other services in 1995 included:

- Orthopaedics services, which comprised 14% of the hospitals admissions, with special emphasis on Hip and Joint Replacement; Spinal Fusion and Laminectomies.
- Women's services accounted for 21% of the hospitals admissions. Normal Deliveries accounted for 80% of all births in the hospital. There were 2,500 deliveries per year.
- Oncology Services represented about 14% of the hospital's admissions. This represented approximately a 2% increase from the prior year.
- Rehabilitation Service accounted for 19% of the hospital's admissions.
- Other services accounted for 10% of the hospital's admissions. These included services in the areas of general acute mental health, and the Neonatal Intensive Care Unit.

SCAM's case mix index for 1995 was over 1.51. The hospital case mix index is a statistic which measures the acuity of illness for a specific condition as established by the Health Care Financing Administration (HCFA). A value over 1.00 specifies above average acuity. Its payor mix distribution in 1995 was: 40% Medicare, 20% Preferred Provider Organizations (PPO), 10% Health Maintenance Organizations (HMO) which were shared risk, 8% Full Risk capitation, 15% Indemnity and 7% Medicaid. SCAM's Medicare discharges for 1995 were 4,500, the highest number in the county.

Competitive Environment

With increased penetration of managed care, the health care industry faced many challenges in the delivery of health care services. These challenges were further accentuated by the continuous mergers and affiliations of health care systems and managed care organizations. The objective of these mergers was primarily to enable the firms to survive and retain market share by prevailing as the ultimate provider of choice. Providers were forced to compete and demonstrate efficiency in the allocation of resources as well as being able to provide cost effective care while assuming accountability for outcomes.

This case was prepared by Silvia Midency under the supervision of Robin Cooper.

Providers of care continued to experience reduced length of stays coupled with lowered per diem reimbursements. The resulting lowered revenues forced hospitals to find ways to delivered health care at lower costs while still maintaining outcome levels.

Managed Care had introduced new forms of reimbursement, new control over the delivery of health care through the introduction of "gatekeepers", and changed the relative power of every group involved in the health care delivery process. Reimbursement had shifted from cost based, to per diem, to capitation approaches. Prior to managed care, hospitals were reimbursed on cost based procedures. Under such procedures, it was difficult for a hospital to lose money. In contrast, with capitation, the hospital carried most, if not all, of the risk associated with delivering care. Consequently, an inefficient hospital was at risk of bankruptcy.

The "Gatekeeper" concept introduced a new level of authorization for services which transferred autonomy for the demand of services from the consumer to utilization management committees which must now determine the need of services, thus changing the relative power of consumers, physicians and hospitals.

The New Decision Support System

The parent company to SCAM decided in 1994 to purchase a decision support system to assist its four hospitals in evaluating their cost structures while simultaneously integrating cost and clinical data. The decision support system was to be implemented across all hospitals. St. Catherine of Alexandria, the largest hospital in the group, was selected to be the pilot site.

The project was coordinated through the Corporate Office, the firm's central administration. The team consisted of a financial analyst, decision support manager, clinical coordinator, and case management. The team was under the direction of the hospital's Chief Financial Officer.

The decision support system was an integrated system. It had the ability to combine the hospital's cost structure with its clinical data and evaluate the hospital's performance. The decision support system interfaced with the hospital's existing main frame systems such as Medical Records, Patient Billing, Payroll and the General Ledger in order to access the hospital's data. The primary purpose of this integration was to provide the hospital with clinical, financial, and cost information within one system. The database was structured to allow multiple users at each site to access cost information and report in a way that facilitated analysis and process reengineering. Procedure standardization was introduced to provide for benchmarking and cost comparison among the hospitals. Each procedure was identified by a unique procedure code.

The decision support system was a managerial tool that focused on cost control within departments and provided for accountability and performance evaluation of department managers. The system was expected to support the following functions:

Development of Critical Pathways and Product Lines

Case Management/Utilization and Quality Management

Clinical Process Improvement—Treatment Protocol Development

Profitability Analysis

Standard and Actual Costing

Service Line and Center Variance Analysis

Flexible Budgeting

Productivity Management

Activity Based Performance Measurement

The Project was divided into two phases to facilitate implementation. Phase I, the initial phase, encompassed developing the basic patient data base and financial structures. During this phase existing data elements such as patient demographics (name, date of birth, age and medical history) and clinical information were used for the patient database. Financial structures were kept simple during this phase to enable early completion. The existing financial structures included information such as payor type (Medicare, HMO, PPO), number of patients admissions charges per admission, and number of procedures performed. The immediate goal was to provide case mix and patient utilization reporting. In Phase II, the refinement phase, the teams were to identify new patient data elements and the financial structures were to be analyzed for site and or department specific charges.

Phase I: Implementation of System

Department Cost Management (DCM), a subsystem of the decision support system, was a control program primarily used by ancillary and routine hospital departments. Ancillary and routine hospital departments were stand alone departments, such as radiology, lab, pathology, which were utilized in the course of a patient's treatment. DCM was designed as a standard cost accounting system focusing on the control and management of the unit costs of the outputs, or products as they were called, of these departments.

Department Costing The general ledger and the payroll system recaptured all revenue and expenses for each individual department. The individual departments were set up as cost centers rather than revenue centers since patient discharges, not tests and procedures, generated revenues under fixed price and prospective payment systems. A unique general ledger number was assigned to each individual department within the general ledger and payroll system. Expenses for each individual department were further subclassified in accordance with the nature of the expense. Subclassifications included such categories as: Salaries & Wages, Benefits, Management and Supervision, Purchased Services, and Professional Fees.

The existing department's structure was analyzed and each department was designated as a direct or indirect department. There were 70 direct departments, and 60 indirect. A direct department was revenue producing. It created services and procedures (patient charges) that could be tied to a specific patient. For example, radiology and pathology were direct departments. Indirect departments were nonrevenue producing and did not generate patient charges. They provided services that could not be specifically traced to an individual patient. For example, medical records, depreciation, housekeeping, and administration were indirect departments.

Each direct department budget was allocated to a number of different products based on the unit cost and the budgeted volume. The unit cost of each product was viewed as the amount of resources required to produce it. These resources included labor, supplies, equipment, facilities and overhead. Each direct department's expenses were classified into Variable and Fixed. Variable expenses were those expenses that depended on the patient volume and the number of tests requested by a physician (i.e. lab, x-rays, etc). Fixed expenses were all other expenses.

Direct department's expenses were classified into seven categories: Variable Labor (VL), Variable Supplies (VS) and Variable Other (VO). Fixed Direct Labor (FDL), Fixed Direct Equipment (FDE), Fixed Direct Facility (FDF) and Fixed Direct Other (FDO). The expenses of the indirect departments were classified as fixed indirect expenses (FI). The selection of these cate-gories were driven by the budgetary requirements of the hospital's cost management software. In particular, they allowed the software to predict departmental costs at different levels of patient activity.

Product Costing The hospital's products were differentiated into two separate categories for purposes of product costing. These categories were End products and Intermediate products. End products were defined as patient discharges. Intermediate products were all stand-alone procedures (ancillary services), such as radiology and pathology, which were ordered during a patient's stay in the hospital.

In the implementation phase—Phase I—all direct department's variable and fixed direct expenses were allocated down to each procedure code level by use of the department's charge master. A charge master is a dictionary which displays all procedures with their appropriate charge codes for a specific department. Allocation of these expenses were made using a cost-to-charge ratio approach. The cost-to-charge ratio methodology is based on the relationship of total expenses to revenues for a specific department (Exhibit 1).

The costs of the indirect departments, such as utilities, depreciation, administration were allocated to the product unit in two steps. The first step assigned overhead expenses to the direct departments via a step-down method. This method allowed for the use of different allocation measures chosen to most accurately reflect the consumption of resources. For example, utilities were allocated to each department based on square footage because area was a significant determinant of utility consumption. The second step allocated overhead expenses from the direct departments down to each department's procedure code level using the same cost to charge ratio.

A hospital like SCAM produced a very large number of different products or procedure codes. Some of these procedures were infrequently performed and not considered worth costing separately. Consequently, they were grouped together into product groups that were treated as if they were a single product. This grouping process was designed to produce a manageable level of complexity during the costing process.

Once expenses were allocated to the intermediate products (product unit level), total costs for a patient discharge were then accumulated in the patient's database to produce the cost of a patient discharge—that is an end product. By categorizing end products into product lines, the decision support system could report product line profitability and costs could be reported (Exhibit 2).

Phase II: Refinement of System

During Phase II, the refinement phase, the cost to charge method of expense allocation was replaced by the Relative Value Unit (RVU) approach. A RVU was assigned to each charge code level (intermediate product) to indicate the relative amount of resources used by that product within a cost category (Exhibit 3). The RVU approach enabled costs to be captured without having to actually measure every single activity performed to complete the procedure.

While in theory the software could accommodate a different RVU for each expense category and department, only two types of RVU were used for each department. The first RVU type consisted of a weighting based upon acquisition costs. This RVU was used for variable supplies. The second type of RVU was the labor minutes required to complete the service being delivered. This RVU was used for all other cost categories. RVU's were developed by each department's manager.

RVUs were developed using an 80/20 approach. This meant RVUs would be developed for those intermediate products which represented the highest revenue and highest volume (80% of all procedures) by selecting the most common procedure/charge code as the benchmark and assigning it a value. The remaining costs of the 20% of all procedures not given an RVU measure were reallocated based on an adjusted cost to charge ratio basis. These CCRs were adjusted to reflect a closer relationship to the relative value units of the group procedures.

Once RVUs had been assigned, the product volume was multiplied by the RVU to determine the total weighted RVUs for each product. The department budget for that cost category (VL, VS etc.) was then divided by the total department weighted RVUs to determine a standard cost per RVU. The standard cost per RVU was then multiplied by the RVU assigned to each product to yield a standard cost per intermediate product. The cost of intermediate products was then summed for each patient encounter to give the cost of the encounter.

Comparing the Two Cost Systems

With the initiation of Phase II, the question arose about the degree to which the two systems would report different product costs both at the intermediate and end levels. To begin the exploration of this issue, a single case—John Smith—was selected for manual calculation (Exhibit 4). The procedure chosen was an angioplasty, a commonly performed and significant revenue generator for SCAM.

An angioplasty was chosen as the test case because, in the near future, the hospital was going to have to bid on a contract to perform angioplasties for an HMO and it wanted that bid to be as competitive as possible. To enable this comparison to be undertaken, additional information on the patient, John Smith, had to be collected. The information included the summary budget for the first quarter of 1966 for the departments that provided services for the patient (Exhibit 5) and the RVUs for the procedures performed on the patient and the total RVUs for each department. The information for the Room and Board and Central Supplies departments were the last to be received. (Exhibit 6). This information was considered sufficient to compute the cost of John Smith's stay (Exhibit 7).

Total Cost:$7,000,000

Charge Code	Description	Volume	Unit Charge	Total Charges	% Charges	Total Costs	Cost per Unit
1	Chest X-Ray	50,000	$150	$7,500,000	37.50%	$2,625,000	$52.50
2	Skull X-Ray	25,000	$200	$5,000,000	25.00%	$1,750,000	$70.00
3	GI Series	25,000	$300	$7,500,000	37.50%	$2,625,000	$105.00
	Total	100,000		$20,000,000		$7,000,000	

EXHIBIT 1　Sample Calculation, X-Ray Department, Cost to Charge Ratio Approach

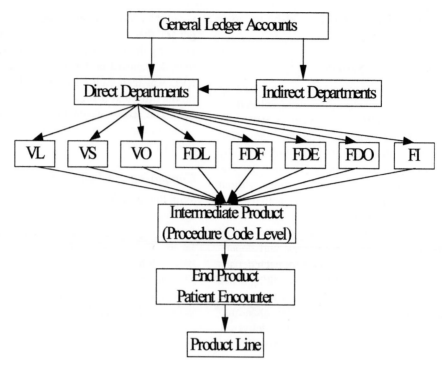

EXHIBIT 2 **The Structure of the Product Costing System**

Total Cost: $7,000,000

Charge Code	Description	Volume	RVUs Minutes	Total RVU Minutes	% RVU Minutes	Total Cost	Unit Cost per RVU
1	Chest X-Ray	50,000	20	1,000,000	23.53%	$1,647,059	$32.94
2	Skull X-Ray	25,000	40	1,000,000	23.53%	$1,647,059	$65.88
3	GI Series	25,000	90	$2,250,000	52.94%	$3,705,882	$148.24
	Total	100,000	120	4,250,000		$7,000,000	

EXHIBIT 3 **Sample Calculation, X-Ray Department, Relative Value Unit Approach**

John Smith a 49 year old man was admitted to St. Catherine of Alexandria Medical Center on July 1, 1995, for a scheduled Angioplasty.

Total charges for the admission were as follows:

Room and Board	$6,038
Central Supplies	166
Clinical Lab	2,690
Cardiac Cath Lab	21,135
Cardiology	771
Pharmacy	2,373
TOTAL	$33,173

The patient was admitted to the hospital as an inpatient stay and spent a total of three days following the procedure. The expected hospital reimbursement for this procedure was $9,200 for the case.

EXHIBIT 4   Case Summary, Patient: John Smith

	Room & Board	Central Supplies	Clinical Lab	Cardiac Cath Lab	Cardiology	Pharmacy
Charges						
Charges Outpatient	$0	$275,488	$1,742,847	$1,714,185	$674,012	$2,725,857
Charges Inpatient	2,085,705	1,512,687	4,230,406	2,076,432	720,289	9,274,704
Total Charges	$2,085,705	$1,788,175	$5,973,253	$3,790,617	$1,394,301	$12,000,561
Direct Expenses						
Salaries & Wages (VL)	$400,844	$72,146	$278,959	$175,000	$42,925	$217,195
Other Salaries (FDL)	80,639	13,330	101,956	40,000	26,080	68,626
Employee Benefits (FDO)	182,267	48,149	163,753	31,764	27,825	100,673
Professional Fees (FDO)	13,749	0	46,926	0	23,148	0
Supplies (VS)	38,673	315,000	207,354	110,000	30,794	910,944
Purchased Services (FDO)	4,956	20,298	84,132	49,383	9,909	9,879
Rental & Leases (FDE)	477	75,000	5,736	252	3,249	3,000
Utilities (FDO)	1,641	258	1,536	294	252	789
Other Expenses (FDO)	777	5,889	7,356	1,591	1,296	2,913
Indirect Expenses (FI)	$642,211	$200,000	$375,000	$900,000	$250,000	$350,000
Total Cost	$1,366,234	$750,070	$1,272,708	$1,308,284	$1,036,478	$1,663,719

EXHIBIT 5   Total Cost Summary, First Quarter Fiscal Year 1996

Department
Room and Board

	Nursing Time Minutes	Supplies
Room 373	540	100
Room 373	540	100
Room 373	540	100
Room 373	540	100
Critical Care Assessment	540	100
All Other patients	1,248,900	233,100
Total RVUs	1,251,600	233,600

Department
Central Supplies

	Labor Handling Minutes	Supplies
Restraint Wrist Disposable	10	450
Pack Transducer	30	1,560
Dressing Gauze 4X4 10 Per/PKG	10	210
Intermittent Unfusion Plug	20	275
Set-Vol Infusion 3 sites	30	560
Set IV Secondary	20	175
Level Lock Cannula	20	75
All Other patients	1,013,960	25,108,600
Total RVUs	1,014,100	25,111,905

EXHIBIT 6   John Smith, RVU Analysis

Department	Variable Cost	Fixed Costs
Room and Board	$_____	$_____
Central Supplies	$_____	$_____
Clinical Lab	$ 234	$ 597
Cardiac Cath Lab	$2,917	$2,378
Cardiology	$ 48	$ 147
Pharmacy	$ 209	$ 204
Total Cost	$	$

EXHIBIT 7   John Smith, RVU Reported Cost

THE CO-OPERATIVE BANK

We were prepared to make bold, innovative decisions to enhance our profitability. But if you are going to be bold, you had better be sure your facts are correct.

Terry Thomas, Managing Director, The Co-operative Bank

History

In 1994, the co-operative movement celebrated the 150th anniversary of its founding. A small group of people, in 1844, had started a grocer's shop in Rochdale, England (near the city of Manchester):

> to provide the local community with a source of pure, unadulterated goods at fair prices; their guiding principle was that the co-operative should exist for the benefit of the people it served, sharing its profits among them in proportion to their purchases.

The founders of the co-operative movement articulated a strong statement of mission and ethical standards (see Exhibit 1). The movement spread throughout the country and was an active force, even 150 years later. In 1994, U.K. co-operative societies generated a turnover of £6 billion, mostly in food retailing, farming, food production, milk sales, funeral supplies, general retailing, car sales and financial services.

The Co-operative Bank

The Co-operative Bank (The Bank) was founded in Manchester in 1872 as a department of the Co-operative Wholesale Society (CWS), a central organization formed by co-operative societies across the country, who were, by then, the dominant retailing force in the U.K. Exhibit 2 summarizes recent financial statistics for the Co-operative Bank. During its first 75 years, The Bank functioned mainly to serve the treasury needs of CWS's operations. Personal accounts were not emphasized though The Bank did attract some personal customers from employees of co-operative societies and local authorities (municipalities).

From the late 1940s through 1971, The Bank began to expand its branch network to support the needs of the CWS and the increasing number of other co-operative societies and local authorities that were bringing their business to The Bank. During this time, the co-operative societies were generating large amounts of cash from their highly successful trading operations and, by 1971, The Bank's deposits had grown to more than £300 million.[1] With this expansion of banking activities, CWS managers realized that they needed to separate the banking business from all their other activities. In 1971, an Act of Parliament established The Bank as a separate legal entity, with the CWS holding the entire issue of share capital. Previously, The Bank's results and financial position had been consolidated with those of the CWS.

Lewis Lee, the first Chief Executive of the newly structured bank, strengthened and broadened The Bank's management expertise by recruiting several senior and middle managers from the larger UK clearing banks. An immediate challenge emerged when The Bank's strong deposit base declined rapidly as the co-operative movement (which supplied 96% of deposits) was confronted with strong competitive pressure on its trading activities. The Bank's managers recognized the need for immediate and radical actions.

To replace the lost retail deposits, The Bank began to pursue, much more aggressively, deposits from personal customers. It became the first UK bank to introduce free banking for customers who maintained credit balances in their current accounts. Over the next ten years, the number and size of personal accounts increased sharply and, while deposits never regained their 1971 highs, the reliance on deposits from the co-operative sector was sharply reduced to 4% of the total.

The Bank pursued a similarly aggressive policy for the asset side of the balance sheet. In 1971, loans to the co-operative movement represented 90% of assets. By the 1990s, this percentage had declined to about 10%–12%, with the remaining assets evenly split between the Personal and Corporate sectors. In 1975, The Bank's broadened customer base for both assets and deposits enabled it to obtain status as a settlement bank so that it could now perform clearing activities and settlements. It was the first new settlement bank in 39 years and the first ever to achieve this status from internal growth.

The Bank, during the 1970s and 80s, also broadened

This case was prepared by Professors Srikant Datar and Robert S. Kaplan with extensive assistance from Robin Webster of The Cooperative Bank.

Copyright © 1995 by the President and Fellows of Harvard College. Harvard Business School case 195–196.

---

[1]This amount was far greater in inflation-adjusted terms, than The Bank's deposits in 1994.

the range of products and services for personal and corporate customers. It introduced credit cards and launched several sophisticated savings products. This broadened mix of product and services, coupled to an increasingly stringent regulatory environment, created demands for more capital, demands that the CWS found difficult to supply given the heavy demands for investment from all its other operations. Therefore, The Bank had to devise a strategy to generate sustainable capital growth from its own operations.

Terry Thomas was appointed Managing Director in 1988, after a 15-year career at The Bank. Thomas had joined The Bank in 1973 as its first Marketing Manager, and had taken on increasing general management responsibilities, including election to the Board in 1983. He took command of a bank that had successfully managed the transition from an almost total reliance on the cooperative movement to a viable, broad-based retail clearing bank. But new challenges had to be faced.

The UK financial services market had entered a period of radical change and restructuring. Government legislation to deregulate the financial sector was blurring traditional industry boundaries. Constraints on Building Societies' operations had been relaxed and they were now competing aggressively for products, such as current accounts, credit cards, and personal loans, that had historically been provided only by banking institutions. One of the UK's largest Building Societies, Abbey National, had even changed its status to become a bank in early 1989. New players with radically different cost structures were also entering the financial services market. First Direct was a postal/telephone/ATM service bank that had no branches. Several companies formed just to offer credit cards. And large retailers, like Marks and Spencer, were now marketing credit products to their considerable customer base.

Customer expectations and behavior were changing as well. Customers were more willing to switch banks, and to take products from several institutions. They were becoming more price sensitive and vocal in their demands for service, including expanded use of electronic banking through telephones and ATMs. The introduction and expansion of electronic technology was transforming all existing cost structures. Significant over-capacity began to appear and institutions were competing aggressively on price for business in all sectors.

While profitability had continued to grow for The Bank through the UK's economic boom of the early and mid-1980s, the UK's worst recession in more than 50 years hit the bank hard. The Bank recorded losses in 1990 and 1991, particularly in loans made to the small and medium-sized enterprises that were now a significant share of the asset base. Significant losses were also occurring with personal customers, who were under great financial pressure from record levels of unemployment in the country.

Thomas recognized that the Bank had to rethink its operating philosophy for the current and future competitive environment. Before undertaking any redirection, however, Thomas wanted to re-affirm the bank's fundamental values. The twenty most senior managers met to develop a Mission Statement (see Exhibit 3) that stressed the bank's responsibility to its customers, its employees, and its communities. The Mission Statement was enhanced by a research program culminating with a statement of Our Ethical Policy (see Exhibit 4). The Ethical Policy statement was informed by questionnaires sent to 30,000 current customers and a study of co-operative values over the past 150 years. The Mission and Ethical Policy statements created a far greater awareness of the bank's values and position in the marketplace. While some customers closed their accounts in protest, a much higher number of new personal and corporate accounts were opened after publicizing these statements.

Thomas's initial steps to restructure the Bank's operations were accomplished through consolidation of personal and corporate account processing tasks. Back office tasks of personal banking operations, previously processed in branches, were consolidated into a Personal Customer Service center. Customers could call this center for the most up-to-date information regarding their accounts and could perform a variety of transactions over the telephone. Similarly many corporate banking tasks were consolidated into Regional Processing Centers. These new centers created 200 new jobs, but they also required eliminating 1,000 jobs (out of a total employee base of nearly 4,300) principally in retail branches. Laying off workers was a sensitive issue for a bank with such close ties to the co-operative and trade union movements. The Bank offered attractive retirement packages and was able to achieve the 1,000 job reduction entirely through voluntary retirements. Most of the terminations, however, were junior, low-level employees and the bank was now operating with a disproportionate number of middle managers.

The Bank also increased its cross-selling activities to existing customers, and began to offer a much wider array of products for customers. Among its major new products were:

VISA Gold Card	A "free for life" (no annual fee) credit card aimed at high net worth individuals
VISA Affinity Cards	Credit cards for specialized groups of customers (for example, The Royal Society for the Protection of Birds)
Pathfinder	A high interest-bearing current account for personal customers, based on a plastic card with no checkbook
Delta	A point of sale debit card/ ATM card/check guarantee card hybrid

Major new services introduced by the bank included:

| Telephone banking | Comprehensive remote banking through a centralized operation for personal and corporate customers |
| Independent financial advice | Investment advice for customers, selling products provided by other financial institutions |

Some of these products, particularly Visa Gold and Visa Affinity credit cards, were highly successful. In 1990, the Bank was not an issuer of Gold cards, but two years later, it had become the largest issuer of Visa Gold cards in the U.K., and by 1994 was the largest issuer in all of Europe.

Despite the new products and headcount reduction, the bank's cost-to-income ratio was high, especially when compared to building societies, with whom it was increasingly in direct competition.[2] Also, The Bank was still a small player in the U.K.'s corporate and personal markets.

Project SABRE

Terry Thomas recalled the bank's situation in late 1992.

In 1988 we had identified the need to be much more focused, in terms of both market niches and our operations. We began to concentrate on those niches and segments where we had particular advantages, and we had taken a number of steps to re-structure our operations. However, these were first steps in a process of transforming our business, and in order to continue and accelerate this process,

we needed better information to help us make some important decisions.

I felt we had too many products for our customer base. But none of us could agree on which were the profitable or unprofitable products and customers. Some thought the corporate sector was the most profitable by contributing a large number of profitable personal accounts. Others justified the full-line consumer product strategy by asserting that unless you offer a wide range of products the customers won't come to you in the first place. How should we balance the benefits of a wide product range against the costs? Should we promote these extra services or just have the capability to provide these extra services to the extent that certain customers want them? Or should we be outsourcing many of these services if we cannot do them effectively internally?

I can remember many unproductive meetings when all we did was argue what the numbers were. Each player came to the table with his or her own set of numbers. Human nature being what it is, each of us believed my set of numbers was right and yours must be wrong, especially if yours say my products are losing more money than I think. We never actually got around to arguing or discussing, given any particular set of numbers, what are we going to do?

I wanted to run the bank on the facts and not on perceptions. Having a set of numbers derived by a systematic process to which everyone agrees cuts out the arguing and focuses attention on action plans. It is not very difficult, really, then to make innovative and bold decisions.

In early 1993, Thomas launched Project SABRE (Sales And Business REengineering), a project with several related streams aimed at improving the cost income ratio and the service to customers. A key element of the project was to develop information that would enable the bank to address five corporate needs:

1. Overhead reduction
2. Reengineering of business processes, particularly those that did not add value to customers
3. Product profitability
4. Customer profitability
5. Segment profitability

John Marper, Executive Director of Finance, recognized that the Bank's cost structure, particularly those costs traditionally considered "fixed"—such as in centralized services like technology, transmission, and finance—had to be attacked. "If you are going to attack the fixed cost base, you need to have a better cost system, especially one that can relate the fixed costs to products."

The Bank's existing cost system was a traditional responsibility accounting system that measured expenses for geographic and departmental cost centers.

---

[2]The cost-to-income ratio is defined in the U.K. as the ratio of all costs (which exclude the provision for bad debts) to net interest revenue earned plus commissions.

Central headquarters expenses, such as information systems and document transmission, were allocated to operating segments using high-level drivers related to the volume and size of the businesses. The bank measured product revenues using fee income and net interest (equal to gross interest minus funding costs). But the estimated costs of producing these revenues were not identified.

Following a pilot exercise in The Bank's check clearing center, managers became interested in activity-based costing (ABC) as a promising methodology for assigning the bank's operating expenses to its varied products and customers. An ABC team, consisting of Robin Webster, Senior Manager (and later Head of Project SABRE), Dennis Goodman, Head of MIS [Management Information Systems], Steve Kemp, Senior Business Analyst, and eight middle managers from different areas of the bank, began model building and process data gathering. The bank also brought in Gemini Consulting to assist in the model development and to advise on the reorganization and action implications from the study in conjunction with internal management.

The bank's project team had to make several choices as it began considering the implementation of activity-based costing. How should it define resource pools? What activities should it define? Should it analyze costs by product or by customer? The bank divided its fiscal year into 13 four-week periods. Over what period should it collect the data for an initial historical analysis?

The team concluded that three periods would be reasonably representative to understand the bank's cost structure. They chose to do the analysis for March–May, 1993, the most recent three periods for which data were available.

The ABC team scanned the general ledger and identified about 210 resource cost pools, divided into three broad resource categories:

OPERATIONAL STAFF (85)	INFRASTRUCTURE (85)	MISCELLANEOUS (40)
Personal network— Staff	Personal network	Outsourced processing fees
Processing centers— Staff	VISA administration	Stationery costs Personal
Personal Accts. Opening	Processing centers ATM network	checkbooks VISA statements

The numbers in parentheses indicate the number of resource pools in each broad resource category. The rows in Exhibit 5 identify the major resource cost pools that service the personal banking side of The Bank's business.

Once the resource cost pools were specified, the ABC team spent eight weeks out in the operational areas identifying activities and mapping them on brown paper pasted around the project work room. The team used their knowledge, supplemented with interviews, to identify 235 activities or tasks undertaken at the bank. Examples of activities were open customer accounts, maintain customer accounts, accept checks, process transactions, close accounts, handle customer queries, issue check books, market and sell products, money market transfers, Visa transactions, ATM transactions, encode, train, process loan applications, manage risk, recover money, and prepare financial statements and management reports. The columns of Exhibit 5 identify the eighteen principal activities related to The Bank's personal banking business.

With the resource pools specified and activities selected and defined, the ABC team then asked each area of the bank to match resource costs to the activities (see the cell entries in Exhibit 5). For example, to trace staff costs to activities, all employees of the bank from senior management to the clerical staff filled out time sheets identifying the time they spent on various activities. The employees' compensation (salary and benefits) was then assigned to each activity in proportion to the time spent. Computer costs were assigned based on the amount of computer time required to perform various activities. By aggregating all of the resource pool costs assigned to each activity, the ABC team derived the total costs of each activity (see Total activity costs row in Exhibit 5).

The next step traced the costs of each activity to the different bank products. The tracing was accomplished by defining activity cost drivers for each activity (see first two columns in Exhibit 6). The activity cost driver represented the event that triggered the performance of each activity, such as a deposit that was processed or an account that was opened. The team collected information about the quantities of each activity cost driver that occurred during the estimation period (March–May 1993). These data came from various sources: the bank's automated information system (for data such as the number of Visa transactions, checks processed, and cash deposited), manual records (for data like the number of personal accounts opened), and statistical sampling procedures (for data not recorded such as the number of customer queries and complaints handled).

Activity cost driver rates (see the last column in Exhibit 6) were calculated by dividing the cost of each activity by the quantity of the associated activity cost driver. The activity cost driver rate could now be used to trace activity costs to individual products and customers.

The project team identified approximately 50 products or groups of closely related products. Corporate products included business loans, corporate current accounts, and leases. Personal banking products included personal loans and advances, current accounts and Visa accounts. Product costs were calculated by determining the quantity of each activity cost driver used by each of the products, multiplying these quantities by the associated activity cost driver rate, and summing across all the activities used by the individual products.

Exhibit 7 summarizes the distribution of activity costs, including funding charges, to various personal banking products (current accounts, ultra account, personal loans, Visa cards and other personal banking products). The last row of Exhibit 7 calculates the product cost as the sum of the activity costs used by individual products.

Not all operating expenses were assigned to banking products. The project team categorized the costs of 10 large activities as sustaining costs—costs of activities that were not directly related to any products, but rather that supported the organization as a whole. No activity cost drivers were defined for these activities, which included accounting, finance, strategy, planning, human resource management, and information technology development activities. These sustaining costs accounted for 15% of the bank's operating expenses.

Product profitability was calculated by subtracting the cost of all activities undertaken to support a particular product (bottom row of Exhibit 7) from the net interest revenue earned from each product plus the fees derived for performing various services for customers. For asset and liability products (such as loans, current accounts, and savings), the bank used a transfer interest rate to represent the rate at which excess funds could be invested or needed funds borrowed on the money mar-

kets.[3] The transfer rate used for most products was the LIBOR[4] rate + 1/4% (which equaled 6 1/4% during the initial estimation period); however, where funds were invested or borrowed specifically for certain products ("matched"), the actual matched rate was used.

Robin Webster, the manager leading the ABC study, described the bank's motivation for calculating product profitability for both asset and liability products:

> In addition to fee income, the bank makes money from asset and liability products in two ways: (1) by accessing sources of funds from liability products; and (2) by lending at higher risk-adjusted rates for our asset products. Using transfer rates allows us to see how well we are doing on both sides of the balance sheet. Are we raising funds from liability accounts at a net cost below our LIBOR borrowing cost? If so, and even without good lending opportunities, we could profit by investing these funds at the LIBOR rate. Are our lending operations healthy? Could we borrow money from the markets at the base rate and still turn a profit from our lending and related fee-generating activities?

Exhibit 8 shows the profitability of the individual personal banking products.

Product Decisions

The Bank had always regarded the provision of independent financial advice and the sale of associated investment products as a highly profitable business. The ABC analysis (see Exhibit 8), however, indicated that this business was only generating small profits on the basis of the activity costs that could be directly assigned to it, even with no allocation of the 15% of expenses classified as "sustaining costs." This came as a particular surprise because the Bank had targeted financial advice and new investment products as a growth area in the deregulated environment.

The analysis showed that several other products were failing to generate adequate returns to pay for the sustaining costs and to support hoped-for improvements in the Bank's cost-income ratio aspirations. For example, The Bank's basic and core product, personal current accounts ("Current Account Plus"), was at best breaking even after considering sustaining costs. This finding

---

[3]For example, the net interest revenue on business loans equaled the actual interest received minus the transfer rate. For liabilities, like corporate deposits and current accounts, net interest revenue equaled the transfer rate minus the interest actually paid.

[4]LIBOR is the London Inter Bank Offer Rate.

was consistent with conventional wisdom at the Bank, and also in the U.K. banking market, where many banks were openly commenting in the press that current accounts were unprofitable. The Bank began contemplating several courses of action to improve the profitability of current accounts.

On a more positive note, all three Visa accounts were revealed to be highly profitable products. The Gold Card is a free for life card that carries a slightly lower interest rate than the Classic Card (which is an ordinary Visa Card) and the Affinity Card. The Affinity Card is attractive to some customers because a portion of the income earned on the Affinity Card is given to specified charities. The Bank saw a clear message to focus its limited marketing resources into growing its personal current accounts and Visa account businesses.

Customer Profitability

The ABC team wanted to extend the analysis to individual customers, but the bank's information systems, many dating back to the 1960s, could not readily access customers' transactions data. The team performed a limited study of customer-specific expenses, based on a sample of current accounts. They did not need to study other products in detail, since most savings accounts had fewer than two transactions per quarter, all loan products had a predictable 12 transactions per year, and credit card costs were found to be mostly constant per account.

The team determined that 55% of current account expenses were related to processing transactions, and 45% were related to maintaining accounts. The maintenance-related costs were divided by the number of accounts, and assigned equally to each account. For assigning transactions-related expenses, the team split customers into three segments—Low, Medium, and High—based on the annual turnover of funds in their accounts. From a month-long sample of customer transactions, they assigned transactions-related expenses to these three segments in the ratios of: 15%, 40% and 45%.

The revenue side was simpler. The team identified, for each product, the income earned from credit balances and fees by individual customers. By matching this income with the assigned cost, the team could now estimate the profitability of each customer.

Next, the Bank identified the entry product (the first product bought by a customer). The five main entry products were Current Accounts, VISA Gold, VISA Affinity cards, VISA Classic and the Pathfinder savings account. All subsequent sales of other products (cross sales) were assigned to the entry product. The results showed that the vast majority of cross sales originated from Current Accounts.

The customer profitability analysis revealed that up to half of all current accounts, particularly those with low balances, were unprofitable. Managers at the Bank began to debate several questions about current accounts. How can it make current accounts attractive to profitable customers? Should The Bank combine and enhance its current account products with features such as service level warranties and restructured charges? Should the Bank aggressively market these accounts using a special sales force backed by an advertising campaign in local newspapers and on television?

How should the Bank discourage unprofitable customers? Should the Bank alter its tariff to give a wide differential between customers taking credit within approved overdraft limits, and those overdrawing accounts outside approved limits where the greatest risk of loss existed, and which prompted high levels of intervention activity?

The Bank segmented Visa customers into profitable and unprofitable customers. The most profitable customers were customers with large unpaid balances that generated interest income, and customers who transacted frequently, thereby generating high processing fees. The Bank developed a profile of the profitable customers, and its marketing was being redirected to attract the customers with profitable behavior.

David Fawell, Marketing Manager, faced an interesting decision:

> Excluding sustaining costs, both current account and Visa customers are profitable, as I thought. But with pressure to reduce our operating expenses, I have only a limited amount of funds to market these products. I'm not sure whether these funds should be directed to prospective personal current account customers or to Visa account customers? Or should I spread the funds across both types of prospects?

Overhead Reduction and Business Process Reengineering

In addition to decisions about products and customers, the initial information from Project SABRE helped to refocus The Bank from a functionally oriented organization to a process-oriented organization. Activity costs provided a metric to evaluate the effects of business process reengineering decisions. Managers were now attempting to identify which processes were adding value to the customer and which were not, and how the efficiency of different processes could be improved. Improving efficiency would enable the bank to either take costs out of the system, or to use the extra capacity to generate more revenue.

Deeper analysis showed that much of the cost base had a high element of costs that were, in the short to medium term, fixed (for example, computer systems and bank branches) and that radical solutions were required to impact on these costs. In 1994, the Bank outsourced its computer development and ATM network, and began serious negotiations to outsource its London check clearing center with a view to eliminating excess capacity and replacing fixed with variable costs.

Next Steps

While stimulated by the interesting findings of the first-pass ABC analysis, many bank managers were still unsure about the action implications. A newly introduced product like foreign currency exchange seemed to be unprofitable. Should it be discontinued or should it be retained as part of a full-service package for current account customers? Also, would department managers, accustomed to high autonomy and control over their operations, be willing to reengineer their organization to facilitate process flows, and eventually to down-size their operations to achieve a lower cost-to-income ratio. Some managers expressed concern that as profitability improved, from better selection of products and customers, the organization's commitment to reorganize and improve would start to diminish.

Robin Webster and Steve Kemp were disappointed that such a large amount of expenses (15% of costs) had been classified as sustaining costs, where they could not be driven down to products and customers. They felt that these sustaining expenses could be reduced but because they had been treated as "fixed," independent of products and customers, they would not be targets for cost reduction. Ken Lewis, Executive Director, Group Resources, concurred. He observed that the bank's people costs had been traced readily and easily to activities that related to products and customers, but that property and information technology resources had been largely classified as business-sustaining. Lewis believed that significant opportunities existed to downsize sustaining costs by making better decisions about the types of properties the bank owned and leased, and the level and extent of information technology the bank deployed. Decisions on information technology could be critical. Unmanned, totally automated kiosks were starting to perform activities formerly done by the bank's labor-intensive branch network.

EXHIBIT 1 Founding Statement of International Co-operative Alliance*

August 22, 1895

The time has come for gathering together the scattered parts of the great co-operative movement, one in aim and one in principle into a strong international alliance.

It is to carry this great idea into execution that the International Co-operative Alliance has been resolved upon. Without interfering in local or national matters or narrowing in any way the independence of each association or national union, the alliance will form a link uniting cooperators who are pursuing very various objects in different countries.

It will thus secure mutual support to each and all, produce a more powerful volume of co-operative opinion than can be created by separate action, help to carry cooperation more successfully foward to new developments, and create means by which cooperators will be enabled steadily to learn from one another by an interchange of opinions, or reports, and of publications.

In carrying out this program the alliance will be an added cause of peace through the inhabited world.

The objects of the alliance are[†]:

(1) To bring into relation of mutual helpfulness those who are seeking in different countries and in various ways to end the present deplorable warfare between Capital and Labor, and to organize industrial peace based on co-partnership of the worker.

(2) To promote the formation or aid the development in each country of a central institution for helping working people to establish and maintain self-governing workshops and for assisting employers and employed to establish just and harmonious profit-sharing arrangements.

(3) To form an international means of connection and communication between these central institutions through which they may render one another mutual assistance.

(4) Generally to promote the employment of the profits of productive industry.

From draft outline of a plan for an International Alliance of the friends of cooperative production, to be considered at an inaugural meeting at the Crystal Palace on Monday, August 22, 1895 at 3:00 P.M.
[†]*From ICA archives.*

EXHIBIT 2 Selected Financial Statistics: 1990–1994 (£000,000)

	1990	1991	1992	1993
Deposits	2,621	2,438	2,707	2,983
Loans and advances	2,597	2,408	2,637	2,740
Profit (loss) before taxes	(14.9)	(6.0)	9.8	17.8
Pre-tax return on shareholder funds	(9.4%)	(4.0%)	6.7%	12.0%

EXHIBIT 3 Mission Statement—1988

We, the Co-operative Bank Group, will continue to develop a successful and innovative financial institution by providing our customers with high quality financial and related services whilst promoting the underlying principles of co-operation which are . . .

1. Quality and Excellence

To offer all our customers consistent high quality and good value services and strive for excellence in all that we do.

2. Participation

To introduce and promote the concept of full participation by welcoming the views and concerns of our customers and by encouraging our staff to take an active role within the local community.

3. Freedom of Association

To be non-partisan in all social, political, racial and religious matters.

4. Education and Training

To act as a caring and responsible employer encouraging the development and training of all our staff and encouraging commitment and pride in each other and the Group.

5. Co-operation

To develop a close-affinity with organizations which promote fellowship between workers, customers, members and employers.

6. Quality of Life

To be a responsible member of society by promoting an environment where the needs of local communities can be met now and in the future.

7. Retentions

To manage the business effectively and efficiently, attracting investment and maintaining sufficient surplus funds within the business to ensure the continued development of the Group.

8. Integrity

To act at all times with honesty and integrity and within legislative and regulatory requirements.

EXHIBIT 4 Our Ethical Policy—1992

The Bank's position is that

1. It will not invest in or supply financial services to any regime or organization which oppresses the human spirit, takes away the rights of individuals, or manufactures any instrument of torture.
2. It will not finance or in any way facilitate the manufacture or sale of weapons to any country which has an oppressive regime.
3. It will encourage business customers to take a proactive stance on the environmental impact of their own activities.
4. It will actively seek out individuals, commercial enterprises and non-commercial organizations which have a complementary ethical stance.
5. It will not speculate against the pound using either its own money or that of its customers. It believes it is inappropriate for a British clearing bank to speculate against the British currency and the British economy using deposits provided by their British customers and at the expense of the British tax payer.
6. It will try to ensure its financial services are not exploited for the purposes of money laundering, drug trafficking or tax evasion by the continued application and development of its successful internal monitoring and control procedures.
7. It will not provide financial services to tobacco product manufacturers.
8. It will continue to extend and strengthen its Customer Charter, which has already established new standards of banking practice through adopting innovative procedures on status inquiries and customer confidentiality, ahead of any other British bank.
9. It will not invest in any business involved in animal experimentation for cosmetic purposes.
10. It will not support any person or company using exploitative factory farming methods.
11. It will not engage in business with any farm or other organization engaged in the production of animal fur.
12. It will not support any organization involved in blood sports, which it defines as sports which involve the training of animals or birds to catch and destroy, or to fight and kill, other animals or birds.

We will regularly re-appraise customers' views on these and other issues and develop our ethical stance accordingly.

EXHIBIT 5 Personal Sector Products—Matrix of Costs by Resource and Activity*

RESOURCE COST POOLS	TOTAL RESOURCE COSTS	PROVIDE ATM SERVICES	CLEAR DEBIT ITEMS	BRANCH OPERATIONS DEBIT ITEMS	ISSUE PERSONAL CHEQUE BOOK	CLEAR CREDIT ITEMS	BRANCH OPERATIONS CREDIT ITEMS	LENDING CONTROL & SECURITY	CUSTOMER INQUIRIES	CUSTOMER CORRESPON-DENCE	MARKETING AND SALES ACTIVITY	COMPUTER PROCESSING
Account management center	£ 1,557,280	£ 0	£ 2,388	£ 66,293	£ 0	£ 509	£ 0	£ 5,647	£ 903,565	£196,803	£ 134	£ 49,745
Account opening teams	368,355	0	0	0	0	0	0	0	0	0	0	0
ATM network	111,031	111,031	0	0	0	0	0	0	0	0	0	0
Branch operations	3,475,959	95,229	40,756	487,269	0	11,641	545,606	5,709	306,263	460,845	1,478,735	0
Clearing operations	833,575	20,099	650,287	1,291	0	135,744	1,394	4,791	0	2,109	25	2,339
Collections	968,256	0	0	36	0	0	1,168	912,190	41,378	10,578	0	0
Collections fees	329,205	0	0	0	0	0	0	329,205	0	0	0	0
Outsourced fees	2,120,071	104,151	0	0	0	0	0	41,611	37,796	3,109	0	22,061
Financial advisors	1,214,383	0	0	0	0	0	0	0	9,799	3,601	81,970	0
Information technology	1,669,453	0	0	65,293	0	0	0	67,261	0	0	1,765	1,535,134
Marketing fees and staff	884,380	16,236	0	0	0	0	0	0	0	279	867,865	0
Postage	713,474	92,397	0	0	107,706	0	0	0	0	48,019	0	0
Regional processing centers	485,102	25,023	328,709	61,263	0	70,107	0	0	0	0	0	0
Stationery	277,746	0	0	0	156,243	0	0	0	0	0	0	24,728
Telesales	129,235	0	0	0	0	0	0	0	0	0	129,235	0
VISA stamps and statements	433,491	0	0	0	0	0	0	0	0	0	0	0
Other	55,671	26,136	0	2,655	0	0	0	14,349	0	863	2,317	7,240
Total activity costs	£15,626,667	£490,302	£1,022,140	£684,100	£263,949	£218,001	£548,168	£1,380,763	£1,298,801	£726,206	£2,562,046	£1,641,247

RESOURCE COST POOLS	STATEMENTING & POSTAGE	ADVISE ON INVESTMENTS & INSURANCE	PROCESS VISA TRANSACTIONS	ISSUE VISA STATEMENTS	OPEN AND MAINTAIN HANDYLOANS	OPEN AND CLOSE ACCOUNTS	ADMINISTER MORTGAGES
Account management center	£ 0	£ 0	£ 138,792	£ 0	£ 0	£193,404	£ 0
Account opening teams	0	0	0	0	0	294,181	74,174
ATM network	0	0	0	0	0	0	0
Branch operations	0	40,930	0	0	0	2,976	0
Clearing operations	15,364	0	0	0	0	132	0
Collections	0	0	0	0	0	2,906	0
Collections fees	0	0	0	0	0	0	0
Outsourced fees	0	0	942,629	0	846,806	0	121,908
Financial advisors	0	1,119,013	0	0	0	0	0
Information technology	0	0	0	0	0	0	0
Marketing fees and staff	0	0	0	0	0	0	0
Postage	455,736	0	0	9,616	0	0	0
Regional processing centers	0	0	0	0	0	0	0
Stationery	3,989	0	92,786	0	0	0	0
Telesales	0	0	0	0	0	0	0
VISA stamps and statements	0	0	0	433,491	0	0	0
Other	2,111	0	0	0	0	0	0
Total activity costs	£477,200	£1,159,943	£1,174,207	£443,107	£846,806	£493,599	£196,082

*Numbers disguised to maintain confidentiality.

EXHIBIT 6 Personal Sector Products: Activity Cost Driver Quantities and Rates*

ACTIVITY DESCRIPTION	ACTIVITY COST DRIVER	TOTAL ACTIVITY COST	QUANTITY OF ACTIVITY COST DRIVER	COST PER UNIT OF ACTIVITY COST DRIVER
Provide ATM service	ATM transactions	£ 490,302	1,021,963	£0.48
Clear debit items	Number of debits processed	1,022,140	5,110,299	0.20
Branch operations for debit items	Number of branch counter debits	684,100	762,111	0.90
Issue personal cheque book	Number of books issued	263,949	40,628	6.50
Clear credit items	Number of credits processed	218,001	871,004	0.25
Branch operations for credit items	Number of branch counter credits	548,168	512,986	1.07
Lending control and security	Number of interventions	1,380,763	765,591	1.80
Customer inquiries	Number of telephone minutes	1,298,801	7,205,560	0.18
Customer correspondence	Number of customer letters	726,206	221,204	3.28
Marketing and sales activity	Number of accounts opened	2,562,046	62,120	41.24
Computer processing	Number of computer transactions (electronic impulses)	1,641,247	16,112,471	0.10
Statementing and postage	Number of statements issued	477,200	1,724,285	0.28
Advise on investments and insurance	Hours of advice given	1,159,943	32,956	35.20
Process VISA transactions	Number of VISA transactions	1,174,207	5,125,248	0.23
Issue VISA statements	Number of VISA statements issued	443,107	1,714,258	0.26
Open/maintain handyloans	Number of Handyloan accounts	846,806	201,521	4.20
Open and close accounts	Number of accounts opened/closed	493,599	57,951	8.52
Administer mortgages	Number of mortgages	196,082	18,609	10.54
		£15,626,667		

Numbers disguised to maintain confidentiality.

EXHIBIT 7 Matrix of Activity Costs Used by Personal Sector Products*

ACTIVITY	TOTAL	CURRENT ACCOUNT PLUS (1)	FREE-FLOW (2)	PERSONAL LOANS (3)	MORT-GAGES (4)	VISA CLASSIC (5)	VISA AFFINITIES (6)	VISA GOLD (7)	HANDY-LOAN/ FASTLINE (8)	INDEPENDENT FINANCIAL ADVICE AND INSURANCE (9)	PATH-FINDER (10)	DEPOSIT PRODUCTS (11)
Provide ATM services	£ 490,302	£ 403,360	£ 4,873	£ 0	£ 0	£ 25,410	£ 7,729	£ 15,447	£ 921	£ 0	£ 22,515	£ 10,047
Clear debit items	1,022,140	921,643	31,915	0	0	33,792	10,397	14,296	0	0	10,071	26
Branch operations for debit items	684,100	487,796	9,774	1,770	0	90,131	35,775	44,617	6,151	0	5,985	2,101
Issue personal checkbook	263,949	252,663	11,286	0	0	0	0	0	0	0	0	0
Clear credit items	218,001	91,982	2,432	4	0	53,731	20,381	45,284	1,149	0	3,004	34
Branch operations for credit items	548,168	506,273	14,964	0	0	3,131	103	807	0	0	3,807	19,083
Lending control and security	1,380,763	532,918	26,288	91,501	20,825	540,563	6,809	143,906	5,387	4,798	4,528	3,240
Customer inquiries	1,298,801	850,569	26,974	97,014	324	107,052	14,749	57,630	5,959	21,053	84,287	33,190
Customer correspondence	726,206	462,178	15,510	64,409	970	56,701	2,439	23,598	6,332	13,277	58,797	21,995
Marketing and sales activity	2,562,046	673,641	4,189	815,211	0	202,552	54,000	197,334	41,210	398,548	85,366	89,995
Computer processing	1,641,247	1,215,933	54,979	113,403	0	31,292	11,317	19,256	38,131	0	49,563	107,373
Statementing and postage	477,200	336,094	18,687	19,179	66	15,241	1,433	49,277	4,430	4,088	22,740	5,965
Advise on investments and insurance	1,159,943	0	0	0	0	0	0	0	0	1,159,943	0	0
Process VISA transactions	1,174,207	223,320	0	18,672	0	468,257	177,895	270,904	15,159	0	0	0
Issue VISA statements	443,107	0	0	0	0	235,406	94,017	113,684	0	0	0	0
Open/maintain handyloans	846,806	0	0	0	0	0	0	0	846,805	0	0	0
Open and close accounts	493,599	188,373	2,786	104,346	0	51,505	1,078	35,397	11,934	0	63,062	35,118
Administer mortgages	196,082	10,596	815	17,117	121,907	0	1,631	0	0	0	13,042	30,974
Total activity costs	£15,626,667	£7,157,339	£225,472	£1,342,626	£144,092	£1,914,764	£439,753	£1,031,437	£983,569	£1,601,707	£426,767	£359,141

Numbers disguised to maintain confidentiality.

EXHIBIT 8 Profitability Analysis of Personal Sector Products*

ACTIVITY	CURRENT ACCOUNT PLUS	FREEFLOW	PERSONAL LOANS	MORT-GAGES	VISA CLASSIC	VISA AFFINITIES	VISA GOLD	HANDY-LOAN/ FASTLINE	INDEPENDENT FINANCIAL ADVICE AND INSURANCE	PATH-FINDER	DEPOSIT PRODUCTS	TOTAL
Net interest	£5,283,472	£1,041,384	£4,530,963	£331,027	£2,856,713	£463,204	£ 808,592	£1,811,526	£ 0	£ 261,717	£960,437	£18,349,035
Net commission	3,593,898	358,867	780,608	147,909	2,101,002	686,117	1,562,720	65,987	1,549,634	4,284	(1,141)	10,849,885
Bad debts	(782,000)	(130,000)	(1,192,000)	(274,000)	(882,000)	(182,000)	(508,000)	(274,000)	0	0	0	(4,224,000)
Gross profit	8,095,370	1,270,251	4,119,571	204,936	4,075,715	967,321	1,863,312	1,603,513	1,549,634	266,001	959,296	24,974,920
Activity costs (from Exhibit 7)	7,157,339	225,472	1,342,626	144,092	1,914,764	439,753	1,031,437	983,569	1,601,707	426,767	359,141	15,626,667
Direct profit	938,031	1,044,779	2,776,945	60,844	2,160,951	527,568	831,875	619,944	(52,073)	(160,766)	600,155	9,348,253
Allocated infrastructure costs	1,014,145	36,845	204,822	4,213	156,768	22,086	81,053	20,864	263,078	65,066	59,685	1,928,625
Net profit	£ (76,114)	£1,007,934	£2,572,123	£ 56,631	£2,004,183	£505,482	£ 750,822	£ 599,080	£(315,151)	£(225,832)	£540,470	£ 7,419,628

*Numbers disguised to maintain confidentiality.

MANUFACTURERS HANOVER CORPORATION: CUSTOMER PROFITABILITY REPORT

Manufacturers Hanover Announces New Structure to Sharpen Its Approach to Customers and Markets: Streamlined, Flatter Organization Redeploys Executives Closer to Customers and Provides Greater Flexibility

(News Release, May 15, 1990)

Company

Manufacturers Hanover Corporation (MHC), after several difficult years of credit loss recognition, primarily from Latin American lending, had emerged with a strengthened financial position. The company now was attempting to profit from its strong North American multinational customer base. With total assets in excess of $60 billion (down from a high of more than $75 billion in 1985), MHC was the eighth largest commercial bank in the U.S. Tangible equity as a percentage of assets had rebounded from a low of 2.9% at year end 1987 to 5.2% by the end of 1989. Exhibit 1 summarizes recent financial performance and ratios.

Thomas S. Johnson, formerly President of the Chemical Banking Corporation, was hired in December 1989 as President of MHC and heir-apparent to John F. McGillicuddy, Chairman and Chief Executive Officer. The reorganization announced in May 1990 gave Johnson major responsibility for the global banking group of MHC, which encompassed six major market and product segments. The six group executives reporting to

This case was prepared by Professor Robert S. Kaplan.
Copyright © 1990 by the President and Fellows of Harvard College. Harvard Business School case 191-068.

Johnson headed the North America markets, Europe, Asia, merchant banking, trading and treasury, and Financial Institutions and Distribution groups. The remainder of the bank's operations were organized into three other major market groups: Developing Markets (including Third World countries), Regional Banking, and Operating Services (also called GEOSERVE), a unit formed in 1989 to handle all the bank's information and transactional services such as cash management, funds transfer, corporate trust, securities processing, and trade services.

The Focus on Customers

The deregulated banking environment of the 1980s led to greatly expanded products offered by commercial banks for customers. These products generated fee-based income, an attractive alternative to the shrinking interest-rate margins earned on traditional lending activities. MHC's Trading and Treasury group engaged in interest rate swaps, foreign exchange transactions, private placements, underwriting, and securitization. Merchant Banking provided financing for leveraged buyouts (LBOs), mergers and acquisitions, venture capital, and equity investment. MHC found that its credit customers provided an excellent base for marketing these fee-based products.

Herb Aspbury, Group Executive for the North American Markets Group, described the changing banking environment.

In the past, corporate lending was the primary driver of bank profitability. The margins we earned on commitments and actual lending were so attractive that any credit-worthy loan we could make was bound to be profitable. The 1980s turned our world upside down. Relationships that had been highly profitable in the 1960s and 1970s became unattractive as profits margins from commercial lending contracted. In addition, commercial lending was consuming our scarcest resource: equity. The new fee-based services, offered by our product groups, provided profitable new opportunities for the bank without requiring heavy equity commitments.

Most of our multinational companies, however, do not want to shop each of their individual financing transactions. These companies had become "overbanked," and they wanted to reduce the number of financial institutions that called on them. By dealing with only a limited number of banks, companies recognized that some business they give to a bank is a reward for providing other key products and services. The commercial lending units, therefore, had to become responsible for marketing the entire bank.

Customers were also becoming more sophisticated about our own performance with them. Many of them surveyed their treasury managers worldwide and gave us an annual report card on how well MHC served their company. We were in a position where our customers were grading us but we couldn't grade our customers.

MHC's financial system was focused on profit center reporting, treating its geographical and product groups as separate reporting entities. Each department manager attempted to meet budgeted profitability goals. Up through the 1970s, this system reflected well the underlying economics of the bank. Commercial lending enjoyed high interest-rate margins that encouraged strong growth in lending activities. The auxiliary merchant and investment banking services were limited in scope and did not contribute greatly to overall bank profitability.

The banking world of the 1980s, however, required interdependencies among the different banking groups, and traditional profit center reporting no longer captured well the underlying economics of the bank. Commercial lending to a large multinational company might be unprofitable because of razor-thin margins and a heavy commitment of equity capital to support the lending relationship. But the lending activity became the entry point for a wide range of profitable merchant banking, treasury, trading, and corporate trust activities that the bank could perform for the client company.

Aspbury recalled the changes in thinking required by the new circumstances.

We had too many people chasing too many accounts: 1,200 separate corporate relationships. We took a hard look at whether each of these relationships led to other ser-

vices for the bank. Many didn't. We terminated relationships with several hundred companies, either by raising our lending margins or, more decisively, by curtailing lending activities altogether. We forced our lending officers to be realistic about their customers. For some companies, we were second or third-tier lenders, and we got none of their fee-based product business. With a scarcity of equity capital, there was no way these customers could be profitable lending at 10 basis points over LIBOR.[1] The reduction in number of clients served enabled us to cut the number of people in the lending group from 600 to 300.

But this was only the start of what needed to be done. The various groups of the bank had now become completely interdependent. The North American Markets Group, with profitable relationships with U.S.-based companies, needed the European Group to support our U.S. companies' overseas activities, making calls and perhaps accepting low-margin business there. And we, in the U.S., had to service the European Group's clients that were expanding into North America.

I felt the need for a system that could regularly tell me the total profitability of individual customers to MHC, accumulating the profits earned in all the MHC groups. That way, each group would be more willing to support and promote the work that earned profits in the operating statements of other groups.

Profit Center Reporting

Business units were evaluated by a business Profit Center Report (see Exhibit 2). *Interest income*, the main revenue source, represented the interest received from commercial loans. Loan fees were interest-based fees earned by granting various forms of credit to customers. *Interest expense* was calculated either using an internal transfer pool rate or a market rate; the particular rate chosen was determined by the terms of the loan.

Operating income, representing noninterest-based fees, was added to the net interest margin, and *operating expenses* (salary and benefits of departmental personnel, occupancy charges, equipment, and other departmental expenses such as telephone, travel, etc.) were subtracted to obtain the *net contribution before interoffice*. This net contribution figure was the key performance measure for lending groups.

Cynthia Warrick, Senior Vice-President of the North American Markets Group and one of eight officers reporting directly to Herb Aspbury, commented on the value of the Profit Center Report.

---

[1]LIBOR was the acronym for London Interbank Offered Rate, the interest rate in London at which banks loaned to each other (comparable to the Federal Funds rate in the U.S.).

This report is all right for an officer working with credit-intensive companies in which all the action takes place within the lending activity. For example, last year we arranged the financing for a major acquisition by one of my customers. We earned a $7,000,000 agent's fee and everything was booked within my profit center.

But an officer like Maryann Sudo handles 12 large multinational relationships, and many of their banking activities are in corporate trust, cash management, and international financing. Maryann's customers frequently show low profitability for lending activities, but the business she generates in other banking products with these companies could be highly profitable to the bank as a whole. Another one of my officers, Gerry Hannon, showed a moderate contribution margin for a large company last year, but his work with this customer led to our European Group's booking and syndicating a major financing transaction with the company's Turkish subsidiary. Herb and I believe that Gerry should get some recognition and reward for the fee the bank earned from this transaction.

In 1986, Herb Aspbury attempted to overcome the limitations of the traditional profit center report by developing a Customer Profitability Report (CPR). The first step was to recognize differences in effort required by officers to handle individual customers. Warrick commented on the difficulties this created.

Officers were asked to fill out time sheets to record how much of their time was spent on each customer. It was a time-consuming job and very tedious. And the people didn't really believe the numbers at the end.

But even the crude results from this early model contained some surprises. Warrick recalled a large midwestern food processor with whom MHC had a long, close relationship.

We knew that the company didn't pay us well for their credit facilities and other services, but the CPR made it clear that the profits we were earning were far too low for the effort we were expending with them. We took a much harder stance on receiving compensation from them for certain services and were able to bring that company to a satisfactory level of profitability.

With other companies, we had a medium-level credit but no other business. We told our officers that if they could not develop additional MHC business with these companies, we would exit the relationship.

Some company relationships showed up as highly profitable. The report confirmed that we wanted to continue to work closely with these companies. But this profitability would never have been revealed if we looked only at the lending relationship. One company's risk-adjusted

ROE for commercial lending was only in the 8% to 10% range, but MHC served as the company's stock transfer agent, and did LBO work, private placements, and interest-rate swaps for their affiliates. Overall, the relationship with the company was among the most profitable the bank had.

John Poplawski was the Senior Vice-President of the Management Reporting Group of the Controllers department. Poplawski had supervised the development of the CPR system as well as the standard unit cost system for all of the bank's transactional products. He had encouraged the commercial lending divisions to participate in the development of CPR but initially found that only Herb Aspbury's North American Markets Group (NAM) actively supported the concept. He recalled that the early CPR reports had large gaps.

The International people initially performed customer profitability studies only on an as-needed or special study basis. They felt this was adequate for their needs, so they stayed out of the CPR system. Unfortunately, the NAM people thought the report would be perfect the first time it appeared and didn't recognize all the difficulties of linking a diverse, worldwide bank's operations into a single report. The officers themselves were not always aware of all of the transactions that a given company had with the bank. The officers also griped a lot about the time survey they had to complete. They thought it tedious and a complete waste of time.

The Loan Pricing Model

Bill Maass, Vice-President and Planning Officer of the Global Bank, had joined NAM in mid-1988 as Planning Officer. He inherited responsibility for refining the Customer Profitability Report. He saw an opportunity to integrate the CPR with a Loan Pricing Model that an outside consulting company had recently introduced into the bank. The Loan Pricing Model (LPM) was designed to determine the profitability of proposed loan transactions. Maass decided to update the model so that a risk-adjusted return on equity (ROE) figure could be produced flexibly and comprehensively.

Suppose we have an existing line of credit with a major corporation. The company comes to us asking for a large increase in the line, say from its present level of $20 million up to $100 or $125 million, and they want to do this with a 25 basis point spread. We would like to know what the impact will be on our profitability and return on equity. Equity is our scarcest resource, and the amount of equity required for a loan depends on its riskiness. The Loan

Pricing Model enables us to evaluate various alternatives for supplying the credit. It's also good for incremental decision analysis, including whether we should retain the loan, syndicate it, or sell it off.

Maass adapted the consultant's simple spread-sheet program into an interactive model that ran on a desk-top computer. Exhibit 3 presents a description of the data inputs required for the LPM.

The model calculated the *risk-adjusted assets (RAA)* of the facility as the sum of the following:

100% × Loans outstanding
90% × Acceptances
40% × Unused commitments (original tenor > 1 year)
20% × Unused commitments (original tenor ≤ 1 year)
10% × Unused lines of credit
80% × Standby letters of credit (financial)
50% × Standby letters of credit (performance)
30% × Commercial letters of credit

The RAA figure was used for several calculations. MHC had developed a risk-adjusted loan loss provision by specifying a percentage, varying by facility grade, to be applied against the RAA of the facility. This loan loss provision was an expense to be deducted from the proposed revenue from the facility.

Maass also decided to use the RAA to allocate departmental expenses to the facility. In response to the opposition from lending officers to filling out customer-specific time reports, he eliminated the effort reporting system. In its place, Maass used a loan's RAA as a surrogate measure of the effort required to develop and monitor loans. He divided budgeted departmental direct expenses by the planned RAA for the period to obtain a ratio of expense dollars per RAA $. This ratio was used in the LPM to assign departmental expenses to loans. The expense ratio was increased for loans rated as requiring a high level of effort and decreased for loans that required a low level of effort.

The RAA was also used to estimate the amount of bank equity required for proposed facilities. Banks need to have a certain amount of equity to support the risk-adjusted assets of loans and commitments. In the original LPM, the consultant had assumed that risk-adjusted equity was a fixed percentage of risk-adjusted assets. Maass developed a finer partition based on the riskiness of the credit.

FACILITY GRADE	RISK-ADJUSTED EQUITY (RAE)%
1–3	2.0%
4–5	3.4
6–7	5.0
8–10	7.0

The risk-adjusted equity recognized that more capital is required for riskier loans.

The LPM then calculated the income, the risk-adjusted ROE, and the value added or destroyed by the proposed facility (see Exhibit 4). Officers were encouraged to run the model at both 0% utilization and 100% utilization so that they could price the loan to have approximately the same profitability, independent of utilization. If the ROE was below 16%, the officer could contemplate selling off part of the facility. This would reduce income and possibly even ROE, but since the smaller facility would require less bank equity, the total amount of value destroyed would decrease. Maass explained how the current pricing structure for lending led to more loan syndication and sales.

> Ten years ago, facilities were richly priced so that more retention was always more profitable. Now, pricing is so thin that more of a loan could be worse, as revealed by the value added/destroyed calculation. The interactive LPM encourages officers to do more sensitivity analysis on the terms of the deal and on the degree and terms of syndication so that they can determine the optimal amount of the loan for MHC to retain.

The revised Loan Pricing Model led naturally to a more accurate Customer Profitability Report. Maass stated,

> For the LPM, the officer estimates the size and utilization of the facility as well as projected expenses. For the CPR, we use the actual utilization of the facility and the actual departmental expenses. The CPR also evaluates the total relationship we have with the customer, including non-credit revenue streams, not just the incremental lending alternatives that get considered in the LPM. But technically, the profitability and ROE calculations are the same in the two models.

The CPR Information System

Hilary Gammage, Vice-President, was the Product Manager for CPR. She was responsible for accessing all the bank's data bases, providing the information processing for the report, and developing its form and distribution.

Conceptually, the CPR seems like a simple concept, but to get this report to work requires an enormous amount of effort. A customer may have a dozen legal entities reflecting domestic subsidiaries, plus all of its international operations. Each entity has its own distinct ID code and each ID code could include dozens of transaction accounts, representing Demand Deposit Accounts (DDA), Loan Accounts, etc. One of the biggest jobs I have is just getting the data to *connect*, to recognize all the accounts the bank has with a given customer. We're still dependent on the knowledge of the account manager and department head for many of these relationships. And in linking with the bank's systems domestically and around the world, we discovered that different units had different cut-off dates for operations, and different ID numbers for the same customers.

For some transactions, the loan may have originated in one location, be funded out of a second location, and sent to the customer in yet a third location. We have to be able to pull together the threads from all these transactions. Our proof that we have all transactions is to tie to the bank's legal books, but that still doesn't tell us things are linked correctly. Another "linking" problem is attaching the appropriate expenses to each transaction. Loan provisions can be calculated from customer data using Bill Maass's model, but direct and operating expenses don't come with customer tags attached to them. Correct alignment of costs to revenues is a big analysis job and initially needed a lot of local involvement. We also have to link with the Commercial Loan and Exposure databases to get detailed information on opening and closing loans and facility grades and amounts. We access the GEOSERVE database for the profitability of the customer's products supplied by GEOSERVE. And we need to hook up with the Merchant Banking and Treasury and Trading information systems to be able to track the fees they are earning from individual customers. Even today, the CPR reports are far from complete, but we're getting better at including more of a customer's transactions with us in a single report.

Poplawski reinforced the difficulty of linking all the bank's information systems.

Initially, we couldn't get the cooperation of the International Groups for CPR. But now, with the emphasis on cost control and centralized reporting, they want to participate in the system, and that has made it a lot easier to link overseas operations to NAM's customers.

Current Status

The CPR system had been operating in Aspbury's North American Markets group for two years and was generally well accepted despite several remaining limitations. Exhibit 5 shows a sample CPR report for a large customer. Aspbury was looking ahead to getting wider bank acceptance for the concept.

I sense some resistance to applying the CPR report more widely in the bank because it can expose unprofitable operations, especially in other groups. It will force the bank to confront why it is operating in certain geographical areas and in certain product lines.

We also need to get a longer time-line for evaluating our profitability with customers. Right now, we're running the model quarterly to stay current on our activities, but even a calendar year may be too short for evaluating customer relationships. In any given year, a company may not use any of its commercial banking relationships. If the company represents a key relationship for us, we need to be patient.

Maryann Sudo, a Vice-President and Relationship Manager in NAM, noted problems she still had with the report.

After each report is issued, we must spend time supplementing and correcting the numbers. Sometimes we can't reconcile to the RAA reported for the customer. We also have to call up the Trust Department to get the profitability of their activities with our customers, and the overseas operations are just beginning to come on to the system. But the systems people seem committed to correcting the errors and making the report work.

At the end of the day, however, the way we use the report is pretty simple. We either increase or decrease our business with the customer, change prices, or even drop companies. We detected two customers in the Midwest who just used us for our credit facilities, which were priced at low margins. Both companies, it turned out, had spread their banking business too thin, across too many banks. We told these customers that we couldn't continue in this way, calling on them several times a year and tying up equity in thinly priced loan commitments.

Interestingly, neither company wanted to terminate their relationship with us. The companies agreed to have us work with them by phone, or when they made trips to New York, helping us to reduce our expenses. We pulled out of both credit facilities. The companies started to use our fee-based services, such as cash management and foreign exchange, much more actively and we see some potential for attractively priced financing. These changes have transformed companies with a 2% ROE into profitable relationships.

We are beginning to use the CPR concept to price out prospective business. For example, we might agree to lend to a Mexican subsidiary of a U.S. company at a competitive price when we have the expectation that the business will lead to some debt/equity swaps. Another customer has asked for a lower price for cash management services. Our enthusiasm in responding to such a request would be determined by the existing ROE of the customer relationship.

Cynthia Warrick, Sudo's manager, also strongly supported the CPR report.

Herb Aspbury keeps pushing us on knowing the profitability of our customer relationships. Some of my officers never turn in a proposal now without a customer profitability report accompanying the analysis. But we're still not picking up enough of the data. One of our largest customers shows only a 3% ROE and an equity value destroyed of almost $6 million. But the company has all its corporate trust work done by the bank, and the profitability from that isn't yet in the report.

We probably should revisit the expense distribution method. Officers now annotate their CPR reports to note major discrepancies between actual effort and the amount allocated based on RAA. I think we need more accuracy here, but I don't want to return to filling out time sheets. Account managers know in general where they spend most of their time and effort. Perhaps they can just estimate the percentage of effort spent with each of their customers to give us a better picture of the different relationships.

I'm sure we'll solve these data problems in the near future. The big issue that the bank needs to resolve is whether we should double-count the revenues from transactions in each group or whether we should negotiate some fee-splitting arrangement. We're currently advising a major U.S. client on financing for a new venture in Hungary. The bank will earn a large advisory fee for this service, plus a syndication fee when the credit is booked out of the London office, and the normal interest-rate spread on the credit itself. The fees could total $1 million this year. Gerry Hannon, in my region, sourced the transaction with his client and did much of the upfront work, but the transaction will take place in Europe. Who should get credit for the fees?

Herb Aspbury wants to measure success through the profitability of the global relationship. Fee splitting can be too arbitrary. But other group executives want a formal fee-splitting arrangement, perhaps formula-based by type of product, feeling that people will be more motivated if their recorded income is "real" rather than a shadow amount. The bank's bonus compensation is based on recorded profitability, and many top bank executives feel that pay-for-performance could become compromised if too much attention is paid to "shadow profits."

Richard Copeland, Vice-President and Planning Officer of the Developing Markets group, described the problems of attempting to assign profits to the various banking groups.

You might have a Brazilian loan that is funded out of London but managed out of New York. You can transfer the loan revenue from London to New York, but then you should pass back, as well, the expenses from London to New York for operating the loan. And the adjustments should be made on the balance sheet too, to recognize equity commitments.

The choice of how to recognize profits really comes down to two alternatives. Number 1, we can attempt to match expenses against revenues and charge out for services provided to other MHC units; or, Number 2, each unit keeps its own expenses and we fee-split the revenues on deals involving multiple departments. I think we're likely to choose Number 2. Expenses are too difficult to apportion, and charging for services based on costs puts operating units into a cost center mentality that provides the wrong kind of motivation.

The current thinking in the bank was to customize the fee-splitting arrangement by type of product. A marketing officer might make the initial contact for a private placement and then bring in the product specialist, who would place the security with investors. The marketing officer might get 30% of the total fee reflected in his P&L for this work. For a more specialized product, where greater expertise was required by the product specialist, the marketing percentage would be lower, closer to 20%.

Large deals of a special nature, such as receiving advisory fees in excess of $500,000, would be shared on a case-by-case basis. All participants would provide their own judgments about their individual contributions to the deal with the percentages reviewed and finalized at the senior executive level.

Copeland summarized the issues involved.

Tom Johnson keeps emphasizing the importance of teamwork and increasing the ROE of the entire global bank, regardless of where the revenue is earned. But integrating this goal into the messy details of profit and revenue measurement and incentive compensation still needs to be worked out.

We now understand that we must have a Global Customer-Product Profitability Report, similar to what the North American Markets Group initiated. But we will need different reports for the bank's individual profit centers. The bank executives seem chastened by the experience of a large Wall Street investment firm that had allowed double-counting of revenues for all its units. Each SBU thought it was very profitable, but overall expenses continued to grow, and the company as a whole became highly unprofitable and almost failed. If the bank is to focus on ROE, it must know which businesses are pulling their weight and which are not, and which products are the most profitable for the bank given its scarce resources of people and capital.

Product people and marketing people are now having intense discussions about fee-splitting. This dialogue, however, may be what Tom Johnson intends to happen. Our companies want a single relationship with MHC, not to have 20 different people calling on them. In the fee-splitting arrangements currently being discussed, the sharing percentages for the marketing units for most corporate finance products vary between 20% and 30%, so it may not be a big deal which number gets selected for each product.

A marketing officer, however, remained skeptical about the equity of any formula-based fee-splitting arrangement.

I prefer the shadow profitability approach rather than any formula-based scheme. I may work four months on a deal with one of my customers, pulling my product colleagues along, but end up getting credit for only 20% of the fees. This doesn't begin to reflect the contribution I feel I made to the success of the transaction.

EXHIBIT 1

MANUFACTURERS HANOVER CORPORATION:
CUSTOMER PROFITABILITY REPORT
Selected Financial Data

	1989	1988	1987	1986	1985
Income Statement Summary					
Total interest revenue	$6,888	$6,637	$6,324	$6,538	$7,322
Total interest expense	5,254	4,645	4,413	4,506	5,210
Net interest revenue	1,634	1,992	1,911	2,032	2,112
Credit loss provision	1,404	502	2,236	859	623
Noninterest revenue	1,532	1,908	1,433	1,428	1,063
Noninterest expense	2,124	2,120	2,346	2,157	1,955
Income (loss) before extraordinary items	($588)	$ 752	($1,140)	$ 411	$ 407
Balance Sheet Summary					
Total loans	$39,145	$49,024	$55,617	$56,273	$58,466
Credit loss reserve	2,677	2,346	2,652	1,008	814
Total assets	60,479	66,710	73,348	74,397	76,526
Total deposits	41,994	41,714	45,176	45,544	46,261
Long-term debt	3,400	8,136	8,473	7,357	7,867
Shareholders' equity	3,381	3,251	2,704	3,766	3,547
Selected Ratios					
Total equity/total assets	5.59	4.87	3.69	5.06	4.64
Tangible equity/total assets	5.17	4.16	2.90	4.26	3.69
Loss reserve/total loans	6.84	4.78	4.77	1.79	1.39
Number employees (full-time equivalent)	20,034	23,094	28,669	29,912	31,814

EXHIBIT 2

MANUFACTURERS HANOVER CORPORATION: CUSTOMER PROFITABILITY REPORT
North American Division
Monthly & Year-To-Date Comparison
Financial Summary
(units are thousands $)

RUN DATE : 19-JAN-90
FUN TIME : 20:38
CENTER : 68339 MIDWEST/GREAT LAKES / WARRICK   FOR THE PERIOD ENDING : DECEMBER 31, 1989

| MONTH-TO-DATE 12/31/89 | | | | | | | YEAR-TO-DATE 12/31/89 | | | | | |
| RETURN ON EARN ASSETS | | | | VARIANCE | | | | | VARIANCE | | RETURN ON EARN ASSETS | |
ACTUAL %	PLAN %	12/31/89 ACTUAL	12/31/89 PLAN	FAVORABLE/(UNFAV) $	%		12/31/89 ACTUAL	12/31/89 PLAN	FAVORABLE/(UNFAV) $	%	ACTUAL %	PLAN %
10.20	9.78	3,141	4,653	(1,511)	(32)	Interest income on loans	45,567	56,921	(11,354)	(20)	10.72	10.10
.01	.03	5	12	(7)	(62)	Tax-free interest adjustment	65	181	(116)	(64)	.02	.03
.35	.58	109	275	(166)	(60)	Total domestic loan fees	2,690	3,297	(607)	(18)	.63	.59
10.56	10.38	3,255	4,940	(1,685)	(34)	Total interest income & fees	48,322	60,399	(12,077)	(20)	11.37	10.72
1.81	.91	558	434	(124)	(29)	Transfer pool expense (net)	10,512	6,260	(4,251)	(68)	2.47	1.11
.45	.43	139	204	65	32	Other interest expense	1,501	2,494	993	40	.35	.44
5.29	6.37	1,629	3,032	1,404	46	LIBOR interest expense	23,010	36,371	13,361	37	5.41	6.45
5.74	6.80	1.768	3,236	1,468	45	Total interest expense	24,511	38,865	14,354	37	5.77	6.90
7.55	7.71	2,326	3,671	1,345	37	Total funding cost	35,023	45,125	10,102	22	8.24	8.01
3.01	2.67	928	1,269	(340)	(27)	Net interest margin	13,299	15,274	(1,975)	(13)	3.13	2.71
3.01	2.67	928	1,269	(340)	(27)	Funds profit	13,299	15,274	(1,975)	(13)	3.13	2.71
2.61	2.77	803	1,321	(518)	(39)	Total operating income	19,321	15,847	3,475	22	4.55	2.81
.77	.59	236	279	43	15	Salary & benefits	2,734	3,175	441	14	.64	.56
.17	.10	51	50	(2)	(3)	Occupancy	596	599	2	0	.14	.11
.03	.06	10	26	16	60	Equipment	201	314	113	36	.05	.06
.22	.20	69	97	28	29	Other operating expenses	394	1,158	764	66	.09	.21
1.19	.95	367	452	85	19	Total operating expense	3,925	5,246	1,321	25	.92	.93
4.43	4.49	1,364	2,137	(773)	(36)	Net cont. before interoffice	28,695	25,875	2,821	11	6.75	4.59
.26	.00	81	0	(81)	0	Total interoffice expense	1,042	0	(1,042)	0	.25	.00
4.17	4.49	1,284	2,137	(854)	(40)	Net income before taxes	27,653	25,875	1,779	7	6.51	4.59
4.17	4.49	1,284	2,137	(854)	(40)	Net income after taxes	27,653	25,875	1,779	7	6.51	4.59
		100,800	85,826	14,974	17	Reference rate loans	125,871	92,285	33,587	36		
		207,031	397,147	(190,116)	(48)	LIBOR loans	242,793	390,773	(147,981)	(38)		
		20,266	45,650	(25,384)	(56)	Money market loans	16,957	46,642	(29,685)	(64)		
		8,817	0	8,817	0	CD-based loans	11,655	0	11,655	0		
		1,525	4,639	(3,114)	(67)	Tax-exempt loans	2,083	5,741	(3,658)	(64)		
		21,436	21,621	(185)	(1)	Fixed rate loans	22,757	22,512	245	1		
		2,656	5,539	(2,883)	(52)	G/L overdraft balances	4,078	5,539	(1,461)	(26)		
		240	0	240	0	Principle adjustments	(1,109)	0	(1,109)	0		
		0	0	0	0	Deferred income FASB 91	0	0	0	0		
		362,771	560,422	(197,651)	(35)	Total loans	425,085	583,492	(138,407)	(25)		
		60,405	70,671	(10,266)	(15)	Total demand deposits	58,301	69,559	(11,258)	(16)		

EXHIBIT 3

MANUFACTURERS HANOVER CORPORATION:
CUSTOMER PROFITABILITY REPORT
Data Input for Loan Pricing Model

To use the Loan Pricing Model, the lending officer entered a number of parameters describing the proposed financing transaction.

1. *Facility Type*[1]
   Line of credit
   Revolving credit
   Term loan
   Standby letter of credit
   Commercial letter of credit
   Banker's acceptance

2. *Facility Grade*
   A numeric grade (from 1 to 10) reflecting the company's risk classification. Similar in concept to a bond rating, most of North American Markets group's customers were in the 4 or 5 category.

3. *Facility Amount and Usage Percentage*
   The size of the facility requested and the officer's estimate of the amount that would actually be used. As more of a facility was used by a company, MHC had to supply more capital to support the loan. Typical pricing for a facility to a highly rated customer could be 10 basis points on the commitment amount and Libor plus 1/4 on the amount actually used.

4. *Tenor*
   Length of commitment; facilities for less than one year were considered less risky than facilities in excess of a year. This split reflected guidelines established by the Federal Reserve Board.

5. *Pricing Index and Spread (in Basis Points)*
   Reference rate
   Libor
   Certificate of deposit
   Money market

6. *Fees (in $ or Basis Points)*
   Amount earned (or paid) as agent, arranger, underwriter, syndicator, or originator; fees could be earned based on commitment, actual usage, and on loan prepayment.

7. *Effort Required (Low, Medium, or High)*
   Officer entered relative amount of effort required for the proposed transaction.

---

[1]A *facility* is the general term used by bankers to describe an agreement or commitment from the bank to lend money when a company needs it. A loan would be the amount actually borrowed by the company under the facility arrangement.

EXHIBIT 4

MANUFACTURERS HANOVER CORPORATION: CUSTOMER PROFITABILITY REPORT
LMP Calculation of ROE and Value Added/Destroyed

Revenues:	Loan spread	[Interest rate spread × outstanding balance]
	Value of balances	
	Loan fees	[fees in lieu of compensating balances, facility fees, interest-related commitment fees, loan orgination fees, agent and syndication fees]
	Equity credit[1]	[Risk-adjusted equity × equity credit rate]
Expenses:	Risk-adjusted loan loss provision	
	Departmental expense allocation (based on RAA and estimated effort required)	
	Expenses of loan syndication and sales	
	Income taxes	

Income = revenues − expenses

ROE = income/risk-adjusted equity.

Value Added/(Destroyed)

MHC estimated that it needed a 16% ROE for its common stock to trade at book value. Loans with an ROE in excess of this 16% rate were considered to add value to stockholders, and loans that yielded less than 16% were destroying stockholder value. A final calculation revealed the amount of stockholder value that was added or destroyed by the proposed transaction.

$$\text{Market-to-book ratio} = \frac{\text{ROE} - \text{corporate growth rate [8.4\%]}}{16\% \text{ [hurdle rate]} - 8.4\% \text{ [growth rate]}}$$

Market value	= (market-to-book ratio) × book value
Book value	= Risk-adjusted equity
Value added/ (destroyed)	= market value − book value

[1]The equity credit reflects a credit for that portion of the facility funded with interest-free equity.

EXHIBIT 5

MANUFACTURERS HANOVER CORPORATION

Customer/Product Profitability Reporting

FAMILY	FAMILY CREDIT GRADE 5		FAMILY DEPT. 425		12-MONTH PERIOD ENDING 06/30/90	RUN DATE 09/20/90	($000)
	NAD1	MHBD	Subtotal	ITA	BIS	OTHER	
On & off balance sheet							
Loans outstanding	$20,918	$1	$20,919		$8,195		
Acceptances							
Standby L/C S							
Commercial L/C S	2,111		2,111				
Unused commitments	65,838		65,838				
Unused lines	27,548		27,548				
Risk-adjusted assets	50,642	1	50,642				
Risk-adjusted common equity	1,801	4	1,805				
Income statement							
Net interest income	$203	– $0	$203		$647		
Domestic loan fees	76		76				
Commitment fees	24		24				
L/C fees	3		3				
Agent fees							
Syndication fees							
Other fees (credit only)	– 3		– 3				
Noncredit fees	258	33	291		17		
Value of balances required for							
credit: excess/(deficient)	21	0	21		89		
Required for noncredit	339		339				
(Deficient)	– 329	– 0	– 329				
Additional value	49		49				
Equity credit	174	0	174				
Total revenue	815	33	848				
Expenses							
Risk-adjusted loan loss provision	$152	$0	$152				
Direct	152		152				
Net interoffice (credit & general)	64		64				
Net interoffice (noncredit)	220		220				
Corporate overhead	66		66				
Other balance sheet charges	41	0	41				
Pre-tax income	120	33	154				
Net income	70	21	91				
Return on equity	4	521	5				
Value added/(destroyed)	– $2,872	268	– 2,604				

(continued)

EXHIBIT 5 *(cont.)*

FAMILY	FAMILY CREDIT GRADE 5	FAMILY DEPT. 425	12-MONTH PERIOD ENDING 06/30/90	RUN DATE 09/20/90	($000)
Investment banking					
Acquisition finance					
Risk exposure					
Foreign exchange					
Structured finance					
Private placement					
ESOPS					
Mergers & acquisitions					
Corporate advisory					
Capital markets					
L S & S (bid notes)	−7				
Agent bank services					
Other					
Total	−7				
BIS					
AIM					
Sovereign risk group					
Total					
ITA					
Bond trustee					
Comm. paper issuance					
Escrow					
Other corporate trust					
Dividend reinvestment					
Reorganization					
Other stock transfer					
Coupon paying					
Institutional custody					
Master trust					
Other instit. asset					
Total					
Cash management					
Collection services	15				
Disbursement services	71				
Interplex					
Total	86				
Total MHC revenue	1,593				

10

Stage IV:
Integrated Cost Systems

Many companies now have developed Stage III activity-based cost systems, and are using them, as discussed in chapters 4–9, to improve profitability through operational and strategic activity-based management. Typically, these ABC systems are retrospective. They are refreshed periodically, say annually or quarterly, based on operating performance during the most recent period.[1] The ABC systems usually reside on personal computers or PC networks, and depend on data downloaded from networks or legacy systems; some data may even require manual entry. In general, these ABC systems are an add-on to the organization's financial reporting and budgeting systems.

In parallel with the development of stand-alone, Stage III ABC systems, many companies are also investing in enterprise resource planning (ERP) systems. These systems integrate and coordinate all the major business functions: purchasing, manufacturing, marketing, sales, logistics, and order fulfillment, plus support services such as human resources and accounting. For example, with an ERP system, a salesperson's order anywhere in the world triggers a shipment from a regional warehouse or schedules the order into production in an appropriate factory. The system then automatically updates inventory levels, material purchases, production schedules, customer information and accounting data. The ERP system has a common data structure and a centralized data warehouse that permits data to be entered and accessed from anywhere in the world. With ERP systems delivering on-line, real-time information about all aspects of a company's operations, managers can envision receiving continuous information about the cost and profitability of their operations.

Managers naturally would like to incorporate their stand-alone ABC systems into such ERP systems where they can support cost-based decision making across a wide range of organizational activities. They also want the ABC systems to be prospective; to provide information about future operations, not just to report on the cost and profitability of past operations. This is the vision for Stage IV. In this chapter, we describe how companies can achieve these goals through integrated ABC and ERP systems.

---

[1]We have indicated, however, in chapter 5 how even Stage III (nonintegrated) ABC systems can operate with budgeted rather than historical data.

CHALLENGES OF SYSTEM INTEGRATION

An integrated Stage IV system, particularly one installed on an ERP platform, will give companies the capability to access daily expenses for activities and process, and daily quantities of activity cost drivers. In principle, rather than waiting a month to get a report on actual cost driver rates, an integrated Stage IV system could calculate daily *actual* activity cost driver (ACD) rates, providing even faster feedback to employees for their learning and improvement activities. For example, the system can report that yesterday the organization's expenses for the resources that *handle customer orders* was $12,468. And the number of orders handled yesterday was 253. Therefore the cost driver rate of $42.98 could be applied to each order received yesterday. If today's expenses for these resources turned out to be $13,491 and the quantity of orders received were 228, the cost driver rate applied to today's orders would be $59.17. This is real-time, objective information. But it is very, very wrong.

Three different sources of variation exist that cause actual ACD rates to fluctuate in the short-term in ways that are unrelated to the underlying economics and productivity of activities and business processes.

1. Spending fluctuations.
2. Volume fluctuations.
3. Fluctuations in productivity and yields.

These three sources of variations affect, respectively, the numerator, the denominator, and the ratio itself of the ACD rate calculation. Allowing short-term fluctuations from these three sources to affect calculated ACD rates will introduce errors when estimating the underlying rate, and mask underlying improvement or deterioration in activities and business processes. Managers who fail to understand these issues may set inappropriate priorities for process improvement initiatives and make incorrect decisions about products and customers.

The period over which activity driver quantities are determined is a function of the frequency with which the activity is performed, the degree of statistical fluctuation in the efficiency and yield, and the ability to control for the effects of spending, usage, and productivity fluctuations. The period chosen should be long enough to capture a sufficient number of the performances of the activity to average out the fluctuations. If the degree of fluctuation is small relatively few observations are required. If it is high then more observations and hence a longer time period are required. Therefore, activities that are performed in high volume each day, and where spending fluctuations are easily controlled for, could be candidates for daily reporting and frequent updating. The costs of activities, like maintenance, that are performed infrequently, may not be updated for a year or even longer.

Companies in Stage III typically use historical, post-period data for their ABC systems. Cost estimates and assignment from such Stage III models have distortions from temporary spending fluctuations, from timing differences in expense recognition, from underutilization of resource capacity, from fluctuations in activity volumes, and from minor, temporary variations in underlying process efficiency. These errors exist but managers accept these limitations because the activity cost driver estimates are still likely to be far more accurate than continuing to operate with Stage II cost systems that use only volume-based drivers. Also, many Stage III cost systems use aggregate data, estimated over three-, six-, or twelve-month periods, for which short-term fluctuations tend to average out. The only substantial error in estimating activity-cost driver rates over these long periods of time arises from failure to reflect unused capacity costs.

With the advent of integrated ERP systems, the time period for estimation shrinks and all the temporary, nonrecurring and timing factors become imbedded in the activity cost driver rates, leading to fluctuations in these rates that are unrelated to the underlying efficiency and productivity of the activities. In effect, migrating a Stage III ABC system to an ERP environment, with daily rather than annual calculations, will enable managers to receive distorted product cost and efficiency information every single day, rather than just once a year (as in a traditional Stage II) system. This is a good example where a higher quantity of more frequent data will actually provide less useful information to managers.

DIFFERENCES BETWEEN ABC AND OPERATIONAL LEARNING AND IMPROVEMENT SYSTEMS

ABC systems and operational learning and improvement systems have different characteristics, as summarized in Exhibit 10–1. By separating the two managerial systems, the functionality of each system can be developed and customized for its particular mission. In particular, we can see several major differences in the design and scope of the two systems, as summarized in Exhibit 10–1.

As this table makes abundantly clear, the requirements for the two types of systems are so different that it would be impossible for a single system to perform both functions well. In Stage III systems (described in chapters 3–9), organizations can experiment with new approaches that meet the requirements of the two functions, without the added burden of integration and compatibility between the two new systems. By recognizing the distinct differences between the two systems, managers avoid the errors made by firms that have tried to go to Stage IV too quickly. Typically, these firms have not achieved their objective because they used an ABC system—that failed to reflect capacity and resource usage concepts—as an operational control system to focus employees' attention on reducing monthly cost driver rates. At-

EXHIBIT 10-1

	OPERATIONAL LEARNING & IMPROVEMENT	ACTIVITY-BASED COSTING
Cost of Resources Used	Actual	Standard
Frequency of Updating	Continual	Periodic (Quarterly, Semiannual or Annual)
Measurement Demands	Highly accurate	Estimates sufficient; more accuracy (duration and intensity drivers) only when cost-justified
Scope of System	Responsibility center	Entire value-chain: from suppliers and product development through operations, administration, customers, and post-sales service
Focus of system	Resource spending: costs of resources supplied	Resource usage: costs of resources used
Cost variability	Emphasis on short-term fixed and variable costs	Degree of variability identified via attributes but not a central feature; Costs become variable as resource supply adjusts to resource demand
Applicability	Most useful in repetitive, predictable processes; less useful in highly discretionary and judgmental activities	Universally applicable: can adjust type of cost driver used (transaction, duration, and direct charging) to nature of underlying process
Complementary systems	Nonfinancial measures (quality, cycle times)	Needs-based customer segment analysis; Competitor and strategic information

tempting to have a system that is satisfactory as a Stage III ABC system take on additional roles, such as operational control and learning, or inventory valuation for financial statements, will compromise the functionality of the system for its main purpose: to calculate reasonably accurate costs for a complete set of organizational activities and processes, and of the products produced and customers served. Such systems are better viewed as activity-based enhanced Stage II systems. They have not been freed of the constraints of trying to perform all three functions of cost systems simultaneously. Consequently, they do not deliver the benefits of Stage III systems, let alone those of Stage IV.

ABC and operational control systems are, of course, not unrelated. We have seen, in operational ABM, that the ABC system provides the front-end justification for reengineering improvement programs to reduce or eliminate inefficiencies in organizational activities. Once such programs are launched, the operational control system provides the continual measurement to help employees improve activity efficiencies. A subsequent ABC model can identify whether the efficiency and the productivity have been captured through increased capacity and lower cost driver rates, and whether the additional capacity has been exploited either through lower resource supply or by higher activity volumes being handled by the existing resources.

ABC AND FINANCIAL REPORTING

As ABC systems get integrated into the mainstream, periodic reporting systems of the firm, managers will naturally ask whether the ABC system can be used to generate cost of goods sold and inventory valuations for financial reporting purposes. The answer is yes but with precautions.

The answer is yes, because an activity attribute can be developed that identifies ABC costs that are assigned to products but that cannot be assigned for financial reporting purposes. For example, the ABC cost might include the interest costs associated with the capital dedicated to that product. Conversely, the ABC system may not assign to products certain facility-sustaining costs that financial reporting requires to be allocated to products. The first correction is trivial, requiring only an extra activity attribute field to identify noninventoriable activity costs. The second correction, however, should be done by financial accountants, outside the ABC system so as to avoid any confusion. They can pick an arbitrary cost driver, such as direct labor, conversion costs, or total ABC costs, for allocating costs required by GAAP but not traceable via cause-and-effect relationships from resources to activities to products.

The primary motivation for having the ABC systems generate GAAP costs arises from concerns that, if the two systems are quite separate, they can report different profit figures. In this case, managers will face ambiguity about which system should be used to evaluate and reward their actions. Managers do act to maximize their reported performance, whatever measurement scheme is chosen. Unfortunately, the problem is not solved by using the ABC system to report GAAP costs. The addition of costs that are excluded by GAAP and the subtraction of costs that should be excluded by ABC principles mean that the two systems will likely always report somewhat different profits and balance sheets.

One hopeful sign on the horizon may lead to a significant lessening of this problem. As companies move to the lean enterprise, drastically lowering their levels of inventory relative to cost of goods sold, accountants can use extremely simple methods, perhaps a simple markup over purchase price (essentially a material-related overhead percentage that includes all nonmaterial costs), for allocating costs to inventory. While the individual product costs calculated in this manner for external reporting (which should be inaccessible to managers anyway) will be wrong, the cost of goods sold and inventory valuations will be sufficiently accurate for financial reporting purposes, especially for companies with low inventories and stable product mixes.

FUNGIBLE RESOURCES

Our capacity costing examples in chapter 5 adopted a simplifying assumption, that the resources supplied could perform only a single activity, *handle customer orders*. With this simplifying assumption, which may be met in practice for some activities, we could measure capacity at either the resource level or the activity level.

In general, however, many resources can perform multiple activities. For example, the same set of resources in the customer administration department might be called upon not only to handle customer orders, but also to maintain credit information on customers, handle customer complaints, measure customer satisfaction, and follow up with customers who pay their bills slowly. When resources can perform multiple activities, capacity must be measured at the resource level, not the activity level. Continuing in the above example, the number of customer orders that could be handled in a period is not a unique number; the capacity for this activity depends upon all the other activity demands made on the resources supplied. If few complaints must be addressed during the period, then many orders can be processed. Conversely, the time available to handle orders will be severely diminished during periods when many customer complaints must be processed, many credit checks must be performed, and many requests are received for customer satisfaction evaluations.

In this more general case, the costing can be well handled by estimating the practical capacity of the resources supplied. Capacity is generally measured by the hours of time available to perform a task. Even for machines, the basic measure is hours of machine time available for productive use.[2]

For Stage IV ABC systems, we can consider a new procedure for assigning resource expenses to activities, one that explicitly incorporates the capacity of the resources supplied, as well as the underlying efficiency with which individual activities are performed. You do not get something for nothing, however, and several new pieces of information will be required to implement the improved approach.

First, the ABC team must estimate the practical capacity of the resources supplied to perform the related activities. The second set of new information is the estimated (standard) time required to perform each activity. Of course, if the ABC model is already using duration drivers to assign activity costs, then this information will already be available (the length of time to handle a customer order, process a complaint, or perform a credit check).[3] Usually, however, organizations will be using many transactional drivers. Recall that one of the conditions for transactional drivers to be adequate is if the time required to perform each instance of the activity is approximately the same.[4] The new requirement is an estimate of the time required to perform each instance of the activity. Let us call this the *unit time estimate*. The unit times for each activity can then be multiplied by the cost of each hour to obtain the activity cost driver rate.

At the end of each period, the ABC system calculates the quantity demanded of each activity, multiplies by each activity's cost driver rate, and sums to obtain the total cost of the resources used during the period. The difference between this amount and the budgeted expenses for the resources represents the cost of unused resource capacity. Students can test their understanding of this approach by working a simple numerical exercise at the end of the chapter.

---

[2]Alternative measures of capacity—number of units that can be processed, gallons and pounds of material that can be converted, or number of operations performed—can be derived from the time-based capacity measure by dividing the available time by the time per unit to process a product unit, convert a gallon or pound of material, or perform a standard operation.

[3]Of course, if the first stage resource driver is itself duration based, then the Stage III system will automatically adjust for the different activity loads each year. The issue being discussed here arises only when a workload percentage, based upon interview data, is used. A duration-based first stage resource driver, however, does not adjust automatically for practical capacity.

[4]The other condition is that the cost of performing the activity is relatively small, so that more detailed measurements, via duration drivers or direct charging, is not warranted.

STAGE IV: INTEGRATING ABC AND OPERATIONAL LEARNING AND IMPROVEMENT SYSTEMS

In Stage IV (see Exhibit 10–2) we integrate activity-based cost systems and systems for operational learning and improvement. Each of these two systems has been customized, in Stage III, to meet the specific needs of managers for activity-based management and for monitoring and improving organizational activities and processes. In Stage IV, linkages and feedback loops between the two systems get established. The budgeting process identifies the practical capacity of the resources supplied to perform activities. The ABC-budgeting process also identifies the resources expected to vary with short-term fluctuations in activity volumes and develops a flexible budget for the supply and spending on these flexible resources. Finally, the Stage IV ABC system specifies estimates of the unit times required to perform different support activities. These estimates provide a standard that can be tested against actual practice.

Once the supply of resources has been determined for operating units, the operational learning and improvement system monitors actual supply and spending against the budgeted amounts. It also can monitor whether realized demands may be approaching the practical capacity of the committed resources. Such capacity monitoring may provide an early signal when bottlenecks are developing. The monitoring may also provide feedback on the accuracy of the capacity estimates. If activity demands exceed the estimated capacity, without encountering delays and backlogs, the organization learns that the actual capacity of the resources to perform work is higher than previously estimated. This information can be fed back to the activity-based cost system to revise upwards the rated practical capacity of the resources.

During the period, the operational learning and improvement system also monitors closely the efficiency and productivity of the resources. As organizational processes become more efficient and productive, through employees' improvement efforts, the system should detect increases in the number of transactions that the existing resources can handle (capacity increases) or decreases in the standard unit times required to perform organizational activities (for example, to handle a customer order, or to process a customer complaint). Stage IV operational learning and improvement systems track the two critical inputs used to estimate an activity cost

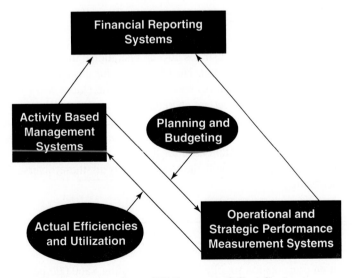

EXHIBIT 10–2   Stage IV: Integrated Cost Systems

driver rate: the resource costs of supplying an hour of time to perform the activity, and the actual time required to perform the activity. Either manually or automatically, using expert systems, the systems should attempt to detect when there has been a permanent shift in:

1. The capacity of the resources supplied,
2. The cost of supplying an hour of productive time on the resource, or
3. The efficiency (time required) in performing the activity.

When such a permanent shift has been detected, this information can be fed back to the ABC system to update the appropriate activity cost driver rate. In this way, the ABC system is kept current with permanent improvements made in organizational activities and processes.

SUMMARY

When companies have achieved their desired functionality in Stage III systems, they can migrate to an integrated set of financial, cost, and performance measurement systems that build upon the low-cost availability of information from enterprise resource planning systems. In Stage IV, the operational improvement system monitors continually the organization's resource spending, and the efficiency, quality, and responsiveness of departments and processes. The ABC system reports periodically the cost of activities and processes, and the cost and profitability of products, services, and customers.

The systems are integrated in that both the operational improvement and the ABC system provide the basis for the periodic financial reports to external constituencies. Further, the operational improvement system updates the ABC system's cost driver rates based on sustainable changes in activity efficiency and capacity.

We have now completed the articulation of our blueprint (see Exhibit 1–1) for migrating to Stage IV integrated systems, in which ABC, operational learning and improvement, and periodic financial reporting are performed in an integrated and comprehensive approach. One final topic remains for companies to achieve all the benefits from their new cost and performance measurement systems. In the final chapter, we show how activity-based costing can become the foundation for an organization's budgeting, decision-making, and transfer-pricing processes.

CASES

The *Shionogi & Co., Ltd.* case illustrates how an operational improvement system and a product costing system can be interconnected. The other cases for this chapter explore the integration of activity-based costing with enterprise-wide systems. The *Queensferry Telecommunications Division* illustrates the problems that are encountered when Stage III systems are used for multiple purposes. The rationale of first developing the Stage III capability and then evolving to Stage IV is demonstrated by this case. The *AT&T Paradyne* case documents how one organization developed an integrated system used for financial reporting, product costing, monthly feedback, and target costing. How well the system performs these diverse functions is the main topic for discussion.

NUMERICAL EXERCISE ON COSTING THE USE OF FUNGIBLE RESOURCES

Assume that an organization supplies resources, costing $560,000 per period, to perform three activities:

- Handle customer orders,
- Process customer complaints, and
- Perform customer credit checks.

A Stage III ABC system estimated that the percentage of time spent by the people resources are 50%, 30%, and 20%, respectively. The actual quantities of demanded work are:

- 7,000 customer orders,
- 200 customer complaints, and
- 350 credit checks.

1. Calculate the costs assigned and the activity cost driver rates for the three activities.

Suppose now that the front-line people who actually perform the various customer support activities can supply 8,000 hours of useful work during the period. Assume also that the $560,000 of expenses are committed for the upcoming period; they are not expected to vary based on the actual number of customer orders processed, complaints handled, or credit checks performed. Finally, the unit times to perform the three activities are:

ACTIVITY	UNIT TIME (HOURS)
Handle Customer Orders	0.72
Process Customer Complaint	3.60
Perform Credit Checks	4.11

2. Assuming the same quantity of demands as before (7,000 orders, 200 complaints, and 350 credit checks), calculate the new activity cost driver rates and the costs assigned to the three activities.
3. Explain any difference between the costs assigned to the activities and the budgeted expenses of $560,000.

SHIONOGI & CO., LTD.: PRODUCT AND KAIZEN COSTING SYSTEMS

Shionogi & Co., Ltd. (Shionogi) was founded in 1878 as a wholesaler of traditional Japanese and Chinese medicines by Gisaburo Shiono. Following the progress and spread of Western medicinal science, Shionogi expanded its operations by importing pharmaceuticals from Europe and the United States. In addition, it initiated an in-house research and development program and started the production and marketing of its own products. The Shiono family continued to play a key role in the management of the firm; for example, in 1992, Yoshihiko Shiono, a descendant of the founder, became President.

The firm incorporated in 1919, and by 1995 had sales of ¥238 billion of which ¥203 billion came from sales of pharmaceutical products. Other businesses included animal health products, agro-chemicals, industrial chemicals, diagnostics, and clinical testing services. The firm was recognized world-wide for the quality of its antibiotics and other pharmaceutical products.

Shionogi was a research and development oriented pharmaceutical manufacturer. In 1995, it dedicated over 11.4% of sales to research and development, an amount over two times its net income. The firm's major pharmaceutical product categories were antibiotics and biological preparations (37% of sales), circulatory and respiratory system drugs (17%), nervous system drugs (10%), "other" pharmaceutical products (21%), and non-pharmaceutical and diagnostics (15%). Shionogi's strategy traditionally focused on selling ethical products to hospitals and general practitioners.

In 1992, Shionogi took its first major step toward internationalization. It acquired a world wide hard-gelatin capsule production and marketing network from Eli Lilly and Company, a major American pharmaceutical company, with which Shionogi had a long-standing relationship. The agreement also covered Shionogi's purchase of Lilly's share in Japan Elanco Company, Limited, a 50/50 joint venture on hard-gelatin capsules in Japan.

The Japanese Pharmaceutical Industry

In 1995, the world's pharmaceutical industry was dominated by American firms such as Merck, Bristol-Myers Squibb, Johnson and Johnson, and Pfizer and European firms such as Glaxo, Roche, SmithKline Beecham, and Hoechst. These firms were considerably larger than their Japanese counterparts. For example, Merck was the largest American firm with sales of about $6.5 billion and Glaxo was the largest European firm with sales of about $7 billion.

The Japanese pharmaceutical industry consisted of about four hundred companies. These companies ranged in size from the large international firms such as Takeda, Sankyo, and Yamanouchi to small domestic ones, such as Kyorin and Nippon Shinyaku. Takeda was by far the largest Japanese firm in the industry with 1995 pharmaceutical sales of approximately ¥580 billion. Sankyo, the second largest, had sales of ¥400 billion. Yamanouchi, the third largest, had sales of ¥280 billion. In 1995, Shionogi was the sixth largest Japanese pharmaceutical firm and about number 30 in the world.

In recent years, Shionogi's position had dropped from third to sixth place in the Japanese pharmaceutical industry due to a lack of successful products which had caused their relative sales ranking to decrease. This decrease was not as serious as it might at first sound because the third through seventh firms were relatively similar in terms of sales. Shionogi top management viewed this set back as temporary and expected the firm to regain rapidly its previous ranking with the introduction of a number of new products. These new products included several antibiotics that were currently undergoing trials.

Pharmaceutical Manufacturing

The firm's pharmaceutical products were manufactured at four production facilities (see Exhibit 1). Two of these facilities, Kuise and Settsu were located close to Osaka. The other two, Kanegasaki and Akoh were located some distance from Osaka. Kanegasaki was located on the Iwate prefecture, about 500 miles north of Osaka. Akoh was located in the Hyogo prefecture, about 70 miles west of Osaka.

There were three major steps in the production of

Professor Robin Cooper of the Peter F. Drucker Graduate Management Center at the Claremont Graduate School prepared this case.

pharmaceuticals; bulk manufacturing, formulation, and packaging. Bulk manufacture consisted of producing large volumes of the active pharmaceutical ingredients. It was performed at two of the firm's facilities, Kuise and Kanegasaki. Formulation consisted of blending the bulk materials and then converting them into tablets, injectable solutions, freeze dried preparations, or ointments. These procedures were performed at the Kuise and Settsu facilities. Finally, packaging was undertaken at the Kuise, Settsu, and Akoh plants.

The Shionogi Cost System

The Shionogi cost system had been under development for approximately 20 years. Its continuous evolution reflected the demand for increasingly accurate product costs as the competitive and regulatory environment that the firm faced became more complex. Kouichi Saeki, the firm's resident specialist in cost accounting, commented:

> Compared to average Japanese practice, ours is a very accurate system. It is not an activity-based system but shares many of the same principles. To achieve the high level of accuracy we require, we have maintained the cost accounting function in the plants, not at headquarters, where it is located in most Japanese firms. Only by locating the cost accounting function in the plants can the system be kept sufficiently up-to-date to maintain the accuracy that Shionogi requires.

The system was, according to Saeki, not technically a standard cost system since no time studies were performed. Rather, it should be considered a "precisely determined forecast-based cost system." Despite this technicality, the system was referred to, inside the firm, as a standard cost system and the costs it reported as standard costs.

Budgetary standards were established based upon the actual data collected for the last month of the previous fiscal year (see Exhibit 2). The budgetary standard for a given product was modified if a significant change was expected in the cost of that product in the new fiscal year. For example, if the product's production volume was expected to change dramatically, then its budgetary standard was modified accordingly. Similarly, if the firm expected to purchase a new piece of equipment during the year, or expected to incorporate a major change in a production process, then the budgetary standards were set to reflect the weighted average anticipated operating efficiencies for the year. For example, if at the end of last year, actual performance for a given

process was 100 and in the middle of the new year it was expected to fall to 80, then the standard was set at 90 (see Exhibit 3).

Under the budgetary standard approach, the reported costs of products could vary quite widely from year to year depending upon the anticipated circumstances. It was this annual variation in reported product costs, that Saeki identified as the major difference from a classical standard cost system. In such a standard cost system, product costs were not subjected to such frequent revisions. According to Saeki, the advantage of the budgetary standard approach was that, "It more accurately reflected the economic realities of the coming year".

The cost system was linked directly to the firm's financial reporting system. The budgetary standards were used as the basis for inventory valuation and product costing. For example, if the firm had 500 cases of the antibiotic Shiomarin on hand at year end, then the value of inventory of that product for financial reporting purposes was 500 times the budgetary standard cost of a case. For tax purposes, manufacturing variances from the firm's budgetary standard costs were prorated between cost of goods sold and inventory.

The conceptual work on the new system began in 1974 when the four categories of cost elements recognized by the then existing system were increased to nine. The original four categories were raw material, packaging material, labor, and other expenses. The additional five cost categories were developed by splitting the category, "other expenses" into six new ones; utilities, equipment repair, testing, subcontracting, other production expenses, and overhead.

The utilities category contained the costs of the various forms of energy consumed in the firm's production facilities including compressed air, vacuum, waste water, steam, and air conditioning. Equipment repair captured the cost of repairing the production and research equipment. Testing included all the costs associated with checking the quality of raw materials and products such as the purity of the chemicals manufactured. Subcontracting represented the cost of bulk chemicals and formulations manufactured by subcontractors for Shionogi.

Other production expenses included items that could be identified directly by the various departments. For example, it included the costs of the small supplies, such as gloves, that were used by each department. The consumption of these supplies was monitored at the department level hence, the ability to assign them directly to each department.

Overhead included all non-production expenses. It was further subdivided into direct and indirect categories depending upon the function of the department that was generating the costs. The costs of the technical development departments were treated as direct overhead because they could be unambiguously associated with a production department. For example, the costs of the technical development staff inventing and testing a new improved production process for a specific production department could meaningfully be assigned to that department In contrast, the costs of service departments, such as General Affairs, that supplied common services were considered indirect overhead.

These new categories were identified so that costs could be more accurately assigned first to departments, and then to products. Reporting highly accurate product costs, the primary objective of the cost system, required that the accuracy of both the first stage of cost allocation, in which costs were assigned to the departments, and the second stage, in which costs were assigned to products, had to be improved. An increase in system sophistication was required because, as the level of automation in the plant increased, the accuracy of assigning the other expenses to the production departments via direct labor hours, the basis used by the old system, became more and more questionable. This accuracy problem was further compounded by a shift in the nature of the work performed by the labor force from direct labor "touch" operations to more indirect labor activities, such as technical development and process monitoring.

In the new system, three types of departments were recognized; production, service, and indirect. Production departments were directly involved in the manufacture of pharmaceutical products. Service departments performed equipment repair, supplied utilities, or provided testing services. Indirect departments either provided technical development support to the production departments or common services such as General Affairs.

The number of each type of department, at each production location, was a function of the size and complexity of the facility. Overall, there were 21 production, four repair, and 15 utilities departments. With the exception of Kuise, there were only two indirect departments at the production plants; General Affairs and Warehousing. In contrast, at Kuise there were ten indirect departments including three for technical development (Bulk Manufacturing, Formulation, and Packaging), in addition to seven indirect departments that provided common services (Quality Control, Produc-

tion Planning, Accounting, Personnel, General Affairs, Warehousing, and Engineering). While these departments served all of the production facilities only the three technical development ones had a small number of personnel located at the other three plants. These individuals all reported to Kuise, not to personnel at the plants at which they worked.

Of the 21 production departments, five were dedicated to bulk chemical production, 12 to formulation, and four to packaging. Each of these production departments was responsible for a single major production process. Thus, the ability to generate accurate departmental costs was equivalent to being able to generate accurate process and hence product costs. Therefore, the second stage of cost allocation, from departments to products, was very simple, typically being a one to one relationship. However, when joint products were produced did this stage become complex.

The identification of the three types of departments allowed the assignment of costs in the first stage of cost allocation to be undertaken in two steps. In the first step, the direct costs (which included directly assigned overhead, raw material, packaging material, and labor) were assigned to all three types of departments. In the second step, the direct costs of the service and indirect departments were allocated to the production departments using a two-tier procedure.

In the first tier of this procedure, the direct costs of the service departments were allocated to the indirect and production departments. This tier started with the costs of the repair department and allocated them to the other service departments as well as to the indirect and production departments. Next the costs of the utility's departments were allocated next, followed by the costs of the testing departments. Three different bases were used to allocate the direct costs of the service departments to the indirect and production departments. For the repair costs, the repair material costs plus a charge for the time spent in the repair department was used. For utility costs, the actual use of each utility was measured and used as the basis for the allocation procedure. Finally, the costs of the testing departments were allocated directly to the products using the number of test hours per product. Once a department's costs were allocated, no costs could be allocated back to it, thus avoiding the problem of reciprocal services (see Exhibit 4).

Sometimes, the utility allocation procedures were more complex. If a single meter was used to measure the consumption of a utility by several departments, then the charge for that meter was allocated to the appropriate departments using a separate procedure. For example, when the electricity consumption for multiple departments was measured on a single electricity meter, a usage matrix was developed that estimated the percentage use of electricity by each department. This usage matrix was used to allocate the metered electricity costs to the departments within the metering point. The same general technique was used for the expenses associated with water usage and air conditioning. Three bases were used to establish usage matrixes; head count, space utilization, and machine hour usage. Head count was used for utilities such as electricity, water, and gas. Space was used to allocate utilities such as air conditioning and heating. Finally, machine hours was used to allocate such utilities as compressed air.

When the first tier of the procedure was complete all of the cost of the service departments had been allocated to either the indirect or the production departments. In the second tier of the procedure, the costs of the indirect departments, including their share of the service department costs, were allocated to the production departments (see Exhibit 5). The nature of the allocation process depended upon whether the departments' costs were treated as direct or indirect overhead. Direct overhead, the costs of the technical development departments, was driven directly to the production departments based upon usage. This procedure was relatively straightforward since production oriented technical development expenses were monitored at the process level and thus were directly assignable to the production departments. Indirect overhead, the costs of the departments that supplied common services, were allocated to the production departments using the ratios of the processing costs (direct production department costs plus allocated Service department costs but excluding allocated Technical Development department costs) of the production departments.

In the final step, product costs were determined by assigning the fully loaded production department costs to products based upon direct manufacturing expenses. Thus, wherever possible production costs were assigned directly (as material, labor, testing, and subcontracting). Finally, for the costs that could not be meaningfully assigned to products, they were allocated using the cost of processing. The process of generating production costs is shown in Exhibit 6.

Uses of Cost Information

There were three major uses of cost information at Shionogi. The first was to help guide the firm's kaizen activities, the second was to help set product prices, and the third was to help manage the firm's product mix.

Kaizen and Standard Costing The purpose of the firm's kaizen program was primarily to reduce material costs. This focus was driven by the cost structure of the firm's products: 70–75 percent of the cost of a typical product consisted of raw material and packaging material. The kaizen program and the standard cost system were used to reinforce each other. Shionogi identified two sets of standards. The first set was the budgetary standards created by the cost system and the second was called the "updated" standards. These updated standards did not form part of the firm's financial reporting process, they were used solely for the managerial purpose of measuring the progress of the firm's kaizen program.

No adjustments for expected kaizen savings were incorporated into the budgetary standards. In contrast, the updated standards were revised as frequently as necessary (up to several times a year) to reflect the results of the firm's kaizen program and were used to monitor its effectiveness (see Exhibit 7). Any difference between the two standards was due to either kaizen improvements that had not yet been reflected in the budgetary standards or anticipated changes in the production process that had not yet been reflected in the updated standards (see Exhibit 8).

Standard setting was considered a very important task at Shionogi. There were five standard setting functions, one for each of the five major manufacturing activities. They were located in the appropriate department:

Manufacturing Activity	Location
Bulk Manufacturing	Chemical Process Technical Development Department
Formulation	Formulation Technical Development Department
Packaging	Packaging Technical Development Department
Testing	Quality Control Department
Equipment	Engineering Department

The personnel responsible for setting standards were selected from among the most highly knowledgeable, skilled, and reliable workers in the technical development staff. Many were holders of a master's degree in chemistry or pharmacy. They were usually assigned from the day they joined the firm to a technical development department. Sometimes, standard setters were temporarily assigned to the production floor to increase their in-depth understanding of the production process. This increased knowledge was considered valuable because it allowed them to set more accurate standards.

The operational control roles of the cost system and the kaizen costing programs clearly intersected. Great care was taken to ensure that the two systems did not create conflicting signals. Upper management did not permit cost reduction pressures to be created by setting the budgetary standards at unrealistic levels compared to the current actual. This constraint was placed on the standard setting group to avoid any temptation on their part to influence the direction of the kaizen process by the way they set the budgetary standards.

At Shionogi variance analysis was not used solely at the management level to identify production problems. It was also used at the production supervisor level to help workers improve efficiency. For every lot that was manufactured, actual performance was compared to the updated standards to generate usage variances. The importance of these variances to the kaizen program was highlighted by their availability to production supervisors. On-line availability of the kaizen variances was considered important by management as they felt it caused the work force to become highly cost conscious. Workers were neither rewarded nor punished for creating variances. However, overall performance, including variances, was taken into account in reviews that lead to both promotion and pay raises.

Supervisors were expected to try to analyze the cause of significant negative variances. If the cause was within their control, the supervisors were expected to take the appropriate action to correct the problem. If it was not under their control, then they were expected to ask the technical development staff to help resolve the problem. To help them achieve this objective, production supervisors had on-line access to the updated standards and the actual production results for each lot and hence the kaizen variances. Access however, was limited to variances specified in terms of units produced, supervisors were not provided with access to variances specified in monetary terms. More detailed financial analysis, including some data expressed in monetary terms, was available but not on-line. These reports were available to management and some production supervisors.

The dynamic nature of the kaizen process was illustrated by the interaction between the workforce and the technical development departments. The work force reported to the appropriate technical development department after every lot was completed to discuss the effectiveness of their kaizen activities. The workers were expected to identify the portion of the variance that was due to kaizen. Once the standard setter and the workers responsible for that chemical process had agreed on the level of kaizen improvement, the updated, but not the budgetary standards, were adjusted accordingly.

Modifying updated standards required three steps. First, the technical development department tested a new process in the laboratory or pilot plant to see if it achieved the anticipated improvement. Second, once the improvement was confirmed, the technical development staff asked the production staff to run the new process on the production line, and checked the result. Finally, when the anticipated result was attained, the production staff repeated the same process on their own and confirmed the improved result by themselves. When all three steps were successfully completed, the management authorized the new standards as official and the firm's databases were modified accordingly.

The primary function of the standards—to create downward pressure on costs—required that the standards were carefully set. There was no point in setting standards that could not be achieved. Rather, standards were set to create achievable targets that require stretching on the part of the workforce. Consequently, the primary role of the standard setter was to ensure that the standard setting process achieved its objective. That is, both budgetary and updated standards reflected the most up to date information. The budgetary standards were revised on an annual basis and the updated standards were revised on a monthly or as needed basis.

If the new updated standard created negative variance in the future, because it was too difficult to achieve consistently, it was reduced to more accurately reflect sustainable levels of performance. Thus, the variances determined from the updated standards were expected to be either zero or slightly positive due to kaizen activities that were yet to be reflected. However, natural variations in the yield of the chemical processes sometimes caused these variances to be small but negative.

The price of drugs in Japan was established by legislation. The National Health Insurance (NHI) reimbursement prices of new pharmaceutical drugs in Japan were set by the Ministry of Health and Welfare (MHW).

Sometimes, these prices were based upon the manufacturer's production costs. The cost reported by the firm's standard cost systems required two major adjustments before they could be used to help set the price of a new drug. The first adjustment reduced the amount of depreciation charged to the drug during its first few years of production. The cost system, in accordance with Japanese financial accounting practices, used an accelerated depreciation charge. Consequently, in the first few years of a products life, very high depreciation charges were allocated to it. This high depreciation charge was further compounded by the low volume of sales that most new drugs achieved in their first few years. Therefore, a second adjustment for more realistic long-term production volumes was required to generate an adjusted cost that could be used for cost-plus pricing and price negotiations in general.

Product Mix Decisions   The cost information generated by the firm's standard cost system was also used to support product mix decisions such as sourcing and discontinuance of products. Often, however, the information provided by the standard cost system was insufficient to support such decisions and special cost studies were required. The primary purpose of these special studies was to determine the split between variable and fixed costs for the specific formulation under review. A formulation was a specific dosage for a given product. For example, the product Shiomarin was packaged in the following formulations; 250mg, 500mg, and 1gram.

Raw material, packaging material, utilities and subcontracting expenses were always considered variable when making product mix decisions. A portion of labor was considered variable if, either part-time labor was used in the manufacturing process or if the decision to out source a manufacturing process was considered permanent. While Shionogi employees had lifetime employment contracts, permanent out sourcing allowed the work force to be reassigned to other production areas. Therefore treating them, at least partially, as a variable cost was considered more appropriate. If the out sourcing decision was considered short-term, then the labor costs were considered fixed and ignored for decision making purposes.

Shionogi normally would not sell a formulation at a loss. However, it would occasionally sell a loss-making formulation as long as it had a positive contribution; that is, if its selling price exceeded its variable cost. Only occasionally would a formulation create this situation because the typical product's variable costs were so high. Consequently, if a product had a positive contribution, it was usually profitable. If a drug was unprofitable, Shionogi would negotiate with the MHW to try to increase the NHI reimbursement price sufficiently to make the drug profitable. Shionogi took its social responsibility to provide drugs seriously and would only withdraw drugs as a last resort.

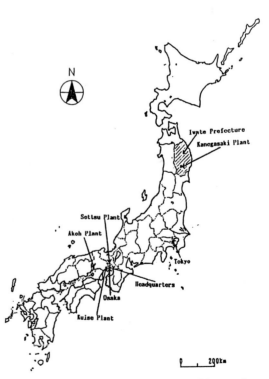

EXHIBIT 1   The Manufacturing Plants of Shionogi & Co., Ltd. in Japan

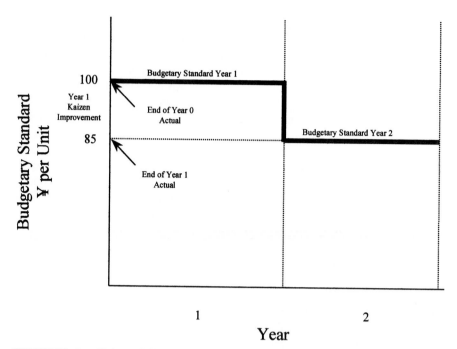

EXHIBIT 2 **Shionogi & Co., Ltd., Setting Budgetary Standards with no Expectation of Change During the Coming Year**

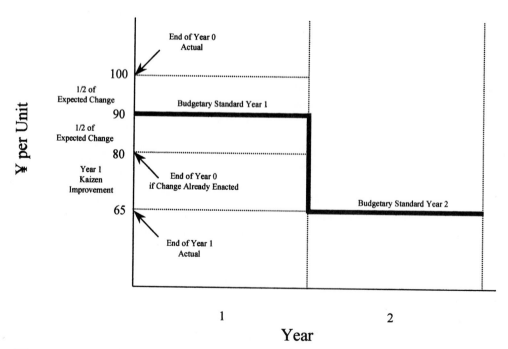

EXHIBIT 3 **Shionogi & Co., Ltd., Setting Budgetary Standards with an Expectation of Change Midway During the Coming Year**

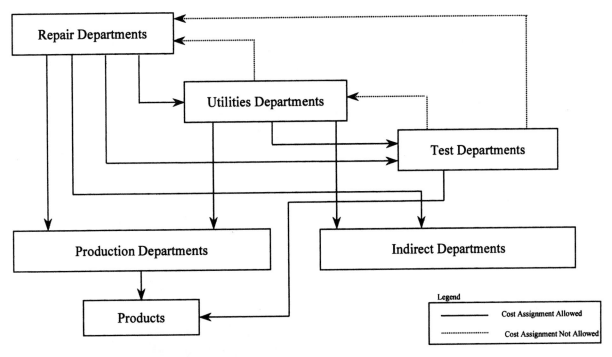

EXHIBIT 4   Shionogi & Co., Ltd., Reciprocal Allocation of Service Departments

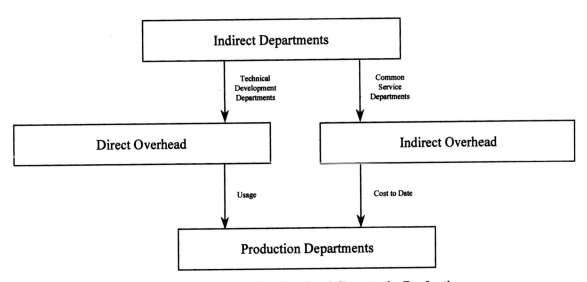

EXHIBIT 5   Shionogi & Co., Ltd., Allocating Overhead Costs to the Production Departments

	Cost Element	Standard Quantity	*	Budgeted Rate
Material Cost	Raw Materials	Standard Quantity		Budgeted Unit Price
	Packaging Materials	Standard Quantity		Budgeted Unit Price
Labor Cost	Labor Cost	Direct Operating Time		Budgeted Wage Rate
Overhead Cost	Utility Expenses	Machine Hours		Budgeted Burden Rate
	Repair Charges	Machine Hours		Budgeted Burden Rate
	Cost of Testing	Time for Testing Operations		Budgeted Burden Rate
	Amount Paid to Subcontractors	Quantity Required		Budgeted Price
	Direct Overhead	Direct Operating Time		Budgeted Burden Rate
	Indirect Overhead	Cost of Processing		Budgeted Burden Rate

EXHIBIT 6   Shionogi & Co., Ltd., The Process of Generating Product Costs

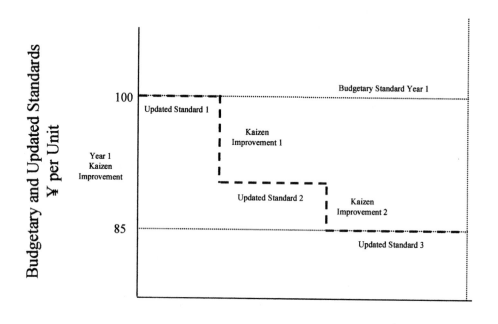

Year 1

EXHIBIT 7   Shionogi & Co., Ltd., Setting Updated Standards with No Expectation of Change During the Coming Year

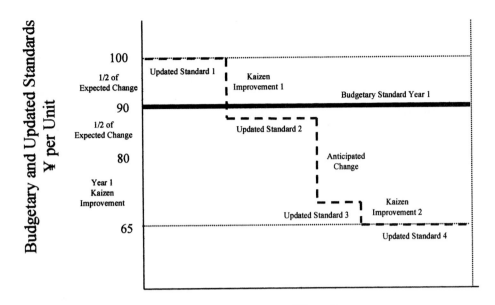

Year 1

EXHIBIT 8   Shionogi & Co., Ltd., Setting Updated Standards with an Expectation of Change Midway During the Coming Year

HEWLETT-PACKARD: QUEENSFERRY TELECOMMUNICATIONS DIVISION

We implemented cost driver accounting primarily to influence the manufacturability of our products. We wanted our engineers to understand the economic consequences of their design choices. We wanted to ensure that our products were both competitively priced and profitable.

Jim Rigby, Division Controller

Queensferry Telecommunications Division (QTD) was established in South Queensferry, Scotland, in 1965. Within the broader Hewlett-Packard organization structure, QTD was a part of the Microwave and Communications Group, which in turn was a part of the Test and Measurement Sector. QTD's main business was the design and manufacture of electronic test and measurement equipment for the international telecommunications industry. In 1990, QTD produced eight different product lines containing over 100 different products. These products were designed to monitor, measure, and find faults in telephone lines. In 1990, QTD employed

approximately 640 people and was expected to generate revenues of about $100 million.

From the outset, QTD was committed to high quality and customer satisfaction. The emphasis on high quality encouraged a vertically integrated production structure, with the division doing much of the low-level fabrication activity (e.g., sheet metal work) in-house. The emphasis on customer satisfaction led to relatively long product life cycles and a commitment to support products long after they ceased to be produced.

During the 1980s, the telecommunications industry switched from analog to digital technology. This switch reduced product life cycles and accelerated the ongoing shift toward automated production. The switch also allowed several firms with digital circuit design experience to enter the telecommunications market.

The Cost Driver Accounting System

Cost driver accounting (CDA) was initially developed by Hewlett-Packard (HP) at its Roseville Network Division in California. It had spread rapidly and voluntarily throughout the organization, and, by 1990, over half of HP's facilities had adopted CDA. The CDA project at

This case was prepared by Professor Robin Cooper and Professor Kiran Verma of MIT.

Copyright © 1990 by the President and Fellows of Harvard College. Harvard Business School case 191-067.

QTD began in 1989, and the system was installed for fiscal year 1990, which ran from November to October.

At QTD, CDA was expected to provide the following benefits:

1. Encourage design for manufacturability.
2. Improve QTD's understanding of its true cost structure, thereby facilitating manufacturing cost reduction.
3. Encourage management to support Total Quality Control methodology and eliminate waste.
4. Provide improved information to monitor production performance.
5. Provide improved product cost information to support pricing and other strategic decisions.

The CDA was well received at QTD. As Harry McCarter, Production Supervisor, commented,

> In the old days, the only way to reduce the cost of a product was to reduce its labor content. Material and engineering costs were designed into the products and were effectively fixed. Using CDA we can design products so that their material, engineering, and labor costs are minimized.

System Design   In CDA, allocation bases such as direct labor hours were replaced with cost drivers that both captured the underlying economics of manufacture and made it easier for product designers to understand those economics. The cost driver accounting system at QTD contained eight drivers, one for each of the seven major production processes and one for materials procurement. The CDA system recognized three distinct processes in board assembly: automatic insertion, manual insertion prior to wave solder, and manual insertion post wave solder. Automatic insertion was performed for two types of components: integrated circuits, and axial components such as resistors and capacitors. Prior to wave soldering, components that could not be inserted automatically due to size or position on the board were inserted manually. In post wave solder, components that would be destroyed by the wave solder process were manually inserted. For all three board assembly processes, the number of insertions was used to drive costs to the products.

In the fourth production process, the wave soldered boards were tested automatically. The cost driver used to assign test costs to products was number of parts tested. This driver was selected because it captured the complexity of the testing process. An alternative driver, test hours, was not considered appropriate because the length of testing did not vary proportionately with the number of parts tested.

The loaded boards were assembled into completed products in the fifth production process. There were three assembly and test production units in which products were assembled and then tested. Different types of instruments were built in each unit depending on the technology used in the product line. One department assembled products just for British Telecom, while the other two assembled the remaining seven product lines. Because assembly was mostly a manual process, labor hours were used to assign assembly costs to products in these departments.

Instrument testing, the sixth process, was an integral part of assembly. Instruments were tested during assembly and on completion. Test hours were used to drive testing costs to the products. The assembly and test unit managers were dissatisfied with this driver for two reasons. First, some tests were automatic while others were manual. These two types of tests consumed different resources. Second, standard tests were designed to ensure that the instrument was operating properly, while special tests were designed to find the cause for an instrument to fail a standard test. The amount of standard testing was captured well by the number of test hours assigned to each instrument. But testing was effectively random, and the CDA averaged the cost of special testing across all products. Management was still working on identifying better drivers for special testing.

The sheet metal for the cabinets was cut to size, shaped, and prepared in the fabrication department. This was the seventh production process recognized by the CDA. Fabrication was a process scheduled for outsourcing in the near future, and rather than spend time trying to identify a more appropriate drive, management decided to use direct labor hours to drive metal fabrication costs to products.

Procurement activities included purchasing, material handling, and storage. The costs of these activities were driven to the products using direct material costs. There was general dissatisfaction with this driver because procurement contained a number of distinct processes, each requiring a different driver. In the next six to nine months, management expected to complete a special study to determine additional drivers for the procurement process.

Setting the Rates

Cost driver rates were determined twice a year. Each department manager was interviewed to identify how much of the department budget related to each production process and hence driver. For example, as shown in Exhibit 1, out of a total budget of $751,800, the quality assurance manager expected to spend $4,000 on the autoinsert process. The total cost of each driver was determined by summing all department costs. This total cost was then divided by the budgeted total driver quantity to give the driver rate. For example, for the second half of fiscal 1990, the cost driver rate of $0.07 per automatic insertion (as per Exhibit 2) was obtained by dividing the total cost of automatic insertion of $248,100 (as per Exhibit 1) by the budgeted total driver quantity of 3,695,200 automatic insertions.

Variance Analysis

Rigby commented on the objectives of variance analysis at QTD.

> Variance analysis has always formed part of our management control process. Our departmental managers are experienced in determining the reasons behind spending, efficiency, and cost variances, and then utilizing this knowledge in future planning cycles. The ability to manage and control to planned levels has always been an integral measure of a manager's performance and ability at QTD.
>
> Since installing cost-driver—based rates, all levels of management have a finer appreciation of the impact of operating at different levels of planned capacity. They now recognize the need to modify our cost structure according to activity levels or face the consequences, an erosion of margin.
>
> I view the variance report as the beacon that highlights the issues needing explanation and action. We benefit by our ability to recognize, and react to, changes in cost, volume, and profit plans.

In both the U.S. and the U.K., generally accepted accounting principles required that the cost-of-goods-sold figures for financial accounting purposes reflect both the standard costs of manufacturing and any significant variances. Since the cost driver accounting system reported standard costs, variances were required for inventory valuation purposes. Variances were also used to help evaluate the monthly performance of department managers. For example, how well they managed spending was evaluated via departmental spending variances.

The process of evaluating the managers of the three assembly and test production units highlighted a shortcoming in the existing design of the cost driver accounting system, which treated the three units as if they were a single unit. Consequently, the variances were computed as if there was only one assembly and test area. The unit managers were unhappy with this approach be-

cause they felt that the cost structures of the three units were different and therefore each unit should be evaluated individually. This dissatisfaction caused accounting to determine separate rates for each of the three units. As the managers had suspected, the cost driver rates for the second half of 1990 turned out to be quite different (see Exhibit 3).

Unit B's rates were particularly high because it was currently introducing many new products. At present, these new products were being produced in low volumes but were expected to be produced in much higher volumes in the future. The current low production volumes led to high cost driver rates because Unit B was staffed with a full complement of personnel even though it was producing below capacity.

A full complement of personnel was maintained because of HP's corporate policy against layoffs. As Rigby commented.

> One of the challenges of our business is to manage the reduction in the direct labor force without having any forced redundancies. I am pleased to say that HP has never been forced to lay people off. This is an impressive achievement considering that the technology is moving at such a rate that demand for manufacturing people is literally decreasing daily. Our adoption of CDA has increased this tendency by demonstrating the financial advantages of choosing automatic over manual insertion.

Rigby strongly felt that the three assembly units should be treated as a single entity in the CDA.

> I'm not at all keen to have three different sets of driver rates for assembly. Basically, because of the scale of the operation, we have split production into three separately managed units. However, it is the same basic process. Unit C benefits greatly from the injection that we get from the British Telecom Contract, so it has the lowest rates. Reporting three different sets of rates will create trouble. I do not want to have engineers telling me that they want their product, when it's launched, to be manufactured in units A, B, or C because the cost structure is inherently different. That's why I want to report only one set of driver rates.

Variance analysis was also performed for each of the eight cost driver processes identified by the cost driver accounting system. The following variances were calculated every month for each driver:

- The *spending variance* captured the difference between actual purchases and budgeted purchases for the month.
- The *volume variance* captured the difference between the actual quantity of cost driver units consumed in the month and the budgeted quantity calculated at the standard rate for that cost driver.

The British Telecom Contract

In 1984, QTD bid aggressively for a major contract with British Telecom. This bid was for a new product that was significantly different from the other products produced at QTD. The British Telecom product consisted of printed circuit boards that were rack mounted and did not require any cabinets or special assembly. The request-for-bid was given to two companies with the expectation that they would share in the business if their quotes were competitive. Despite bidding aggressively by pricing the contract on an incremental basis, the QTD bid was higher than its competitors. Consequently, it was awarded only $3 million of the British Telecom business that year.

The original contract was thought to be a one-time deal. However, in subsequent years, British Telecom placed requests-for-bids every year to the two companies. The amount of work offered to each firm was based on the bid price and the reliability of delivery achieved in the prior year. In the last six years QTD had been awarded business ranging from $3 million to $12 million per year.

The ability to meet British Telecom's delivery requirements was a major consideration in being awarded the contract. Since QTD did not know for sure whether an order would be placed, how big the order was going to be, or when it would be placed, it was forced to budget for an anticipated level of activity that included an estimate of the size of the contract.

At the end of fiscal 1989, British Telecom placed an order with QTD for $13 million production in fiscal 1990. In the first quarter of fiscal 1990, however, Telecom postponed delivery of $8 million of its purchase until the last quarter of 1990. This postponement caused production levels in the first half of fiscal 1990 to drop below budgeted levels (see Exhibit 4). The second quarter was the worst hit, even though actual volume in the second quarter exceeded that of the first quarter. Rigby commented,

> When the production volumes dropped in the first half of the year, we began to encounter volume variances. These variances were not significant in the first quarter, but by the second quarter they were very high. In a perfect world, spending would drop to offset lower production volumes. However, in environments like ours where we retain our employees, it is almost impossible for spending to be cut back when volume drops in a period.

The total volume variance for the first quarter was $43,000 unfavorable. The unfavorable volume variance for the second quarter was nearly $1,000,000 (see Exhibit 5). A variance of this magnitude was thought likely to attract the attention of the auditors and therefore require restatement of year-end inventory values. To avoid reporting large variances in the second half of fiscal 1990, QTD management decided to compute the cost driver rates for the second half of fiscal 1990 using lower production volumes that reflected the postponement of the British Telecom contract.

The postponement of the contract and its impact on the firm caused Rigby to question the cost driver accounting system. He voiced his concerns in a meeting with Finlay McKenzie, General Manager of QTD.

JR The British Telecom contract is different from our core business. We price it incrementally and, therefore should cost it incrementally. Averaging cost driver rates across the two types of business makes our core business look a lot more profitable than it really is. I think we should develop two sets of cost driver rates, one for the core business and the other for the British Telecom contract. I did a quick analysis of the British Telecom Contract, and its driver rates are very different (Exhibit 6).

FM I don't know how you can say that the British Telecom business is different from our core business. The way I look at it, our core business consists of two elements: base business, consisting of small orders from a wide base of customers, and big deals, which are large orders from the national telecommunications firms. Big deals range from $0.5 million to $4.0 million. The British Telecom contract is simply a larger version of a big deal.

JR That's not right, Finlay. We don't discount other big deals to the same extent that we discount the British Telecom contract. Besides, even though we get business from British Telecom every year, its size and uncertainty make it inherently more risky than the core business.

FM Again, I don't agree. The British Telecom contract has been with us for the last five years and will probably be with us for the next 10. There is no difference between our winning four $2 million big deals and getting an $8 million order from British Telecom. The risks are just the same. The British Telecom contract is a cash cow. It funds the development of new products for our core business. The cost system as designed reflects the reality of our business.

EXHIBIT 1

QUEENSFERRY TELECOMMUNICATIONS DIVISION

Department Overhead Analysis by Process: Second Half Fiscal 1990 Budgets Revision

$(000)

	AUTO INSERT	PRELOAD	BACKLOAD	AUTOTEST	INSTRUMENT ASSEMBLY	INSTRUMENT TEST	PANEL FAB	PROCURE	TOTAL $
Quality	4.0	1.2	1.0	4.0	49.5	532.6	13.4	146.1	751.8
Manufacturing management	11.0	56.4	21.3	24.8	49.6	162.7	24.6	38.8	389.2
Materials management	10.9	22.1	13.0	3.8	28.9	61.4	14.2	1,995.9	2,150.2
Fabrication							441.6		441.6
Assembly	146.7	557.3	218.3	8.9	609.7	1,193.7	39.0		2,773.6
Engineering	75.5	97.7	21.8	110.4	74.1	44.4	—	67.0	490.9
Total	248.1	734.7	275.4	151.9	811.8	1,994.8	532.8	2,247.9	6,997.3

EXHIBIT 2

QUEENSFERRY TELECOMMUNICATIONS DIVISION

Manufacturing Cost Driver Rates

Fiscal 1990

		RATES	
PROCESS	DRIVER	FIRST HALF STANDARD	SECOND HALF STANDARD
Autoinsert	Parts Inserted	$ 0.09	$ 0.07
Manual insert Prewave solder	Parts inserted	0.23	0.24
Manual insert Postwave solder	Parts inserted	0.70	0.75
PC autotest	Parts tested	0.04	0.04
Instrument assembly	Labor hours	50.84	58.34
Instrument test	Test hours	63.36	82.60
Fabrication	Labor hours	59.69	40.88
Procurement	% of direct material	26.68%	26.51%

EXHIBIT 3

QUEENSFERRY TELECOMMUNICATIONS DIVISION

Cost Driver Rates for the Instrument Assembly and Instrument Test Departments
for the Second Half of Fiscal 1990

| | INSTRUMENT ASSEMBLY | | | | INSTRUMENT TEST | | | |
	UNIT A	UNIT B	UNIT C	TOTAL	UNIT A	UNIT B	UNIT C	TOTAL
Quality	22.1	14.1	13.3	49.5	272.8	146.2	113.6	532.6
Manufacturing management	27.4	10.1	12.1	49.6	83.4	50.3	29.0	162.7
Materials management	13.9	7.2	7.8	28.9	26.0	19.5	15.9	61.4
Fabrication	—	—	—	—	—	—	—	—
Assembly	321.7	131.4	156.6	609.7	405.5	434.9	353.3	1,193.7
Engineering	24.7	24.7	24.7	74.1	14.8	14.8	14.8	44.4
Total	409.8	187.5	214.5	811.8	802.5	665.7	526.6	1,994.8
Number of operations	7.21	2.32	4.39	13.92	8.82	4.47	10.86	24.15
Cost per operation	$56.84	$80.94	$48.89	$58.34	$91.03	$148.93	$48.51	$82.60

EXHIBIT 4

QUEENSFERRY TELECOMMUNICATIONS DIVISION

Budgeted and Actual Spending and Production Levels
for the First Half of Fiscal Year 1990

| | SPENDING ($ THOUSANDS) | | | | VOLUME (THOUSANDS) | | | |
| | BUDGET | | ACTUAL | | PLAN | | ACTUAL | |
	Q1	Q2	Q1	Q2	Q1	Q2	Q1	Q2
Autoinsert	$214	$225	$207	$203	1,946	2,662	1,566	1,709
Manual insert prewave solder	422	441	396	373	1,672	2,120	1,389	1,325
Manual insert postwave solder	160	167	149	141	210	257	173	168
PC autotest	91	91	91	58	1,866	2,505	1,891	1,936
Instrument assembly	415	433	384	392	8.1	8.6	9.0	6.4
Instrument test	918	966	860	891	13.4	16.5	13.7	12.8
Lower-level fabrication	292	315	264	402	5.1	5.0	6.2	6.0
Procurement	1,191	1,227	1,190	1,288	4,267	4,800	4,150	3,860
Total	$3,703	$3,865	$3,541	$3,748				

EXHIBIT 5

QUEENSFERRY COMMUNICATIONS DIVISION
Manufacturing Overhead Variances
for the First Half of Fiscal Year 1990
$(000)

	SPEND VARIANCE		VOLUME VARIANCE	
	Q1	Q2	Q1	Q2
Autoinsert	7	22	(34)	(86)
Manual insert prewave solder	26	68	(65)	(183)
Manual insert postwave solder	11	26	(26)	(62)
PC autotest	—	33	1	(23)
Instrument assembly	31	41	46	(112)
Instrument test	58	75	19	(234)
Lower-level fabrication	28	(87)	47	54
Procurement	1	(61)	(31)	(251)
	162	117	(43)	(898)

EXHIBIT 6

QUEENSFERRY TELECOMMUNICATIONS DIVISION
Driver Rates for British Telecommunications Contract
for the Second Half of 1990

	BUDGETED ($000)	DRIVER VOLUMES	DRIVER RATES
Autoinsert	85.3	1,797.2	0.05
Manual prewave solder	46.0	1,099.0	0.04
Manual postwave solder	18.5	53.4	0.35
PC auto test	82.8	2,382.8	0.04
Instrument assembly	214.5	4.39	48.89
Instrument test	526.8	10.86	48.51
Lower-level fabrication	54.2	1.9	28.50
Procurement	265.0	2,485.0	10.66%

AT&T PARADYNE

Our Design and Manufacturing Engineering groups are using Activity-Based Cost (ABC) along with quality and cycle time information to make life-cycle cost decisions.

ABC/ABM *Team Leader*

The Company

AT&T acquired Paradyne Corporation, a company specializing in the data communications equipment, in February, 1989. Operating as a wholly owned AT&T subsidiary, AT&T Paradyne designed and produced medium- and high-speed data communications equipment that provided the interface between telephone networks and computers. AT&T Paradyne, in 1994 employed approximately 3,000 team members and generated about $500 million in sales.

The company faced intense competition in all of its market segments—digital service units, modems, net-

work management systems and services, multiplexers, and channel extension devices. No competitor had more than one-third of any market, each product market had a different leader, and, in most cases, five or six competitors represented 95% of the market.

The company's headquarters was located in Largo, about midway up the western (Gulf) coast of Florida, in a 525,000 square foot facility. Product research and development were done both at the Largo facility and at AT&T Bell Laboratories facilities in Middletown, New Jersey.

Total Quality Management

AT&T Paradyne's General Management Team (GMT), consisting of the President and direct reports, launched a Total Quality Management program shortly after the AT&T acquisition in 1989. The GMT created a Mission Statement:

"To be recognized by our customers as the leader in providing quality data communications products and services world-wide."

Professor Robert S. Kaplan prepared this case.
Copyright © 1995 by the President and Fellows of Harvard College. Harvard Business School case 195-165.

Customer focus and quality values had become integrated into business practices and the daily work of team members. Senior executives led the rollout of continuous improvement practices which included an explicit model of cooperative Customer-Supplier relations. The business planning process was renamed the "Strategic Quality Management Process" to emphasize the goals of customer satisfaction, team member satisfaction, and achievement of excellent shareholder returns. Customer Value Added, People Value Added, and Economic Value Added became the primary quality metrics for this process. The Customer Value Added process used formal competitor comparisons and benchmarking to measure AT&T Paradyne's value to its customers, relative to both competitors and, through benchmarking, best-in-class companies.

By 1994, the company had identified ten Customer Satisfaction Predictors (CSP). The CSP's were selected as quality indicators of critical business processes (see Exhibit 1):

Business Process	Customer Satisfaction Predictors
Build and Develop Products	Field Product Failures
	New Products Late
	New Product Cycle Time
Maintenance and Repair	Install & Service Defects
	Service Call Cycle Time
Installation	Order Defects
	Units Shipped Late
Sales Support	Order Cycle Time
	Product Problem Response
Order Management	Invoice Defects

Charts for each of the ten CSP metrics, showing monthly results and trends, along with target and annual challenge goals, were clearly displayed on the walls of all AT&T Paradyne's worldwide facilities. The CSP's had also been imbedded into an incentive plan for all team members. Team members could earn an annual bonus based on performance measured by a weighted average of targets: 60% on achieving targeted levels for the CSP's and 40% on achieving a target level for AT&T Paradyne's MOI—Measured Operating Income. The CSP metrics signaled the quality of the overall products or service provided. Each operational area collected and maintained its own internal metrics that linked local operational quality and time-based performance to the company-wide CSP metrics.

The People Value Added (PVA) mission was to

"Create an environment wherein all team members are empowered partners sharing responsibility for supporting business strategies."

Seven initiatives and associated metrics had been formulated to fulfill the PVA mission:

- Strategic Planning: Performance and Planning
- Empowerment/Teaming: Adequacy of Communications
- Diversity: Charter and Mission
- Sourcing/ Transformation of Talent: Lateral Career Planning
- Continuous Learning and Development: Continuous Performance Improvement
- Team Member Well-Being: Partners in Improvement Survey
- Reward and Recognition

Measures had been defined and data were being collected along each of these seven initiatives.

Amidst the intense commitment to quality and emphasis on responsiveness to customers, team-members, suppliers and shareholders, the manufacturing finance community at AT&T Paradyne launched an intiative to improve dramatically the quality of the financial data they provided.

Developing an Activity-Based Cost Model

AT&T Paradyne's manufacturing cost system in 1990 was still based on the traditional approach of assigning materials and production overhead to products as percentage markups over materials cost and direct labor. The distortions from continuing to use a direct-labor based system, however, had become painfully obvious to everyone. Fifty years ago, the assembly of electronic components on printed circuit boards had involved mostly hand insertion of components. By the mid-1970s, most components were placed by automatic through-hole insertion, though many circuit boards still required a large number of components to be manually placed. During the past few years, a new technology. Surface Mount Technology (SMT), had been introduced in which electronic components were automatically mounted and then soldered on printed circuit boards that had been prepared with a tacky solder paste. AT&T Paradyne's cost system had not been capturing this dramatic change in technology. In 1990, production overhead was being applied at a rate over 500% of direct labor costs. But even worse, the direct labor routing data in the Materials Requirements Planning System (MRP) had become obsolete and would have required a major effort to bring up to date. With direct labor shrinking in importance, managers made the decision to eliminate direct labor reporting and manual labor routing maintenance and move to an activity-based system whereby costs would be accumulated by production process and applied based on the actual activity volumes in each process.

In 1991, a finance and a materials manager developed a simple ABC model that used only two drivers: volume — measured by number of units, and, for non-volume related expenses, part numbers. The cost per part number of about $1,000 led to very high reported costs for low volume products with many unique components. Managers and engineers concurred that the $1,000 per part number cost was ⎧ simplistic and grossly over-costed ⎫ several minor
⎪uct costs were
⎪eliminated en-
⎪system. Thus,
⎪t only for in-
⎭ory valuation

⎧eam includ-
⎪ystems, and
⎪he system.
⎪model that
⎪rivers such
⎪s, and test
⎪and pur-
⎭acquisi-

⎧ext two
⎪zed and
⎪heering
⎪ted ac-
⎪target
⎪d ex-
⎪ment.
⎪the
⎭eam

es
n
s
een

- Magnetics, Fuses, Switches, Wire, Cable
- Printed Wire Boards, Plastic, LCD, Memory switches
- Labels, Manuals, Cabinets, Packaging
- Integrated circuits
- ASICS, Oscillators, Active devices
- Subcontracted OEM
- Dropped Shipped Parts
- Passive devices

Material acquisition costs were assigned to separate activity cost pools for each of the eight commodity types. Initially, the materials acquisition cost was allocated as a percentage markup over materials purchase cost. Managers determined, however, that materials acquisition activity was driven more by the number of purchase orders and receipts rather than by the costs of the materials ordered. The system now calculated a standard cost per piece received for each of the eight commodity groups. In this way, commodities ordered in high volumes under long-term contracts had lower assigned acquisition costs than commodities ordered in low volumes under arrangements where the ordering cost was high.

Engineers and managers considered the current system for assigning materials acquisition cost to be greatly superior to the company-wide average percentage markups used previously. The system signaled the benefits from outsourcing some of the purchasing function. For selected supply items, such as nuts, bolts, and packaging materials, purchasing managers had authorized vendors to maintain and continually replenish supplies in the factory. Since no activities by purchasing people were required, these items received no materials acquisition burden.

But managers could still see room for improvement. The purchasing from preferred suppliers had been streamlined (36 vendors supplied 86% of the parts purchased), but the system did not recognize the lower cost of ordering from these preferred vendors. Nor did it reflect the much higher effort required to order a new part versus an existing part. And freight costs could not be traced to the method of transportation used. Currently all freight costs were assigned to the receiving commodity cost pool, based on number of receipts, and included in the cost per piece received.

Production costs were the direct and indirect costs associated with converting raw materials and purchased parts into a finished product. Production activities included inserting or placing electronic components onto printed circuit boards, assembling boards into housings, and testing components, boards, and the finished products. Production costs were accumulated in production activity cost pools in the plant, such as Surface Mount Technology (SMT), automated insertion (AI), and pre-wave hand insertion (see list of production cost pools in first column of Exhibit 3). Many costs, such as machine expenses and the costs of employees dedicated to production centers, could be traced directly to each of the production cost pools. The costs of indirect manufacturing departments (referred to internally as "vertical load), such as Manufacturing Management, Supply Line Management, Training Management, and Quality Management were assigned to production and support cost pools based on the percentage of actual support performed by the people in these manufacturing support departments. Thus, actual total costs assigned to the each production cost pool included its directly traceable actual production center costs plus a percentage (held constant through the year) of the costs of the manufacturing support departments. A standard rate for each production cost pool was estimated each year by dividing total budgeted expenses by the expected quantity of activity in the production cost pool. The last column in Exhibit 3 shows the budgeted cost driver rates for the production cost pools in 1994.

Support costs were the indirect costs associated with production activities. Support costs were assigned to major product groups based on monthly surveys of effort. The support costs assigned to product groups were then driven down to individual product units by an appropriate activity cost driver:

Support Cost Activity	Activity Cost Driver
Vendor Tooling	Units Manufactured
Master Schedulers	Units Manufactured
Planners	Units Manufactured
Traffic/Shipping/Warehouse	Units Shipped
QA Audit	Units Audited
Process and Test Engineering	Number of Engineering Change Revisions

Monthly Reporting

At the end of each month, the financial system accumulated actual expenses for each of the production and support departments. The actual monthly expenses assigned to each production cost pool were divided by the cost pool's actual activity cost driver quantities to ob-

tain the actual monthly cost driver rate for each activity; see Exhibit 4. The system also produced a graphical presentation of the monthly trends in the activity cost driver rate for the year (see Exhibit 5 for the Surface Mount Technology cost report). A similar calculation and presentation was prepared for the materials acquisition cost driver rates for the eight commodity classes (see Exhibit 6 for the report on integrated circuits (IC's)). When actual production volumes were well below those forecasted in the annual budget (as had occurred in the first six months of the year, see Exhibits 5 and 6) production center managers were expected to reduce their spending by eliminating weekend shifts and overtime, working fewer shifts during the week, and reducing the use of temporary workers.

The monthly charts on cost driver rates were posted and widely circulated in the plant to provide visibility to the plant's continuous improvement efforts. Whenever possible, the ABC team collected and displayed information on best-in-class competitor costs as well as "reach" objectives for these activities to serve as targets for local team members' process cost reductions.

An early success was achieved when the high cost of testing had led design engineers to examine closely how much functional testing was really required. They were able to replace a 72 hour heat stressing test with a more intensive two hour test that subjected boards to rapid extremes of severe heat and cold. Only 10% of products continued to be tested using the traditional 72 hour process, and when these products were replaced, the large burn-in ovens could be eliminated off the factory floor. Planners were also more aware of the benefits of batching as many boards as possible in the heat/cold stressing process. One cost team member reported:

> The acceptance of the ABC model has created awareness and focus among all team members on the opportunities for total cost reduction. Before, employees never saw financial results. Now they can see monthly how their activities affect product costs.

One of the unique aspects of the AT&T Paradyne ABC system was its assignment of monthly actual costs to each of the major product groups. Rather than apply the actual monthly activity cost driver rate to all products that used a given production center, the system calculated separate rates, based on budgeted utilization, for each major product group using the procedure shown in the calculations below:

PRODUCT GROUP	PLANNED ACTIVITY VOLUME	%	ASSIGNED ACTUAL EXPENSES	ACTUAL ACTIVITY VOLUMES	ACTUAL COST DRIVER RATE
A1	3,000,000	50%	$100,000	2,000,000	$0.050
B2	2,000,000	33%	66,667	2,100,000	0.032
C3	1,000,000	17%	33,333	900,000	0.037
Total	6,000,000	100%	$200,000	5,000,000	$0.040

In this procedure, the actual monthly expenses (of $200,000) of the production activity cost pool are assigned to the three product groups using percentages derived from the percentage of capacity each group was expected to use. These percentages represented an implicit contract between each product group and manufacturing for use of the supplied capacity, since many expenses, such as equipment costs and occupancy were committed for the year.

The monthly cost driver rate for each product group, as shown in the last column of the above calculation, is obtained by dividing the assigned product group expenses by the actual cost driver quantity for that month for each group. In the numeric example, the A1 product group has a high cost driver rate because its actual activity volume was only 2/3 of that forecasted, while the B2 product group has a cost driver rate much lower than the average because its activity volume was 5% higher than the forecast. The ABC Project Team had initially implemented this approach, because, with the ABC system also being used for valuing inventory, they wanted all factory expenses to be applied to products. The team now advocated this approach because they felt that product groups that used less capacity than had been forecasted should be penalized, whereas product groups with sales higher than expected should be rewarded. Several product group managers had already started to phase out mature products based on the low profitability or even losses being reported from the ABC system.

Target Costing

Opportunities for cost reduction with AT&T Paradyne's manufacturing process technology, as with many discrete part manufacturing processes, were greatest during the initial product design phase. Decisions, such as product functionality, number of components, type of components, and use of common versus unique components, were made early in the life cycle of the product

and basically locked in 80–90% of the product's manufactured cost. Opportunities for cost reduction once the product had been released for production to the manufacturing departments were much more limited.

AT&T Paradyne engineers and managers had recently started to use the ABC information to work together in a target costing process (see Exhibit 7). The target costing process started with marketing managers estimating the price at which a new product with specified features and functionality could be sold to achieve a significant market position. The product team then subtracted the desired gross margin for the new product from the projected average selling price to obtain the desired or targeted manufacturing cost for the product. The manufacturing associate team determined an attainable target manufactured cost including materials, materials acquisition, production and support costs. The product team and the manufacturing associate team then interlocked on a target cost. New product engineers and manufacturing engineers worked to reduce existing materials and process costs to achieve the targeted cost for the new product.

New-product manufacturing engineers (NPME) worked with product design engineers to lower the manufacturing costs of new products. Nick Katte, a NPME, recalled the difficulty of implementing target costing with the old costing system:

> We were told to reduce costs by 10%, but the cost system calculated product costs as materials and direct labor plus a burden rate in excess of 500% on direct labor. No one believed these numbers and it was hard to get the product design engineers' attention for cost reduction opportunities.
>
> Now, using the ABC methodology, we have the numbers that an SMT component costs $0.024 to place while an automatic (through-hole) insertion costs $0.08 and a post-wave solder hand-insertion costs about $1.[1] By knowing

---

[1] Unit cost numbers are for illustration purposes only. They do not reflect actual company data

the differences in costs per insertion, we can work better with the product design engineers, encouraging them to replace components requiring hand assembly with SMT components. We can establish targets to reduce, in the next version of a given product, the number of hand assembled components from 100 to, say, 30. We can also influence them to reduce the number of functional tests they specify if the tests are not really adding value to the process.

Mark Studebaker, the product design engineer, who worked with Nick Katte concurred:

> The difference in placement cost between these components are now highly visible. Before, engineering people and factory people had different mental models of factory cost and we were working at cross purposes, forcing us to do lots of special studies to get better estimates of costs that we could agree on. Now we're all very much on the same page and pointing in the same direction about the impact of design decisions on manufacturing costs.

The cost information could also be used to choose between alternative vendors of components. For example, Intel chips, with more standard technology, were easier to place using SMT. But these chips offered less functionality. Marketing and design engineers were now having discussions about whether customers would value the added functionality that came from a more expensive design or whether the standard chips that were less expensive and easier to place would be adequate.

Mark Studebaker expressed a concern, however, that the ABC information might encourage too much tinkering with product designs:

> The design engineer's job is change — new products, and redesigned products for cost reduction. ABC is a tool that encourages change; it gives us more cost drivers to play with. But change is difficult and expensive, and we may not be recognizing all the costs of change, such as the costs of engineering change notices and changes in the design configuration of the product.

> We should attempt to measure the cost for each PAR [Part Approval Request — the process of approving a new part] or the cost of adding a new vendor. These costs would have a greater impact on engineer's decision than amortizing overhead expenses in piece part costs.

> But my bottom line is that the mushiness and error in the old system led to fruitless debate so we're way ahead of where we were three years ago.

Individuals designated as Product Managers had profit and loss (P&L) responsibility for a set of key products. They functioned in a matrix organization serving as a liaison among marketing, sales, engineering, manufacturing, technical documentation, and finance. Product managers were supposed to track down problems and opportunities with products under their responsibility: One product manager commented:

> ABC was a cultural change for us. It has enabled us to be very specific about costs so that we focus engineers to only put components in if they were really needed. Every insertion or placement is a potential point of failure. Engineers like to over-design products; they buffer the design — just-in-case — to be sure that the product will more than comply with government specifications. But they were not seeing the cost consequences from this design philosophy; they were not designing boards with placement and failure costs in mind.

> ABC makes it clear that placement of components is a big cost to us; it gives us a very specific picture of what it costs to manufacture a board. We can sit down with engineering and encourage them to use fewer components, use components that are easier to place, and reduce the number of vendors we purchase from. By giving us information for examining every design decision carefully, ABC has the potential for great cost avoidance. We'll be able to do an even better job when we start to get data from the field about specific component failure rates.

The impact on design decisions extended beyond electronic components. Purchasing and Manufacturing Engineering people started to focus on reducing packaging materials costs. They identified the lowest cost packaging and the lowest total cost vendors. The number of vendors was reduced and AT&T Paradyne established partnering relationships with them — bringing them onsite to manage and reduce packaging costs, and tailoring packaging requirements to vendor's machinery to reduce vendor's production costs and thereby obtain lower prices for packaging materials. A manufacturing engineer commented on the impact of these efforts.

> We reduced the number of different boxes we use from 700 to about 140. And we try, as much as possible, when designing a new product, to use an existing box, already produced in high volumes. This avoids the added engineering and tooling costs associated with newly designed boxes. The fewer number of boxes require less ordering, handling, and storing as well. Team members used to ask us why they were handling so many different containers when one or two would seem to do the same job? They were right. For our standard "873" part number packages, we have moved the vendor on site so these boxes go directly into our inventory without any ordering or handling on our part.

The design decision on components and packaging materials had enabled AT&T Paradyne to reduce the number of suppliers from 1,800 in 1992 to 300 in 1994. The group doing post-wave solder hand insertion of components had been reduced from 48 people in 1991 to six people in 1994. The streamlining of suppliers and processes had enabled cycle times to be reduced from 42 days in 1992 to 12 days in mid-1994. Half the products were now being produced with a one day cycle time with a goal to achieve one day cycle time for 100% of the products by year-end. The ABC Team Leader identified other potential savings:

> Manufacturing management is also analyzing whether all activities being performed are benefiting the product or the customer. We currently have six machines for testing circuit boards. By being more careful about what functional tests get specified, we could eliminate the need for one machine, sell it, and use the freed-up space in the factory to bring a process, like repair, currently done externally back into the factory. A similar savings could also be realized if we eliminate the need for one of our automatic insertion machines.

> For the activities we continue to perform, the ABC information enables us to benchmark our processes, to identify how competitive our activities are compared to the industry best.

An ABC team member noted:

> Many decisions have been taken to improve our processes. While none of the decisions were made exclusively using ABC-supplied information, it was certainly an influence in each decision. ABC added the cost dimension to time and quality considerations. It provided focus on the cost of activities and it encouraged team members to find innovative ways to reduce costs.

The Road Ahead

Several initiatives were underway to expand the scope of activity-based management at AT&T Paradyne. A Purchasing Manager, admitted:

> Our new sourcing strategy to reduce the number of suppliers did not come from ABM. ABM is brand new for me. I'm still learning about what it can do for me. I see ABM as a great tool to go forward as it gets fine-tuned. I would like to be able to see the space costs of different components and materials. I could see spreading ABM to our key suppliers and perhaps using ABM when selecting a single-source supplier which will include considerations of technology, quality, service, and, also, price.

Marketing, selling, and distribution expenses were being addressed by a Cost-to-Serve project that would identify the costs of selling through different channels: direct sales, indirect sales that used distributors and

value-added-resellers, and royalty sales.[2] The project would also trace the expenses of the sales engineers and field engineers who supplied post-sales support to the different channels.

The cost-to-serve project, and the product cost ABC model, would provide inputs into a new Economic Value Added (EVA) decision support model. The EVA project team had already interviewed customers, marketing, sales, and service support to identify the distribution of costs across 15 steps involved in the sales process. The EVA model would calculate profitability by channel, product line, and by customer and allow managers to assess the impact on company EVA of pricing and discounting policies.

And the product costing model was still undergoing continual refinement. Future versions of the model were expected to assign non-volume related costs differentially to new versus used parts, preferred versus restricted parts, and the cost of adding new suppliers. The existing ABC model was being benchmarked against the models being developed at similar companies, such as Digital Equipment Corporation and Hewlett-Packard. In July 1994, AT&T Paradyne hosted an ABM conference at a hotel near the Largo facility, where representatives from other AT&T business units and independent companies, both manufacturing and service, presented the current status of their ABC/ABM initiatives. A cost team member reflected on the progress during the past two years:

> The AT&T Paradyne ABM effort has produced a new cost model with wide acceptance in the company. People are using it on an every-day basis for designing new products and for improving existing products and processes. I am proud that we built the model using existing people at AT&T Paradyne, with no consultants, and on an existing computer system. Also the system is not just used for special studies like many other ABC models. We obtain monthly reports on the actual incurred costs of products and processes allowing us to also use the numbers to value inventory for external reporting.

> It's certainly not a perfect system and we need to continue to improve it. This will be a long journey and we have only traveled 10% of the way; 90% is still ahead of us. I am confident, however, that we will never turn back.

---

[2]Royalty sales occurred when AT&T Paradyne provided proprietary technology to an external company. In return, it received a stream of royalties and brand recognition from the external company's sales of products that used this technology.

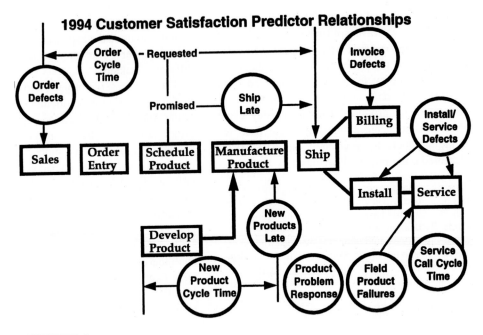

EXHIBIT 1

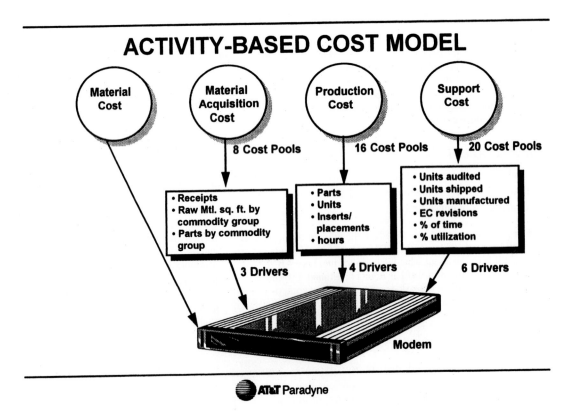

EXHIBIT 2

Production Cost Pools: Annual Expenses ($000) and Activity Cost Drivers

Budget for Year	Traceable Cost	Manufacturing Support	Metrology Support	Engineering Support	Total Expense	Activity Cost Driver (ACD)	Quantity of ACD	Standard Cost: ACD
Surface Mount Technology	$ 3,000	$ 325	$ 5	$ 250	$ 3,580	# Placements	150,000	0.024
Budlite	200	70	0	70	340	# Parts	800	0.425
Pre-Wave Hand Insertion	800	200	15	40	1,055	# Parts	15,000	0.070
I.C.T.	1,600	150	120	150	2,020	# Std. Hours	60	33.667
Functional Test	1,400	150	30	500	2,080	# Std. Hours	75	27.733
Assembly: Product A1	700	130	40	100	970	# Parts	4,000	0.243
Assembly: Product E5	600	70	25	70	765	# Parts	600	1.275
Automatic Insertion	300	100	0	80	480	# Parts	6,000	0.080
Post-Wave Hand Insertion	500	200	15	60	775	# Insertions	800	0.969
Assembly: Product D4	600	70	10	75	755	# Parts	2,500	0.302
Assembly: Product B2	200	64	16	70	350	# Units	750	0.467
Assembly: Product C3	150	45	5	50	250	# Parts	60	4.167
ESS	300	150	0	200	650	# Std. Hours	20	32.500
Burn Oven	20	50	5	25	100	# Units	40	2.500
Wave Solder	350	100	0	70	520	# Units	230	2.261
Total	$10,720	$1,874	$286	$1,810	$14,690			

Note: Financials are for illustration purposes only and do not reflect actual company results.

EXHIBIT 3

Monthly Accruals: June

	Activity Cost Driver (ACD)	Planned Quantity	Actual Quantity	Planned Spending	Actual Spending	Cost Driver Rate ($/ACD)			Volume Actual vs. Plan	Spending Actual vs. Plan
						Plan	Actual	Difference		
Surface Mount Technology	# Placements	12,500	13,000	$ 300	$ 275	0.024	0.021	-0.003	104%	92%
Budlite	# Parts	70	50	30	25	0.429	0.500	0.071	71	83
Pre-Wave Hand Insertion	# Parts	1,250	800	90	65	0.072	0.081	0.009	64	72
I.C.T.	# Std. Hours	5	5	170	150	34.000	30.000	-4.000	100	88
Functional Test	# Std. Hours	10	15	175	135	17.500	9.000	-8.500	150	77
Assembly: Product A1	# Parts	350	300	80	70	0.229	0.233	0.005	86	88
Assembly: Product E5	# Parts	50	60	60	40	1.200	0.667	-0.533	120	67
Automatic Insertion	# Parts	500	450	40	30	0.080	0.067	-0.013	90	75
Post-Wave Hand Insertion	# Insertions	70	80	65	50	0.923	0.625	-0.298	114	77
Assembly: Product D4	# Parts	200	160	60	45	0.300	0.281	-0.019	80	75
Assembly: Product B2	# Units	60	60	30	20	0.500	0.333	-0.167	100	67
Assembly: Product C3	# Parts	5	5	20	20	4.000	4.000	0.000	100	100
ESS	# Std. Hours	10	5	55	50	5.500	10.000	4.500	50	91
Burn Oven	# Units	5	15	10	5	2.000	0.333	-1.667	300	50
Wave Solder	# Units	20	25	45	45	2.250	1.800	-0.450	125	100
Total				$1,230	$1,025					

Note: Financials are for illustration purposes only and do not reflect actual company results.

EXHIBIT 4

AT&T PARADYNE
S.M.T. COST PER PLACEMENT

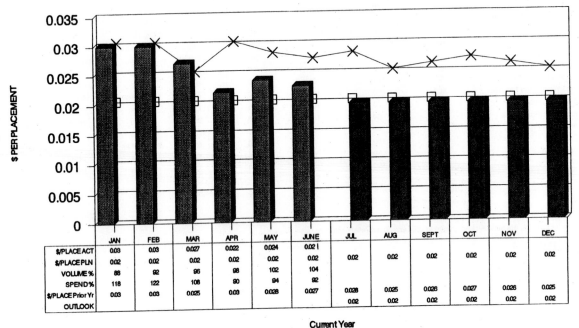

	JAN	FEB	MAR	APR	MAY	JUNE	JUL	AUG	SEPT	OCT	NOV	DEC
$/PLACE ACT	0.03	0.03	0.027	0.022	0.024	0.02						
$/PLACE PLN	0.02	0.02	0.02	0.02	0.02	0.02	0.02	0.02	0.02	0.02	0.02	0.02
VOLUME %	88	92	96	98	102	104						
SPEND %	118	122	108	90	94	92						
$/PLACE Prior Yr	0.03	0.03	0.025	0.03	0.028	0.027	0.028	0.025	0.026	0.027	0.026	0.025
OUTLOOK							0.02	0.02	0.02	0.02	0.02	0.02

Current Year

| $/PLACE ACT | $/PLACE PLN | $/PLACE Prior Yr | OUTLOOK |

YTD ACTUAL = $.026
YTD PLANNED = $.0.02
YTD PRIOR YR = $.033

Note: Financials are for illustration purposes only
and do not reflect company results.

EXHIBIT 5

AT&T PARADYNE COMMODITY CLASS #4
IC's

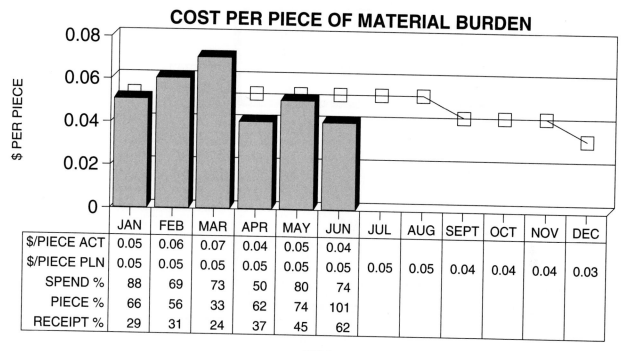

COST PER PIECE OF MATERIAL BURDEN

	JAN	FEB	MAR	APR	MAY	JUN	JUL	AUG	SEPT	OCT	NOV	DEC
$/PIECE ACT	0.05	0.06	0.07	0.04	0.05	0.04						
$/PIECE PLN	0.05	0.05	0.05	0.05	0.05	0.05	0.05	0.05	0.04	0.04	0.04	0.03
SPEND %	88	69	73	50	80	74						
PIECE %	66	56	33	62	74	101						
RECEIPT %	29	31	24	37	45	62						

1994

■ $/PIECE ACT ⊟ $/PIECE PLN

Note: Financials are for illustration purposes
only and do not reflect company results.

YTD ACTUAL = $.05 YTD
PLANNED = $.05

EXHIBIT 6

TARGET COST PROCESS FLOW

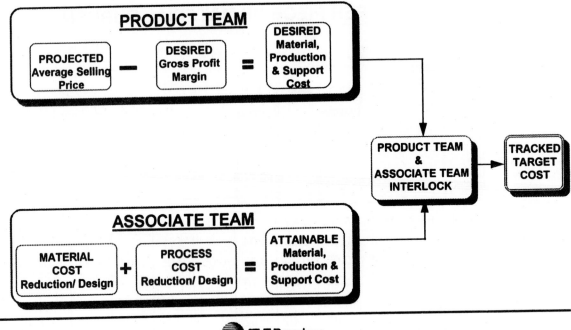

EXHIBIT 7

11

Stage IV: Using ABC for Budgeting and Transfer Pricing

We conclude the book by showing how an ABC system can be used for budgeting, What-If analysis, and transfer pricing. By using ABC for budgeting, a practice we refer to as activity-based budgeting, managers determine the supply of resources to operating units and responsibility centers based on the demands for activities that these units are expected to supply. Activity-based budgeting is an extremely important application; it is the process by which costs, previously thought to be "fixed", are made variable.

What-If analysis enables managers to assess the consequences from major changes in product and customer mix. Transfer pricing allows current ABC information on production costs and capacity utilization to be incorporated into the operating, pricing, and selling decisions of decentralized organizational units.

At the time of this writing, however, we do not have cases that illustrate actual company experiences with using ABC systems in these more advanced ways. So this chapter represents a vision about the future for ABC and integrated systems.

WHY ACTIVITY-BASED BUDGETING?

Conventional budgeting practice is an iterative, negotiating process between heads of responsibility centers and senior executives. Responsibility center managers continually seek more resources while senior executives continually attempt to control increases in the spending authorized for their decentralized units. The result is that the budget for the next year builds from the baseline of the previous year, plus or minus a few percent depending upon the outcome of the negotiations between senior executives and local management. Activity-based budgeting offers the opportunity for such discussions to be based more upon facts, and less upon power, influence, and negotiating ability. We could even refer to activity-based budgeting as *zero-based budgeting* since it develops budgets from the ground (product and customer) level.

If implemented successfully, activity-based budgeting demolishes conventional thinking about fixed and variable costs. Is it interesting to know how much more an organization will spend in the middle of the year; should it increase production from 2,000 units of a product to

2,001 units? Sure, it is of some interest, but, as we have repeatedly discussed, this narrow concept of a variable cost encompasses very few organizational resources. And the resources that are most variable or flexible within short periods of time represent mostly resources the organization purchases from outside suppliers:

- Vendors from whom it purchases materials,
- Utility companies from whom it purchases energy,
- Manpower agencies from whom it purchases temporary, part-time workers, and
- Individual labor suppliers from whom it purchases labor hours as needed or pays for on a piecework basis.

Left unaddressed by conventional variable or marginal cost thinking is the entire organizational infrastructure of (i) personnel—front-line employees, engineers, salespersons, managers—with whom the organization has a long-term contractual commitment (either explicit or implicit), (ii) equipment and facilities, and (iii) information systems supplying computing and telecommunications. What determines the level of spending on resources for this infrastructure? Decisions to acquire new resources or to continue to maintain the current level of these committed resources are most likely made during the annual budgeting process. Once the authorization to acquire and maintain organizational resources has been made, of course, the expenses of these resources appears fixed and unrelated to local, short-term decisions about product mix and customer expansion or contraction. The time to make spending on these resources variable is during the budgeting process. Activity-based costing gives managers the information they need during the budgeting process to acquire, supply, and maintain only those resources needed to perform the activities expected to be demanded in upcoming years.

The Activity-Based Budgeting Process

Activity-based budgeting (ABB) is simply activity-based costing performed in reverse (see Exhibit 11–1). Recall that the ABC process starts from assigning resource expenses down to activities, and, via activity cost drivers, down to cost objects like products, services, and cus-

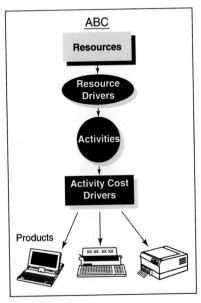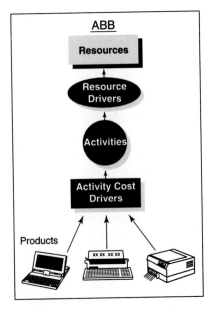

EXHIBIT 11–1   ABC Reverses Causal Relationship in an ABC Model

tomers. Costs flow (on a conventional diagram) from north to south. In activity-based budgeting, the analysis flows from south to north.

Activity-based budgeting follows the following sequence of steps:

1. Estimate next period's expected production and sales volumes by individual products and customers.
2. Forecast the demand for organizational activities.
3. Calculate the resource demands to perform the organizational activities.
4. Determine the actual resource supply to meet the demands.
5. Determine activity capacity.

We discuss each, briefly, in turn.

1. Estimate Next Period's Production and Sales Volumes

The organization starts with estimates of expected production and sales volumes and mix. The estimates include not only the products and services that will be sold, but also the individual customers (or customer types) expected to buy the products and services. The estimates should include in addition to the total production of products and sales to customers the production and sales ordering process. For example, the budget should include the number of production runs for each product, the frequency of materials orders and receipts, the number of customer orders, the method of shipment, and so on. So the demand estimates must include both the total production volume and also the details of how the forecasted volume will be produced, such as the number of batches and production runs.

2. Forecast the Demand for Organizational Activities

The budgeting exercise continues by forecasting the demand for organizational activities required to meet the forecasted volume and mix of products, services, and customers. This process should be identical to that used in conventional budgeting for calculating budgets for purchases of materials, the utilization of machines, and the supply of direct labor, based on the forecasted production mix for the upcoming year. Activity-based budgeting extends the conventional exercise by forecasting the demands for all indirect and support activities: ordering, receiving and handling materials; processing customer orders, complaints, and requests for technical support; scheduling and setting up for production runs; and all other activities identified in the activity dictionary. The activity-based budgeting exercise estimates the expected *quantity* for all activity cost drivers: how many setups, how many customer orders, how many engineering change notices, how many products and customers to support, and so on. To accomplish this objective, the budgeting team must certainly know the volume of production and sales. But it must also estimate how the production and sales volume will be achieved; that is, knowledge of the underlying processes that will be used to produce the products and services, and market, sell, and service customers. For example, Exhibit 11–2 shows the calculation for the number of truck shipments, based on the total number of units to be shipped, and the average shipment size. Thus, starting from forecast of product and customer demands, we obtain a forecast for the quantity of activities that must be performed during the upcoming budgeting period.

3. Calculate the Resource Demands to Perform the Organizational Activities

With knowledge of the expected *quantity* of demands for activities, the budgeting team then estimates the resources that must be supplied to perform the demanded level of activities. The forecast of resource supply requires the budgeting team to understand the underlying *efficiency* of performing activities. The team must know how many resources, and of what types, must be

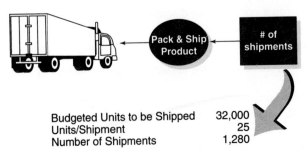

Budgeted Units to be Shipped	32,000
Units/Shipment	25
Number of Shipments	1,280

EXHIBIT 11-2   **Estimating the Demand for Truck Shipments**

supplied to handle the demanded quantity of activities. Exhibit 11–3 shows the mapping from an activity demand for shipments to the resource demand for trucks.

As another example, if the production schedule calls for 2,400 production runs, and each run requires a setup that averages 40 minutes, then machine and personnel resources capable of performing 1,600 hours of setup activity must be supplied. If each production run requires 20 minutes of scheduling and quality assurance (QA) activities, then 800 hours of scheduling and QA resources must be provided to meet this demand. With fungible resources that support multiple activities the total demand becomes the sum of the resource demands from all the activities performed by the fungible resources.

4. Determine the Actual Resource Supply to Meet the Demands

In the next step, the budgeting process converts the demand for resources to perform activities (calculated in the third stage above) into an estimate of the total resources of each type that must be supplied. Exhibit 11–4 shows how the demand (from Exhibit 11–3) for 1.6 truck shipments per period translates into a required estimated resource supply of 2 truckloads per period.

In general, each resource has a particular resource spending profile (see Exhibit 11–5). These profiles capture how the supply of each resource changes with activity volume. The activity-based budgeting process uses three basic profiles: flexible, committed-fixed, and committed-step function.

For flexible resources, such as energy used for machine operations or labor paid hourly or based on actual production, the supply can be matched closely to the demand for these re-

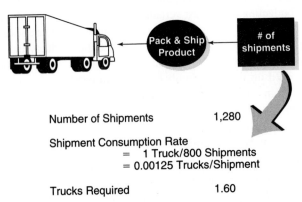

Number of Shipments	1,280

Shipment Consumption Rate
    = 1 Truck/800 Shipments
    = 0.00125 Trucks/Shipment

Trucks Required	1.60

EXHIBIT 11-3   **Estimating the Demand for Trucks**

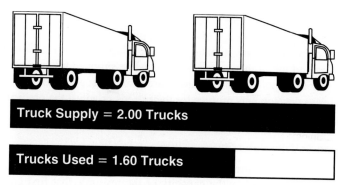

EXHIBIT 11–4   Link from Resource Demand to Resource Supply

sources. This profile leads to resource supply costs that are essentially linear with demand. At the other extreme, for committed-fixed resources such as plant floor space, any demand that is less than the capacity of the committed resources can be met by the existing supply without additional spending.[1] Therefore, this profile shows no spending changes with demand. In between these extremes, we have committed-step resources where the supply of the resource increases in definite steps as demand increases.[2]

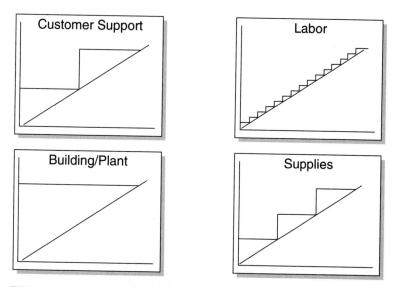

EXHIBIT 11–5   Resource Supply Patterns Differ for Different Resources

---

[1] Any demand that exceeds the practical capacity of the committed fixed resources cannot be satisfied. Managers must adjust the forecasted product–customer mix until the demand can be met with the existing supply; or managers must authorize a capital expenditure to increase the supply of the constraining resource.

[2] These three profiles capture a lot of the observed variation in resource supply behavior, but by no means all. For example, resource supply often displays different profiles when demand is increasing than when it is decreasing. For example, managers may be less willing to release highly skilled individuals when demand decreases than they are to hire new ones when demand increases. In addition, some resources may initially be committed, but become flexible above a certain level. For example, floor space is limited to existing buildings until all space is occupied. Then demands for additional space can be used to adapt to almost any demand level. There are many different resource supply behavior profiles that are encountered in practice.

The estimation of resource supply is undertaken for each resource used by an activity. In general, when multiple resources must be supplied to perform a given activity, the activity-based budgeting model must estimate the relationship between the demands for activities and the derived demand for all the resources that must be supplied to perform that activity. Activity-based budgeting attempts to approximate future resource supply; not to try to model it perfectly. Users can always develop new profiles for their needs or adjust the predicted supply of the three basic resource types after the initial budgeting calculation.

5. Determine Activity Capacity

When all an activity's resources have been identified, the user can determine the practical capacity of the activity, which is the capacity of the resource that first constrains the ability of the firm to perform the activity. For example, suppose activity A consumes two resources, R1 and R2. The predicted demand for activity A is 100 units which converts to a required supply of $220 and $360 of R1 and R2, respectively. Activity A uses $2 of R1 and $3 of R2 each time it is performed. Therefore, the activity driver rate for Activity A is $5 ($2 + $3) and the activity's practical capacity is 110 units (220/2). This practical capacity means that the predicted demand for 100 units of Activity A will result in unused capacity of 10 units (110 − 100) at a cost of $50 ($5 × 10), and a surplus capacity of resource R2 of $30 ($360 − $3 × 110). There is no unused capacity predicted for resource R1. Therefore, the total cost of unused capacity is $80.

This example shows that in activity-based budgeting we identify two forms of capacity, one at the activity level and the other at the resource level. When the resources are fungible, the unused capacity at the resource level requires a calculation for each activity that uses the resource. Say Activity B also consumes resource R2. The total demand for Resource R2 is $500 ($300 for Activity A and $200 for activity B). The resource supply profile requires a supply of resource R2 of $550. The practical capacity of Activity A consumes $330 of Resource R2 and the practical capacity of Activity B consumes $210 of Resource R2. Therefore, the unused capacity of Resource R2 is now only $10 ($550 − ($330 + $210)). Nothing stops the fungible resource from setting the practical capacity of an activity. If the resource supply profile of R2 had been such that the level of resource R2 available for Activity A was below $330, then resource R2 would have been the constraining resource, the practical capacity of Activity A would be lower, and surplus capacity would emerge for Resource R1.

The concept of separate capacities at the resource and activity levels does not emerge in retrospective (Stage III) systems that assign resource costs based upon interviews about percentage of time required for different activities. Systems that use percentage estimates typically assume that 100% of the supplied resources are required to support practical capacity.[3] Therefore, it is only at the activity level that unused capacity emerges in retrospective models. This simplification introduces some distortion into the reported costs as the driver rates are too high by the amount of unused resources that are included in the activity cost. In prospective Stage IV systems, unused capacity must be identified at the resource level if ABB is to be meaningfully undertaken.[4] For the purposes of costing outputs, it is expedient to still define capacity at the activity level even though the ability to define it at the resource level exists.

---

[3]Theoretically, if the interviewed individuals identified the unused capacity at the resource level (e.g., an individual is busy only 80% of the time) then a retrospective ABC could identify capacity at both activity and resource levels. We rarely encounter such responses.
[4]This statement only holds true when unused capacity at the resource level is significant.

Using Activity-Based Budgeting

Several modifications are required to the budgeting process as the company becomes more efficient (operational ABM) and, also, as it changes the demand for activities through strategic ABM. First, the costs of performing the activity can decrease, and second, an activity, such as inspections or moving material, may be performed less often. These two improvements can easily be reflected in the computation of resource supply, practical capacity of the activities, and resource capacity by changing the estimated requirement for activity cost driver quantities, and the changed relationship between activities performed and resources required for these activities. Including such improvements before they have been achieved obviously risks developing over optimistic activity-based budgets. Consequently, any proposed improvements should be subjected to considerable scrutiny to ensure that they are plausible.[5]

Activity-based budgeting is most useful for resources performing repetitive activities, especially activities triggered by demands from products, services, and customers. In addition to this derived demand for organizational resources, the budgeting team must also estimate the quantity of discretionary spending for the upcoming year. This spending, on product and customer support, will typically represent elements of product and customer sustaining expenses, plus spending at higher hierarchical levels (brand and product-line sustaining; channel, business unit, and region-sustaining). This analysis of discretionary spending will complement the activity-based budgeting process for the resources required to perform the more repetitive and predictable unit, batch, order, and some product and customer-sustaining activities.

Once the activity-based budget has been determined, managers will authorize the supply of resources to meet the demand for the upcoming year. At that point, users can run their ABC model in the traditional direction, north to south, to calculate activity cost driver rates for the coming period. These prospective driver rates can be used in the several ways identified in the ABM chapters, such as motivating continuous improvement and learning programs; making product and customer-based decisions on pricing, order size and order acceptance, and helping engineers design new products.

In practice, of course, activity-based budgeting will not be a simple exercise. The organization will have to specify far more details; about how production and sales demands will be met, about the underlying efficiency of all organizational activities, and about the spending and supply pattern of individual resources. When performed successfully, however, managers will have much greater control over their cost structure, particularly over their so-called fixed costs.

WHAT-IF ANALYSIS

Managers use activity-based budgeting to determine resource supply and spending levels for future periods and to calculate the expected future costs of products, services, and customers. Complementary to activity-based budgeting is What-if analysis that helps managers predict the consequences of decisions taken about individual products, customers, and suppliers.

Consider introducing a new product or customer. As long as the change in activity volumes caused by the new product or customer can be handled with available capacity, the existing activity cost driver rates can be used to report the cost of the product. This analysis assumes that the quantity of flexible resources, such as material and power for machines, will vary, but that the supply of committed resources will not change. The ABC model reports the cost of all

---

[5]A relatively straightforward extension to this procedure is required to model the interaction between primary activities, the secondary activities that support the primary activities, and the resources that are required to perform the secondary activities.

the resources used for the new product or customer. This will be especially useful if the product or customer is not a one-time incremental order; that is, the product and customer will be sustained for at least several periods. But a manager wishing to price an order for a new product or customer below full cost can strip away the cost of resources that are not expected to be utilized by other products or that will not be eliminated in the near future.

If the anticipated changes in activity volumes for new products or customers, however, requires additional capacity to be supplied, then a mini activity-based budgeting exercise is undertaken. The exercise incorporates the additional cost of supplying new committed resources, the incremental costs of the flexible resources (e.g., materials and energy), and the normal cost of using already supplied resources. Understanding both the total cost and the incremental costs—of materials, energy, plus newly-supplied resources—helps managers make better decisions on order acceptance and price and delivery terms. The process of associating increments of resource supply with particular products or customers also produces a more effective resource acquisition process.

What-If analysis also helps in decisions about the use of common components. Consider a proposal to increase the use of common components, and decrease the use of unique components (those used for only a single product). The What-If analysis permits managers to assess the change in resource requirements from increasing the production volumes of the common components and reducing or eliminating the use of many unique components.

Similarly, if engineers are contemplating changing the design of a common component, a What-If model identifies every product that uses the common component, the total volume of that common component, and the quantities of activities and resources currently required for its production. The model can simulate the new activity-resource profile for the redesigned common component and calculate the revised resource cost. If the redesign is accomplished, the revised cost can easily be imbedded into the reported cost of all products that use the redesigned component.

A third class of decisions relates to changes in operating processes. For example, the introduction of a new production machine will change the demand for activities and resources. Process improvements in any primary or secondary activity will reduce the demands for resources required to perform the activity. A What-If analysis allows managers to model the impact of the operating change and assess the benefits on product and customer costs.

Such What-If analyses enable managers to explore the resource supply implications of decisions taken about products, customer, and operating processes. The existing ABC model, either retrospective (past period's costs) or prospective (future period's costs), provides the starting point for analysis. The What-If analysis enables managers to translate an ABC resource usage model into implications for changes in resource supply and spending. The forecasted spending changes provide the fact-based benefits case for proposed changes in products, customers, and processes.

TRANSFER PRICING

We close the book by illustrating how managers with real-time access to an ABC model of resource demand and resource supply now have a mechanism to allow continual communication of economic information between managers in dispersed and organizationally separate units. This facilitates better decision making on the allocation and management of existing capacity resources to meet the demands from dispersed marketing and sales units.

Transfer pricing issues arise when two organizational units interact by having one unit acquire the output from the other unit. Historically, transfer pricing has been one of the most difficult and controversial problems for senior managers to resolve. Economics and accounting scholars have demonstrated, using simple deterministic examples, that in perfectly competitive markets, the optimal transfer price should be the market price. In this situation, costs play no role other than to allow each division to calculate its own profitability from producing or acquiring the transferred product. When the transferred product cannot be acquired in perfectly competitive markets, the scholars recommend using the long-run marginal cost of supplying the transferred good.[6] This long-run marginal cost reflects the opportunity cost to the selling division of supplying an additional unit of the transferred product. In practice, considerable controversy has arisen about how to calculate long-run marginal cost.

Companies have evolved several cost-based methods for transfer pricing. At one extreme, some companies allow the selling division to calculate a fully-absorbed product cost (using the usual arbitrary overhead allocation scheme from a Stage I or Stage II cost system), and add a profit margin so that the division could appear to be a profit center. At the other extreme, managers interpreted the marginal cost rule to include only the short-term variable costs associated with producing an extra unit of the product.

Activity-based costing allows managers to use a two-tier approach to transfer pricing. Consider a manufacturing division, treated as a cost center, that produces and distributes products to several profit-center marketing divisions which market and sell the products to customers. The problem is how to assign the cost on the internal transfer from a manufacturing plant to a marketing division. First, the ABC transfer-pricing approach assigns unit-level costs (such as materials and labor) reported in the manufacturing division to each marketing division based on standard costs and the actual quantities of each individual product it orders. In addition, the marketing division is charged the manufacturing division's standard batch-level costs based on the actual number of batches required for each product the marketing division ordered. This procedure gives managers of the marketing division the flexibility to decide, for example, whether to accept a small order from a customer, or how much of a discount he or she was willing to grant for large orders. As a cost center, the manufacturing division's manager has the motivation to reduce actual unit and batch-level costs below the standard ABC costs.

In the second calculation, the product and facility-sustaining expenses are charged to marketing divisions on an annual basis, based on budgeted information about which products they wanted to sustain in the product line. The charges for facility-sustaining expenses are based on marketing divisions' budgeted use of the capacity of the manufacturing division's facilities. Managers in the marketing divisions have an incentive to monitor the product and facility-sustaining costs to ensure that they do indeed stay "fixed" and not creep upwards each period. Should one or more of them request a change in production capacity, the responsibility for the fixed cost increment becomes clearly traceable and assignable.

With the transfer pricing process, managers in the marketing division can plan their product mix with knowledge of the cost impact of their decisions. When they propose increases in variety and complexity, they know the added costs that they will be charged because of the increased demands on manufacturing facilities. They can identify which products cover only their unit and batch-level expenses, and hence fail to make a profit contribution that covers their annual product-sustaining and plant-level expenses.

In summary, activity-based transfer prices enable marketing divisions (those typically engaged in marketing and selling processes) to see the long-run marginal costs—at the unit, batch, product-sustaining, and facility-sustaining levels—of their decisions on product volume,

---

[6]J. Hirschleifer, "On the Economics of Transfer Pricing," *Journal of Business* (July 1956), pp. 172–184; J. Hirschleifer, "Economics of the Divisionalized Firm," *Journal of Business* (April 1957), pp. 96–108; and D. Solomons, *Divisional Performance: Measurement and Control* (Homewood IL: Irwin, and Financial Executives Research Foundation, 1965), pp. 160–228.

order size, and mix (i.e., strategic ABM). Manufacturing divisions get signals about cost behavior reflecting the volume, variety, and complexity of the tasks they have been assigned, and can attempt to lower the costs incorporated in the transfer prices through improved efficiencies at the unit, batch, and product-sustaining levels (i.e., operational ABM). Producing and marketing–selling divisions now share a common (and valid) language about cost behavior, and their efforts and decisions become synchronized to enhance overall organizational profitability.

SUMMARY

In activity-based budgeting, the resources to be supplied to all organizational departments and business processes are determined based on the forecasted demands for these resources by products, services, and customers. Using What-If capabilities in their ABC system, managers contemplate the resource implications from major changes in product design, product mix, and relationships with suppliers and customers. And the ABC information can be used for transfer pricing to communicate between operations departments and marketing and sales units the economics of product sourcing and customer sales decisions. These are all examples of how integrated Stage IV cost and performance measurement systems can provide timely, valid information to managers to help them meet the challenges of their highly competitive environment.